Handbook of the Economics of Climate Change

Volume 1

INTRODUCTION TO THE SERIES

The aim of the *Handbooks in Economics* series is to produce a definitive source, reference, and teaching supplement in different branches of the subject for use by professional researchers and graduate students. The series continues to bring out new handbooks in core areas and also seeks to expand into new areas that reflect modern developments in the methodology and the practice of economics.

STEVEN DURLAUF, SANJEEV GOYAL, and ROSA MATZKIN

Handbook of the Economics of Climate Change

Volume 1

Editors

Lint Barrage
ETH Zurich

Solomon Hsiang
Stanford University

ELSEVIER

N·H

North-Holland

An imprint of Elsevier

North-Holland is an imprint of Elsevier
Radarweg 29, PO Box 211, 1000 AE Amsterdam, Netherlands

First edition 2024

ISBN: 978-0-443-31324-0
ISSN: 0169-7218

For information on all North-Holland publications
visit our website at https://www.elsevier.com/books-and-journals

Publisher: Zoe Kruze
Acquisitions Editor: Jason Mitchell
Editorial Project Manager: Sneha Apar
Production Project Manager: Abdulla Sait
Cover Designer: Gopalakrishnan Venkatraman
Typeset by MPS Limited, India

Contents

List of Contributors

Tamma Carleton Department of Agricultural and Resource Economics, University of California, Berkeley, CA; National Bureau of Economic Research, Cambridge, MA, United States

Simon Dietz London School of Economics and Political Science (LSE), Houghton St, London WC2A 2AE, United Kingdom

Esther Duflo National Bureau of Economic Research; Department of Economics, Massachusetts Institute of Technology, Cambridge, MA, United States

Christian Gollier Toulouse School of Economics, University of Toulouse-Capitole, Toulouse, France

Bård Harstad Stanford University, Stanford, California, United States

Dylan Hogan Columbia University School of International and Public Affairs, New York, United States

B. Kelsey Jackb National Bureau of Economic Research, Cambridge, MA, United States; Haas School of Business, University of California, Berkeley, CA, United States

Svenn Jensen Oslo Business School, Oslo Metropolitan University, Oslo, Norway

Matthew J. Kotchen Yale University and NBER

Wolfram Schlenker Harvard Kennedy School of Government and NBER, Cambridge, United States

Christian Traeger Department of Economics, University of Oslo, Oslo, Norway

Guglielmo Zappalà Department of Agricultural and Resource Economics, University of California, Berkeley, CA, United States

Preface

In recent years, the topic of climate change has risen to the forefront of policy debates, academic research, and business decision-making. Interest among economists in the topic has risen just as markedly. As shown in Fig. 1, the number of economics papers published each year on the topics of climate change and carbon emissions has risen dramatically over time.

The early days of the literature, starting in the 1970s, saw few papers on the topic but many were groundbreaking in their content. Due to his early pioneering work at this time, William Nordhaus is widely thought of as the "father" of the economic analysis of climate change, warning that climate change could affect economic growth (Nordhaus and Tobin, 1972, Nordhaus, 1974), producing the first estimates of global carbon taxes that could stabilize greenhouse gas concentrations (Nordhaus, 1977), and developing the first optimizing integrated assessment model (IAM) of the economy and the climate (Nordhaus, 1975, 1980). In parallel, Martin Weitzman published his seminal work evaluating the optimal regulation of pollution under uncertainty in 1974 (Weitzman, 1974).

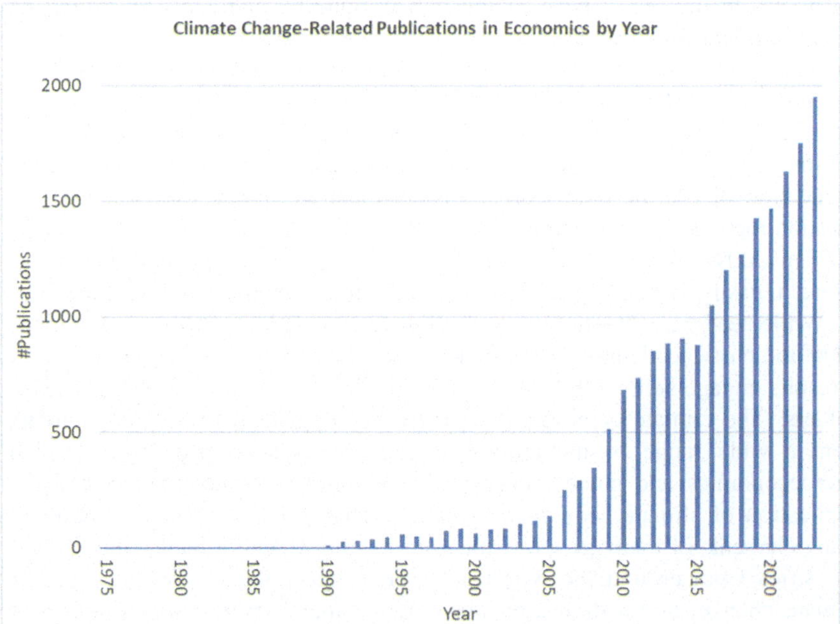

FIG. 1 Number of climate-change related publications in economics by year. Obtained from Web of Science search for articles or book chapters in the economics category with keywords "climate change" or "carbon dioxide" or "carbon emissions.".

As attention to climate change grew in the 1980s, more economists tackled these questions (e.g., Edmonds and Reilly 1983), and by the early 1990s, a substantial literature of integrated climate-economic and energy-economic modelers studying greenhouse gas emissions control policies had developed such that multi-model comparison studies on climate policy options (e.g., Energy Modeling Forum (EMF), 1993) and IAM reviews were being published (e.g., Tol and Fankhauser 1998). Empirical analysis of climate change impacts took off, slowly, following the groundbreaking 1994 study by Mendelsohn et al. (1994), and Scott Barrett published his seminal game-theoretic analysis of self-enforcing environmental agreements that same year (Barrett, 1994).

After decades of the field's intellectual development, the economics of climate change emerged further on the global stage with the 2006 publication of Sir Nicholas Stern's controversial "The Economics of Climate Change" from the UK's Prime Minister's Cabinet Office for HM Treasury (Stern, 2006). The publication of the "Stern Review", as it was known, was the highest profile analysis by the government of a major economy and it arrived at the stark and somewhat new conclusion that mitigation of climate change was an urgent economic investment. The publicity and controversial findings of the Stern Review attracted many new thinkers to the questions of climate change economics, and the Review's assumptions triggered widespread debate about many key issues in the field—most famously a critique by Nordhaus regarding the unconventional discount rate used by Stern (Nordhaus, 2007). The interest stimulated by the Stern Review—along with other key events of the time such as the entry into force of the Kyoto Protocol and the European Union's greenhouse gas emissions trading scheme in 2005, the awarding of the Nobel Peace Prize to the Intergovernmental Panel on Climate Change and Al Gore in 2007, and the publication of Martin Weitzman's "dismal theorem" paper which called into question the use of cost-benefit analysis to evaluate "fat-tailed" climate change risks in 2009—greatly accelerated the growth of climate change economics research, easily visible in Fig. 1 as the break in the trend around the time.

While academic attention towards climate change has grown steadily since 2006, the past decade has also brought an accelerated sense of urgency and, as a result, engagement with a wider community and a broader set of stakeholders. The climate economics literature has expanded to include scholars from a wide range of methodological backgrounds ranging from applied microeconomics and game theory to finance and macroeconomics, and the application of climate economics in policy-making has expanded throughout many elements of many governments. For example, central banks and finance ministries from around the world are increasingly engaged on the topic of climate change, as illustrated by the growing memberships of organizations such as the Network for Greening the Financial System (counting 138 members at the time of this writing) or the Coalition of Finance Ministers for Climate Action (counting over 90 member countries at the time of this writing); numerous countries around the world are considering or using a social cost of carbon (SCC) in policy-making, as exemplified by the US Federal Government recently adopting sophisticated estimates from the academic economics research community (Environmental Protection Agency, 2023); government agencies are beginning to view support of climate change action as part of their mandate, as shown by the US Securities and Exchange Commission adoption of rules that mandate disclosure of climate-related risks (Securities and Exchange Commission, 2024) and similar disclosure requirements under the European Union's Corporate Sustainability Reporting Directive (European Comission, 2024); and governments are considering how economic impacts of climate change and climate policy will alter their ability to function, as indicated by the US government evaluating the exposure of the federal budget to the risks of climate change (Office of Management and Budget, 2024) and governmental analyses of the fiscal implications of climate policy elsewhere in the world (e.g., Swiss Federal Department of Finance, 2024; Denmark GreenREFORM model Organization for Economic Co-Operation and Development (OECD), 2022). Non-governmental economic organizations, including organs of the United Nations, the Organization for Economic Cooperation and Development, the International Monetary Fund, the World Bank, and regional development banks are similarly, if not more, engaged on the issue of climate change. The demand for expertise in the economics of climate change has never been greater.

This Handbook aims to address this growing demand and is the first part of a two-volume new Handbook on the Economics of Climate Change that seeks to facilitate entry into the literature to a broad audience of students, practitioners, and researchers. This Volume 1 provides an overview of *core* issues, methods, and topics in the economics of climate change. Volume 2 will present surveys of key *new frontiers* in the field, including emerging literatures that explore interactions between the climate and climate policy with economic forces and topics such as the macroeconomy, financial markets, trade, human health, innovation, mitigation technologies, and economic development.

Volume 1 of the Handbook of the Economics of Climate Change provides seven chapters written by internationally recognized experts in the field which introduce readers to these core issues in the economics of climate change.

Chapter 1, "*Introduction to Integrated Assessment Modeling of Climate Change*" by Simon Dietz provides an introduction to and overview of climate-economic modeling, focusing on Integrated Assessment Models that are used to analyze interactions between the climate system and the global economy and to evaluate climate policy ideas holistically.

Chapter 2, "*Empirical Approaches to Climate Change Impact Quantification*" by Dylan Hogan and Wolfram Schlenker reviews the growing set of empirical approaches used to measure the causal impacts of climate change.

Chapter 3, "*Discounting*" by Christian Gollier provides an overview of the economic theory of discounting, which guides how policy can account for future intergenerational impacts of climate change today, drawing from public economics, decision theory, and asset pricing theory to do so.

Chapter 4, "*Adaptation to Climate Change*" by Tamma Carleton, Esther Duflo, Kelsey Jack and Guglielmo Zappala review what we understand about populations' ability to protect themselves from the adverse effects of climate change, focusing on how this knowledge can inform policy.

Chapter 5, "*On International Cooperation*" by Bard Harstad reviews what we understand about the game-theoretic concepts that determine how international climate treaties are developed, rationalizing past treaties and suggesting future directions.

Chapter 6, "*Climate Policy Options*" by Matthew Kotchen overviews how domestic policies create incentives to reduce greenhouse gas emissions, providing a theoretical foundation for a broad array of both proposed and actual policies observed around the world.

Finally, Chapter 7, "*Uncertainty in Climate-Economic Modeling*" by Svenn Jensen and Christian Traeger explores the role of uncertainty in climate-economic modeling, particularly in determining the social cost of carbon and guiding policy decisions.

We believe that the chapters of Volume 1 provide an accessible and informative foundation for anyone looking to become more engaged with the economic analysis of climate change, whether they are experienced economic researchers, policy-makers, or students. As the United Nations, individual governments, and non-governmental organizations move to address both the causes and consequences of climate change, many more individuals will need to engage with the ideas and challenges discussed in these chapters. We hope that compiling this volume will support our rapidly growing community.

Lint Barrage
ETH Zurich

Solomon Hsiang
Stanford University

References

Barrett, S., 1994. Self-enforcing international environmental agreements. Oxford economic papers 46 (ement_1), 878–894.

Edmonds, J., Reilly, J., 1983. Global Energy and CO2 to the Year 2050. The Energy Journal 4 (3), 21–47.

Energy Modeling Forum (EMF) 1993, Global Climate Change: Impacts of Greenhouse Gas Control Strategies, Executive Summary. URL (accessed September 2024): [https://web.stanford.edu/group/emf-research/docs/emf12/WP1201.pdf].

Environmental Protection Agency 2023, Report on the Social Cost of Greenhouse Gases: Estimates Incorporating Recent Scientific Advances URL (accessed September 2024) [https://www.epa.gov/system/files/documents/2023-12/epa_scghg_2023_report_final.pdf].

European Comission 2024, Corporate Sustainability Reporting, URL (accessed October 2024) [https://finance.ec.europa.eu/capital-markets-union-and-financial-markets/company-reporting-and-auditing/company-reporting/corporate-sustainability-reporting_en].

Mendelsohn, R., Nordhaus, W.D., Shaw, D., 1994. The impact of global warming on agriculture: a Ricardian analysis. The American economic review 753–771.

Nordhaus, W.D., 1974. Resources as a Constraint on Growth. American Economic Review 64 (2), 22–26.

Nordhaus, W.D. 1975, Can We Control Carbon Dioxide?, IIASA Working Paper 75–63.

Nordhaus, W.D., 1977. Economic Growth and Climate: The Carbon Dioxide Problem. American Economic Review 67 (1), 341–346.

Nordhaus, W.D. 1980, Thinking about Carbon Dioxide: Theoretical and Empirical Aspects of Optimal Control Strategies, Cowles Foundation Discussion Paper 565, Yale University.

Nordhaus, W.D., 2007. A review of the Stern review on the economics of climate change. Journal of economic literature 45 (3), 686–702.

Nordhaus, W.D. and Tobin, J. 1972, Is Growth Obsolete?, in Economic Research: Retrospect and Prospect, Vol. 5, Economic Growth, NBER Books, Chicago IL, 1–80.

Office of Management and Budget 2024 "The Federal Government's Budget Exposure to Financial Risk Due to Climate Change" (accessed September 2024) [https://www.whitehouse.gov/wp-content/uploads/2024/03/climate_budget_exposure_fy2025.pdf].

Organization for Economic Co-Operation and Development OECD (2022) "Denmark's GreenREFORM model to assess the economic and fiscal impacts of climate policies" (accessed September 2024) [https://www.oecd.org/en/publications/ipac-policies-in-practice_22632907-en/denmark-s-greenreform-model-to-assess-the-economic-and-fiscal-impacts-of-climate-policies_5661304e-en.html].

Securities and Exchange Commission 2024 "The Enhancement and Standardization of Climate-Related Disclosures for Investors" [https://www.sec.gov/rules-regulations/2024/03/s7-10-22].

Stern, N., 2006. Stern Review: The economics of climate change. Cambridge University Press.

Swiss Federal Department of Finance 2024 "Fiscal Sustainability Report for Switzerland" (accessed September 2024) [https://www.newsd.admin.ch/newsd/message/attachments/87128.pdf].

Tol, R.S.J., Fankhauser, S., 1998. On the representation of impact in integrated assessment models of climate change. Environmental Modeling & Assessment 3, 63–74.

Weitzman, M.L., 1974. Prices *vs.* Quantities. The Review of Economic Studies 41 (4), 477–491. https://doi.org/10.2307/2296698.

Weitzman, M.L., 2009. On modeling and interpreting the economics of catastrophic climate change. The review of economics and statistics 91 (1), 1–19.

Chapter 1

Introduction to integrated assessment modeling of climate change

Simon Dietz*
London School of Economics and Political Science (LSE), Houghton St, London WC2A 2AE, United Kingdom
**Corresponding author. e-mail address: S.Dietz@lse.ac.uk*

Chapter Outline

1 Introduction

The starting point for climate economics is surely the observation that climate change is a negative externality. That is, economic activities such as burning fossil fuels have unintended, harmful side effects on the climate and in turn human well-being, which are not accounted for in market prices. So, those causing the harm do not bear the full cost of their actions. An economist then wants to know how big the externality is, how much it will cost to internalize it, and how the externality is optimally internalized: what is the optimal amount of climate change? You can imagine estimating a marginal benefit/damage function, a marginal abatement cost function, and locating where these functions intersect.

Handbook of the Economics of Climate Change, Vol. 1. https://doi.org/10.1016/bs.hesecc.2024.10.002

It is never easy to estimate environmental externalities and optimal pollution, but still climate change is an externality with a difference (Stern, 2007). First, it is truly global in scope. Greenhouse gases (GHGs) are well mixed in the atmosphere, which implies that the marginal effect of a GHG emission is independent of where it takes place, and an emission has consequences everywhere. Second, climate change is a very long-term, persistent problem. This principally stems from the long atmospheric residence time of carbon dioxide, by far the most important GHG. After 100 years, roughly 40 % of a pulse emission of CO_2 will remain in the atmosphere (Ciais et al., 2013). Third, climate affects many aspects of human well-being, so GHG emissions produce impacts on many dimensions or in many "sectors", so to speak. Fourth, and partly as a function of (1)-(3), the impacts of climate change are highly uncertain. Best-case scenarios foresee mild consequences of planetary warming, worst-case scenarios typically invoke notions of a global "catastrophe". The range of outcomes spreads as one moves through the causal chain from emissions to climate responses to economic impacts. In the social sciences, climate change has become known as a "wicked" or even "super wicked" problem for these (and other) reasons (Levin et al., 2012).

To quantify the value of the externality and the optimal amount of climate change, economists have built formal models called Integrated Assessment Models or IAMs. Various definitions exist for IAMs. The word "integrated" is key because it indicates that modeling the economic costs and benefits of climate action requires integrating knowledge across multiple disciplines, at least physical climate science and economics. Some definitions also highlight that IAMs are built to inform decision- and policy-making, thus making the field an applied science (Weyant et al., 1996; Schneider, 1997). Because climate change is an externality with a difference, Integrated Assessment Modeling is hard. Besides finding an appropriate structure to represent the key processes, calibrating the model parameters (and sometimes the initial conditions) presents many difficulties. It is particularly important to think about how to reflect uncertainty, and not to overlook the fact that some value judgements are being made. More on these later.

This chapter has several purposes. The first is to provide further insight into what an IAM is made of and how it works. That is covered in Section 2. The second purpose is to review the IAM literature – key findings, the general evolution of ideas, and how the consensus has shifted. This will be tackled in two parts. The first part is in Section 2.5 and covers the literature from pioneering work in the early 1990s to roughly the early 2010s. During this period, the basic structure of IAMs was similar and fairly stable. The end of this section is an opportune moment to cover critiques of IAMs, which are thus taken up by Section 3. In recent years, the IAM literature has branched out in multiple directions and become more heterogeneous, partly in response to critiques, partly in response to new policy questions. Section 3.4 explores some of these new branches. Lastly, Section 4 concludes with some thoughts on future directions for IAMs, based on the question; what might IAMs still be useful for?

Before moving into Section 2, a brief clarification is in order about the scope of IAMs covered in this chapter. In fact, there are many varieties of IAM. They differ greatly in scope. For example, the term IAM is often used to describe models that focus on the costs of emissions abatement and are used to calculate paths that minimize the cost of a pre-determined climate objective (i.e., perform cost-effectiveness analysis). A large class of energy models is used for this purpose, regularly synthesized by Working Group III of the Intergovernmental Panel on Climate Change (IPCC) among others. Another example is the set of IAMs used to estimate the environmental/human impacts of climate change without undertaking any economic valuation. The Inter-Sectoral Impact Model Intercomparison Project (ISIMIP) coordinates a lot of this work. However, this chapter will deal almost exclusively with the subset of IAMs built to perform cost-benefit analysis.

2 Anatomy of an IAM

Fig. 1 is a diagrammatic representation of an IAM. It corresponds most closely to William Nordhaus' DICE model but it can describe most other IAMs with at most minor modifications.

2.1 Consumption and utility

Most IAMs are social planning models. The planner's objective is to maximize social welfare, which is a function of the flows of utility accruing to individuals over time. Most models maximize the discounted sum of population-weighted utilities:

$$W = \sum_{t=0}^{T} u_t N_t (1 + \rho)^{-t}, \tag{1}$$

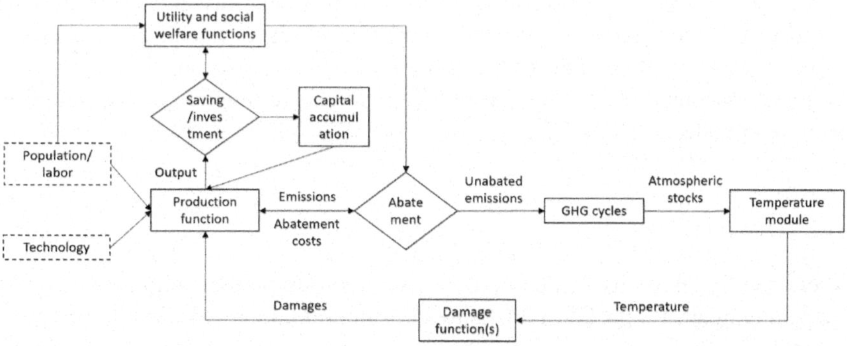

FIG. 1 Flow diagram of a typical IAM. Rectangles with dashed lines denote exogenous variables. Rectangles with solid lines denote functions converting inputs to outputs. Diamonds denote control variables.

where W is social welfare, u is individual utility, N is population, ρ is the utility discount rate or pure rate of time preference, and here time proceeds in discrete steps until some terminal period T. Most IAMs are numerical and solve a finite-time problem like this.

There are several things to note about the social welfare function or SWF (1). First, this represents a globally aggregated model like DICE. Some IAMs are regionally disaggregated, in which case one would not only sum the product of utility and population across time-periods but also across regions, potentially subject to a set of regional welfare weights. Furthermore, Eq. (1) corresponds to regions' objective under full cooperation. The strategic behavior of regions is beyond the scope of this chapter (see Chapter 7 of this volume by Harstad). Second, some IAMs are stochastic, in which case one would calculate the expected value of (1). The resolution of uncertainty over time and how this is accounted for in decision-making is complicated and discussed further in Sections 3 and 5. Third, the distinction between a social planner as the person maximizing (1) and a representative agent is subtle and leaves space for debates about how to interpret utility and the utility discount rate. Fourth, the inclusion of population makes this a "classical/total utilitarian" SWF. Some IAMs omit population from the SWF, solving an "average utilitarian" problem instead. The pros and cons of these different population principles are discussed in Dasgupta (2001) and Blackorby, Bossert and Donaldson (2005). The inclusion of population is non-trivial, as a growing population is equivalent to discounting at a lower rate (Kelly and Kolstad, 2001) – if population grows at constant rate g_n then future utility is effectively discounted at rate ρ - g_n. Fifth, a number of other variants of (1) have been proposed, which apply alternative theories of utility. For example, individual utilities may be combined non-linearly, with higher weight on individuals with lower utilities, as in Prioritarianism (Adler and Treich, 2015). A critical level may be added to utility, an attractive property if population is endogenous (Blackorby, Bossert and Donaldson, 2005). A sustainability constraint may be added to (1) such that the utility discount rate is set to zero if present utility exceeds future welfare (Dietz and Asheim, 2012). And so on.

Instantaneous utility in (1) is usually an iso-elastic function of consumption of an aggregate good, c:

$$u_t = \frac{c_t^{1-\eta}}{1-\eta}, \tag{2}$$

where η is the elasticity of marginal utility of consumption. If climate change is happening against a backdrop of rising consumption, then diminishing marginal utility of consumption, $\eta > 0$, implies discounting future consumption and it is a standard result that in a risk-free setting (1) and (2) yield the "Ramsey rule" $r = \rho + \eta g_c$, where r is the consumption discount rate and g_c is the growth rate of consumption per capita (see Gollier, 2012, and Chapter 3 of this volume). In a regionally disaggregated model, $\eta > 0$ also implies aversion to consumption inequality across space. Therefore, if one sums utility across regions, the social planner will want to equalize regional incomes, all else equal. Many scholars regard this as a problem because the IAM will then generate unrealistic transfers from rich to poor countries, conflating climate policy with wider redistribution objectives. It can be nullified by the use of so-called "Negishi weights" (after Negishi, 1960)[1] or by explicitly restricting redistribution (Dennig et al., 2015). In a stochastic model, $\eta > 0$ implies constant relative risk aversion.

These three different interpretations of η – intertemporal inequality aversion, intra-temporal inequality aversion and risk aversion – create ambiguity about what kind of empirical evidence (if any) should be used to calibrate it (Groom and Maddison, 2019). In practice, most scholars have chosen a value of η in the interval 1–2, usually towards the lower end of the interval, although without any modifications to the basic preference structure in Eqs. (1) and (2) this is inconsistent with large observed premia on risky assets like stocks (the "equity premium puzzle"; Mehra and Prescott, 1985), which is relevant for models that are stochastic. Therefore, it is particularly useful that so-called "recursive" IAMs permit disentangling of risk aversion from inter-temporal inequality aversion in globally aggregated models, because then risk aversion can be raised without also raising inter-temporal inequality aversion (see Section 3.4). Analogous disentangling of inter- and intra-temporal inequality aversion is possible in regionally disaggregated models (Anthoff and Emmerling, 2019).

An important subset of IAMs writes utility not as a function of one good but rather of more than one good, usually two, with the second good being some generic environmental good (Hoel and Sterner, 2007; Drupp and Haensel, 2021). This structure allows for imperfect substitution between material and environmental goods, and in turn the possibility of changing relative prices along the model paths. Where there is a constant elasticity of substitution (CES) between the material and environmental goods, the utility function would be written as

$$u_t = \frac{1}{1-\eta}\left[\gamma_c c_t^{\frac{\sigma_c-1}{\sigma_c}} + (1-\gamma_c)G_t^{\frac{\sigma_c-1}{\sigma_c}}\right]^{\frac{(1-\eta)\sigma_c}{\sigma_c-1}}, \tag{2'}$$

where G denotes the environmental ("green") good, γ_c is the weight of material consumption in utility and σ_c is the elasticity of substitution between the two goods.

[1] Negishi weights are an example of welfare weights in (1) which set the social marginal utility of consumption equal across regions within each period by weighting regional utilities by the inverse of their marginal utility, normalized so the weights sum to one (Nordhaus and Yang, 1996; Stanton, 2011).

2.2 Production and emissions

Fig. 1 also follows the logic of DICE in how it represents production. The genius of DICE lay in linking a neoclassical growth model with a simple climate model, thus providing a conceptually grounded and coherent way of thinking about the co-evolution of the economy and the climate in the long run. Output Y is produced by combining capital K and labor L given total factor productivity or TFP A:

$$Y_t = A_t K_t^{\alpha} L_t^{1-\alpha} \frac{(1 - \Lambda_t)}{(1 + D_t)}, \tag{3}$$

where α is the capital share. $(1 - \Lambda_t)$ is the abatement cost multiplier and $(1 + D_t)$ is the damage multiplier. Damages will be discussed later.

Eq. (3) is a Cobb-Douglas production function. Labor (which is usually set equal to population) is standardly exogenous, growing at a decreasing rate in the future to replicate the expected completion of the global demographic transition by the end of this century (United Nations, 2022). A few papers have started to think about endogenous population. Mejean et al. (2020) consider the possibility that climate catastrophes could reduce global population. Dietz and Lanz (2022) model the effect of climate change on fertility choice, which requires a more complex pair of welfare/utility functions than (1) and (2). TFP standardly grows at an exogenous rate too, which in DICE is gradually decreasing. Some papers have considered endogenous technical change within this framework. For example, Dietz and Stern (2015) analyze a version of DICE where A is increased by spillovers from capital investment, in the tradition of Arrow (1962) and Romer (1986), and is decreased by knowledge depreciation and climate damages.

Being a neoclassical growth model, the capital stock evolves endogenously, increased by investment I and decreased by depreciation δ:

$$Y_t = C_t + I_t, \tag{4}$$

$$K_t = (1 - \delta) K_{t-1} + I_{t-1}. \tag{5}$$

where C is consumption. The saving or investment rate I/Y is one of the two control variables in the model.

GHG emissions are a by-product of economic activity. The easiest way to think about this is to write them as the product of output and an emissions intensity coefficient, which may be changing over time, most likely falling due to autonomous decarbonization. Structural change out of manufacturing into services would be one source of this. However, one must be careful here not to ignore GHGs other than CO_2, and non-industrial GHG emissions sources/sinks such as agriculture and land use. According to one recent source, non-CO_2 GHGs account for more than 25 % of radiative forcing based on 100-year Global Warming Potential, while sources of GHGs other than fossil-fuel combustion account for 23 % on the same basis (World Resources Institute, 2022). The latest version of DICE (Barrage and Nordhaus, 2024) accounts for these issues in approximately the following way:

$$E_t = (1 - \mu_t)(\chi_t Y_t + E_t^{LAND} + E_t^{NON-CO2}), \tag{6}$$

where E stands for total unabated GHG emissions, μ is the emissions control rate, the other control variable in the model, χ is the CO_2 emissions intensity of industrial output, E^{LAND} represents CO_2 emissions from land use, and $E^{NON-CO2}$ represents emissions of other GHGs, for example methane emissions from oil and gas production, livestock and waste. E^{LAND} and $E^{NON-CO2}$ are exogenous, but they can be abated. A model with an explicit agriculture sector using land as a factor of production would be another option, given the importance of agriculture to non-industrial and non-CO_2 emissions, in which case one would have at least a two-sector economic model (see Section 3.4 for further discussion of multi-sectoral models).

The emissions control rate and abatement costs are linked via a total abatement cost function:

$$\Lambda_t = \phi_t \mu_t^{\varphi}, \tag{7}$$

where ϕ_t is a cost coefficient that can fall over time due to technical progress. The exponent φ is usually set above two, which reflects the assumption of increasing marginal abatement costs.

Some IAMs deviate more significantly from the production/emissions structure in (3)-(7). "Analytical" IAMs, whose goal is to simplify the overall optimization problem to derive closed-form analytical solutions, often treat the whole economic growth process as exogenous, as do "social-cost" IAMs that focus on modeling damages in detail. Output and even emissions are exogenous in such models. These IAMs will be discussed in Section 3.4. Modelers can turn to established scenario frameworks for internally consistent output/population/emissions scenarios, such as the Shared Socio-economic Pathways (SSPs) (Riahi et al., 2017) or the probabilistic RFF-SPs (Rennert et al., 2022). Conversely, some IAMs specify a richer production structure in which energy enters the production function (e.g., Golosov et al., 2014; Hassler and Krusell, 2018). For example, we could rewrite the production function (3) as

$$Y_t = A_t K_t^{\alpha} L_t^{1-\alpha-\nu} X_t^{\nu} \frac{(1 - \Lambda_t)}{(1 + D_t)}, \tag{3'}$$

where X is an energy composite with production share ν that is itself a CES combination of clean/renewable and dirty/fossil energy:

$$X_t = \left[\gamma_d X_{d,t}^{\frac{\sigma_X - 1}{\sigma_X}} + (1 - \gamma_d) X_{c,t}^{\frac{\sigma_X - 1}{\sigma_X}} \right]^{\frac{\sigma_X}{\sigma_X - 1}}.$$

In this formulation, CO_2 emissions from fossil-fuel burning are a direct function of fossil energy use X_d, and decarbonization requires substitution of fossil with clean energy X_c, which is governed by an elasticity of substitution σ_X and fossil share γ_d. Further disaggregation of clean and dirty energy types is possible.

This opens up a range of new insights and calibration possibilities (since empirical estimates are available of the elasticity of substitution between energy types), but again care needs to be taken not to reduce the entire climate problem to substituting away from burning fossil fuels for energy – while this is the primary economic problem, other emissions sources and abatement mechanisms exist (which is why it can be useful to retain the abatement cost multiplier in Eq. (3′), suitably recalibrated on abatement potential and costs outside the energy sector). A production structure like this also makes it possible to model the effects of fossil-fuel scarcity. Fossil energy can be modeled as an exhaustible resource that can also be costly to extract, using additional equations for depletion, the scarcity constraint and extraction costs. This enables an examination of the interplay between optimal fossil-fuel extraction and CO_2 abatement, including the so-called "green paradox", which suggests that pricing carbon could accelerate fossil-fuel production and combustion in the short term, as fossil-fuel producers bring forward extraction in anticipation of future climate policy that will destroy their products' value. van der Ploeg (2013) provides an overview of the approach and issues. In practice, most IAMs do not explicitly model fossil fuels. In DICE, fossil-fuel scarcity is handled via a constraint that total cumulative CO_2 emissions do not exceed the carbon embodied in remaining fossil-fuel resources, but the constraint tends not to bind (Barrage and Nordhaus, 2024). The reason is the abundance of coal.

Eq. (7) admits exogenous technical progress in emissions abatement technologies. Endogenous technical progress could be handled in this framework by introducing a functional relationship between the cost coefficient and cumulative past abatement (Goulder and Mathai, 2000; Bramoullé and Olson, 2005). Such a relationship is often characterized as "learning by doing", although saying so risks overlooking what is in reality quite a complex set of drivers of falling unit abatement costs, including economies of scale in manufacturing (Grubb et al., 2021). Endogenous technical progress via R&D investment would require a richer model (e.g., Popp, 2004; Acemoglu et al., 2012).

2.3 Climate

The climate module of an IAM usually comprises (a) one or several GHG cycles and (b) a temperature module. The former converts GHG emissions into atmospheric concentrations, while the latter converts atmospheric concentrations via radiative forcing into global mean temperature change. However, it turns out that in some models a useful shortcut is possible, directly from emissions, cumulated over time, to temperatures (see below).

Most simple models of the GHG cycle partition the system into a series of reservoirs or boxes, between which GHGs are exchanged. These boxes can be interpreted as GHG sinks, e.g., the atmosphere, the biosphere and the oceans. Sometimes, however, a box is a mathematical abstraction rather than corresponding precisely to an actual physical component of the climate system, as in the key model of Joos et al. (2013). GHG diffusion between different boxes can be represented by a system of equations:

$$\boldsymbol{m}_{i,t} = \boldsymbol{A}_i \boldsymbol{m}_{i,t-1} + \boldsymbol{b} E_{i,t}, \tag{8}$$

where $\boldsymbol{m}$ is a vector of stocks of GHG i with a length equal to the number of boxes, $\boldsymbol{A}$ is a transition matrix with elements describing the diffusion speed of the GHG from one box to another, and $\boldsymbol{b}$ is a vector of emissions shares flowing into each box. The length of $\boldsymbol{m}$ varies from model to model. DICE traditionally had three boxes for CO_2. The model of Joos et al. (2013) has four. By contrast, it is sufficient to use one box for methane (CH_4), a powerful GHG with a much shorter atmospheric residence time.

If $\boldsymbol{A}$ and $\boldsymbol{b}$ are constant, the GHG cycle is linear, i.e., it is not state-dependent. However, some GHG cycles are state-dependent. In particular, the effectiveness of the biosphere and the oceans at removing atmospheric CO_2 decreases with climate change, a positive feedback in the system. Some climate modules, notably the FaIR model (Leach et al., 2021) that is used by Working Group I of IPCC on physical climate science to make some climate projections, include a mechanism whereby elements of $\boldsymbol{A}$ are state-dependent.[2]

The stock of GHGs can be converted into an atmospheric concentration M using

$$M_{i,t} \equiv \mathbf{d}_i' \boldsymbol{m}_{i,t}, \tag{9}$$

where $\boldsymbol{d}'$ is a vector that performs the mapping by assigning weights to the contribution of each stock to M.

The next stage is to estimate radiative forcing as a function of the atmospheric concentration. Here, the functional form depends on the GHG. A general expression capable of nesting the forcing relationships of different GHGs (see Myhre et al., 2013) as special cases is provided by the FaIR model:

$$F_{i,t} = f_{1,i} \ln\left(\frac{M_{i,t}}{\underline{M_i}}\right) + f_{2,i}\left(M_{i,t} - \underline{M_i}\right) + f_{3,i}\left(\sqrt{M_{i,t}} - \sqrt{\underline{M_i}}\right), \tag{10}$$

where F is forcing, $\underline{M}$ is the pre-industrial concentration, and f_1, f_2 and f_3 are coefficients. The basic idea here is that, depending on the GHG, forcing is either a concave or linear function of atmospheric accumulation, and if concave it is best represented by either a logarithmic or square-root relationship. For CO_2, most IAMs only include a logarithmic term. For CH_4 and nitrous oxide,

[2] In FaIR, diffusion of CO_2 out of the atmosphere depends on cumulative CO_2 emissions and temperature.

the forcing-concentration relationship is well approximated by the square-root term. For the many other relatively trivial GHGs, the relationship is linear.

The last step is from forcing to global mean temperature change. This is also generally done using a system of equations, which is referred to in climate science as an Energy Balance Model or EBM. An EBM explains changes in global mean temperature by imbalances in the Earth's energy budget. The imbalance in this case is F from (10), the anthropogenic greenhouse effect. The EBM simulates heat diffusion between heat boxes, i.e., relatively homogeneous vertical layers of the atmosphere/ocean. The system can be represented as

$$T_t = \boldsymbol{l}'\left(\boldsymbol{J}\boldsymbol{h}_{t-1} + \boldsymbol{k}\sum_i F_{i,t}\right), \tag{11}$$

where $\boldsymbol{h}$ is a vector of heat boxes, $\boldsymbol{J}$ is a matrix of heat diffusion rates, $\boldsymbol{k}$ apportions forcing to each heat box and $\boldsymbol{l}'$ maps heat in the system's boxes into global mean temperature T. The number of heat boxes tends to range from one to three, where the first/top box is the atmosphere and uppermost ocean layer, and subsequent boxes are layers of the deep ocean. The basic purpose of using more than one heat box is to create some thermal inertia in the system, so that temperatures respond to emissions with an appropriate lag. DICE has two. The latest version of FaIR has three.

As mentioned above, it turns out that for some IAM applications, especially where there is a pressing need to minimize the number of state variables in the model (e.g., for analytical modeling), a shortcut is possible. Both observational data and simulation modeling results from complex Earth System Models indicate that there is a nearly linear relationship between temperature and cumulative CO_2 emissions (Matthews et al., 2009; Zickfeld et al., 2009; Collins et al., 2013). Climate scientists have named the constant coefficient that multiplies cumulative CO_2 emissions to give temperature the "Transient Climate Response to cumulative carbon Emissions" (TCRE). The physical reasons why TCRE is constant both with respect to time and atmospheric CO_2 are discussed in Dietz and Venmans (2019). With this shortcut, steps (8)-(11) can be skipped with little loss of fidelity by simply writing

$$T_t = \xi \sum_{s=0}^{t} E_s \tag{11'}$$

where ξ is the TCRE. There are two things to watch out for here. The first is that (11′) ignores the short time delay between a CO_2 emission and the resulting constant/peak warming response. The delay is of the order of ten years. It is straightforward to introduce a delay into (11′), but the delay is ignorable if the interest is in long-run properties. The second is that the linear temperature response to emissions only applies to CO_2. One way of dealing with non-CO_2 emissions in the framework of (11′) is by assuming total warming is a fixed fraction of warming induced by CO_2 alone, e.g., 10 %

higher (Allen, 2016). Accordingly, one would multiply the TCRE coefficient by a fixed factor (say 1.1) and then run the rest of the IAM with CO_2 only. This will likely mis-estimate efficient abatement of non-CO_2 emissions, however, as they will always be proportional to CO_2.

2.4 Damages

Perhaps the most important component of an IAM is the damage function or set of damage functions. After all, without damages there is no reason to control emissions. Unfortunately, this has historically also been the most speculative IAM component, in large part because the body of theory and evidence on which modelers can rely has been meagre.

So far in this chapter we have been mostly working within the framework of DICE, in which damages enter the production function as a multiplier, $1/(1 + D_t)$. This immediately implies several assumptions. First, damages are proportional to output. Second, there is Cobb-Douglas substitutability between climate damages and the rest of production. Note, this is not the same as assuming natural and produced capital are perfect substitutes either in production or consumption/utility, as has sometimes been claimed. Drupp and Haensel (2021) have a precise discussion of this. Third, damages explicitly reduce the level of output, rather than the growth rate.

In many IAMs, damages are a polynomial or power function of global mean temperature. It can be helpful to think in terms of a polynomial. Thus, in general:

$$D_t = \psi_n T_t^n + \psi_{n-1} T_t^{n-1} + \cdots + \psi_2 T_t^2 + \psi_1 T_t + \psi_0 \tag{12}$$

The choice of the order of the polynomial is highly consequential – very different perspectives on the impacts of warming can be formalized in this way. The standard assumption is order two: quadratic. This was originally just an assumption but it may nonetheless be a good approximation of the aggregate damage-warming relationship obtained using detailed empirical estimates of damages at the sectoral level (Hsiang et al., 2017). However, other scholars have advocated, literally or effectively, for polynomials of much higher order. Their argument, which largely predates the accumulation of empirical evidence on damages at fine scales, is as follows. Suppose the first few degrees of warming cause damages of at most a few percent of output. Knowing this permits a quadratic function to be calibrated, but then a quadratic damage function is not convex enough to generate very large damages at high temperatures. Assuming high temperatures have the capacity to cause damages of tens of percent of output, this requires a polynomial of much higher order (or a power function with a large exponent). Weitzman (2012) proposed a damage function including T raised to almost the seventh power, for example. Note that writing damages as $1/(1 + D_t)$ ensures the damage multiplier is strictly positive at finite temperatures. Otherwise, consumption can be non-positive and utility can be undefined. This problem is a manifestation of Weitzman's Dismal Theorem (Weitzman, 2009), which is further discussed in the next section. Bounding the utility function is another solution. The problem is generally more acute the higher the order of the polynomial.

There are several important departures from (12) in the literature. Going back to early work by Fankhauser (1995), Nordhaus (1991), Tol (1995) and others, some IAMs include a set of damage functions, one for each of several damage sectors (e.g., agriculture, coastal, energy use, etc.). Neglected for a while except in a specific branch of the literature using multi-sectoral models (see Section 3.4 for a discussion), this sector-by-sector approach has recently been revived by some of the new social-cost IAMs (Rennert et al., 2022; United States Environmental Protection Agency, 2023). It allows calibration on sector-level data and can support diverse functional forms, but incorporating interactions between sectors is challenging and so the question arises; are total damages equal to the sum of sectoral damages, or more or less than them? Related to this, some IAM papers, usually building on DICE, partition damages into so-called "market" and "non-market" components, which are then combined with a utility function extended to two goods like (2′), thus permitting more flexible assumptions about substitutability (Sterner and Persson, 2008; Drupp and Haensel, 2021). Building on recent empirical results in macroeconomics (Dell, Jones and Olken, 2012; Burke, Hsiang and Miguel, 2015), some IAMs have written the growth rate of output, not level losses as in (3), as a function of temperature (Ricke et al., 2018). This choice is also highly consequential because growth damages compound over time. It is not a dichotomy though – options exist for implementing mixed growth/levels damages or in other words imperfect persistence of damages (Dietz et al., 2021; Kikstra et al., 2021). When damages work at least partly on the growth rate, then the assumption that the level of output depends only on the level of temperature is also relaxed, although this latter assumption could also be relaxed more directly by specifying damages as a function of temperature *change* (Tol, 1997). On a similar theme, some work has made the depreciation rate of capital dependent on climate, motivated by the idea that natural disasters destroy capital (Bretschger and Karydas, 2018). Lastly, new applications with Dynamic Stochastic General Equilibrium (DSGE) models make possible the implementation of damages as stochastic shocks (Cai and Lontzek, 2019). This is arguably a more direct way of modeling climate "disasters", cascading/compounding impacts and more generally moving away from smooth, long-term trends, something that some scholars are calling for (e.g., Zscheischler et al., 2018).

2.5 Optimization and comments on solving IAMs

This archetypal model would be optimized by simultaneously choosing the emissions control rate μ_t and the investment/saving rate I_t/Y_t for all t to maximize the SWF (1). The terminal period T is set sufficiently far in the future to avoid terminal-value problems on policy-relevant timescales. The problem is constrained by the initial values of the state variables, N_0, A_0, K_0, E_0^{LAND}, $E_0^{NON-CO2}$, $\boldsymbol{m_0}$ and $\boldsymbol{h_0}$.[3] It is also subject to the equations of motion (5), (8) and (11) (or (5) and (11′)). Additional constraints are sometimes imposed. This can be for conceptual reasons, e.g., a constraint on fossil fuel resources as mentioned above, or they can be imposed simply to help locate the optimum. The latter constraints are where science meets art and tend, sadly, to be poorly documented.

A model such as this can be solved using a variety of off-the-shelf, non-linear programming algorithms. Recursive IAMs are solved using a different set of dynamic programing methods that are generally much more complex and computationally demanding. In the above model, quantities are computed, not prices, but prices can still be calculated using shadow prices. Notably, the optimal carbon tax is the negative of the ratio of the marginal welfare cost of emissions to the marginal value of capital or consumption, where the marginal values are the change in (1) with respect to each. This is also an opportune moment to mention that while the whole problem thus far has been cast as one of social planning, it is relatively straightforward to establish conceptual equivalence between this problem and a decentralized market equilibrium where firms face a Pigouvian carbon tax based on the marginal damage caused by their emissions (Golosov et al., 2014). More complex model structures are equivalent to more complex markets.

All this amounts to using the IAM to solve for the optimal schedule of emissions/taxes. But often IAMs are not run with the purpose of calculating optimal policies, because in fact some policy questions call on the modeler to look away from the optimum. This is particularly true of the literature devoted to estimating the social (i.e., marginal) cost of GHGs. The social cost of a GHG can be estimated on any emissions path. All that is required is that the model be run twice, the second time with an incremental emission in whatever year is of interest. The difference in social welfare due to the marginal emission, suitably normalized in money terms (Anthoff, Hepburn and Tol, 2009), is the social cost of the GHG. There is demand in various countries/institutions for estimates of the social cost of GHGs. Moreover, policymakers have been particularly interested in estimates of the social cost of GHGs on the most likely emissions path (Rennert et al., 2022), which is unlikely to be optimal from society's point of view due to coordination problems, market failures, policy failures, etc. Therefore, this literature has converged on using exogenous emissions paths. Section 4 provides further discussion of issues of policy application/usefulness like this.

[3] Assuming changes in the exogenous state variables are explicitly modeled; alternatively, the entire time series of these variables constitute boundary conditions.

Lastly, the length of the model's time step can matter. Longer time steps save on computation. Early versions of the DICE model had a ten-year time step, while early versions of the PAGE model had a variable time step including later periods that were several decades long (Hope, 2006). However, long time steps can generate optimal solutions that are a poor approximation of the equivalent solution with a short time step of, say, one year (Cai, Judd and Lontzek, 2012). Shorter time steps are therefore recommended. DICE now runs with a five-year time step. Many models are annual.

3 The first generation of IAMs: conceptual development and results

The first IAM results began to appear in the early 1990s. Nordhaus, building on a program of research originating in the 1970s, published results from the first version of the DICE model in Nordhaus (1992, 1993a, 1993b, 1994). The key message was that GHG emissions should be reduced, but only modestly. Using the emissions control rate and temperature change as measures of policy stringency, Fig. 2 illustrates this result. The optimal emissions control rate starts at about 10 % in 1995 and increases to about 15 % by 2100. This reduces warming, but only a little. In 2100, global mean temperature is reduced by about 0.2 °C relative to the no-policy baseline and is still more than 3 °C above pre-industrial. The modest level of optimal emissions control can be contrasted with what is required in this first version of DICE to stabilize emissions at the 1990 level and even more so what is required to limit warming to 1.5 °C. The carbon tax rate corresponding to the optimal emissions control path starts at about USD3/tCO_2 in 1995, increasing to USD11/tCO_2 in 2100.[4]

Most other analyses produced similar results. Using the FUND model, Tol (1997) estimated optimal warming in 2100 of around 3.5 °C, like Nordhaus just a few tenths of a degree below the no-policy baseline. Peck and Teisberg (1992) generated very similar results with their CETA model. Across the wider – but still small – literature of the time, optimal carbon taxes and social costs of carbon (optimal or not) were mostly in the range USD3–10/tCO_2 (Fankhauser and Tol, 1997). The best estimate from the first version of the PAGE model was at the top of this range (Plambeck and Hope, 1996).

Thus, the first wave of studies agreed that GHG emissions should be controlled but not drastically. Optimal near-term emissions control rates should be modest and possibly increased in the medium and long term. Later, Nordhaus would characterize this result as a "climate-policy ramp" (Nordhaus, 2007). This metaphor he developed in order to draw a contrast with the analysis of the Stern Review on the Economics of Climate Change, a British government report originally published in 2006 (Stern, 2007). The Stern Review used the PAGE

[4] All carbon taxes and other monetary amounts are reported in 2022 prices in this chapter, adjusting for inflation from the IAM's base year using US GDP deflator data from the World Bank.

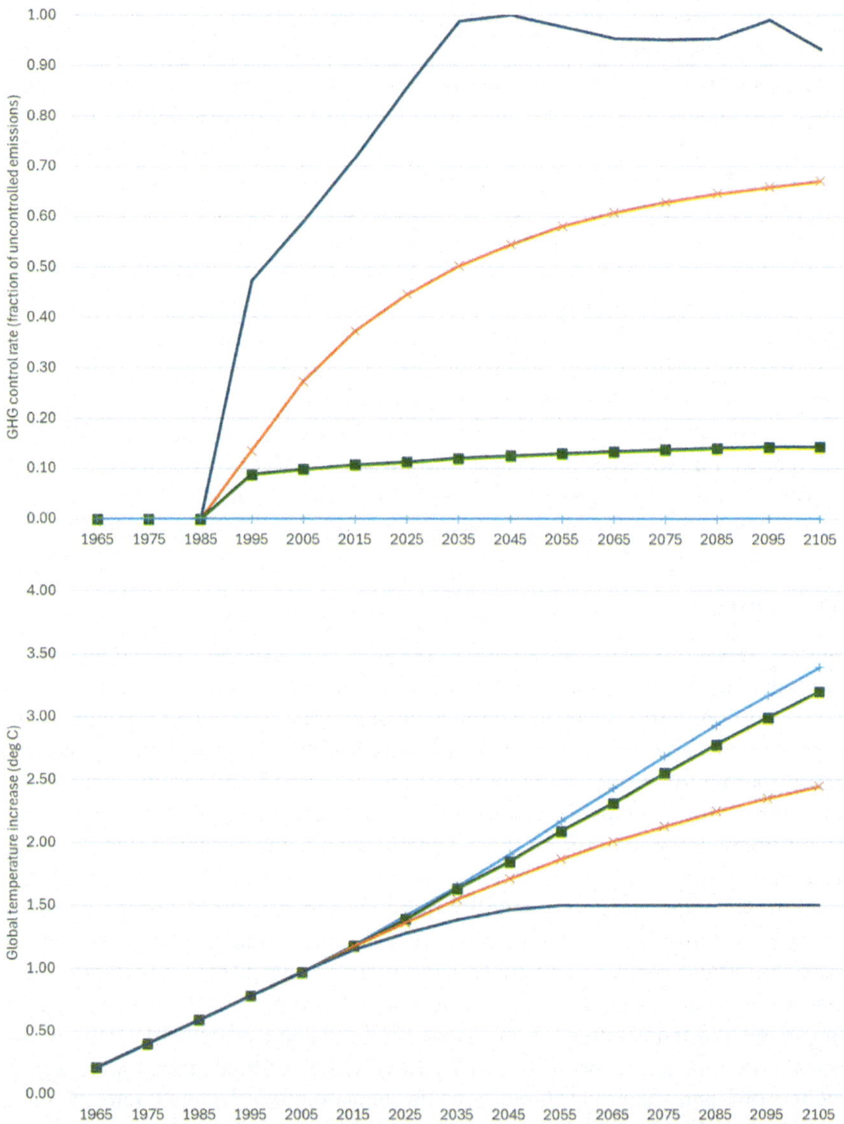

FIG. 2 Optimal GHG control rates (top) and global mean temperatures above pre-industrial (bottom) in the DICE model. The four paths are no-policy/uncontrolled emissions (+), optimal emissions (squares), emissions stabilization (crosses) and limiting warming to 1.5 °C (–) (note this last run is also constrained to limit the warming rate to 0.2 °C per decade). *Reproduced from data in Nordhaus (1992).*

IAM (2002 version) to estimate marginal and total damage costs on exogenous emissions paths. It did not estimate the optimal emissions path per se. It reported a marginal damage cost of around USD140/tCO_2 on the no-policy baseline,[5] which was clearly much higher, perhaps an order of magnitude higher, than most of the previous literature. The Review concluded atmospheric GHGs should be stabilized at around 450–550ppm, requiring rapid emissions reductions in the near term. For context, the composite atmospheric GHG stock was estimated at 472 ppm in 2021 (European Environment Agency, 2024).

The Stern Review was not the first IAM study to estimate higher climate damages and imply higher optimal emissions reductions (e.g., Cline, 1992). However, it was the most prominent and so a great deal of attention immediately focused on why its conclusions were so different. As Geoffrey Heal put it in a 2009 article reflecting on the Stern Review,

"we have probably seen more economics articles on climate change in the last year and a half than in all preceding history" (Heal, 2009, p4).

The resulting literature was very helpful in shedding light on the key sensitivities in first-generation IAMs and moving the literature forward.

3.1 Discounting

One key sensitivity is the discount rate (see Chapter 3 of this volume by Gollier for further discussion). Indeed, the debate about appropriate discount rates for analysis of long-term issues like climate change was given added impetus by the Stern Review and often labeled "Stern versus Nordhaus" at this time. It stands to reason that the discount rate is an important driver of IAM results, since emissions abatement involves short-run costs and delivers a stream of benefits far into the future, with the majority of those benefits then being distant in time from the abatement costs. Adopting a "prescriptive" approach and a particular ethical position, Nicholas Stern set the utility discount rate $\rho = 0.1\%$ and the elasticity of marginal utility $\eta = 1$. By contrast, at the time Nordhaus' preferred values, based on a "descriptive" approach that sought to match the consumption discount rate with estimated returns to capital, were $\rho = 1.5\%$ and $\eta = 2$. Supposing constant, deterministic consumption/capita growth of 2 % (in fact growth was not the same in the Stern Review's PAGE scenarios as it was in DICE), this generates a difference in the consumption discount rate of 3.4 % points, which is a large difference indeed. Numerous IAM results exhibit strong sensitivity to the discount rate (see Fig. 4 for an illustration with DICE). Over time, the consensus on appropriate discounting parameters appears to have shifted towards Stern (Drupp et al., 2018; Office of Management and Budget, 2023). The prescriptive approach generally points towards low rates, while

[5] The Stern Review's marginal damage cost exhibited strong sensitivity to the emissions path on which it was calculated. On low emissions paths, the initial marginal damage cost was up to 50 % lower.

declining equilibrium real interest rates have made adherents of the descriptive approach more predisposed to low rates (Bauer and Rudebusch, 2023).

3.2 Uncertainty

Another key sensitivity is the treatment of uncertainty. This was in fact an overlooked difference between Stern and Nordhaus, as Stern ran the PAGE model under uncertainty and estimated marginal and total damages in terms of changes in expected utility, whereas Nordhaus' default analysis was deterministic, based on best guesses of each parameter individually. However, the issue was brought to the fore by the contributions of Martin Weitzman (2007, 2009, 2012). Weitzman was motivated by the long right tail of the distribution of equilibrium climate sensitivity, i.e., how much temperature would increase in equilibrium after doubling the atmospheric CO_2 concentration relative to pre-industrial (Fig. 3). He noticed that climate scientists could not rule out equilibrium climate sensitivities of 10 °C or more and speculated that so much warming would have catastrophic impacts in the sense of driving consumption towards zero. With a "fat tail" on the equilibrium climate sensitivity and damages approaching 100 % of consumption, technically it can follow that the expected social cost of carbon is unbounded; what he called the "Dismal Theorem" (Weitzman, 2009; see Buchholz and Schymura, 2012, for a particularly creative and clear restatement of the mathematical intuition).

But while there are various ways to negate the Dismal Theorem *stricto sensu* (Millner, 2013), Weitzman's work had broader relevance in highlighting the importance of formally modeling uncertainty and appropriately considering the shapes of the distributions of key parameters, particularly those that might be strongly skewed. Accordingly, his work was central in stimulating several new avenues of research. These included tracing through the implications of possible catastrophic damages, usually represented by polynomial or power damage functions of higher order (Weitzman, 2012). These naturally give rise to a higher social cost of carbon, stronger optimal emissions abatement or proportional changes in related output variables such as the total welfare cost (Dietz, 2011; Ackerman and Stanton, 2012; Anderson et al., 2014). But the implications of uncertainty run deeper than just randomizing and otherwise changing parameters.

Another avenue of research contemplated the same climate science as Weitzman but took a close interest not so much in the shape of individual distributions in Fig. 3, but rather in the co-existence of multiple distributions (in fact, the Dismal Theorem was also influenced by this property). The state of knowledge this represents is second-order uncertainty, often known as "ambiguity". In decision theory, it is often argued though not universally agreed that decision-makers, e.g., a global social planner, should be ambiguity-averse or otherwise take precautionary action under second-order uncertainty (Gilboa, 2009). Several papers have explored the implications of ambiguity/second-order uncertainty for climate policy in IAMs, using different theoretical

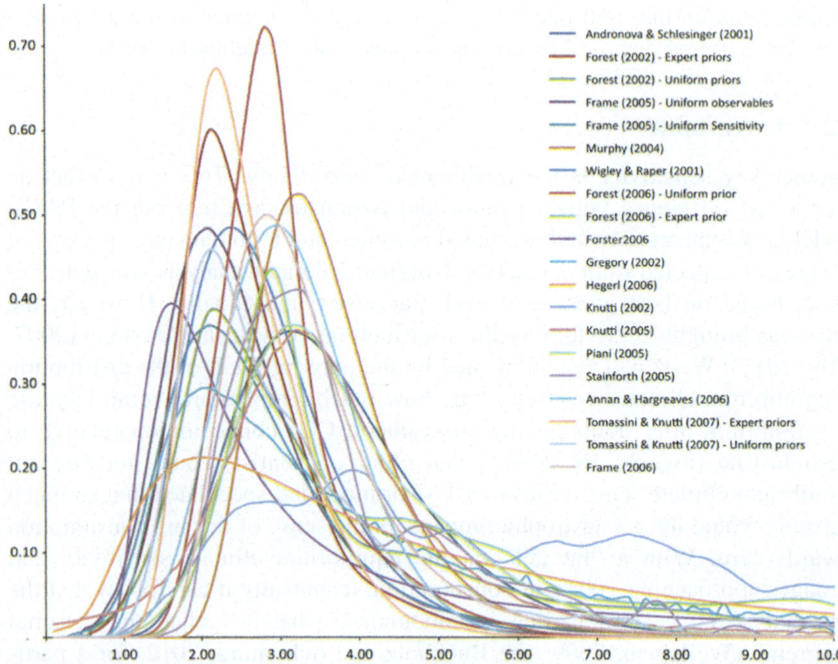

FIG. 3 Probability density functions for the equilibrium climate sensitivity according to various published studies from the 2000s. All distributions have a long right tail of estimates of high climate sensitivity with low probability. Multiple distributions are indicative of uncertainty about the true distribution. *Reproduced from Milner, Dietz and Heal (2013).*

frameworks (Athanassoglou and Xepapadeas, 2012; Milner, Dietz and Heal, 2013; Lemoine and Traeger, 2014). These papers also estimate a higher social cost of carbon, and stronger optimal emissions abatement.

A third avenue of research overlooked (or did not consider normatively relevant) the existence of second-order uncertainty but was nonetheless interested in the implications of first-order uncertainty, i.e., risk. A key issue in this regard is how uncertainty is resolved over time. The early IAM literature took simple approaches to this. One is conceptually to compute optimal emissions for different values of the model's parameters, thus solving a deterministic problem repeatedly, and then to calculate the expectation of optimal emissions. Another is conceptually to compute optimal emissions under uncertainty and to assume commitment to the optimal path after uncertainty is fully resolved. In practice, where exogenous emissions scenarios are used, this dichotomy translates into estimating the social cost of carbon either as the disutility of expected damages (e.g., Anthoff, Tol and Yohe, 2009), or the expected disutility of damages (e.g., Stern, 2007). For a given model and parameter vector, the latter approach yields a higher social cost of carbon (Dietz, Hope and

Patmore, 2007) and stronger optimal emissions abatement. The difference can be thought of as a climate risk premium. But neither approach is satisfactory. They are opposite ends of a spectrum. The former assumes all uncertainty is resolved before emissions are optimized, once and for all. The latter assumes no uncertainty is resolved before emissions are optimized, once and for all. In reality, the state of uncertainty changes over time (it may tend to gradually decrease but can also increase) and the planner can change policy as it does so. This dynamic has been picked up by the literature on recursive IAMs, briefly discussed in Section 3.4.

3.3 Spatial inequality

Although the marginal warming effect of GHGs is the same regardless of where they are emitted, the impacts of that warming are by no means the same everywhere. People's physical exposure to climate change varies significantly from place to place. Additionally, a wide body of literature from across the social sciences has documented how vulnerability to climate change depends negatively on development – development reduces the socio-economic impacts of given changes in physical climate.

To explore spatial inequality in an IAM first requires the model to be regionally disaggregated, of course. First-generation IAMs that are spatially disaggregated only disaggregate to a limited extent. RICE, the regionally disaggregated counterpart to DICE, divided the world into 12 regions at this time, FUND divided it into 16 regions, and PAGE eight regions. More recent work on spatial inequality using first-generation IAMs by Dennig et al. (2015) and Anthoff and Emmerling (2019) has developed methods of further disaggregating these large regions, into quintiles of the regional income distribution and countries respectively. Social-cost IAMs, discussed in Section 3.4, have at least country-level resolution and are well suited to studying spatial inequality in principle. Spatial IAMs, also discussed in Section 3.4, typically have very fine spatial resolution, e.g., 1° latitude × 1° longitude. There is usually no inequality within the smallest spatial unit of the IAM, although it is possible to specify an income distribution within each unit, as Dennig et al. (2015) did.

The spatial distribution of damages is another key ingredient. This mostly flows from the damage function parameters for each spatial unit. Some studies have explicitly parameterized the relationship between damages and income, however, by means of an income elasticity of damages (e.g., Anthoff and Tol, 2012; Dennig et al., 2015; Anthoff and Emmerling, 2019). While this relationship is difficult to calibrate and may not be estimated with high statistical confidence, it is nonetheless pedagogically helpful for thinking through what differential vulnerability to climate change means in an IAM. A positive elasticity means that absolute damages are increasing in income. An elasticity of one is the special case where absolute damages are increasing in income, but relative damages are constant as income rises. This special case is in fact baked into damage functions of the multiplicative sort that do not consider income-dependence (Eqs. 3 and 12, for example). An elasticity of zero means that absolute damages are independent of income. A negative elasticity means that absolute damages are higher in poor countries. After accounting for any income-dependence and assuming that Negishi weights are not being used, the weight given to damages in aggregate welfare then depends on the concavity of the utility function in Eq. (2), i.e., inequality aversion. Even if damages are constant relative to income (unit elasticity), damages in poor countries are given higher weight by concave utility functions. A prioritarian SWF has the same effect (Adler et al., 2017). This is why early IAM papers framed the issue in terms of so-called "equity weighting" (Azar and Sterner, 1996; Fankhauser, Tol and Pearce, 1997; Anthoff and Tol, 2010). Anthoff and Emerling (2019) have proposed a welfare function that disentangles intertemporal inequality aversion from spatial inequality aversion, unlike Eq. (2), which conflates them via the parameter η.

Overall, this strand of the literature finds that the social cost of carbon is higher once spatial inequality is accounted for, considerably so. The size of the effect is potentially comparable to that of Nordhaus-Stern variations in the discount rate (Dennig et al., 2015). It is important to emphasize that the literature analyzes spatial inequality *together with* intertemporal inequality. IAMs are dynamic models, and it is the evolution of spatial inequality that matters most, not spatial inequality today. Growth makes possible the "Schelling conjecture" that poor countries' "best defense against climate change may be their own continued development" (Schelling, 1992, p6). It is an empirical question though: a major driver of the higher social cost of carbon in models with spatial inequality is the possibility that, even though average incomes rise, some people become poorer in the future than they are today (Dennig et al., 2015).

3.4 Imperfect substitutability of environmental goods

In the adroitly titled "An even Sterner Review", Sterner and Persson (2008), building on Hoel and Sterner (2007), also contributed to the literature on the Stern Review. In fact, it is possible to see their paper as another contribution to the discounting debate, but it deserves to be in a category of its own. Sterner and Persson's point is as follows. Suppose we are evaluating the costs and benefits of GHG abatement against a development path where consumption of material goods is growing faster than consumption of environmental goods. There is plenty of evidence to support this ordering of growth rates. Then, environmental goods become more scarce and, if the two goods are imperfect substitutes, the relative price of environmental goods increases. Climate change contributes to this increasing relative scarcity of the environment via non-market damages. Increasing relative scarcity in turn increases the welfare cost of climate damages and makes GHG abatement more attractive. This dynamic can only be *explicitly* modeled in an IAM with multiple goods entering the utility function, such as (2′). Damages then also have to be unbundled, with separate functions/parameters for each good.

Taking the DICE model and unbundling environmental goods from aggregate consumption based on some illustrative assumptions (i.e., not attempting a rigorous calibration), Sterner and Persson showed that the optimal emissions path looks fairly similar to that generated using Stern's discounting assumptions (see Fig. 4). Subsequently, Drupp and Haensel (2021) have pursued the same task of incorporating two goods and limited substitutability into DICE, investigating the issues more thoroughly. Their headline estimate is about a 50 % increase in the social cost of carbon, and a reduction in optimal peak temperature of 0.6 °C (though optimal peak warming is still above 3 °C without any further changes). Note that a wider literature in the 2000s and 2010s has explored the substitutability of environmental goods (e.g., Gollier, 2010; Traeger, 2011; Baumgärtner et al., 2015; Drupp, 2018), so the two papers discussed here are less isolated than they might seem.

3.5 Levels versus growth damages

As discussed in Section 2, the standard, DICE-like damage function assumes that climate change reduces the level but not the growth rate of

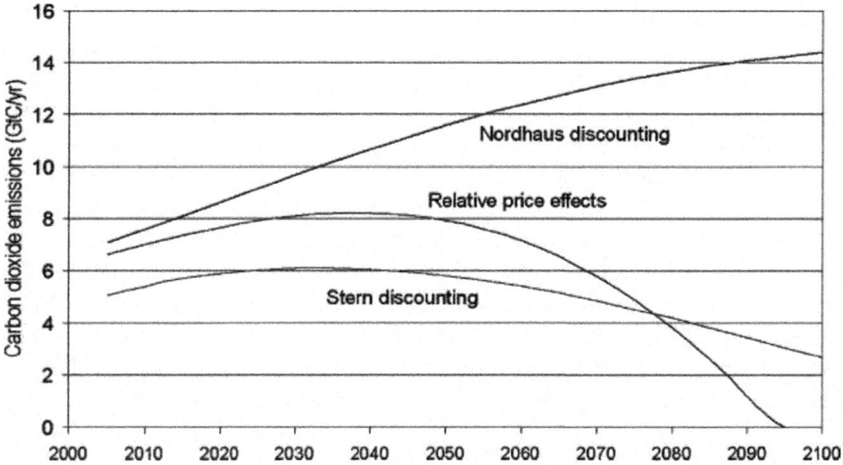

FIG. 4 Optimal unabated CO_2 emissions in the DICE-2007 model under alternative discounting assumptions ("Nordhaus/Stern discounting") and in an extended DICE-2007 model with two goods, material consumption and an environmental good ("Relative price effects"). Nordhaus discounting represents $\rho = 3$ % initially, decreasing to 2.3 % in 2100. Stern discounting represents $\rho = 0.1$ % (constant). The Relative price effects run sets ρ equal to Nordhaus discounting and uses the utility function in Eq. (2') instead of (2). The elasticity of marginal utility $\eta = 1$ in all cases. *From Sterner and Persson (2008).*

GDP. This default assumption is highly consequential given that impacts on GDP growth compound over time, gradually driving a wedge between the projections made using these different formulations. The implications of levels versus growth damages have been explored in the DICE model by Dietz and Stern (2015), and Moore and Diaz (2015). The former paper adapted the production function in DICE to incorporate endogenous growth from spillovers to capital accumulation, alongside a partitioning of climate damages between the level of output and capital/TFP, i.e., keeping the overall value of damages D_t the same. These changes alone increased the social cost of carbon in the initial period by about 70 %. Moore and Diaz (2015) also adapted the DICE model, applying damages to TFP growth or capital depreciation, and dividing the world into two regions (rich and poor), which enabled calibration of damages on the empirical work of Dell, Jones and Olken (2012). These changes had a bigger effect, increasing the social cost of carbon by a factor of close to seven and bringing optimal temperatures from over 3.5 °C in 2100 to below 2 °C. It is a well-known feature of Dell, Jones and Olken (2012) that their estimated climate impacts are much larger in poor countries, so the large effects in Moore and Diaz (2015) are driven by depressed growth in those countries and the welfare consequences of them (see Fig. 5), linking this contribution to the literature on spatial inequality. Ricke et al. (2018) conducted a similar analysis, feeding temperature projections taken directly from complex climate models through a set of growth-damage functions based on Dell, Jones and Olken (2012) as well as Burke, Hsiang and Miguel (2015). They estimated large damages, including a median global social cost of carbon of USD549/tCO_2. Their results also showed that global damages and patterns of country-level damages depended sensitively on the precise specification of growth damages (i.e., whether differentiated between rich and poor countries or pooled, and whether lagged or not). At the time of writing, the debate about levels versus growth damages remains very active and without settlement (see recent contributions by Newell, Prest and Sexton, 2021; Casey, Fried and Goode, 2023; Nath, Ramey and Klenow, 2024), which makes it important for future modeling to respond to advances in knowledge.

3.6 Adaptation IAMs

Whether damages affect GDP levels or growth, a common feature of almost all damage functions is that the role of adaptation is already accounted for and implicit. This not only makes assumptions about adaptation opaque, but adaptation can also be thought of as a choice variable, alongside mitigation. A small number of papers responded to this by attempting to decompose damages into adaptation costs and residual damages, such that adaptation is a choice associated with cost and benefit functions, the latter in terms of avoided

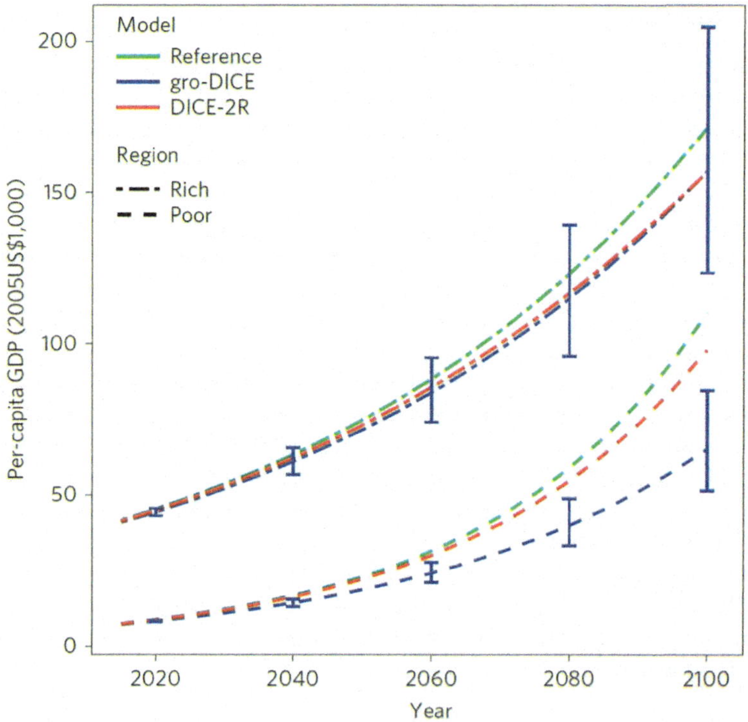

FIG. 5 GDP per capita for the rich and poor world regions in the extended DICE model of Moore and Diaz (2015). The reference run excludes damages. The DICE-2R and gro-DICE runs include damages under no-policy baseline emissions. DICE-2R uses standard levels damages as per Eq. (3); gro-DICE uses growth damages based on Dell, Jones and Olken (2012), which involves applying damages to the TFP growth rate instead. The error bars show uncertainty in the estimates arising from a change in the growth damage parameters of +/− one standard error (i.e., the 68 % confidence interval).

damages (de Bruin, Dellink and Tol, 2009; Agrawala et al., 2011).[6] It is difficult to find empirical counterparts for the key parameters governing adaptation costs and benefits at the global level, something that has held back this branch of the literature, but these studies have been helpful in clarifying that although adaptation and mitigation are substitutes as climate policy tools, they are only partially so and the optimal combination involves deploying both, with some disagreement about sequencing/timing (see Chapter 5 of this volume by Carleton et al. for a much more extensive discussion of adaptation to climate change).

[6] In fact, the PAGE model has always had the capability of choosing the level of adaptation to reduce damages (Plambeck and Hope, 1996; Hope, 2006).

3.7 Summary

The initial phase of development of IAMs from the early 1990s to about the early 2010s was characterized by a relatively small number of relatively homogeneous IAMs. Most early studies estimated a gentle optimal climate policy ramp, but this early consensus was disturbed by the Stern Review in particular. Subsequent avenues of research – what the first generation of IAMs was used for – were arguably shaped primarily by three factors: (i) the particular modeling assumptions of Stern versus Nordhaus and other previous studies, (ii) the state of climate science at the time, (iii) what was possible to do in first-generation IAMs. These three factors came together to direct a lot of attention to the SWF and utility function, i.e., how time, uncertainty, spatial inequality and environmental substitutability were represented. It is possible to identify a trend towards higher optimal emissions abatement and higher social costs of carbon (Tol, 2023), broadly in line with international climate goals (Haensel et al., 2020). The literature essentially established a set of sufficient rather than necessary conditions for ambitious optimal emissions abatement. High optimal emissions abatement can be obtained in, for example, (i) a globally aggregated, deterministic model with a low discount rate, or (ii) a globally aggregated, stochastic model with tail risk of high climate damages but run with a high discount rate, or (iii) a regionally disaggregated, deterministic model with a high discount rate, and so on.

4 Critiques of IAMs

IAMs have been frequently criticized and this is a good moment to discuss some of those criticisms, because they provide background context for more recent model developments.

One set of criticisms is essentially a rejection of the normative legitimacy of welfare economics as applied to climate policy by IAMs (Gardiner, 2004). Alternative normative/political frameworks that have been applied to climate change include capability theory (Schlosberg, 2012), human rights (Caney, 2008), virtue ethics (Jamieson, 1992), the precautionary principle (Hartzell-Nichols, 2017), and climate justice (Schlosberg and Collins, 2014), noting that these are not mutually exclusive. These criticisms are important, but they are outside the scope of this chapter. In the view of this author, a degree of ethical pluralism in climate policy, i.e., drawing from multiple frameworks, is perfectly defensible (Dietz, Hepburn and Stern, 2009).

Another set of criticisms attacks IAMs based on the strongly held intuition that IAMs' valuation of climate damages and their prescribed optimal emissions reductions are too low. As should be evident by now, many assumptions in an IAM can drive low damage valuations and low optimal emissions reductions. It follows that these critiques include: excessively high discount rates; insufficient treatment of uncertainty, especially catastrophic risk;

misspecification of abatement costs and clean technology development leading to overestimated costs; misspecification of the climate module leading to a climate response to emissions that is too slow/mild; and misspecification of damages leading to underestimation. Thus, in a sense, many of the developments in the literature outlined above were born out of critiques from within the IAM paradigm, accompanied by practical remedies. It is important to avoid portraying an overly simplistic, straw-person version of the IAM literature, which ignores the role of debate from within.

But the critiques cannot simply be dismissed at this point. Damages are a major reason why. They have often been central to criticisms that IAMs are wrong on climate policy (Ackerman et al., 2009; Pindyck, 2013; Stern, 2013). To some, it is self-evident that damages in IAMs are too low, because they are inconsistent with the impacts described by climate science (Heal, 2009; Stern, 2013). The argument is, however, not so straightforward to make. First, the kinds of scientific study that critics have in mind do not provide contradictory economic estimates – they generally estimate physical and environmental effects of climate change. That leaves open a wide spectrum of economic responses, beyond the immediate province of scientific expertise per se. Second, it is impossible to completely validate IAMs' damage estimates, even in today's climate. Important reasons why include that we don't observe a counterfactual world without climate change, which would serve as a baseline against which we could measure changes, and that we don't directly observe many types of damage even in the actual world (e.g., non-market damages). Therefore, it is fair to say nobody knows what "true" damages are. Third, some critiques are potentially based on a misperception that enormous losses of global GDP due to climate change – many tens of percent – are a necessary condition for high optimal emissions abatement. In turn, such critiques are based on the firmly held belief that optimal emissions abatement is truly high. But Haensel et al. (2020) showed that DICE can prescribe optimal warming consistent with the United Nations' Paris Agreement's 1.5 °C target when damages are assumed to be "only" 6.7 % of GDP at 3 °C, provided other assumptions on discounting, the climate module, etc. are conducive. The Stern Review (Stern, 2007) delivered a similar result.

Nonetheless, there are clear grounds for suspicion that damages have been underestimated in *most* studies, particularly early studies. One is that studies building damage estimates sector-by-sector (the so-called enumerative approach) or otherwise using empirical data for damage estimation usually end up with missing damage channels/mechanisms. Although including these missing mechanisms could in principle reduce damage estimates, it is much more plausible that doing so would increase them.[7] In addition, it seems

[7] Since the 2013 version, Nordhaus has made a subjective upwards adjustment to damages in DICE to account for missing damages. This adjustment started at 1.25 times the coefficient on the

reasonable to assume that extremely large increases in global mean temperature (say 10 °C) would be immensely damaging (Weitzman, 2009; Ackerman, Stanton and Bueno, 2010), and although these lie far outside the realm of probable warming, even a very small probability of such outcomes would be sufficient to weigh heavily on the social cost of carbon, as Weitzman's work shows. Lastly, estimates of the social cost of carbon have increased over time (Tol, 2023), very likely due in part to more studies with higher damages.

While several papers have proposed ways to assume larger climate damages, the inability to constrain the specification of damages with empirical evidence – in effect the freedom to make almost whatever assumption one likes – has been a clear weakness. It contributes greatly to the criticism that IAMs lack robustness to uncertain/contested input assumptions, and not just those relating to the damage function (Pindyck, 2013). A counterargument is that this is largely a feature of our underlying knowledge about climate change and optimal responses, IAMs or not. To the extent that we are still uncertain about the temperature response to GHGs, for example, this is very much a problem for climate science (Hsiang and Kopp, 2018). Uncertainty about the correct discount rate is largely driven by differences in value judgements and in what way value judgements are relevant – arguably formal economic modeling plays a constructive role here in making the consequences of these differences transparent.

Still, it leaves open the critique that IAMs give a misleading impression of precision and knowledge (Schneider, 1997; Pindyck, 2013), and that it is better to set climate-policy guardrails in the spirit of the precautionary principle and use economics to evaluate how to respect those guardrails instead (Ackerman et al., 2009; Stern, Stiglitz and Taylor, 2022). Section 4 returns to this issue. On the topic of using IAMs to make policy recommendations, Stern, Stiglitz and Taylor (2022) make the point that the climate externality interacts with several other market failures and constraints in the economy, and that this could plausibly affect model results. In general, and for reasons of tractability, the IAM literature has tended to treat the climate externality in isolation. Exceptions include Barrage (2020), who studies optimal carbon taxation with preexisting distortionary capital and labor taxes in an extended DICE model, and Rezai and van der Ploeg (2016b), who study carbon taxation and renewables subsidies in an IAM with a positive innovation externality associated with learning-by-doing alongside the climate externality.

5 Recent advances and how the field has evolved

Section 2.5 discussed various developments in the IAM literature in the 2000s and 2010s, within the context of what we might call first-generation models

---

(footnote continued)
quadratic term in the damage function (Nordhaus, 2014) and has now risen to 0.5 % of GDP at 3 °C warming (Barrage and Nordhaus, 2024).

(e.g., DICE, FUND and PAGE). These models are still in use, have been developed significantly since their original versions, and can still be useful (see Section 4). Therefore, this period of scholarship has not come to a definitive end. However, the 2010s did see the development of several new classes of IAM, of which this section provides an overview. These new classes of IAM have emerged either in response to shortcomings of first-generation models, thus in response to critiques of the sort aired in the previous section (and that could not easily be overcome by tweaking first-generation models as described in Section 2.5), or they have emerged to address new policy questions or exploit developments in adjacent sub-fields of economics like economic geography. In general, a key feature of the contemporary IAM literature is that it has become more heterogeneous.

5.1 Recursive IAMs

Recognizing the importance of uncertainty and the limitations of the early literature in analyzing it, a class of models emerged in the 2010s that have been called "recursive IAMs" (Lemoine and Rudik, 2017). They are so called because solving a problem under uncertainty in which the planner receives new information and adjusts climate policy in response requires recursive dynamic programming methods.[8] Lemoine and Rudik (2017) introduce the approach and review the literature up to the mid-2010s. Note that Kelly and Kolstad (1999) built a recursive IAM well ahead of its time.

The essence of the planner's problem in a recursive IAM is a sequence of choices over the control variables, one choice in each period, where current utility is known but future utility remains uncertain. The decision problem can be written as a Bellman equation, where in each period the planner chooses climate policy to maximize welfare as the sum of current flow utility and discounted expected welfare in the next period. Since next period's problem is also the sum of current utility and discounted expected welfare in the next-but-one period, a recursive problem is set up, so one works backwards from the end of the model horizon, ensuring that every period's controls are optimal given future controls. Although elegantly simple in principle, such planning problems are hard to solve computationally. In particular, the recursive dynamic construction of the problem suffers from the curse of dimensionality, i.e., the exponential increase in computational complexity as the number of state variables increases. This has significantly constrained the complexity of IAMs that can be solved in this way – most recursive

[8] This is not to be confused with the sense of the word "recursive" in the literature on computable general equilibrium (CGE) models. In these models, recursive means that agents make decisions based only on current prices. Agents are myopic because they assume prices will remain unchanged in the future. In recursive IAMs, agents are forward-looking. CGE modelers have adopted various strategies in practice for mimicking aspects of forward-looking behavior by recursive/myopic agents. Readers are referred to Babiker et al. (2009) for a discussion of these issues. CGE models are covered in more detail later in this section.

IAMs are simplified versions of DICE, where the number of state variables is reduced to around four or five, usually by simplifying the climate module (as explained above, DICE has five state variables in the climate module alone).

Appropriately, recursive IAMs have generated rich but nuanced insights into the role of uncertainty in optimal climate policy (see Chapter 8 of this volume by Traeger). Starting with the simplest insight, controlled comparisons with deterministic models show that, in general, uncertainty increases the social cost of carbon and optimal emissions reductions, particularly where the uncertainty applies to damages (Crost and Traeger, 2014) or represents stylized tipping points in the climate system (Lemoine and Traeger, 2014; Cai and Lontzek, 2019). The role of uncertainty about economic growth is more ambiguous (Jensen and Traeger, 2014; Cai and Lontzek, 2019).

Crost and Traeger (2013) showed using a recursive dynamic version of DICE with uncertainty about damages that optimal emissions are lower than the expected value of optimal emissions across many deterministic runs of the same model. The result is intuitive: climate policy under this latter approach, which the reader will recall was taken by some of the earlier literature, is too lax because taking expectations over optimal solutions to the deterministic problem implies the planner has the luxury of waiting for uncertainty to be resolved, thus underestimating the "insurance" motive for emissions abatement.

Kelly and Tan (2015) analyzed optimal emissions in a similar recursive dynamic version of DICE, where uncertainty applies to the equilibrium climate sensitivity instead. Unlike most other recursive IAMs, their model allows for learning about the true value of the uncertain parameter, rather than simply reacting to stochastic realizations of the parameter value while maintaining constant beliefs about it. They found optimal emissions are higher when the planner can learn about the uncertain parameter and update their beliefs, compared to a situation where the planner cannot learn. This is also intuitive: without the possibility of learning, climate policy is too strict because the insurance motive is overestimated. Fitzpatrick and Kelly (2017) provide a complementary result. They analyzed a policy constraint on temperature consistent with the Paris Agreement temperature goals, also in a recursive dynamic DICE model with uncertain equilibrium climate sensitivity and learning. In such a model, there is a welfare cost of inflexibility associated with having to stick to a pre-determined climate goal despite new information being revealed as time passes. We might extend this result to speculate that first-generation approaches to uncertainty, where the planner chooses the optimal path in the first period under uncertainty and does not then deviate from that path (e.g., Stern, 2007), are similarly costly.

Recursive IAMs are particularly suited to analyzing the effects of economic and/or climate shocks that are discontinuous and/or irreversible in nature (e.g., Cai and Lontzek, 2019, see Fig. 6). These shocks are naturally represented by various kinds of stochastic process. Recursive IAMs also enable risk

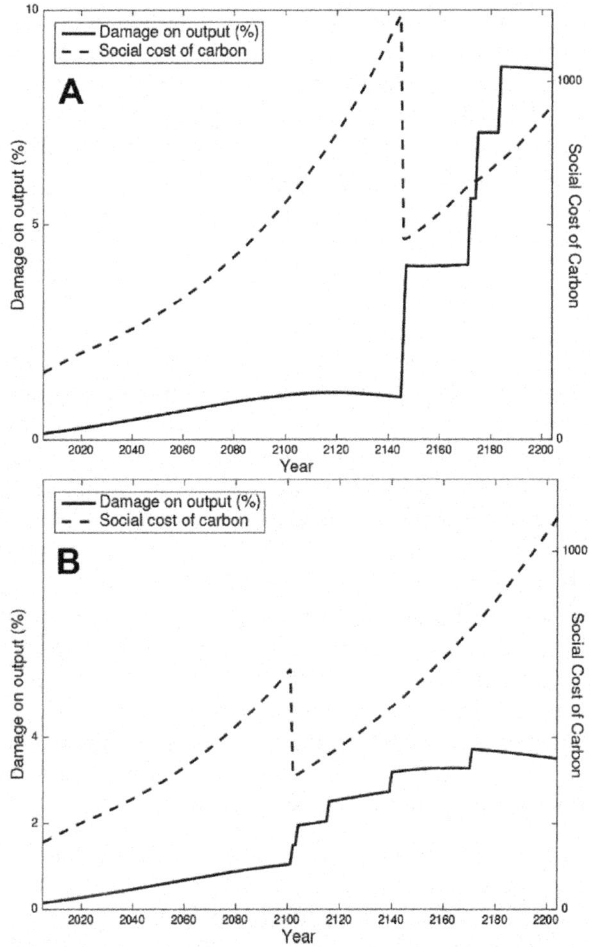

FIG. 6 Two example runs from the recursive version of DICE built by Cai and Lontzek (2019), in which rising output causes rising temperatures, which can in turn cause a stylized climate tipping point to be crossed, in 2146 in run A and 2102 in run B. Once the tipping point is crossed, damages (solid line) occur via a series of jumps of different heights and intervals. The social cost of carbon (dashed line) falls after the tipping point is crossed in Cai and Lontzek (2019) under the assumption that once crossed, damages are irreversible. However, note the possibility of crossing a tipping point strongly increases the *ex ante* SCC in their study.

and time preferences to be disentangled, using the formulation of Epstein and Zin (1989)/Weil (1990). Doing so has been shown to have a large effect on the social cost of carbon and optimal emissions reductions (Crost and Traeger, 2014; Cai and Lontzek, 2019; Daniel, Litterman and Wagner, 2019; Hambel, Kraft and Schwartz, 2021), but results seem to suggest this comes more from effectively reducing the intertemporal discount rate than from a risk premium introduced by ramping up risk aversion. Given the perceived importance of climate risks, this might be paradoxical. Lemoine and Traeger (2016), Barnett, Brock and Hansen (2020), and Rudik (2020) incorporate ambiguity in recursive IAMs. As advances in computational economics such as high-performance computing and machine learning enable more complex models to be solved, expect to see recursive IAMs used to integrate a wider range of uncertainties, while making fewer simplifications.

5.2 Analytical IAMs

First-generation IAMs are too complex to yield closed-form analytical solutions for key variables such as emissions and carbon prices, so they are solved numerically. This has led to the criticism that IAMs are "black boxes" whose internal workings are hidden and poorly understood. Such a criticism applies with even more force to most of the other classes of model discussed in this section, which are, in general, more complex than the first-generation IAMs.

As a response, several "analytical IAMs" have been developed, which can be solved analytically with a view to obtaining transparent policy rules. The idea is that a policymaker or any other non-expert model user should be able to clearly see what exogenous parameters the IAM's results depend on and how the results change when these parameters are varied. An analogy would be the Taylor rule for the nominal interest rate in monetary policy. The literature was spawned by Golosov et al. (2014), who derived a surprisingly simple formula for the optimal carbon tax/social cost of carbon from a quite general IAM under a set of particular assumptions. Suppose that:

1. The SWF is average utilitarian or equivalently population does not grow, which means population is dropped from Eq. (1);
2. The utility function in (2) is logarithmic ($\eta \approx 1$);
3. Damages enter the production function multiplicatively as in (3);
4. Moreover, assuming temperature responds instantly to increases in atmospheric CO_2, then damages can be written as a negative exponential function of the atmospheric stock of CO_2, $1 - D(M_{CO2,t}) = \exp[-\psi(M_{CO2,t} - \underline{M_{CO2}})]$;
5. The CO_2 cycle is linear;
6. Capital fully depreciates in each period, where a period is a decade.

Then the optimal carbon tax/social cost of carbon τ is

$$\tau_t = Y_t \psi \frac{1 + \rho}{\rho + \delta_{CO2}} \tag{13}$$

Note this corresponds to Eq. (11) in Golosov et al. (2014) using the notation of this paper, assuming ψ does not vary over time and, for the sake of simplicity, that there is a one-box model of the carbon cycle with a decay rate for atmospheric CO_2 of δ_{CO2}. What is notable about this formula is that τ is a constant proportion of output, therefore it grows at the same rate as the economy, and it depends transparently on just three parameters: it is decreasing in the utility discount rate ρ, increasing in the damage function coefficient ψ, and decreasing in δ_{CO2}.

Getting to an expression for the optimal carbon tax as simple as this requires numerous assumptions, including the seven stated above, as well as wider assumptions embedded in the model structure outlined in Section 2. Therefore, naturally attention turned to relaxing some of these assumptions. Two papers that have worked directly to generalize the optimal carbon tax rule in Golosov et al. (2014) are Rezai and van der Ploeg (2016a), and van der Ploeg and Rezai (2021). Across these two papers, the authors examine a range of extensions. Here I will focus on some of the more conceptually and quantitatively important extensions (as revealed by their analysis).

Population growth at rate g_n coupled with the SWF in (1) leads to

$$\tau_t \approx Y_t \psi \frac{1 + \rho - g_n}{\rho - g_n + \delta_{CO2}}, \tag{13'}$$

which is intuitive given that population growth in a classical/total utilitarian SWF effectively lowers the discount rate to ρ-g_n, as mentioned above. The optimal carbon tax is increasing in g_n and if g_n is non-constant, which we expect it to be, then τ is no longer a constant proportion of output.

Now relaxing the assumption of logarithmic utility (i.e., allowing $\eta \neq 1$) gives

$$\tau_t \approx Y_t \psi \frac{1 + \rho - g_n + (\eta - 1)(g_c - g_n)}{\rho - g_n + (\eta - 1)(g_c - g_n) + \delta_{CO2}}. \tag{13''}$$

This is decreasing in the elasticity of marginal utility of consumption, which is also intuitive because in this globally aggregated, deterministic set-up, an increase in η just serves to increase the consumption discount rate. But of course the scope of the result is limited by ignoring spatial inequalities and risk/uncertainty. Again, the constancy of τ with respect to output is unlikely to hold.

One of the assumptions in Golosov et al. (2014) that draws from the basic model in this chapter is that damages affect the level of output. However, we know from studies with numerical IAMs that shifting damages on to the growth rate of output can greatly increase the social cost of carbon. This was formalized in van der Ploeg and Rezai (2021) by parameterizing the degree of persistence of damages on TFP. For the case of complete/perfect persistence, i.e., what is sometimes called "pure growth damages",

$$\tau_t \approx Y_t \psi \frac{[1 + \rho - g_n + (\eta - 1)(g_c - g_n)]^2}{[\rho - g_n + (\eta - 1)(g_c - g_n)][\rho - g_n + (\eta - 1)(g_c - g_n) + \delta_{CO2}]} \tag{13'''}$$

What this implies is that if damages affect the growth rate rather than the level of output, then the optimal carbon tax is $(1 + r_n)/r_n$ larger, where $r_n = \rho - g_n + (\eta - 1)(g_c - g_n)$, the population-adjusted consumption discount rate. As r_n will be in the region of a few percent, $(1 + r_n)/r_n$ will be a large number and it becomes analytically clear that pure growth damages will generate a very large increase in the optimal carbon tax.

A couple of further extensions are also worth reporting here. First, a linear, one-box carbon cycle is not a good model of CO_2 accumulation. Golosov et al. (2014) considered more complex removal dynamics but their carbon cycle still assumed linearity/state-independence. van der Ploeg and Rezai (2021) instead considered the TCRE model, in which temperature is a linear function of cumulative CO_2 emissions, which implicitly represents a non-linear, state-dependent carbon cycle with a positive feedback, as discussed above. This also requires rewriting damages as a function of temperature instead of atmospheric CO_2. Going back to the simple case of (13) for ease of comparison, the optimal carbon tax with the updated climate is

$$\tau_t = Y_t \hat{\psi} \frac{1 + \rho}{\rho}, \tag{13''''}$$

where $\hat{\psi} = \xi\psi$ is the product of the TCRE and the damage function coefficient. Thus, just updating the climate module does not appear to alter the basic result in Golosov et al. (2014) that the optimal carbon tax is a constant proportion of output. However, this is only true for the minimal extension where atmospheric CO_2 is substituted by temperature in the damage function (Dietz and Venmans, 2019), which amounts to assuming damages are close to linear in temperature. As such, it is a stronger assumption than the counterpart in Golosov et al. (2014), assumption #4 above: this allows for convexity in the damage function as long as it is approximately exactly offset by the concave relationship between atmospheric CO_2 and warming. Both formulations assume an instantaneous temperature response to emissions, which overlooks the roughly decade-long delay in this response. Traeger (2023) derives an analytical expression for the effect of the delay and estimates it reduces the optimal carbon tax by 20–40 %.

Second, suppose the overall optimization problem is no longer unconstrained welfare maximization but rather welfare maximization subject to a binding temperature constraint such as well below 2 °C or 1.5 °C as in the Paris Agreement. Working from the TCRE model of (13''''), the optimal carbon tax is the sum of the unconstrained optimal carbon tax and a Hotelling-like term, which grows at the discount/interest rate and reflects optimal intertemporal use of the cumulative CO_2 emissions budget. The expression is somewhat complex and can be found in van der Ploeg and Rezai (2021; Equation 10).

These results give a flavor of what is possible in analytical IAMs. Other important contributions to this strand of the literature include van den Bijgaart,

Gerlagh and Liski (2016), Gerlagh and Liski (2018), Dietz and Venmans (2019), and Traeger (2023). Barrage (2014) has also evaluated the performance of the Golosov et al. (2014) pricing rule numerically.

5.3 Social-cost IAMs

The US government has been using estimates of the social cost of carbon in cost-benefit analysis of federal regulations since 2008. This is surely one of the most important policy applications of IAMs given the importance of the US geopolitically and as a GHG emitter, i.e., given the potential scope of climate policy that could be influenced. An Interagency Working Group was set up to provide harmonized estimates of the social cost of carbon based on the three principal first-generation IAMs: DICE, FUND and PAGE (Interagency Working Group on Social Cost of Carbon, 2010). Recognizing the shortcomings of first-generation IAMs and with the particular purpose of estimating the social cost of carbon (thus being much less interested in optimal paths per se), the Interagency Working Group then commissioned the National Academy of Sciences, Engineering and Medicine to produce a report on how to improve the estimates (National Academies of Sciences, Engineering, and Medicine, 2017). This report made a number of recommendations, including:

- Taking an integrated, modular approach to build better models and draw more readily on multi-disciplinary expertise.
- Using a simple Earth system model to serve as the climate module, which "satisfies well-defined diagnostic tests".
- Building a damages module with transparent calibration, suitable disaggregation, and which can leverage the emerging empirical literature on climate damages.

Following the NASEM report, a pair of modeling groups in the US built IAMs that focused on implementing these recommendations. I will therefore call these IAMs "social-cost IAMs". One group has built the GIVE model (Rennert et al., 2022), the other the DSCIM model (Rode et al., 2021; Carleton et al., 2022; United States Environmental Protection Agency, 2023). Independently of the US social cost of carbon process, another group including this author has built the META model, which also belongs to this class (Dietz et al., 2021). Following the above recommendations, one distinctive feature of social-cost IAMs is their modularity – modules (formally, subsets of the system of equations constituting a full IAM) can be relatively easily coupled and uncoupled. This facilitates controlled model inter-comparisons (e.g., alternative damage modules as in United States Environmental Protection Agency, 2023), and easy extensions, for example, incorporation of various tipping points as additional modules (Dietz et al., 2021). It has been supported by the development of a bespoke scientific computing framework in the Julia language, Mimi.jl. Another distinctive feature is spatial disaggregation to at least the country level, which all three models mentioned here achieve (DSCIM has approximately 24,000 county-like regions). This enables the inequality implications of climate change to be relatively thoroughly explored (but see spatial IAMs below). Moreover, it facilitates calibration of country-level damages on the results of empirical studies that are often at this level of spatial disaggregation.

Initial results from social-cost IAMs have suggested high social costs of carbon, towards the upper end of the range of estimates in the literature. The most recent estimates from the GIVE and DSCIM models are in United States Environmental Protection Agency (2023). For a central, near-term consumption discount rate of 2 %, the social cost of carbon in both models is USD190/ tCO_2. The two models' convergence on the same value is noteworthy. Partly it comes from using the same input socio-economic and emissions scenarios, as well as the same climate module, but the two models treat damages differently, so it is therefore somewhat surprising. Analysis by Rennert et al. (2022) indicates that the most important reason for the higher social cost of carbon in the GIVE model relative to DICE-2016 is actually a reduction in the discount rate, with damages being a distant second. It is unclear how generalizable this result is, however. Note that neither the GIVE nor DSCIM estimates for the United States Environmental Protection Agency (2023) include so-called equity weighting, as the rules of the time for US federal cost-benefit analysis did not allow it. This is, however, a natural capability of social-cost IAMs and is now allowed under new federal rules (OMB, 2023).

5.4 Spatial IAMs

Building on theories and methods from economic geography, in recent years spatial equilibrium IAMs have been built to explore the implications of climate change for the distribution of economic activity and people around the world. Desmet and Rossi-Hansberg (2024), who have been at the forefront of this branch of the literature, provide a review and label these "spatial IAMs" for short. Although spatial disaggregation has been achieved in other IAMs, notably social-cost IAMs but even in first-generation IAMs, spatial IAMs are distinctive in exploring the equilibrium effects of climate change over space much more thoroughly. To start with, these models are usually much more spatially disaggregated than other IAMs, often to the level of 1°x1° grid cells (Conte et al., 2021; Desmet et al., 2021), which, to give a sense of complexity, gives around 17,000 grid cells that include some land. More importantly, households and firms are able to move across space in response to differences in local factors such as the cost of goods, amenities, availability of factors of production, and innovation/ technology. Climate change affects local land availability, amenities and firm productivity, depending on the model (it can also potentially affect population size). Localities trade goods with each other according to comparative advantage and product differentiation. The ability of households and firms to move depends on frictions such as migration, trade and transportation costs. Fixed physical

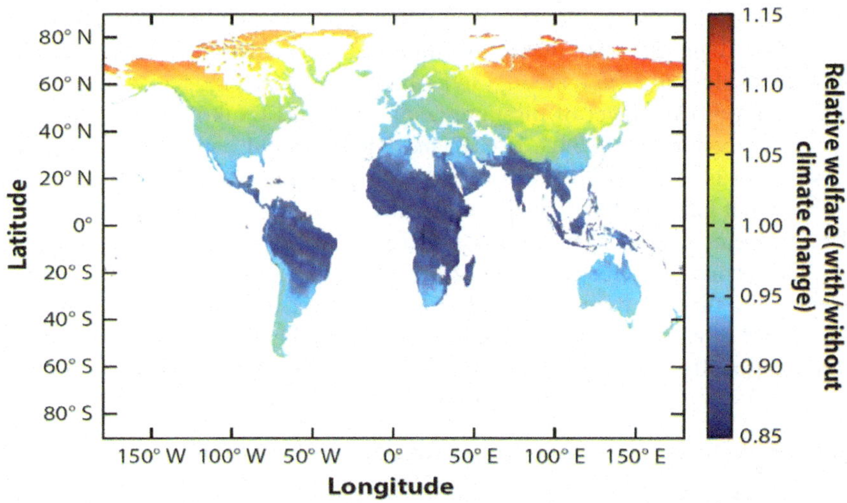

FIG. 7 Map of welfare costs of climate change on no-policy baseline emissions scenario. *From Cruz and Rossi-Hansberg (2024), as adapted and reproduced in Desmet and Rossi-Hansberg (2024).*

infrastructure and local knowledge clusters generated by forces of agglomeration are also in a sense frictions – they are not cheap to rebuild elsewhere.

Like the earlier branch of the IAM literature, spatial IAMs are motivated by the heterogeneity of climate impacts across space. Broadly speaking, simulations with spatial IAMs tell a story of a poleward advance of economic activity and people, especially in the Northern Hemisphere, in search of more benign local climates in a warming world (Desmet and Rossi-Hansberg, 2015; Cruz and Rossi-Hansberg, 2024; see Fig. 7). This is a potentially important form of adaptation at the global level, but it depends on barriers to migration and trade. Migration and trade appear to be partial substitutes as adaptation margins. Models also simulate a parallel retreat from coastlines exposed to sea-level rise (Desmet et al., 2021), with agglomeration effects and other frictions making this retreat more interesting and complex than in other models. Adaptation through relocation can be highly effective in this context too, although overall the welfare cost of sea-level rise is much smaller than that of the direct temperature channel (Desmet and Rossi-Hansberg, 2024), a result corroborated by social-cost IAMs (United States Environmental Protection Agency, 2023). Social-cost IAMs simulate the defense of coastlines from sea-level rise where it is economic to do so, which spatial IAMs so far do not do.

Spatial IAMs enable an investigation into how much damage/welfare estimates might be biased by averaging in IAMs with coarser spatial resolution. The more spatial disaggregation, the more a model can track the effect of climate change on spatial inequality. If this correlates with income inequality it can have first-order welfare implications globally, as explained above. And the more spatial disaggregation, the more capacity there is to adapt through spatial reallocation of firms and households within larger spatial units, which would also affect damages and in turn welfare. Cruz and Rossi-Hansberg (2024) provide results suggesting the bias in globally aggregated models is quite large. But even a modest level of disaggregation to World Bank regions (similar to the disaggregation in FUND, PAGE and RICE) would eliminate most of the bias except in the very long run.[9] Conte, Desmet and Rossi-Hansberg (2022) use a spatial IAM to study the effects of introducing a unilateral carbon price in the European Union, showing that spatial reallocation can lead to counter-intuitive economic effects of adding carbon costs to the EU economy. However, at the time of writing, spatial IAMs have not been used to estimate the social cost of carbon or optimal emissions. Optimal emissions in particular are computationally highly challenging to calculate in spatial IAMs.

5.5 Short-run macroeconomic models with climate

In 2018, Katheline Schubert observed that "almost no space is given to environmental issues in short-term macroeconomics. Environmental issues are perceived as affecting the long term and the structure of economies rather than the current situation" (Schubert, 2018, p117). The IAM literature largely reflects this perception – DICE is the quintessential model of long-run growth coupled to a simple climate model, and all the IAMs discussed so far in this chapter can be fairly described as long-run models. But the situation is changing fast, as models are built to study the relationship between short-run macroeconomic fluctuations, business cycles and climate policy. This relationship works both ways: (i) macroeconomic volatility has implications for the design of climate policy and (ii) climate policy could affect macroeconomic volatility, with implications for monetary and macroprudential policy in turn. DSGE models are the core tools used to study macroeconomic volatility. Where these are extended to generate GHG emissions and where climate shocks affect the economy, one has yet another type of IAM (sometimes called Environmental DSGE or E-DSGE models). Annicchiarico et al. (2022) have written a recent review of this emerging literature. Recursive IAMs can also be classed as DSGE models, although the focus of that branch of the literature is more on the long run.

The introduction to this chapter characterized the basic task of climate economics as estimating the optimal control of GHG emissions, where marginal benefits equal marginal costs. While benefits do not vary much over the business cycle due to the long atmospheric residence time of CO_2, costs do, in particular because CO_2 emissions are strongly procyclical (Doda, 2014). Thus, the question

[9] Depending on the time horizon, estimating damages at the 1°x1° resolution produces damages that are 1.5–2x larger than when damages are averaged at the world level. Averaging damages at the level of World Bank regions produces damages that are similar to the 1°x1° resolution this century, although the two methods diverge after 2100.

arises how climate policy ought to reflect the business cycle. Real-business-cycle (RBC) models have been used to analyze this (Fischer and Springborn, 2011; Heutel, 2012; Angelopoulos, Economides and Philippopoulos, 2013). RBC models depart minimally from the neoclassical model of long-run growth. Hence, an RBC model coupled to a simple climate model can look very similar to the DICE-like IAM presented in Section 2, but with two main differences. First, there needs to be some source of volatility. Typically, this source is exogenous, autocorrelated shocks to TFP in the production function, although shocks can be introduced in other ways (e.g., Dissou and Karnizova, 2016). Second, a core aim of business-cycle research is to study fluctuations in employment. This is standardly achieved in RBC models by adding labor/leisure as a second argument of the utility function. The representative household now obtains utility not only from consumption but also from leisure (equivalently disutility from labor), and the resulting trade-offs mean that employment responds to the productivity shocks. To study policy instrument choice (e.g., carbon taxation versus cap-and-trade), it is necessary to model the problem as a decentralized economy.

A well-known limitation of RBC models is that they predict nominal shocks have no real effects. There are no market imperfections (aside from the climate externality in this case), so nominal shocks simply change all prices proportionally and real relative prices and quantities are unaffected. However, this is contradicted by a large body of empirical evidence showing that nominal shocks do indeed have real effects. New Keynesian (NK) models allow for real effects of nominal fluctuations by introducing nominal rigidities, i.e., barriers to the adjustment of prices or wages, as well as imperfections in the goods or labor markets. Therefore, they depart more from the DICE-like IAM of Section 2. In a typical NK model, a continuum of monopolistic firms each produces a single good. Firms set prices to maximize discounted profits, but this is subject to a price adjustment equation that constrains their ability to adjust prices in the face of shocks. There is often no capital in such models: production equals labor. Households and firms are affected by inflation, which the central bank controls by using a monetary policy rule to set interest rates. Annicchiarico and Di Dio (2015) developed a model similar to this, although theirs has capital. Coupling an NK model to a simple climate model makes it possible to study the relationship between climate and monetary policy (Annicchiarico and Di Dio, 2017), an area of rapidly increasing interest for central banks (see Section 4).

Studying the implications of climate change for financial stability, whether it be so-called "transition risk" that comes from decarbonization or "physical risk" that comes from climate damages, and conversely studying the implications of financial market imperfections for climate policy, requires introducing a financial market with frictions and financial regulation to the model (Benmir and Roman, 2020; Diluiso et al., 2021; Carattini, Heutel and Melkadze, 2023). These papers build on an emerging literature in macroeconomics that has been inspired by the Global Financial Crisis of 2007–8 and resulting Great Recession. The lesson learned from this episode is that financial market frictions can be an important source of volatility in the real economy. These papers further extend the analysis to include dirty and clean firms, which enables them to analyze the effects of various monetary policy tools that could discriminate in favor of clean firms.

Three other features of DSGE models with a coupled climate are worth noting, compared to long-run growth models with a coupled climate. First, in short-run macroeconomic models the time step is typically a quarter rather than a full year. Second, many of the models in the literature have been built to describe regions rather than the world economy, e.g., the United States or the EU Area. This raises the question of whether to model a closed or open economy (Annicchiarico and Diluiso, 2019). Third, the economy is typically assumed to be in a steady state and the interest is in perturbations around the steady state, whereas in long-run IAMs there is usually an explicit interest in transitioning to a new steady state. In the future, expect to see papers emerging that introduce heterogeneous agents to the kinds of model featured in this section (Benmir and Roman, 2022).

5.6 Multi-sectoral general equilibrium models

The IAMs discussed in this chapter typically have one explicit, aggregated production sector, as in Eq. (3). A parallel literature has sought to integrate climate change in models with multiple production sectors. The larger part of this literature studies the consequences of imposing pre-determined climate objectives on the economy – cost-effectiveness analysis of climate mitigation – and is therefore outside the scope of this chapter, as explained in Section 1. However, some of this literature has studied climate damages in a multi-sectoral framework and it is important that this part of the literature does not fall between the cracks.[10]

Traditionally this literature starts with a computable general equilibrium (CGE) model of the economy, which simulates the interactions between firms in multiple sectors, households and governments, assuming agents maximize their profit/utility objectives and subject to all factor and goods markets clearing, i.e., general equilibrium. The model is calibrated on input-output Social Accounting Matrices. There are many commonalities with the DSGE models discussed in the previous sub-section, but CGE models have more sectoral disaggregation, at the expense of being either static or at most partially dynamic, and deterministic. The models are solved numerically, hence the term "computable". CGE models have a long tradition of use in estimating the economic effects of fiscal policy, trade policy, etc., and many are maintained by national governments and multilateral institutions (e.g., the IMF, OECD and

[10] This literature in fact dates back to the mid-2000s; its inclusion in this section is convenient but it is an imperfect fit from a chronological point of view.

World Bank).[11] In the context of climate change, the key step is to implement climate damages in the model as a set of exogenous shocks to factor availability (capital, labor or land), factor productivity, or demand (e.g., expenditure on energy, health or infrastructure), and simulate their propagation across sectors and value chains. CGE models are not used to calculate optimal emissions paths due to their complexity.

The comparative advantage of multi-sectoral models is that they can simulate the indirect effects of climate damages beyond the (market) sector and region in which they occur, thus directly tackling the issue identified earlier in this chapter that adding up damages sector-by-sector may mis-estimate total damages. By doing so, multi-sectoral models can also generate results on the changing sectoral composition of output, trade patterns, etc., which are important in their own right. In multi-sectoral general equilibrium models, substitution in response to changes in relative prices, in this setting due to climate damages, is a key mechanism. It is often referred to as "market-driven", "autonomous" or "reactive" adaptation to climate change.

Early contributions to the literature using CGE models include Bosello, Roson and Tol (2006) on health impacts, and Darwin and Tol (2001) and Bosello, Roson and Tol (2007) on sea-level rise. Building on these studies, Eboli, Parrado and Roson (2010), Bosello, Eboli and Pierfederici (2012) and Roson and van der Mensbrugghe (2012) simultaneously analyzed impacts in multiple sectors. More recent contributions include Dellink, Lanzi and Chateau (2019), Kompas, Pham and Che (2018), and Takakura et al. (2019). These studies also include impacts in multiple sectors. The set of impact sectors is fairly common across studies (especially agriculture, energy, health, sea-level rise and tourism) and is gradually expanding. A sketch of key results from these CGE studies is as follows. The overall level of damages and their distribution across countries/regions is similar to the center of the remaining IAM literature (Rose et al., 2022). It is unclear how important this result is, however, because CGE studies are usually not fully independent of the wider literature, for example calibrating shocks on some of the same underlying studies. Agriculture and health impacts are particularly important, although these findings may be sensitive to which impacts are included and which are not. Despite their comparative advantage, there has not in fact been much focus in the CGE literature on the contribution of indirect effects relative to direct effects. Bosello, Eboli and Pierfederici (2012) found that general-equilibrium adjustment mechanisms reduce the overall impact of climate change compared to direct, first-round effects, but not always, while Dellink, Lanzi and Chateau (2019) found the converse result in a dynamic setting, emphasizing the channel

[11] CGE models arguably have a comparatively low profile in academic journals in economics, and this might be a reason why.

of reduced capital accumulation leading to lower future growth (which is a mechanism present in the standard one-sector model).

In the last few years, similar multi-sectoral models have been developed outside the applied CGE literature, which have the primary intention of studying indirect, general-equilibrium effects. Examples include Nath (forthcoming), who builds a static, three-sector model of the world economy, which distinguishes agriculture, manufacturing and services. He studies the potential for adaptation through reallocation of production between agriculture and manufacturing/services, as well as across countries. He finds the potential is large but the subsistence role of food,[12] combined with trade barriers, acts as a barrier to adaptation. Dietz and Lanz (2022) set up a dynamic, two-sector model (agriculture and non-agriculture) without spatial disaggregation. They also highlight the potential for adaptation through reallocating resources from non-agriculture to agriculture but estimate a large opportunity cost of doing so. Casey, Fried and Gibson (2024) build a dynamic, five-sector model (construction, mining, agriculture, manufacturing, services) with the purpose of studying how the differential production of consumption versus investment goods across sectors matters (for example, the construction sector produces investment goods, while agriculture produces consumption goods). Intuitively, if climate change has a greater effect on sectors producing investment goods, then the overall impacts of climate change are smaller in the short run but higher in the long run.

6 Conclusions

This chapter has documented the evolution of IAMs from a small set of relatively similar models built to study welfare-maximizing paths of global temperatures, emissions and emissions prices, to a much larger and more heterogeneous set of models whose purposes are also broader. It is worth taking stock by asking what IAMs might still be useful for.

One reason for asking the question is that the international community has, since at least the 2015 UN Paris Agreement, had a target for global mean temperature: "Holding the increase in the global average temperature to well below 2 °C above pre-industrial levels and pursuing efforts to limit the temperature increase to 1.5 °C above pre-industrial levels" (UNFCCC, 2015, Article 2). The Paris Agreement and subsequent negotiated texts make further statements about what an emissions path looks like that meets these temperature goals. Thus, countries have convened and agreed a partial answer to the question IAMs were originally built to analyze. For their part, as Section 2.5 has described, IAMs did not originally provide support for temperature goals as low as those contained in the Paris Agreement, but over the years more and more papers have been

[12] Formally, consumer preferences are non-homothetic and the substitutability between food and other goods is low.

published that do lend support to the Paris goals, and the IAM literature has essentially characterized a set of sufficient conditions for them to be welfare-improving and perhaps maximizing.

Views differ on whether climate economists should consider the question of optimal temperature to have been answered, and what remaining scope there is to use IAMs to inform emissions and emissions price paths. There is certainly widespread demand from policymakers for advice in setting emissions targets on various timeframes, for example at the national level, and in setting emissions prices for price-based policy instruments and for cost-benefit analysis of new policies, regulations and large infrastructure projects. But still it is not obvious what role the IAMs discussed in this chapter should play. Writing at a time when damages were very imprecisely estimated by first-generation IAMs, Dietz and Fankhauser (2010) made a pragmatic case for taking climate targets as given and using information on abatement costs *only* to establish optimal emissions and emissions prices that meet the target. This amounts to cost-effectiveness analysis rather than cost-benefit analysis. The case primarily rests on abatement costs being more precisely estimated than damage costs. Kaufman et al. (2020) and Stern and Stiglitz (2021) make similar arguments. Specifically with reference to emissions prices, this has become known as the "target-consistent pricing" approach and is now government practice in the UK, for example. Aldy et al. (2021) provide the opposite perspective. Among the reasons given for preferring cost-benefit analysis/the social cost of carbon, they worry that taking the target as given when the target is a political decision makes derived targets and prices arbitrary and subject to arbitrary change. They are also worried that target-consistent pricing will not work in the United States for legal reasons. This goes a long way to explaining the use of the social cost of carbon in the United States and in turn why so much effort has been invested in the United States in developing the new class of social-cost IAMs to estimate it, as described in Section 3.4. The United States' social cost of carbon will likely remain a key focal point for IAMs, particularly of the social cost type, although the United States is not alone, with countries such as Canada, France and Germany also using a social cost of carbon in policy.

Even if the overall target is taken as given, cost-effectiveness analysis implicitly values damages at zero. That is because the cost-effective path is the solution to the problem of minimizing abatement costs only, not abatement costs plus damage costs. If damages are positive-valued, however, the optimal carbon price path should be different. Dietz and Venmans (2019) illustrated this using an analytical IAM by comparing optimal price paths under cost-effectiveness analysis and cost-benefit analysis with a common temperature constraint. By ignoring damages, the cost-effective price path starts too low and grows more quickly, meaning emissions reductions are backloaded. Overall, the debate here perhaps shows that, firstly, many policy questions about appropriate emissions targets and prices remain open, despite the high-level framework of the Paris Agreement, and that, secondly, IAMs can still make useful contributions to policy design, particularly price levels and paths. Despite their high level of abstraction, it is noteworthy how much analytical IAMs have contributed to our understanding of the characteristics of optimal price paths, not so much the current level but more especially the future growth rate and the relationship with GDP.

Outside these core climate policy applications, Section 3.4 described the growing interest in climate change among central banks. In the domain of monetary policy, climate change and climate policy may impact inflation in various ways. Climate damages may be inflationary, e.g., through the effect of climate shocks on food prices ("climateflation"). Decarbonization may be inflationary, e.g., through the effect of a green investment boom on aggregate demand ("greenflation"). Dependence on fossil fuels may also be inflationary, e.g., through the effect of fossil-fuel price shocks ("fossilflation") (Schnabel, 2022). In the domain of financial stability, central banks are concerned that physical and/or transition risks could be systemic. These issues of monetary policy and financial stability should continue to fuel the development of short-run macroeconomic models with climate, and related recursive IAMs. IAMs can be applied to questions of fiscal policy too. So far, IAMs have seen limited application to fiscal policy, mostly to taxation rather than public spending and mostly using energy models that are outside the scope of this chapter (Siegmeier et al., 2018). However, there is a substantial literature showing that climate and fiscal policy interact and there is surely scope to deploy IAMs productively in this space, following the examples of Barrage (2020, 2024). Doing so requires a sufficiently rich description of the government in IAMs and how it interacts with firms and households.

IAMs with a more detailed description of damage mechanisms, including social-cost IAMs, spatial IAMs and multi-sectoral models, raise the prospect of using IAMs more for planning climate adaptation. Early adaptation IAMs, briefly discussed in Section 2.5, were helpful for thinking in the broadest terms about where adaptation fits in global climate policy, but they were too abstract/aggregated to generate specific insights on where to allocate scarce resources. Social-cost IAMs, spatial IAMs and multi-sectoral models offer much more promise in this regard.

All kinds of IAM but especially first-generation IAMs and analytical IAMs still have a role to play in helping to understand key relationships at the heart of the climate-economy interaction. One can draw a distinction between prognostic models built for forecasting and diagnostic models built for understanding. Experience has shown that first-generation and analytical IAMs have their limitations as forecasting tools: the low level of disaggregation and detail in such models generates a set of parameters, on which results depend sensitively but for which there are no empirical counterparts. This was a key point of the critiques discussed in Section 3 and which is still more-or-less valid. On the other hand, these models are perhaps more useful as diagnostic models than some of the more complex IAM varieties, because they are less of a black box, and they can be calibrated to mimic the behavior of more complex models corresponding to key IAM components, e.g., the climate system or damages (thus partially countering the critiques). One diagnostic use of first-generation and analytical IAMs has been to apply new ideas from economic theory, for example welfare and decision theory. There remains scope for further work in this area.

References

Acemoglu, D., et al., 2012. The environment and directed technical change. Am. Economic Rev. 102 (1), 131–166.

Ackerman, F., et al., 2009. Limitations of integrated assessment models of climate change. Climatic Change 95, 297–315.

Ackerman, F., Stanton, E.A., Bueno, R., 2010. Fat tails, exponents, extreme uncertainty: simulating catastrophe in DICE. Ecol. Econ. 1657–1665. https://doi.org/10.1016/j.ecolecon.2010.03.013

Ackerman, F., Stanton, E.A., 2012. Climate risks and carbon prices: revising the social cost of carbon. Economics: Open-Access, Open-Assessment E-Journal. https://doi.org/10.5018/economics-ejournal.ja.2012-10

Adler, M., et al., 2017. Priority for the worse-off and the social cost of carbon. Nat. Clim. Change 7 (6), 443–449. https://doi.org/10.1038/nclimate3298

Adler, M.D., Treich, N., 2015. Prioritarianism and climate change. Environ. Resour. Econ. 62 (2), 279–308. https://doi.org/10.1007/s10640-015-9960-7

Agrawala, S., et al., 2011. Plan or react? Analysis of adaptation costs and benefits using integrated assessment models. Clim. Change Econ. 2 (3), 175–208.

Aldy, J.E., et al., 2021. Keep climate policy focused on the social cost of carbon. Sci. (N. York, N. Y.) 373 (6557), 850–852.

Allen, M.R., 2016. Drivers of peak warming in a consumption-maximizing world. Nat. Clim. Change 6 (7), 684–686.

Anderson, B., et al., 2014. Uncertainty in climate change modeling: can global sensitivity analysis be of help? Risk Anal. 34 (2), 271–293 (Wiley Online Library).

Angelopoulos, K., Economides, G., Philippopoulos, A., 2013. First-and second-best allocations under economic and environmental uncertainty. Int. Tax. Public. Financ. 20, 360–380.

Annicchiarico, B., et al., 2022. Business cycles and environmental policy: a primer. Environ. Energy Policy Economy 3 (1), 221–253.

Annicchiarico, B., Di Dio, F., 2015. Environmental policy and macroeconomic dynamics in a new Keynesian model. J. Environ. Econ. Manag. 69, 1–21.

Annicchiarico, B., Di Dio, F., 2017. GHG emissions control and monetary policy. Environ. Resour. Econ. 67, 823–851.

Annicchiarico, B., Diluiso, F., 2019. International transmission of the business cycle and environmental policy. Res. Energy Economics 58, 101112.

Anthoff, D., Emmerling, J., 2019. Inequality and the social cost of carbon. J. Assoc. Environ. Resour. Economists 6 (2), 243–273.

Anthoff, D., Hepburn, C.J., Tol, R.S.J., 2009. Equity weighting and the marginal damage costs of climate change. Ecol. Econ. 68 (3), 836–849.

Anthoff, D., Tol, R.S.J., 2010. On international equity weights and national decision making on climate change. J. Environ. Econ. Manag. 60 (1), 14–20.

Anthoff, D., Tol, R.S.J., 2012. Schelling's conjecture on climate and development: a test. In: Hahn, R.W., Ulph, A. (Eds.), Climate Change and Common Sense: Essays in Honour of Tom Schelling. Oxford University Press, Oxford, pp. 260–274.

Anthoff, D., Tol, R.S.J., Yohe, G.W., 2009. Risk aversion, time preference, and the social cost of carbon. Environ. Res. Lett. 4 (2), 024002.

Arrow, K.J., 1962. The economic implications of learning by doing. Rev. Economic Stud. 29 (3), 155–173 (JSTOR).

Athanassoglou, S., Xepapadeas, A., 2012. Pollution control with uncertain stock dynamics: when, and how, to be precautious. J. Environ. Econ. Manag. 63, 304–320. https://doi.org/10.1016/j.jeem.2011.11.001

Azar, C., Sterner, T., 1996. Discounting and distributional considerations in the context of global warming. Ecol. Econ. 19 (2), 169–184.

Babiker, M., et al., 2009. Forward-looking versus recursive-dynamic modeling in climate policy analysis: a comparison. Economic Model. 26 (6), 1341–1354.

Barnett, M., Brock, W., Hansen, L.P., 2020. Pricing uncertainty induced by climate change. Rev. Financial Stud. 33 (3), 1024–1066.

Barrage, L., 2014. Sensitivity analysis for Golosov, Hassler, Krusell, and Tsyvinski (2014): "Optimal taxes on fossil fuel in general equilibrium". Econometrica Suppl. Mater. 82, 1.

Barrage, L., 2020. Optimal dynamic carbon taxes in a climate–economy model with distortionary fiscal policy. Rev. Economic Stud. 87 (1), 1–39.

Barrage, L., 2024. Fiscal costs of climate change in the United States.

Barrage, L., Nordhaus, W.D., 2024. Policies, projections, and the social cost of carbon: Results from the DICE-2023 model. Proc. Natl. Acad. Sci. 121 (3), e2312030121.

Bauer, M.D., Rudebusch, G.D., 2023. The rising cost of climate change: evidence from the bond market. Rev. Econ. Stat. 105 (5), 1255–1270.

Baumgärtner, S., et al., 2015. Ramsey discounting of ecosystem services. Environ. Resour. Econ. 61, 273–296.

Benmir, G., Roman, J., 2020. Policy interactions and the transition to clean technology. Working Paper No. 337. London.

Benmir, G., Roman, J., 2022. The distributional costs of net-zero: a heterogeneous agent perspective.

Blackorby, C., Bossert, W., Donaldson, D., 2005. Population Issues in Social Choice Theory, Welfare Economics, and Ethics. Cambridge University Press (Econometric Society Monographs), Cambridge, UK.

Bosello, F., Eboli, F., Pierfederici, R., 2012. Assessing the economic impacts of climate change. Rev. Energy Environ. Economics. https://doi.org/10.2139/ssrn.2004966

Bosello, F., Roson, R., Tol, R.S.J., 2006. Economy-wide estimates of the implications of climate change: human health. Ecol. Econ. 58 (3), 579–591.

Bosello, F., Roson, R., Tol, R.S.J., 2007. Economy-wide estimates of the implications of climate change: sea level rise. Environ. Resour. Econ. 37, 549–571.

Bramoullé, Y., Olson, L.J., 2005. Allocation of pollution abatement under learning by doing. J. Public. Econ. 89 (9–10), 1935–1960.

Bretschger, L., Karydas, C., 2018. Optimum growth and carbon policies with lags in the climate system. Environ. Resour. Econ. 70, 781–806.

Buchholz, W., Schymura, M., 2012. Expected utility theory and the tyranny of catastrophic risks. Ecol. Econ. 234–239. https://doi.org/10.1016/j.ecolecon.2012.03.007

Burke, M.B., Hsiang, S.M., Miguel, E., 2015. Global non-linear effect of temperature on economic production. Nature 527, 235–239. https://doi.org/10.1038/nature15725

Cai, Y., Judd, K.L., Lontzek, T.S., 2012. Open science is necessary. Nat. Clim. Change 2 (5), 299.

Cai, Y., Lontzek, T.S., 2019. The social cost of carbon with economic and climate risks. J. Political Economy 127 (6), 2684–2734.

Caney, S., 2008. Human rights, climate change, and discounting. Environmental Politics Vol. 17. Taylor & Francis, pp. 536–555.

Carattini, S., Heutel, G., Melkadze, G., 2023. Climate policy, financial frictions, and transition risk. Rev. Economic Dyn. 51, 778–794.

Carleton, T., et al., 2022. Valuing the global mortality consequences of climate change accounting for adaptation costs and benefits. Q. J. Econ. 137 (4), 2037–2105.

Casey, G., Fried, S., Gibson, M., 2024. Understanding climate damages: consumption versus investment. European Economic Review 167, 104799.

Casey, G., Fried, S., Goode, E., 2023. Projecting the impact of rising temperatures: the role of macroeconomic dynamics. IMF Economic Rev. 71 (3), 688–718.

Ciais, P., et al., 2013. Carbon and other biogeochemical cycles. In: Stocker, T.F. (Ed.), Climate Change 2013: The Physical Science Basis. Contribution of Working Group I to the Fifth Assessment Report of the Intergovernmental Panel on Climate Change. Cambridge University Press, Cambridge, United Kingdom and New York, NY, USA.

Cline, W.R., 1992. The Economics of Global Warming. Peterson Institute.

Collins, M., et al., 2013. Long-term climate change: projections, commitments and irreversibility. In: Stocker, T. (Ed.), Climate Change 2013: The Physical Science Basis. Contribution of Working Group I to the Fifth Assessment Report of the Intergovernmental Panel on Climate Change. Cambridge Univ Press, Cambridge, UK and New York, NY, USA, pp. 1029–1136. https://doi.org/10.1017/CBO9781107415324.024

Conte, B., et al., 2021. Local sectoral specialization in a warming world. J. Economic Geogr. 21 (4), 493–530.

Conte, B., Desmet, K., Rossi-Hansberg, E., 2022. On the geographic implications of carbon taxes.

Crost, B., Traeger, C.P., 2013. Optimal climate policy: uncertainty versus Monte Carlo. Econ. Lett. 120 (3), 552–558.

Crost, B., Traeger, C.P., 2014. Optimal CO_2 mitigation under damage risk valuation. Nat. Clim. Change 4 (7), 631–636. https://doi.org/10.1038/nclimate2249

Cruz, J.L., Rossi-Hansberg, E., 2024. The geography of global warming. Rev. Economic Stud. 91 (2), 899–939.

Daniel, K.D., Litterman, R.B., Wagner, G., 2019. Declining CO_2 price paths. Proc. Natl Acad. Sci. 116 (42), 20886–20891.

Darwin, R.F., Tol, R.S.J., 2001. Estimates of the economic effects of sea level rise. Environ. Resour. Econ. 19, 113–129.

Dasgupta, P., 2001. Human Well-Being and the Natural Environment. Oxford University Press.

de Bruin, K.C., Dellink, R.B., Tol, R.S.J., 2009. AD-DICE: an implementation of adaptation in the DICE model. Climatic Change 95 (1–2), 63–81.

Dell, M., Jones, B.F., Olken, B.A., 2012. Temperature shocks and economic growth: evidence from the last half century. Am. Economic Journal: Macroecon. 4 (3), 66–95 (American Economic Association).

Dellink, R., Lanzi, E., Chateau, J., 2019. The sectoral and regional economic consequences of climate change to 2060. Environ. Resour. Econ. 72, 309–363.

Dennig, F., et al., 2015. Inequality, climate impacts on the future poor, and carbon prices. Proc. Natl. Acad. Sci. 112 (52), 15827–15832.

Desmet, K., et al., 2021. Evaluating the economic cost of coastal flooding. Am. Economic J.: Macroecon. 13 (2), 444–486.

Desmet, K., Rossi-Hansberg, E., 2015. On the spatial economic impact of global warming. J. Urban. Econ. 88 (C)), 16–37.

Desmet, K., Rossi-Hansberg, E., 2024. Climate change economics over time and space. Annu. Rev. Econ. 16, 271–304.

Dietz, S., 2011. High impact, low probability? An empirical analysis of risk in the economics of climate change. Climatic Change 108 (3), 519–541. https://doi.org/10.1007/s10584-010-9993-4

Dietz, S., et al., 2021. Economic impacts of tipping points in the climate system. Proc. Natl. Acad. Sci. 118 (34), e2103081118.

Dietz, S., Asheim, G.B., 2012. Climate policy under sustainable discounted utilitarianism. J. Environ. Econ. Manag. 63 (3), 321–335. https://doi.org/10.1016/j.jeem.2012.01.003

Dietz, S., Fankhauser, S., 2010. Environmental prices, uncertainty, and learning. Oxf. Rev. Economic Policy 26 (2), 270–284. https://doi.org/10.1093/oxrep/grq005

Dietz, S., Hepburn, C., Stern, N., 2009. Economics, ethics and climate change. In: Basu, K., Kanbur, R. (Eds.), Arguments for a Better World: Essays in Honor of Amartya Sen. Volume II: Society, Institutions and Development. Oxford University Press, Oxford, pp. 365–386.

Dietz, S., Hope, C., Patmore, N., 2007. Some economics of dangerous climate change: reflections on the Stern Review. Glob. Environ. Change. Elsevier 17 (3), 311–325. https://doi.org/10.1016/j.gloenvcha.2007.05.008

Dietz, S., Lanz, B., 2022. Growth and adaptation to climate change in the long run. CESifo Working 411.

Dietz, S., Stern, N., 2015. Endogenous growth, convexity of damages and climate risk: how Nordhaus' framework supports deep cuts in carbon emissions. Economic J. 125 (583), 574–602. https://doi.org/10.1111/ecoj.12188

Dietz, S., Venmans, F., 2019. Cumulative carbon emissions and economic policy: in search of general principles. J. Environ. Econ. Manag. London 96, 108–129. https://doi.org/10.1016/j.jeem.2019.04.003

Diluiso, F., et al., 2021. Climate actions and macro-financial stability: the role of central banks. J. Environ. Econ. Manage. 110, 102548.

Dissou, Y., Karnizova, L., 2016. Emissions cap or emissions tax? A multi-sector business cycle analysis. J. Environ. Econ. Manag. 79, 169–188.

Doda, B., 2014. Evidence on business cycles and CO_2 emissions. J. Macroecon. 40, 214–227.

Drupp, M., 2018. Limits to substitution between ecosystem services and manufactured goods and implications for social discounting. Environ. Resour. Econ. 69, 135–158.

Drupp, M., et al., 2018. Discounting disentangled. Am. Economic J.: Economic Policy 10 (4), 109–134.

Drupp, M., Haensel, M., 2021. Relative prices and climate policy: how the scarcity of nonmarket goods drives policy evaluation. Am. Economic J.: Economic Policy 13 (1), 168–201.

Eboli, F., Parrado, R., Roson, R., 2010. Climate-change feedback on economic growth: explorations with a dynamic general equilibrium model. Environ. Dev. Econ. 15 (5), 525–533.

Epstein, L.G., Zin, S.E., 1989. Substitution, risk aversion, and the temporal behavior of consumption and asset returns: a theoretical framework. Econometrica: J. Econometric Soc. 57 (4), 937–969.

European Environment Agency, 2024. Atmospheric greenhouse gas concentrations. Available at: https://www.eea.europa.eu/en/analysis/indicators/atmospheric-greenhouse-gas-concentrations#:~:text=. The total concentration of greenhouse, CO2 equivalents in 2021.

Fankhauser, S., 1995. Valuing Climate Change: The Economics of the Greenhouse. Earthscan, London.

Fankhauser, S., Tol, R.S.J., 1997. The social costs of climate change: the IPCC second assessment report and beyond. Mitig. Adapt. Strateg. Glob. Change 1 (4), 385–403.

Fankhauser, S., Tol, R.S.J., Pearce, D.W., 1997. The aggregation of climate change damages: a welfare theoretic approach. Environ. Resour. Econ. 10 (3), 249–266. https://doi.org/10.1023/A:1026420425961

Fischer, C., Springborn, M., 2011. Emissions targets and the real business cycle: intensity targets versus caps or taxes. J. Environ. Econ. Manag. 62 (3), 352–366.

Fitzpatrick, L.G., Kelly, D.L., 2017. Probabilistic stabilization targets. J. Assoc. Environ. Resour. Economists 4 (2), 611–657.

Gardiner, S.M., 2004. Ethics and global climate change. Ethics 114 (3), 555–600.

Gerlagh, R., Liski, M., 2018. Carbon prices for the next hundred years. Economic J. 128 (609), 728–757.

Gilboa, I., 2009. Theory of Decision Under Uncertainty. Cambridge University Press, Cambridge, UK.

Gollier, C., 2010. Ecological discounting. J. Environ. Econ. Manag. 145 (2), 812–829.

Gollier, C., 2012. Pricing the Planet's Future: The Economics of Discounting in an Uncertain World. Princeton University Press.

Golosov, M., et al., 2014. Optimal taxes on fossil fuel in general equilibrium. Econometrica: J. Econometric Soc. 82 (1), 41–88.

Goulder, L.H., Mathai, K., 2000. Optimal CO_2 abatement in the presence of induced technological change. J. Environ. Econ. Manag. 39, 1–38.

Groom, B., Maddison, D.J., 2019. New estimates of the elasticity of marginal utility for the UK. Environ. Resour. Econ. 72 (4), 1155–1182.

Grubb, M., et al., 2021. Induced innovation in energy technologies and systems: a review of evidence and potential implications for CO_2 mitigation. Environ. Res. Lett. 16 (4), 043007.

Haensel, M., et al., 2020. Climate economics support for the UN climate targets. Nat. Clim. Change 10 (8), 781–789.

Hambel, C., Kraft, H., Schwartz, E., 2021. Optimal carbon abatement in a stochastic equilibrium model with climate change. European Economic Review 132, 103642.

Hartzell-Nichols, L., 2017. A Climate of Risk: Precautionary Principles, Catastrophes, and Climate Change. Routledge, New York, NY.

Hassler, J., Krusell, P., 2018. Environmental macroeconomics: the case of climate change. In: Dasgupta, P., Pattanayak, S.K., Smith, V.K. (Eds.), Handbook of Environmental Economics 4. Elsevier, pp. 333–394.

Heal, G.M., 2009. The economics of climate change: a post-stern perspective. Climatic Change 96, 275–297.

Heutel, G., 2012. How should environmental policy respond to business cycles? Optimal policy under persistent productivity shocks. Rev. Economic Dyn. 15 (2), 244–264.

Hoel, M., Sterner, T., 2007. Discounting and relative prices. Climatic Change 84 (3–4), 265–280 (Springer).

Hope, C., 2006. The marginal impact of CO_2 from PAGE2002: an integrated assessment model incorporating the IPCC's five reasons for concern. Integrated AssessmentJ. 6, 16–56.

Hsiang, S., et al., 2017. Estimating economic damage from climate change in the United States. Sci. (N. York, N. Y.) 356 (6345), 1362–1369.

Hsiang, S., Kopp, R.E., 2018. An economist's guide to climate change science. J. Economic Perspect. 32 (4), 3–32.

Interagency Working Group on Social Cost of Carbon, 2010. Technical Support Document: Social Cost of Carbon for Regulatory Impact Analysis—under Executive Order 12866.

Jamieson, D., 1992. Ethics, public policy, and global warming. *Sci. Technol. Hum. Values*. Sage Publ. 17 (2), 139–153.

Jensen, S., Traeger, C., 2014. Optimal climate change mitigation under long-term growth uncertainty: stochastic integrated assessment and analytic findings. Eur. Economic Rev. 69, 104–125.

Joos, F., et al., 2013. Carbon dioxide and climate impulse response functions for the computation of greenhouse gas metrics: a multi-model analysis. Atmos. Chem. Phys. 13 (5), 2793–2825.

Kaufman, N., et al., 2020. A near-term to net zero alternative to the social cost of carbon for setting carbon prices. Nat. Clim. Change 10 (11), 1010–1014.

Kelly, D.L., Kolstad, C.D., 1999. Bayesian learning, growth, and pollution. J. Economic Dyn. Control. 23 (4), 491–518 (Elsevier).

Kelly, D.L., Kolstad, C.D., 2001. Malthus and climate change: betting on a stable population. J. Environ. Econ. Manag. 41, 135–161.

Kelly, D.L., Tan, Z., 2015. Learning and climate feedbacks: optimal climate insurance and fat tails. J. Environ. Econ. Manag. 72, 98–122.

Kikstra, J.S., et al., 2021. The social cost of carbon dioxide under climate-economy feedbacks and temperature variability. Environ. Res. Lett. 16 (9), 094037.

Kompas, T., Pham, V.H., Che, T.N., 2018. The effects of climate change on GDP by country and the global economic gains from complying with the Paris climate accord. Earth's Future 6 (8), 1153–1173.

Leach, N.J., et al., 2021. FaIRv2. 0.0: a generalized impulse response model for climate uncertainty and future scenario exploration. Geoscientific Model. Dev. 14 (5), 3007–3036.

Lemoine, D., Rudik, I., 2017. Managing climate change under uncertainty: recursive integrated assessment at an inflection point. Annu. Rev. Resour. Econ. 9, 117–142.

Lemoine, D., Traeger, C., 2014. Watch your step: optimal policy in a tipping climate. Am. Economic J.: Economic Policy 6 (1), 137–166 (American Economic Association).

Lemoine, D., Traeger, C., 2016. Ambiguous tipping points. J. Economic Behav. Organ. 132 (B), 5–18.

Levin, K., et al., 2012. Overcoming the tragedy of super wicked problems: constraining our future selves to ameliorate global climate change. Policy Sci. 45, 123–152.

Matthews, H.D., et al., 2009. The proportionality of global warming to cumulative carbon emissions. Nature 459 (7248), 829–832 (Nature Publishing Group).

Mehra, R., Prescott, E.C., 1985. The equity premium: a puzzle. J. Monetary Econ. 15 (2), 145–161.

Mejean, A., et al., 2020. Catastrophic climate change, population ethics and intergenerational equity. Climatic Change 163 (2), 873–890.

Millner, A., 2013. On welfare frameworks and catastrophic climate risks. J. Environ. Econ. Manag 65. Elsevier, pp. 310–325.

Milner, A., Dietz, S., Heal, G., 2013. Scientific ambiguity and climate policy. Environ. Resour. Econ. 55, 21–46.

Moore, F.C., Diaz, D.B., 2015. Temperature impacts on economic growth warrant stringent mitigation policy. Nat. Clim. Change 5, 127–131.

Myhre, G., et al., 2013. Anthropogenic and natural radiative forcing. In: Stocker, T.F. (Ed.), Climate Change 2013: The Physical Science Basis. Contribution of Working Group I to the Fifth Assessment Report of the Intergovernmental Panel on Climate Change. Cambridge University Press, Cambridge, UK and New York, NY, USA, pp. 659–740.

Nath, I.B., n.d. Climate change, the food problem, and the challenge of adaptation through sectoral reallocation. *Journal of Political Economy*.

Nath, I.B., Ramey, V.A., Klenow, P.J., 2024. How much will global warming cool global growth? w32761.

National Academies of Sciences, Engineering, and Medicine, 2017. Valuing Climate Damages: Updating Estimation of the Social Cost of Carbon Dioxide. The National Academies Press, Washington, DC. https://doi.org/10.17226/24651.

Negishi, T., 1960. Welfare economics and the existence of an equilibrium for a competitive economy. Metroeconomica 12, 92–97.

Newell, R.G., Prest, B.C., Sexton, S.E., 2021. The GDP-temperature relationship: implications for climate change damages. J. Environ. Econ. Manage. 108, 102445.

Nordhaus, W.D., 1991. To slow or not to slow: the economics of the greenhouse effect. Economic J. 101 (407), 920–937.

Nordhaus, W.D., 1992. An optimal transition path for controlling greenhouse gases. Sci. Am. Assoc. Advancement Sci. 258, 1315.

Nordhaus, W.D., 1993a. Optimal greenhouse-gas reductions and tax policy in the "DICE" model. Am. Economic Rev. 83 (2), 313–317.

Nordhaus, W.D., 1993b. Rolling the "DICE": an optimal transition path for controlling greenhouse gases. Resour. Energy Econ. 15 (1), 27–50 (Elsevier).

Nordhaus, W.D., 1994. Managing the Global Commons: The Economics of Climate Change. MIT Press, Cambridge, MA.

Nordhaus, W.D., 2007. A review of the "stern review on the economics of climate change". J. Economic Lit. 45 (3), 686–702.

Nordhaus, W.D., 2014. Estimates of the social cost of carbon: concepts and results from the DICE-2013R model and alternative approaches. J. Assoc. Environ. Resour. Economists 1, 273–312. https://doi.org/10.1086/676035

Nordhaus, W.D., Yang, Z., 1996. A regional dynamic general-equilibrium model of alternative climate-change strategies. Am. Economic Rev. JSTOR, pp. 741–765.

Office of Management and Budget, 2023. Circular No. A-4. Washington, DC, USA.

OMB, 2023. Circular No. A-4.

Peck, S.C., Teisberg, T.J., 1992. CETA: a model for carbon emissions trajectory assessment. Energy J. 13 (1), 55–77.

Pindyck, R.S., 2013. Climate change policy: what do the models tell us? J. Economic Lit. 51 (3), 860–872.

Plambeck, E.L., Hope, C., 1996. PAGE95: an updated valuation of the impacts of global warming. Energy Policy 24 (9), 783–793.

Popp, D., 2004. ENTICE: endogenous technological change in the DICE model of global warming. J. Environ. Econ. Manag. 48 (1), 742–768.

Rennert, K., et al., 2022. Comprehensive evidence implies a higher social cost of CO_2. Nature 610 (7933), 687–692.

Rezai, A., van der Ploeg, F., 2016a. Intergenerational inequality aversion, growth, and the role of damages: Occam's rule for the global carbon tax. J. Assoc. Environ. Resour. Economists 3 (2), 493–522. https://doi.org/10.1086/686294

Rezai, A., van der Ploeg, F., 2016b. Second-best renewable subsidies to de-carbonize the economy: commitment and the Green Paradox. Environ. Resour. Econ. 66, 409–434.

Riahi, K., et al., 2017. The Shared Socioeconomic Pathways and their energy, land use, and greenhouse gas emissions implications: an overview. Glob. Environ. Change 42, 153–168. https://doi.org/10.1016/j.gloenvcha.2016.05.009

Ricke, K.L., et al., 2018. Country-level social cost of carbon. Nat. Clim. Change 8 (10), 895–900.

Rode, A., et al., 2021. Estimating a social cost of carbon for global energy consumption. Nature 598 (7880), 308–314.

Romer, P.M., 1986. Increasing returns and long-run growth. J. Political Economy. JSTOR, pp. 1002–1037.

Rose, S., et al., 2022. Cross-working group box ECONOMIC I estimating global economic impacts from climate change. In: Pörtner, H.-O. (Ed.), Climate Change 2022: Impacts, Adaptation and Vulnerability. Contribution of Working Group II to the Sixth Assessment Report of the Intergovernmental Panel on Climate Change. Cambridge University Press, Cambridge, UK and New York, NY, USA, pp. 2495–2499.

Roson, R., van der Mensbrugghe, D., 2012. Climate change and economic growth: impacts and interactions. Int. J. Sustain. Economy 4 (07), 270–285. https://doi.org/10.1504/IJSE.2012.047933

Rudik, I., 2020. Optimal climate policy when damages are unknown. Am. Economic J.: Economic Policy 12 (2), 340–373.

Schelling, T.C., 1992. Some economics of global warming. Am. Economic Rev. 82 (1), 1–14 JSTOR.

Schlosberg, D., 2012. 'Climate justice and capabilities: a framework for adaptation policy'. Ethics Int. Aff. 26 (4), 445–461.

Schlosberg, D., Collins, L.B., 2014. From environmental to climate justice: climate change and the discourse of environmental justice. *Wiley Interdiscip. Reviews: Clim. Change* 5 (3), 359–374.

Schnabel, I., 2022. A new age of energy inflation: climateflation, fossilflation and greenflation: Speech by Isabel Schnabel, Member of the Executive Board of the ECB, at a panel on "Monetary Policy and Climate Change" at The ECB and its Watchers XXII Conference. Frankfurt am Main, Germany.

Schneider, S.H., 1997. Integrated assessment modeling of global climate change: transparent rational tool for policy making or opaque screen hiding value-laden assumptions? Environ. Modeling Assess. 2, 229–249.

Schubert, K., 2018. Macroeconomis and the environment. *Rev. de. l'OFCE* 157 (3), 117–132.

Siegmeier, J., et al., 2018. The fiscal benefits of stringent climate change mitigation: an overview. Clim. Policy 18 (3), 352–367.

Stanton, E.A., 2011. Negishi welfare weights in integrated assessment models: the mathematics of global inequality. Climatic Change 107, 417–432.

Stern, N., 2007. The Economics of Climate Change: The Stern Review. Cambridge University Press, Cambridge, UK.

Stern, N., 2013. The structure of economic modeling of the potential impacts of climate change: grafting gross underestimation of risk onto already narrow science models. J. Economic Lit. 51 (3), 838–859.

Stern, N., Stiglitz, J.E., 2021. *The social cost of carbon, risk, distribution, market failures: an alternative approach*. Working Paper 28472.

Stern, N.H., Stiglitz, J.E., Taylor, C., 2022. The economics of immense risk, urgent action and radical change: towards new approaches to the economics of climate change. J. Economic Methodol. 29 (3), 181–216.

Sterner, T., Persson, U.M., 2008. An even Sterner review: introducing relative prices into the discounting debate. Rev. Environ. Econ. Policy 2 (1), 61–76 (Oxford University Press).

Takakura, J., et al., 2019. Dependence of economic impacts of climate change on anthropogenically directed pathways. Nat. Clim. Change 9 (10), 737–741.

Tol, R.S.J., 1995. The damage costs of climate change toward more comprehensive calculations. Environ. Resour. Econ. 5, 353–374.

Tol, R.S.J., 1997. On the optimal control of carbon dioxide emissions: an application of FUND. Environ. Modeling Assess. 2, 151–163.

Tol, R.S.J., 2023. Social cost of carbon estimates have increased over time. Nat. Clim. Change 13 (6), 532–536.

Traeger, C.P., 2011. Sustainability, limited substitutability, and non-constant social discount rates. J. Environ. Econ. Manag. 62 (2), 215–228 (Elsevier).

Traeger, C.P., 2023. ACE—analytic climate economy. Am. Economic J.: Economic Policy 15 (3), 372–406.

UNFCCC, 2015. *Paris Agreement.*

United Nations, 2022. World Population Prospects 2022: Summary of Results. New York, NY.

United States Environmental Protection Agency, 2023. Report on the Social Cost of Greenhouse Gases: Estimates Incorporating Recent Scientific Advances. Washington, DC.

van den Bijgaart, I., Gerlagh, R., Liski, M., 2016. A simple formula for the social cost of carbon. J. Environ. Econ. Manage. 77. FEEM Working Paper, pp. 75–94. https://doi.org/10.1016/j.jeem.2016.01.005.

van der Ploeg, F., 2013. Cumulative carbon emissions and the Green Paradox. Annu. Rev. Resour. Econ. 5, 281–300.

van der Ploeg, F., Rezai, A., 2021. Optimal carbon pricing in general equilibrium: temperature caps and stranded assets in an extended annual DSGE model. J. Environ. Econ. Manag. 110, 102522.

Weil, P., 1990. Nonexpected utility in macroeconomics. Q. J. Econ. 105 (1), 29–42.

Weitzman, M.L., 2007. A review of the "stern review on the economics of climate change". J. Economic Lit. 45 (3), 703–724 (American Economic Association).

Weitzman, M.L., 2009. On modeling and interpreting the economics of catastrophic climate change. Rev. Econ. Stat. 91 (1), 1–19 (MIT Press).

Weitzman, M.L., 2012. GHG targets as insurance against catastrophic climate damages. J. Public. Economic Theory 14 (2), 221–244.

Weyant, J., et al., 1996. Integrated assessment of climate change: an overview and comparison of approaches and results. In: Bruce, J.P., Lee, H., Haties, E.F. (Eds.), Climate. Cambridge University Press, Cambridge, UK.

World Resources Institute, 2022. World Greenhouse Gas Emissions: 2019. Available at: https://www.wri.org/data/world-greenhouse-gas-emissions-2019.

Zickfeld, K., et al., 2009. Setting cumulative emissions targets to reduce the risk of dangerous climate change. Proc. Natl. Acad. Sci. 106 (38), 16129–16134 (National Acad Sciences).

Zscheischler, J., et al., 2018. Future climate risk from compound events. Nat. Clim. Change 8 (6), 469–477.

Chapter 2

Empirical approaches to climate change impact quantification

Dylan Hogan[a] **and Wolfram Schlenker**[b,*]
[a]*Columbia University School of International and Public Affairs, New York, United States,*
[b]*Harvard Kennedy School of Government and NBER, Cambridge, United States*
[*]*Corresponding author. e-mail address: wolfram_schlenker@hks.harvard.edu*

Chapter Outline

1 Introduction

Human history is intrinsically linked to weather and climate fluctuations. For the longest time, humans were primarily engaged in foraging, pastoralism, or agricultural settlements across the globe, with potential trade between them (Spielmann and Eder, 1994). These activities are directly affected by weather and climatic events that impacted natural vegetation, leading to significant effects on food shortages, conflict, migration and societies at large. Büntgen et al. (2011) use tree-ring reconstructions over two and a half centuries in Europe and argue that "Wet and warm summers occurred during periods of Roman and medieval prosperity. Increased climate variability from ≈ 250 to 600 C.E. coincided with the demise of the western Roman Empire and the turmoil of the Migration Period." Similarly, Behringer (1999) observed that

Handbook of the Economics of Climate Change, Vol. 1. https://doi.org/10.1016/bs.hesecc.2024.10.006

cooling during the Little Ice Age lead to increased prosecution for witchcraft, "because a part of society held the witches directly responsible for the high frequency of climatic anomalies."

The Industrial Revolution partially decoupled human systems from environmental fluctuations, but it also initiated a feedback loop in which humans increasingly contribute to anthropogenic climate change. In recent decades, a natural science literature has emerged that focused on the consequences of anthropogenic greenhouse gas emissions on the climate. More recently, empirical studies have begun to explore the economic impacts of observed climate change. This chapter aims to discuss recent advances in this area.

Economists have long advocated for the use of benefit-cost analysis in environmental regulation (Arrow et al., 1996). Quantifying the economic implications of any regulation, or the absence thereof, is crucial when evaluating various policy options. Many countries have started conducting benefit-cost analyses to assign a shadow value to greenhouse gas emissions, and these values have been trending upward (Tol, 2023). In the U.S., the EPA initially devoted limited resources to empirically estimating the economic costs of climate change; however, a 2007 Supreme Court ruling mandated the agency to evaluate and incorporate the non-zero cost of carbon emissions (Freeman and Vermeule, 2007). This ruling jump-started the EPA's work on benefit-cost analysis of climate change, which became part of the Interagency Working Group on the Social Cost of Carbon (Pizer et al., 2014). The initial iteration of the SCC had to rely on simplified assumptions about how greenhouse gas emissions would lead to climate change and ultimately affect the economic system.[1] A subsequent review by the National Academies of Sciences, Engineering, and Medicine (2017) on the Social Cost of Carbon (SCC) recommended an integrated modular approach consisting of four major components: (i) socioeconomic and emissions projections, (ii) climate modeling, (iii) estimation of climate impacts and damages, and (iv) discounting net monetary damages.

Our chapter focuses on the third component and the lessons learned over the past four decades, during which there has been exponential growth in empirical papers examining the economic impacts of climate change. Fig. 1 displays the publication rate from 1980 to 2023. To make the different data sources that cover various sets of journals comparable, we normalize the graph to show the fraction of articles that appeared in a particular year relative to the entire 44-year period from 1980 to 2023. Depending on the citation database used, between one-eighth and one-sixth of the articles published over the last 44 years have appeared in the last year (2023) alone. As a result, we now have

[1] The evolution of Integrated Assessment Models is outline in the first chapter of this handbook. One pioneering model is DICE (Nordhaus, 1992), which has recently been updated (Barrage and Nordhaus, 2024).

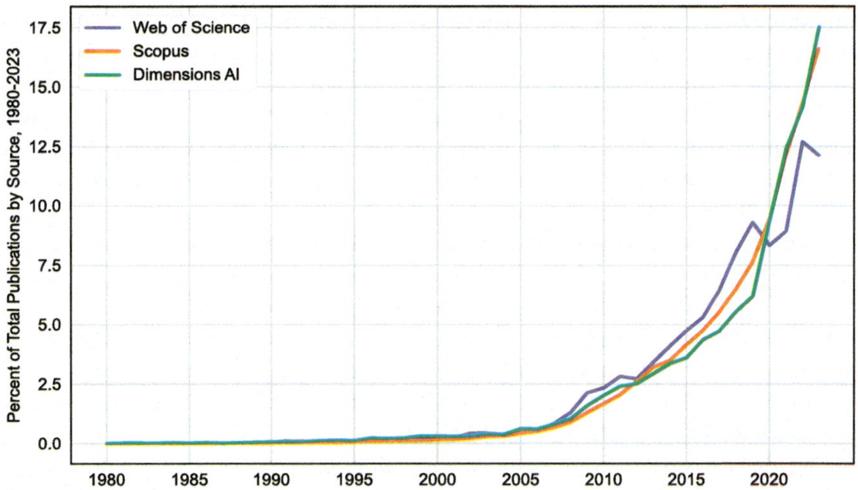

FIG. 1 Publication rate over time. *Notes*: Figure displays the fraction of articles that were published each year relative to the entire period 1980–2023. The three lines use article counts from Dimensions AI, Scopus, and Web of Science. Each ran a search of all articles that included "Climate Impact" and "Economics" in the title or the abstract.

many more micro-level studies on how various sectors are impacted by changing climatic conditions. The emergence of this field has provided further insights into how changing climatic conditions will affect human well-being and has allowed for a refinement of the social cost of carbon. The EPA's latest proposed revision (National Center for Environmental Economics, US EPA, 2023) relies on estimates from the GIVE model (Rennert et al., 2022) as well as DSCIM by the Climate Impact Lab, both of which incorporate more recent empirical damage functions.

The significant growth in empirical studies has also contributed to a broader general awareness. Recent research has not only focused on the average (or aggregate) impact but has also explored the wide range of impacts that vary significantly across different regions. While there is an emerging consensus that climate change is real and human-made, discrepancies remain regarding optimal policy responses, partly due to equity concerns and whether such policies would be regressive (Dechezleprtre et al., 2022).

Our chapter is certainly not the first to address the empirical estimates of climate change. It builds on earlier work that has explored the economics of climate change (Hsiang, 2016; Auffhammer, 2018), the use of various weather data sets (Auffhammer et al., 2013), the implications of using weather panel variation in climate impact assessments (Dell et al., 2014; Kolstad and Moore, 2020), as well as climate damage functions more broadly (Diaz and Moore, 2017).

A common theme in these empirical studies is the selection of the source of variation. Every study in this rapidly developing field faces an empirical challenge brought on by the endogeneity of climate. For example, consider a hypothetical scenario in which we observe the same city under two different climates — one with climate change and one without. In this idealized case, the difference in any outcome, whether it be mortality or crop yields, would represent the causal effect of climate change. However, we cannot observe a city with two different climates at the same point in time, which is known as the Fundamental Problem of Causal Inference (Holland, 1986). In some areas of economics, one solution is to randomize a climate change treatment across two groups of cities. Obviously, without innovations in geoengineering and questionable research ethics, this is not a viable strategy for studying climate change. Moreover, a naive regression of mortality on average temperature risks conflating the effect of temperature with other variables correlated with temperature across space, such as income and institutional quality, among many others.

We discuss various sources of identification in Section 2.1 before presenting how statistical models using historical data are then used to project future impacts in Section 2.2. Section 2.3 concludes with implications for the social cost of carbon. Section 3 discusses what we believe are important lessons learned from recent empirical studies, presenting ten lessons in Sections 3.1–3.10 before Section 4 concludes.

Throughout this chapter, we frequently use corn yields and their response to weather fluctuations to illustrate our points. The motivation is twofold: first, commodity crops like corn are mostly grown under rain-fed conditions and are strongly influenced by climatic events. There is a long history in both statistics—dating back to Wright (1928) and the discussion of instrumental variables—and in economics, where weather-induced yield shocks are often used as instruments. Corn yields, therefore, serve as an example with a well-established literature. Second, agricultural impacts are generally the second-largest after temperature-induced mortality, making it crucial to understand their effect as an important component of the social cost of carbon. However, it should be emphasized that many other sectors, besides agricultural yields, are affected by climate change—our example should not be taken as an indication that these constitute the only or even the most important economic impacts.

2 Empirical estimates of the effect of climate change

Empirically estimating the impact of changing climatic conditions generally involves two steps: The first is to estimate the response function, which shows how various sectors of interest are affected by climatic conditions using historical data, as discussed in Section 2.1 below. The second step is to use the estimated response function to simulate a counterfactual world where climatic conditions have changed, which is discussed in Section 2.2. We conclude by discussing the implications for the Social Cost of Carbon in Section 2.3.

2.1 Review of core empirical methodologies

We provide an overview of common empirical strategies for estimating the impact of climate change on various aspects of society and the economy. The methodologies covered in this section have been applied to questions across different geographies – from individual cities or countries to global effects – and to various outcomes of interest, including impacts on humans (e.g., health and conflict), economic systems (e.g., energy consumption and sectoral productivity), and aggregate economic indicators such as GDP. Together, these studies offer insight into the diverse ways in which climate and weather affect society today, as well as our potential future under climate change. The evolution of the econometric approaches applied in these studies, along with the climate science they rely on, is crucial for understanding the evolution of predicted impacts and the evolution of policies that mitigate climate change and facilitate adaptation to climate change.

The distinction between climate and weather is essential for understanding the methods that follow. Weather refers to the atmospheric conditions in a specific place at a specific time, including factors like temperature, humidity, precipitation, wind speed, and atmospheric pressure. Weather conditions change frequently and can vary significantly from day to day or season to season. In contrast, climate refers to the long-term patterns and averages of weather conditions in a region over an extended period (typically 30 years or more). More generally, climate can be viewed as the underlying distribution from which weather realizations are drawn. Researchers studying the impacts of climate change use observations of weather and climate from the historical record to predict the economic effects of changes in the climate, i.e., changes in the distribution of weather outcomes. As we discuss Section 3 below, the results of an econometric analysis of climate impacts are often sensitive to the specification of weather and climate variables, to the extent that these predictions can vary significantly in magnitude or even change in sign.

Most of the approaches we discuss in this section draw from quasi-experimental tools to estimate plausibly causal effects of climate, each with identification assumptions that influence the interpretation of the econometric results. However, alongside questions of identification, there is a trade-off between what is identified and what is desired (Donaldson, 2022). For example, econometric methods that exploit randomness in the weather system may yield a causal interpretation of weather that differs from that of climate due to adaptation (Mérel et al., 2024).

This chapter is not the first publication to review these concepts. Hsiang (2016), Auffhammer (2022), and Kolstad and Moore (2020) are three examples of papers that provide comprehensive discussions of the approaches outlined below. We review them here to provide a reference for the discussion of lessons learned from recent analyses in Section 3.

For the remainder of the chapter, we will repeatedly use an empirical example, shown in Fig. 2, to illustrate how different sources of identification

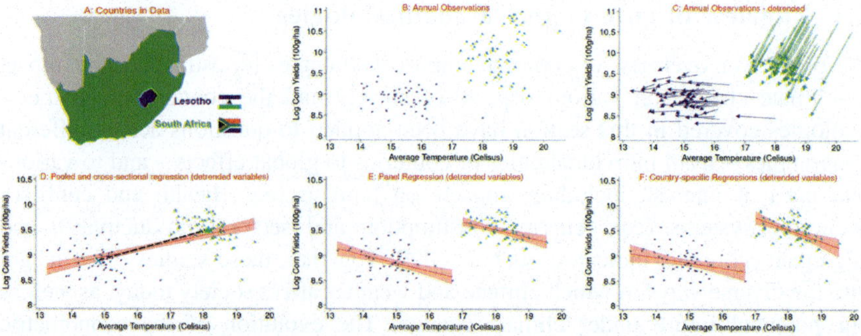

FIG. 2 Corn yields and average temperature in Lesotho and South Africa. *Notes*: Figure displays log maize yields and average temperature over the growing season November-May for Lesotho (X) and South Africa (▲) during the years 1961–2022.

can yield vastly different results regarding how temperature influences corn yields. Yield data (production per unit of land area) are taken from the FAO for both South Africa and Lesotho.[2] Panel A shows the location of the two countries: Lesotho is an "island" surrounded by South Africa. It has a higher average altitude (2161 m) than South Africa (1200 m) and, consequently, lower average temperatures.[3] This is depicted in Panel B, which presents a scatter plot of average temperatures (x-axis) against average yields (y-axis) over 62 years (1961–2022). Lesotho is not only colder but also less productive. The two sets of points (blue crosses for Lesotho and green triangles for South Africa) form disjoint sets.

Before contrasting various sources of identification and discussing whether it is better to compare across countries or within countries, Panel C highlights the importance of being cautious about spurious correlations between two trending variables. Historically, annual temperatures fluctuated around a constant mean, implying they were independently and identically distributed (i.i.d.) around the long-term average. However, in recent decades, clear warming trends have emerged. For example, since roughly 1980, the United States has experienced a decrease in heating-degree days (cold days when heating is required) and an increase in cooling-degree days (hot days when cooling is required).[4] As a result, the i.i.d. assumption is no longer valid. It is imperative to remove the trend to avoid spurious correlations between trending

[2] Data was downloaded from https://www.fao.org/faostat/ for all available years (1961–2022) at the time of writing.

[3] We will discuss the major available data sources in further detail below. For this example, we use ERA5-Land. Daily temperature records are weighted by the maize-growing area in each grid cell and averaged over the maize-growing season from November to March. A more detailed description of how the data is aggregated can be found in Hogan and Schlenker (2024).

[4] See for example Figure A12 in Schlenker and Taylor (2021).

variables. A well-known teaching example is the myth told to children that the stork delivers babies. Interestingly, there is a highly significant correlation between the stork population and birth rates (Höfer et al., 2004), the reason being that both are trending over time — the stork population declines in many areas as did birth rates.

Panel C therefore demeans both variables. It does so by using restricted cubic splines in time with three knots.[5] The arrows in Panel C show the transition from the raw data in Panel B to the detrended values.[6] Note how, in South Africa, the picture changes drastically for the years with the highest temperatures: while these years were associated with the highest yields in Panel B, they show lower (detrended) yields in Panel C. This is because both yields (due to technological progress) and temperatures (due to climate change) have been trending upwards in South Africa, leading to a false positive correlation. Once the trend is removed, the highest average temperatures (net of the trend) tend to correspond with lower yields (net of the trend). Lesotho has also experienced warming, and removing the trend causes the arrows to point to the left, indicating colder temperatures. At the same time, yields in Lesotho have not trended upward significantly over time, so the arrows do not point down much after the trend is removed. The trend should be group-specific to account for heterogeneity in observed trends. For macroeconomic indicators like GDP, authors often use growth rates (the first difference in the log of the outcome variable) because GDP is difference-stationary rather than trend-stationary.[7] Going forward, we will focus on detrended variables in our empirical example (panels D-F of Fig. 2) to avoid spurious correlations between trending variables.

2.1.1 Cross-sectional models

Cross-sectional research designs estimate the effect of climate by comparing economic outcomes across different locations, while controlling for observable non-climate confounding variables. The following linear model is typical in cross-sectional analyses of climate impacts:

$$y_i = \alpha + \mathbf{C}_i\boldsymbol{\beta} + \mathbf{X}_i\boldsymbol{\gamma} + \epsilon_i, \tag{1}$$

[5] Resulting in two variables of time.

[6] We simply regress each variable on the two spline variables of time and then deduct the predicted value to remove the trend.

[7] Note that taking a first difference reduces the order of the polynomial of the time trend by one. For example, taking the first difference of a model with group-specific linear time trends is equivalent to a model in first differences with group fixed effects. Newell et al. (2021) caution against using both time trends and region-by-year fixed effects simultaneously, as the latter will also absorb the trends in various regions. They argue that having time trends of lower order or no time trend at all might increase out-of-sample predictive performance. However, returning to the stork example, a reduced out-of-sample predictive performance of a spurious correlation between two trending variables is not necessarily a bad thing if the correlation isn't causal.

where y_i is the outcome of interest for location i, $\mathbf{C}_i$ is a vector representing moments of the climate distribution, $\mathbf{X}_i$ is a vector of non-climate covariates, and ϵ_i is an error term. This often includes a non-linear function of variables like average temperature and precipitation to reflect the changing marginal effect of climate on the outcome. While the regression model is still linear in all parameters, the variables themselves are often non-linear transformations. For example, studies assessing the effect of rainfall on agricultural productivity may specify average precipitation as a quadratic function to capture the benefits of moderate rainfall patterns relative to arid or flood-prone climates. The elements of $\boldsymbol{\beta}$ represent the marginal effect of each moment of the climate distribution on the outcome. The identifying assumption is that, after conditioning on observable characteristics $\mathbf{X}_i$, there is no correlation between the climatic variables and the error term.

Mendelsohn et al. (1994) first estimated the Ricardian (or hedonic) framework, which applies the cross-sectional research design to estimate the marginal effect of climate on agricultural land prices in the US. This approach departed from earlier studies that relied on empirical or experimentally derived production functions. The innovation of the Ricardian approach is that it implicitly captures farmer adaptation to climate, whether through crop choice, technological change, changes in agricultural land use (e.g., conversions from farming to livestock or forestry), or transitions away from agriculture to other productive uses. The key theoretical assumption underlying the Ricardian approach is that land markets capitalize the net present value of all future land uses once the land is put to the optimal use, implying that changes in land value reflect farm profitability net of climate impacts and adaptive responses. In contrast, production-function approaches model adaptive margins directly and require ample data on farmer behavior to measure shifts in the production function along each dimension. Conceptually, the Ricardian approach avoids this challenge by focusing on the outer envelope of the production functions, where farm profit is maximized (Auffhammer, 2022).

The empirical implementation of Mendelsohn et al. (1994) follows the structure of equation (1). They regress farmland values from the 1978 and 1982 Census of Agriculture on quadratic functions of temperature and precipitation for four months, chosen to represent each season, while controlling for various county characteristics, including latitude, soil quality, population density, and income per capita. The estimated coefficients capture the direct effects of climate on crop yields, as well as the indirect substitution of inputs, agricultural practices, or other adaptations to climate differences across space. Their results suggest that the agricultural sector in the US would experience *net benefits* from climate change under their preferred model, based on a simplified projection of temperature and precipitation from the IPCC. However, the approach and its implementation in Mendelsohn et al. (1994) have drawn criticism, some of which could lead to changes in the sign of predicted climate change impacts.

The cross-sectional research design is prone to omitted variable bias. For example, Schlenker et al. (2005) revisit the Mendelsohn et al. (1994) analysis, incorporating additional data on irrigation. Access to subsidized irrigation water is a critical input for agriculture in the drier western portion of the United States, yet it is highly subsidized: Wahl (1989) estimates that 86 % of the project costs of the U.S. Bureau of Reclamation are subsidized. This access is highly correlated with climate, with hotter climates receiving more subsidized water, which capitalizes into farmland values (Schlenker et al., 2007). Thus, without including subsidized irrigation in $\mathbf{X}_i$ in equation (1), a valuable underpriced input, estimates of the marginal effect of climate are biased: they capture not only the effect of temperature (negative) but also the access to a subsidized input (positive). Lacking sufficient data on irrigation use and cost, Schlenker et al. (2005) reanalyze the hedonic model, focusing only on dryland agriculture. Their results consistently predict large, negative damages from climate change. Several other omitted variables have been proposed since Mendelsohn et al. (1994) was published, including the costs of adaptation (Quiggin and Horowitz, 1999), expectations of future climate (Severen et al., 2018), and nonfarm spillovers on farmland markets (Ortiz-Bobea, 2020), highlighting the vulnerability of cross-sectional analysis to endogeneity concerns.

Panel D of Fig. 2 presents both a pooled regression (red line) and a cross-sectional regression linking average outcomes in each country (black dashed line between the larger cross and triangle, symbolizing the average temperature and yield in each of the two countries).[8] Both regressions suggest that higher temperatures are beneficial for yields, as indicated by the positive slopes of the lines. However, one concern is that the higher yields in South Africa may be due to other factors correlated with climate that differ between the two countries. For example, fertilizer use is much higher in South Africa (24 kg per hectare) than in Lesotho (3 kg per hectare), and the higher yields in South Africa might result from this increased fertilizer use rather than the beneficial effect of higher temperatures. Indeed, both panel regressions (Panel E) and country-specific regressions suggest that warmer-than-normal temperatures result in lower-than-normal yields, which is the opposite of what is observed in Panel D.

2.1.2 Panel models

Panel data sets include repeated observations of groups over time. In climate impact modeling, these groups are generally spatial units (locations). Panel models almost always include group (location) fixed effects, which flexibly control for time-invariant omitted variables that commonly affect cross-sectional analyses. They sometimes also include period fixed effects to absorb

8 Since we only have two countries, we are left with two observations and cannot estimate a confidence band for the cross-sectional relationship.

time-varying shocks that are common to all units. Conceptually, fixed effects regressions estimate the marginal effect of weather from within-unit period-to-period (e.g., year-to-year or month-to-month) variation in both weather and the dependent variable. The linear panel model with group fixed effects can be expressed as:

$$y_{it} = \alpha_i + \mathbf{W}_{it}\boldsymbol{\beta} + \mathbf{X}_{it}\boldsymbol{\gamma} + \epsilon_{it} \tag{2a}$$

where y_{it} is the outcome of interest in location i and time t, $\mathbf{W}_{it}$ is a vector of weather variables, and $\mathbf{X}_{it}$ is a vector of time-varying controls. The unit fixed effects α_i absorb any confounding effects caused by unobserved factors that are constant over time within each unit, such as differences in soil quality. Including this group-specific intercept term is equivalent to removing the unit-specific mean from the dependent and independent variables.[9]

Panel E of Fig. 2 relies on panel variation, examining whether yields in each country are higher or lower than the country-specific average when temperatures are above or below the country-specific average. Here, we observe that the relationship completely reverses compared to the cross-sectional or pooled analysis in panel D: the red line now slopes downward, indicating that higher-than-average temperatures lead to lower-than-average yields in each country. A panel model forces the slopes to be the same across all groups (countries in this example) while allowing for different intercepts (group fixed effects). The idea is that all other time-invariant factors, such as soil quality differences, will be absorbed by the country fixed effects. The statistical advantage of using weather fluctuations around a mean – at least for detrended variables – is that they are exogenous and random (Dell et al., 2014). However, a major potential downside is that while this random and unexpected variation is defensible in statistical terms, it also means that the response of agents to these unexpected weather shocks may differ significantly from their response to a permanent shift in the climate. For example, farmers might not install irrigation systems in response to a hot and dry year, both because it takes time and is costly, but they might do so if conditions are permanently altered, suggesting that long-term adaptation possibilities are greater than short-term ones.[10] Conversely, the opposite scenario is also possible—an agent might be able to respond to a one-time shock in a way that is not sustainable in the long term, suggesting that short-term adaptation possibilities might be greater than

[9] Taking the average for group (location) i we get $\frac{1}{T}\Sigma_t y_{it} = \alpha_i + \frac{1}{T}\Sigma_t \mathbf{W}_{it}\boldsymbol{\beta} + \frac{1}{T}\Sigma_t \mathbf{X}_{it}\boldsymbol{\gamma} + \frac{1}{T}\Sigma_t \epsilon_{it}$. A necessary condition under OLS to minimize the sum of squared residuals is that the errors sum to zero for each constant (here group i) or $\frac{1}{T}\Sigma_t \epsilon_{it} = 0$. Using the notation for group means $\overline{y_i} = \frac{1}{T}\Sigma_t y_{it}$ we get $\alpha_i = \overline{y_i} - \overline{\mathbf{W}_i}\boldsymbol{\beta} + \overline{\mathbf{X}_i}\boldsymbol{\gamma}$, which upon substitution in equation (2a) gives the revised regression equation $[y_{it} - \overline{y_i}] = [\mathbf{W}_{it} - \overline{\mathbf{W}_i}]\boldsymbol{\beta} + [\mathbf{X}_{it} - \overline{\mathbf{X}_i}]\boldsymbol{\gamma} + \epsilon_{it}$. This showcases why a panel model is often called a "within" model, as it is equivalent to demeaning the dependent and independent variables.

[10] The next chapter in this handbook provides a more detailed discussion of adaptation (Carleton et al., 2024b).

long-term ones. For example, a farmer might be able to pump groundwater to irrigate fields during a hot year but could not sustain this during prolonged drought conditions as the aquifer becomes depleted.

In summary, a major issue with panel models is that the parameter of interest, β, represents the marginal effect of weather rather than climate. This distinction is crucial because the response to short-term weather fluctuations differs from the impact of long-term climate changes. For example, Bakkensen and Barrage (2018) examine the effects of hurricanes on economic growth and stress that response to hurricane *risk* (ex-ante exposure as measured in the cross-section) can lead to an increase in the savings rate with positive effects on economic growth, while hurricane *strikes* (realizations that are used in panel studies) reduce growth due to the damage they inflict.

In climate impact studies, β estimates reflect short-run (or intensive margin) adaptations to immediate weather conditions. However, they typically do not account for long-run (or extensive margin) adaptations that affect climate sensitivity over time. For example, while β might capture an individual's decision to stay indoors during an exceptionally hot day, it does not encompass long-term adaptations such as the widespread adoption of air conditioning. To address this limitation, several econometric approaches have been developed to account for and quantify long-run adaptations in panel models, which will be discussed in Section 3.

A common extension to the standard panel model is to estimate a two-way fixed effect model that not only includes group (location) fixed effects, but also temporal fixed effects δ_t absorb common shocks in each period. The revised regression equation becomes

$$y_{it} = \alpha_i + \mathbf{W}_{it}\boldsymbol{\beta} + \mathbf{X}_{it}\gamma + \delta_t + \epsilon_{it} \tag{2b}$$

This has implications for the meaning of "within-variation" which is now net of both group and period fixed effects.[11]

Just as unit fixed effects match the spatial unit of observation (e.g., counties, states, or countries), time fixed effects often correspond to the temporal resolution of the data. The most common time unit is years, as most panel data track units from year to year. However, the recent growth in high-frequency, remotely sensed variables (discussed further in Section 3) has enabled the measurement of social and economic outcomes at monthly or even daily scales. In such cases, it may be important to include temporal fixed effects to account

[11] Using the notation of footnote 9 and the notation $\frac{1}{T}\sum_t \delta_t = \overline{\delta}$ we get a revised regression equation $[y_{it} - \overline{y}_i] = [\mathbf{W}_{it} - \overline{\mathbf{W}}_i]\boldsymbol{\beta} + [\mathbf{X}_{it} - \overline{\mathbf{X}}_i]\gamma + [\delta_t - \overline{\delta}] + \epsilon_{it}$. A two-way fixed effect model with both location and time fixed effect is equivalent to (i) running the model that is demeaned by each group (location) with temporal fixed effects, (ii) demean all variables by period and include again location-specific fixed effects, or (iii) by the Frisch-Waugh-Lovell theorem, first running a regression of the dependent and independent variables on location and period fixed effects and use the residuals net of group and period fixed effects.

for seasonality, typically in the form of month or month-of-year fixed effects. Omitting these seasonality controls can bias the weather coefficient by conflating within-year trends with the true effect of weather.

In settings where most of the variation comes from year-to-year fluctuations (e.g., a study of weather shocks in a smaller country that experiences common shocks), it may be preferable to replace time period-specific fixed effects (intercepts) with linear or quadratic time trends. These trends remove broader trends from both the dependent and independent variables while preserving part of the year-to-year fluctuations. Including period fixed effects for small geographic areas is problematic because weather variables, particularly temperature, are often highly correlated within the same area and are measured with error — especially since they tend to be interpolatied between weather stations. As a result, period fixed effects for small geographic areas may remove much of the true signal, leaving predominantly noise as weather variation. This noise will bias the coefficients towards zero and lead to standard errors that are too small. The appropriate set of controls should balance potential sources of bias and variance in the weather coefficients, depending on the available data and the underlying data-generating process.

An example that illustrates the potential drawbacks of including regional fixed effects is Deschnes and Greenstone, 2007. The authors were among the first to utilize a panel approach for analyzing climate impacts. Their paper linked county-level agricultural profits to measures of temperature and precipitation, and the regression included state-by-year effects. State-by-year fixed effects could be useful for controlling for price feedback of regionally grown crops or state policy changes that are correlated with weather, as they capture time-varying shocks common to all counties within a state. However, in smaller states with limited within-state variation, these fixed effects can absorb a substantial portion of the overall variation in weather. Consider the smaller state of Maryland: if counties in northern Maryland are warmer than usual in a particular year, the same is true for counties in Southern Maryland as well. In general counties in Maryland have highly correlated temperature shocks. The inclusion of state-by-year fixed effects can lead to weather variables that are in large part noise. While we would expect the standard errors to enlarge as identifying variation is removed, if the remaining variation is mostly noise, the standard errors will be too small. Intuitively, if all the variation that is left is noise, the regression equation sees changes in the exogenous variables (the noise) that have no effect on the dependent variable and hence predicts a precise zero. Fisher et al. (2012) show in Table 2 that state-by-year fixed effects in the particular weather data result in a signal-to-noise ratio of 1:7, i.e., the remaining variation was in large part (87 %) noise.[12]

[12] They argue that state-by-year fixed effects should, in theory, increase the magnitude of the coefficient on temperature if they capture regional price variations, which move inversely to production fluctuations. For instance, if a freeze affects the orange crop in Florida, leading to a reduction in output, regional prices for oranges will increase. This price increase will partially offset the reduction in profits due to lower output.

While panel models effectively control for many sources of omitted variables bias, they remain susceptible to bias from time-varying factors that influence the outcome and are correlated with $\mathbf{W}_{it}$ or $\mathbf{X}_{it}$. Weather variation is often assumed to be exogenous due to its random atmospheric origins. However, weather variables drawn from the same climate distribution are typically correlated, which can introduce bias if not all relevant variables are included. For instance, while studies interested in temperature effects usually control for rainfall (which is correlated with temperature), this may not be sufficient. Proctor et al. (2022) highlight that soil moisture, which historically correlates with temperature, can bias temperature coefficients if the regression equation does not account for soil moisture. Moreover, the historic correlation does not hold under climate change, leading to biased estimates as the reduced-form estimate on temperature is no longer appropriate. In a different context, relative humidity is often cited as a potential omitted variable in the temperature-mortality relationship. Wet-bulb temperature, which combines temperature, relative humidity, wind speed, and solar radiation, is considered a more relevant metric for assessing weather's impact on mortality because it reflects the role of sweat evaporation. In arid climates, the human body regulates heat exposure more efficiently through sweating compared to humid climates, where high wet-bulb temperatures exceeding skin temperature can be fatal (Wilson et al., 2024). Omitting relative humidity may therefore bias estimates of the temperature-mortality relationship. Although some argue that such estimates can still predict future climate impacts, this assumes that weather variable correlations remain constant, which is problematic given shifting climatic patterns and feedback loops, e.g., through changes in cloud formation. Furthermore, historical data on temperature and rainfall are generally more reliable than relative humidity measurements, particularly at finer scales. Consequently, focusing exclusively on locations with reliable humidity data—typically high-income countries—limits the ability to explore weather effects across diverse global climates and income levels.

2.1.2.1 Non-linear effects of weather

Modeling outcomes as a linear function of weather variables assumes a constant marginal effect of weather across its range. This assumption is often unrealistic in climate studies. For instance, a one-degree increase in temperature from 35°C to 36°C is likely more detrimental to human health and crops than the same increase from 20°C to 21°C. Additionally, rising temperatures from extreme cold can be beneficial for various outcomes. While the same non-linearity might be present in cross-sectional studies discussed in the previous section, they are often harder to identify given the limited number of spatial units, such as the roughly 3000 counties in the United States. In contrast, panel models track the same units over time — such as these 3000 counties over 50 years — resulting in a total of 150,000 observations. This extensive dataset helps in identifying and analyzing extreme events that occur infrequently. To identify non-linear effects, we can generalize equation (2b) to incorporate flexible functions of weather variables, allowing for varying marginal effects across different weather conditions.

$$y_{it} = \alpha_i + f(\mathbf{W}_{it}) + \mathbf{X}_{it}\gamma + \delta_t + \epsilon_{it} \tag{2c}$$

In modeling weather effects, f represents a linear-in-parameters function of the weather variables $\mathbf{W}_{it}$. There are several common approaches to specify the function $f(\mathbf{W}_{it})$. Polynomials, splines, and step functions are frequently used in climate impact studies, each with distinct advantages and disadvantages:

Polynomials: These functions offer a parsimonious way to model non-linearity and require fewer observations to estimate. However, they are sensitive to extreme values, which can distort the function's shape. Increasing the polynomial's order can mitigate this, but it may lead to overfitting and require more parameters.

Splines: These consist of piecewise linear or non-linear (e.g., cubic) segments fitted between control points (knots). Splines provide a smooth, continuous function at each knot and are less sensitive to extreme values than polynomials. They balance flexibility and stability but might be sensitive to the number of chosen knots or knot location.

Step Functions: These non-parametric bins offer high flexibility but require assumptions about the number of bins, which can affect interpretation. Too many bins can lead to noisy results due to high correlation among bin categories, while too few bins may miss important non-linearities. Step functions assume that the effect within each bin is constant and changes abruptly at bin boundaries, which may not accurately reflect real-world continuous responses.

Capturing non-linearity in response functions requires careful construction of the weather variables $\mathbf{W}_{it}$. For some outcomes, relevant non-linearity occurs at a daily or sub-daily scale and is specific to the local context of the study. Conversely, other outcomes are often measured using weather averages over longer time horizons or larger geographic areas. For instance, while individuals and crops may respond to local temperature shocks on a sub-daily basis, mortality rates and crop yields might only be available annually (temporal aggregation) and aggregated at the county level (spatial aggregation). Therefore, the construction of weather variables should align with the data generating process (DGP) by targeting non-linear weather effects at the relevant spatial and temporal scales. In practice, this might involve calculating polynomial terms for daily, or even sub-daily (e.g., hourly), weather data at the station or pixel level and then averaging these terms across space and time to reflect the true exposure influencing outcomes like mortality or crop yields. The key is to derive the non-linear transformation of weather variables *before* aggregation across time or space, not the other way around. This approach is more suitable if the unit of response pertains to overall county climate rather than localized conditions or specific time periods.

2.1.2.2 Heterogeneity across space and time

As discussed, a key feature of the panel approach is its use of stochastic weather variation to identify causal response functions, which does not capture slow-moving adaptation to climate. To investigate long-run responses, researchers sometimes examine changes in weather sensitivity across different climates and time periods. Spatially, under climate change, locations with currently cooler climates may begin adopting adaptation strategies similar to those found in currently warmer climates. Comparing weather sensitivities across locations with different climates can provide insights into the benefits of such adaptations. To at least partially account for changing adaptation possibilities, recent studies have begun to allow group-specific sensitivities to temperature fluctuations to systematically vary with covariates, most notably average temperature and/or income (Butler and Huybers, 2013; Carleton et al., 2022). The idea is to model whether places can become less sensitive to temperature fluctuations as they become warmer or richer, for example, through defensive investments. Panel F of Fig. 2 illustrates the yield-temperature relationship separately for each country, allowing both the intercept and the slope to vary by country. In our example, the warmer country (South Africa) appears more sensitive to temperature fluctuations, possibly indicating a non-linear yield-temperature relationship where warming has a greater impact on places that are already hotter. It should be noted that allowing climate sensitivity to vary with an average characteristic of a group is, once again, a cross-sectional analysis that may suffer from the potential downsides discussed earlier. For example, the sensitivity might be higher in areas with hotter average climates not necessarily because they are hotter, but because they could have different institutional setups.

Temporally, researchers can assess how weather sensitivity evolves by dividing the sample into different sub-periods and comparing the marginal effects of weather across these sub-periods. This approach helps to determine if sensitivity to weather fluctuations decreases over time as new adaptation strategies become available, whether through technological advances or economic growth. For example, the sensitivity of human mortality to very hot temperatures has decreased following the widespread adoption of air conditioning (Barreca et al., 2016). Similarly, Barreca et al. (2015) analyzed state-by-month data on mortality and temperature in the US to estimate differences in the marginal effect of heat exposure by climatic zone and time period. They found that before 1960, regions with more high-temperature days were less sensitive to extreme heat compared to colder regions, suggesting that individuals in warmer climates had invested in costly adaptations like air conditioning. After 1960, sensitivities converged as the cost of air conditioning decreased, making adaptation to extreme temperatures more accessible.

However, it is important to note that the cross-sectional and temporal differences in temperature sensitivity examined in this study are not random.

Thus, while the decline in air conditioning costs is a compelling explanation for changes in the temperature-mortality relationship, the approach remains susceptible to time-invariant variables that may influence the marginal effect of temperature across different regions, similar to issues in traditional cross-sectional research designs. On top of that, it is also succeptible to time-varying omitted variables that covary with the adoption of air conditioning. An alternative explanation is provided by Mullins and White (2020), which link changes in sensitivity to hot temperatures to access to healthcare. This research uses the idiosyncratic roll-out of Community Health Centers (CHCs) across US counties in the 1960s and 1970s as a source of identification and finds that improved access to healthcare facilities was a major driver. In an supplementary analysis the authors find that acute care facilities are especially effective at mitigating the effect of cold temperatures on human mortality, highlighting the importance of health care access as air conditioning has no effect on the effect of cold temperatures. It highlights the potential for omitted variable bias in panel settings, where better access to healthcare facilities correlated with the adoption of air conditioning.

2.1.3 *Long differences*

Recent observed warming trends have provided researchers with the opportunity to examine how individuals respond to instances of climate change. The advantage of this approach is that it allows for the investigation of responses to actual changes in climate. However, a challenge arises because many areas exhibit only minor changes, making it unclear whether individuals recognized these changes as a permanent shift in climate, prompting adaptation, or if they were experiencing decadal cycles.

The long differences strategy aims to balance the time-series identification of panel models with the climate treatment interpretation of cross-sectional analysis. Instead of leveraging high-frequency changes in the independent and dependent variables, as is typical in standard panel models, long differences methods focus on period-to-period changes over more extended time horizons, such as decades. For example, consider a panel data set containing observations of an outcome and weather variables for each county i in year t. For each multi-year time period τ, let $\overline{Z}_{i\tau} = \frac{1}{\tau}\sum_{t\in\tau} Z_{it}$. Then the long differences model is

$$\overline{y}_{i\tau} = \alpha_i + \overline{\mathbf{W}}_{i\tau}\beta + \overline{\mathbf{X}}_{i\tau}\gamma + \overline{\delta}_\tau + \overline{\varepsilon}_{i\tau} \tag{3a}$$

where β represents the marginal effect of changes in *average* weather conditions taken for each multi-year period to the corresponding change of the average in the outcome variable. While the long differences equation appears similar to equation (2b), the interpretation of β changes as the data are aggregated over longer periods and $\overline{\mathbf{W}}_{i\tau}$ becomes a better approximation of local climate $\mathbf{C}_i$. Thus, as the length of the time period τ increases, β incorporates longer-run effects of changes in climate as well as adaptation investments that materialize over the long run. When the data are aggregated to only two periods (τ_1 and τ_2), the long differences model can be rewritten in first differences:

$$\bar{y}_{i\tau_2} - \bar{y}_{i\tau_1} = \tilde{\delta} + (\overline{\mathbf{W}}_{i\tau_2} - \overline{\mathbf{W}}_{i\tau_1})\boldsymbol{\beta} + (\overline{\mathbf{X}}_{i\tau_2} - \overline{\mathbf{X}}_{i\tau_1})\gamma + \epsilon_i \quad (3b)$$

where $\tilde{\delta} = \bar{\delta}_{\tau_2} - \bar{\delta}_{\tau_1}$ is the average trend across the sample and $\boldsymbol{\beta}$ is the marginal effect of the observed trend between τ_1 and τ_2 on the outcome variable of interest. This approach has the advantage of controlling for location-specific time-invariant unobserved heterogeneity — note that α_i drops out in equation (3b) — while relying on longer-run variation that accounts for gradual forms of adaptation. As with other methods, the long differences strategy is also susceptible to omitted variable bias, particularly with respect to trending variables that are correlated with both weather trends and the outcome of interest. Additionally, this approach requires a sufficiently large data set to calculate long-run trends in the variables and enough spatial variation in these trends to accurately estimate marginal effects. It also relies on the assumption that agents perceive changes as long-term rather than as decadal fluctuations.

For example, Burke and Emerick (2016) estimate equation (3b) using data on agricultural yields and average weather in the US. Their main specification compares two periods, 1980 and 2000, calculating 5-year centered averages of weather variables to characterize local climate. The effectiveness of equation (3b) depends on spatial variation in trends; however, one concern is that observed climate trends are relatively small compared to future projections from climate models. Burke and Emerick (2016) address this by showing that trends over the sample period are of a similar magnitude to expected trends for 2030 and exhibit significant spatial heterogeneity. They find that the marginal effects estimated from their long differences approach are smaller in some specifications (and larger in others) compared to those from a baseline panel model, but the differences are not statistically significant. They argue that if adaptations available to farmers take place over decades rather than years, the marginal effect of gradual climate changes will be less pronounced than the impact of unexpected year-to-year variability. Thus, they interpret the statistically similar coefficients from the long differences and panel models as evidence that there has been limited long-run adaptation in US agriculture during the study period.

Returning to our example of yields in South Africa and Lesotho from Fig. 2, the trend in average temperature over the growing season was 0.195°C per decade for South Africa and 0.25°C per decade for Lesotho. The corresponding trends in log corn yields per decade were 0.24 for South Africa and −0.02 for Lesotho, although, as previously mentioned, the latter is not statistically significant. In this example, the country with the lower observed temperature trend (South Africa) had a higher growth rate in yields, suggesting that warming may be detrimental to yield growth. With only one trend per group, the analysis reverts to a purely cross-sectional approach, which carries the same potential pitfalls discussed earlier, specifically, if there are other trending variables that are corelated with the climate trends. This raises the question of what drives the differences in trends and whether they are correlated with other factors. For instance, recent studies have found that cropland intensification and irrigation in the United States can reduce the upper tail of the temperature distribution (Mueller et al., 2016; Braun and Schlenker, 2023). Therefore, there may be an important feedback loop between economic activity and observed climate trends, making these trends endogenous. Although such feedback is also present in panel variation, year-to-year weather fluctuations are generally much larger than observed trends, suggesting that feedback loops likely account for a smaller fraction of the observed variation.

Kolstad and Moore (2020) argue that trends in average weather vary depending on the length of the time period analyzed. Specifically, they highlight that temperature changes over long periods (e.g., more than a century) tend to be more pronounced, yet often revert to a common trend (e.g., the Little Ice Age had similar effects across European countries). This raises concerns about including regional fixed effects, as they might absorb much of the common variation. Conversely, changes over shorter periods (e.g., 30–50 years) exhibit more variation within regions. For instance, Burke and Emerick (2016) employed state fixed effects, which forced their analysis to rely only on differences in warming trends within states. There is a trade-off: while longer periods provide stronger signals, they rely on differences across larger geographic areas, which may have confounding trends that need to be controlled for in $\boldsymbol{X}_{i\tau}$. Furthermore, Kolstad and Moore (2020) note that studies using long differences to date often consider timescales that are too short to distinguish permanent climate shifts from low-frequency natural variability in the climate system. If observed historical trends are solely attributable to inter-annual oscillations, farmers might not invest in long-term adaptation strategies that are only advantageous under permanent climate change.

2.1.4 Spatial first differences

Spatial first differences (SFD) is a recent empirical strategy proposed by Druckenmiller and Hsiang (2018), where identification comes from differences in the independent and dependent variables between close neighbors. The motivation behind this approach is that omitted variable bias might be more severe when comparing units that are far apart. By focusing on direct neighbors, the expectation is that other potential confounders vary smoothly in space and do not covary with the variable of interest, such as climate, thereby reducing omitted variable bias. This method is analogous to using first differencing in time series analysis, except that the difference occurs across two spatial units rather than across time. Starting with the standard cross-sectional regression in equation (1), the SFD design regresses the difference in outcomes between location i and its adjacent neighbor $i - 1$ on the corresponding differences in climate variables and covariates.

$$y_i - y_{i-1} = (\mathbf{C}_i - \mathbf{C}_{i-1})\boldsymbol{\beta} + (\mathbf{X}_i - \mathbf{X}_{i-1})\boldsymbol{\gamma} + (\epsilon_i - \epsilon_{i-1}) \tag{4}$$

where $\boldsymbol{\beta}$ represents the marginal effect of climate on the outcome of interest. The advantage of SFD over standard cross-sectional analysis is that it implicitly controls for unobserved heterogeneity from confounding factors that are common between two spatially adjacent observations or vary slowly across space. As a result, the core identifying assumption differs from the pure cross-sectional design where all units are compared to each other. If unobserved variation exists on a larger spatial scale (e.g., subsidized irrigation water access in the Western US but not in the Eastern US), comparing neighbors helps alleviate this problem. Conversely, if unobserved variation occurs on a finer scale (e.g., polluted neighborhoods within cities, which are correlated with socio-economic characteristics), the spatial first difference approach might amplify the correlation.

SFD is typically implemented by assigning neighbors along a single cardinal direction (e.g., North-South or East-West). A natural robustness check is to test for stability in $\boldsymbol{\beta}$ across multiple directions or to pool various neighbors. An alternative is to include difference to all neighbors. Additionally, subsequent research has expanded this method to panel models, where authors take first differences for each year.

The identifying variation in the SFD regression arises from "high-frequency" changes between spatial units. Therefore, this approach is best suited for estimating relationships between variables that exhibit substantial variation between neighbors. A potential concern is insufficient residual variation when the spatial units (e.g., locations) are small relative to the changes in climate across space. For instance, if neighboring zip codes have very similar climates, estimates of $\boldsymbol{\beta}$ may be imprecise due to minimal variation in the spatial difference in climate. Conversely, geographically large spatial units (e.g., countries) are more likely to violate the core identification assumption, as other differences between units may correlate with climate and the outcome.

Additionally, in the presence of spatial spillovers, the estimates obtained from SFD may be biased due to a violation of the Stable Unit Treatment Value Assumption (SUTVA). For example, if the climate in one location ($\mathbf{C}_i$) influences the outcome in a nearby location (y_{i+1}) due to flows of capital, goods, or people, then $\boldsymbol{\beta}$ will capture a combination of local and distant climate effects. However, it should be noted that traditional approaches are also biased in the presence of spatial spillovers. The advantage of the SFD design is that it lends itself to including spatial lags, the analog to including temporal lags in time series analysis (Druckenmiller and Hsiang, 2018).

2.2 Future projection of climate impacts

Causal estimates of the marginal effect of climate are most helpful to policymakers when used to predict future impacts under climate change. Methodologies for simulating future climate impacts have evolved alongside the econometric approaches for estimating the marginal effect of climate described in the previous section. Early studies in the climate impacts literature often employed spatially uniform climate change scenarios, where temperature and precipitation were shifted by the same amount in every location. For instance, Mendelsohn et al. (1994) considered a 5°F increase in average temperature and an 8 % increase in precipitation, based on early estimates from the Intergovernmental Panel on Climate Change (IPCC). However, these underlying IPCC estimates, which reflect changes in global average conditions, are coarse approximations of projected warming in specific locations, with higher latitudes generally warming more than lower latitudes and highly heterogeneous precipitation changes varying from wetter to drier conditions.

To account for spatially and temporally heterogeneous climate change, subsequent climate impact analyses utilized outputs from general circulation models (GCMs). GCMs are numerical models that simulate physical processes in the atmosphere, ocean, and land surface to predict changes in climate based on projected future emissions. These models operate on a three-dimensional grid covering the globe. In their simplest form, GCMs project future weather conditions by calibrating initial conditions that represent the current state of the climate and then applying the laws of fluid motion to model interactions between grid cells over time. Emissions influence this process through their impact on radiative forcing, which measures the effect of human activities (such as greenhouse gas and aerosol emissions) on the amount of downward-directed radiant energy received by Earth's surface.

Despite their grounding in deterministic mathematical equations (Auffhammer et al., 2013), GCMs can sometimes disagree on the magnitude or direction of future changes in key aspects of the climate. This disagreement arises from the complexity of the relationships modeled. GCMs are computationally intensive, which means the spatial resolution of their grid cells is often too coarse to capture important physical processes that occur at smaller scales, such as cloud formation. As a result, properties within a grid cell are averaged using empirical or theoretical methods in a process known as "parameterization," which introduces uncertainty into the climate projections. Additionally, many feedback mechanisms in the climate system — such as those between water vapor and warming or clouds and radiation – are challenging to model accurately, further limiting the precision of GCM outputs. Consequently, different GCMs may produce divergent responses to the same emissions scenario, making projections from a single model potentially misleading (Burke et al., 2015a). To address this issue, recent studies often use multiple GCMs to estimate climate impacts, thereby capturing uncertainty across the modeled feedback loops.

However, with dozens of climate modeling institutions worldwide, projecting impacts using every model can be challenging due to differences in input emissions scenarios and output data formats. The Coupled Model

Intercomparison Project (CMIP) provides a standardized framework for generating and studying GCM outputs. The latest phase, CMIP6, offers standardized scenarios of future population and economic development, known as Shared Socioeconomic Pathways (SSPs), along with their emissions implications. These SSPs range from ambitious mitigation efforts to scenarios of continued emissions growth.[13] For example, CMIP6's most ambitious mitigation scenario (SSP1–2.6) aligns with the lower end of the Paris Agreement's goal to limit the increase in global average temperature to 1.5°C above preindustrial levels. As discussed in Section 2.2.2, by projecting impacts using multiple GCMs under consistent emissions scenarios, climate impact researchers can better capture both uncertainty in the projected climate variables and statistical uncertainty in the response functions.

2.2.1 *Calculating future impacts*

Given a plausibly causal estimate of the marginal effects of various components of climate (temperature, precipitation, etc.) on an outcome of interest, denoted as $\boldsymbol{\beta}$, the projected impacts of climate change are calculated by multiplying these coefficients by projected changes in the relevant climate variables over time. For example, assuming a linear model, let β^T represent the marginal effect of temperature. The predicted impact of temperature in location i in 2100 is given by $\beta^T[T_{i,2100} - T_{i,\text{hist}}]$, where $T_{i,2100}$ is the projected temperature in 2100 and $T_{i,\text{hist}}$ is the average temperature over the historical period. The temporal resolution of $T_{i,2100}$ should match the temporal resolution of the data $T_{i,\text{hist}}$ used in the estimation. For example, if β^T was estimated using a measure of extreme heat based on daily data, the future temperature projection should also be using the same measure of extreme heat based on daily data data.[14]

It is common practice for both $T_{i,2100}$ and $T_{i,\text{hist}}$ to be simulated outputs from the GCM. This is because GCM simulations, which are generally calibrated to match global averages, are often regionally biased for the current climate, e.g., by either under- or over-predicting the current average temperature, leading to discrepancies in statistical characteristics (e.g., mean, variance, etc.) between observed and modeled temperatures in the historical period. If the model is linear in the climate variable, the implicit model bias drops out once the difference $[T_{i,2100} - T_{i,\text{hist}}]$ is taken.

On the other hand, if the regression equation relies on a non-linear transformation $f()$ of a climatic variable, but is still linear in parameters $\boldsymbol{\beta}$ as specified in equation (2c), the predicted temperature impact in our above example

[13] The SSPs are closely related to Representative Concentration Pathways (RCPs), which were the scenarios used in CMIP5. The SSPs and RCPs are similar in terms of radiative forcing levels projected for 2100. For instance, SSP5–8.5 aligns with RCP8.5.

[14] If a model is linear in average temperature, the temporal resolution does not matter.

$\beta^T [f(T_{i,2100}) - f(T_{i,\text{hist}})]$ will be biased if T_i is biased.[15] It is therefore important to correct for possible biases. As discussed following equation (2c), the non-linear transformation should be applied at the finest spatial scale before aggregating the data. Bias correction should ideally be performed on the same geographic scale at which the non-linear transformation is applied, both in the historic data as well for future projections. This poses an issue if the historic data (e.g., the PRISM data for the US) is at a much fine scale than future projections. Outputs from raw model runs conducted under CMIP6 are spatially coarse (e.g., a few degrees in latitude and longitude), which limits their ability to capture spatial details that may be important for estimating regional climate impacts.

There have been various community efforts to use post-processing techniques for bias-correcting and spatially downscaling raw GCM output. For example, NASA Earth Exchange Global Daily Downscaled Projections (NEX-GDDP-CMIP6) address biases in GCM simulations by applying an algorithm that maps the quantiles of each GCM in CMIP6 to a reference historical dataset (GMFD). Specifically, for each GCM, climate variable, and day, the algorithm generates a cumulative distribution function (CDF) for the observed reference dataset and the historical simulations. It then compares these two CDFs, establishing a mapping between quantiles of observed and simulated data. This mapping is used to translate GCM values in any quantile to the corresponding observed values in the same CDF quantile. This translation is applied to de-trended future simulations, assuming that the CDF of the GCM simulations remains stable across historical and future periods after flexibly removing the long-run trend in the climate variable. The trends are then added back to the adjusted GCM climate variables.

In a second step, the bias-corrected projections are spatially downscaled by merging the observed historical spatial climatology at the high resolution of the reference dataset with the relative changes at each time step simulated by the GCMs. This process involves estimating "scaling factors" that represent the difference between the bias-corrected GCM data and the reference climatologies. These scaling factors are downscaled through statistical interpolation to the resolution of the reference data and applied to the reference climatologies at a lower spatial scale. Together, the bias-correction and spatial downscaling procedures preserve the local statistical properties of the historical dataset, which helps to avoid biases in climate impacts projections based on empirically derived response functions.

[15] Consider the following hypothetical example to illustrate this point. Assume the observed average temperature in a location is 15°C and is predicted to increase by +2°C to 17°C by 2100. Assume the GCM is biased in this location and is under-reporting temperatures by 1°C, i.e., reporting historic average temperatures of 14°C and projected future temperatures of 16°C. In case of a linear model, this poses no problem as the bias drops out: for example, if $\beta^T = 3$, the predicted impact is $3[17 - 15] = 3 \times 2 = 6 = 3 \times 2 = 3[16 - 14]$. On the other hand, if there is a nonlinear transformation like $f(T) = T^2$, this is no longer true as $3[17^2 - 15^2] = 3[289 - 255] = 3 \times 64 = 192 \neq 180 = 3 \times 60 = 3[259 - 196] = 3[16^2 - 14^2]$.

2.2.2 Characterizing uncertainty

Not surprisingly, there is significant uncertainty when predicting outcomes several decades into the future, and future climate impacts are no exception. Economic studies often focus on two primary sources of uncertainty: statistical uncertainty in the underlying response functions and uncertainty in the future trajectory of climate variables. We discuss them first before alluding to other sources of uncertainty.

Statistical uncertainty is typically captured either through Monte Carlo simulations or bootstrapping. Monte Carlo simulations involve randomly sampling a set of coefficients representing the marginal effect of climate from the empirical multivariate normal distribution, which is characterized by the variance-covariance matrix obtained from estimating the response function. Each sampled set of coefficients is then used to produce a projection, estimating the impact in each year simulated by the GCM, as discussed above. By repeating this process many times, the range of predicted impacts (e.g., 5th and 95th percentiles) represents the uncertainty associated with estimating the response function.

Bootstrapping, on the other hand, involves repeatedly drawing observations from the dataset with replacement and then re-estimating the response function for each bootstrap sample. Each bootstrapped response function is used to calculate impacts in a manner similar to the Monte Carlo procedure. While bootstrapping does not rely on the large sample properties of ordinary least squares (OLS), it can be substantially more computationally intensive with large datasets because the response function must be re-estimated with each iteration.

Climate uncertainty arises from imperfect predictions of future climate change and is generated from two main sources. The first source is uncertainty from differences in future emissions trajectories. The SSPs described above partially account for emissions uncertainty by outlining scenarios that cover a range of plausible futures. By comparing projected impacts under high emissions scenarios (e.g., SSP5–8.5) and low emissions scenarios (e.g., SSP1–2.6) across one or more models, we can assess, in partial equilibrium, the benefits of climate mitigation on the outcome of interest. Note that the emission trajectory depends on mitigation policies and is hence a policy choice.

The second source of uncertainty comes from differences in GCM predictions given the same emissions inputs. As discussed, parameterizing local (i.e., within grid cell) climate dynamics requires statistical or theoretical methodologies that may differ across modeling groups. Consequently, each model in the CMIP6 ensemble produces different predictions of future climate. One natural approach to accounting for climate model uncertainty is to generate projections with multiple models and report the distribution of predicted impacts. However, the CMIP ensembles are "ensembles of opportunity" rather than a systematic sample of potential climate futures (Rasmussen et al., 2016; Carleton et al., 2022). There is weather uncertainty due to the choice of initial conditions, yet modeling groups often only report the mean ensemble outcome. A sample of means from different modeling groups tends to understate the true uncertainty. This is because the variability across different models' initial conditions and their corresponding responses can lead to a broader range of possible outcomes than what is captured by ensemble means. Thus, the true distribution of a given climate variable in the future may not be well approximated by the empirical distribution of that variable across available GCMs. In particular, "tail risks," which have low probability but large potential economic consequences, are not well represented in the CMIP6 ensemble (Rasmussen et al., 2016).

Recent studies by Rode et al. (2021) and Carleton et al. (2022) generate a surrogate model mixed ensemble (SMME) (Rasmussen et al., 2016), which combines CMIP5 GCMs with scaled versions of some models called surrogates to better reflect the tails of the future temperature distribution. The climate projections using the SMME outputs are then probability-weighted according to a projection of global mean surface temperature from a probabilistic simple climate model. This process uses probability weighting to enure that the distribution of mean surface temperatures is the same under the SMME translation as in the simple climate model that is computationally cheaper to run and hence can be evaluated repeatedly to obtain the distribution of future mean surface temperatures. It generates estimates of future impacts that account for uncertainty due to modeling approaches across GCMs as well as the under-sampling of tail risks in the GCM distribution.

Beyond model and climate uncertainty, there are many other sources of uncertainty, notably, whether the econometric model was specified correctly, whether the estimated relationships are stable over time, whether there are omitted variables (whose correlation with the included weather variable changes over time), and whether there are endogenous policy responses or adaptation strategies that are not modeled. For a further discussion of uncertainty, we refer the interested reader to the chapter by Traeger (2024).

2.3 Estimating social cost of greenhouse gases

While estimates of future damages from climate change are valuable for addressing specific sectoral impacts and identifying affected regions and sub-populations, many governments rely on a single metric to assess the monetary benefits of greenhouse gas mitigation policies: the social cost of carbon (SCC). The SCC represents the net present value of the future cost to society from an additional ton of carbon dioxide emitted into the atmosphere, summed across all sectors, individuals, and years.

As with any optimal Pigouvian tax, the SCC should be derived at the optimal level, which involves solving for the optimal emission scenario. When empirical climate impact studies use GDP and emission growth as given and evaluate the implied damages, they derive the cost under *one* specific emission scenario, which may not be the optimal scenario. Unless damages are constant regardless of the emission scenario — a highly questionable assumption — the optimal SCC requires solving for the optimal emission scenario.

The chapter by Dietz (2024) provides an overview of integrated assessment models (IAMs) that endogenize the relationships between the economy, emissions, the climate, and damages. There is a natural connection between the two sub-fields: empirical climate impact studies continuously refine how various sectors are influenced by changing climate conditions, which can then be incoporated in the latest IAMs to solve for the optimal emission scenario.

The first estimates of the social cost of carbon (SCC) published by the US Environmental Protection Agency (EPA) relied on the DICE (Nordhaus, 1992), FUND (Tol, 1997) and PAGE (Hope et al., 1993) model as well its respective revisions. All three models originated in the 1990s and initially used highly simplified damage functions. A core component in the SCC calculation is the damage function, which maps changes in global mean surface temperature to monetary impacts. For instance, early versions of the DICE model calibrated the damage function as a simple quadratic function of temperature.

The EPA's latest proposed revision (National Center for Environmental Economics, US EPA, 2023) relies on estimates from the GIVE model (Rennert et al., 2022) as well as the DSCIM model by the Climate Impact Lab, both of which incorporate recent advances in estimating empirical damage functions. In the DSCIM model, the largest effect is on human mortality (Carleton et al., 2022). This paper illustrates the significant progress made in the field of empirical climate damage functions. It monetizes the projected mortality impacts of climate change using the value of statistical life and fits a time-varying damage function derived from with micro-level mortality data across the globe. They do so by combining the empirical damage functions with a simple climate model (FAIR), which estimates the GMST implications from a pulse of carbon dioxide, to calculate the future mortality costs of a marginal ton of carbon dioxide in the atmosphere. The model establishes a link between the global mean surface temperature (GMST) from general circulation models (GCMs) to globally aggregated mortality impacts in 5-year intervals. The discounted stream of future mortality costs represents the "partial" social cost of climate change on the global mortality burden, as it does not account for general equilibrium responses to the climate-induced change in mortality. Bressler (2021) extends the DICE integrated assessment model (IAM) to include the direct effects of climate on mortality in general equilibrium by incorporating empirical damage functions from Carleton et al. (2022) alongside other damage function estimates.

2.4 A reference guide to estimating climate impacts

In this section, we provide an example workflow for estimating climate impacts. Specifically, we guide you through the process of aggregating weather data, linking it to an outcome of interest, and simulating climate impacts, referencing some of the most commonly used datasets in the field.

2.4.1 Choosing a climate dataset

Table 1 lists commonly used weather datasets at regional and global scales, along with their spatial and temporal resolutions. Climate data come at individual weather stations or are provided in grid format, covering large regions or the globe with equally sized grid cells, each containing a weather observation. The grid format has become the standard in climate impacts literature for several reasons.

First, while weather stations provide accurate weather data for specific locations, their records are often incomplete as stations may go in and out of operation. Second, the spatial distribution of weather stations is nonrandom and may be endogenous to the empirical relationships being studied. This means that the quality and consistency of station data could be correlated with the outcome of interest, introducing non-classical measurement error, which can bias the estimated coefficients.

Gridded weather datasets provide uniform weather records through statistical interpolation or "reanalysis" of available weather station data using climate models. Statistically interpolated products work best in regions with a relatively dense network of weather stations. For example, the Parameter-elevation Regressions on Independent Slopes Model (PRISM) dataset offers daily weather measurements at a 4 km resolution for the continental U.S., far exceeding the spatial resolution of any currently available reanalysis dataset. This fine-scale precision is possible thanks to the incorporation of around 20,000 weather stations into its statistical parameterization.[16]

In areas where statistical methods are less accurate, reanalysis datasets leverage the physical properties of the climate system to generate weather records with limited data, similar to how a global climate model (GCM) predicts future climate. Reanalyses integrate weather measurements from stations or satellites in a process called "data assimilation," which merges observational data with the physics-based model to reduce (but not eliminate) systematic biases. Although the computational demands of reanalysis can limit its spatial resolution, newer datasets, such as ERA5-Land, have significantly improved in this regard.

Despite their reliance on climate models, reanalysis data generally perform well in climate impact analyses, particularly in data-sparse regions and for capturing weather extremes that may be critical drivers of outcomes. Reanalysis also provides estimates at spatial and temporal resolutions that surpass those of statistically interpolated products offering global coverage (e.g., CRU). However, it's important to note that both interpolation methods can smooth weather data across time and space, unlike raw weather station data.

---

[16] See https://prism.oregonstate.edu/documents/PRISM_datasets for details on the statistical parameterization.

TABLE 1 Frequently used climate datasets for climate impacts analysis.

Dataset	Type	Spatial Coverage	Spatial Resolution (km)	Temporal Coverage	Temporal Resolution
NOAA	Weather Stations	Global	Point	Varies	Daily
PRISM	Statistical	Continental US	4	1895–Present	Daily
ERA5(-Land)	Reanalysis	Global	31 (9)	1950–Present	Hourly
GMFD	Reanalysis	Global	31	1948–2016	Daily
BEST	Statistical	Global	56	1880–Present	Daily
CRU	Statistical	Global	56	1901–Present	Monthly
UDEL	Statistical	Global	56	1900–2017	Monthly

Notes: Table provides a list of common climate datasets used in empirical analysis of climate impacts. Spatial resolutions are provided in kilometers, but note that these resolutions are approximations, as grid cell size varies with latitude due to the curvature of Earth's surface.

2.4.2 Aggregating climate data to administrative regions

The second step, after selecting the appropriate climate dataset, is to aggregate the data to the temporal and spatial scales consistent with the outcome of interest. As mentioned earlier, carefully constructing the weather variables is crucial for specifying non-linear response functions. The transformation and aggregation of raw weather observations from climate datasets should align with the underlying Data Generating Process (DGP), ensuring weather effects are targeted at the relevant scales.

For instance, if the DGP suggests that the outcome responds to local weather exposure on a daily basis, then any nonlinear transformation (e.g., polynomial terms, splines, or step functions) should be applied at the pixel-day level before aggregating these transformed terms to match the temporal scale of the outcome data.

To further clarify, let's assume that, conditional on fixed effects and time-varying controls, excess mortality is a quadratic function of daily average temperature at the location of exposure (e.g., weather station or grid cell). Furthermore, assume we have mortality observations at the county-year level. In this case, the appropriate county-year aggregation of raw temperature data for this DGP would involve the following non-linear construction of temperature:

$$f(T_{cy}) = \beta_1\left(\frac{1}{P(c)D(y)}\sum_{p\in P(c)}\sum_{d\in D(y)} T_{pd}\right) + \beta_2\left(\frac{1}{P(c)D(y)}\sum_{p\in P(c)}\sum_{d\in D(y)} T_{pd}^2\right) \tag{5}$$

where p is a climate data pixel among $P(c)$ pixels residing in county c, and d is one of the $D(y)$ days in year y. Note that the nonlinear transformation of the second term in $f()$ occurs before the aggregation in time and space. Other transformations, such as splines and step functions, follow a similar procedure where each term is calculated at the pixel level and then aggregated separately to match the spatial and temporal units of the outcome variable.

The function in equation (6) applies uniform weights to pixels within a county, assuming that each pixel is equally relevant for determining the outcome of interest. However, this assumption may be flawed if weather in specific areas of the county is the primary driver of the outcome. Ignoring this spatial variation can introduce measurement error in the aggregated weather terms. For example, country-level averages of temperature in the United States could significantly misestimate human exposure to extreme temperatures as humans often concentrate in urban area or cities.

To better capture relevant weather exposure when averaging over large spatial units, recent studies have utilized high-resolution satellite data to more precisely isolate weather exposure in $f()$, weighting pixels based on independent measures of exposure. Fig. 3 demonstrates the value of this approach using precipitation data for Illinois. The state boundary is outlined in red.

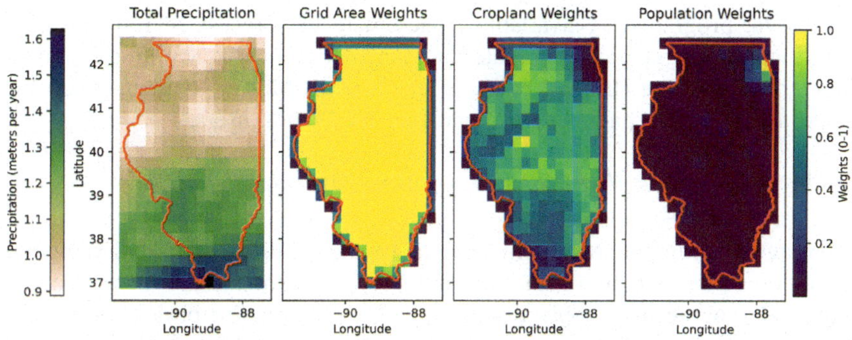

FIG. 3 Weighting Climate Data to Illinois State Boundary. *Notes*: The figure displays maps with the Illinois state boundary outlined in red. The left map shows total precipitation for 2022, with the corresponding scale on the left. The remaining three maps display grid weights, using the scale shown on the right. The second map illustrates the share of a grid cell that overlaps with the state of Illinois: grid cells that fall entirely within the state are shown in yellow (indicating a weight of 1). The third map represents the share of cropland within each grid cell based on FAO's Global Agro-Ecological Zones. The fourth map uses population data from LandScan, showing the share of the state's population within each grid cell.

The first (left) map shows total rainfall in 2022, obtained from ERA5, with the grid cells represented by squares. There is substantial spatial variation, with rainfall totals ranging from 0.9 to 1.6 m. The legend on the left provides the scale for rainfall totals.

The second map displays grid cell weights (ranging from 0 to 1) based on the share of each cell that overlaps the administrative region. For many of the grid cells, this closely resembles the uniform weighting assumption mentioned earlier — cells that fall entirely within Illinois are shown in yellow (weight of 1). This result occurs because the grid size in ERA5 is relatively small compared to the size of Illinois. For climate datasets with larger grid sizes, fewer cells would fully lie within the state, leading to a different weighting distribution.

The third and fourth maps display weights based on satellite-derived measures of cropland and population, using data sources that offer much higher resolution (30 arc-seconds) than the climate data. These weights are constructed by calculating the share of cells' area that is cropland and the share of the state's population in each climate grid cell. The third map focuses on weather exposure in areas where crops are grown, while the fourth map highlights areas where most humans live, with the concentration of the population in Chicago (upper right corner) clearly visible. Each weighting assumption results in a different estimate of total rainfall in Illinois, demonstrating the significant impact that the choice of weighting method can have on the analysis.

Several programs are available to automate the process of transforming, weighting, and aggregating climate data across time and space. For example, the `stagg` package (Liddell et al., 2025) is available for R users, while the `xagg` and `aggfly` packages are available for Python users.[17]

2.4.3 Estimating the nonlinear panel model with a statistical package

After aggregating the raw climate data to match the spatial and temporal resolution of the outcome data, the final step is to estimate the model using a statistical program and apply the estimated coefficients to project future climate impacts. The two most commonly used programs for estimating econometric models are Stata and R. While both can handle all the models discussed in this chapter with their core functionalities, several user-developed packages make panel model estimation more efficient. Notably, the `reghdfe` package in Stata and the `fixest` package in R have become the standard tools for economists working with fixed effects models.[18] One key component is to cluster the errors or account for the spatial correlation of the error terms (see Section 3.3).

2.4.4 Predicting future impacts

The parameter estimates obtained from the regression can then be combined with GCM output to project future climate damages, as described in Section 2.2.1. As discussed earlier, for nonlinear panel models, the GCM data must be bias-corrected and downscaled to align with the corresponding historical climate dataset. The climate predictions from the GCMs should then be aggregated to the same spatial and temporal resolution as the outcome data (e.g., county-year) through the same process used for the historical data, before calculating future damages.

3 Lessons learned

The previous section outlined various modeling approaches that empirical studies have employed. We now turn to some key specification issues that have emerged over the past several decades of climate impacts analysis.

3.1 Importance of temperature extremes

Several articles have shown that temperature extremes have the strongest effects on various sectors, with the detrimental effects of extreme heat often

[17] More information on the packages is available in the documentation at their respective Github pages: `stagg`: https://github.com/tcarleton/stagg, `xagg`: https://github.com/ks905383/xagg, `aggfly`: https://github.com/dylanhogan/aggfly

[18] Documentation for these packages is available at https://scorreia.com/software/reghdfe/ for `reghdfe` and at https://lrberge.github.io/fixest/ for `fixest`.

having the single largest impact. This has been observed in studies on corn, soybean, and cotton yields (Schlenker and Roberts, 2009), mortality (Barreca et al., 2015; Carleton et al., 2022), energy consumption (Auffhammer and Aroonruengsawat, 2011), student test scores (Park et al., 2020), and innovation in agricultural seed varieties (Moscona and Sastry, 2023).

Two locations with the same average temperature can still experience very different exposures to temperature extremes, as shown in Fig. 4. This figure illustrates the temperature distribution of two locations with an identical annual average temperature of 13.2°C (55.8°F). The first location is ther PRISM grid whose centroid falls within Central Park in New York City, specifically the Northern Meadows.[19] The second location is situated just south of Half Moon Bay in the Bay Area, California, chosen because it matches the average temperature of Central Park. Despite having the same mean temperature, New York exhibits much more variability in temperature extremes, both hot and cold. If temperature extremes are the primary factor, these two locations would not be comparable, even though they share the same average temperature. It is hence important to capture temperature fluctuations within a year or even day. For instance, energy consumption is likely higher in New York due to the need for heating during cold winter months and air conditioning during hot summer months.

The impact of temperature extremes can be obscured not only by using average annual temperatures but also by focusing on daily averages that overlook within-day temperature variations. The studies mentioned earlier in this section all rely on daily data, but they do so in different ways. One approach bins daily average temperatures by including indicator variables for various temperature ranges, e.g., Barreca et al. (2015). However, since most weather datasets provide both daily minimum and maximum temperatures, this method overlooks the within-day distribution of temperatures.[20] This within-day distribution captures how much temperatures vary within a day, where two locations with the same average temperature can have very different minimum and maximum temperatures. It is analogous to what was shown for a year in Fig. 4. The difference between minimum and maximum temperatures is called the diurnal range, and a meta-analysis found that a higher diurnal range negatively affects human mortality (Cheng et al., 2014).[21] Given the importance of temperature extremes, another set of studies uses minimum or

[19] The PRISM climate group at Oregon State University (https://prism.oregonstate.edu/) provides daily minimum and maximum temperatures or the contiguous United States on a $\frac{1}{24}$ degree grid in both longitude and latitude, a roughly 2.5mile (4 km) grid size. While PRISM averages all available weather stations and hence can be influenced by the set of available weather stations that are available at a time, another product keeps the set of weather stations constant through time (https://zenodo.org/records/10625288).

[20] The daily average temperature is the arithmetic mean of minimum and maximum temperature, i.e., it is not weighted by how long temperatures were at various levels.

[21] A day with a constant 68°F (20°C) is much less taxing on the body than a hypothetical day with a minimum temperatures of 32°F (0°C) and a maximum temperature of 104°F (40°C).

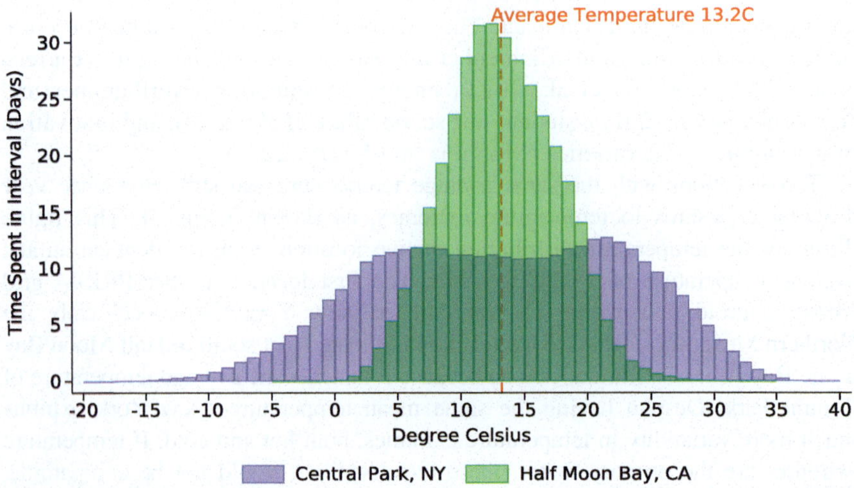

FIG. 4 Temperature distribution in New York City and Bay Area. *Notes*: Figure displays the temperature exposure for each 1°C interval in two PRISM grids counting partial days between the daily minimum and maximum temperatures for the years 1980–2023. The grid centroid (73.95834 W,40.79167 N) is located in the North Meadow of Central Park, NY, while grid centroid (122.4167 W, 37.4167 N) is located just south of Half Moon Bay, CA. The latter grid was chosen as it has the same average annual temperature (13.2°C in both cases), yet note how New York has much more density in the tails (both cold days in the winter and hot days in the summer).

maximum temperatures as separate variables or derives degree days based on maximum temperatures alone, e.g., Moscona and Sastry (2023). A more parsimonious model that accounts for within-day distribution was proposed by Snyder (1985), who fits a sinusoidal function to the reported minimum and maximum temperatures of the day to approximate the within-day temperature distribution, e.g., used by Schlenker and Roberts (2009). Finally, some studies rely on datasets that provide repeated within-day observations, such as ERA5-Land, which reports hourly data, and the North American Reanalysis Datasets, which provides data every three hours.

Tack et al. (2015) find that using the within-day approximation between minimum and maximum temperatures provides much better out-of-sample forecasts of Kansas wheat yields than relying on daily average temperatures. Hogan and Schlenker (2024) test different temporal aggregations of ERA5-Land data, which provides hourly observations. Their findings suggest that deriving degree days based on the 24 hourly data or using a sinusoidal approximation between the daily minimum and maximum temperatures – while disregarding the hourly values — yield comparable results. Both provide better predictive power than simply using the daily average temperature and disregarding the diurnal range. Together, these studies indicate that, at least for agriculture, using both minimum and maximum temperatures improves model fit, but additional within-day observations do not offer significant additional gains.

Given the importance of within-day temperature distribution, we will recap the approach that relies on daily minimum and maximum temperatures in more detail. Consider an arbitrary bound b. Researchers generally aim to determine what fraction f of the day's temperatures exceed this bound. If the bound is below the minimum temperature T_{min} of the day, the entire day's temperatures are above it, so $f = 1$. Conversely, if the bound exceeds the maximum temperature T_{max}, none of the day's temperatures are above the bound, so $f = 0$. If the bound b falls within the day's temperature range $[T_{min}, T_{max}]$, the fraction of the day's temperatures that exceed b is given by $f = \frac{\bar{t}(b)}{\pi}$ where $\bar{t}(b) = acos\left(\frac{2b - T_{max} - T_{min}}{T_{max} - T_{min}}\right)$. This formula allows for easy calculation of the fraction of a day's temperatures that fall into the interval $[b_0, b_1]$, which is simply $f = \frac{\bar{t}(b_0) - \bar{t}(b_1)}{\pi}$, the difference in the fraction spent above the two respective bounds. See D'Agostino and Schlenker (2016) for a formal derivation.

Another commonly used measure is degree days, which assesses not only the duration but also the extent to which temperatures exceed a certain bound b. For example, a temperature of 31°C results in one degree day above 30°C, while a temperature of 32°C results in two degree days above 30°C. Analytically, degree days above a bound are represented by the area (integral) under the temperature curve that is above the bound, as illustrated by the green area in Fig. 5. The interpolation process involves several implicit assumptions: that minimum temperatures occur in the morning, maximum temperatures occur in the afternoon, that these temperatures are always 12 h (half a day) apart, and that temperatures follow a sinusoidal approximation between the minimum and maximum temperatures.[22]

As described above, the dependent variable is often available only at a higher spatial and temporal scale. It is crucial to *first* derive the nonlinear transformation and then aggregate over time and space. This is because the average of a nonlinear function can differ significantly from applying the nonlinear function to an average.

---

[22] The formula to derive degree days *above* a threshold – sometimes also called cooling degree days $CDD(b)$ as they capture how cooling is required for the amount of heat – is:

$$CDD(b) = \begin{cases} \frac{T_{max} + T_{min}}{2} - b & \text{if } b \le T_{min} \\ \left[\frac{T_{max} + T_{min}}{2} - b\right]\frac{\bar{t}(b)}{\pi} + \frac{T_{max} - T_{min}}{2\pi} sin(\bar{t}(b)) & \text{if } b \in (T_{min}, T_{max}) \\ 0 & \text{if } b \ge T_{max} \end{cases}$$

Similarly, if we are interested in degree days *below* a threshold, the formula for heating degree days is

$$HDD(b) = \begin{cases} 0 & \text{if } b \le T_{min} \\ \left[b - \frac{T_{max} + T_{min}}{2}\right]\left[1 - \frac{\bar{t}(b)}{\pi}\right] + \frac{T_{max} - T_{min}}{2\pi} sin(\bar{t}(b)) & \text{if } b \in (T_{min}, T_{max}) \\ b - \frac{T_{max} + T_{min}}{2} & \text{if } b \ge T_{max} \end{cases}$$

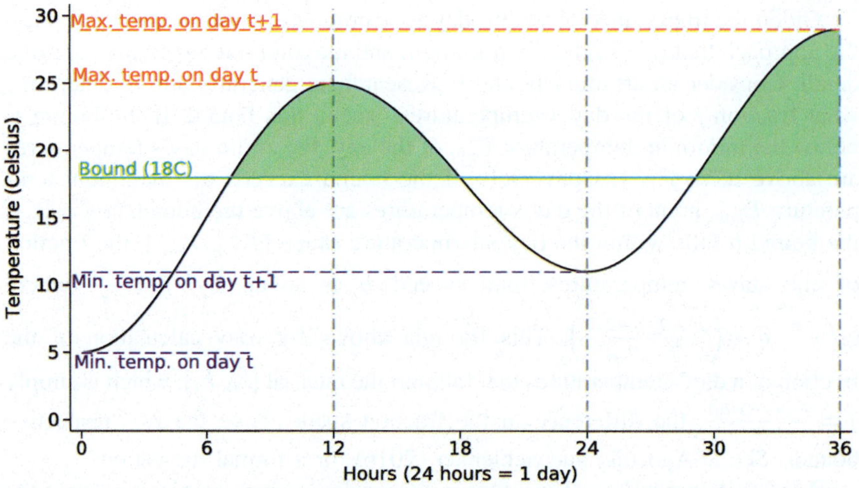

FIG. 5 Construction of degree days. *Notes*: Figure shows the approximation of Snyder (1985) to calculate degree days when only the minimum and maximum temperature are known. He fits a sinusoidal curve between the minimum and maximum temperature. The graph extends this logic by fitting a sinusoidal curve between a day's maximum temperature and the next day's minimum temperature. Degree Days above 18°C are shown as green area.

3.2 Modeling non-linearity

The previous section highlighted that locations with the same average temperature can have very different exposures to temperature extremes. A growing body of research has found that temperature extremes — primarily heat but also, in some cases, extreme cold — account for a significant portion of the year-to-year variation in outcomes.

Fig. 6 illustrates the impact of extreme heat on corn yields using observed temperatures during the growing season from April to September (183 days) in a panel setting (Schlenker and Roberts, 2009). It highlights common approaches to modeling non-linearities. A key challenge in empirical studies of climate change effects is that outcomes of interest are often recorded at aggregated temporal levels, such as monthly or annual mortality rates or annual crop yields. Consequently, climate data must be aggregated over time to match the temporal scale of the outcome variable. A common assumption is time separability, where empirical models assume that what matters is the duration of exposure to various temperatures, without considering the sequence in which these temperatures occurred. This implies that three consecutive hot days are treated the same as three hot days separated by a week of cooler temperatures. This assumption holds better for some sectors than others, as the impact of successive exposure to temperature extremes can vary. For instance, in agriculture, models sometimes account for the fact that the effects of temperature extremes can differ depending on the growth stage of the crops

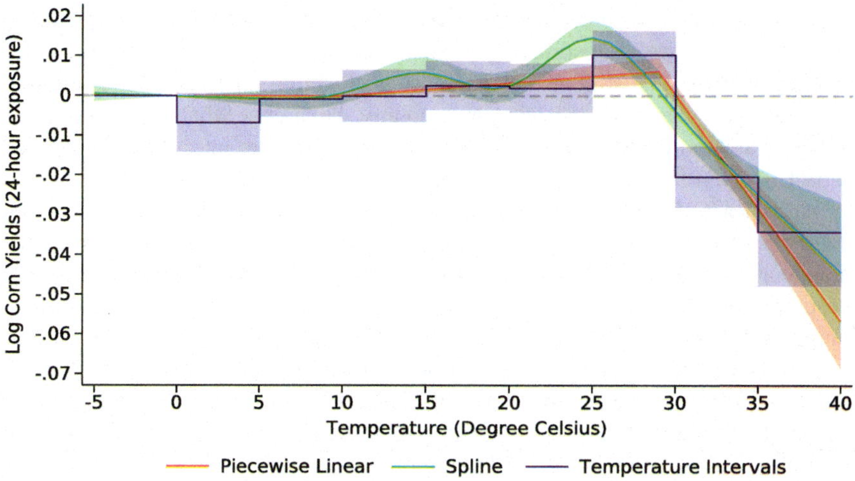

FIG. 6 Modeling nonlinearity. *Notes*: Figure displays the relationship between annual log corn yields and observed temperatures during the growing season April-September (183 days), accounting for the within-day temperature distribution. The graph shows the effect of a 24-hour (one day) exposure to various temperatures on annual log yields. It uses counties east of the 100 degree meridian (except Florida) for the years 1980–2020 that had at least 20 observations, resulting in 70,471 observations. All models control for a quadratic in season-total precipitation as well as county-specific quadratic time trends. Errors are clustered at the state level.

(Welch et al., 2010; Tack et al., 2015). For human mortality, consecutive hot days (heat waves) might amplify the effects on mortality and economic output compared to when these days are spaced out (Miller et al., 2021).[23]

One empirical approach is to bin the data by counting the amount of time temperatures fall within a certain range, as shown by the blue lines in Fig. 6. The 95 % confidence intervals are represented by shaded bands. The regression equation estimates an indicator variable that captures the average effect for each temperature interval. Since the total time across various temperature categories must equal the length of the growing season, one category has to be omitted to avoid perfect collinearity – all impacts are measured relative to that omitted category.

In the case of Fig. 6, the omitted category is freezes (time below 0°C), so all other effects measure the impact of 24-hour (one day) exposure to various temperatures relative to freezes. The graph uses 5°C intervals, with temperatures above 35°C top-coded into the highest interval. The regression also includes a quadratic

[23] In their baseline model, the exposure measure increases by one for each consecutive day that temperatures exceed a given threshold and drops to zero as soon as temperatures fall below the threshold. For instance, with a threshold of 80°F, a sequence of daily temperatures over a week (78, 81, 76, 72, 85, 74, 90) would yield an exposure measure of (0, 1, 0, 0, 1, 0, 1). Conversely, if the same temperatures are arranged so that the three days above 80°F occur consecutively, such as (78, 76, 81, 85, 90, 72, 74), the exposure measure would be (0, 0, 1, 2, 3, 0, 0).

term for season-total precipitation and county-specific quadratic time trends. Moreover, since we are estimating a panel model, each location (county) has a separate intercept that shifts the entire response function up and down. The figure does not show the predicted level in a county, but rather what happens if temperatures are shifted from one interval (x-value) to another interval: the predicted impact is given by the corresponding difference in y-values.

An artifact of using binned categories is that the marginal effect is assumed to be zero for all temperatures within the same interval, with a discontinuous change at the interval borders. In reality, responses are likely continuous across temperatures. Another empirical challenge is that the time spent in various temperature categories is highly correlated. For example, locations with a lot of time in the [20,25)°C category likely also have significant time in the [15,20)°C and [25,30)°C categories. As a result, there is significant multicollinearity, especially among the intermediate categories, which can lead to fluctuations in the individual coefficients.

A second approach uses restricted cubic splines with 7 knots (5°C, 10°C, 15°C, 20°C, 25°C, 30°C, 35°C). The relationship is assumed to be linear below the smallest knot (5°C) and above the largest knot (35°C), while it is approximated by third-order polynomials between the knots, which are forced to be continuous and differentiable. With 7 knots, there are 6 parameters to estimate.[24]

As we repeatedly stressed, it is important to evaluate the non-linear transformation before aggregating across days and grids. In this example we folow the approach depicted in Fig. 5, where we fit a sinusoidal function between the minimum and maximum temperatures of the day (assumed to span 12 h), as well as a sinusoidal function between the maximum temperature and the minimum temperature on the next day (again assumed to span 12 h). The spline function is then evaluated every 30 min, or 48 times per day at each grid, before it is summed over all days of the growing season (April-September), and then averaged over all grids within a county, with the cropland area used as the weight. The regression result is shown as the green line in Fig. 6. The relationship, similar to the intervals shown in blue, exhibits some variability for intermediate values but becomes strikingly linear in the upper tail above roughly 26°C, not just above the highest knot (35°C) where it is forced to be linear by design.

Fig. 5 depicts a third response function in red that follows the concept of degree days from the agronomic literature. Degree days are piecewise linear in temperatures. The breakpoints at 10°C and 29°C are taken from what was

[24] The linear terms below the smallest knot and above the largest knot result in 2 parameters, while the $k-1$ intervals between the k knots have $3(k-1)=3k-3$ parameters for the third-order polynomials, totaling $3k-1$ parameters. There are two restrictions at each of the k knots: one for continuity (restriction on the intercept) and one for differentiability (restriction on the first derivative), resulting in $2k$ restrictions. Therefore, the net number of parameters is $[3k-1]-2k=k-1$.

previously found to give the best fit (Schlenker and Roberts, 2009). The model is parsimonious: while the binned approach had eight indicator variables for various temperature ranges and the spline model used six variables, the degree days model has only two variables: degree days between 10–29°C (sometimes called growing degree days as they are beneficial for crop growth) and degree days above 29°C (sometimes called killing degree days as they are harmful for crop growth). The linearity in the upper temperature tail was also observed in the flexible spline model. Despite having fewer variables than the binned model, the degree days model has been shown to provide superior out-of-sample predictions (Schlenker and Roberts, 2009; Tack et al., 2015).

In summary, various modeling options have been used in the past to capture the non-linear effect of extreme temperatures. The most important take away is to allow for nonlinearity in the response function. Especially the upper tail of the temperature distribution has been found to play an outside role, e.g., in agriculture (Schlenker and Roberts, 2009), mortality (Deschenes and Greenstone, 2011), energy (Auffhammer and Aroonruengsawat, 2011), labor supply (Graff Zivin and Neidell, 2014), or the amenity value of climate (Albouy et al., 2016) While the three response functions in Fig. 6 look similar, the parsimonious piecewise linear model gives the best out-of sample forecast in the case of agriculture. On the other hand, no significant difference was found in out-of-sample prediction error among the three specifications for mortality.

3.3 Spatial correlation of error terms

Our discussion on Spatial First Differences in Section 2.1.4 highlighted that omitted variables might vary smoothly across space. Therefore, taking differences between neighboring areas can help eliminate these omitted variables. Similarly, in common panel and cross-sectional analyses, errors that include these omitted variables are likely to be highly spatially correlated. It is imperative to adjust the standard errors for spatial correlation to avoid underestimating them, which could lead to misleadingly small standard errors and artificially high confidence levels.

There are two approaches to dealing with spatial correlation of the error term. The first approach is to estimate the spatial dependence and incorporate it into a weighted regression (feasible generalized least squares - FGLS) to obtain a more efficient estimator (Anselin, 2013). However, if the weighting matrix is misspecified, the estimator can become biased. Additionally, it is common practice to row-standardize the weighting matrix to ensure its invertibility. This standardization, however, has significant implications for how neighboring units influence a spatial unit. Consequently, the economics profession has largely favored the second approach of using the unweighted, though less efficient, OLS estimator and adjusting the standard errors to account for spatial correlation.

One implementation for addressing spatial correlation is to cluster the standard errors. This approach allows for correlation among units within each cluster but assumes no correlation across clusters. Many modern statistical packages use a Huber-White sandwich estimator to derive the variance-covariance matrix, which does not impose a constant correlation among all units within a cluster.[25] The choice of clustering level and the number of clusters is an ongoing debate (Abadie et al., 2023). If the number of clusters is too small — with a common recommendation being at least 30 to 50 clusters — the clustering approach might be unreliable.

A second approach is to use a group bootstrap that samples years, as year-to-year weather is relatively random, yet there is clear spatial correlation within each year. This method requires a sufficient number of years in the dataset to be effective.

Another more structural approach is to impose a correlation structure, either by assuming a common correlation between units up to a distance cutoff or by allowing this correlation to decline linearly with distance until it reaches zero at the cutoff. This method was first proposed by Conley (1999) and is sometimes referred to as Conley standard errors. Subsequent extensions have adapted this approach to account for panel data structures, where errors are allowed to be correlated only within a cluster for a given year, and have also considered serial correlation (Chen and Conley, 2001).[26]

We conclude with an example: adjusting for spatial correlation in county-level panel analyses in the US has increased standard errors by a factor of six (Schlenker and Roberts, 2009). While the original study employed a version of Conley standard errors that account for spatial correlation within a year, clustering errors by state in STATA gives comparable standard errors.

3.4 Levels versus growth effects

GDP has a high degree of serial correlation and it is common in macroeconomics to examine GDP growth rates rather than GDP levels.[27] Consequently, top-down climate impact studies that examine how climatic events affect GDP often use *growth rates* as the dependent variables. For example, authors have analyzed the effects of natural disasters, especially hurricanes, on GDP growth rates (Noy, 2009; Strobl, 2011; Loayza et al., 2012). Dell et al. (2012) investigate the impact of weather fluctuations on economic growth, and their paper has inspired a substantial body of follow-up research that explores the advantages of top-down (GDP regression) and bottom-up approaches for estimating impacts across various sectors.

---

[25] This approach is an extension of White (1980), which originally addressed heteroskedasticity, to allow for correlation of errors within clusters.

[26] The latest code by Solomon Hsiang for handling spatial and serial correlation in a panel setting is available on his website: https://www.globalpolicy.science/code.

[27] There is a substantial time series literature on unit roots. A shock to a random walk is persistent and affects the entire growth path, resetting it.

While the original article argued that heat is only detrimental to poor countries, Burke et al. (2015b) highlight the importance of nonlinear temperature response functions (see Section 3.2). They find a hill-shaped response function between temperatures and GDP growth rates. Since hotter countries tend to be poorer, they exhibit greater sensitivity to temperature fluctuations; however, this sensitivity is not necessarily due to their economic status but rather to the nonlinear effects of temperature.[28] The later article underscores that hotter countries are much more affected by climate change, a finding that is confirmed by bottom-up approaches.

We defer interested readers to the chapter on integrated assessment models (Dietz, 2024) but would like to highlight one specific example that illustrates how the choice between growth and level effects can profoundly impact results. Generally, models incorporating growth effects find larger impacts and recommend more stringent mitigation policies. For instance, Dietz and Stern (2015) endogenize growth in the DICE model and identify stronger incentives for immediate action. Similarly, Moore and Diaz (2015) incorporate growth effects in the DICE model through two pathways: total factor productivity growth and capital depreciation. This adjustment significantly slows GDP growth in poorer regions but has more modest effects in wealthier countries. In this model, optimal climate policy stabilizes global temperature change below 2°C by eliminating emissions in the near future, implying a social cost of carbon several times larger than previous estimates.

A growth effect is more severe than a level effect of the same magnitude, as it resets the entire future growth path rather than impacting just one period in isolation. For example, if a permanent negative growth effect of $x\%$ is assumed, it will lower the outcome this year by $x\%$, and this reduction will propagate into all future years due to its permanent nature. At a 3 % discount rate, the discounted net effect of this growth impact is 33 times as harmful as a one-time level effect of $x\%$ in the contemporaneous period.[29] Nath et al. (2024) find an intermediate case, rguing that the effect is persistent (extending beyond the current period) but not permanent, meaning it eventually phases out over time.

One way to test for persistence is to include lagged variables in the model. In a growth specification, if a level effect is present, the first lag should fully offset the contemporaneous effect. However, a challenge in the empirical literature is that the inclusion of lags often leads to a significant increase in standard errors. Consequently, researchers cannot reject the hypothesis that the combined cumulative effect differs from the contemporaneous effect or that the cumulative effect is different from zero (Schlenker and Auffhammer, 2018).[30]

---

[28] The dummy for poor countries is no longer significant

[29] The discounted effect of an annuity is $\frac{1}{r} = \frac{1}{0.03} = 33$.

[30] Moreover, while level and growth models yield very different results, (Newell et al., 2021) find that out-of-sample prediction tests cannot consistently identify a superior model. They also highlight the sensitivity of results to the chosen time trend.

We provide an example in Table 2, which regresses corn yields on a piecewise linear function of temperature and a quadratic in season-total precipitation — the red line in Fig. 6. Corn, being an annual crop planted in the spring and harvested in the fall, is expected to exhibit a level effect: weather conditions in a given year impact the crop yields of that year but do not directly affect future yields. Although there could be some indirect spillovers – such as a good crop yield depleting the soil and potentially lowering yields in subsequent years — the model typically treats it as a level effect with no lags. Column (1a) replicates the standard model for the period 1980–2020 with contemporaneous terms only, while column (1b) introduces one lag of each variable. As anticipated, none of the lagged terms are statistically significant.

Columns (2a) and (2b) replicate the same analysis using a growth model, where the dependent variable is the difference in log yields between the current and previous periods, representing the growth rate.[31] Note that the coefficients for the last three variables in column (2a) is very similar to column (1a), which is expected given the random nature of year-to-year weather fluctuations in the sample. The one exception is the moderate degree days in the 10–29°C range, which becomes statistically insignificant in column (2a) and is also notably smaller compared to column (1a).

The last three coefficients in columns (1a) and (2a), especially degree days above 29°C, account for over 90 % of the predicted impacts. In the growth model of column (2a), which assumes a permanent shift in the yield trajectory, the implied impact is 33 times greater than in column (1a),[32] which assumes a one-time reduction in yields. This highlights how a growth model with only contemporaneous weather terms can imply much larger impacts than a level model.

Column (2b) re-runs the growth model, adding one lag of each weather variable. The lagged coefficients show the opposite sign and similar magnitude, indicating that yields recover from the initial effect and return to the previous growth path. This underscores the appropriateness of a level effect in this context and warns against using growth models with only contemporaneous terms, as they might excessively inflate damage estimates when a level model would be more suitable.

3.5 Modeling adaptation

In Section 2.1, we demonstrate that the variation in the climate system used to estimate β affects the type of adaptation captured in the marginal effect of climate. Panel studies, which utilize high-frequency temporal variation in both independent and dependent variables, tend to capture only those adaptation

---

[31] If $y_t = y_0 e^{\rho t}$, then $y_{t+1} = y_t e^{\rho} \Leftrightarrow \log(y_{t+1}) = \log(y_t) + \rho$ and the growth rate $\rho = \log(y_{t+1}) - \log(y_t)$.

[32] Again assuming an interest rate of 3 %.

TABLE 2 Level and growth model for US corn yields.

	Level Model		Growth Model	
	(1a)	(1b)	(2a)	(2b)
Degree Days 10–29°C (1000)	0.340***	0.346***	0.114	0.110
	(0.091)	(0.094)	(0.114)	(0.112)
First Lag		0.063		−0.244***
		(0.050)		(0.075)
Degree Days 29°C (100)	−0.581***	−0.577***	−0.677***	−0.602***
	(0.067)	(0.070)	(0.082)	(0.072)
First Lag		0.039*		0.602***
		(0.022)		(0.055)
Precipitation (m)	0.964***	0.984***	1.098***	1.112***
	(0.222)	(0.223)	(0.346)	(0.325)
First Lag		0.132		−0.807***
		(0.093)		(0.200)
Precipitation Squared (m^2)	−0.729***	−0.738***	−0.811***	−0.809***
	(0.178)	(0.176)	(0.284)	(0.254)
First Lag		−0.066		0.650***
		(0.062)		(0.161)
Observations	67,161	67,161	67,161	67,161
R-squred	0.787	0.787	0.263	0.431

Notes: Table regresses log yields in counties east of the 100 degree meridian (except Florida) for the years 1980–2020 on two degree day variables as well as a quadratic in precipitation over the growing season April-September. Columns (1a) and (1b) use log yield as the dependent variable, while columns (2a) and (2b) use the growth rate in log yields as the dependent variable. Columns (a) only use the contemporaneous weather variables, while columns (b) also add the first lag. All regressions include county-specific quadratic trends. Errors are clustered at the state level.

decisions occurring on a short time scale. For example, such studies might reflect decisions to stay indoors on a hot day or to irrigate crops during a drought. Conversely, methods that incorporate slow-moving or time-invariant differences in climate encompass long-term adaptation decisions critical for forecasting future impacts, such as the installation of new air conditioning systems or irrigation technologies.

However, while these methodologies inherently account for some form of adaptation in the marginal effect of climate, they do not directly measure the extent of short- or long-run adaptation or its associated costs. Therefore, this section provides a detailed discussion on how to identify adaptation to climate change within the methodologies outlined in Section 2.1 and summarizes recent empirical methods for quantifying adaptation in climate impact studies.

For a comprehensive review of adaptation to climate change within the economics literature, including a systematic evaluation of studies employing these methodologies, the reader is encouraged to consult the next chapter in this handbook (Carleton et al., 2024b).

3.5.1 When panel models account for long-run adaptation

Several studies have applied theoretical frameworks to describe the conditions under which panel models account for both short- and long-run adaptation. Hsiang (2016) and Deryugina and Hsiang (2017) use the Envelope Theorem to demonstrate that if the outcome of interest results from a maximization problem (e.g., agricultural profits) that is continuous and differentiable with respect to available adaptive actions, then the marginal effect of climate equals the marginal effect of a similar change in weather. Additionally, using the Gradient Theorem, they show that the sequence of marginal effects obtained from panel regressions can be aggregated across sequential climate values to estimate non-marginal climate changes. A note by McIntosh and Schlenker (2004) emphasizes that non-linear panel models rely again on the mean of the exogenous variables.[33] Mérel et al. (2024) build on this literature to identify the necessary and sufficient conditions for these results to hold under expected outcome maximization.[34] They find that, in this more general case, short-run and long-run responses coincide at mean weather when the marginal effect of adaptive actions depends linearly on weather. This implies that while adaptation can alter the magnitude of the marginal effect of weather on the outcome, it does not affect the convexity of the response function. It is important to note that the key assumptions underlying these results—namely a maximized outcome and a continuous adaptive margin—apply only to a subset of climate impact studies.

For panel studies that do not account for long-run effects, the distinction between weather and climate becomes a crucial caveat when interpreting the estimated marginal effect of weather, especially for projecting future impacts of warming. Future projections of climate damages may be biased if long-run

---

[33] Only linear models are strictly "within" models, where the mean of the exogenous variables does not play a role. In contrast, consider a quadratic model: the mean reenters because the square of the demeaned variable differs from the demeaned squared variable.

[34] They include both the demeaned squared variable (which measures long-term adaptation possibilities) and the square of the demeaned variable (which measures the additional cost of deviating from the expected climate).

adaptation is not considered, and the direction of this bias can be ambiguous. Impacts may be overstated if significant adaptations are only feasible in the long run. For instance, a farmer might switch crops or alter other agricultural practices over time (Deschenes and Greenstone, 2007). Conversely, impacts could be understated if effective short-run adaptations are limited in the long run, such as the depletion of groundwater used for irrigation (Blanc and Schlenker, 2017). The following sections discuss modifications to core empirical strategies that incorporate and quantify long-run adaptations in panel data analyses.

3.5.2 *Cross-sectional heterogeneity in the marginal effect of weather*

As discussed in Section 2.1.2, comparing the marginal effect of weather across different climates, whether spatially or temporally, can offer insights into the extent of long-run adaptation. An increasingly popular approach, based on this intuition, involves estimating heterogeneity in the marginal effect of weather by interacting weather variables with long-run averages of those variables, which represent the climate in a given location. This regression can be expressed as:

$$y_{it} = \alpha_i + f(\mathbf{W}_{it}) + f(\mathbf{W}_{it}) \times \mathbf{C}_i + \mathbf{X}_{it}\gamma + \delta_t + \epsilon_{it} \tag{6}$$

where the interaction term $f(\mathbf{W}_{it}) \times \mathbf{C}_i$ mediates the sensitivity of the outcome to weather based on the climate of location i (Butler and Huybers, 2013). If locations optimize their adaptation decisions based on their local climates, then differences in sensitivities across those locations reflect the benefits of adaptation. For instance, if Houston, with its hotter climate, has invested in widespread air conditioning, whereas Seattle, with its relatively cooler climate, has not, then the sensitivity to an equally hot day should be greater for Seattle than for Houston. Equation (6) models the difference in sensitivity across climates as a linear cross-sectional relationship. However, this approach is prone to similar omitted variable bias as the cross-sectional research design and is thus rarely causally identified. Some of this omitted variable bias can be mitigated by including additional interaction terms in equation (6). For example, in global climate impact regressions of mortality and energy consumption, Carleton et al. (2022) and Rode et al. (2021) include a time-invariant income interaction term to control for the confounding effect of local wealth on the influence of climate on weather sensitivity of outcomes. Similarly, Hultgren et al. (2022) include time-invariant irrigation measures in their analysis of global agricultural impacts. Note also that including non-climate interaction terms can present challenges when projecting future climate impacts, as an "exogenous" projection of each additional variable is necessary to characterize the marginal effect of climate in the future.

It is important to note that the difference in climate sensitivities estimated in equation (6) reflects only the benefits of adaptation, not the costs. Failing to account for adaptation costs results in underestimated future impacts of climate change. Adaptation costs are incurred as agents invest in technologies to reduce the marginal effect of climate and through changes in the average level of the outcome. For example, in agriculture, adaptation costs may include the installation of an irrigation system and the cost, in terms of yield, from replacing a yield-maximizing crop varietal with a climate-resistant alternative. Given the specification of the interaction term between weather shocks and the average climate $f(\mathbf{W}_{it}) \times \mathbf{C}_i$, the adaptation cost can be empirically recovered (Schlenker et al., 2013). Carleton et al. (2022) extend the theoretical framework from Guo and Costello (2013) and Schlenker et al. (2013) to empirically estimate adaptation costs from the climate-mortality relationship, as estimated from a version of equation (6), finding that adaptation costs account for a substantial share of the future mortality costs of climate change.

3.5.3 *Evaluating adaptation related policies*

Several studies have exploited exogenous variation in adaptation-related policies to causally identify changes in the marginal effect of weather. For example, Mullins and White (2020) study the impact of preventative healthcare in the US on the temperature-mortality relationship, combining panel variation in temperature with the idiosyncratic roll-out of Community Health Centers in the 1960s and 1970s. They find that access to preventative healthcare reduces the temperature sensitivity of mortality by about 14 %, suggesting that improved access to primary care may be an effective adaptation mechanism for climate change. Using a similar strategy, Colmer and Doleac (2023) examine whether the effect of temperature on violent behavior is mediated by concealed carry restrictions, finding that temperature sensitivity declines by between 2.9 % and 4.2 % under stricter gun control regimes. Conceptually, these studies apply a difference-in-differences strategy where the outcome of interest is the marginal effect of weather. While this approach can provide critical insights into the policy-relevant drivers of climate sensitivity, it also comes with drawbacks relative to the methods discussed above. For example, policy variation is usually local relative to the global impacts of climate change, which limits the external validity of these studies. Moreover, results from these studies often cannot easily inform climate projections.

3.6 Informing empirical models with insights from other fields

We have outlined various sources of identification for econometric studies linking an outcome of interest to weather shocks, climate averages, or climate trends. These statistical studies can sometimes be informed by findings from plant physiology, epidemiology, physics (such as conservation of mass and energy), or economic theory (such as open access for resources). We highlight some examples below.

3.6.1 Biophysical crop models

In the agricultural context, studies have drawn on insights from the agronomic literature, which utilizes calibrated process-based crop models. These models are analogous to what economists might term structural models: they require the calibration of key parameters but allow for the simulation of counterfactual scenarios (e.g., a warming world). Agronomic experiments conducted in controlled environments have provided valuable insights into crop physiology, plant growth, and nutritional content.

Crop modelers have predicted changes in yield under changing climatic conditions before the recent emergence of statistical studies, e.g., see Rosenzweig and Parry (1994). The crop-modeling community has established the Agricultural Model Intercomparison and Improvement Project (AgMIP) that brings together agronomists to study how various inputs—including weather—affect crop yields. It aims to harmonize inputs and assumptions across various biophysical models to make outputs comparable. Asseng et al. (2015) conducted an interesting experiment where they provided various crop modeling groups, as well as one statistical modeler, with information on different inputs (including weather) from actual, but unknown-to-the-modeler, locations. Each group was asked to predict three outcomes for maize: days until anthesis (flowering), days until maturity, and maize yields. They then compared these predictions to actual outcomes, as shown in Appendix Figures S4 and S5 of their article. While biophysical models were better at predicting crop stages like flowering and maturity, the very parsimonious statistical model was among the best at predicting yields.

Combining model outputs from biophysical models with weather variables used in statistical models gives superior out-of-sample forecasts compared to using either econometric or biophysical models alone (Roberts et al., 2017). Biophysical (process-based) models excel at capturing the temporal evolution of how of precipitation, vapor pressure deficit, and solar radiation affect yields, while statistical studies are better at accounting for the damaging effects of extreme heat. Consequently, revised econometric models have focused on accurately capturing the effects of soil moisture (Ortiz-Bobea et al., 2019; Proctor et al., 2022), which is influenced by both precipitation (positively influences water supply) and temperature (positively affects water demand by crops and negatively affects water supply through evaporation). Ideally, process-based and econometric studies should complement each other. Process-based models and field experiments are well-suited for examining the potential contributions of various inputs on crop growth. However, field experiments are often conducted under ideal conditions (other factors are kept at their ideal levels), which might differ from real-world conditions on farms and omit other constraints farmers might face, such as liquidity constraints and present-bias in inter-temporal decision making. Using observational field-level data can verify whether the results hold up under actual growing conditions and sometimes reveal hypotheses that can be tested in the lab. For instance, the sensitivity to extreme temperatures was first identified in statistical studies and subsequently verified in crop models (Schauberger et al., 2017).

3.6.2 Human physiology

Similarly, there are important findings on how much heat stress the human body can endure before overheating becomes dangerous. Sherwood and Huber (2010) find that wet-bulb temperatures rarely exceed 31°C in the locations where humans live. They argue that prolonged exposure to wet-bulb temperatures above 35°C will induce hyperthermia and potentially lead to death due to overheating. The occurrence of dangerous levels of heat stress is predicted to significantly increase (Vecellio et al., 2023). Recent empirical studies on mortality have incorporated humidity into their estimates (Wilson et al., 2024). Controlling for humidity has shifted the demographic most affected from the elderly to infants.

In the context of temperature-induced mortality, studies in the medical literature have explored possible channels underlying heat-induced mortality and provided guidance on statistical specifications. Semenza et al. (1996) investigated the 1995 Chicago heat wave by interviewing 339 relatives, neighbors, or friends of those who died and matching them with 339 control interviews. They found that individuals with medical conditions who were socially isolated and lacked access to air conditioning were more likely to die. This finding has been subsequently confirmed in statistical studies linking the decrease in temperature-induced mortality to the widespread adoption of air conditioning (Barreca et al., 2016). Additionally, changes in the seasonal pattern of cardiovascular mortality have been documented and linked to temperature trends (Seretakis et al., 1997). The authors found that the ratio of cardiovascular mortality rates in the months with the highest rate to the month with the lowest rate, what they term peak-to-trough ratio, declined from 1937 to 1970.[35] They attribute this to increased availability of heating and cooling. However, this trend stalled as hotter summers, driven by climate change, increased temperature-induced mortality, while less cold winters contributed to a decrease in mortality.

3.6.3 Natural laws

Other studies use physical laws, such as conservation of mass and energy, to construct superior data. Hsiang (2010) demonstrates that the intensity and occurrence of hurricanes are often under-reported, particularly in earlier periods. Wind speeds are only measured at certain points and do not change discontinuously along a hurricane's path. To address this issue, Hsiang

---

[35] The idea is similar to a triple-difference strategy in economics that compares summer to winter trends in mortality.

constructs the Limited Information Cyclone Reconstruction and Integration for Climate and Economics (LICRICE) database, which estimates a hurricane's center, minimum central surface air pressure, and maximum sustained surface wind speed. It does so by using physical laws like conservation of energy. Since damages have been shown to respond to a high-order polynomial of wind speed, accurately measuring wind speed is crucial. Hsiang's approach, by improving the precision of wind speed data, reduces attenuation bias.

3.7 Omitted variables

Various weather outcomes (heat, rain, humidity, water stress) are all correlated. For example, extreme heat is often associated with dry conditions, as evaporative cooling (the process by which energy is absorbed as water transitions from liquid to gas, drawing heat from the air) limits the upper tail of the temperature distribution (Braun and Schlenker, 2023). The correlation between extreme heat and low water availability explains the strong negative impact these conditions have on crop yields. As temperatures rise, plant water demand increases, but water supply becomes limited due to soil moisture depletion (as implied by the lack of evaporative cooling that would have otherwise moderated the temperature rise). Thus, extreme heat signals conditions where plants require water the most, but it is least available. A regression that includes only a measure of extreme heat will, therefore, capture the combined effects of both heat and water stress (Ortiz-Bobea et al., 2019; Haqiqi et al., 2021).

This presents an empirical challenge in any analysis, even in panel studies, as various weather measures covary over time, leading to time-varying omitted variables. As long as the correlation between the weather variables included in the model and the omitted variables remains constant over time—i.e., remains the same during the estimation period and under changing climate conditions — the included weather variables should still correctly identify the overall net effect. This includes both the direct effect of the weather variable and the indirect effects through its correlated variables. However, these correlations between weather variables may change in the future. For instance, there is ongoing debate about whether warming will lead to a drier world or whether increased precipitation from greater cloud coverage will alter the water cycle (McColl et al., 2022).

Bilal and Känzig (2024) adopt a different approach by linking the time series of global GDP to the global average temperature for each year. It is important to note that warming is heterogeneous, meaning that a 1°C rise in global mean temperature does not equate to a uniform 1° increase across all regions. Higher latitudes tend to experience greater warming, while lower latitudes warm less. Therefore, the sensitivity of global GDP to global temperature fluctuations needs to be adjusted to make it comparable to its sensitivity to local temperature fluctuations.

The authors find that temperature fluctuations in this aggregated time-series model (one observation per year) result in greater sensitivities compared to using a country-level panel model that links local temperature to local GDP. One possible explanation they offer for this observed difference is that global temperature shocks "predict a large and persistent rise in extreme climatic events that cause economic damage, including extreme temperature, wind, and precipitation." Since the climate system is influenced by macro-scale phenomena (e.g., oceans releasing heat during El Niño events), the authors argue that global average temperature is a more effective variable to capture overall climate system dynamics than including all weather measures separately.

For example, maize yields in Zimbabwe have been shown to be strongly influenced by the Southern Oscillation (El Niño), a warming of sea surface temperatures in the eastern Pacific, which is geographically distant but still affects the African climate through teleconnections (Cane et al., 1994). However, implicit in the argument to rely on global average temperature is again the assumption that the correlation between global average temperature and extreme climate events remains constant between the estimation period and a future world under climate change.

In case the correlation between weather variables changes, modeling each variable separately becomes important for predicting the correct climate impacts (Proctor et al., 2022). Studies therefore have to be careful to include all relevant weather variables, which is empirically challenging.

3.8 Interlinkages across space and time

When estimating climate impacts, panel studies typically rely on local weather variations to identify parameters of interest, often accounting for time fixed effects. However, the world is interconnected through trade across regions and over time via storage. On the positive side, production shortfalls or disruptions in one region can be mitigated by switching to imports from other regions, providing a natural hedge as long as the weather shocks are not correlated. At the same time, production is often concentrated in certain areas: for example, Taiwan produces over 60 % of the world's semiconductors and over 90 % of the most advanced ones,[36] while the U.S. produces more than 40 % of the world's maize (corn). If a cyclone were to disrupt chip production in Taiwan, or if a heat wave in the Corn Belt reduced corn production, global prices would adjust.

The global price feedback is captured in the temporal fixed effects, and hence not counted as a direct climate impact. In case of global price feedback, one has to be careful about the inclusion of year fixed effects. Similarly, in case of regional price feedbacks, one has to be careful about the inclusion of region-by-year fixed effects. Moreover, price feedbacks can reverse the effect in specific sectors and shift them to others. For instance, demand for agricultural commodities is highly

[36] The Economist, March 6, 2023. "Taiwan's dominance of the chip industry makes it more important".

inelastic, meaning a production shortfall (which by itself reduces farmer profits) might be more than offset by a simultaneous increase in the price farmers receive for their remaining crops. In this case, the climate impact shifts to consumers, who must pay higher prices to meet their dietary needs.

This highlights how the response to short-term weather shocks can differ significantly from that to a permanent shift in climate, where higher prices may lead to an expansion of the growing area. The realignment is not limited to shifts within a sector but can also occur between sectors, particularly if labor is mobile and can move between them. For instance, temperature-driven reductions in the demand for agricultural labor in India have been shown to result in a shift toward employment in the manufacturing sector (Colmer, 2021).

Modeling how economies and agents realign in a world with a different climate requires a more structural approach. A growing body of literature on spatial equilibrium models simulates these effects. Regions best suited for specific economic activities (agriculture, manufacturing, etc.) may realign. As a result, not only might the total area devoted to these activities expand or contract, but their spatial distribution could shift (Cruz and Rossi-Hansberg, 2024). Costinot et al. (2016) argue that comparative advantages in agriculture evolve, leading to a reallocation of areas where crops are grown. An impact study that focuses solely on direct local effects risks missing these adjustments and potentially overstating the net impact once adaptation measures are accounted for.

Nath (2020) extends this argument by estimating how comparative advantages of various sectors are evolving across countries under climate change. He examines the effect of weather fluctuations on both the agriculture and manufacturing sectors, analyzing the global reallocation of production. Nath argues that developed countries have a comparative advantage in food production and should expand their agricultural output, but trade restrictions hinder this realignment. In developing countries, a significant portion of the labor force is employed in agriculture. A focus on domestic production in these regions may drive even more people into the agricultural sector to meet demand, despite a relative disadvantage in that sector.

3.9 Uncertainty and expected impacts

As summarized above, many damage functions are highly non-linear. As a result, expected damages can differ significantly from damages evaluated at the expected level of climate change. Early climate assessments evaluated damage functions for specific climate change scenarios. For example, Mendelsohn et al. (1994) examined the effects of a $+5$°F temperature increase and an 8 % rise in precipitation. Increased availability of climate projections now allow researchers to integrate damage functions over a range of possible outcomes. A first step in this direction is the use of bias-corrected projections from various climate models, such as NASA's Global Daily Downscaled Projections (NASA NEX-GDDP), which provide a set of possible outcomes over which climate damages are averaged (see Section 2.2.1 for discussion).

However, these projections represent the predicted average outcomes of each model and may underestimate the variability of future outcomes (see Section 2.2.2). More sophisticated approaches therefore use weighted averages of climate models and model surrogates to ensure that the distribution of possible future climate changes aligns with the distribution of Global Mean Surface Temperature (GMST). For an example, refer to Fig. 1a in Hsiang et al. (2017).

Integrating over the full range of possible outcomes is particularly important when considering fat tails. If there is a significant probability of tail events and the impact function is non-linear, these extreme events could dominate the overall magnitude of the predicted impacts (Weitzman, 2013, 2014). In this context, climate policy can be viewed as an insurance policy that reduces the probability of these extreme tail events, much like home insurance protects against the destruction of a house by rare but extreme events (such as fires), even though it has no impact during average years.

When translating predicted impacts into a social cost of carbon, the discount factor plays a crucial role as the SCC is the discounted sum of future impacts. Traeger's chapter in this Handbook discusses the importance of uncertainty. Here, we highlight one aspect of uncertainty that has strong implications for empirical studies on climate impacts and how they influence the social cost of carbon: if there is uncertainty about discount rates, the equivalent discount rate is not simply the average of all discount rates r, but rather the average of all discount factors $\beta = \frac{1}{1+r}$.[37] Uncertainty regarding the appropriate discount rate for long-term benefits shifts the equivalent discount factor toward the lower end of the distribution (Newell and Pizer, 2004; Weitzman, 2001).

3.10 Remote sensing: the data frontier

In the last two decades, the availability of remotely sensed data for climate change research has surged. The key advantages of these data are: (1) access to information that would otherwise be difficult or costly to obtain; (2) higher spatial and temporal resolution (e.g., monthly or daily) compared to data collected manually; and (3) global coverage, which provides valuable data for systematically understudied regions (Donaldson and Storeygard, 2016). However, with these novel datasets come new econometric challenges, as we encounter systematic biases in remotely sensed data that require both theoretical and empirical scrutiny. In this section, we discuss recent advancements in remote sensing data relevant to estimating climate change impacts and review empirical approaches that maximize the utility of these data in practice.

---

[37] As an illustrative example, if the discount rate is either $r = 0\%$ or $r = 10\%$ with equal probability, the average discount factor for a benefit that occurs in 100 years $0.5[1 + (\frac{1}{1.1})^{100}] = 0.500036283$, which is equivalent to discounting at 0.695 % over 100 years as $\frac{1}{1.00695})^{100} = 0.500036283$.

Satellite measurements of environmental and economic outcomes are increasingly utilized in the economics literature, with recent applications addressing climate-related research questions. As discussed in Section 2.4, satellite datasets (often referred to as rasters) that provide high-resolution, global-scale measurements of population and cultivated land cover are frequently used to correctly derive the exposure to climate variables in impact analyses. These rasters can be used to assign weights to climate grid cells or weather stations within a geographic unit (e.g., a US county). The weighted average of all weather measurements within that unit can more accurately reflect the weather exposure relevant to the outcome of interest. For example, in the context of county-level agricultural yields, weighting weather grid cells by the percentage of cropland within each cell provides a more precise estimate of weather exposure for crops than a simple unweighted average.[38] Similarly, for health or other human-related outcomes, high-resolution population weights can better capture the weather exposure relevant to humans.[39]

Other datasets can be used to measure outcomes with high temporal and spatial frequency. For instance, satellite scans of nighttime lights are sometimes employed as a proxy for economic activity (Jean et al., 2016). Linsenmeier (2023) compiles data on nightlights to study long-run economic activity. He does so by linking this remotely-sensed outcome to temperature variability, using a spatial first differences, i.e. following equation (4) above. He finds that day-to-day temperature variability lowers long-run economic activity, while seasonal variability has a smaller but still negative effect. Inter-annual variability increases economic activity at low temperatures but has a negative impact at high temperatures.

In the agricultural context, vegetation indices provide promising remote observations of crop yields. Wuepper et al. (2023) study the effect of institutional quality, specifically a measure of economic freedom (freemarket reforms), on crop yields. The outcome variable is the high resolution Enhanced Vegetation Index (EVI), which has been shown to be a good proxy for crop yields. The authors construct annual discontinuities at administrative boundaries and then link these discointinuities in a panel setting to measure of economic freedom. An additional point on a ten-point institutional quality index increases the discontinuity in yields by about 2.2 % over five years. Hogan and Schlenker (2024) use monthly EVI measurements over the growing season to compare weather-yield relationships in Sub-Saharan Africa across different climate datasets, finding that panel models estimated on global daily data outperform those using monthly data in out-of-sample predictions.

[38] For U.S. cropland, the USDA Cropland Data Layer is the standard dataset used for weighting climate grids. For global analyses, several options are available, including the FAO Global Agro-Ecological Zones Version 4 and the Spatial Production Allocation Model. Additionally, the FAO provides the Global Map of Irrigated Areas, offering high-resolution data on the areas equipped for irrigation worldwide.

[39] See Oak Ridge National Laboratory's LandScan dataset.

Other satellite measurements with potential climate applications include forest cover (Hansen et al., 2013), air pollution (Currie et al., 2023), and freshwater availability (Carleton et al., 2024a).

It is important to note that most of these datasets are pre-processed versions of raw satellite scans of Earth's surface. The methods used to produce these datasets for economic analysis vary, ranging from spatiotemporal averaging over satellite "swaths" to complex machine learning models with underlying assumptions that may affect subsequent empirical analysis. Therefore, understanding the processing methods is crucial before applying these datasets to climate impact studies.

Additionally, the size of many satellite datasets can pose a computational challenge, especially when they need to be merged with socioeconomic data at lower spatial and temporal scales. To address this, Rolf et al. (2021) developed a pre-processing methodology that reduces raw satellite imagery into a lower-dimensional set of general-purpose features. These features can be combined with training data to predict out-of-sample observations at significantly lower computational costs (e.g., on a laptop or desktop). They demonstrate that their framework can predict a wide range of economically relevant variables (e.g., forest cover, house prices, road length) with accuracy comparable to complex deep neural networks applied to the same raw satellite images.

Finally, it is important to reiterate that satellite observations can exhibit biases relative to in-situ measurements. These biases arise from both classical and systematic measurement errors, which can obscure causal relationships. Proctor et al. (2023) investigate this measurement error in the context of causal inference and demonstrate that a common error-correction methodology, known as multiple imputation, can account for such errors when a researcher has a relatively small amount of labeled data for calibration. Through simulations and re-analysis of prior studies using remotely sensed data, they show that failing to account for measurement error can substantially bias point estimates and increase uncertainty in various empirical settings. Their findings also indicate that multiple imputation outperforms other error-correction methods in reducing bias, whether remotely sensed variables are used as dependent or independent variables.

4 Conclusion

In this chapter, we introduce the core methodologies used by economists to estimate relationships between climate and key socioeconomic outcomes, including those related to human health, energy, agriculture, conflict, migration, and overall economic well-being. We cover the practical aspects of climate impact analysis, from acquiring, transforming, and aggregating climate data to addressing uncertainty in future damage predictions. Additionally, we review significant topics from several decades of empirical research to guide new researchers toward the forefront of this field, while highlighting ten key lessons for obtaining robust empirical impact estimates.

References

Abadie, A., Athey, S., Imbens, G.W., Wooldridge, J.M., 2023. When should you adjust standard errors for clustering?*. The Quarterly Journal of Economics 138 (1), 1–35. https://doi.org/10.1093/qje/qjac038

Albouy, D., Graf, W., Kellogg, R., Wolff, H., 2016. Climate amenities, climate change, and american quality of life. Journal of the Association of Environmental and Resource Economists 3 (1), 205–246. https://doi.org/10.1086/684573

Anselin, L., 2013. Spatial Econometrics: Methods and Models. Springer Science & Business Media.

Arrow, K.J., Cropper, M.L., Eads, G.C., et al., 1996. Is there a role for benefit-cost analysis in environmental, health, and safety regulation? Science 272 (5259), 221–222. https://doi.org/10.1126/science.272.5259.221

Asseng, S., Ewert, F., Martre, P., et al., 2015. Rising temperatures reduce global wheat production. Nature Climate Change 5 (2), 143–147. https://doi.org/10.1038/nclimate2470

Auffhammer, M., 2018. Quantifying economic damages from climate change. Journal of Economic Perspectives 32 (4), 33–52. https://doi.org/10.1257/jep.32.4.33

Auffhammer, M., 2022. Climate adaptive response estimation: short and long run impacts of Climate Change on residential electricity and natural gas consumption. Journal of Environmental Economics and Management 114, 102669. https://doi.org/10.1016/j.jeem.2022.102669

Auffhammer, M., Aroonruengsawat, A., 2011. Simulating the impacts of climate change, prices and population on California's residential electricity consumption. Climatic Change 109 (1), 191–210. https://doi.org/10.1007/s10584-011-0299-y

Auffhammer, M., Hsiang, S.M., Schlenker, W., Sobel, A., 2013. Using weather data and climate model output in economic analyses of climate change. Review of Environmental Economics and Policy 7 (2), 181–198. https://doi.org/10.1093/reep/ret016

Bakkensen, L., Barrage, L., 2018. Climate Shocks, Cyclones, and Economic Growth: Bridging the Micro-Macro Gap. NBER Working papoer 24893. https://doi.org/10.3386/w24893.

Barrage, L., Nordhaus, W., 2024. Policies, projections, and the social cost of carbon: results from the DICE-2023 model. Proceedings of the National Academy of Sciences 121 (13), e2312030121. https://doi.org/10.1073/pnas.2312030121

Barreca, A., Clay, K., Deschenes, O., Greenstone, M., Shapiro, J.S., 2016. Adapting to climate change: the remarkable decline in the US temperature-mortality relationship over the twentieth century. Journal of Political Economy 124 (1), 105–159. https://doi.org/10.1086/684582

Barreca, A., Clay, K., Deschnes, O., Greenstone, M., Shapiro, J.S., 2015. Convergence in adaptation to climate change: evidence from high temperatures and mortality, 1900–2004. American Economic Review 105 (5), 247–251. https://doi.org/10.1257/aer.p20151028

Behringer, W., 1999. and Witch-hunting: the Impact of the Little Ice Age on Mentalities. Climatic Change 43 (1), 335–351. https://doi.org/10.1023/A:1005554519604

Bilal, A., Känzig, D.R., 2024. The Macroeconomic Impact of Climate Change: Global vs. Local Temperature. NBER working Paper 32450. https://doi.org/10.3386/w32450.

Blanc, E., Schlenker, W., 2017. The use of panel models in assessments of climate impacts on agriculture. Review of Environmental Economics and Policy 11 (2), 258–279. https://doi.org/10.1093/reep/rex016

Braun, T., Schlenker, W., 2023. Cooling Externality of Large-Scale Irrigation. NBER Working Paper 30966. https://doi.org/10.3386/w30966.

Bressler, R.D., 2021. The mortality cost of carbon. Nature Communications 12 (1), 4467. https://doi.org/10.1038/s41467-021-24487-w

Burke, M., Dykema, J., Lobell, D.B., Miguel, E., Satyanath, S., 2015a. Incorporating climate uncertainty into estimates of climate change impacts. The Review of Economics and Statistics 97 (2), 461–471. https://doi.org/10.1162/REST_a_00478

Burke, M., Emerick, K., 2016. Adaptation to climate change: evidence from US agriculture. American Economic Journal: Economic Policy 8 (3), 106–140. https://doi.org/10.1257/pol.20130025

Burke, M., Hsiang, S.M., Miguel, E., 2015b. Global non-linear effect of temperature on economic production. Nature 527 (7577), 235–239. https://doi.org/10.1038/nature15725

Butler, E.E., Huybers, P., 2013. Adaptation of US maize to temperature variations. Nature Climate Change 3 (1), 68–72. https://doi.org/10.1038/nclimate1585

Büntgen, U., Tegel, W., Nicolussi, K., et al., 2011. 2500 Years of European climate variability and human susceptibility. Science 331 (6017), 578–582. https://doi.org/10.1126/science.1197175

Cane, M.A., Eshel, G., Buckland, R.W., 1994. Forecasting Zimbabwean maize yield using eastern equatorial Pacific sea surface temperature. Nature 370 (6486), 204–205. https://doi.org/10.1038/370204a0

Carleton, T., Crews, L., I. Nath, I., 2024a. Agriculture, Trade, and the Spatial Efficiency of Global Water Use. Working Paper.

Carleton, T., Duflo, E., Jack, K., Zappalá, G., 2024b. Adaptation to climate change. Handbook of Climate Economics.

Carleton, T., Jina, A., Delgado, M., et al., 2022. Valuing the global mortality consequences of climate change accounting for adaptation costs and benefits*. The Quarterly Journal of Economics 137 (4), 2037–2105. https://doi.org/10.1093/qje/qjac020

Chen, X., Conley, T.G., 2001. A new semiparametric spatial model for panel time series. Journal of Econometrics 105 (1), 59–83. https://doi.org/10.1016/S0304-4076(01)00070-7

Cheng, J., Xu, Z., Zhu, R., Wang, X., Jin, L., Song, J., Su, H., 2014. Impact of diurnal temperature range on human health: a systematic review. International Journal of Biometeorology 58 (9), 2011–2024. https://doi.org/10.1007/s00484-014-0797-5

Colmer, J., 2021. Temperature, labor reallocation, and industrial production: evidence from India. American Economic Journal: Applied Economics 13 (4), 101–124. https://doi.org/10.1257/app.20190249

Colmer, J., Doleac, J.L., 2023. Access to guns in the heat of the moment: more restrictive gun laws mitigate the effect of temperature on violence. The Review of Economics and Statistics 1–40. https://doi.org/10.1162/rest_a_01395

Conley, T.G., 1999. GMM estimation with cross sectional dependence. Journal of Econometrics 92 (1), 1–45. https://doi.org/10.1016/S0304-4076(98)00084-0

Costinot, A., Donaldson, D., Smith, C., 2016. Evolving comparative advantage and the impact of climate change in agricultural markets: evidence from 1.7 million fields around the world. Journal of Political Economy 124 (1), 205–248. https://doi.org/10.1086/684719

Cruz, J., Rossi-Hansberg, E., 2024. The economic geography of global warming. The Review of Economic Studies 91 (2), 899–939. https://doi.org/10.1093/restud/rdad042

Currie, J., Voorheis, J., Walker, R., 2023. What caused racial disparities in particulate exposure to fall? New evidence from the clean air act and satellite-based measures of air quality. American Economic Review 113 (1), 71–97. https://doi.org/10.1257/aer.20191957

D'Agostino, A.L., Schlenker, W., 2016. Recent weather fluctuations and agricultural yields: implications for climate change. Agricultural Economics 47 (S1), 159–171. https://doi.org/10.1111/agec.12315

Dechezleprtre, A., Fabre, A., Kruse, T., Planterose, B., Chico, A.S., Stantcheva , S., 2022. Fighting Climate Change: International Attitudes Toward Climate Policies. NBER Working Paper 30265. https://doi.org/10.3386/w30265.

Dell, M., Jones, B.F., Olken, B.A., 2012. Temperature shocks and economic growth: evidence from the last half century. American Economic Journal: Macroeconomics 4 (3), 66–95. https://doi.org/10.1257/mac.4.3.66

Dell, M., Jones, B.F., Olken, B.A., 2014. What do we learn from the weather? The new climate-economy literature. Journal of Economic Literature 52 (3), 740–798. https://doi.org/10.1257/jel.52.3.740

Deryugina, T., Hsiang, S., 2017. The Marginal Product of Climate. NBER Workinhg Paper 24072. https://doi.org/10.3386/w24072.

Deschenes, O., Greenstone, M., 2007. The economic impacts of climate change: evidence from agricultural output and random fluctuations in weather. American Economic Review 97 (1), 354–385. https://doi.org/10.1257/aer.97.1.354

Deschenes, O., Greenstone, M., 2011. Climate change, mortality, and adaptation: evidence from annual fluctuations in weather in the US. American Economic Journal: Applied Economics 3 (4), 152–185. https://doi.org/10.1257/app.3.4.152

Diaz, D., Moore, F., 2017. Quantifying the economic risks of climate change. Nature Climate Change 7 (11), 774–782. https://doi.org/10.1038/nclimate3411

Dietz, S., 2024. Introduction to integrated climate-economic modeling. Handbook of Climate Economics.

Dietz, S., Stern, N., 2015. Endogenous growth, convexity of damage and climate risk: how Nordhaus' framework supports deep cuts in carbon emissions. The Economic Journal 125 (583), 574–620. https://doi.org/10.1111/ecoj.12188

Donaldson, D., 2022. Blending theory and data: a space odyssey. Journal of Economic Perspectives 36 (3), 185–210. https://doi.org/10.1257/jep.36.3.185

Donaldson, D., Storeygard, A., 2016. The view from above: applications of satellite data in economics. Journal of Economic Perspectives 30 (4), 171–198. https://doi.org/10.1257/jep.30.4.171

Druckenmiller, H., Hsiang, S., 2018. Accounting for Unobservable Heterogeneity in Cross Section Using Spatial First Differences. NBER WOrking paper 25177. https://doi.org/10.3386/w25177.

Fisher, A.C., Hanemann, W.M., Roberts, M.J., Schlenker, W., 2012. The economic impacts of climate change: evidence from agricultural output and random fluctuations in weather: comment. American Economic Review 102 (7), 3749–3760. https://doi.org/10.1257/aer.102.7.3749

Freeman, J., Vermeule, A., 2007. Massachusetts v EPA: from politics to expertise. The Supreme Court Review 2007, 51–110. https://doi.org/10.1086/655170

GraffZivin, J., Neidell, M., 2014. Temperature and the allocation of time: implications for climate change. Journal of Labor Economics 32 (1), 1–26. https://doi.org/10.1086/671766

Guo, C., Costello, C., 2013. The value of adaption: climate change and timberland management. Journal of Environmental Economics and Management 65 (3), 452–468. https://doi.org/10.1016/j.jeem.2012.12.003

Hansen, M.C., Potapov, P.V., Moore, R., et al., 2013. High-resolution global maps of 21st-century forest cover change. Science 342 (6160), 850–853. https://doi.org/10.1126/science.1244693

Haqiqi, I., Grogan, D.S., Hertel, T.W., Schlenker, W., 2021. Quantifying the impacts of compound extremes on agriculture. Hydrology and Earth System Sciences 25 (2), 551–564. https://doi.org/10.5194/hess-25-551-2021

Hogan, D., Schlenker, W., 2024. Non-linear relationships between daily temperature extremes and US agricultural yields uncovered by global gridded meteorological datasets. Nature Communications 15 (1), 4638. https://doi.org/10.1038/s41467-024-48388-w

Holland, P.W., 1986. Statistics and causal inference. Journal of the American Statistical Association 81 (396), 945–960. https://doi.org/10.1080/01621459.1986.10478354

Hope, C., Anderson, J., Wenman, P., 1993. Policy analysis of the greenhouse effect: an application of the PAGE model. Energy Policy 21 (3), 327–338. https://doi.org/10.1016/0301-4215(93)90253-C

Hsiang, S., 2016. Climate econometrics. Annual Review of Resource Economics 8 (2016), 43–75. https://doi.org/10.1146/annurev-resource-100815-095343

Hsiang, S., Kopp, R., Jina, A., et al., 2017. Estimating economic damage from climate change in the United States. Science 356 (6345), 1362–1369. https://doi.org/10.1126/science.aal4369

Hsiang, S.M., 2010. Temperatures and cyclones strongly associated with economic production in the Caribbean and Central America. Proceedings of the National Academy of Sciences 107(35), 15367–15372. https://doi.org/10.1073/pnas.1009510107.

Hultgren, A., Carleton, T., Delgado, M., et al., 2022. Estimating Global Impacts to Agriculture from Climate Change Accounting for Adaptation. SSRN Working paper 4222020. https://doi.org/10.2139/ssrn.4222020.

Höfer, T., Przyrembel, H., Verleger, S., 2004. New evidence for the Theory of the Stork. Paediatric and Perinatal Epidemiology 18 (1), 88–92. https://doi.org/10.1111/j.1365-3016.2003.00534.x

Jean, N., Burke, M., Xie, M., Davis, W.M., Lobell, D.B., Ermon, S., 2016. Combining satellite imagery and machine learning to predict poverty. Science 353 (6301), 790–794. https://doi.org/10.1126/science.aaf7894

Kolstad, C.D., Moore, F.C., 2020. Estimating the economic impacts of climate change using weather observations. Review of Environmental Economics and Policy 14 (1), 1–24. https://doi.org/10.1093/reep/rez024

Liddell, T., Boser, A.S., Orofino, S., Mangin, T., Carleton, T., 2025. Stagg:: a data pre-processing R package for climate impacts analysis. Environmental Modelling & Software 183, 106202. https://doi.org/10.1016/j.envsoft.2024.106202

Linsenmeier, M., 2023. Temperature variability and long-run economic development. Journal of Environmental Economics and Management 121, 102840. https://doi.org/10.1016/j.jeem.2023.102840

Loayza, N.V., Olaberría, E., Rigolini, J., Christiaensen, L., 2012. Natural disasters and growth: going beyond the averages. World Development 40 (7), 1317–1336. https://doi.org/10.1016/j.worlddev.2012.03.002

McColl, K.A., Roderick, M.L., Berg, A., Scheff, J., 2022. The terrestrial water cycle in a warming world. Nature Climate Change 12 (7), 604–606. https://doi.org/10.1038/s41558-022-01412-7

McIntosh, C.T. , Schlenker , W., 2004. Identifying non-linearities in fixed effects models. Working Paper.

Mendelsohn, R., Nordhaus, W.D., Shaw, D., 1994. The impact of global warming on agriculture: a ricardian analysis. The American Economic Review 84 (4), 753–771.

Miller, S., Chua, K., Coggins, J., Mohtadi, H., 2021. Heat waves, climate change, and economic output. Journal of the European Economic Association 19 (5), 2658–2694. https://doi.org/10.1093/jeea/jvab009

Moore, F.C., Diaz, D.B., 2015. Temperature impacts on economic growth warrant stringent mitigation policy. Nature Climate Change 5 (2), 127–131. https://doi.org/10.1038/nclimate2481

Moscona, J., Sastry, K.A., 2023. Does directed innovation mitigate climate damage? Evidence from U.S. agriculture*. The Quarterly Journal of Economics 138 (2), 637–701. https://doi.org/10.1093/qje/qjac039

Mueller, N.D., Butler, E.E., McKinnon, K.A., Rhines, A., Tingley, M., Holbrook, N.M., Huybers, P., 2016. Cooling of US Midwest summer temperature extremes from cropland intensification. Nature Climate Change 6 (3), 317–322. https://doi.org/10.1038/nclimate2825

Mullins, J.T., White, C., 2020. Can access to health care mitigate the effects of temperature on mortality? Journal of Public Economics 191, 104259. https://doi.org/10.1016/j.jpubeco.2020.104259

Mérel, P., Paroissien, E., Gammans, M., 2024. Sufficient statistics for climate change counterfactuals. Journal of Environmental Economics and Management 124, 102940. https://doi.org/10.1016/j.jeem.2024.102940

Nath, I.B., 2020. The Food Problem and the Aggregate Productivity Consequences of Climate Change. NBER Working Paper 27297. https://doi.org/10.3386/w27297.

Nath, I.B., Ramey, V.A., Klenow, P.J., 2024. How Much Will Global Warming Cool Global Growth? Working Paper.

National Academies of Sciences, Engineering, and Medicine, 2017. Valuing Climate Damages: Updating Estimation of the Social Cost of Carbon Dioxide. National Academies Press.

National Center for Environmental Economics, US EPA, 2023. EPA Report on the Social Cost of Greenhouse Gases: Estimates Incorporating Recent Scientific Advances. Technical Report EPA-HQ-OAR-2021-0317.

Newell, R.G., Pizer, W.A., 2004. Uncertain discount rates in climate policy analysis. Energy Policy 32 (4), 519–529. https://doi.org/10.1016/S0301-4215(03)00153-8

Newell, R.G., Prest, B.C., Sexton, S.E., 2021. The GDP-temperature relationship: implications for climate change damages. Journal of Environmental Economics and Management 108, 102445. https://doi.org/10.1016/j.jeem.2021.102445

Nordhaus, W.D., 1992. An optimal transition path for controlling greenhouse gases. Science 258 (5086), 1315–1319. https://doi.org/10.1126/science.258.5086.1315

Noy, I., 2009. The macroeconomic consequences of disasters. Journal of Development Economics 88 (2), 221–231. https://doi.org/10.1016/j.jdeveco.2008.02.005

Ortiz-Bobea, A., 2020. The role of nonfarm influences in ricardian estimates of climate change impacts on US agriculture. American Journal of Agricultural Economics 102 (3), 934–959. https://doi.org/10.1093/ajae/aaz047

Ortiz-Bobea, A., Wang, H., Carrillo, C.M., Ault, T.R., 2019. Unpacking the climatic drivers of US agricultural yields. Environmental Research Letters 14 (6), 064003. https://doi.org/10.1088/1748-9326/ab1e75

Park, R.J., Goodman, J., Hurwitz, M., Smith, J., 2020. Heat and learning. American Economic Journal: Economic Policy 12 (2), 306–339. https://doi.org/10.1257/pol.20180612

Pizer, W., Adler, M., Aldy, J., et al., 2014. Using and improving the social cost of carbon. Science 346 (6214), 1189–1190. https://doi.org/10.1126/science.1259774

Proctor, J., Carleton, T., Sum, S., 2023. Parameter Recovery Using Remotely Sensed Variables. NBER working Paper 30861. https://doi.org/10.3386/w30861.

Proctor, J., Rigden, A., Chan, D., Huybers, P., 2022. More accurate specification of water supply shows its importance for global crop production. Nature Food 3 (9), 753–763. https://doi.org/10.1038/s43016-022-00592-x

Quiggin, J., Horowitz, J.K., 1999. The impact of global warming on agriculture: a ricardian analysis: comment. American Economic Review 89 (4), 1044–1045. https://doi.org/10.1257/aer.89.4.1044

Rasmussen, D.J., Meinshausen, M., Kopp, R.E., 2016. Probability-weighted ensembles of U.S. county-level climate projections for climate risk analysis. Section: Journal of Applied Meteorology and Climatology. https://doi.org/10.1175/JAMC-D-15-0302.1

Rennert, K., Errickson, F., Prest, B.C., et al., 2022. Comprehensive evidence implies a higher social cost of CO_2. Nature 610 (7933), 687–692. https://doi.org/10.1038/s41586-022-05224-9

Roberts, M.J., Braun, N.O., Sinclair, T.R., Lobell, D.B., Schlenker, W., 2017. Comparing and combining process-based crop models and statistical models with some implications for climate change. Environmental Research Letters 12 (9), 095010. https://doi.org/10.1088/1748-9326/aa7f33

Rode, A., Carleton, T., Delgado, M., et al., 2021. Estimating a social cost of carbon for global energy consumption. Nature 598 (7880), 308–314. https://doi.org/10.1038/s41586-021-03883-8

Rolf, E., Proctor, J., Carleton, T., Bolliger, I., Shankar, V., Ishihara, M., Recht, B., Hsiang, S., 2021. A generalizable and accessible approach to machine learning with global satellite imagery. Nature Communications 12 (1), 4392. https://doi.org/10.1038/s41467-021-24638-z

Rosenzweig, C., Parry, M.L., 1994. Potential impact of climate change on world food supply. Nature 367 (6459), 133–138. https://doi.org/10.1038/367133a0

Schauberger, B., Archontoulis, S., Arneth, A., et al., 2017. Consistent negative response of US crops to high temperatures in observations and crop models. Nature Communications 8 (1), 13931. https://doi.org/10.1038/ncomms13931. (Publisher: Nature Publishing Group).

Schlenker, W., Auffhammer, M., 2018. The cost of a warming climate. Nature 557 (7706), 498–499. https://doi.org/10.1038/d41586-018-05198-7

Schlenker, W., Hanemann, W.M., Fisher, A.C., 2005. Will U.S. agriculture really benefit from global warming? Accounting for irrigation in the hedonic approach. American Economic Review 95 (1), 395–406. https://doi.org/10.1257/0002828053828455

Schlenker, W., Hanemann, W.M., Fisher, A.C., 2007. Water availability, degree days, and the potential impact of climate change on irrigated agriculture in California. Climatic Change 81 (1), 19–38. https://doi.org/10.1007/s10584-005-9008-z

Schlenker, W., Roberts, M.J., 2009. Nonlinear temperature effects indicate severe damages to U.S. crop yields under climate change. Proceedings of the National Academy of Sciences 106 (37), 15594–15598. https://doi.org/10.1073/pnas.0906865106

Schlenker, W., Roberts, M.J., Lobell, D.B., 2013. US maize adaptability. Nature Climate Change 3 (8), 690–691. https://doi.org/10.1038/nclimate1959

Schlenker, W., Taylor, C.A., 2021. Market expectations of a warming climate. Journal of Financial Economics 142 (2), 627–640. https://doi.org/10.1016/j.jfineco.2020.08.019

Semenza, J.C., Rubin, C.H., Falter, K.H., Selanikio, J.D., Flanders, W.D., Howe, H.L., Wilhelm, J.L., 1996. Heat-related deaths during the July 1995 heat wave in Chicago. New England Journal of Medicine 335 (2), 84–90. https://doi.org/10.1056/NEJM199607113350203

Seretakis, D., Lagiou, P., Lipworth, L., Signorello, L.B., Rothman, K.J., Trichopoulos, D., 1997. Changing seasonality of mortality from coronary heart disease. Journal of the American Medical Association 278 (12), 1012–1014. https://doi.org/10.1001/jama.1997.03550120072036

Severen, C., Costello, C., Deschnes, O., 2018. A forward-looking ricardian approach: do land markets capitalize climate change forecasts? Journal of Environmental Economics and Management 89, 235–254. https://doi.org/10.1016/j.jeem.2018.03.009

Sherwood, S.C., Huber, M., 2010. An adaptability limit to climate change due to heat stress. Proceedings of the National Academy of Sciences 107 (21), 9552–9555. https://doi.org/10.1073/pnas.0913352107

Snyder, R.L., 1985. Hand calculating degree days. Agricultural and Forest Meteorology 35 (1), 353–358. https://doi.org/10.1016/0168-1923(85)90095-4

Spielmann, K.A., Eder, J.F., 1994. Hunters and farmers: then and now. Annual Review of Anthropology 23, 303–323.

Strobl, E., 2011. The economic growth impact of hurricanes: evidence from U.S. coastal counties. The Review of Economics and Statistics 93 (2), 575–589. https://doi.org/10.1162/REST_a_00082

Tack, J., Barkley, A., Nalley, L.L., 2015. Effect of warming temperatures on US wheat yields. Proceedings of the National Academy of Sciences 112 (22), 6931–6936. https://doi.org/10.1073/pnas.1415181112

Tol, R.S.J., 2023. Social cost of carbon estimates have increased over time. Nature Climate Change 13 (6), 532–536. https://doi.org/10.1038/s41558-023-01680-x

Tol, R.S.J., 1997. On the optimal control of carbon dioxide emissions: an application of FUND. Environmental Modeling & Assessment 2 (3), 151–163. https://doi.org/10.1023/A:1019017529030

Traeger, C., 2024. Uncertainty. Handbook of Climate Economics.

Vecellio, D.J., Kong, Q., Kenney, W.L., Huber, M., 2023. Greatly enhanced risk to humans as a consequence of empirically determined lower moist heat stress tolerance. Proceedings of the National Academy of Sciences 120 (42), e2305427120. https://doi.org/10.1073/pnas.2305427120

Wahl, R.W., 1989. Markets for Federal Water: Subsidies, Property Rights, and the Bureau of Reclamation. RFF Press, New York.

Weitzman, M.L., 2001. Gamma discounting. American Economic Review 91 (1), 260–271. https://doi.org/10.1257/aer.91.1.260

Weitzman, M.L., 2013. Tail-Hedge discounting and the social cost of carbon. Journal of Economic Literature 51 (3), 873–882. https://doi.org/10.1257/jel.51.3.873

Weitzman, M.L., 2014. Fat tails and the social cost of carbon. American Economic Review 104 (5), 544–546. https://doi.org/10.1257/aer.104.5.544

Welch, J.R., Vincent, J.R., Auffhammer, M., Moya , P.F., Dobermann, A., Dawe, D., 2010. Rice yields in tropical/subtropical Asia exhibit large but opposing sensitivities to minimum and maximum temperatures. Proceedings of the National Academy of Sciences 107(33), 14562–14567. https://doi.org/10.1073/pnas.1001222107.

White, H., 1980. A heteroskedasticity-consistent covariance matrix estimator and a direct test for heteroskedasticity. Econometrica 48 (4), 817–838. https://doi.org/10.2307/1912934

Wilson, A.J., Bressler, R.D., Ivanovich, C., et al., 2024. Age-dependent vulnerability to humid heat: evidence from wet-bulb temperature exposure. Working Paper.

Wright, P.G., 1928. The Tariff on Animal and Vegetable Oils. Macmillan.

Wuepper, D., Wang, H., Schlenker, W., Jain, M., Finger, R., 2023. Institutions and Global Crop Yields. NBER Working Paper 31426. https://doi.org/10.3386/w31426.

Chapter 3

Discounting☆

Christian Gollier*
Toulouse School of Economics, University of Toulouse-Capitole, Toulouse, France
**Corresponding author. e-mail address: christian.gollier@tse-fr.eu*

Chapter Outline

1 Introduction

Our collective failure to reduce our emissions of greenhouse gases over the last three decades is a clear illustration of the free-riding problem associated with the climate externality. But it also raises the issue of whether human beings are short-termists by ignoring the grave consequences of their behaviour on the welfare of their peers who will live on this planet in the future. Whether this statement is true or not depends upon what are our individual and collective responsibilities towards future generations, and upon how these responsibilities should be translated into our collective values system. I refer here to the valuation of our natural assets (biodiversity, renewable and non-renewables resources, …), or of

☆ This research has also been funded by the French Agence Nationale de la Recherche under grant ANR-17-EURE-0010 (Investissements d'Avenir program).

Handbook of the Economics of Climate Change, Vol. 1. https://doi.org/10.1016/bs.hesecc.2024.10.007

our emissions of persistent pollutants such as CO_2 and mercury. The estimation of the carbon value, which economists have been referring to as the social cost of carbon, has been a focal issue for climate economists since the beginning of this century, following the seminal work by Bill Nordhaus. At the core of this experts' debate lies the problems of cost-benefit analysis and discounting.

One of the most basic missions of economists is to evaluate actions from the point of view of a predefined objective, most often utility or welfare. For an act to be desirable, one should obviously ensure that the welfare benefit of this act exceeds its welfare cost. One key difficulty of this evaluation comes from the observation that most human, corporate and governmental acts entail benefits and costs that are scattered over a potentially long duration. Typically, an investment imposes an immediate cost and a flow of delayed benefits. Even if all benefits and costs can be valued under a one-dimensional monetary scheme, they remain different by nature, because we typically don't consider that one future dollar has the same value as an immediate dollar, even in the absence of inflation. In this cost-benefit analysis, most people penalize delayed dollars just because they cannot be spent immediately. They discount the future.

When one discounts a sure benefit of 100 materializing in one year at a constant discount rate of 5 %, its present value should be $100/1.05 = 95.24$.[1] With such a discount rate, a project that costs x today and that generates a sure benefit of 100 next year is socially desirable if and only if x is smaller than 95.24, i.e., its Net Present Value (NPV) $-x + 100/1.05$ is positive. But if this benefit of 100 materializes only in a century, its present value should be reduced to $100/1.05^{100} = 0.76$. With such a discount rate, one should not be ready to pay more than 0.76 to get 100 in one hundred years. This simple exercise illustrates the crucial role of discounting in the valuation of long-dated impacts. Even a small discount rate compresses the present values of distant impacts, sometimes up to the point where these impacts can be completely ignored in the traditional cost-benefit analyses used by economists to evaluate public and private investments and policies. This is why economists are often at odds with other scientists and ecologists on various sustainability issues. Remember that until the end of 2023, the official discount rate used in the United States to evaluate public policies was set at the incredibly high real rate of 7 % (with an alternative rate at 3 % for sensitive analysis, whatever that means). This rate has been reduced since then to 2 % (OMB, 2023). In the United Kingdom, the public discount rate is 3.5 % (Treasury, 2018), and it is 2.25 % in the Netherlands (Rijksoverheid, 2020). In this survey, I try to answer the question of where this rate should be set, and on what ethical basis.

This survey has three parts. I first determine the efficient discount rate in the artificial context without any uncertainty. In the second part of the survey,

[1] This means that the discount factor equals 0.9524 in this case. More generally, the discount rate r is associated to the discount factor $(1 + r)^{-t}$ for maturity t.

I reevaluate this analysis in the context of risk and uncertainty. Finally, in Part III, I discuss different implementation of the theory of discounting in different countries, and for its application to climate change.

2 Part I: Discounting under certainty

2.1 Why do we discount the future?

In the absence of any uncertainty, economists have identified three reasons for why benefits materializing in the more distant future should be more heavily penalized in their valuation process: impatience, temporal arbitrage, and inequality aversion.

The celebrated "marshmallow test" in psychology is an impressive illustration of human beings' preferences for immediate rewards compared to delayed ones. In short, people are impatient. Since Samuelson (1937), economists have recognized this trait of human behaviour by describing individual intertemporal preferences as a discounted sum of the flow of temporal utility. Thus, an increase in future utility has a lower impact on welfare today than the same increase in current utility. It is often assumed that this rate of impatience, or "rate of pure preference for the present", is constant over time, yielding an exponential discount factor.[2] But climate economists have extended the model from an intertemporal framework to an intergenerational one. By doing this, they have transformed individual impatience, a perfectly reasonable human trait, into collective racism towards future generations, an attitude that many experts find morally unacceptable, as documented in Broome (1992) and Gollier (2013). It is indeed ethically questionable to measure intergenerational welfare with a lower weight for more distant generations. How could one punish people for being born later? In a survey of 180 economic experts, Drupp et al. (2018) observed that our profession continues to accept penalizing future generations by discounting their felicity at an average rate of 1.1 % per year, with a standard deviation for this "rate of pure preference for the present" of 1.47 % in this sample. In this survey, I will ignore this ethically questionable "agism" by setting the rate of pure preference for the present to zero. The intergenerational welfare will thus be measured by the unweighted sum of the flow of generational utility.[3] I will come back to this issue in Section I.4.

[2] Exponential discounting is important for the intertemporal consistency of the decision process. The alternative "hyperbolic discounting" framework generates a time-consistency problem: A dynamic strategy considered as optimal today may become suboptimal with the passing of time, even in the absence of any new information. The anticipation of switching strategy in the future makes the immediate action incoherent with future choices (Laibson, 1997). For example, with hyperbolic discounting, it may be intertemporally optimal to smoke one last cigarette today if one stop smoking tomorrow. But as tomorrow becomes today, the same argument can be applied to smoke one "last" cigarette again. This consumption is intertemporally incoherent.

[3] Mathematical economists have often criticized this approach by the unbounded nature of this welfare function in any infinite horizon model. But we know that the lifetime of Earth is limited by the one of the Sun, which is finite.

A second argument to discount the future is based on the opportunity cost of capital. Keep in mind here that the discount rate of a project can be interpreted as the minimum rate of return required to invest in that project. Keep also in mind that an action aimed at improving the future should not be evaluated in a vacuum. There exists a myriad of other possible actions to make the world better in the future: beyond the reduction of emissions of CO_2 which will reduce climate damages in the future, one could also reduce public debt, or make various investments that will improve our ability to create valuable goods in the future. If there exists a scalable investment in the economy that generates a sure payoff of 4 dollars in 35 years from now for every dollar invested today,[4] this means that one can secure a sure rate of return of 4 % per year for safe investments with a 35-year maturity. Therefore, it would make no sense to invest in any safe project with a 35-year maturity yielding a rate of return smaller than 4 %. This is particularly true if funding this alternative project must be made by divesting from the scalable one, as such a substitution would destroy future value for zero benefit today. The simple way to observe the rate of return of the best safe investment opportunity in the economy is to look at the interest rate. If financial markets are efficient, the interest rate is also the cost of capital of risk-free corporations, which are therefore incentivized to invest in their safe investments up to the point where their marginal rate of return equals this cost of capital. In short, this paragraph justifies using the interest rate as the rate at which risk-free benefits and costs should be discounted. The new official public discount rate of 2 % used in the United States relies on this argument (OMB, 2023).

The third argument to discount the future is based on both our collective beliefs in long-term economic growth and inequality aversion, as described in the next section.

2.2 A model-free argument for discounting

When examining an action that yields a sacrifice for someone and a benefit for someone else, as is the case for fighting climate change, there is a clear conflict of interest between them, yielding a social dilemma. This is why many classical philosophers such as John Locke, Jean-Jacques Rousseau, Immanuel Kant and John Rawls have recommended using the concept of the veil of ignorance to determine an ethically reasonable attitude to this kind of social dilemma. Let us put people under a veil of ignorance about who will be on the sacrifice side and who will be on the benefit side of the action. This creates a sense of impartiality when determining whether this action should be performed or not.

[4] Something growing at 4 % has an accumulated value of $\exp(0.04t)$ or 1.04^t depending upon whether one uses a continuous-time or a discrete-time approach. I prefer the continuous-time approach, yielding $4 \simeq \exp(0.04 \times 35)$.

Let us apply this resolution of social dilemma to the following example, inspired by Okun (1975). Croesus consumes twice as many goods and services as John. One contemplates a policy aimed at increasing the aggregate prosperity of the community. The problem is that the policy is detrimental to the poor John, and beneficial for the wealthy Croesus. More specifically, the policy generates $x > 1$ additional dollars for Croesus for each dollar lost by John. Clearly, the policy makes the community more prosperous, but at the same time more unequal. It is also clear that one would reject such a policy if $x = 1$, as it would not even raise GDP in this case. This rejection defines the concept of inequality aversion. Okun was not only interested whether one is inequality-averse. He was also interested in measuring the intensity of our inequality aversion. In this framework (which reverses Okun's "leaky bucket" experiment where income is transferred from the wealthy to the poor), the respondents to this experiment under the veil of ignorance are requested to elicit the minimum value of x that would make them willing to accept the policy. Inspired by estimations of the degree of inequality aversion existing in the literature (see for example Gollier (2013)), suppose that we come to a consensus that, to be socially acceptable under the veil of ignorance, the minimum benefit accruing to Croesus for each dollar lost by John should be $x = 4$ dollars. This is a measure of our collective degree of inequality aversion.

How is this analysis linked to discounting? Consider an economy which grows at 2 % per year. This means that consumption will double every 35 years. This is typically what happened in the western world over the last century. Now, contemplate an investment that would generate a single sure benefit of x dollars in 35 years for each dollar invested today. Under the veil of ignorance, what should be the minimum benefit x in the future to compensate for the dollar lost today? You certainly recognize here the analogy with the issue examined in the previous paragraph, as one asks a current John to sacrifice something for the benefit of a future Croesus who will consume twice as much as the present John. Under the consensus of $x = 4$, I can claim that the value today of generating 4 dollars in 35 years is one dollar. In other words, the discounted value of 4 dollars in 35 years should be 1 dollar. As seen in the previous section, this corresponds to a discount rate of 4 %. This is the discount rate that should be used in an economy growing at a sure annual rate of 2 %.

Observe that this moral argument supporting a discount rate of 4 % if the economy is certain to grow at 2 % per year is model-free. It just relies on the impartiality concept of the veil of ignorance and on a degree of inequality aversion which is experimentally estimated. We discount the future because future generations will be wealthier than us, so that investing for the future makes our society more intergenerationally unequal. The socially desirable level of the discount rate should be interpreted as the minimum rate of return of safe projects that compensates for the fact that implementing them would raise intergenerational inequalities.

2.3 Discounted expected utility and the Ramsey rule

Since Ramsey (1928), economists have argued that discounting is rational in a growing economy under (intertemporal) inequality aversion. In fact, Ramsey provided a model to support the intuition presented in the previous section. I hereafter describe this model and its implicit and explicit moral foundations. Observe first that the veil of ignorance substitutes a context of (intertemporal) inequality into a context of risk. Without knowing the generation to which one will belong, the unequal levels of consumption between generations make one's situation uncertain. This raises the deep question of how to evaluate welfare under uncertainty, a fundamental issue examined by decision theorists over the last three centuries (Gollier, 2001). Although this classical decision theory often fails to pass the test of observed human behaviours, the Expected Utility (EU) theory has a strong normative appeal associated with its underlying "independence axiom". This axiom states that if one prefers outcome X to outcome Y under certainty, one also prefers a lottery that gives X with probability p over lottery that gives Y with probability p, independent of the alternative Z that materializes with probability $1 - p$ in these two lotteries. This axiom forces the additivity of the welfare functional with respect to the states of nature.

Under EU, if John and Croesus consume respectively C_0 and C_t, then under the veil of ignorance, before knowing who will be Croesus, they will both enjoy a welfare equalling.

$$V_0 = \frac{1}{2}U(C_0) + \frac{1}{2}U(C_t),$$

where $U(C)$ is the utility level attained by an individual consuming C. I assume that U is increasing and concave. The concavity of U, a key property usually referred to as decreasing marginal utility, is synonymous to risk/inequality aversion. Indeed, if C_t is larger than C_0, a marginal transfer of consumption from t to 0 reduces risk/inequality and increases welfare V_0 if and only if U is concave. This is the definition of risk/inequality aversion. Economists typically use the family of power utility functions $U(C) = C^{1-\gamma}/(1-\gamma)$, in which $\gamma > 0$ is an index of relative risk/inequality aversion.

Observe that under the veil of ignorance, the indifference towards a policy that generates 4 dollars to Croesus consuming C_t for each dollar extracted from John consuming C_0 means that

$$U'(C_0) = 4U'(C_t). \tag{1}$$

Under the power specification, if Croesus consumes twice as much as John ($C_0 = 1$ and $C_t = 2$), this means that $1 = 4 \times 2^{-\gamma}$, or $\gamma = 2$. Thus, the thought experiment presented in the previous section is compatible with this EU model if we calibrate it with a degree of relative inequality aversion of 2.

In this model, it is interesting to measure the marginal rate of substitution between consumption in the two states/dates/individuals *0* and *t*. Let

$$PV = \frac{\partial V_0}{\partial C_t} \Big/ \frac{\partial V_0}{\partial C_0} = \frac{U'(C_t)}{U'(C_0)} \tag{2}$$

denote the willingness to sacrifice consumption in *0* to increase consumption in *t* by 1, i.e., the present value of a sure unit benefit materializing at *t*. Replacing $U'(C)$ by $C^{-\gamma}$ and C_t by $C_0 e^{gt}$ where g is the growth rate of consumption over time, we can replace Eq. (2) by

$$PV = \exp(-\gamma g t). \tag{3}$$

Since the present value of 1 in t years is related to the discount rate through equation $PV = \exp(-r_f t)$, this means that the efficient discount rate is

$$r_f = \gamma g. \tag{4}$$

This discount rate is efficient as a signal describing how people are willing to exchange future consumption against present one. This discount rate is such that the following two statements are equivalents, whichever marginal project X is considered:

- Project X has a positive NPV;
- Project X raises intertemporal welfare.

Eq. (4) is the Ramsey rule: The socially desirable discount rate is equal to the product of the degree of inequality aversion γ by the growth rate of consumption g. We recognize here the two ingredients that I used in the previous section to build a normative argument to discount the future. If $\gamma = 2$ and $g = 2\ \%$, we get a discount rate of 4 %. Notice that in an economy experiencing a negative growth, the inequality aversion argument goes in reverse, yielding a negative discount rate.

2.4 Aggregation of heterogenous time preferences

In the economic literature, the Ramsey rule is more generally written as

$$r_f = \delta + \gamma g, \tag{5}$$

where δ is the rate of pure preference for the present which corresponds to the rate at which the flow of utility is discounted. This parameter measures the degree of impatience in society. Eq. (5) is derived as in the previous section when one uses the following intertemporal welfare function:

$$V_0 = U(C_0) + e^{-\delta t} U(C_t). \tag{6}$$

Although I personally support calibration $\delta = 0$ for moral reasons, it appears that I am not representative of the profession. In particular, experimental and observational evidence suggests that most people are impatient ($\delta > 0$), with a large heterogeneity in individual degrees of impatience

(Frederick, Loewenstein and O'Donoghue, 2002). There is now an extensive literature exploring the role of disagreement in social intertemporal preferences. A very competent recent literature review can be found in Millner and Heal (2023). With Richard Zeckhauser, I contributed to this literature by examining the case of a community of immortal individuals with heterogenous degrees of impatience (Gollier and Zeckhauser, 2005). I consider here the simplest case with an analytical solution. The n individuals have to share a cake whose size can vary over time. Its size is C_t in date t, and individual i consumes c_{it} of it at that time, with $\sum_i c_{it} = C_t$ for all t. At date 0, the community organizes a Pareto-efficient intertemporal allocation of the cake among its members. The issue is that some members are more impatient than others, so that it is efficient to frontload their consumption in the first few periods in exchange for the others to consume more in the future. The issue is about the preferences of the community towards a transfer of the cake's size over time. The Pareto-efficient intertemporal allocation of consumption associated to the Pareto-weights $\{w_i\}_{i=1,\dots,n}$ is the solution of the following program:

$$U(C_t, t) = \max_{c_{1t},\dots,c_{nt}} \sum_{i=1}^{n} w_i e^{-\delta_i t} \frac{c_{it}^{1-\gamma}}{1-\gamma} \quad s.t. \quad \sum_{i=1}^{n} c_{it} = C_t, \tag{7}$$

for all t, where δ_i is the rate of pure preference for the present of individual i, and γ is the index of relative aversion to consumption fluctuations over time, which is assumed to be identical within the community. Solving this problem yields

$$c_{it} = C_t \frac{w_i^{1/\gamma} e^{-\frac{\delta_i t}{\gamma}}}{\sum_{j=1}^{n} w_j^{1/\gamma} e^{-\frac{\delta_j t}{\gamma}}} = C_t \frac{w_i^{1/\gamma} e^{\frac{(\delta_{at}-\delta_i)t}{\gamma}}}{\sum_{j=1}^{n} w_j^{1/\gamma}}, \tag{8}$$

where δ_{at} is defined as follows:

$$\delta_{at} = -\frac{\gamma}{t} \ln\left(\frac{\sum_{i=1}^{n} w_i^{1/\gamma} e^{-\frac{\delta_i t}{\gamma}}}{\sum_{i=1}^{n} w_i^{1/\gamma}}\right) \tag{9}$$

Observe from Eq. (8) that the share of the cake allocated to individual i is locally increasing with time when i has a rate of impatience δ_i that is smaller than δ_{at}. More patient people get a larger fraction of the cake later in time, leaving more of it to more impatient ones in the short term.

Now, the collective intertemporal preferences should be based on the sum of temporal discounted utilities $U(C_t, t)$, i.e., on

$$V_0 = \sum_{t=0} U(C_t, t). \tag{10}$$

Now, combining the last three equations yields

$$U(C_t, t) = k e^{-\delta_{at} t} \frac{C_t^{1-\gamma}}{1-\gamma}. \tag{11}$$

These two equations tell us that δ_{at} is nothing else than the collective rate of pure preference for the present. This is the δthat should be plug into the Ramsey Eq. (5) to determine the discount rate that should be used by the community to evaluate a sure payoff materializing in t years. Although all members of the community have a constant rate of pure preference for the present, the community will use a rate of pure preference for the present that is decreasing with maturity t. Indeed, it is easy to check from Eq. (9) that δ_{at} is between the smallest and the largest δ_i, that it equals to its weighted mean when t tends to zero, and that it tends to the smallest one when t tends to infinity. In other words, individuals are exponential discounters but the community is an hyperbolic discounter. The intuition is simple: Because more patient people transfer their consumption rights to the future, their own time preferences will play a bigger role when contemplating a partial transfer of the cake longer into the future. For extra-long maturities, most of the cake is consumed by the most patient member of the community, implying that it is only her own rate of impatient that matters in the long run.

Hyperbolic discounting implies that decisions and valuations are time-inconsistent. Because the next period intertemporal welfare function V_1 is not proportional to $V_0 - U(C_0, 0)$ as is the case under exponential discounting, the investment/saving decision that will be made next year is not the one that is optimally planned this year. Because, from the point of view of today, the optimal investment decision this year is optimal only conditional to following the optimally planned investment strategy in the future, this raises a time-consistency issue. By analogy to a drug addiction that can be explained by hyperbolic discounting, taking a last pill today may be optimal conditional on stopping tomorrow. But when tomorrow comes, the same argument can be made to pursue the addiction. In the framework of Gollier and Zeckhauser (2005), a community which would use the same Pareto-weights across time would face that inconsistency issue.[5]

Millner and Heal (2023) survey the many issues and extensions related to the aggregation of heterogeneous time preferences: resolution of the time-inconsistency problem, voting procedures, axiomatic approach to constraining the Pareto-weights, adding uncertainty, and so on. More recently, Eden (2023) characterizes the collective time preferences in an economy with overlapping generations. This is a very rich area of research.

2.5 Other extensions

Thus, intertemporal inequalities are critically important to justify discounting, which in turn plays a critical role in the practice of sustainable policy evaluation. It is therefore a puzzle that most policy evaluations are performed with

[5] This problem would be eliminated if the group would revise these weights over time, with the coefficient w_{it+1} used to weight the utility of individual i at date $t+1$ being equal to $w_{it}e^{-\delta_i}$.

a very limit integration of *intra*-generational inequalities. This puzzle can be explained by the limited understanding by most decision-makers about the role of inequalities to justify discounting. As we discount the prosperous future, we should also impose lower weights to value benefits accruing to wealthier people within the same period, in the spirit of my original Croesus and John story: four dollars of benefit accruing to Croesus should be valued as one dollar accruing to John. Coherence requires to use the same intensity of inequality aversion in proceeding to the selection of the discount rate and the intragenerational weights for benefit-cost analysis.

In this simple model, I implicitly assumed that people consume a single good, say rice or potatoes. Hopefully, the real world is of course more sophisticated. This is because one believes that more rice will be available in the future that one kilogram of rice in the future is valued less than one kilogram of rice today. But consider for example the value of the service of an ecosystem that is expected to shrink in the future. In that context, one should value more one future unit of this service in the future than in the present. In order to discount this time-transfer of units of specific goods and services, one could use Ramsey rule (4) where g would be the growth rate of consumption of the specific good under scrutiny, which could be positive or negative. The idea that each good or service in the economy could have its own discount rate was first developed by Malinvaud (1953), and then extended by Guesnerie (2004), Hoel and Sterner (2007), Sterner and Persson (2008), and Gollier (2010) in the case of uncertainty.

However, the growth rate of the consumption of a specific good or service is not the only ingredient to determine its specific discount rate. We may well have less of the service of an ecosystem in the future, but this service could be substituted by something else so that the future value of the service does not grow over time. For example, if one expects that a specific future benefit will see its societal valuation grows at a specific rate x, for example because of the anticipation of an increase in its relative scarcity with limited substitutability, then one could use a corrected rate r_f $-x$ to discount this future benefit, in exchange for ignoring its intrinsic value growth. A recent paper by Drupp et al. (2024) illustrates this idea in the case of ecosystem services. Potentially because of economic growth or because of pollution or excessive extraction of natural resources associated with these services, the relative scarcity of some of these services are expected to grow, yielding an increase in their societal value. A key ingredient of this argument is the income-elasticity of the demand for these services, which is associated to their degree of substitutability.

3 Part II: Discounting under uncertainty

3.1 Stochastic discount factor

The Ramsey rule has a clear and transparent normative foundation. Under certainty, it offers a simple framework to evaluate sustainability policies.

Things are more complex in the case of uncertainty. We need to recognize two sources of uncertainty, the one surrounding future consumption C_t and the one surrounding the future benefit B_t of the project under scrutiny. Under EU and the veil of ignorance about both the state of nature and the generation to which everyone will belong, the present value PV of this future uncertain benefit must be such that

$$\frac{1}{2}u(C_0 + PV) + \frac{1}{2}Eu(C_t) = \frac{1}{2}u(C_0) + \frac{1}{2}Eu(C_t + B_t), \tag{12}$$

so that one would be indifferent to get PV immediately or lottery B_t in the future. At the margin, that is for a marginal project, this condition is equivalent to

$$PV = E[e^{-\rho_t t}B_t] \text{ with } e^{-\rho_t t} = m_t = \frac{u'(C_t)}{u'(C_0)}, \tag{13}$$

where $\rho_t = \gamma g_t$ is the stochastic discount rate, m_t is the stochastic discount factor (SDF), and

$$g_t = \frac{1}{t}\ln\left(\frac{C_t}{C_0}\right) \tag{14}$$

is the stochastic annualized growth rate of consumption between 0 and t. Eq. (13) is ubiquitous in the modern asset pricing literature, with m_t denoting the stochastic discount factor, the price kernel or the Arrow-Debreu price. Under uncertainty, pricing a future payoff consists in using the Ramsey rule state by state to determine the present state-specific value of the future benefit. The value today of the future lottery B_t is just equal to the expectation of this stochastic present value. As soon as C_t is uncertain, the discount factor m_t and the discount rate ρ_t are stochastic, i.e., contingent to the state. But the message is exactly the same as in the first part of this paper, except for the fact that the underlying valuation procedure needs to be implemented state by state.

Let me illustrate this approach with a simple example. Assume that γ equals 2 and that there are only two possible states of nature. The growth rate is constant but unknown at time 0. This uncertainty will be fully resolved only after investment decisions will be made. In the normal state, the growth rate is $g_n = 2.33\,\%$, whereas in the "degrowth" state, the growth rate is $g_d = -1\,\%$. The probability of degrowth is $p = 10\,\%$, so that the expected growth rate is $2\,\%$. In this context, let us value a benefit that takes value B_{tn} and B_{td} respectively in states n and d. The SDF approach consists in discounting each of these two contingent benefits at the Ramsey rates ρ_t of $4\,\%$ and $-2\,\%$ respectively. The two contingent present values PV_n and PV_d are then weighted by their respective probability to obtain the present value of the project. In Table 1, I calculated the present value of various projects that differ on their maturity and risk profile by using formula (13).

TABLE 1 Present value *PV* and risk-adjusted discount rates R_t for four different projects that differ on their maturity *t* and on their contingent payoffs (B_{tn}, B_{tc}). They all have an expected future value of \$1000. We assume that there is a normal scenario with a consumption growth rate of 2.33 % forever and one degrowth scenario with a consumption growth rate of −1 % forever. The probability of degrowth is 10 %.

	Project 1	Project 2	Project 3	Project 4
t	1	100	100	100
B_{tn}	1000	1000	500	1100
B_{td}	1000	1000	5500	100
PV_n	954	9	5	10
PV_d	1020	7389	40,640	739
PV	961	747	4068	83
R_t	3.98 %	0.29 %	−1.40 %	2.49 %

Consider first a project (project 1) that generates for sure 1000 dollars next year. We see in Table 1 that its present value of this project equals 961 dollars. This corresponds to discounting the future benefit at a risk-free rate of 3.98 %. For a maturity of 100 years (project 2), this sure future benefit of 1000 dollars has a contingent PV of 9 dollars in the normal state and of 7389 dollars in the degrowth state, yielding a present value of 747 dollars. This is equivalent to using a risk-free discount rate that equals 0.29 %. Interestingly enough, these risk-free discount rates are decreasing with maturity and are smaller than the Ramsey rate of 4 % that would have been obtained by using the expected growth of 2 % in the Ramsey rule. We will see why in the next section.

In projects 3 and 4, the future benefit is contingent to the state, but its expected future value is 1000 dollars as in the first two projects. In Project 3, the future benefit is much larger in the bad state of nature than in the good one, so that it provides some insurance against the macroeconomic catastrophe described by the degrowth state. Because of its huge PV contingent to the bad state, the present value of project 3 (4068 dollars) is much larger than its expected future benefit (1000 dollars). If one defines the risk-adjusted discount rate R_t as the rate that should be used to discount the future expected benefit to get PV, this risk-adjusted discount rate is here equal to −1.40 %. Finally, Project 4 exhibits a positive correlation between its future benefit and future consumption. The value of Project 4 today is a small 83 dollars, which is compatible with a risk-adjusted discount rate of 2.49 %. In the next section, I provide an economic logic to these large discrepancies in present values and discount rates.

These 4 projects demonstrate that, although the value today of a future benefit is the expectation of its stochastic present value, which suggests risk-neutrality, the investor's risk attitude plays a critical role in its valuation. They also illustrate the simplicity of the generalization of the intuitive Ramsey rule and methodology to the case of uncertainty.

3.2 Risk-adjusted discount rates: Prudence and risk-aversion

In the asset-pricing literature and in the practice of finance and capital budgeting, it is a tradition to measure the present value of an uncertain future benefit as the expectation of that future benefit discounted at a risk-adjusted rate R_t. This has already been used in the example described in Table 1. This risk-adjustment can be obtained by rewriting formula (13) as follows:

$$PV = e^{-R_t t} E[B_t] \text{ with } R_t = \frac{-1}{t} \ln\left(\frac{E[B_t e^{-\rho_t t}]}{E[B_t]}\right). \tag{15}$$

The second equation above tells us that the risk-adjusted discount factor *exp* $(-R_t t)$ is a weighted average of the state-contingent discount factors *exp* $(-\rho_t t)$, where the weights correspond to the contingent net benefit B_t of the specific project under scrutiny.

This approach with a risk-adjusted discount rate R_t that is specific to the project seems to be more complex than the stochastic discount factor (SDF) approach. In particular, it perverts the intuitive simplicity of the Ramsey rule that prevails in the SDF approach. But as we will see in the next section, there exists a special case in which the risk-adjusted discount rate approach is in fact much easier than the SDF one.

From formula (15), the rate R_{ft} to be used in this uncertainty context to evaluate any risk-free benefit equals

$$R_{ft} = \frac{-1}{t} \ln\left(E\left[e^{-\rho_t t}\right]\right). \tag{16}$$

It is easy to check that, for any time horizon $t > 0$, this risk-free rate R_{ft} is smaller than the expected contingent Ramsey rate $R_{f0} = E[\rho_t]$. When t tends to zero, the risk-free discount rate tends to R_{f0}, so that for small maturities, the uncertainty surrounding the risk-free discount rate is unaffected by the uncertainty surrounding consumption growth. On the contrary, for large maturities, R_{ft} tends to the smallest possible discount rate among the different contingent ρ_t. These results are general as they do not depend upon the distribution of the contingent discount/growth rates. They are described in Weitzman (1998, 2001).

The property that the uncertainty surrounding future consumption reduces the rate at which risk-free benefits should be discounted relies on the notions of prudence and precautionary savings. From formula (13), the present value of a unit benefit materializing in t years equals $Eu'(C_t)/u'(C_0)$. This is larger than $u'(EC_t)/u'(C_0)$, i.e. uncertainty reduces the risk-free discount rate, if and only if marginal utility is a convex function of consumption (Leland, 1968; Drèze and Modigliani, 1972), a property called prudence (Kimball, 1990). Notice that all concave power utility functions have a convex marginal utility. Prudence is supported by the observation that an increase in the uncertainty surrounding someone's future incomes raises her optimal (precautionary) saving, as stated by John M. Keynes. The reduction of the risk-free discount rate is the asset-pricing version of this idea: The uncertainty surrounding the future should induce us to invest more for that future. This is done by reducing the risk-free discount rate. This explains why the discount rates of projects 1 and 2 in Table 1 are less than 4 %. This concludes our discussion about how the macroeconomic uncertainty affect the risk-free discount rate.

Let me now turn to the issue of how the uncertainty surrounding the net benefit should affect the rate at which its expected value should be discounted. Under this approach in which one discounts the expected future benefit, the only way to value the impact of a project on the aggregate risk is through the adjustment of the discount rate. Intuitively, comparing two projects with the same net benefit, but the first one raises the aggregate risk whereas the second one reduces it, risk-averse people should value more this second project. This should be done by using a smaller discount rate for this second project. To illustrate, a smaller discount rate should be used by Caribbean States for valuing more stringent anti-hurricane building norms, or by Western States to value strategic oil and gas reserves and military capacity, compared for example to projects to expand public transportation networks. Formulas (13) and (15) clearly show that the riskiness of the future benefit affects its present value only if it is statistically linked to the uncertainty surrounding the stochastic discount rate ρ_t, thus to the uncertainty surrounding future aggregate consumption C_t. Said differently, if B_t is uncertain but $B_t|C_t$ is independent of C_t, then its present value is equal to its expected future value discounted at the risk-free rate R_{ft}. Risk that are not statistically linked to the aggregate risk should not be priced. This is due to the property of the EU model that risk is a second-order effect (Segal and Spivak, 1990). In other words, when B_t and C_t are independent, the risk premium of kB_t is proportional to k^2 in the small.

Suppose alternatively that $C_t$and B_t covary positively, which implies that $\rho_t$and B_t covary positively too, under risk aversion. This implies that

$$R_t = \frac{-1}{t}\ln\left(\frac{E[B_t e^{-\rho_t t}]}{E[B_t]}\right) \geq \frac{-1}{t}\ln\left(\frac{E[B_t]E[e^{-\rho_t t}]}{E[B_t]}\right) = R_{ft}. \tag{17}$$

Under risk aversion, the risk-adjusted discount rate R_t should be larger than the risk-free rate whenever C_t and B_t covary positively. This condition defines a project that raises the aggregate risk borne by the representative agent. This undesirable feature justifies penalizing this project by discounting the expected benefit at a risk-adjusted rate R_t which is larger than the risk-free rate R_{ft}. If C_t and B_t covary negatively, we get that the associated project specific discount rate R_t should be smaller than the risk-free rate R_{ft}. In practice, because aggregate consumption is itself generated by a portfolio of different investments (in human and physical capital), it happens that most projects covary positively with C_t, as in Project 4 in Table 1, so that the risk adjustment of the project-specific discount rate is in general positive. But counterexamples are easy to find, such as gold, military defence, intensive care units, and most investments in self-insurance (earthquake-resistant building norms, adaptation to climate change, ...). Project 3 in Table 1 shares this insurance feature. It explains why its risk-adjusted discount rate (−1.40 %) is smaller than the risk-free discount rate (0.29 %) associated with maturity $t = 100$ years.

3.3 Consumption-based capital asset pricing model (CCAPM)

Under the risk-adjusted discount rate approach summarized in formula (15), the present value of future benefit B_t is equal to its expected future value discounted at a rate R_t which is specific to its statistical link with g_t. This sensitivity of the discount rate to the risk profile of the benefit is a key insight of this asset pricing model. In order to specify this relationship, it is useful to calibrate the above model in the special case where the income-elasticity of benefit B_t is a constant β, so that $B_t = \xi_t C_t^\beta$ with $\beta \in \mathbb{R}$ and ξ_t is an independent random variable. A positive (negative) β signals a project that increases (decreases) the aggregate risk. Under that specification, we obtain that

$$R_t = -\frac{1}{t}\ln\left(\frac{E\left[e^{(\beta-\gamma)g_t t}\right]}{E\left[e^{\beta g_t t}\right]}\right). \tag{18}$$

Observe that this discount rate is a function of the project-specific β. Let's further assume that$g_t$is normally distributed with mean μ_t and volatility σ_t. In this framework, using the SDF approach would be difficult given the infinite number of states of nature. It is noteworthy that the timing of the resolution of the uncertainty is irrelevant to value a claim B_t maturing at t. Only the joint distribution of (C_t, B_t) matters. This result is specific to the Discounted Expected Utility model. Using Stein's Lemma,[6] Eq. (18) implies that

$$R_t = -\left(\left((\beta-\gamma)\mu_t + 0.5(\beta-\gamma)^2 t\sigma_t^2\right) - \left(\beta\mu_t + 0.5\beta^2 t\sigma_t^2\right)\right) = R_{ft} + \beta\pi_t \tag{19}$$

with

$$R_{ft} = \gamma\mu_t - 0.\ 5\gamma^2 t\sigma_t^2 \text{ and } \pi_t = \gamma t\sigma_t^2, \tag{20}$$

where π_t is the aggregate risk premium. It tells us by how much the discount rate should be adjusted for a project that duplicates the aggregate risk ($\beta = 1$).

6 It states that if x is normally distributed with mean μ and standard deviation σ, then $E[\exp(kx)]$ equals $\exp(k\mu + 0.5k^2\sigma^2)$ for all $k \in \mathbb{R}$.

Observe that we recover here the two basic properties of asset pricing: the risk-free rate is reduced by the uncertainty surrounding the future aggregate consumption, and the risk-adjustment of the project-specific discount rate has the same sign as the project's beta.

The calibration of the CCAPM pricing rules (20) requires information on the mean and the standard deviation of g_t, the annualized growth rate of consumption between 0 and t defined by Eq. (14). This calibration is particularly challenging in the case of maturities relevant for sustainability issues such as climate change. Christensen, Gillingham and Nordhaus (2018) used 13 probabilistic expert forecasts to perform this task for the growth of the global real per-capita GDP between 2010 and 2100. Their procedure to aggregate these 13 beliefs implies a normal distribution for g_{90} with mean $\mu_{90} = 2.1\ \%$ and standard deviation $\sigma_{90} = 1.1\ \%$. Plugging these parameters into (20) and using $\gamma = 2$ as before, we get

$$R_{f90} = 2.\ 4\% \text{ and } \pi_{90} = 1.\ 8\%. \tag{21}$$

Under this CCAPM framework, the evaluator with a project maturing in 90 years should be given these two tutelar discounting parameters to evaluate the risk-adjusted discount rate using the estimation of the project's beta. Notice that, by definition, the beta of a project is nothing else than the income-elasticity of its net benefit. Sectoral betas could be estimated by an OLS regression of the log added value of the sector over the log GDP/cap. For example, using US data between 1997 and 2018, Gollier, van der Ploeg and Zheng (2023) estimated a sectoral beta of the rail transportation sector of 2.27, and a sectoral beta for hospitals of −0.32. Any expected benefit materializing in 90 years should be discounted at a rate of 6.49 % and 1.82 % respectively for railways and for hospitals.

3.4 Classical CCAPM

We could reproduce the same procedure for other maturities in order to generate a term structure for the risk-free discount rate R_{ft} and the aggregate risk premium π_t. This requires determining the risk profile of C_t or g_t. The most standard calibration assumes that C_t follows a geometric Brownian motion with trend μ and volatility σ. It implies that g_t is normally distributed with mean $\mu_t = \mu$ and standard deviation $\sigma_t = \sigma/t$. In this special case, the CCAPM formula (20) simplifies to

$$R_{ft} = \gamma\mu - 0.5\gamma^2\sigma^2 \text{ and } \pi_t = \gamma\sigma^2. \tag{22}$$

This continuous-time CCAPM formula has been pioneered by Rubinstein (1976), Lucas (1978) and Breeden (1979). An interesting feature of this version of the CCAPM is that it yields risk-free discount rates and aggregate risk premia that are independent of the time-horizon, i.e., it yields flat term structures of risk-adjusted discount rates and risk premia. This is because the variance of $\ln(C_t/C_0)$ grows proportionally with the time horizon t in the case of a geometric Brownian process for consumption. More generally, when $\ln(C_{t+1}/C_t)$ is an i.i.d. process (not necessarily gaussian), the term structures of the risk-free discount rates and of the aggregate risk premia are flat.

The Brownian process is too simple to represent the real world. For example, growth expectations are fluctuating over time, with periods of growing or diminishing expectations. Since this pioneering standard CCAPM innovation of the 70 s, the asset pricing literature has generalized the above formula to other stochastic processes for C_t, such as auto-regressive models allowing for business cycles, or such as models with discontinuous regime switches, and more generally to all affine models. They all generate special cases of the CCAPM formula (20).

3.5 Asset pricing puzzles and their implications in the discounting debate

The strong ethical foundation of the CCAPM makes it an attractive benchmark for policy evaluation. However, the standard version of the CCAPM presented in the previous section failed to explain observed asset prices on financial markets. Indeed, over the last century or so, the annual growth rate of real GDP per capita in the western world had a mean around $\mu = 2\ \%$ and a volatility around $\sigma = 3\ \%$. Combining these parameters with $\gamma = 2$ in the calibration of formula (22) yields

$$R_{ft} = 3.82\% \text{ and } \pi_t = 0.18\%. \tag{23}$$

Observe first that the precautionary motive reduces the Ramsey discount rate of 4 % to 3.82 %. In other words, the macroeconomic uncertainty has a very small impact on our willingness to invest in risk-free projects. The risk-free rate puzzle (Weil, 1989) comes from the comparison between this risk-free discount rate and the real interest rate observed on markets in the past, which has been around 1 % in the western world during the last century or so (Kocherlakota, 1996; Jordà et al., 2019). This huge discrepancy between the efficient discount rate and the observed interest rate is a puzzle because at equilibrium, the interest rate is the cost of capital of risk-free corporations. To maximize their profit, they will use it as a discount rate to evaluate their own risk-free investment projects. The fact that risk-free projects have been evaluated by financial market players at such a small rate of 1 % means that they have been much more long-termist over the period than what would have been socially desirable. Why did our great grand-parents save and invest so much in such fast-growing economies for the benefit of future generations that happened to be so much wealthier than them anyway? The ethical approach yielding a discount rate for risk-free project at 3.82 % clashes with the approach based on the opportunity cost of capital that yields a risk-free discount rate around 1 %. Much of the discounting debate over the last 3 decades has been about which is right and which is wrong among these two approaches, the predicted rate by the model or the observed rate on the market.

The estimation (23) of an aggregate risk premium of $\pi_t = 0.18\%$ is also puzzling. It means that a claim on aggregate consumption ($\beta = 1$) should be penalized for the risk that it bears by adjusting the discount rate upward to 4 % from the risk-free rate $R_{ft} = 3.82\%$. This penalty is surprisingly low. It happens that a portfolio of diversified equity has a beta around 3 (Bansal and Yaron, 2004), so that we should observe an expected excess return compared to the interest rate, which is referred to as the equity premium, around 0.54 %. Kocherlakota (1996) and Jordà et al. (2019) estimated that the observed equity premium in the western world has been 6 % on average. This means that financial markets suggest an aggregate risk premium of 2 %, which is more than 10 times larger than its value of 0.18 % predicted by the model. This large discrepancy is usually referred to in the literature as the equity premium puzzle. Contrary to my conclusion above for safe assets, markets seem to have been much more short-termist than socially desirable when contemplating risky investments.

3.6 Infrequent macro catastrophes

As shown by Barro (2006, 2009), the two asset pricing puzzles that prevail when the CCAPM is calibrated using a geometric Brownian process for consumption can be solved by adding to that process the possibility of infrequent macroeconomic catastrophes. In continuous time, this can be done by mixing a geometric Brownian process with a Poisson process. In discrete time, this can be done by assuming that each year, the annual change in log consumption is $N(\mu,\sigma^2)$ with probability $1\text{-}p$, which corresponds to business-as-usual, or is equal to $ln\,(1\text{-}k)$ with probability p, which corresponds to a catastrophe. Parameter k is the loss expressed as a share of aggregate consumption. Because the probability p of catastrophe is small, these events may not be in the data. Maybe, in spite of two world wars and a great depression, we have been lucky enough over the last century to have escaped the kind of catastrophes that could prevail in the future: civilizational crisis, climate change, outbreak of a new epidemic without a vaccine, and so on. These potential events are in our mind, but they are not in the data. This magnifies the macroeconomic risk. It reduces the risk-free rate because of the precautionary investment motive, and it raises the risk premium because of risk aversion. This has thus the potential to solve both the risk-free rate puzzle and the equity premium puzzle.

Because changes in log consumption are i.i.d., the term structure of risk-adjusted discount rates R_t are flat. Using Eq. (18), we obtain that

$$e^{-R_t} = \frac{(1-p)e^{(\beta-\gamma)\mu+0.5(\beta-\gamma)^2\sigma^2} + p(1-k)^{\beta-\gamma}}{(1-p)e^{\beta\mu+0.5\beta^2\sigma^2} + p(1-k)^{\beta}}. \tag{24}$$

To illustrate, let me calibrate this discounting system with $\gamma = 2$, $\mu = 2\,\%$, $\sigma = 3\,\%$ as before, with the additional parameters of the catastrophe: $p = 1\,\%$ and $k = 50\,\%$. With a 1 % probability every year, consumption drops by 50 %.

The plausibility of this catastrophe reduces the expected growth rate of consumption to 1.33 %. The risk-free rate also goes down to $R_{ft} = 0.71\%$, and the risk premium goes up to $\pi_t = 2.45\%$. We see that in spite of the low probability of catastrophes, their plausibility has a dramatic effect on the efficient discounting system. Basically, if one could agree on the realism of this calibration, the two asset-pricing puzzles are solved: equilibrium market returns are efficient and can be predicted by using the CCAPM incremented with infrequent macro catastrophes. Macroeconomic catastrophes are a fact of human history, and extreme events are much more frequent than what is assumed under the assumptions of the classical CCAPM with a Brownian motion. For these reasons, this classical calibration of the CCAPM should be definitely discarded to calibrate an efficient discounting system.

We have seen that when one calibrates pricing rule (18) with a normal distribution for the annualized growth rate g_t, the risk-adjusted discount rate R_t is a linear function of the income-elasticity β of the net benefit of the project. Eq. (24) illustrates the fact that this linearity is specific to this gaussian framework. In Fig. 1, I draw the non-linear relationship between R_t and β under the calibration described in the previous paragraph. Martin (2013) links the shape of this curve to the higher cumulants of the distribution of g_t. The concavity of $R_t(\beta)$ that emerges from this calibration is due to the negative skewness of the distribution of the annualized growth rate of consumption. Using the linear approximation based on the risk-free rate and the aggregate risk premium would have the effect of potentially vastly overestimating the risk-adjustment of the discount rate for betas larger than 1.

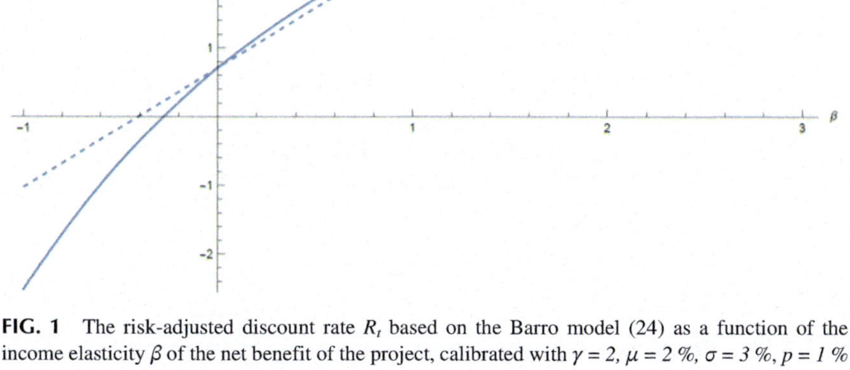

FIG. 1 The risk-adjusted discount rate R_t based on the Barro model (24) as a function of the income elasticity β of the net benefit of the project, calibrated with $\gamma = 2$, $\mu = 2\ \%$, $\sigma = 3\ \%$, $p = 1\ \%$ and $k = 50\ \%$. The dashed curve corresponds to the linear extrapolation based on the efficient discount rates at $\beta = 0$ and $\beta = 1$.

3.7 Parametric uncertainty

Shaping a stochastic process that fits our collective beliefs about our future prosperity for the decades and centuries to come is an extraordinary challenge on which this whole exercise of characterizing the term structures of risk-adjusted discount rates is based. This process is by nature ambiguous and deeply uncertain. In other words, our future risks are uncertain. How should this second layer of risk affect our estimation of short, medium and long term discount rates? I explored the problem of making the parameters of the growth process uncertain in Gollier (2016). Consider the simplest example in which the annual growth rate of consumption is binary and i.i.d. conditional to parameter p. Every year, with probability $1\text{-}p$, consumption will grow at 2 %, and with probability p, it will go down by 1 %. What is the effect on the macroeconomic risk of introducing some parametric uncertainty on the loss probability p? Because expected (marginal) utility is linear in probabilities, a white noise on p does not affect $Eu'(C_1)$, so it does not affect the efficient discount rates for a one-year maturity. Notice however that for longer maturities, this white noise on p affects the distribution of C_2. Compare for example two contexts, one in which $p = 0.5$ with certainty, and one in which p is either 0.9 or 0.1 with equal probabilities. In the first context, the probability getting two consecutive positive (negative) growth years is 25 %. If you do the math in the case of an uncertain p, you will obtain that the probability of this event is increased to 41 %. It illustrates the fact that observing a low-growth outcome in the first period is bad news for C_1, but it is also bad news for the future because of the Bayesian update of the probability distribution, for the worse. This parametric uncertainty increases the fatness of the tails of the distribution of future log consumption. This point has been made first by Halevy and Feltkamp (2005). By raising the long-run macro uncertainty, it reduces the long-term risk-free discount rate under prudence and it raises the long-term aggregate risk premium under risk aversion.

The simplest illustration of this effect is obtained by assuming that conditional to μ, $ln\,(C_{t+1}/C_t)$ is i.i.d. $N(\mu,\sigma^2)$. Suppose also that our prior beliefs on μ are $N(\mu_0, \sigma_\mu^2)$. In that case, Eq. (18) can be solved by using Stein's Lemma twice to obtain

$$\begin{aligned} R_t &= -\frac{1}{t}\ln\left(\frac{E\left[e^{(\beta-\gamma)g_t t}\right]}{E\left[e^{\beta g_t t}\right]}\right) = -\frac{1}{t}\ln\left(\frac{E\left[e^{(\beta-\gamma)\mu t+0.5(\beta-\gamma)^2\sigma^2 t}\right]}{E\left[e^{\beta\mu t+0.5\beta^2\sigma^2 t}\right]}\right) \\ &= -\frac{1}{t}\ln\left(\frac{e^{(\beta-\gamma)\mu_0 t+0.5(\beta-\gamma)^2\sigma_\mu^2 t^2+0.5(\beta-\gamma)^2\sigma^2 t}}{e^{\beta\mu_0 t+0.5\beta^2\sigma_\mu^2 t^2+0.5\beta^2\sigma^2 t}}\right) \\ &= R_{ft} + \beta\pi_t \end{aligned} \tag{25}$$

with

$$R_{ft} = \gamma\mu_0 - 0.5\gamma^2(\sigma^2 + t\sigma_\mu^2) \text{ and } \pi_t = \gamma(\sigma^2 + t\sigma_\mu^2). \tag{26}$$

Observe that the risk-free discount rate and the aggregate risk premium are respectively linearly decreasing and linearly increasing with maturity t. Risk-adjusted discount rates are thus asymptotically unbounded. Observe also that parametric uncertainty does not affect short-term discount rates. These results are related to Weitzman (1998, 2001) who showed that parametric uncertainty leads to an asymptotic risk-free discount rate that is equal to the smallest plausible conditionally efficient discount rate. Here, using the Ramsey rule, the smallest plausible discount rate is obtained when assuming that μ is $-\infty$, in which case the conditionally efficient discount rate R_{ft} equals $-\infty$ too.

What do we learn from this analysis with parameter uncertainty? First, economists should recognize that for time horizons relevant for most sustainability issues such as climate change, realism should force us to recognize that some of the parameters driving the growth process are uncertain. Second, this parametric uncertainty does not matter much for valuing short- and medium-term projects, and this property may explain why our profession has not focus much on this issue until recently. Third, this issue appears to be key to value long-term projects. This represents a challenge for economists because the calibration of this uncertainty is complex for obvious reasons. This is why our ability to tackle sustainability problems and to provide credible policy recommendations remain limited. More than ever, our evaluations of extra-long-term projects should be accompanied by a transparent description of our representation of the planet's stochastic future.

3.8 Other social welfare functions

Under the veil of ignorance and recognizing the merits of the independence axiom, there exists a strong scientific and moral basis for using EU as the intergenerational welfare function. But, following for example Olijslagers and Van Wijnbergen (2024), let me consider two prominent extensions of the EU model for discounting: ambiguity aversion and Epstein-Zin preferences. Both preference functionals violate the independence axiom as they are non-linear in probabilities.

The Ellsberg paradox (Ellsberg, 1961) suggests that even in a static framework, many people value a lottery yielding \$100 with an unknown probability p that is equally likely to be either 0.9 or 0.1 less than a lottery that yields \$100 with a sure probability of 0.5. This "ambiguity aversion" has been formalized in the literature in different ways, but its most convincing version has been provided by Klibanoff, Marinacci and Mukerji (KMM, 2005). As in the previous section, suppose that the distribution of C_t is ambiguous in the sense that its distribution is parametrized by θ whose distribution F represents our prior beliefs on this second-order risk. But contrary to Section II.6, suppose that the representative consumer is averse to the parametric ambiguity. I apply the smooth ambiguity aversion model of KMM which takes the following form:

$$V_0 = \frac{1}{2}U(C_0) + \frac{1}{2}\phi^{-1}\left(\int \phi(E[U(C_t)|\theta])dF(\theta)\right), \tag{27}$$

where the concavity of function $\phi(.)$ measures the degree of ambiguity-aversion. Gierlinger and Gollier (2011) characterized the conditions under which the ambiguity surrounding future consumption growth reduces the risk-free discount rate, as suggested by the intuition. This model violates the compounding of probabilities that is so fundamental to probability theory. In this model, receiving 100 with probability $p=0.9$ or $p=0.1$ with equal probabilities is not equivalent to receiving 100 with $p=½$. Indeed, because ϕ is non-linear, intertemporal welfare V_0 is negatively affected by a mean-preserving spread in the probability of C_t. Although real people may violate it in some circumstances, I find it hard for policy-makers to make the same trivial mistake to shape optimal policies. More discussion on this issue may be found in Traeger (2014).

The other alternative to EU initiated in the 70 s is aimed at disentangling risk aversion from inequality aversion. Epstein and Zin (1989) offered a definitive representation of the so-called "recursive preferences". In the simpler case of two consumption dates, it simplifies to

$$V_0 = \frac{1}{2}U(C_0) + \frac{1}{2}U(\chi_t) \tag{28}$$

where χ_t is defined as follows:

$$V(\chi_t) = EV(C_t). \tag{29}$$

Under this representation, the concavity of function U measures inequality aversion, whereas the concavity of function V measures risk aversion. When U and V are not identical, this model violates the impartiality principle of the veil of ignorance by treating differently the economic uncertainty surrounding C_t and the generational uncertainty surrounding the generation to which one will belong. The typical calibration of the two utility functions are such that $U(C) = C^{1-\rho}/(1-\rho)$ and $V(C) = C^{1-\gamma}/(1-\gamma)$, where ρ and γ are the indices of respectively relative inequality aversion and relative risk aversion. In the geometric Brownian case with trend μ and volatility σ, the CCAPM formula (22) must be generalized as follows in that case:

$$R_{ft} = \rho\mu - 0.5(\rho\gamma + \gamma - \rho)\sigma^2 \text{ and } \pi_t = \gamma\sigma^2. \tag{30}$$

As anticipated, the aggregate risk premium is governed by risk aversion, whereas the Ramsey term in the risk-free rate is governed by inequality aversion, the precautionary term mixing the two ingredients. But again, under the impartiality principle implemented by the veil of ignorance, there is no reason to differentiate ρ from γ. Bansal and Yaron (2004) generalized this model by examining the case of mean-reverting processes for μ and σ.

II.8 Summary of reasonable calibrations of the efficient discounting system.

To sum up, I described in this survey four calibrations of the efficient risk-sensitive discounting system, as documented in Table 2. If one eliminates the classical CCAPM for the reasons mentioned above, we have a relatively convergent consensus for an aggregate risk premium around 2 %. The only

TABLE 2 Three calibrations of the CCAPM discounting system (19), and their comparison with observed asset returns on financial markets. The "classical CCAPM" is greyed because of its absence of realism in using a geometric Brownian representation of the macroeconomic uncertainty.

	Risk-free rate	Risk premium	Discount rate for average project
Classical CCAPM	$R_{ft} = 3.82\%$	$\pi_t = 0.18\%$	$R_t(\beta = 1) = 4.00\%$
CCAPM calibrated using (Christensen et al., 2018)	$R_{f90} = 2.40\%$	$\pi_{90} = 1.80\%$	$R_{90}(\beta = 1) = 4.20\%$
CCAPM with catastrophes à la (Barro, 2006, 2009)	$R_{ft} = 0.71\%$	$\pi_t = 2.45\%$	$R_t(\beta = 1) = 3.16\%$
Financial markets	$R_{ft} = 1.00\%$	$\pi_t = 2.00\%$	$R_t(\beta = 1) = 3.00\%$

remaining issue is related to the choice of the risk-free discount rate. A risk-free rate between 1.00 % and 2.50 % seems to be reasonable.[7] For very long maturities, there is an argument relying on parametric uncertainties that supports using a smaller risk-free discount rate and a larger aggregate risk premium.

4 Policy issues

4.1 Public policy evaluation in practice

Arrow and Lind (1970) have demonstrated that public investments should be discounted at the risk-free interested rate when their net benefits are uncorrelated to aggregate consumption. This paper was published a few years before the emergence of the modern asset pricing literature initiated by Rubinstein (1976) and Lucas (1978). Many experts from the early 70 s to today took the Arrow-Lind theorem literally and ignored its restricted domain of applicability to zero CCAPM beta projects. This may explain why most countries continue to use a single discount rate for public policy evaluation. Gollier, van der Ploeg and Zheng (2023) document that 24 % of respondents in a sample of around a

[7] Personally, for mature economies with efficient financial markets, I support a solution in which the short-term risk-free discount rate is indexed on the short-term return of the sovereign debt, or on the Ramsey rule using the prediction of the short-term growth rate of GDP/cap. This would have the additional benefit to make the public investment policy more Keynesian.

thousand economic experts around the world continue to support using a single discount rate. Without any additional adjustment for the risk profile of each project, using a single discount rate generates a vastly inefficient allocation of public capital, with an overinvestment in risky projects, and an under-investment of safer ones, in particular in projects that reduce aggregate risks.

The tradition to use a single discount rate for public project evaluation contributed to the many misunderstandings surrounding discounting (Lucas, 2014). In particular, it is not clear which single discount rate should be used. The unicity of the public discount rate is incompatible with the multiplicity of expected rates of return that prevails in the real world. Using the market interest rate, or its predicted level from consumption-based models characterized by the Ramsey rule, would underestimate the average efficient risk-adjusted discount rate because the average beta of public projects is positive and probably close to 1. Using this approach is likely to generate too many public projects passing the test of a positive net present value. Given the limitation of public funds, this will require using a (random) rationing scheme, a very inefficient allocation rule. Other countries, such as the U.S. until recently, preferred using the average cost of capital in the economy as the reference for their public discount rate.

In the United Kingdom, the discount rate is based on the Ramsey rule, with a calibration containing a rate of pure preference for the present of 1.5 %, an inequality aversion of 1 and a growth rate of 2 %, yielding a discount rate of 3.5 % per annum (Treasury, 2018). A smaller discount rate is used in the health sector to take account of the expected increase in the relative value of life. For maturities greater than 30 years, the guidance specifies a stepwise decreasing discount rate motivated by Weitzman (2001). The discount rate is 3.0 % for years 31–75 and it falls to 1 % for maturities larger than 300 years.

In the United States, the official discount rate has been 7 % over the last three decades, with an alternative rate of 3 % that should be used for sensitivity analysis (OMB, 2003). The Office of Management and Budget has recently imposed an extraordinary reduction of the official discount rate to 2 % (OMB, 2023). This rate is based on the average real risk-free interest rate over the last 30 years. It should be revised every three years on this basis. The OMB recommends taking care of the riskiness of the project by discounting at 2 % the flow of certainty equivalent net benefits. This strategy is based on the following version of Eq. (15):

$$PV = e^{-R_{ft}t} B_t^c \text{ with } B_t^c = \frac{E[B_t e^{-\rho_t t}]}{E[e^{-\rho_t t}]}, \tag{31}$$

where $B_t^c \in \mathbb{R}$ is the certainty equivalent net benefit, i.e., at the margin, $Eu(C_t + B_t^c) = Eu(C_t + B_t)$. Observe that this OMB guidance is not in the tradition of public and private investment capital budgeting. There is a considerable risk of incoherence between the choice of the risk-free discount rate $R_{ft} = E[e^{-\rho_t t}] = 2\%$, and the estimation of the certainty equivalent B_t^c based on the statistical relation between the net benefit B_t and the stochastic Ramsey discount rate ρ_t. I have shown that a risk-free rate of 2 % is compatible with observed economic growth only if low-frequency catastrophe events are included in the probabilistic description of the future. If evaluators are not required to include them, it is likely that they will be confronted to the well-known equity premium puzzle, with certainty-equivalent net benefits almost equal to their expectations, an outcome incompatible with observed risk pricing in the real world. The jury is still out.

As a last example, let me consider the case of France. France is currently the only country in the world to impose a public discounting system based on the CCAPM formula $R_t = R_{ft} + \beta\pi_t$. For short maturities, the current tutelar risk-free rate is $R_{ft} = 1.2\%$ and the tutelar aggregate risk premium is $\pi_t = 2\%$ (Guesnerie, 2023). However, in practice, many evaluators find it difficult to estimate the beta of their projects, so that most of them use the average rate of $R_t = 3.2\ \%$. Guidelines to estimate the income-elasticity of projects' net benefits should be improved (Cherbonnier and Gollier, 2021).

4.2 Application to climate change

The debate about the efficient discounting system reemerged two decades ago in the context of climate change and the necessity to estimate the impact of our climate inaction. The Social Cost of Carbon (SCC) is defined as the present value of the flow of marginal climate damages generated by emitting one ton of CO_2 today. Because of the long maturity of this flow, the choice of the discount rate is crucial for the determination of the SCC. For example, EPA (2023) estimated the SCC for 2020 at \$120, \$190 and \$340 for a reference discount rate of 2.5 %, 2 % and 1.5 %, respectively. In the early years of the development of climate economics, the debate of the discount rate to be used for the SCC was mostly focused on the Ramsey rule. It culminated in 2007 and the years after the publication of the Stern report (Stern, 2006). Nicholas Stern used the EU framework to calibrate an intergenerational welfare function under certainty with an index of relative inequality aversion of 1 and a growth rate of consumption of 1.3 %. Stern also used a rate of pure preference for the present of 0.1 %. Thus, from the Ramsey rule, he implicitly used a discount rate of 1.4 %, yielding a SCC estimate that was one order of magnitude larger than previously estimated. Of course, the estimation of the SCC requires to measure the flow of damages generated by one ton of CO2 emitted today. This task requires in turn to understand the interaction between the economy and its environment. The first attempt to build such an "integrated assessment" model was made by William Nordhaus (Nordhaus, 1994; Nordhaus, 2013) three decades ago. This model was named DICE. Although DICE was run under certainty, Bill Nordhaus typically used a discount rate around 4–5 %, on the basis of the opportunity cost of (risky) capital rather than on the Ramsey rule. This exercise generated a small estimation for the SCC. More recently, as documented above, EPA mostly sided for a discount rate à la Stern, and therefore for a much larger SCC, around \$200 per tCO_2.

Relying on the Ramsey rule for the climate discount rate is fundamentally misleading, because climate damages are risky. Remember that the Ramsey rule is useful to estimate the rate at which risk-free benefits and costs should be discounted. And because there is no a priori reason to believe that the risk profile of the climate damage duplicates the risk surrounding the return of productive capital in the economy as assumed by Nordhaus, using the average return on equity is also potentially misleading. As claimed in this survey, using the Ramsey rule to estimate the SCC is correct only if the "climate beta", i.e., the income-elasticity of the marginal climate damage, is zero. But abating CO_2 emissions would have an insurance effect if this damage is negatively correlated with GDP, i.e., when the climate beta is negative. In that context, abating CO_2 would not only reduce the expected damage. It would also have a larger social benefit in the worst states of nature (low GDP), yielding a hedging value for the action. This insurance benefit should be recognized in that case by using a climate discount rate smaller than the risk-free discount rate. Using a discount rate smaller than the interest rate would typically generate a very large estimation for the SCC, implying that most efforts to abate CO2 emissions would be socially desirable.

There are some reasons to believe in this negative climate beta story. Indeed, if the main source of aggregate risk is due to the climate damage function or to the climate sensitivity parameter, then a worse climate scenario yields at the same time a low future GDP (due to the large average climate damage), and a large benefit of the abating effort today (due to the large marginal climate damage). This negative climate beta would raise the SCC.

But there is another effect that goes in the opposite direction as it generates a positive climate beta. Suppose that the main source of aggregate risk comes from the unknown future productivity growth. In that context, there will be a positive statistical relationship between the future benefit of decarbonation and GDP. Indeed, a larger positive shock on productivity will generate at the same time a larger GDP and more emissions. Because the damage function is convex, this generates a larger marginal climate damage, and thus a larger future benefit to the mitigation effort today. This yields a positive climate beta, a larger climate discount rate, and a smaller SCC. In that context, fighting climate change raises the macroeconomic risk. Its valuation should be revised downwards.

Given the fact that uncertainty surrounds both the intensity of the climate problem and the productivity growth, the sign of the climate beta is ambiguous. Dietz, Gollier and Kessler (2018) were the first to address this question. They simulated the DICE model by randomizing various parameters of this integrated assessment model (IAM). They regressed the log marginal damage with respect to the log GDP/cap to estimate the climate beta assuming that DICE is a correct representation of the climate/economic dynamics of the world. They obtained a climate beta that is positive and close to 1. The main reason for this result is that DICE, as many other IAMs, is based on the hypothesis that climate damages are proportional to GDP. This is an obvious channel for a climate beta equalling 1. Notice also that much of the impacts of climate change are related to human life, health, morbidity and life expectancy. The income-elasticity of the value of statistical life being close to 1 (Hammitt and Robinson, 2011), so is the climate beta. However, one must be aware of the possibility for the climate beta to be much smaller than 1, in particular if one magnifies the uncertainty surrounding the climate damage function and the climate sensitivity parameter.

In their survey, Gollier, van der Ploeg and Zheng (2023) documented that most economists continue to believe that the rate at which climate damages should be discounted to measure the SCC should be close to the risk-free discount rate. This suggests a consensus for a zero climate beta. This is inconsistent with what is modelled in our IAMs. More research efforts should be made in the coming years to estimate the climate beta and to rationalize the climate discount rate in order to estimate the social cost of carbon.

5 Conclusion

The reader of this survey may feel some disappointment at the end of this journey in the discounting kingdom. Already in 1968, William Baumol commented that "*few topics in our discipline rival the social rate of* discount *as a subject exhibiting simultaneously a very considerable degree of knowledge and a very substantial level of ignorance*" (Baumol, 1968). Although some progresses have been made in knowledge, such as a new scientific consensus for using risk-adjusted discount rates, the discipline is still struggling to determine the rate at which one should discount climate damages, ecological impacts, or the benefit generated by transportation, education, energy and health infrastructures. The recent decision of the OMB to continue to recommend a single public discount rate in the United States illustrates that lack of achievement perfectly. The consequences are dire, in particular for the misallocation of our portfolio of actions and efforts to improve the future and for making our world more sustainable.

There exist multiple paths for improvement in this discounting field. Within the discounted expected utility (DEU) model, there are issues related to using different discount rates for different goods and services with different growth rates in consumption or different degrees of substitutability. There are also issues related to the aggregation of preferences and of unequal levels of consumption, as I assumed here a single representative consumer. Should we adjust the rate at which we discount a future benefit not only on its risk profile but also on its distribution among different social classes? There also remain many issues related to the aggregation of time preferences when people differ on their degree of impatience or on their life expectancy. And, recognizing that the CCAPM failed to satisfy the practitioners of cost-benefit analysis, what alternative evaluation strategy could we recommend as a better compromise between efficiency and simplicity? Finally, there are also many important open questions about discounting when we explore decision frameworks outside DEU. Researchers willing to disentangle risk aversion from the aversion to consumption fluctuation over time or intergenerational inequality aversion should think beyond the Epstein-Zin model that has its own puzzles, such as the large value accruing to an early resolution of uncertainty. Non-exponential discounting of the flow of utility generates the terrible issue of time-inconsistent preferences that should also be addressed adequately.

References

Arrow, K.J., Lind, R.C., 1970. Uncertainty and the evaluation of public investment decision. Am. Economic Rev. 60, 364–378.

Bansal, R., Yaron, A., 2004. Risks for the long run: a potential resolution of asset pricing puzzles. J. Financ. 59, 1481–1509.

Barro, R.J., 2006. Rare disasters and asset markets in the twentieth century. Q. J. Econ. 121, 823–866.

Barro, R.J., 2009. Rare disasters, asset prices, and welfare costs. Am. Economic Rev. 99, 243–264.

Baumol, W.J., 1968. On the social rate of discount. Am. Economic Rev. 58, 788–802.

Breeden, D., 1979. An intertemporal asset pricing model with stochastic consumption and investment opportunities. J. Financial Econ. 7, 265–296.

Broome, J., 1992. Counting the Cost of Global Warming. White House Press, Cambridge.

Cherbonnier, F., Gollier, C., 2021. Risk-adjusted social discount rates. Energy J. 43, 19–41.

Christensen, P., Gillingham, K., Nordhaus, W., 2018. Uncertainty in forecasts of long-run economic growth. Proc. Natl. Acad. Sci. 115, 5409–5414.

Dietz, S., Gollier, C., Kessler, L., 2018. The climate beta. J. Environ. Econ. Manag. 87, 258–274.

Drèze, J.H., Modigliani, F., 1972. Consumption decisions under uncertainty. J. Economic Theory 5, 308–335.

Drupp, M.A., et al., 2024. Accounting for the increasing benefits from scarce ecosystems. Science 383, 1062–1064.

Drupp, M.A., Freeman, M.C., Groom, B., Nesje, F., 2018. Discounting disentangled. Am. Economic J.: Economic Policy 10, 109–134.

Eden, M., 2023. The cross-sectional implications of social discount rates. Econometrica 91, 2065–2088.

Ellsberg, D., 1961. Risk, ambiguity, and the savage axioms. Q. J. Econ. 75, 643–669.

EPA, 2023. Supplementary Material for the Regulatory Impact Analysis for the Final Rulemaking, "Standards of Performance for New, Reconstructed, and Modified Sources and Emissions Guidelines for Existing Sources: Oil and Natural Gas Sector Climate Review", EPA Report on the Social Cost of Greenhouse Gases: Estimates Incorporating Recent Scientific Advances, U. S. Environmental Protection Agency.

Epstein, L., Zin, S., 1989. Substitution, risk aversion and the temporal behavior of consumption and asset returns: a theoretical framework. Econometrica 57, 937–969.

Frederick, S., Loewenstein, G., O'Donoghue, T., 2002. Time discounting and time preference: a critical review. J. Economic Lit. 40, 351–401.

Gierlinger, J., Gollier, C., 2011. Socially efficient discounting under ambiguity aversion, TSE Discussion Paper.

Gollier, C., 2001. The Economics of Risk and Time. MIT Press.

Gollier, C., 2010. Ecological discounting. J. Economic Theory 145, 812–829.

Gollier, C., 2013. Pricing the Planet's Future. The Economics of Discounting in an Uncertain World. Princeton University Press.

Gollier, C., 2016. Evaluation of long-dated assets: The role of parameter uncertainty. J. Monetary Econ. 84, 66–83.

Gollier, C., Zeckhauser, R., 2005. Aggregation of heterogeneous time preferences. J. Political Economy 113, 878–896.

Gollier, C., van der Ploeg, R., Zheng, J., 2023. The discounting premium puzzle: survey evidence from professional economists. J. Environ. Econ. Manag. 122.

Guesnerie, R., 2004. Calcul économique et développement durable. Rev. Economique 55, 363–382.

Guesnerie, R., 2023. Guide de l'évaluation socioéconomique des investissements publics. France Stratégie.

Halevy, Y., Feltkamp, V., 2005. A Bayesian approach to uncertainty aversion. Rev. Economic Stud. 72, 449–466.

Hammitt, J.K., Robinson, L.A., 2011. The income elasticity of the value per statistical life: transferring estimates between high and low income populations. J. Benefit-Cost Anal. 2, 1–27.

Hoel, M., Sterner, T., 2007. Discounting and relative prices. Climatic Change 84 (2007), 265–280.

Jordà, O., Knoll, K., Kuvshinov, D., Schularick, M., Taylor, A.M., 2019. The rate of return on everything, 1870–2015. Q. J. Econ. 134, 1225–1298.

Klibanoff, P., Marinacci, M., Mukerji, S., 2005. A smooth model of decision making under ambiguity. Econometrica 73 (6), 1849–1892.

Kocherlakota, N.R., 1996. The equity premium: it's still a puzzle. J. Economic Lit. 34, 42–71.

Kimball, M.S., 1990. Precautionary saving in the small and in the large. Econometrica 58, 53–73.

Laibson, D., 1997. Golden eggs and hyperbolic discounting. Q. J. Econ. 112 (2), 443–477.

Leland, H.E., 1968. Saving and uncertainty: the precautionary demand for saving. Q. J. Econ. 465–473.

Lucas, R., 1978. Asset prices in an exchange economy. Econometrica 46, 1429–1446.

Lucas, D., 2014. Rebutting Arrow and Lind: why governments should use market rates for discounting. J. Nat. Resour. Policy Res. 6, 85–91.

Malinvaud, E., 1953. Capital accumulation and efficient allocation of resources. Econometrica 21 (2), 233–268.

Martin, I., 2013. Consumption-based asset pricing with higher cumulants. Rev. Economic Stud. 80, 745–773.

Millner, A., Heal, G., 2023. Choosing the future: markets, ethics, and rapprochement in social discounting. J. Economic Lit. 61, 1037–1087.

Nordhaus, W., 1994. Managing the Global Commons: The Economics of Climate Change. MIT Press.

Nordhaus, W., 2013. The Climate Casino: Risk, Uncertainty, and Economics for a Warming World. Yale University Press.

Okun, A.M., 1975. Equality and Efficiency: The Big Tradeoff, Brookings Institution, Washington DC.

OMB, 2003. Circular N. A-4 To the Heads of Executive Department Establishments, Subject: Regulatory Analysis, Tech. rep., Washington: Executive Office of the President.

OMB, 2023. Circular No. A-4, U.S. Office of Management and Budget, November 9, 2023.

Olijslagers, S., Van Wijnbergen, S., 2024. Discounting the future: on climate change, ambiguity aversion and Epstein–Zin preferences. Environ. Resour. Econ. 87, 683–730.

Ramsey, F.P., 1928. A mathematical theory of saving. Economic J. 38, 543–559.

Rijksoverheid, 2020. Rapport Werkgroep discontovoet 2020, Tech. rep., Dutch Ministerie van Financien.

Rubinstein, M., 1976. The valuation of uncertain income streams and the pricing of options. Bell J. Econ. 7 (2), 407–425.

Samuelson, P.A., 1937. A note on the measurement of utility. Rev. Economic Stud. 4, 155–161.

Segal, U., Spivak, A., 1990. First order versus second order risk aversion. J. Economic Theory 51, 111–125.

Stern, N., 2006. The Economics of Climate Change: The Stern Review. Cambridge University Press.

Sterner, T., Persson, M., 2008. An even Sterner report: introducing relative prices into the discounting debate. Rev. Environ. Econonomics Policy 2 (1), 61–76.

Traeger, C.P., 2014. Why uncertainty matters: discounting under intertemporal risk aversion and ambiguity. Economic Theory 56, 627–664.

Treasury, 2018. Green Book: Central Government Guidance on Appraisal and Evaluation, Technical report, UK Treasury.

Weil, P., 1989. The equity premium puzzle and the risk-free rate puzzle. J. Monetary Econ. 24, 401–421.

Weitzman, M.L., 1998. Why the far-distant future should be discounted at its lowest possible rate. J. Environ. Econ. Manag. 36 (3), 201–208.

Weitzman, M.L., 2001. Gamma discounting. Am. Economic Rev. 91, 260–271.

Chapter 4

Adaptation to climate change☆

Tamma Carleton[a,b,*], Esther Duflo[b,c], B. Kelsey Jack[b,d], and Guglielmo Zappalà[a]

[a]*Department of Agricultural and Resource Economics, University of California, Berkeley, CA, United States,* [b]*National Bureau of Economic Research, Cambridge, MA, United States,* [c]*Department of Economics, Massachusetts Institute of Technology, Cambridge, MA, United States,* [d]*Haas School of Business, University of California, Berkeley, CA, United States*

**Corresponding author. e-mail address: tcarleton@berkeley.edu*

Chapter Outline

1 Introduction

As the impacts of anthropogenic climate change accelerate, adaptation plays an increasingly critical role in shaping human well-being now and into the future. Climate adaptation is generally defined as any behavior, investment or other decision taken in direct response to realized or anticipated changes in the

☆ We are grateful for constructive feedback from Fiona Burlig, Simon Dietz, Kyle Emerick, Ishan Nath, Katherine Wagner, members of the Coase Project, and the Editors, Lint Barrage and Solomon Hsiang. Kathryn McMahon provided excellent research assistance.

Handbook of the Economics of Climate Change, Vol. 1. https://doi.org/10.1016/bs.hesecc.2024.10.001

climate. While adaptation often refers to decisions that ameliorate the adverse impacts of climate change, adaptive behavior can also include actions that allow individuals to exploit beneficial opportunities that arise with an evolving climate. These adaptation decisions occur within a broader socioeconomic fabric in which many environmental, economic, political, and cultural conditions shape the constraints and opportunities that individuals, communities, and governments face as they navigate climate change. As a result, conditions exogenous to climate change itself – such as social services and available technolgoies – are important in determining the degree and nature of adaptation.

Unlike mitigation of the greenhouse gas emissions responsible for climate change, adaptation to its impacts is generally construed as a set of private decisions. Under perfect market conditions, individuals should make adaptive choices that best respond to short- and/or long-run changes in the climate. Such a setting leaves little room or justification for adaptation policy. Hence, most research in climate economics has focused on quantifying the manner and extent of private adaptation. However, in practice, private adaptation is constrained by many frictions, including imperfect information and inaccurate beliefs, as well as limits to property rights, credit markets, and insurance, which often disproportionately affect low income individuals and countries. Moreover, some adaptation investments have increasing returns to scale or involve public goods and externalities and cannot or will not be undertaken by individuals. Thus, a critical role for adaptation policy emerges, as intervention can ameliorate climate damages in contexts where market failures preclude individuals from making optimal adaptive decisions. More broadly, climate change is projected to worsen inequality, due both to the spatial distribution of exposure and to unequal spending on adaptation. Public policies governed by equity motives may therefore also justify adaptation interventions, even in the absence of market failures.

This chapter reviews the economic literature on climate change adaptation, with a focus on how this body of work can inform adaptation policy. We begin by defining two core channels of adaptation – ex post responses to realized weather shocks and ex ante investments undertaken before weather is experienced – using a simple conceptual model of private adaptation decisions. We demonstrate how the decision environment, including prices, income, and associated markets, shapes adaptation choices and outcomes. We next link these channels to two policy-relevant motivations for studying adaptation, each of which has molded a stream of adaptation literature. The first is composed of research quantifying climate damages, which has sought to account for adaptation using a variety of reduced form and structural strategies. The second stream has studied adaptation more directly, aiming to understand the impacts and effectiveness of various adaptation behaviors, technologies and interventions. We review both literatures through a single unifying framework that helps illustrate opportunities for further research progress and synthesis across subfields. Finally, as climate damages mount, so does interest in effective and cost effective adaptation interventions. We therefore discuss frameworks for policy evaluation and conceptual justifications for policy intervention – which are rarely made explicit in existing studies – as well as potential limitations and pitfalls of public sector intervention. Throughout the chapter, we highlight weaknesses of current research and opportunities for improvement; we conclude with a final section that summarizes these opportunities and priorities for future work.

2 Defining adaptation: two channels of adaptive decision-making

The term "climate adaptation" is invoked across the economics literature in various ways with distinct meanings. To clarify definitions and fix ideas, we categorize uses of the term into two groups, which form two "channels" of adaptation: ex ante and ex post.

We begin by presenting a simplified but general conceptual framework in which decision-makers face exogenous changes in the climate and choose adaptive actions to maximize welfare. The framework encompasses both ex post and ex ante adaptation channels and serves to demonstrate differences between the channels and to elucidate key measurement objectives in the literature. It also highlights the critical role of external factors, which are orthogonal to climate change itself, that shape the adaptation decision environment and therefore influence both channels of adaptation.

Consider an agent facing a simple dynamic utility maximization problem in which she faces exogenous weather realizations, $\boldsymbol{c}_t$ in each period t, that may impact her utility. Period t weather $\boldsymbol{c}_t$ is drawn from a steady-state climate distribution $\boldsymbol{C}$, as in Hsiang (2016).[1] For example, one possible functional form linking weather and climate is $\boldsymbol{c}_t = \boldsymbol{C} + \varepsilon_t$, where ε_t are random, mean-zero, i.i.d. shocks. Other functional forms are possible, but we will assume throughout that the parameters describing the steady state climate reflect expected weather; that is, that $\mathbb{E}[\boldsymbol{c}_t] = \boldsymbol{C}$.

Under a steady state climate $\boldsymbol{C}$, there are two ways the agent can respond to weather-induced utility shocks. First, she can choose quantities of each element in a vector of goods or services $\boldsymbol{b}$ that are available to her as the weather event is occurring or after it has arrived. For example, she may increase energy use to cool her home during a heat wave, increase irrigation water applications to her farm under drought, or switch sectors of employment in response to climate-induced productivity shocks. The choice of adaptive actions $\boldsymbol{b}$ is thus not anticipatory, but instead reactive; we call these adaptive actions "ex post" adaptation, following, for example, Lemoine (2023).

[1] Weather and climate are denoted as vectors because they can compose many possible variables and moments of the distribution, such as drought, cooling degree days, rainfall, etc.

Second, she can choose quantities from another vector of goods or services $\boldsymbol{k}$ that require up front investment before weather realizations occur. For example, if she is a farmer, she must choose which seeds to plant and whether to take up crop insurance before growing season weather is realized. Similarly, if she represents a local government, she must make infrastructure investments, such as bridges and sea walls, in anticipation of future sea levels and storm surges. Her decisions about these durable investments are made based on her information set, which includes her expectations about weather realizations that will occur in the future. In practice, the relevant time horizon for such expectations depends naturally on the durability of the decision; for example, for a farmer planting annual crops, the relevant horizon is a single year, but for an educational investment the time horizon may be a lifetime. These adaptive actions $\boldsymbol{k}$ we call "ex ante" adaptation.

Here we assume that decisions regarding durable investments $\boldsymbol{k}$ must be made during a single pre-period, before weather is realized and utility is impacted.[2] These durable investments then persist into future periods, but depreciate through time at rate δ. After this pre-period, in each period $t \in [0, ..., \infty)$, the agent then solves:

$$\max_{\boldsymbol{b}_t, w_t} u(\boldsymbol{c}_t, \boldsymbol{b}_t, w_t; \boldsymbol{k}(1-\delta)^t) \text{ s.t. } \boldsymbol{p}_t \boldsymbol{b}_t + w_t \leq y_t, \tag{1}$$

where w_t is a numeraire consumption good and y_t is exogenous income. Note that weather $\boldsymbol{c}_t$ is known with certainty before the ex post adaptation choice $\boldsymbol{b}_t$ is made, and that, in contrast, $\boldsymbol{k}$ is taken as given and unchangeable in period t, so that its iterative law of motion is $\boldsymbol{k}_t = \boldsymbol{k}(1-\delta)^t$ for all t. The indirect utility function in period t is therefore $u(\boldsymbol{c}_t, \boldsymbol{b}_t^*, y_t - \boldsymbol{p}_t \boldsymbol{b}_t^*; \boldsymbol{k}_t)$, where we have substituted in the budget constraint and where $\boldsymbol{b}_t^* = \boldsymbol{b}^*(\boldsymbol{c}_t, y_t, \boldsymbol{p}_t; \boldsymbol{k}_t)$ represents the utility-maximizing choice of $\boldsymbol{b}$ in time t.

Now consider the choice of $\boldsymbol{k}$ during the pre-period. The agent must make this choice before knowing the weather realizations $\boldsymbol{c}_t$, but with full knowledge of $\boldsymbol{C} = \mathbb{E}[\boldsymbol{c}_t]$.[3] Suppose for simplicity that prices $\boldsymbol{p}_t$ (the price vector in period t for ex post adaptations) and $\boldsymbol{r}$ (the price vector in the pre-period for ex ante adaptations), as well as income y_t, are deterministic and known with certainty during the pre-period. She then solves:

$$\max_{\boldsymbol{k}} \sum_{t=0}^{\infty} \beta^t \mathbb{E}[u(\boldsymbol{c}_t, \boldsymbol{b}_t^*, y_t - \boldsymbol{p}_t \boldsymbol{b}_t^*; \boldsymbol{k}(1-\delta)^t)] \text{ s.t. } \boldsymbol{rk} \leq \bar{y} \tag{2}$$

---

[2] The assumption of a pre-period in which durable investments are made is also used in the dynamic framework in Lemoine (2023).

[3] Of course, in practice durable investments can be made at any time, and agents must decide as the climate changes continuously when, if at all, to invest in long-run adaptive capital. To maintain tractability, we abstract from this timing decision here, but point readers to Fried (2022); Bilal and Rossi-Hansberg (2023); Krusell and Smith (2022), among others, where it is handled explicitly.

where $\mathbb{E}[\cdot]$ indicates expectations over the uncertain weather distribution, given information available in the pre-period, and $\bar{y}$ indicates income available in the pre-period (noting that all other future variables, such as prices and income, are deterministic). The agent's decision over $\boldsymbol{k}$ influences her utility in all future periods $t = 0, \ldots, \infty$, due to its durability. Her optimal choice $\boldsymbol{k}^*(\boldsymbol{C}, \bar{y}, y_{t=0,\ldots\infty}, \boldsymbol{p}_{t=0,\ldots\infty}, \boldsymbol{r}; \delta)$ represents the value of $\boldsymbol{k}$ that maximizes her expected stream of utility over all periods. Note that $\boldsymbol{k}^*$ depends not on the weather, but on the climate (i.e., expected value of the weather in all t), as this ex ante decision must be made before weather is realized.

We are interested in assessing the impacts of climate change. Following the literature (e.g., Deryugina and Hsiang, 2017; Hsiang, 2016; Lemoine, 2023; Rudik et al., 2024), we consider the steady-state impacts of changing the climate, evaluated in a future period t, after ex post adaptations have taken place and allowing for ex ante adaptations to adjust in expectation of a new climate. This mirrors the empirical literature reviewed in Section 3.1, much of which seeks to estimate the total damages from climate change in a given year — for example, the year 2100. Recall that the steady-state climate is $\boldsymbol{C}$, from which all weather realizations $\boldsymbol{c}_t$ are drawn. Since each period's decision problem for t is a static problem with optimal actions that satisfy the first-order conditions from Equation (1), the expected impact of climate change in t is simply the total derivative of the expected value of the indirect utility in period t, i.e., $u_t = u(\boldsymbol{c}_t, \boldsymbol{b}_t^*, y_t - \boldsymbol{p}_t\boldsymbol{b}_t^*; \boldsymbol{k}_t)$, with respect to the steady-state climate:

$$\frac{d\mathbb{E}[u_t]}{d\boldsymbol{C}} = \underbrace{\frac{\partial u_t}{\partial \boldsymbol{c}_t}\frac{d\boldsymbol{c}_t}{d\boldsymbol{C}}}_{\substack{\text{direct effect of}\\ \text{weather}}} + \underbrace{\frac{\partial u_t}{\partial \boldsymbol{b}_t}\frac{\partial \boldsymbol{b}_t^*}{\partial \boldsymbol{c}_t}\frac{d\boldsymbol{c}_t}{d\boldsymbol{C}}}_{\substack{\text{ex post response}\\ \text{to weather}}} + \underbrace{\frac{\partial u_t}{\partial \boldsymbol{k}}\frac{d\boldsymbol{k}^*}{d\boldsymbol{C}}}_{\substack{\text{ex ante adaptation}\\ \text{to climate}}} \tag{3}$$

where all partial derivatives are evaluated at $\boldsymbol{c}_t = \mathbb{E}[\boldsymbol{c}_t] = \boldsymbol{C}$ and expectations are formed using information available in the pre-period.[4] The expression in Equation (3) makes clear that the overall impacts of climate change (lefthand side) can be decomposed into the direct effects of changing weather realizations, holding fixed all adaptive decisions (first term), and two terms capturing the impacts of the two channels of adaptation: one for ex post decisions (second term) and one for ex ante (third term). We discuss each of these channels in turn below, as well as the importance of exogenous conditions (e.g., income y and

[4] Evaluating the derivative of payoffs at mean weather is equivalent to evaluating the derivative of expected payoffs over the full distribution of weather only under the functional form assumptions detailed in Mérel et al. (2024) – i.e., that actions $\boldsymbol{b}_t$ and $\boldsymbol{k}$ interact linearly with weather within $u(\cdot)$. Like Lemoine (2023); Deryugina and Hsiang (2017); Carleton et al. (2022) and many others, we make that assumption here in order to simplify the notation of the stylized framework we present. This assumption does not have bearing on the qualitative interpretations of Equation (3) made throughout the chapter.

prices $\boldsymbol{p}$ and $\boldsymbol{r}$, as well as market structure, information, and other factors) that shape adaptation choices and thus the impacts of climate change.

Before considering each channel of adaptation, we note that this framework is highly stylized and therefore omits many key features of adaptation. For example, the dynamic decision problem in Equation (2) involves no savings nor credit constraints, and both ex post and ex ante decisions are assumed to be made under perfect information regarding the weather, the impacts of weather on utility, and the steady state climate. Additionally, the object of interest is assumed to be utility itself, in which case the Envelope Theorem implies that $\frac{\partial u_t}{\partial \boldsymbol{b}_t} = \frac{\partial u_t}{\partial \boldsymbol{k}} = 0$ in Equation (3) and the two adaptation terms drop out (Deryugina and Hsiang, 2017; Guo and Costello, 2013; Hsiang, 2016). In contrast, most applied work investigates a component of utility or profits that is impacted by the weather, such as crop yields or human health, rendering the two latter terms on the righthand side of Equation (3) nonzero and critical for assessing climate change impacts. Throughout the remainder of the chapter, we highlight literature that empirically and/or theoretically expands upon this simplified framework to investigate more complex models of adaptation.

2.1 Channel 1: Ex post response to a climate shock

Ex post adaptation captures how individuals, households, or governments respond to weather realizations either as they are occurring or after they arrive. The role of ex post adaptation in shaping welfare under climate change can be seen in the second term on the righthand side of in Equation (3). This effect includes three components.

The vector of partial derivatives $\frac{\partial \boldsymbol{b}^*}{\partial c}$ captures any behavior changes taken in response to the weather. To the extent that these partial derivatives are nonzero, they reflect ex post adaptations agents pursue to respond to the weather shocks they experience. When empirical papers investigate the adoption and use of ex post adaptation technologies – for example, how much irrigation water is applied during drought events or how much energy is used during heat events – they are assessing this partial derivative. How such adaptations influence utility is captured in $\frac{\partial u}{\partial \boldsymbol{b}}$. We note that this effect can be composed both of direct utility benefits or harms from changing decisions $\boldsymbol{b}$, as well as utility benefits that arise from lowering the welfare effects of an adverse weather shock. Studies that assess impacts of adaptation decisions on welfare-relevant outcomes, such as agricultural profits or consumption, are either quantifying this term alone, or this term in combination with how the adoption decision changes with the weather, i.e., $\frac{\partial \boldsymbol{b}^*}{\partial c}$. Finally, $\frac{dc}{dC}$ captures how weather changes due to climate change. Studies that investigate ex post adaptation under the current climate distribution do not account for this final term, although its inclusion is critical to making insights regarding adaptation relevant to the future under long-run climate change.

2.2 Channel 2: Ex ante investment based on beliefs

Many adaptive decisions are anticipatory, requiring an ex ante adjustment before weather realizations occur. Thus, agents must choose the optimal vector of durable goods $\boldsymbol{k}^*(\cdot)$ to maximize the expected stream of discounted utility, facing unknown future weather. This uncertainty arises because weather is inherently unpredictable, even when the climate distribution itself is known. However, in many settings, particularly with rapidly evolving climate change, the climate distribution from which weather is being drawn may also be uncertain. In either case, ex ante decisions must be made based on agents' expectations, as long as adaptation technologies or investments are long-lived. The effects of ex ante adaptation on welfare under climate change can be seen in the last term on the righthand side of Equation (3), which is composed of two parts.

First, the vector of partial derivatives $\frac{d\boldsymbol{k}^*}{d\boldsymbol{C}}$ captures ex ante behavior changes taken in response to changes in the expectation of future weather realizations. If such derivatives are non-zero, they reflect ex ante adaptations. As detailed throughout the chapter, these decision adjustments made in response to changing expectations are assessed both implicitly and explicitly in existing literature. How these adaptations influence utility is captured by $\frac{\partial u}{\partial \boldsymbol{k}}$, which, like for ex post adaptation, will include both direct effects of adaptive investments on utility, as well as any benefits realized through reducing harms from adverse weather. In Section 3, we describe how some subsets of the literature successfully identify ex ante adaptation and/or its influence on climate damages. We also highlight how difficult accounting for ex ante adaptation can be and therefore we identify many gaps in the literature. We discuss how ex ante adaptation decisions also affect the set of feasible ex post adaptations (as seen in the decision problem in Equation (1), which complicates separation of the two channels in some empirical settings.

2.3 Exogenous conditions governing the adaptation decision environment

A diverse set of conditions unrelated to climate change itself governs the adaptation decision problems in Equations (1) and (2), influencing choices $\boldsymbol{b}^*$ and/or $\boldsymbol{k}^*$. These external factors include adaptation prices $\boldsymbol{p}$ and $\boldsymbol{r}$, income y, as well as information, market structure, and any market frictions. To see how such features shape adaptation and the impacts of climate change, consider, for example, an exogenous change in the budget constraint y_t in period t. A loosening of the budget constraint changes optimal ex post adaptations $\boldsymbol{b}^*(\boldsymbol{c}_t, y_t, \boldsymbol{p}_t; \boldsymbol{k}_t)$, where $\frac{\partial \boldsymbol{b}^*}{\partial y_t} \geq 0$ for normal goods. The effects of such reoptimization on the impacts of climate change can be seen by taking the derivative of Equation (3) with respect to y_t:

$$\frac{d^2\mathbb{E}[u_t]}{dy_t d\boldsymbol{C}} = \frac{\partial u_t}{\partial \boldsymbol{b}_t} \frac{\partial^2 \boldsymbol{b}_t}{\partial y_t \partial \boldsymbol{c}_t} \frac{d\boldsymbol{c}_t}{d\boldsymbol{C}}, \tag{4}$$

where all variables are defined as in Equation (3).[5] The middle term on the righthand side of Equation (4) quantifies how a marginal relaxation of the budget constraint changes the optimal ex post adaptation actions $\boldsymbol{b}$ in response to weather $\boldsymbol{c}$. When multiplied by $\frac{\partial u_t}{\partial \boldsymbol{b}_t}\frac{d\boldsymbol{c}_t}{dC}$, this indicates how this change in the budget constraint modifies the welfare effects of climate change.[6] An analogous expression can be derived for a change in pre-period income $\bar{y}$, which will alter optimal ex ante adaptation $\boldsymbol{k}^*$. Similarly, changes in prices $\boldsymbol{p}$ and $\boldsymbol{r}$, shifts in expectations $\mathbb{E}[u_t]$, changing preferences $u_t(\cdot)$, and any other features of the decision problem may change adaptation choices and ultimately the welfare effects of climate change.

In discussing the empirical literature on the adoption and efficacy of adaptation strategies in Section 3.2, we use E to indicate an intervention that changes any aspect of the adaptation decision environment, including changes in: prices $\boldsymbol{p}$ and $\boldsymbol{r}$; income y; and any other frictions or market conditions. Here we briefly preview how these features interact with the ex post and ex ante adaptation channels articulated above.

(i) First, prices $\boldsymbol{p}$ and $\boldsymbol{r}$ affect adaptation decisions and outcomes. If adaptation goods are normal goods, $\frac{\partial b_j^*}{\partial p_j} \leq 0$ for any element j of the vector $\boldsymbol{b}$ (or, analogously, for $\boldsymbol{k}$). Price changes induced by the market, by public policies, or by innovation therefore affect adaptation decisions and resulting climate change damages Relatedly, technological innovation can introduce new elements into the vectors $\boldsymbol{b}$ and $\boldsymbol{k}$, effectively reducing their prices from infinite to nonzero, leading to substitution and income effects that reshape adaptation decisions.

(ii) Second, adaptation decisions over $\boldsymbol{b}$ and $\boldsymbol{k}$ will depend on the tightness of the budget constraint y, independent of weather realizations or expectations of future climate. Specifically, demand for adaptation goods that are normal and deliver positive utility will increase with income, even for a given climate. For example, India is projected to see expansive growth in air conditioning installations, regardless of how future climate change unfolds (Birol, 2018), lowering mortality risks from climate change by mitigating the risk of death on extremely hot days. Relatedly, social programs may reduce variability in income, as opposed to its overall

---

[5] In Equation (4) we assume the cross-partials $\frac{\partial^2 u_t}{\partial y_t \partial \boldsymbol{c}_t}$ and $\frac{\partial^2 u_t}{\partial y \partial \boldsymbol{b}}$ are both zero. These are relatively innocuous assumptions – they imply that income has no influence over the direct effects of weather and that income itself does not change the efficacy of the adaptation actions within the vector $\boldsymbol{b}$.

[6] Note that an increase in income changes the welfare effects of climate change both by relaxing the budget constraint, as discussed here, and by raising the lower bound of consumption under a bad weather realization. The importance of the latter channel depends on the shape of the utility function.

level, with corresponding influence over adaptation choices and outcomes, particularly in dynamic settings.

(iii) Finally, a wide array of frictions, including behavioral biases, incomplete information, market structure (e.g., trade costs), and other barriers to optimal adaptation, including credit and financial constraints, influence adaptation decisions. These various frictions are regularly influenced by government policy and they modify adaptation decisions and resulting climate change damages.

A growing body of literature leverages variation in conditions *(i)*, *(ii)*, and/or *(iii)* to identify the adoption and/or efficacy of both ex post and ex ante adaptation decisions. We review this literature in detail in the next section.

3 Why study adaptation? The evolution of the adaptation literature and its policy motivations

The economics literature on adaptation to climate change has emerged largely through two distinct streams, each of which is motivated by very different aims. One body of work emerging largely within environmental economics, but interacting with a broader interdisciplinary scientific community, has focused on quantifying the expected damages from long-run climate change, which has required attention to the costs and benefits of adaptation. The motivating principle in this literature is that accurately assessing the future impacts of climate change requires accounting for the adaptive actions that agents are likely to take as the climate warms. This literature is designed to inform mitigation policy by generating estimates of policy-relevant objects like the social cost of carbon (Carleton and Greenstone, 2022) or optimal carbon taxes (Nordhaus, 1993).

A second stream of literature growing out of both development and environmental economics has focused on identifying the particular interventions that facilitate adaptation to climate change. The motivation in this literature is generally that policy interventions, sometimes directly targeting adaptation, can enable welfare improvements under climate variability and change. This literature seeks to inform adaptation policy by providing insight into what does and does not enable individuals, firms, or local governments to suffer less under climate change.

In this section, we provide a brief intellectual history of each stream of literature and review the methods employed and findings uncovered in each. We show that these two literatures place different emphasis on each of the terms in Equation (3), thus providing distinct insights into the role of adaptation in shaping welfare under climate change. While we highlight weaknesses and strengths of the existing literature throughout the section, recommendations on how the two bodies of work can learn from one another can be found later in Section 5.

3.1 The study of adaptation to inform mitigation policy

One branch of literature studying climate change adaptation is motivated by the goal of estimating the total effect of climate change on a welfare-relevant outcome (e.g., agricultural profits, economic output, health, etc.). This literature is thus focused on quantifying the lefthand side of Equation (3), $\frac{d\mathbb{E}[u_t]}{dC}$. It has long been acknowledged that doing so accurately requires accounting for the adaptive actions that agents will undoubtedly take as climate change gradually unfolds (Deschênes and Greenstone, 2007; Schlenker et al., 2005). Thus, while a growing body of empirical work has quantified the short-run direct effects of weather (previously reviewed in, e.g., Auffhammer, 2018; Carleton and Hsiang, 2016; Dell et al., 2014; Kolstad and Moore, 2020), these studies are of limited relevance for understanding the effects of long-run climate change if people, governments, and firms make adaptive investments or undertake behavior changes in order to cope with a gradual, expected shift in the climate. That is, estimates of the total derivative in Equation (3) must account for both adaptation terms on the righthand side of the expression.[7]

In its pursuit to measure the impacts of climate change inclusive of adaptation, this literature faces a core challenge: the vectors $\boldsymbol{b}$ and $\boldsymbol{k}$ are composed of myriad adaptive actions, many of which are difficult to observe and measure. To confront this challenge, some studies develop methodological and/or theoretical innovations that, under key assumptions, allow climate impacts estimates to *implicitly* account for *all* unobservable changes to choices $\boldsymbol{b}$ and $\boldsymbol{k}$ without enumerating adaptive margins individually. To do so, these studies generally rely on the assumption that agents perfectly optimize their adaptation choices, facing no frictions, distorted incentives, or incomplete information. Other studies *explicitly* model specific elements of the $\boldsymbol{b}$ and/or $\boldsymbol{k}$ vectors that are likely to be first-order in terms of their impacts on climate change damages (e.g., international trade, migration, infrastructure investments). While these studies by construction omit many plausible adaptive margins, they enable researchers to investigate the welfare implications of particular adaptation actions, as well as the barriers and frictions impeding the deployment of those adaptations.

Here we review three sets of methods that contribute to our understanding of climate change damages inclusive of adaptation, each of which navigates this fundamental challenge in a distinct way. First, in Section 3.1.1, we describe reduced form econometric approaches to estimate the damages from climate change. These studies generally take the implicit approach to solving the challenge of many unobservable adaptive actions: their goal is not to

[7] As mentioned in Section 2, when the outcome of interest is an optimized quantity, there are conditions under which the Envelope Theorem can be applied such that the adaptation terms in Equation (3) need not be directly estimated in order to recover accurate estimates of the long-run impacts of climate change (Hsiang, 2016).

identify which specific elements of ***b*** or ***k*** are used or are most effective in mitigating damages, but instead to produce estimates of climate change damages that include all adaptive responses. Second, in Section 3.1.2, we outline a growing set of quantitative general equilibrium models designed to estimate the aggregate damages from climate change. These analyses enumerate specific ex post and/or ex ante adaptation decisions, such as trade and migration, that modify climate damage projections. Finally, in Section 3.1.3, we summarize the body of work using integrated assessment models (IAMs) and process-based models to estimate climate change damages, the social cost of greenhouse gases, and/or optimal carbon taxes. These studies present a mix of implicit and explicit modeling of adaptation. In each section, we describe the methods used to identify adaptation and highlight the key findings on adaptation that have emerged to date.

3.1.1 Reduced form econometric approaches to account for adaptation in climate damage estimation

A rapidly expanding applied econometrics literature has uncovered a multitude of ways that the weather shapes social and economic activity. Increasingly, such analyses are being combined with climate model-generated projections of future weather under climate change to estimate the long-run impacts of climate change. As discussed above, this literature has long endeavored to ensure such estimates account for both ex post and ex ante adaptation channels, largely through attempts to implicitly embed such adaptive actions in empirical estimation, rather than to enumerate adaptive margins explicitly. Here, we outline the key methodologies developed in this space, roughly in chronological order (while acknowledging that different approaches have emerged independently and simultaneously). We then summarize the central findings regarding the nature and extent of adaptation uncovered across this literature. Throughout, we focus on adaptation methods and results; more comprehensive treatments of the large climate econometrics literature can be found in Chapter 2 of this Volume by Hogan and Schlenker (2024) and in prior reviews (e.g., Auffhammer and Schlenker, 2014; Auffhammer, 2018; Carleton and Hsiang, 2016; Dell et al., 2014; Kolstad and Moore, 2020; Massetti and Mendelsohn, 2018).

3.1.1.1 Methodologies

Here we identify the key methodologies used in the climate econometrics literature to assess damages inclusive of ex post and/or ex ante adaptation. With few exceptions noted below, these methods all implicitly account for adaptation, instead of enumerating specific adaptive margins. The benefit of this approach is that adaptive actions do not need to be identified and measured directly. The key drawback is that each methodology relies on assumptions regarding adaptive behavior that are often difficult to validate empirically, as are described within each methodology below.

Long-run climate variation in cross-sectional regression.

The first reduced form econometric estimates of the impacts of climate change utilized cross-sectional variation in the long-run climate. This approach, referred to as the "Ricardian" method, estimates the equilibrium (i.e., long-run) effects of climate change on an outcome, just as other forms of hedonic analyses recover the value of nonmarket attributes by leveraging variation in the market price of an asset. If one assumes that agents have chosen all $\boldsymbol{b}$ and $\boldsymbol{k}$ values so as to optimize the outcome under the current climate, comparisons of outcomes across climates are inclusive of all ex post and ex ante adaptive actions (i.e., the total derivative on the lefthand side of Equation (3)). In its first application, Mendelsohn et al. (1994) regress U.S. farmland values, reflecting the discounted stream of expected future land rents, on long-run average climate conditions to estimate climate damages on agriculture, accounting for adaptation.[8]

While the Ricardian approach implicitly accounts for all adaptive margins under quite general assumptions, it faces two shortcomings that have limited its continued use. First, correlated unobservables pose a considerable threat – many factors correlate spatially with climate and also influence outcomes of interest.[9] Second, an implicit assumption is that the economic assets used as outcome variables (e.g., land values) do not capitalize future climate change, but instead reflect historical climates only. Severen et al. (2018) show that the forward-looking nature of asset markets leads to a misspecified standard Ricardian approach since assets capitalize available information on future climate change, inducing another form of omitted variables bias that they show to be large in the context of U.S. agriculture.

Short-run weather variation in panel fixed effects regressions.

To address omitted variables bias concerns in Ricardian analyses, panel data methods were developed to isolate plausibly random variation in the weather by including time- and location-specific fixed effects (Deschênes and Greenstone, 2007; Schlenker and Roberts, 2009). This approach effectively eliminates the influence of omitted time-invariant characteristics and common time trends (Ortiz-Bobea, 2020), but such regressions only capture agents' short-run responses to realized weather shocks at a particular point in time, thus

[8] See Mendelsohn and Massetti (2017) for a review of the results of cross-sectional climate impact studies on agriculture around the world. The authors conclude that the relationship between farmland value or net revenue and temperature, inclusive of adaptation, is concave, such that the marginal impact of warming is beneficial in cold places and harmful in hotter locations.

[9] For example, access to irrigation shapes agricultural outcomes and correlates with the long-run climate, as has been shown in the U.S. (Schlenker et al., 2005), China (Wang et al., 2009), and Africa (Kurukulasuriya and Mendelsohn, 2008). To partially remedy this challenge, researchers can sometimes leverage longer time series to observe the same spatial unit under different long-run climate regimes in a "repeat-Ricardian" model (Bareille and Chakir, 2023a; Buck et al., 2014).

accounting for ex post (second term in Equation (3)), but not ex ante (third term in Equation (3)) adaptation.[10] These estimates may overstate the total damage associated with climate change if omitted ex ante adaptations successfully reduce long-run damages (Deschênes and Greenstone, 2007), although long-run damages may be underestimated if ex post responses cannot be sustained indefinitely. For example, Blanc and Schlenker (2017) discuss how groundwater pumping might temporarily offset water deficits, but cannot be sustained in the long-term due to resource depletion. The tension between the benefit of low-frequency variation accounting for ex ante adaptation (as in the Ricardian approach) and the cost of less credible identification relative to the panel fixed effects method has been called the "frequency-identification trade-off" (Hsiang and Burke, 2014; Hsiang, 2016).

In some settings, short-run weather variation can be used to generate climate damage estimates inclusive of both ex post and ex ante adaptation. As mentioned in Section 2, when agents are optimizing in a static environment, both adaptation terms in Equation (3) drop out due to the Envelope Theorem and the impacts of short-run weather are identical to impacts of long-run climate change, inclusive of adaptation (Deryugina and Hsiang, 2017; Guo and Costello, 2013; Hsiang, 2016). For this conclusion to hold, however, the outcome of interest must be an optimized quantity (e.g., profits), adaptive actions $\boldsymbol{b}$ or $\boldsymbol{k}$ must be continuously differentiable with respect to the weather $\boldsymbol{c}$, markets and information must be perfect, and agents must rationally optimize without frictions. When adaptation technologies are discontinuous and the choice variables are discrete (e.g., long-lived infrastructure), outcomes are not optimized quantities (e.g., health), and/or frictions impede optimal decision-making, reduced form panel fixed effects regression results no longer reflect ex ante adaptation. Additionally, Mérel et al. (2024) show that restrictions are needed on the functional form of ex ante adaptation in order for standard implementations of the insights from Deryugina and Hsiang, 2017 and Hsiang (2016) to appropriately capture adaptation. Thus, while some papers assume that the conditions necessary to invoke the Envelope Theorem hold, the vast majority of panel fixed effects climate regressions generate climate change impact estimates that do not attempt to account for ex ante adaptation.

While most reduced form econometric methods only implicitly account for adaptation, panel fixed effects estimates are used in some cases to *explicitly* identify ex post adaptation. This is done by using a specific adaptive margin as the outcome variable, thus estimating the extent to which a particular form of ex post adaptation responds to short-run weather shocks. These studies identify *adoption* and *use* of ex post adaptive behaviors and/or technologies (i.e., $\frac{\partial \boldsymbol{b}^*}{\partial \boldsymbol{c}}$),

[10] In non-linear panel models with higher-order polynomials of weather variables, some ex ante adaptation is also implicitly incorporated, by accounting for mean weather (see McIntosh and Schlenker (2005); Lobell et al. (2011); Schlenker (2017); Mérel et al. (2024) for additional methodological details).

but generally do not identify the *effectiveness* of these ex post adaptive measures in mitigating climate damages (i.e., $\frac{\partial u}{\partial b}\frac{\partial b^*}{\partial c}$). For example, Deschênes and Greenstone (2011) show that state-level energy demand responds to heat shocks, but do not link this adaptive behavior directly to its heat-related health benefits. Besides energy use, other ex post adaptation responses that have been investigated include: human migration (e.g., Benveniste et al., 2020; Cai et al., 2016); time use (e.g., Graff-Zivin and Neidell, 2014; Rode et al., 2022); changes in supply-chain relationships (e.g., Balboni et al., 2023; Pankratz and Schiller, 2024); firms' location choices (e.g., Castro-Vincenzi, 2023; Indaco and Ortega, 2021; Jia et al., 2022); and use of agricultural inputs, such as pesticides and fertilizers (Jagnani et al., 2021), land adjustments (Aragón et al., 2021), irrigation investments (Taraz, 2017), and soil and water conservation practices (Tambet and Stopnitzky, 2021).

Heterogeneous short-run weather impacts based on long-run climate.

A newer set of approaches aims to leverage plausibly random weather variation while also accounting for ex ante adaptation. Perhaps the most common method is to estimate heterogeneous treatment effects of within-location weather variation across locations with different long-run baseline climates. The intuition is that ex ante adaptive investments are made based on the expectations people form over their location's weather distribution (as reflected in Equation (2)). Therefore, differences in the marginal effects of a short-run weather shock across distinct climates are assumed to reflect differential adaptive investments made by individuals, firms, and local governments located in different equilibrium climates. Econometrically, this is often implemented as an interaction between a long-run climate variable, which proxies for expectations of local agents, and a short-run weather shock. One of the first applications of this methodology was in the study of temperature's influence over GDP growth (Dell et al., 2012), but the approach has also been applied to tropical cyclone damages (Hsiang and Narita, 2012) and the impact of heat on: agriculture (Butler and Huybers, 2013; Hultgren et al., 2022); mortality (Carleton et al., 2022; Heutel et al., 2021); energy consumption (Rode et al., 2021); labor supply (Rode et al., 2022); and retail sales (Roth Tran, 2023). This approach can also be implemented via two-step estimation, as in Auffhammer (2022) for temperature impacts on electricity consumption in California.

This method faces two challenges. First, the measures used as proxies for climate expectations are not exogenous and only vary cross-sectionally, making it difficult to determine whether the recovered coefficients reflect ex ante adaptation or are simply jointly co-determined by a third unobserved factor. Second, and related, ex ante adaptation is identified using cross-sectional heterogeneity in weather responses under the implicit assumption that preferences and technology are constant across space, so that differences reflect only different choices of $\boldsymbol{b}^*$ or $\boldsymbol{k}^*$, as opposed to differences in utility functions or available technologies. This is an analogous problem to the Lucas critique (Lucas, 1972). A partial solution is to exploit, when available, temporal variation in climatic trends by replacing the time-invariant climate variable with a rolling climatic average, which may help ensure that preferences and/or technologies are more comparable between long-run climates (Mérel et al., 2024). Direct measurement of individual beliefs about the weather distribution – instead of the use of climate variable proxies for expectations – could also help mitigate both challenges, but these beliefs are also likely correlated with unobservables and are themselves seldom observable.

Partitioning long-run climate and short-run weather variation in a single equation.

An alternative set of approaches emerged in parallel to the heterogeneous weather effects methods described above. These "partitioning variation" methods combine variation in weather and climate in a jointly estimated equation to decompose meteorological conditions into a component associated with a long-run climate mean (the response to which is presumed to be inclusive of ex ante adaptation) and a component associated with deviations from it (the response to which is presumed to include only ex post adaptation) (Kelly et al., 2005; Kolstad and Moore, 2020).

This method takes multiple forms. Mérel and Gammans (2021) introduce a "climate penalty" to a panel fixed effects regression, which measures the distance between contemporaneous weather and a location's long-run average climate. Just as in the heterogeneous weather effects models described above, this allows for weather shocks closer to average conditions to differentially impact outcomes relative to shocks that are more unusual (and therefore less expected). Schlenker (2017) adopts a slightly more general approach in which the "climate penalty" reflects the distance between contemporaneous weather and a measure of expectations that is endogenously estimated and may differ from the long-run climate mean. Both Moore and Lobell (2014) and Bento et al. (2023) include 30-year moving averages of climate variables in a panel fixed effects regression alongside weather deviations from those averages to jointly estimate long- and short-run responses to changes in the climate.[11] The authors interpret differences between those responses as an empirical measurement of adaptation. However, this approach has identification challenges and, as implemented in Moore and Lobell (2014), is conceptually inconsistent, as the estimated long-run response does not represent the outer envelope of the short-run response (Mérel and Gammans, 2021). Moreover, it is unclear why the long-run climate would *directly* impact annual outcomes; in other approaches, the long-run climate shapes beliefs and expectations, which influence ex ante adaptive decisions that lower or raise responses to short-run weather shocks.

[11] There are multiple differences between estimation methods in these two papers, but a notable one is that Moore and Lobell (2014) do not include panel unit spatial fixed effects, implying both cross-sectional and temporal variation influence estimated parameters.

Long differences.

A relatively recent method aimed at combining the benefits of both the panel fixed effects model and the Ricardian approach uses medium- to long-run climate *trends* as a source of identification. Using a sufficiently long time series of weather observations, the "long differences" approach estimates the relationship between a time trend in an outcome of interest (e.g., crop yields) and the corresponding trend in climate (e.g., temperature) over the same period, generally leveraging cross-sectional variation in these trends (Burke and Emerick, 2016; Dell et al., 2014).[12] Because the variation is medium- to long-run, ex ante adaptations that are undertaken in response to gradually changing climatology are accounted for.

Results from this approach are often compared against estimates from a short-run weather panel data model (inclusive of only ex post adaptation) to draw conclusions regarding the extent of ex ante adaptation taking place (see Dell et al. (2012) for an application to economic growth and Burke and Emerick (2016) for an application in agriculture).[13] While generally used to implicitly characterize ex ante adaptation, this approach is also used to explicitly identify specific ex ante adaptive actions by placing adaptation choices on the lefthand side of the regression. These studies identify the adoption of ex ante adaptation (i.e., $\frac{dk^*}{dC}$), but generally cannot identify the *effectiveness* of such behaviors in lowering climate damages (i.e., $\frac{\partial u}{\partial k}\frac{dk^*}{dC}$). For example, Cui (2020) and Cui and Zhong (2024) show that cropping patterns respond to long-run trends in temperature in the U.S. and China, respectively, suggesting (but not directly showing) that crop migration and switching may be an important margin of agricultural adaptation. Similarly, Liu et al. (2023) show that long-run increases in temperature restrict labor mobility across sectors in India — a result which contrasts sharply with documented increases in sectoral reallocation following short-run temperature shocks (Colmer, 2021).

This method has two key drawbacks. Most importantly, any unobservable that is correlated with trends in weather and also influences trends in the outcome will bias identification. That is, climatic trends must be spatially randomly assigned, conditional on regression controls. Second, results may be sensitive to how the "difference" is computed between the start and end of the

[12] In long enough time series, changes in the trend itself within a location can be exploited; this is called a "panel" of long differences (Waldinger, 2022).

[13] Hsiang (2016) recommends exploiting climatic variations at many different temporal frequencies and comparing estimated coefficients to those from long differences and from the cross-section. Lemoine (2023) shows that long difference estimates are also identified off of differences in the sequences of transient weather shocks which might also conflate differential rates of climate change. Whether divergent estimates from the long difference and panel estimates are driven by ex ante adaptation or other unobserved factors is a topic of ongoing debate.

period[14]; to avoid this, recent papers estimate trends using all observations over the sample period (e.g., Burke and Tanutama, 2019).

Quasi-random spatial variation in long-run climate.

To mitigate the challenge of non-random variation in long-run climate trends (long differences) or levels (Ricardian approach), a set of recent methodologies has emerged to isolate plausibly random spatial variation in the long-run climate. First, the "spatial first differences" (SFD) method regresses the difference in the long-run average of the outcome between two geographically-adjacent locations on the corresponding spatial difference in the long-run average climate (Druckenmiller and Hsiang, 2018). In essence, this approach substitutes the temporal difference in a classical "first difference" approach with its spatial analog. By limiting cross-sectional variation to spatially adjacent pairs of locations, SFD relies on less restrictive identifying assumptions than the pure cross-section, yet still accounts for ex ante adaptation if agents adapt to their local climatology. However, this approach can suffer from limited variation at higher spatial resolutions where its key identifying assumption becomes more plausible. Moreover, this approach may be subject to violations of the stable unit treatment value assumption (SUTVA) since flows of goods, people, and capital are often inversely related to distance, although models accounting for spatial lags may help allay such concerns (Druckenmiller and Hsiang, 2018). SFD has been applied in agricultural settings in the U.S. (Druckenmiller and Hsiang, 2018; McFadden et al., 2022) and to assess temperature's influence over global economic activity (Linsenmeier, 2023).

Second, a few studies have generated climate impacts estimates inclusive of ex ante adaptation by exploiting quasi-random spatial variation in geologically determined access to groundwater (Blakeslee et al., 2020; Hornbeck, 2012; Hornbeck and Keskin, 2014), and spatial discontinuities in water supplies (Hagerty, 2022). This approach is generally well-identified, but is less generalizable – it relies on context-specific availability of plausibly random spatial variation in climatic conditions.

Accounting for weather forecasts.

A causal interpretation of the panel fixed effects models described earlier requires the assumption that short-run weather variation is plausibly randomly assigned. However, in practice, individuals often access weather forecasts, which can facilitate ex ante adaptation to weather, undermining the assumption of unanticipated random shocks. A growing number of studies,

[14] Long differences in climate and outcome variables are generally computed as $\frac{1}{n}\Sigma_{t\in a} x_t - \frac{1}{n}\Sigma_{t\in b} x_t$, where a and b are multi-period ranges spanning n time periods, with b representing the end of the sample and a the beginning (e.g., in the annual analysis in Burke and Emerick (2016), $n = 5$, a includes years 1978–1982 and b includes years 1998–2002). If there is substantial inter-period variability in climate and/or outcome variables, the choice of n, a, and/or b can influence estimates.

which we further discuss in Section 3.2.2, show that short-run forecasts do influence behavior and thus induce short-run ex ante adaptation.[15] If individuals adjust their behavior in response to forecast information, climate damage estimates that do not account for forecasts represent biased estimates of direct climate effects ($\frac{\partial u}{\partial c}$), as they include some ex ante adaptation effects ($\frac{\partial u}{\partial k}\frac{dk^*}{dC}$) resulting from forecasted weather. The solution proposed in the literature is straightforward – simply add controls for forecast information into a standard panel fixed effects weather regression (Lemoine, 2023). For example, Shrader (2023) adds El Niño Southern Oscillation (ENSO) forecasts to a regression of commercial fishing output on the ENSO index, showing that ex ante adaptive actions taken in response to forecasts substantially reduce direct damages from ENSO. This approach allows researchers to isolate unexpected shocks in realized weather from forecasted weather events that may induce ex ante adaptation, providing valuable information on the nature and extent of adaption.

This approach relies on the assumption that individuals perfectly observe publicly available, and thus measurable, forecasts. Any wedge between individuals' expectations and forecasted meteorological conditions can introduce measurement error into the quantification of ex ante adaptation through forecast control variables. Moreover, while this approach is helpful for identifying climate damages inclusive of short- and medium-run ex ante adaptation, to date this method has not been used to assess ex ante adaptation to longer-run climate change projections.

Accounting for dynamics in adaptive investments.

Most formalizations of adaptation used to inform climate econometric models rely on a static maximization problem in which agents choose adaptive actions in each period with no dynamic linkages (e.g., Carleton et al., 2022; Deryugina and Hsiang, 2017; Hsiang, 2016).[16] However, many ex post and ex ante decisions influence a capital or natural resource stock, implying that decision-making is inherently dynamic. For example, using groundwater for irrigation in response to a heat shock today lowers the stock of groundwater available for adaptation tomorrow. A small set of recent papers propose approaches to incorporate dynamic considerations into reduced form econometric estimation of climate damages and adaptation, though these methodologies have not yet been widely applied.

---

[15] The role of forecasts has been documented in several sectors, including agriculture (Burlig et al., 2024; Du Puy and Shrader, 2024; Rosenzweig and Udry, 2013), health (Shrader et al., 2023), labor supply (Downey et al., 2023; Song, 2024), and financial markets (Lemoine and Kapnick, 2024; Schlenker and Taylor, 2021). Here, we discuss the studies that focus on quantifying climate damages, deferring a discussion of the rest of the literature on forecasts to Section 3.2.2.

[16] Note that Guo and Costello (2013) study adaptation within a dynamic optimization framework, but do not link their model to an estimable reduced form regression method.

First, Lemoine (2023) develops a dynamic optimization model in which ex post and ex ante adaptation influence a capital or resource stock, showing that short-run panel fixed effects models fail to reflect long-run climate impacts, inclusive of adaptation, when such dynamics are ignored. Lemoine (2023) proposes an indirect least squares (ILS) estimator which maintains the same identification strategy as the common panel fixed effects specifications, but can disentangle the direct effects of the weather ($\frac{\partial u}{\partial c}$) from ex post and ex ante adaptation ($\frac{\partial u}{\partial \boldsymbol{b}}\frac{\partial \boldsymbol{b}^*}{\partial c}$ and $\frac{\partial u}{\partial \boldsymbol{k}}\frac{d\boldsymbol{k}^*}{dC}$) without needing to observe either the ex ante adaptation capital stocks or actions. However, without forecast data, this method only captures the dynamics of ex post adaptations, not ex ante.

Second, Rudik et al. (2024) focus on ex ante adaptation in a dynamic setting, reconciling measurements of adaptation from a dynamic spatial general equilibrium model (reviewed in Section 3.1.2) with a reduced form approach. The authors develop a novel dynamic Envelope Theorem method to measure welfare impacts accounting for specific ex ante adaptations (trade and labor reallocation) and apply their method to climate impacts on the U.S. economy.

Accounting for adaptation costs.

All of the methods discussed above aim to recover the benefits of ex post and/or ex ante adaptation (i.e., the second two terms of Equation (3)). However, such benefits come at a cost. In some cases, this cost may manifest as a reduction in the average outcome level – for example, many heat-resilient crop varieties perform suboptimally under average climate conditions, creating a mean-variance trade-off (Schlenker et al., 2013). In other cases, this cost is simply pecuniary, as agents pay for investments or technologies that lower the damages from adverse weather. Generating climate change impact estimates that account only for the benefits, but not the costs, of adaptation will systematically underestimate total damages (Carleton et al., 2022; Mérel et al., 2024; Schlenker et al., 2013).[17] As discussed above, ex post adaptation is generally embedded implicitly within reduced form econometric estimates of climate damages, such that neither benefits nor costs of such adaptations are explicitly identified in the literature. In contrast, a set of studies have developed revealed preference based methods to estimate costs of ex ante adaptations.

Schlenker et al. (2013) first quantified ex ante adaptation costs by showing that the lower sensitivity of U.S. maize yields to extreme temperatures observed in hotter locations (documented in Butler and Huybers (2013) and presumably reflecting ex ante adaptation) comes at the cost of lower average yields. The authors add these average yield "costs" of adaptation in to climate change impact estimates to show that total effects of climate change on yields

[17] As previously discussed, only when the outcome variable of interest is an optimized quantity (e.g., profits, utility) and the change in the climate is marginal, can the Envelope Theorem be invoked to assume that the benefits of adaptation exactly equal its costs, and neither need to be explicitly measured.

rise substantially. Carleton et al. (2022) build on thus intuition and the theory from Guo and Costello (2013) to develop a revealed preference approach to infer adaptation costs associated with the mortality risk from climate change. Adaptation is assumed to be undertaken up to the point where marginal adaptation benefits, obtained from empirical estimates of how the long-run climate impacts mortality's sensitivity to temperature, equal marginal adaptation costs. Total costs of adapting to non-marginal climate change are then calculated by integrating marginal adaptation costs over time, and they include any level effects of the climate on mortality, as well as the value of pecuniary expenditures. The authors find that estimated costs of adaptation are a meaningful share of overall climate change damages and that they are incurred disproportionately by the world's wealthier populations.

These reduced form econometric approaches to assessing adaptation costs rely on strong assumptions regarding agent behavior and the nature of adaptation technologies. Most approaches do not take dynamics into account. Moreover, results from an enumerative approach – in which specific adaptation expenditures are measured and studied directly (e.g., Auffhammer, 2022; Rode et al., 2021; Du Puy and Shrader, 2024) – have yet to be directly compared with the adaptation cost estimates recovered from the revealed preference methods described here. These two approaches are complementary and much could be learned from combining insights from both.

3.1.1.2 Key findings

A growing set of reduced form econometric analyses use the methods articulated above to quantify climate impacts either inclusive of ex post adaptation or of both ex post and ex ante adaptation. Ex post adaptation is implicitly accounted for in nearly all reduced form estimates of climate damages, but isolating its effect from direct climate impacts is generally impossible (i.e., separating the first two terms on the righthand side of Equation (3) is rarely feasible as observable short-run variations in outcomes always include ex post adaptations).[18] In contrast, the methods detailed above often enable researchers to isolate ex ante adaptation effects, shedding light on the extent and economic importance of such preemptive adaptation. Here, we summarize the key findings on ex ante adaptation from this literature; quantitative estimates are provided in Table 1.

Key finding # 1: Ex ante adaptation in U.S. agriculture is minimal, but in global agriculture is substantial.

[18] There are two important exceptions to this claim. First, Lemoine (2023) uses a theoretically-derived indirect least squares estimator to document that ex post adaptations substantially lower climate damages to U.S. county incomes. Second, Bareille and Chakir (2023b) pair a panel fixed effects method with a structural model to show that ex post adaptive use of fertilizer and pesticide on French farms mitigate between one-quarter and two-thirds of the negative impacts of warming on yields.

TABLE 1 Ex ante adaptation in reduced form econometric climate impact studies.

Reference	Estimating equation general form	Sector	Geographical scope	Spatial resolution	Impact of ex ante adaptation
Short-run weather variation in panel fixed effects regressions					
Schlenker and Roberts (2009)	$y_{it} = f(c_{it}; \beta) + \alpha_i + h(t) + \varepsilon_{it}$	Agriculture	U.S.	ADM–2	Accounting for ex ante adaptation has little to no effect on crop yield impacts of climate change
Dell et al. (2012)	$y_{it} = f(c_{it}; \beta) + \alpha_i + h(t) + \varepsilon_{it}$	Income per capita	World	ADM–0	Accounting for ex ante adaptation has no statistically distinguishable effect on aggregate output impacts of temperature
Burke and Hsiang (2015b)		Income per capita	World	ADM–0	Accounting for ex ante adaptation has no statistically distinguishable effect on aggregate output impacts of temperature
Deryugina and Hsiang (2017)		Income per capita	U.S.	ADM–2	Accounting for ex ante adaptation (via nonlinearities within a temperature bin and urban-rural heterogeneity) reduces net present value of income losses from climate change by 51%
Burke and Tanutama (2019)		Income per capita	World	ADM–1/ ADM–2	Accounting for ex ante adaptation (via long differences) increases climate damages
Kalkuhl and Wenz (2020)		Income per capita	World	ADM–1/ ADM–2	Accounting for ex ante adaptation (via cross sectional regressions) reduces climate damages by 50%

Continued

TABLE 1 Ex ante adaptation in reduced form econometric climate impact studies.—Cont'd

Reference	Estimating equation general form	Sector	Geographical scope	Spatial resolution	Impact of ex ante adaptation
Heterogeneous short-run weather impacts based on long-run climate					
Butler and Huybers (2013)	$y_{it} = f(c_{it}, \mathbf{C}_i; \beta_C) + \alpha_i + h(t) + \varepsilon_{it}$	Agriculture	U.S.	ADM−2	Accounting for ex ante adaptation reduces maize yield impacts by 57%
Schlenker et al. (2013)		Agriculture	U.S.	ADM−2	Accounting for ex ante adaptation reduces maize yield impacts by 8%
Heutel et al. (2021)		Health	U.S.	ZIP code	Accounting for ex ante adaptation reduces mortality impacts of climate change by 30%
Rode et al. (2021)		Energy consumption	World	ADM−2	Accounting for ex ante adaptation reduces energy expenditure impacts of a 1oC increase in global mean surface temperature in 2100 by 39%
Carleton et al. (2022)		Health	World	ADM−2	Accounting for ex ante adaptation benefits reduces mortality impacts of climate change by 30%; accounting also for ex ante adaptation costs (via a revealed preference approach) reduces impacts by 19%[1]
Hultgren et al. (2022)		Agriculture	World	ADM−2	Accounting for ex ante adaptation and economic development reduces crop yield impacts of climate change by 47%
Rode et al. (2022)		Labor disutility	World	ADM−2	Accounting for ex ante adaptation reduces labor disutility costs of climate change by 17%

Mérel et al. (2024)	$y_{it} = f(c_{it}; \beta C_{i,t}) + \gamma z_i c_{it} + \alpha_i h(t) + \varepsilon_{it}$	Agriculture	U.S.	ADM–2	Accounting for ex ante adaptation reduces agricultural GDP impacts of climate change by 9–28%
Auffhammer (2022)	(i) $y_{it} = f(c_{it}; \beta_i) + \alpha_i + h(t) + \varepsilon_{it}$	Energy[2]	California (U.S.)	ZIP code	Accounting for ex ante adaptation increases electricity consumption impacts of climate change by 50%
	(ii) $\widehat{\beta_i} = f(C_i; \gamma) + \mathbf{X}'_i + \varepsilon_i$				
Long differences					
Burke and Emerick (2016)	$y_{it} - y_{i,t-\tau} = f((c_i - c_{it-\tau}); \beta) + (\varepsilon_{it} - \varepsilon_{it-\tau})$	Agriculture	U.S.	ADM–2	Accounting for ex ante adaptation has no statistically distinguishable effect on the maize yield impacts of heat exposure
Partitioning long-run climate and short-run weather variation					
Moore and Lobell (2014, 2015)	$y_{it} = f((c_{it} - C_{ip}); \beta) + g(C_{ip}; \gamma) + \alpha_i + h(t) + \varepsilon_{it}$	Agriculture	Europe	ADM–2	Accounting for ex ante adaptation reduces yield impacts of climate change by 7% (wheat), 32% (barley), and 89% (maize)
Bento et al. (2023)	$y_{it} = f((c_{it} - C_{ip}); \beta) + g(C_{ip}; \gamma) + \alpha_i + h(r) + \varepsilon_{it}$	Ozone concentration	U.S.	Ozone monitors	Accounting for ex ante adaptation reduces the ozone impacts of climate change by 44%

Continued

TABLE 1 Ex ante adaptation in reduced form econometric climate impact studies.—Cont'd

Reference	Estimating equation general form	Sector	Geographical scope	Spatial resolution	Impact of ex ante adaptation
Quasi-random spatial variation in long-run climate					
Druckenmiller and Hsiang (2018)	$y_{it} - y_{jt} = f((c_{it} - c_{jt}); \beta) + (\varepsilon_{it} - \varepsilon_{jt})$	Agriculture	U.S.	ADM–2	Accounting for long-run versus medium-run ex ante adaptation has no statistically distinguishable effect on the maize yield impacts of heat exposure
Accounting for weather forecasts					
Shrader (2023)	$y_{it} = f((c_t; \beta) + h(\hat{c}_t; \gamma) + \alpha_i + h(p) + \varepsilon_{it}$	Fisheries	North Pacific Ocean	N/A[3]	Accounting for short-run ex ante adaptation reduces fisheries output impacts of El Niño Southern Oscillation by 31%

Notes: The "Estimating equation general form" column reports a stylized representation of the main empirical specification adopted in each paper, where three dots indicate the same specification as the preceding row. $f(\cdot)$ represents a general functional form of the weather and/or climate variables in the estimating equation, such as high-order polynomials or bins. c_{it} represents weather, C_i represents climate (long-run average weather), i indicates location, and t indicates time. τ is the time interval over which differences are taken in the "long differences" approach. p indicates a weakly larger level of temporal aggregation than t (used in the "partitioning variation" and "accounting for forecasts" approach), and r a one-level higher aggregation in time than p (used in the "partitioning variation"). The "Spatial First Difference" approach (Druckenmiller and Hsiang, 2018) takes the difference on both left- and right-hand side of the estimating equation with j, the unit immediately adjacent in space to i. "Accounting for forecasts" also includes $\hat{c}_t$, which indicates weather forecasts available at time t. Each equation estimates coefficients β and/or γ. α_i indicates unit fixed effects and $h(\cdot)$ indicates a general function of time (t, p or r), which can include spatially explicit time trends and/or time fixed effects. In the "Spatial resolution" column, ADM-0 indicates country, ADM-1 indicates the first administrative unit (e.g., a U.S. state), and ADM-2 indicates the second administrative unit (e.g., a U.S. county). [1] We compare the global estimates of the benefits of climate adaptation in 2100 under RCP8.5 in deaths/100k to a counterfactual that accounts for benefits of income growth only (see Table II in Carleton et al. (2022)). [2]Auffhammer (2022) uses an ex post adaptation margin, residential electricity consumption, as the outcome variable in estimating equation (i). Thus, accounting for ex ante adaptation (i.e., adoption of energy technologies like air conditioning) *increases* use of electricity as an ex post adaptation strategy under climate change. [3] The unit of analysis in Shrader (2023) is vessel-month-year. The estimating equation accounts for vessel-, month-, and year- fixed effects, but the ENSO forecasts and realizations do not vary across space.

Much of the reduced form econometric literature has focused on U.S. maize yields, and Table 1 shows that these studies generally present minimal evidence of within-crop ex ante adaptation. That is, while crop switching and/or crop migration are likely important margins of ex ante adaptation (Cui, 2020), and total agricultural GDP in the U.S. exhibits large benefits from ex ante adaptation (Mérel et al., 2024), it appears that farmers can do to little to lower U.S. maize yield losses from heat (Burke and Emerick, 2016; Druckenmiller and Hsiang, 2018; Schlenker and Roberts, 2009; Schlenker et al., 2013).[19] In contrast, in settings with greater geographical scope, ex ante adaptations appear to substantially reduce crop-specific losses from climate change. For example, Hultgren et al. (2022) show that accounting for ex ante adaptation benefits reduces aggregate global yield losses from climate change by 47 %.

Key finding #2: Ex ante adaptation in aggregate economic output is likely minimal.

Comparisons of climate change impacts on aggregate GDP derived from methods that do (e.g., long differences) versus do not (e.g., panel fixed effects) implicitly account for ex ante adaptation suggest that the benefits from adaptation are minimal. Dell et al. (2012) do not find heterogeneous responses of country-level annual GDP to temperature shocks across distinct baseline climates. They also show that long differences and panel fixed effects approaches recover similar estimates, and that responses to temperature do not become less severe over time in a long panel. Burke and Hsiang (2015b) reach a similar conclusion, also studying country-level GDP responses to temperature and showing limited evidence of ex ante adaptation using variation over time and across space. Burke and Tanutama (2019) use subnational GDP data from 37 countries to show that short-run panel estimates of GDP-temperature relationship are *smaller* than those recovered with long differences, a result that is inconsistent with any substantial ex ante adaptation effects.

Two exceptions suggest that ex ante adaptation may be more substantial than these earlier studies suggest. Kalkuhl and Wenz (2020) use sub-national economic output data across 77 countries and find that projected climate change damages based on panel estimates are about twice as large as those based on cross-sectional ones, suggesting that ex ante adaptation may be considerable in magnitude. However, omitted variables bias in the cross section renders such a comparison difficult to interpret. Kahn et al. (2021) regress country-level economic growth on a measure of weather deviations from baseline climate to show that varying the time interval over which the baseline climate is computed changes output losses from climate change. This suggests ex ante adaptations taken in response to a

[19] An exception to this finding is Butler and Huybers (2013), who use the response heterogeneity approach to uncover evidence of substantial ex ante adaptation within U.S. maize. To our knowledge, this finding has not been reconciled with evidence from other methods indicating that ex ante adaptation is minimal.

shifting long-run climate are considerable. To our knowledge, these findings have not been reconciled with earlier work, leaving uncertainty regarding the extent to which ex ante adaptation has and will continue to mitigate aggregate economic losses from climate change.

Key finding #3: Ex ante adaptation is substantial in nearly all settings outside agriculture and aggregate economic output.

Ex ante adaptation is found to have large impacts on climate damages in nearly all settings other than agriculture and aggregate economic output. This finding is consistent across various econometric methods. Results from papers leveraging the two-stage approach (Auffhammer, 2022), response heterogeneity method (Carleton et al., 2022; Heutel et al., 2021), or from those partitioning the variation in long run climate and weather deviations (Bento et al., 2023) and leveraging forecasts (Shrader, 2023) conclude that accounting for adaptation substantially alters estimates of climate damages across a wide range of outcomes, including mortality, energy consumption, labor disutility, ozone concentrations, and fishery output. The magnitude of welfare benefits from ex ante adaptation in these settings is estimated to be large, ranging from 17 % in a study of global labor disutility (Rode et al., 2022) to 44 % in a study of the elevation of U.S. ozone concentrations in response to temperature (Bento et al., 2023). One important exception to this conclusion is the study of crime, conflict, and suicide. Burke et al. (2018) and Carleton (2017) show that short-run variation in temperature has similar impacts on suicide rates across different temporal and spatial subsamples in Mexico, the U.S., and India, while reviews of the large crime, conflict, and temperature literature similarly show limited evidence of ex ante adaptation (Burke and Hsiang, 2015a; Carleton et al., 2016).

Key finding #4: Ex ante adaptation costs are estimated to be large.

While only a few studies aim to account for ex ante adaptation costs alongside ex ante adaptation benefits, their findings show that such costs dramatically change total climate damage estimates. Three studies in Table 1 provide such estimates — Schlenker et al. (2013); Carleton et al. (2022) and Hultgren et al. (2022) – and all conclude that while adaptation benefits are substantial, they come at a high cost. This implies that studies accounting only for ex ante adaptation benefits will underestimate the welfare effects of climate change and adds urgency to the need for improved methodologies for estimating ex ante adaptation costs.

3.1.2 Adaptation in quantitative general equilibrium models

An expanding literature in trade, macroeconomics, and related fields assesses climate change damages using quantitative general equilibrium models that explicitly enumerate key ex post and ex ante adaptation margins. Such studies are generally focused on informing mitigation policy by estimating aggregate welfare damages from climate change, but their enumerative approach to adaptation also elucidates when and where specific margins of adaptation, or barriers to those margins, are critical to determining welfare under climate change. To maintain tractability, these models generally focus either on adaptation over time (e.g., durable investments) or adaptation margins that link spatial units (e.g., international trade or migration). Here, we review the key findings from this literature, first summarizing insights from studies modeling adaptation over time, and second from those modeling adaptation over space. We highlight the papers that embed both features in dynamic spatial general equilibrium models. Table 2 summarizes key findings on adaptation from this literature. We note that a comprehensive review of the methods employed in these studies is beyond the scope of this chapter; we focus here on results.

3.1.2.1 Adaptation over time

This strand of literature develops macroeconomic quantitative models that focus on intertemporal adaptation margins. These models do not account for spatialno links across geographical units, but they often study different adaptation strategies within one paper, enabling cost-effectiveness comparisons (e.g., comparing ex post and ex ante margins, or comparing public to private adaptation options). This provides a rich analysis of adaptation trade-offs that to date has not been feasible in the reduced form approaches outlined above. Simulations are generally conducted using a calibrated model to draw these conclusions, allowing a wide range of counterfactual analyses, but coming at the cost of structural assumptions that cannot always be verified with appropriate data and empirical evidence. Only few studies, notably Bakkensen et al. (2018), bridge the reduced form-structural gap by combining both approaches.

A first group of papers assesses the macroeconomic effects of natural disasters, often focusing on disaster-prone countries like small island nations, and using either a dynamic small open economy model or a dynamic stochastic general equilibrium (DSGE) model. Together, these papers point to large benefits from intertemporal ex ante adaptation. Marto et al. (2018) study the impact of cyclones in Vanuatu through a dynamic small open economy model, highlighting the trade-off between investing in ex ante resilient capital and spending on ex post international aid after a disaster takes place – they find that ex ante investments are 10% less costly. Cantelmo et al. (2023) reach a similar conclusion in a DSGE model, with ex ante public investment in resilient capital across disaster-prone developing countries being 30% more cost-effective than ex post international aid at reducing welfare losses. Corugedo et al. (2023) expand these approaches with a DSGE model which includes incomplete markets, financial frictions with collateral constraints (which limits borrowing for ex post reconstruction), and a full set of fiscal policy instruments and find modest long-run gains from ex ante adaptation. Bakkensen and Barrage (2018) combine a rich econometric analysis with a stochastic growth model calibrated for 40 vulnerable countries to quantify macroeconomic welfare impacts of cyclone risk accounting for adaptation via

TABLE 2 Adaptation in quantitative general equilibrium models.

Reference	Climate shock	Adaptive margin	Sectoral heterogeneity	Geographical scope	Spatial resolution	Impact of adaptation
Adaptation over time						
Marto et al. (2018)	Cyclones	Public infrastructure investment, public savings in contingency fund	One sector	Vanuatu	ADM–0	Ex ante adaptation reduces public infrastructure damages by 5%, private capital damages by 10%, productivity losses by 4%
Mallucci (2022)	Hurricanes	Disaster clauses	One sector	Seven Caribbean countries	ADM–0	Coupon suspension clauses reduces welfare losses from climate change by 15% Debt reduction clauses reduce welfare losses by 50%
Fried (2022)	Severe storms	Private investment, public disaster aid and adaptation subsidies	One sector	U.S.	ADM–2	Adaptation reduces the welfare cost of climate change by 11%

Cantelmo et al. (2023)	Natural disasters	Ex-ante infrastructure investments, ex-post disaster aid	One sector	average Emerging Market and Developing Economy	ADM–0	Ex ante adaptation reduces welfare loss by 20%
Corugedo et al. (2023)	Natural disasters	Public investment	One sector	Dominica	ADM–0	Ex ante adaptation reduces GDP losses from climate change by 6.5%
Phan and Schwartzman (2024)	Cyclones	Catastrophe bonds, disaster insurance	One sector	Mexico	ADM–0	Adaptation reduces welfare losses from climate change by 25%
Van Der Straten, 2024	Sea level rise / coastal flooding	Private investment	One sector	Florida (U.S.)	ADM–1	Adaptation reduces house price increases by 15%, cost of capital increase by 20%, consumption inequality by 24%
Adaptation over space						
Costinot et al. (2016)	Temperature	Trade, crop specialization	Agriculture, non-agriculture	50 countries, 10 crops	ADM–0	Crop switching restrictions increase welfare losses from climate change by 300% Full trade restrictions increase welfare losses from climate change by 4%

Continued

TABLE 2 Adaptation in quantitative general equilibrium models.—Cont'd

Reference	Climate shock	Adaptive margin	Sectoral heterogeneity	Geographical scope	Spatial resolution	Impact of adaptation
Gouel and Laborde (2021)	Temperature	Trade, crop specialization	Agriculture, non-agriculture	50 countries, 35 crops	ADM–0	Crop switching restrictions increase welfare losses from climate change by 37%. Full trade restrictions increase welfare losses from climate change by 23%
Conte (2023)	Temperature	Trade, migration, crop specialization	Agriculture, non-agriculture	Africa	100x100km grid cell (1°)	Bilateral migration restrictions increase welfare losses from climate change by 8%. Removing trade tariffs reduces welfare losses by 0.18%. Allowing crop switching reduces welfare losses by 2.44%
Nath (2023)	Temperature	Trade, sectoral reallocation	Agriculture, manufacturing, services	17 countries	ADM–0	Fully removing trade frictions reduces welfare losses from climate change by 22%; reducing them to current global openness frontier reduces welfare losses by 13%

Castro-Vincenzi (2023)	Floods	Plant location and capacity	Automotive	World	Plant	Removing plant location and capacity decisions reduces firms' profits due to extreme precipitation by 5–6%
Balboni et al. (2023)	Floods	Suppliers' sourcing in production network	Manufacturing	Pakistan	Firm	Removing changes in sourcing behavior after 2012 floods increases damages in a 2015 flood scenario by 1%
Castro-Vincenzi et al. (2024)	Floods	Suppliers' sourcing in production network	Manufacturing	India	Firm	Allowing free trade increases average real wages with current climate risk by 6.5%
Adaptation over space and time						
Desmet and Rossi-Hansberg (2015)	Temperature	Trade, migration, innovation	Agriculture, manufacturing	World	Latitudes (hemisphere)	Migration restrictions increase welfare losses from climate change by 1.7%. Migration restrictions and trade barriers of 20% increase welfare losses from climate change by 3%

Continued

TABLE 2 Adaptation in quantitative general equilibrium models.—Cont'd

Reference	Climate shock	Adaptive margin	Sectoral heterogeneity	Geographical scope	Spatial resolution	Impact of adaptation
Shayegh (2017)	Temperature	Skill-heterogeneous migration	Agriculture, manufacturing	Africa, West Europe	Continent	Allowing for skilled and unskilled migration, output per capita increases by 3%
Conte et al. (2021)	Temperature	Trade, migration, sectoral specialization	Agriculture, non-agriculture	World	100x100km grid cell (1°)	50% increase in trade costs raises welfare losses from climate change globally, but decreases them in Canada and Siberia
Desmet et al. (2021)	Sea level rise	Trade, migration, innovation	One sector	World	100x100km grid cell (1°)	25% increase in migration, trade, or innovation costs raises welfare losses from climate change by 21%, 21%, and 5%, respectively
Burzyński et al. (2022)	Temperature, sea level rise, extreme weather events	Skill-heterogeneous migration	Agriculture, non-agriculture	World	5x5 km grid cell	Migration restrictions reduce share of extremely poor inhabitants under climate change by 5%

Bilal and Rossi-Hansberg (2023)	Storms, heat waves	Migration, capital investment, forward-looking anticipation	One sector	U.S.	ADM−2	Restricting ex ante anticipation reduces welfare losses from climate change by 0.9% (for workers) to 2.6% (for capitalists). Restricting migration reduces welfare losses by 2.2% (for workers) to 6% (for capitalists)
Rudik et al. (2024)	Temperature	Trade, migration, sectoral labor reallocation	Agriculture, manufacturing, services	U.S.	ADM−1	Allowing trade reduces welfare losses from climate change by 16%. Allowing migration and industry switching reduce welfare losses by 0.1%. All margins jointly reduce welfare losses by 25%

Notes: The table includes all studies that develop a quantitative general equilibrium model for which it is possible to extract estimates of the economic value of adaptation to climate change. In the "Spatial resolution" column, ADM-0 indicates country, ADM-1 indicates the first administrative unit (e.g., a U.S. state), ADM-2 indicates the second administrative unit (e.g., a U.S. county). Rudik et al. (2024) allow for sectoral heterogeneity of climate damages across three sectors (agriculture, manufacturing, services), but they account for a granular set of 20 industries within these three sectors and allow for industry switching and worker unemployment in their calibration. Other studies (e.g., Bakkensen, 2022; Bakkensen et al., 2023; Cruz, 2021; Cruz and Rossi-Hansberg, 2023; Hong et al., 2023) include adaptation within the model, as discussed in the main text, but do not directly quantify the impact of modeled adaptation margins, and are therefore omitted here.

changes in savings and investment. In a global sample, Hong et al. (2023) introduce learning and adaptation into a continuous-time stochastic general equilibrium model with disaster risks, showing that adaptation changes as society learns about climate change and demonstrating that optimal adaptation involves a mix of private adaptation at the firm level and public spending. Finally, Fried (2022) uncovers adaptation benefits of 11% using a dynamic general equilibrium model in the context of severe storms in the U.S., where benefits are derived from both private ex ante adaptation capital investment and public ex post adaptation through U.S. federal disaster policy.

A second stream of papers focuses on adaptation through financial instruments, generally using dynamic small open economy models with a representative agent. Borensztein et al. (2017), Mallucci (2022) and Phan and Schwartzman (2024) study adaptation to climate change in sovereign bond markets, where adaptation is represented as purchasing bonds with disaster clauses (called CAT bonds). These papers highlight the importance of financial frictions, as CAT bonds are highly effective at mitigating welfare effects of hurricanes, but are not readily available in all vulnerable nations. Bakkensen et al. (2023) integrate heterogeneous beliefs and learning as drivers of adaptation to sea level rise where agents make adaptation decisions regarding mortgage leverage and maturities in the collateralized debt market. More pessimistic buyers are more likely to leverage and use longer maturity mortgage contracts to finance the purchase of properties exposed to sea level rise risk.

An important feature that only few papers consider – but which we revisit in detail in Sections 3.2 and 4 – is the role of wealth and income heterogeneity in determining adaptive responses and resulting welfare effects of climate change. Van Der Straten (2024) studies the implications of sea level rise and floods for household wealth and welfare in Florida accounting for adaptation through home ownership and investment in home protection (e.g., stilts). The author introduces credit constraints for low-income households and shows that climate change worsens wealth inequality when adaptation is less accessible for credit-constrained households. Fried (2024) highlights the importance of income inequality in determining U.S. climate damages induced by higher temperatures, as wealthier individuals can invest more heavily in energy and equipment for heating and cooling. She finds that aggregate welfare losses induced by climate change accounting for income heterogeneity are almost four times larger than in a representative agent simulation.

3.1.2.2 Adaptation over space

Recent advances in spatial general equilibrium modeling have enabled investigations into margins of adaptation to climate change that reallocate economic activity across space, such as migration, trade, and knowledge spillovers. These models have progressively implemented more realistic and detailed embeddings of empirically-grounded spatial relationships, and some also include temporal dynamics. As with the models discussed in the previous subsection, the use of counterfactual simulations that restrict or constrain particular margins of adaptation enable insights into the welfare implications of adaptation that are generally infeasible in reduced form approaches. Of course, these models also require structural assumptions that may be difficult to evaluate, particularly at global scale. Here we review key findings from these analyses as they pertain to adaptation, summarizing results in Table 2. We refer the reader to Desmet and Rossi-Hansberg (2024) for a comprehensive review.

There are three major differences in scope between these analyses and the structural literature modeling adaptation only over time (see second two panels in Table 2). First, while the intertemporal adaptation literature has focused on natural disasters, most spatial studies rely on temperature as the major climate shock, with some notable exceptions that include sea level rise (Burzyński et al., 2022; Desmet et al., 2021), storms (Burzyński et al., 2022), and heat waves (Bilal and Rossi-Hansberg, 2023). Second, most of the studies have a global geographical scope, although the spatial unit of analysis varies from country (Costinot et al., 2016; Gouel and Laborde, 2021; Nath, 2023) to grid cell level (Burzyński et al., 2022; Conte et al., 2021; Desmet et al., 2021). Third, these papers introduce sectoral heterogeneity, although often only differentiating between agriculture and non-agriculture.

The first contributions in this literature focused on migration. For example, Desmet and Rossi-Hansberg (2015) introduce dynamic and spatial linkages into a general equilibrium model to quantify the adaptive role of migration, as well as trade and innovation, in a one-dimensional model that focuses on global warming across latitudes. To our knowledge, this was the first paper to document the welfare consequences of restricting the adaptive margins of migration and international trade under climate change. Importantly, the approach includes general equilibrium forces – wage adjustments and agglomeration economies – that render the direction of such restrictions on welfare under climate change ambiguous. On average, the authors find that enabling individuals to move away from the regions most impacted by climate change dominates general equilibrium feedbacks, and that welfare effects of unrestricted adaptive migration are net positive.

More recent work on migration shows conflicting estimates of the magnitude of adaptive gains from migration. While Desmet and Rossi-Hansberg (2015) find that imposing restrictions on migration raises the welfare costs of warming temperatures by 1.7% globally, Rudik et al. (2024) find smaller values for the U.S. Shayegh (2017) models the effect of climate change on fertility rates, income inequality, and human capital accumulation in developing countries with skill-heterogeneous migration as the ex ante adaptation margin. Output per capita increases by 3% when skilled and unskilled migration is allowed. When modeling a broader suite of climate shocks, Burzyński et al. (2022) uncover migration benefits of 6% globally, while Desmet et al. (2021) find very large (21%) global benefits of migration in the case of sea level rise. In the case of storms and heat waves, Bilal and Rossi-Hansberg (2023) find a limited effect of ex ante anticipation and migration on aggregate U.S. losses from climate change, but a sizeable effect on welfare dispersion across counties, particularly for capital owners whose capital stock cannot move. In Africa, migration restrictions are found to increase welfare losses from climate change by 8% (Conte, 2023).

A second focus in this literature has been on agriculture. These models aim to assess how crop choice and international trade in agricultural products influence projected damages from climate change, as existing reduced form analyses ignored both margins of adaptation (Costinot et al., 2016; Gouel and Laborde, 2021). Estimated benefits from these adaptive margins differ across studies. While Costinot et al. (2016) find that shutting down crop switching raises the agricultural welfare losses from climate change by 300%, trade in agricultural goods is shown to be unimportant as an adaptive margin. In contrast, Gouel and Laborde (2021) find that free trade lowers agricultural damages from climate change by 27%, on par with the effects of crop switching.[20] In more recent work, Nath (2023) accounts for non-homothetic preferences and low substitutability between agricultural and non-agricultural production and recovers large adaptive benefits from trade in agriculture that reduce welfare losses from climate change by 22%. However, other recent work on agriculture recovers small (<1%) adaptive benefits from trade within Africa (Conte, 2023).

A third group of recent studies examines the welfare consequences of specific margins of adaptation that involve a spatial dimension at the firm level. These adaptation strategies include plant location choices (Castro-Vincenzi, 2023) and sourcing decisions from suppliers (Balboni et al., 2023; Castro-Vincenzi et al., 2024) in the case of floods globally, in India, and in Pakistan, respectively. These papers tend to find modest (1–6.5%) gains from adaptation, but these aggregate figures mask substantial heterogeneity recovered across regions. Because these studies differ in many dimensions, including spatial extent, sectoral disaggregation, and approaches to empirical calibration, it is difficult to decompose the sources of such large differences in estimated adaptive benefits. As we discuss below in Section 5, such a decomposition would have enormous value for informing emerging adaptation policy discussions.

3.1.3 Adaptation within integrated assessment models and process-based models

A final set of approaches to estimate aggregate global climate damages includes Integrated Assessment Models (IAMs) in which climate, economic activity, and adaptation are endogenously determined, as well as process-based models, in which climate change and/or adaptation are exogenously prescribed. IAMs have been used extensively to inform mitigation policy (Greenstone

---

[20] We note that each set of authors define the adaptive gains from trade slightly differently; we refer the reader to Gouel and Laborde (2021) for a more detailed discussion of the differences between these two papers.

et al., 2013), while other forms of process-based models are used to simulate various exogenous climate change and adaptation scenarios. These models include treatments of ex post and ex ante adaptation that either implicitly embed adaptation (as in the reduced form literature) or enumerate individual elements of $\boldsymbol{b}$ and/or $\boldsymbol{k}$ (as in the quantitative general equilibrium literature). Here, we focus our attention on how these two sets of models have accounted for adaptation; we refer the reader to Diaz and Moore (2017) and to Chapter 1 of this Volume by Dietz (2024) for more comprehensive reviews of IAMs, and to Martinich and Crimmins (2019) for a review of process-based models studying climate change damages.

3.1.3.1 Adaptation in integrated assessment models

The first generation of IAMs, pioneered by the Dynamic Integrated Climate-Economy (DICE) model (Nordhaus, 1992, 1993), did not explicitly include adaptation. Instead, adaptation was accounted for implicitly via "damage functions" – calibrated relationships between aggregate monetized damages from climate change and the magnitude of global mean surface temperature change – that sometimes were estimated inclusive of adaptation and its costs (Manne et al., 1995; Sokolov et al., 2005; Tol, 2006). In this implicit treatment of adaptation, both the costs of adaptation and the cost of residual damages were accounted for, although the two components were rarely distinguished from one another.[21] To help separate these effects, De Bruin et al. (2009) develop the Adaptation in DICE model to include adaptation as an explicit decision variable calibrated from empirical estimates. This model quantifies adaptation benefits that range between 9% and 45% of gross damages.

Other IAM damage functions also implicitly account for adaptation by exogenously imposing a process of adjustment to a changing climate represented through transition costs and transition time (Tol, 1995). This approach relies on modeling assumptions regarding the speed and costs of reducing climate damages through adaptation. For example, Moore and Diaz (2015) model adaptation using an exponential decay curve in which the short-run impacts of temperature on GDP growth declines over time and the long-run effect is zero.

In a third approach, IAMs enumerate adaptation margins explicitly as an endogenous variable that can be set at a specific level or optimized. For example, the World Induced Technical Change Hybrid (WITCH) model endogenously accounts for adaptive effects of learning-by-doing and R&D investments (Bosetti et al., 2006). The Climate Framework for Uncertainty, Negotiation and Distribution (FUND) model considers adaptation to sea level

[21] An important exception is the Policy Analysis of the Greenhouse Effect (PAGE) model, which introduces adaptive policies and their associated costs separately from the damage function (Hope et al., 1993).

rise in the form of coastal protection and/or displacement (Tol, 2007). Diaz (2016) calibrates the Coastal Impact and Adaptation Model (CIAM) to model the economic damages of sea level rise, finding that optimal protection and retreat reduce global damages by a factor of seven. Depsky et al. (2023) expand CIAM and calibrate adaptation to empirical levels (as opposed to optimal levels), finding adaptation benefits of 90–94%. Benveniste et al. (2020, 2022) extend FUND to include international migration and remittances as forms of adaptation, while Dietz and Lanz (2022) develop a new IAM to study adaptation through capital accumulation, demographic change, innovation, land-use change, and sectoral reallocation.

Computable General Equilibrium (CGE) models represent a related but complementary approach to IAMs for climate damage estimation. In contrast with IAMs, CGE models focus on the relations between different economic agents and are more sectorally disaggregated. Early examples study just one sector, such as health impacts (Bosello et al., 2006) or sea level rise (Bosello et al., 2007). These studies allow for ex post adaptation via adjustments to sectoral composition and trade patterns. Multi-regional CGE models link economic activities across sectors and regions through international trade and factor reallocation (Château et al., 2014; Dellink et al., 2019; Takakura et al., 2019). Some studies focus on adaptation in the energy sector, which propagates to the rest of the economy via price adjustments, including the Environmental Impact and Sustainability Applied General Equilibrium (ENVISAGE) model (Roson and van der Mensbrugghe, 2012), the Intertemporal Computable Equilibrium System (ICES) model (Eboli et al., 2010), the Global Responses to Anthropogenic Change in the Environment (GRACE) model (Aaheim et al., 2009, 2012), and the Intertemporal General Equilibrium Model (IGEM) (Jorgenson et al., 2004).

Finally, a set of IAMs has recently emerged with the objective of estimating the social cost of greenhouse gases (US Environmental Protection Agency, 2022). These are sometimes called "SC-IAM"s and they have very heterogeneous treatments of adaptation. Rennert et al. (2022) build and calibrate the Greenhouse Gas Impact Value Estimator (GIVE) model to obtain a measure of the social cost of carbon that accounts for damages to agriculture, energy, mortality, and sea level rise. However, only sea level rise damages obtained from the CIAM account for adaptation. Dietz et al. (2021) develop a meta-analytic IAM (META), which introduces eight climate tipping points but does not explicitly model adaptation. The Data-driven Spatial Climate Impact Model (DSCIM) (Climate Impact Lab, 2023) builds a spatially granular SC-IAM using damage functions across five sectors estimated inclusive of both adaptation costs and benefits (Carleton et al., 2022; Hultgren et al., 2022; Depsky et al., 2023; Rode et al., 2021; Rode et al., 2022).

3.1.3.2 Exogenous adaptation in process-based models

Process-based models combine a structural model with a set of exogenous climate and socioeconomic scenarios to estimate sector-specific climate damages accounting for adaptation costs and benefits. While adaptation is explicitly modeled in such analyses, adaptive adjustments are set exogenously as opposed to being determined endogenously based on optimizing behavior (as in quantitative general equilibrium models or some IAMs). Process-based models offer the advantage of accounting for high levels of complexity and nonlinear interactions (e.g., detailed hydrologic modeling) and of simulating the effects of many adaptation margins simultaneously. However, such models rely heavily on extensive parameterization, which often constrains the scope of the analysis; many papers are limited to studying specific sectors within the U.S.

Three sectors have been the focus of process-based models. The first is public infrastructure, where ex ante infrastructural investments or ex post repairs serve as key margins of adaptation. Analyses specifically investigate: roads (Chinowsky et al., 2013); bridges (Wright et al., 2012); railroads (Chinowsky et al., 2019); and urban drainage systems (Price et al., 2016). In a multi-climate risk multi-sector effort, Neumann et al. (2015) estimate impacts of temperature, precipitation, sea level rise, and coastal storms in the U.S., modeling and quantifying the benefits of multiple margins of adaptation, including abandonment, structure elevation, and a wide range of road, bridge, drainage, and property protection and repair investments. Similar multi-sector studies have focused on adaptation of roads, buildings, airports, railroads, and pipelines to changes in permafrost, precipitation, and precipitation-induced flooding in Alaska (Larsen et al., 2008; Melvin et al., 2017). Overall, these studies find substantial benefits from ex ante and ex post adaptation. In particular, ex ante adaptation is found to substantially reduce estimated climate damages, often with net benefits exceeding those from mitigating greenhouse gases directly, even when accounting for adaptation costs.

Second, process-based models have been used extensively to study the impacts of sea level rise and storm surge on coastal property, where ex ante adaptation margins include property elevation, armor, and abandonment. Examples include the U.S. National Coastal Property Model (Lorie et al., 2020; Neumann et al., 2011, 2015; Yohe et al., 1996) and the global Dynamic Interactive Vulnerability Assessment (DIVA) model (Hinkel and Klein, 2009; Hinkel et al., 2014), which has also been used to study floods in Indonesia and adaptation through spatial planning of new urban areas and flood protection enhancement (Muis et al., 2015).

Finally, agriculture and natural resources compose a third focus. Agronomic process-based models simulate climate damages accounting for adaptation margins including crop choice, production practices, land allocation, and international food trade (Beach et al., 2015; Mosnier et al., 2014). The impacts of climate change on water supply have been studied in municipal and industrial settings, in which adaptation is modeled as ex post reallocation across sectors (Henderson et al., 2015). Additionally, Wobus et al. (2017) assess the impact of changes in snowpack on recreation visits for skiing and snowboarding, where artificial snow-making is the simulated adaptation response.

3.2 The study of adaptation to inform adaptation policy

A completely distinct motivation for studying adaptation, and perhaps a more intuitive one, is to inform policies and programs that influence adaptation directly. To do so, a second body of literature focuses on directly recovering estimates of the second two adaptation terms on the righthand side of Equation (3). In some contexts, the goal may be only to identify interventions that lower damages due to climate change, regardless of the particular adaptation strategy undertaken by individuals, groups, firm, or governments – that is, to recover estimates of the lefthand side of expressions like Equation (4). In other settings, program evaluations are conducted explicitly to assess the demand for and efficacy of specific actions or technologies $\boldsymbol{b}$ or $\boldsymbol{k}$, to change the available information set to improve decisions, or to address market failures that are believed to constrain adaptation. In contrast to the literature reviewed in Section 3.1, this literature has focused less on the quantification of magnitudes and more on signing the impact of specific interventions. We discuss specific motivations behind adaptation policies, as well as their welfare justifications, below in Section 4. Regardless of the specific intervention setting or motivation, studying adaptation interventions directly requires isolating variation in the adaptation decision environment that will induce agents to reoptimize $\boldsymbol{b}^*$ and $\boldsymbol{k}^*$.

In this section, we first review the empirical methods used to isolate variation in adaptation in order to study specific adaptive actions and outcomes. We then review the literature studying adaptation interventions directly, categorizing studies by the source of variation in the adaptation decision environment that they employ or induce. We have chosen to include structural general equilibrium studies, IAMs, and process-based models in Section 3.1, though they contribute substantially to our understanding of the efficacy of specific adaptation margins and interventions. Because these models sit between the climate damages literature and the adaptation interventions literature, we review them only in one place (above).

3.2.1 Methodology

Empirical approaches used to study adaptation directly exploit both quasi-experimental and experimental variation in the decision environment. Here, we overview these methods and highlight a set of key methodological challenges confronting papers in this literature.

3.2.1.1 Direct empirical estimation of ex post and ex ante adaptation

As detailed above in Section 3.1, panel data fixed effects models are widely used to isolate plausibly random variation in the weather that can be leveraged to estimate climate damages. These models are then modified to implicitly account for ex ante adaptation (as previously discussed), but also to generate and study variation in adaptive investments directly. To achieve the latter, studies rely on variation in some factor we denote E which, as described in Section 2.3 above, restricts, enables, or otherwise shapes ex post or ex ante adaptation choices. E may represent a cash transfer (expanding the budget constraint y), a technology subsidy (changing prices of adaptation $\boldsymbol{p}$ or $\boldsymbol{r}$), a vocational training program, or myriad other interventions aimed at modifying adaptation choices and thus outcomes under climate change.

Studies directly investigating adaptive investments fall into one of two broad empirical classes. First, many studies regress a welfare-relevant outcome variable, such as agricultural revenues, household consumption, or health, on a measure of the weather, c, the factor E, and the interaction between these two:

$$u_{it} = \beta E_{it} + \gamma c_{it} + \delta E_{it} \times c_{it} + \alpha_i + \mu_t + \varepsilon_{it}, \tag{5}$$

where E is a source of variation unrelated to climate change and where fixed effects α_i and μ_t can be more elaborately defined if desired. In cases where E is randomized in an experiment, fixed effects may not be necessary and E varies across units i only. We note that Equation (5) is closely related to the "response heterogeneity" econometric approach detailed above in Section 3.1.1 and used to recover implicit estimates of ex ante adaptation. The key distinction between these methods is that E is an intervention exogenous to climate change that modifies adaptation choices, while the response heterogeneity approach interacts a measure of the weather c with a measure of the long-run climate C.[22] This distinction is critical, as E is generally a policy-relevant intervention that can be used to directly address adaptation needs; in contrast, C is determined by the global process of climate change and cannot be perturbed by policymakers seeking to improve adaptive responses to climate change.

The object of interest in Equation (5) is generally δ, which measures how the intervention or factor E influences the direct effect of weather c on a welfare-relevant outcome u. Using the notation from the framework in Section 2, while β recovers the direct welfare impact of the intervention $\frac{du}{dE}$, δ recovers $\frac{\partial^2 u}{\partial E \partial c}$, a measure of how the intervention changes welfare effects of a weather shock. Notably, these two objects are themselves insufficient for quantifying Equation (4), the effects of an intervention on the damages from

[22] In some studies, researchers combine approaches to include interactions with long-run climate C as well as other factors, such as irrigation (Hultgren et al., 2022) or income (Carleton et al., 2022).

long-run climate change – we discuss below how the literature can better bridge this gap. In Equation (5) and its many permutations, variation in E is intended to generate changes in ex post or ex ante adaptive behavior through changes in adaptation prices, income, information, market structure, and other frictions, although specific adaptive margins are not uncovered through estimation of this equation alone.

In panel data fixed effects models with wide spatial and temporal coverage, variation in E is often limited to cross-sectional comparisons only. This leaves many threats to identification of δ. For example, Carleton et al. (2022) estimate a model along the lines of (5) in which E_i is defined as the long-run average income per capita of an administrative unit, the outcome variable u_{it} is the mortality rate, and $\boldsymbol{c}$ is a vector of nonlinear temperature exposure variables in an unbalanced panel from 1968 to 2010 for 11,881 sub-national units in 40 countries. In contrast, RCTs experimentally manipulate E, enabling causal identification of both β and δ, generally with much smaller sample sizes. For example, Macours et al. (2022) estimate a similar specification combining experimental variation in a social protection program in Nicaragua with weather variability to uncover benefits of cash and training in reducing weather damages to consumption and income. They leverage variation from the RCT implemented in 2005 and measure outcomes in two follow-up surveys in 2006 and 2008.[23] Randomization in a sufficiently large sample creates balance on the characteristics of the treatment and control samples, including in their climate history and distribution of weather realizations before and after treatment.[24] This makes inference straightforward: δ in Equation (5) (and (6), below) identifies the causal effect of an adaptation intervention, conditional on a weather draw.

In Equation (5), β represents the marginal effect of the intervention or factor E under average climate conditions (as long as c is defined relative to mean conditions, which is common). Estimation of β and δ jointly therefore enables the researcher to uncover the extent to which aggregate impacts of an intervention manifest through mitigating losses under adverse weather. In contrast, in some panel data regression settings, E may be collinear with fixed effects and therefore its uninteracted effect (first term in Equation (5)) is omitted. This allows the researcher to investigate how the factor or intervention E shapes weather responses, but not its average treatment effect on u. The implications of this difference for adaptation policy are discussed below in Section 5.

---

[23] Their approach differs in that they do not use quasi-random weather variation in the reduced form estimation of Equation (5), but use block averages of self-reported shocks and instrument them with weather variation. Their RCT was implemented in 44 blocks across six municipalities.

[24] Papers reporting on randomized trials conventionally include statistics testing balance on key covariates between treatment and control. For adaptation papers, particular emphasis should be placed on balance on the full distribution of long term weather and short run weather shocks.

While Equation (5) is useful for studying the impact of various interventions on climate damages, it sheds little light on the specific adaptive actions, behaviors, or investments that underlie the impacts (i.e., it says little about individual elements in the $\boldsymbol{b}$ and/or $\boldsymbol{k}$ vectors). That is, these studies recover either $\frac{du}{dE}$ or $\frac{\partial^2 u}{\partial E \partial c}$, but not $\frac{\partial^2 \boldsymbol{b}}{\partial E \partial c}$ – the second term from Equation (4) that determines how an intervention alters a specific adaptive decision. To unpack which ex post or ex ante adaptation decisions are made in response to interventions, a second empirical class of regressions takes the following form:

$$b_{it} = \beta E_{it} + \gamma c_{it} + \delta E_{it} \times c_{it} + \mu_t + \varepsilon_{it}, \tag{6}$$

where all variables are defined as above and b_{it} represents one element of either the $\boldsymbol{b}$ or $\boldsymbol{k}$ vector (e.g., irrigation use, seed varietal choices, etc.). The objects of interest are β, γ, and, in particular, δ, which represents $\frac{\partial^2 b}{\partial E \partial c}$, the key component in Equation (4) used to assess how an intervention changes the welfare impacts of climate change.

This specification is estimated both in panel data settings as well as in randomized experiments and variation in E can be across time and space or be limited to cross-sectional variation only (in which case E would have subscript i only). For example, Cattaneo and Peri (2016) use international migration data to estimate a version of Equation (6) in which migration rate is the outcome variable and E is an indicator for the bottom quartile of the GDP per capita distribution, which reduces the migration propensity under hotter temperatures due to liquidity constraints.[25] In the social protection RCT mentioned previously, Macours et al. (2022) augment their estimation of Equation (5) with a version of Equation (6) estimated for multiple left-hand side variables, including non-agricultural wage work, migration and business creation. This allows the authors to uncover the mechanisms, i.e., the elements in $\boldsymbol{b}$ and $\boldsymbol{k}$, through which the intervention facilitates income and consumption smoothing in response to shocks.

In some cases, the adaptation technologies $\boldsymbol{b}$ and $\boldsymbol{k}$ studied in Equation (6) are purposely designed to reduce climate sensitivity under deteriorating weather conditions (as opposed to raising welfare generally). The question of interest is then how to induce take up or use of the technology or behavior. In such settings, researchers may omit the weather variable c from the regression entirely, estimating average treatment effects of E only. For example, Aker and Jack (2023) show that an agricultural training intervention in Niger dramatically increased adoption of a water-saving agricultural technique using a version of Equation (6) in which c is omitted. This is only useful for understanding adaptation to the extent that there is strong prior evidence that the technology

[25] Benonnier et al. (2022) go one step further and show that irrigation access offsets the temperature-migration liquidity constraint effect.

of interest lowers the welfare cost of weather conditions that will become more frequent under climate change.

Much of the literature estimates versions of Equation (6) in which b represents an ex post adaptation strategy (e.g., energy use, irrigation practices, daily labor decisions), but interventions E may also alter ex ante adaptive decisions $\boldsymbol{k}$. For example, Lane (2024) estimates the effect of eligibility for guaranteed credit lines (E) in Bangladesh, focusing on changes to ex ante agricultural investments as outcome variables, including fertilizer and pesticides investments, input costs, and non-agricultural investments. This is motivated by the fact that guaranteed credit, which provides loan access conditional on a flood, can facilitate adaptation by encouraging farmers to make more costly adaptation choices, which they might have been unwilling to adopt in the presence of weather risk.

For Equations (5) and (6), causally identifying the "adaptation effect" of policy interventions δ requires exogenous variation both in the adaptation environment E and in weather c. Below, we discuss two empirical challenges that this literature confronts while aiming to assess and inform adaptation interventions.

3.2.1.2 Empirical challenge #1: Sources of variation in weather

The identification of weather variation in Equations (5) and (6) relies on the assumption that deviations from long run averages within a location are as good as randomly assigned. In these regressions, identification comes from either variation within location over time (time series variation) or across locations within time (cross sectional variation), or some combination of the two. When these equations are estimated in long panel data settings, weather variation is always time series, as discussed in detail above in Section 3.1. However, in studies that exploit the random or quasi-random roll-out of adaptation interventions, sufficient time series variation is not always available. Such studies, common in the literature that focuses on adaptation intervention, are forced to leverage different sources of variation in the weather, which come with important limitations.

Limited variation in weather.

A key limitation that emerges with better identification of adaptation interventions E is that the range of variation in weather is often constrained. This is true because exogenous variation in access to adaptation typically comes from policy variation or a randomized trial, which often limit the scale of implementation to a single country or sub-country region. In many cases, this implies highly correlated climate histories across locations in the sample, limiting the between-location variation in weather realizations c_{it} used to identify γ and δ. When outcome data come from primary data collection, as is the case for many randomized controlled trials, a single follow up survey is typical.[26] Even when researchers rely on administrative data sources or third party surveys, the number of outcome observations is often limited by infrequent data collection (e.g., decadal censuses) or limited time since the intervention. This constrains the within-location time variation in weather realizations c_{it} that can be used to identify γ and δ. In general, studies focusing on isolating random variation in E rarely investigate or report the resulting variation in c, but this variation is critical to credible identification of δ and to its interpretation. For example, a statistically significant δ may be the result of just a few outlier c shocks, or may be relevant only over a very limited range of c. We suggest possible solutions to this challenge in Section 5.

Variation in weather rarely linked to long-run climate change.

The historical weather shocks studied in the adaptation interventions literature often do not reflect future weather under climate change, limiting their relevance for long-run climate change. While climate impacts studies reviewed in Section 3.1 combine econometric estimation with future projections of climate change to directly assess how weather responses from the historical record will change outcomes under future climate change, studies focused on adaptation rarely make this link explicitly. In other words, while $\frac{\partial u}{\partial \boldsymbol{b}}\frac{\partial \boldsymbol{b}^*}{\partial c}$ (or its counterpart for ex ante adaptation $\boldsymbol{k}^*$) may be identified in Equation (3), $\frac{dc}{dC}$ is often ignored.

Climate models can be used to guide researchers toward studying the weather variation most relevant to a particular region in the future. However, in some cases the models lack the necessary spatial resolution for localized analyses, or they exhibit wide uncertainty bands or substantial disagreement across models (Lee et al., 2021).[27] In any case, such model forecasts are rarely used to inform the type of shock analyzed. Even more problematically, the relevant variation for climate change may not exist in the study observations. For example, in a region that is growing wetter (like many parts of Africa), the adverse weather shocks of the past may have come in the form of droughts, while the adverse shocks of the future might come in the form of floods. If floods are particularly infrequent in the past, then it is with low odds that one appears in the short window during which treatment effects are identified.

This disconnect between the weather shocks analyzed and the changes in weather shocks projected under climate change raises questions about the ability of studies in this literature to inform adaptation interventions that will be effective under long-run climate change. We return to this point to offer recommendations in Section 5.

[26] McKenzie (2012) calls for repeated outcome data collection to reduce noise in stochastic measures like agricultural production or firm profits. The inverse argument can be made – with the same recommendation for repeated outcome measurement – when the interest is in characterizing an important component of the volatility in these outcomes.

[27] This is particularly true for precipitation, which is very widely used as the variable of interest c in the studies investigating adaptation directly.

Functional forms of weather responses.

The functional form used to model weather plays a crucial role in the identification and interpretation of analyses in the adaptation interventions literature, just as it does in the climate damages literature in Section 3.1. Specifically, the estimation of different weather functional forms corresponds to implicit underlying assumptions regarding beliefs and expectation formation. There is a stark contrast between the functional forms used in studies with large spatial and temporal extents versus those with more limited weather variation. When weather variation is minimal, for example due to primary data collection in an RCT, the most common approach is to compute weather shocks as anomalies above or below a certain threshold, often defined in standard deviations from a long-run mean. Using a time-invariant baseline assumes stationarity of the weather distribution. Different time intervals used to compute long-run means imply different assumptions on the belief formation process of the agents and the speed of adjustment to the climate distribution.

Such assumptions regarding belief formation and stationarity are rarely discussed, made explicit, or empirically justified in this literature, and they differ starkly across studies. To demonstrate this heterogeneity, Fig. 1 plots the length of time used to define the long-run climate baseline (y-axis) against the threshold used to define a weather "shock" (x-axis) for all adaptation papers we reviewed that estimate effects of weather anomalies on outcomes of interest ($N = 20$). The time frame over which the long-run mean is computed varies from a decade in Adhvaryu et al. (2024), who study conditional cash transfers in Mexico, to more than sixty years in Rocha and Soares (2015), who study water and sanitation infrastructure in Brazil. Notably, no paper we reviewed includes a robustness analysis in which multiple baseline periods are used to define the long-run mean.[28] Anomalies are constructed in terms of standard deviations or percentile deviations from the long-run mean and similarly vary substantially across papers. The definition of "negative" shocks ranges from those falling in the 5th percentile of the long-run distribution to the 50th percentile, while "positive" shocks range from the 75th to the 97.5^{th} percentile. Only Premand and Stoeffler (2022) show robustness to altering the cut-offs used to compute anomalies. Instead of using discrete shock variables, some studies employ a continuous measure of weather deviations from baseline, such as the degrees of temperature difference from the long-run mean; such studies

[28] While these studies do not investigate adaptation explicitly, Moore et al. (2019) show that climate-related social media posting behavior reacts differently to temperature anomalies depending on how the baseline period is defined. Additionally, Kahn et al. (2021) alter the definition (20-, 30-, or 40-year moving averages) in a cross-country GDP-temperature regression to study adaptation implicitly.

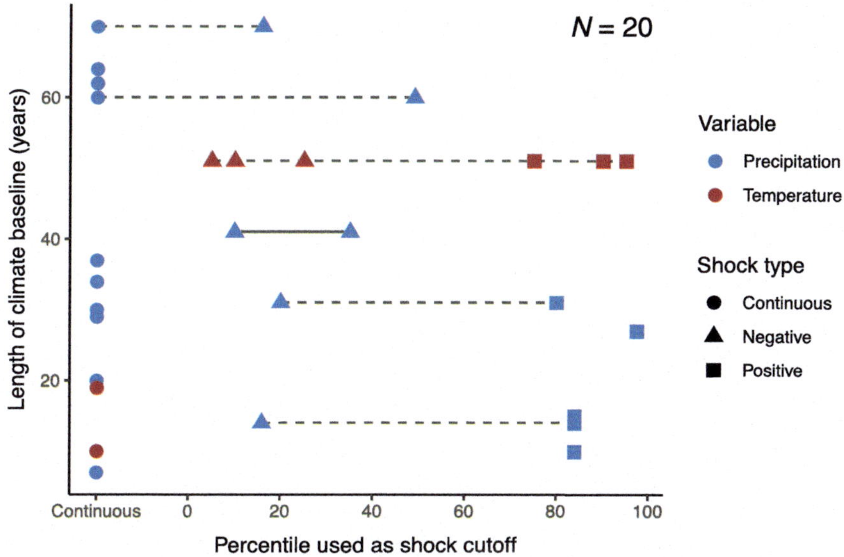

FIG. 1 Weather functional form assumptions in studies of adaptation interventions. Notes: Each point represents one definition of a weather anomaly or shock used in the 20 studies that normalize weather variation with respect to a long-run climate norm (underlying data are reported in Appendix Table A1). Point color denotes the weather variable used (temperature or precipitation). Point shape denotes whether the anomaly captures positive shocks, negative shocks, or is continuous. Dashed lines connect multiple definitions used within the same study. A solid line is used for Premand and Stoeffler (2022), who show robustness across negative shock thresholds at every integer from the 10th to the 35th percentile. Positive and negative shock definitions measured in standard deviations have been assigned percentile values using properties of the normal distribution, such that a positive shock threshold at 1 standard deviation above the mean is assumed to fall at the 84th percentile.

are indicated as "continuous" on the far left of the figure. The baseline period used to define the long-run mean differs substantially across these studies as well.[29]

An example highlighting the implications of highly heterogeneous weather functional form decisions is illustrated in Fig. 2. Specifically, this figure uses monthly maximum temperature data obtained from the European Centre for Medium-Range Weather Forecasts Reanalysis v5 (ERA5) for Punjab, India to plot the total number of positive temperature heat shocks that would be observed in a given sample (y-axis) against the percentile of

[29] Note that the period used to define the long run mean around which anomalies are measured is generally far longer than the length of the panel used to estimate impacts. Of the 20 studies shown in Fig. 1, all but three include time fixed effects, which further de-mean the dataset. This affects interpretation of the γ and δ terms in e.g., Equation (5), which – in the presence of time fixed effects – represent deviations from i's average anomaly over the panel period.

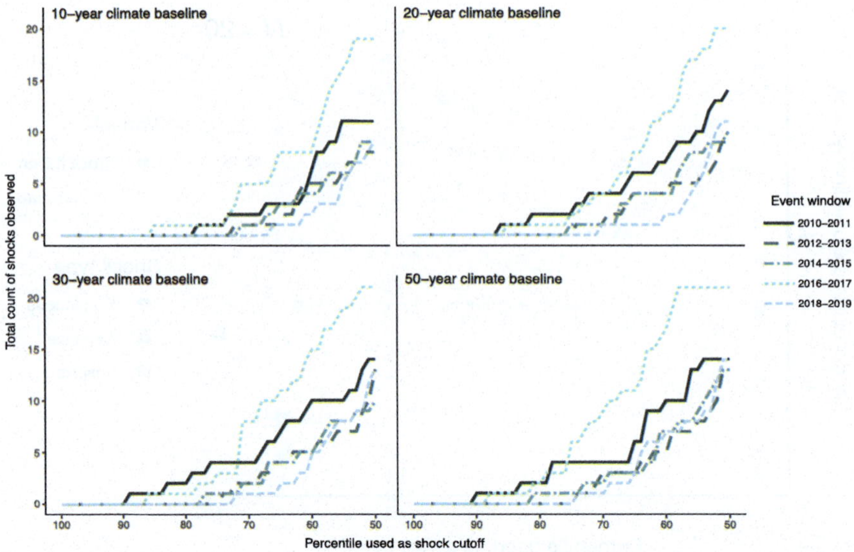

FIG. 2 Sensitivity of weather variation to functional form assumptions. *Notes*: Each line plots the total number of anomalous months observed within a 2-year event window against the threshold used to define the anomaly relative to the historical temperature distribution (in units of percentiles). Percentiles on the x-axis are defined by calendar month and use a dynamic baseline climate period covering the 10, 20, 30, or 50 years preceding the start of a given event window (each subplot uses a different baseline climate time period). Temperature data are daily maximum temperatures obtained from the European Centre for Medium-Range Weather Forecasts Reanalysis v5 (ERA5) for the city of Kapurthala in Punjab, India, and are aggregated to the monthly level.

the long-run distribution used to determine the definition of a shock (x-axis). Each line shows a different possible study window, and each subplot indicates a different time period used to define the climate baseline. These plots show that both the baseline time period and the percentile cutoff chosen dramatically influence the number of shocks observed in a given sample. With shorter baseline periods, a study sample is less likely to contain an extreme shock, particularly if it happens to fall in cooler years. The discrete jumps shown in each panel indicate that the choice of the threshold can considerably influence whether a given location-month falls into "treatment" or "control" weather conditions. This one case study demonstrates the importance of conducting robustness when key functional form choices must be made without empirical justification.

3.2.1.3 Empirical challenge # 2: External validity

Looking to the past to learn about the future presents a natural problem of external validity. This challenge exists in the climate damages literature discussed in Section 3.1, but can be even more pronounced in the literature that focuses explicitly on identifying changes in the adaptation decision environment. As noted earlier, none of the papers that we have identified project adaptation impacts into the future using estimated interaction term(s) and climate model projections. While these projections are important for understanding the intervention's value under future climate change, conducting such a counterfactual confronts several potential pitfalls that need to be overcome.

First, the weather shocks identified in historical data and used to assess adaptation interventions may not represent the types of shocks relevant under future climate change. Second, and related, the relevant adaptation margin may be sensitive to the distribution of shocks. For example, while health care access may reduce the effect of currently extreme temperatures on health (Cohen and Dechezleprêtre, 2022; Mullins and White, 2020; Nyqvist et al., 2023), whether such public services will similarly soften the impacts of the weather shocks that will become more common in the future is unclear. Repeated exposure to adverse conditions like heat and drought may result in a level of malnutrition or disease exposure that renders public health services far less effective than they are today. More extreme temperatures and longer heatwaves may undermine refrigeration for drug supply or the benefits of hospitalization, or conversely, infrastructure and facilities may innovate and adapt themselves to future climate change. In small-scale case studies, the trade-off between in-sample variation for identification and observing the relevant extremes to make informed projections is particularly stark (as illustrated in Fig. 2). While never fully solved, the challenge of using historical weather shocks to inform future projections has been a focus of methodological innovation in the climate damages literature reviewed in Section 3.1 – we discuss approaches to applying these insights to the adaptation interventions literature in Section 5.

3.2.2 *Literature evaluating adaptation interventions*

Here we review the findings of the empirical analyses estimating versions of Equations (5) and (6). We categorize these studies into three groups based on three key sources of variation in the decision environment: *(i)* variation in the costs of adopting specific $\boldsymbol{b}$ or $\boldsymbol{k}$ actions, i.e., lowering prices $\boldsymbol{p}$ or $\boldsymbol{r}$ in Equations (1) and (2); *(ii)* variation in the level or volatility of the income constraint y_t and $\bar{y}$ in Equations (1) and (2); and *(iii)* variation in other determinants of adaptation decisions, such belief updating or weather forecasts. In all of these cases, variation in the decision environment induced by an intervention E causes variation in adaptation decisions, allowing researchers both to study the impacts of adaptation and the effect of interventions to relax constraints to adaptation. We discuss each in turn here.

3.2.2.1 Changes to adaptation technology access or its price p, r

A set of papers using the estimation strategies laid out in Equations (5) and (6) rely on spatial and/or temporal variation in access to or prices of specific adaptation behaviors or technologies to identify the extent and efficacy of adaptation. For example, using long panel datasets, multiple studies have shown that the agricultural yields-temperature relationship is moderated by access to irrigation (Butler and Huybers, 2013; Hultgren et al., 2022). Similarly, the mortality-temperature relationship is moderated by doctors per capita, share of the population with residential electricity, and share with residential air conditioning in the U.S. (Barreca et al., 2016), and by access to health care and quality of the service in Colombia (Helo Sarmiento, 2023). While these papers are informative of how access to particular technologies or resources moderate climate damages, they are prone to endogeneity in E, the variation used to induce changes in $\boldsymbol{b}$ or $\boldsymbol{k}$, complicating interpretation and policy implications. For example, adoption of irrigation may be driven by unobserved heterogeneity in agricultural profitability, access to credit, or farmer characteristics, which may also influence climate sensitivity for other reasons.

To mitigate such endogeneity concerns, a related set of papers uses a similar empirical framework but with *exogenous* variation in an intervention E that improves access to an adaptation technology. Applications in agriculture include randomized access to trial seed packets and training sessions on drought tolerant seeds (Boucher et al., 2021) and a flood-tolerant rice variety (Emerick et al., 2016), which were shown to provide protection against adverse weather events, mitigate long-term drops in farm productivity, and/or encourage ex ante adoption of improved farm practices. In health, exogenous variation in access to technologies that boost baseline health, such as the free provision of vitamin A supplementation, have been shown to reduce damages from negative climate shocks, like tornadoes (Gunnsteinsson et al., 2022). Other examples in health include: the introduction of a community health care worker program in India that moderates the infant mortality-temperature relationship (Banerjee and Maharaj, 2020); the deployment of community health care workers in Uganda that reduces the risk of infant mortality following rainfall deficit seasons (Björkman Nyqvist et al., 2023); the roll-out of primary care services provided by Community Health Centers in the U.S. in the 1960s and 1970s that moderates the mortality-heat and mortality-cold relationships (Mullins and White, 2020); and policies that increase access to health care for low-income households in Mexico in early 2000s also moderate the mortality-heat and mortality-cold relationships (Cohen and Dechezleprêtre, 2022). Using gun control policies in the U.S., Colmer and Doleac (2023) show that more prohibitive concealed-carry laws attenuate the homicide-temperature relationship.

As discussed above in Section 3.2.1, for some technologies that are explicitly designed for adaptation, particularly in already marginalized climates, the empirical strategy may not incorporate the weather variation explicitly, and thus focus on estimating versions of Equation (5) and/or (6) without weather controls or interactions. Examples include studies on the adoption and efficacy of: a flood-tolerant rice variety in India (Dar et al., 2013); salinity-tolerant seeds in Bangladesh (Patel, 2024); and rainwater harvesting technologies in Niger (Aker and Jack, 2023). These papers randomly vary access to adaptation technologies and study the welfare consequences in an experimental setting. By heavily subsidizing the access to these technologies, these studies do not inform what the averted climate damages would be in a counterfactual world where technologies were accessible only at the market price, nor do they directly project adaptation benefits under climate change (as previously discussed).

3.2.2.2 Changes to income *y* or access to social insurance programs that reduce income variability

Instead of lowering the cost of a specific adaptation technology, other papers relax the opportunity cost of adaptation through changes to the budget constraint. With higher incomes, agents solving Equations (1) and (2) re-optimize and make new adaptive decisions $\boldsymbol{b}^*$ or $\boldsymbol{k}^*$. Agents may similarly re-optimize when provided access to social programs, such as subsidized insurance or conditional cash transfers, which smooth y_t over time and/or states of the world.

Variation in income in randomized control trials.

In some cases, variation in the budget constraint comes from a randomized controlled trial. For example, random assignment to treatment generates variation in income constraints through cash transfers in several studies. Transfers are found to mitigate the effect of rainfall anomalies on consumption and food security in Zambia (Asfaw et al., 2017); mitigate welfare effects of rainfall shocks in rural Niger through savings, asset accumulation, and income smoothing in agriculture and off-farm activities (Premand and Stoeffler, 2022); and provide protection against weather shocks in Nicaragua by facilitating income smoothing and diversification of economic activities when bundled with productive investments or vocational training (Macours et al., 2022). Ultra-poor graduation programs, which provide a bundle of support including assets (usually livestock) and training, have a similar effect in moderating the negative impacts of droughts (Hirvonen et al., 2023). Specifically, in contrast to control households, treated households use enhanced household savings to mitigate the adverse effect of drought on diet, nutrition, and intimate partner violence. Anticipatory cash transfers provided to households forecasted to experience extreme floods in Bangladesh reduce the likelihood of spending a day without eating during the flood and increase child and adult food consumption and wellbeing after the flood (Pople et al., 2021). In contrast, however, anticipatory cash transfers in Mongolia do not have any effect on assets, income, adaptive investments, or consumption (Mogge et al., 2024). Cash transfers conditioned on weather realizations have not, to our knowledge, been rigorously evaluated.

Quasi-random variation in income.

Other papers have leveraged quasi-random variation in budget constraints, sometimes borrowing identification strategies from prior published papers. These include studies using the world's largest workfare program, the National Rural Employment Guarantee Scheme in India, to quantify how it: modulates the effect of: temperature on test scores (Garg et al., 2020); temperature on infant mortality (Banerjee and Maharaj, 2020); and adverse monsoon rainfall on conflict (Fetzer, 2020). Other papers have used at-scale cash transfer programs as a source of quasi-experimental variation in income, and find that the roll-out of the PROGRESA/*Oportunidades* conditional cash transfer program in Mexico only modestly decreased the sensitivity of intergroup killings by drug-trafficking organizations to temperature (Baysan et al., 2019), but significantly attenuated the effects of higher same-day temperature on homicides (Garg et al., 2020) and of children's exposure to adverse rainfall shocks on educational and labor market outcomes (Adhvaryu et al., 2024), while also mitigating the impact of drought on households' caloric intake of vegetables, fruits, and animal products (Hou, 2010). Similarly, the roll-out of a large-scale cash transfer in Indonesia, the Program *Keluarga Harapan*, and a randomized experiment of the same program, have been found to reduce the impact of rainfall shocks on suicides (Christian et al., 2019). Knippenberg and Hoddinott (2019) use Ethiopia's Productive Safety Net Program to document a substantial reduction in the impact of drought shocks on food security due to the program, which fully eliminates the adverse impact on food security within two years. Christian et al. (2019) combine exposure to a cyclone with the staggered rollout of the Odisha Rural Livelihoods Program, and find that program participation mitigated negative impacts of the cyclone on household nonfood expenditure and women's consumption, but not on food expenditure. Overall, the majority of studies using random or quasi-random variation in the budget constraint find that higher incomes lead to meaningful reductions in the damages caused by adverse weather.

Cross-sectional variation in income.

In many panel data settings with large spatial and/or temporal scope, quasi-random variation in the budget constraint is not available. Thus, many studies simply use cross-sectional variation in income to identify δ, similar to the use of cross-sectional variation in the long-run climate used in many of the econometric methods discussed in Section 3.1.1. In one of its first applications, Dell et al. (2012) find heterogeneous effects of temperature on GDP growth between poor and rich countries. Subsequent studies with a similar application find contrasting results: Burke and Hsiang (2015b) and Kahn et al. (2021) cannot reject the hypothesis of no differential temperature effects on poor versus rich countries.[30] Carleton et al. (2022) find that GDP per capita moderates the effect of heat on mortality across 40 countries, and Bakkensen and Mendelsohn (2016) find a large income elasticity of damages from cyclones in most of the world, with the exception of the U.S., where damages are high regardless of income. In a meta-analysis, Carleton et al. (2016) show that the conflict-climate relationship is moderated in studies conducted in wealthier regions of the globe. Others find that adaptive behaviors are increasing in income, such as the use of electricity on hot days (Auffhammer, 2022; Rode et al., 2021). However, income may not always be beneficial for mitigating climate damages – Hultgren et al. (2022) shows that staple crop yields are *more* sensitive to heat in wealthier regions of the globe, possible due to seed varietal differences and/or access to subsidized insurance (Annan and Schlenker, 2015), a topic we return to in Section 4.

Identifying specific margins of adaptation.

Evaluation of these variations in financial resources through the estimation of Equation (5) informs the "reduced-form" effect of the policy and its potential climate sensitivity benefits. With additional measurement of the specific changes in $\boldsymbol{b}$ and $\boldsymbol{k}$ induced by a relaxation of the budget constraint, these studies have the potential to offer additional policy-relevant insights by estimating Equation (6) (and thus enabling the calculation of the righthand side of Equation (4)). For example, measurement of the income elasticity and welfare benefits of specific adaptation strategies is informative of agents' preferences across different alternatives. Of course, if strategies are very heterogeneous or otherwise hard to measure, this can be difficult in practice. Additionally, to inform the cost effectiveness of adaptation policies that target a single b or k, studies need to both estimate the effect of an intervention on adaptation (e.g., $\frac{\partial^2 \boldsymbol{b}^*}{\partial E \partial c}$), as well as how that adaptive decision changes a welfare relevant outcome (e.g., $\frac{\partial u}{\partial \boldsymbol{b}}$). For example, Premand and Stoeffler (2022) show that cash transfers in Niger strengthen poor households' ability to mitigate the welfare effects of drought shocks. To understand which adaptive margins are re-optimized after this exogenous change in the decision environment, they show an increase in household capacity to smooth income when shocks occur, with intensification of agricultural activities and more off-farm activities. This suggests that interventions targeting these adjustment margins may provide adaptation benefits consistent with household preferences.

Insights from the consumption smoothing literature.

This collection of studies has some parallels to a long literature in development economics that uses weather shocks as a source of variation to

[30] One possible reason for this discrepancy in findings is functional form; Burke and Hsiang (2015a) estimate a nonlinear relationship between growth and temperature and argue that poor countries are estimated to be more sensitive in Dell et al. (2012) only because they are on average hotter than wealthier nations.

understand both formal and informal ex ante and ex post consumption smoothing strategies. A primary objective of this literature has been to test a null hypothesis of full insurance in the absence of functioning insurance markets, but some papers also analyze heterogeneity in the degree of smoothing. We note two insights from this literature that are particularly relevant for studying climate adaptation.

First, idiosyncratic shocks are more easily insured than are aggregate shocks (Townsend, 1994, 1995). That said, aggregate shocks may also be partially insured, though more often through private actions than through informal risk sharing strategies within villages or among kin (Corno and Voena, 2023; Kazianga and Udry, 2006; Morduch, 1995). For example, even in the absence of formal financial institutions, precautionary savings or buffer stocks can smooth the consumption response to "normal" income fluctuations (e.g., Paxson, 1992; Rosenzweig and Binswanger, 1993), though a changing climate may undermine the effectiveness of these strategies. Ex ante, in addition to precautionary savings, households diversify their income, migrate, marry into families with minimally-correlated shocks, enter into labor contracts that share risk between employers and employees, and a variety of other strategies. Ex post, they adjust labor supply and income sources, migrate, and receive remittances (Jack and Suri, 2014; Kochar, 1999; Yang and Choi, 2007). While these strategies do not always result in full smoothing – i.e., consumption still varies with weather realizations – they do speak to the potential for private actions and investments to make considerable progress toward reducing vulnerability to weather shocks.

Second, this literature has documented the importance of general equilibrium effects of weather shocks and of behavioral responses to those shocks. For example, Jayachandran (2006) shows that weather-induced productivity shocks lead to lower wages, which are further lowered by inelastic labor supply. This acts as a transfer to landowners from laborers, who tend to be poorer, reducing the income volatility of the former and increasing that of the latter. In settings with better-developed infrastructure to support adaptation – more banks and lower migration costs – the wage response to productivity shocks is dampened. Accounting for these general equilibrium and distributional consequences of adaptation can be difficult in smaller-scale partial equilibrium studies.

3.2.2.3 Changes to the broader adaptation decision environment

A third way of studying adaptation choices and their impacts is through policies or other interventions designed to relax frictions in the broader adaptation decision environment. We group such constraints into the following categories: behavioral and informational, associated markets such as credit or insurance, and market structure. In Section 4, we return to the question of whether such frictions or constraints justify policy intervention from a welfare or efficiency standpoint.

Information, beliefs and behavioral biases.

As articulated in Equation (2), ex ante climate adaptation depends directly on beliefs about future weather realizations, which in turn depend on the information environment and on individuals' belief formation processes. As discussed in Section 3.1.1, a growing number of papers show behavioral and market responses to weather forecasts. While these papers help implicitly identify ex ante adaptation when assessing climate change damages, they are also relevant to the study of adaptation interventions: changes in forecast information provide a source of exogenous variation in the decision environment (Burlig et al., 2024; Rosenzweig and Udry, 2014; Du Puy and Shrader, 2024; Molina and Rudik, 2023; Shrader et al., 2023). Some rely on variation in forecast quality. For example, Shrader et al. (2023) use plausibly random variation in the difference between the forecasted and realized temperature to show that improving the accuracy of temperature forecasts reduces mortality in the U.S. Molina and Rudik (2023) find similar results with hurricanes: when forecasted windspeeds are closer to realized windspeeds, total spending (including protective spending and post-hurricane repairs) is lower. In agricultural settings, information about the upcoming growing season is important for ex ante decision-making. Rosenzweig and Udry (2013) find that farmers in India learn about forecast quality: in places where forecasts tend to be inaccurate, farmers respond to them less than in places where they tend to be accurate. In a similar setting, also in India, Burlig et al. (2024) combine variation in weather forecasts with careful measurement of farmer beliefs. In their field experiment, farmers are given information much further in advance than in the typical forecast study – recent innovations in monsoon forecasts allow for rainfall onset forecasts up to six weeks in advance. They find that changing the farmer's decision environment through more accurate information changes farmer investments and – consistent with a Bayesian updating model – the direction of change depends on farmer priors.

Forecasts have also been used as a source of variation in the financial sector, where markets and firm valuations respond to hurricane forecasts (Kruttli et al., 2023) and weather news (Letta et al., 2022), and future weather derivative prices respond both to short-term weather forecasts (Dorfleitner and Wimmer, 2010) and longer-term warming trends (Schlenker and Taylor, 2021), although sometimes risk information is not always fully reflected in valuations (Hong et al., 2019). Lemoine and Kapnick (2024) show that firms react to improvements in ENSO and hurricane seasonal forecast quality, which help them reduce – but not fully eliminate – exposure to the forecastable component of climate risk, although investors still hedge the forecast news,; firms reducing their exposure but only at the cost of reducing their stock market value. Forecasts are likely to affect numerous other domains, including labor markets. Downey et al. (2023) show that employment falls in response to forecasted rainfall and Song (2024) documents that labor supply adjusts to temperature forecasts.

A related literature studies the effect of changes in long-run climate risk information, focusing disproportionately on flood risk in the U.S., and finds that improving information lowers home values and decreases exposure in high-risk regions. Most papers exploit policies and events that work as flood risk signals, which change the decision environment through information and beliefs, such as new floodplain maps (Gibson and Mullins, 2020), individual events like Hurricane Sandy (Addoum et al., 2024; Gibson and Mullins, 2020), and the Home Seller Disclosure Requirement in the U.S. (Lee, 2023). Households learn about their risk through flood maps, experience with extreme events, and information campaigns, and make investments in adaptation accordingly (Mulder, 2022). The market also responds, with flood risk and sea level rise at least partially capitalized into home values (Bernstein et al., 2019; Hino and Burke, 2021; Severen et al., 2018; Shr and Zipp, 2019), though others have shown regressive distributional consequences and persistent over-valuation of risky properties (Baldauf et al., 2020; Gourevitch et al., 2023; Murfin and Spiegel, 2020; Weill, 2023).

The effect of information on adaptation decisions depends on prior beliefs and the learning process. Studying the climate learning process poses significant challenges due to its inherent complexity and the fact that it is not directly observable. While individuals can observe weather events $\boldsymbol{c}$, they cannot directly observe the underlying probability distributions from which these weather events are drawn, i.e., the climate $\boldsymbol{C}$ (Moore, 2017). Early models assume a Bayesian updating process describes how individuals learn about climate change, given observations of weather (Kelly et al., 2005). Since then, a number of studies have shown that Bayesian models of belief formation are inconsistent with the empirical evidence (Deryugina, 2013; Gallagher, 2014; Ji and Cobourn, 2021; Kala, 2017; Moore et al., 2019; Zappalà, 2023). A more recent line of research combines surveys of climate beliefs with adaptive actions and welfare measures to study how beliefs and information provision shape adaptation decision-making. For example, Barrage and Furst (2019) document that climate skepticism delays adaptation, and Bakkensen (2022) show that flood risk misperceptions give rise to market inefficiency. In an agricultural context, Gine et al. (2015) show that farmers' subjective beliefs about the timing of the onset of the monsoon in India determine agricultural decisions. , Burlig et al. (2024), Patel (2023), and Zappalà (2024)go one step further to show that correcting inaccurate beliefs or expectations can change investment decisions and agricultural returns.

Imperfections in associated markets.

In many settings, insurance, credit, land, and labor markets may operate with frictions due to poor contract enforcement, limited liability, or asymmetric information (Bardhan and Udry, 1999). These affect adaptation decisions, and researchers use naturally occurring or induced variation in these markets as a source of variation in adaptation. For example, Burgess et al. (2017) exploit variation in the proximity to bank branches in India to show that bank access is correlated with a lower impact of heat on mortality, due plausibly to a combination of better saving and better borrowing opportunities. Rajan and Ramcharan (2023) show benefits of bank access for drought recovery in the 1950s U.S. Similarly, newer financial technologies may lower risk or otherwise facilitate adaptation. Examples include mobile money services, which decrease the variability of remittances and attenuate consumption losses induced by rainfall shocks in Tanzania (Riley, 2018) and Kenya (Jack and Suri, 2014) and satellite-based index insurance, which increases investment and mitigates both the immediate and longer term consequences of weather shocks (Boucher et al., 2021; Hill et al., 2019; Janzen and Carter, 2019; Stoeffler et al., 2022).[31] Existing financial products may also be tailored to reduce damages from weather risk, such as the contingent loans studied by Lane (2024) and Collier et al. (2024). Access to a line of credit conditional on flooding affects both ex ante investment decisions and ex post consumption smoothing, which echoes other findings on risk-reducing technologies (Emerick et al., 2016). Variation in the functioning of land, labor or other input markets may also be a source of variation in adaptation outcomes, particularly where there are complementarities across markets as in the decision to adopt irrigation (Jones et al., 2022). We discuss the role for government intervention in these and other markets in Section 4.

Market structure.

The very structure of markets – the degree of market integration and competition, fixed costs, and externalities – may also shape private adaptation decisions. A series of papers uses variation in aspects of market structure to understand adaptation, with findings that suggest ample room for improving private adaptation choices, most often through policy intervention. Trade openness and infrastructure are important spatial determinants of adaptation, with insights coming largely from the spatial general equilibrium literature discussed in Section 3.1.2. For example, trade barriers together with subsistence preferences have been shown to prevent low-income countries from reallocating sectoral activities that alleviate the productivity effects of rising temperatures (Nath, 2023). Infrastructure affects trade costs, and improvements to transportation infrastructure have been shown to attenuate the famine-rainfall relationship in India (Burgess and Donaldson, 2010) and reduce volatility in market prices and trade in Rwanda (Brooks and Donovan, 2020) and India (Allen and Atkin, 2022). Transportation infrastructure also determines the cost of ex ante and ex post adaptation. For example, in China, rapid expansion of both air and rail transportation has led to a decline in the share of the

[31] Even when insurance markets are not distorted, a large literature documents low levels of take up at actuarially fair prices that may be partly explained by time inconsistency or credit constraints (Casaburi and Willis, 2018; Cole et al., 2013).

population exposed to extreme temperatures (Barwick et al., 2022). Balboni et al., 2023 provide evidence that firms in Pakistan update their beliefs about flood risk in response to flood events and permanently change their composition of upstream suppliers to less risky transportation routes and less risky locations. Infrastructure and policy may also influence the degree of competition in markets, which can shape private adaptation decisions in, for example, the agricultural sector in India (Kochhar and Song, 2023).

Fixed costs, economies of scale, public goods, and externalities are all important determinants of private adaptation decisions. In many cases, public intervention will be necessary to overcome coordination failures and incentive problems. For example, negative externalities from energy use or groundwater extraction will tend to lead to too much reliance on these adaptation technologies, from a social perspective (Abajian et al., 2023; Auffhammer, 2022; Bruno et al., 2023; Colelli et al., 2022). Policy-induced variation may offer insights into private adaptation incentives. For example, Baylis and Boomhower (2021) find that mandating wildfire-resilient building materials lowers home destruction during fire and potentially reduces wildfire spread – a positive externality. This finding is suggestive of some distortion but leaves open the question of whether regulation is efficient. We discuss this, other policy responses to market failures, and unintended consequences of government intervention in adaptation in Section 4.

3.2.3 *Summary of studies quantifying impacts of specific adaptation interventions and/or constraints*

Fig. 3 summarizes the key characteristics of the subset of the adaptation interventions literature that exploits exogenous variation in interventions E by plotting the distribution of studies across the three categories discussed above. That is, studies that exploit variation in: *(i)* the price of adaptation; *(ii)* the budget for adaptation; or *(iii)* frictions in the adaptation decision environment. Fig. 3 additionally shows how studies are distributed across different outcome sectors, such as agriculture, health, and housing.

This figure shows that most studies have focused on relieving various frictions in the decision environment, particularly credit markets and information provision. Only a handful of studies have investigated how access to insurance or market power shapes adaptation outcomes. Agriculture has been the sector of focus for the majority of studies across all three sources of variation, while cross-cutting metrics such as income or consumption have been more dominant in studies manipulating budget constraints, credit access, and/or information. Interestingly, while ex post adaptation is generally more straightforward to study than ex ante adaptation, given the complexities of expectation formation and dynamics, price interventions are roughly evenly split between those lowering the costs of accessing ex post adaptation strategies versus those that make ex ante adaptation more affordable.

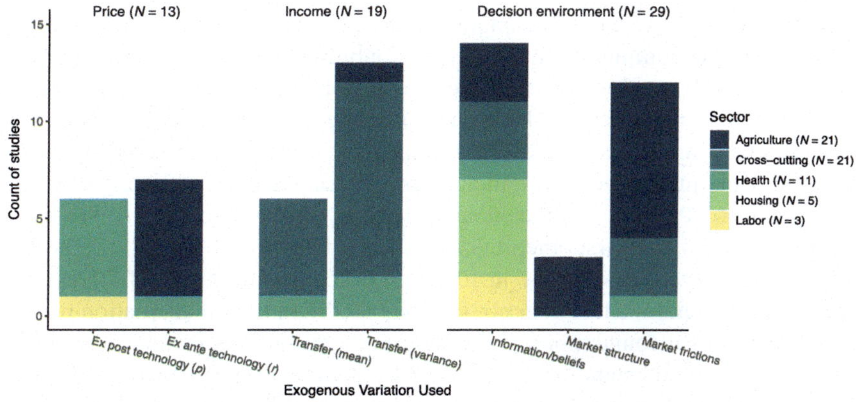

FIG. 3 Summary of variation exploited and sectors studied in papers leveraging exogenous variation in adaptation interventions. *Notes*: Bar chart plots the count of studies (in total 55) that utilize exogenous variation in: the price of ex post or ex ante adaptation technologies (left panel); transfers designed to change the mean or the variance of income (middle panel); or frictions in the decision environment (right panel). In the middle panel, income interventions that benefit all households in a region (e.g., unconditional transfers or workfare programs made available to all) are classified as "transfer (mean)", while those that target only the most vulnerable households (e.g., the poorest or the most shock-exposed) are classified as "transfer (variance)". Color is assigned according to the primary sector represented by the outcome of interest in the study. "Cross-cutting" includes studies that examine changes in income, consumption, expenditures, and/or education. Six papers that consider multiple outcomes or include multiple sources of variation are included in all relevant categories and sectors. Specifically: Banerjee and Maharaj (2020) is included in the price and income categories; Boucher et al. (2021) is included in the price and decision environment categories; Burlig et al. (2024) is included in the information/beliefs and markets' frictions subcategories; Hirvonen et al. (2023) and Knippenberg and Hoddinott (2019) are each included in the transfer (mean) and transfer (variance) subcategories; Patel, 2024 is included in the price and decision environment categories. All other studies appear only once. Underlying data are reported in Appendix Table A2.

4 The role of public policy in shaping adaptation outcomes

Under standard economic assumptions of perfect markets, in which individuals are fully informed and markets are efficient, there is little justification for policy interventions in adaptation to climate change. Under such conditions, individual agents will adapt endogenously to a gradually changing climate, choosing adaptive behaviors and investments that reflect their preferences and budget constraints. The role of the public sector is then to design climate change *mitigation* policies that properly weigh the costs of lowering emissions against the benefits of avoiding climate damages, inclusive of both the costs and benefits of endogenous adaptation.

As the literature reviewed in Section 3.2 makes clear, private adaptation decisions are shaped by budget constraints and prices, and are influenced by a number of associated markets and market frictions. This raises a critical set of questions regarding how, when, and for whom the public sector should intervene in order to guide adaptation outcomes at scales ranging from the individual to the community to the entire economy. Here, we first describe two approaches to adaptation policy choice: *(i)* a standard welfare evaluation that seeks to maximize social welfare incorporating all costs and benefits of a policy under climate change; and *(ii)* a narrow evaluation that considers only the effects of intervention on damages from weather and/or climate change. The second of these is motivated by emerging policy discussions. We then describe how in the first, theoretically-founded approach to policy choice, adaptation interventions can be justified on two grounds: market failures and equity-based social welfare functions. While the literature on adaptation policy and its theoretical foundations is limited, we highlight studies that have contributed to our understanding of each policy justification. Finally, we discuss inefficiencies and unintended consequences of public provision of climate adaptation.

4.1 Two approaches to adaptation policy evaluation

We consider two approaches to adaptation policy – one that corresponds to theoretically-justified welfare maximization, and another guided by pragmatic funding and policy prioritization. In the first approach, adaptation to climate change fits into standard cost benefit analysis that aims to maximize welfare by accounting for the full costs and benefits of an intervention. This raises two measurement challenges. First, when a potential policy intervention explicitly designed for climate change adaptation is assessed, its ancillary costs and benefits on other aspects of the economy, including any externalities due to market failures, must be accounted for. For example, cooling centers use energy that produce global and local pollutants (Abajian et al., 2023; Deschenes, 2022), sea walls change property values with potential distributional implications (Hsiao, 2024), ex post disaster relief may crowd in other public spending (Deryugina, 2017), and adaptation infrastructure may damage the natural environment (Gittman et al., 2016; Rodríguez et al., 2017; Tognin et al., 2021). When planners aim to maximize welfare, cost benefit analysis of adaptation policies should account for these ancillary impacts.

Second, many policies that do not explicitly target climate change adaptation may still have adaptation consequences that ought to be accounted for in policy cost benefit analyses. For example: land use regulations may encourage building in high climate risk areas (Ospital, 2023), raising future climate damages; expanding public health facilities may increase medical service provision following extreme heat events (Mullins and White, 2020), lowering morbidity and mortality effects of heat; and relaxing trade barriers may facilitate adaptive sectoral reallocation (Nath, 2023), mitigating economic damages from climate change. These adaptation-driven impacts may be positive or negative, but if they are ignored in the analysis of long-run policy costs and benefits, such evaluations will be inaccurate. Given uncertainty around future climate, climate adaptation inclusive assessments will result in a range of plausible costs and benefits for any given intervention. Importantly, accounting for the adaption consequences of long-run policies may highlight opportunities for policies themselves to adapt. For example, adjusting existing cash transfer programs to make payouts contingent on weather forecasts or realizations may increase the net benefits of the policy under climate change – by helping increase the resilience of vulnerable populations – without increasing costs.

In the second approach to adaptation policy, climate adaptation is a narrowly defined priority, in which interventions are evaluated based only on their net benefits for reducing the impacts of weather variability and/or long-run climate change. This approach has gained recent traction in policy and funding circles. For example, the Green Climate Fund, the largest climate financing organization dedicated to supporting developing countries, awards adaptation funding based a project's adaptation "impact potential", as opposed to a holistic cost benefit analysis. Similarly, the Adaptation Fund supported by the United Nations Framework Convention on Climate Change is dedicated to adaptation projects in developing countries, where project evaluation is conducted based on a project's potential to reduce climate vulnerability and/or increase adaptive capacity. These and other adaptation financing regimes compare alternative projects based on their ability to cost-effectively flatten the climate damage curve. Measurement challenges aside – and they are myriad – this narrow frame for policy evaluation may prioritize projects with negative consequences in other domains or miss policies that provide large welfare gains but small adaptation benefits. At the same time, this narrow approach to policy evaluation need not focus exclusively on adaptation policies; inexpensive policies with large adaptation co-benefits (e.g., improving access to credit) may rank relatively well.

In spite of the potential pitfalls of this narrow approach to policy evaluation, it also presents some pragmatic advantages: a transparent way to compare policies based on their adaptation benefits can guide spending toward the most cost effective investments. This is closely analogous to wide-ranging efforts to compare the cost per ton of avoided carbon emissions when evaluating the cost-effectiveness of mitigation policy (Gillingham and Stock, 2018; Hahn et al., 2024) (note that it is also similar to how much sector-specific public spending is allocated, in domains such as education, health, and international aid). However, ranking the cost effectiveness of adaptation interventions analogously to mitigation interventions is complicated by the fact that adaptation is not a global public good, so the ranking is context dependent, and that the ideal outcome for comparison is utility or welfare, which is proxied in a diversity of ways so that direct comparison is difficult.[32]

[32] An example of practical guidance on how to do this is offered by Adaptation and Resilience Investors Collaborative, 2024.

This narrow evaluation of impacts also permeates the academic literature. For example, authors often focus on measuring how an intervention E mitigates the damages from a weather shock ($\frac{\partial^2 u}{\partial E \partial c}$), but do not measure or report average treatment effects of the intervention (i.e., impacts of the intervention in a "typical" year or season, $\frac{du}{dE}$). And yet, such mean effects may be economically significant: for example, agricultural technologies often present a mean-variance trade-off, as varietals that have higher average yields are often more sensitive to input use or weather (Gatti et al., 2023). To the extent that adaptation interventions present a similar trade-off, measuring the mean effect is crucial to a holistic welfare accounting. In other cases, interventions more targeted to climate adaptation may receive more credit for their adaptation impacts than broader interventions in which the climate adaptation benefits are harder to isolate. For example, an information intervention that provides households with long range forecasts and changes housing stock decisions gets evaluated as generating large adaptation benefits, while a credit market intervention that has a similar impact on housing stock decisions (and on many other decisions) typically does not.

4.2 Justifications for policy intervention in adaptation

While there is substantial discussion surrounding the need for adaptation funding and policy (UNFCC, 2024), the conceptual justifications for policy intervention in private adaptation decisions are rarely clear. When adaptation interventions are being considered in isolation from other public policies, as they are in the growing number of adaptation financing organizations, no economic justification is provided; it is simply taken for granted that intervention is merited. However, when the decision of whether and how to intervene is faced by a welfare-maximizing social planner, adaptation policies require clear justification on welfare grounds.

Here we articulate two broad classes of justifications for policy intervention on climate adaptation. In the first, we include both policy action that alters the privately optimal amount of adaptation and that substitutes public for private adaptation. By focusing on market inefficiencies, we highlight policy interventions that are justified even under a utilitarian social welfare function. The second set of justifications lends itself to a broader range of policies by describing how alternative welfare functions that are often invoked implicitly in discussions of climate adaptation may also justify policy action.

4.2.1 Policy intervention can be justified when market imperfections distort private adaptation decisions

In the presence of market imperfections or missing markets, private provision of adaptation will be inefficient. Thus, policy can improve welfare by either addressing the market failure directly (e.g., regulating insurance markets to reduce "cream skimming") or by providing or subsidizing a particular adaptive behavior or technology (i.e., an element of $\boldsymbol{b}$ and/or $\boldsymbol{k}$) that is under-adopted due to the market failure.[33] Here we consider a number of market imperfections that potentially distort private adaptation decisions. Research on how these distortions shape adaptation decisions is reviewed above in Section 3.2; below, we focus on studies that uncover the efficacy of policy interventions aimed at mitigating adaptation-distorting market failures. Later, we describe the possible distortions introduced by public policy itself (either because the intervention was not justified by a particular market friction or because its implementation introduces additional market imperfections).

4.2.1.1 Information and beliefs

Information is a public good, and is therefore often underprovided.[34] Individuals may also hold persistent incorrect beliefs in situations where learning is slow or otherwise difficult. Climate change is just such a situation, as discussed in Section 3.2. This suggests a role for the public sector, both in providing accurate climate projections to inform adaptation decision-making and – potentially – in supporting decision-making directly.

Short-run weather forecasts and long-run climate risk assessments are prime examples of the public provision of information to aid decision-making. As detailed in Section 3.2.2, a growing body of work empirically demonstrates the ex ante adaptive benefits of forecasts and climate risk information. However, these studies also highlight that the quality of such information is critical (Molina and Rudik, 2023; Rosenzweig and Udry, 2013; Shrader et al., 2023), suggesting a role for regulation of the quality of information. Moreover, information alone may be insufficient to generate welfare-improving adaptation decisions. As discussed in Section 3.2, learning about climate is challenging, and responses to weather or risk information may be prone to behavioral biases (e.g., Deryugina, 2013; Gallagher, 2014). To date, little work has focused on the potential for other decision support – for example, to help people interpret and respond to climate information – to improve the adaptation benefits from the public provision of information.

Together, the papers in this literature highlight the value of public investment in the availability and accuracy of weather and climate information to facilitate private ex ante adaptation. However, translating these findings into policy prescriptions requires some caution. First, as noted above, forecasts update beliefs about weather, not climate, though work on responses to climate risk or longer-run climate model predictions also show some promise (e.g.,

[33] Of course, over-adoption of adaptation behaviors or technologies is also possible; in this case, taxation or rationing may be justified. Based on the review of available literature, over-adoption appears far less common than under-adoption.

[34] We discuss other public goods separately below. Because of the prominent role of information in shaping adaptation decisions, we consider it separately here.

Schlenker and Taylor, 2021). To the extent that weather becomes more volatile and less predictable with climate change, public investment in better weather or disaster forecasts may support climate adaptation; however, this may not be true if forecast quality deteriorates with climate change, i.e., if forecasts become less accurate as $\frac{dc}{dC}$ becomes large. Second, simpler information – for example, a monsoon onset date – may be easier to forecast accurately, and to communicate to the public, than more complex multi-dimensional forecasts or predictions about multi-faceted risk. This is particularly important in making the leap from relatively short run forecasts that inform labor supply or planting decisions to long run forecasts of climate change that inform migration decisions or educational investments. Finally, information about upcoming weather may be insufficient for successful adaptation if people also lack information on how to best respond to the information – that is, they may also need information about the availability, costs and benefits of adaptation strategies.

4.2.1.2 Public goods and natural monopolies

Where efficient adaptation requires coordination or investment in public goods, or imposes fixed costs, private markets will tend to result in coordination failures, free riding, and under-provision. These classic justifications for public intervention in markets apply to numerous types of climate risks. An obvious case is infrastructure investments: seawalls, elevated highways, and desalinization plants will not be constructed by individual agents. They require raising revenue to finance construction. In some cases, infrastructure is, itself, an adaptation investment, as in the case of seawalls or levees (Benetton et al., 2022; Bradt and Aldy, 2022; Kelly and Molina, 2023). In other cases, such as transportation infrastructure, it changes the decision environment and lowers the cost of adaptation, for example by facilitating migration (Barwick et al., 2022), improving supply chain resilience (Balboni et al., 2023), and reducing uncertainty in market access (Brooks and Donovan, 2020). Other types of publicly provided services, such as water, electricity, or health care, play an important role in household or firm level exposure and vulnerability to climate shocks (Cohen and Dechezleprêtre, 2022; Lin et al., 2021; Mullins and White, 2020; Nyqvist et al., 2023; Ponnusamy, 2022; Rocha and Soares, 2015). Yet, as the climate changes, demand for, supply of, and revenue from these services will change (Flores et al., 2024). As a result, changes to their regulation and/or to forward-looking investments may be necessary to avoid collapse (Abajian et al., 2024).

The costs and benefits of ex ante infrastructure investments for adaptation should be compared with ex post approaches to achieving similar adaptation outcomes (Davlasheridze et al., 2017; Hovekamp and Wagner, 2023), and to regulation-based alternatives such as restrictions on development (Ostriker and Russo, 2024). In spite of the importance of infrastructure for climate adaptation, less research focuses on its cost effectiveness or optimal investment under uncertainty, with the notable exception of the macroeconomic studies outlined in Section 3.1.2. Choices about how to locate transportation and other types of infrastructure require that policy makers consider evolving climate risks rather than the static or historically optimal placement (Balboni, 2023).

Innovation creates public goods, and is likely to play an important role in adaptation to climate change, as structural model simulations highlight (e.g., Desmet et al., 2021; Dietz and Lanz, 2022). However, innovation for adaptation, such as crop breeding research and development, will tend to be undersupplied in the absence of policy intervention (Zilberman et al., 2012). For example, new agricultural technologies have helped reduce agricultural losses in U.S. counties that cultivate crops with large national markets, but lag behind in settings where market signals and government support are weaker (Moscona and Sastry, 2023). At the same time, innovation may respond to catastrophic disasters rather than anticipate them (Auci et al., 2021; Hu et al., 2018; Miao and Popp, 2014; Moscona, 2021; Noy and Strobl, 2023). Innovations may also fail to diffuse without interventions to support their spread (Ben Yishay and Mobarak, 2019). This suggests an important role for policy to support both the supply and diffusion of innovations for adaptation, particularly in contexts where markets provide insufficient incentives on their own.

4.2.1.3 Adaptation externalities

Many adaptation decisions create externalities. When left unregulated, this leads to classic market failures that distort private adaptation markets: goods or services that generate negative externalities (such as air conditioning) will be over-adopted and those that generate positive externalities (such as wildfire fuel management) will be under-adopted. Policy intervention can correct these distortions, either through corrective pricing or regulation, and restore adaptation investments to the socially efficient level. We note that effective internalization of these externalities may, in the case of adaptation technologies with negative externalities, *decrease* adaptation in practice – optimal government intervention will weigh the forgone adaptation benefits against their social costs in determining optimal pricing. Of course, negative externalities can arise from public adaptation investments themselves – here we discuss the literature on private adaptation externalities, but return to the unintended consequences of public adaptation investments in Section 4.3.

The negative externalities imposed by adaptive use of energy and water are perhaps the most studied. Both inputs have been shown to mitigate the harms from a wide range of weather risks, including heat-related mortality (Deschênes and Greenstone, 2011), heat-driven reductions in student learning (Park et al., 2020), and drought and heat-induced crop loss (Hultgren et al., 2022). However, prices of both energy and water fall below their socially efficient levels in many settings, implying adaptive use of these inputs is likely too high. For example, adaptation through changes in final energy use affects greenhouse gas emissions and air pollution (Abaijan et al., 2023; Auffhammer and Aroonruengsawat, 2011; Colelli et al., 2022; Deschenes, 2022); when prices are unregulated, these negative externalities impose unpriced external costs. The standard policy prescription applies: correct the market failure to ensure optimal use of each input. Where, for example, water markets function well, changing water use patterns will be reflected in market signals (Ayres et al., 2021; Rafey, 2023). Without such regulation, extraction and use are likely to be unsustainable, particularly as climate change raises demand (Ayres et al., 2021; Carleton et al., 2024). The examples of energy and water use highlight that while some adaptation externalities are local (within a single aquifer, for example), others are larger scale (air conditioning emits globally harmful greenhouse gases), raising very distinct political economy challenges regarding efficient regulation of the market failure.

Energy and water use are not the only channels through which adaptation generates environmental externalities. Changes to agricultural production or other forms of land use may affect water quality, energy use, or biodiversity (Chakravorty et al., 2023; Renard et al., 2023). Transportation infrastructure may enable supply chains to adjust more fluidly to natural disasters, but such investments have well-documented environmental externalities (Balboni et al., 2023). Other externalities likely exist but are yet unstudied – for example, climate-induced migration may reshape disease transmission and changes to trade networks under climate change may influence the spread of invasive species. In such cases, correcting the market failure may be more challenging and complementary public policy may be needed.

4.2.1.4 Incomplete markets

As discussed in Section 3.2, insurance, credit, land, and labor markets shape private adaptation choices. However, these markets may operate with frictions due to poor contract enforcement, limited liability, or asymmetric information (Bardhan and Udry, 1999). In some cases, intervening in these markets to improve their efficiency will be the best approach to improving adaptation decisions – while also improving welfare in other domains. In other cases, the underlying causes of market inefficiencies are intractable and the adaptation decision should be targeted directly. Which of these is preferred will depend both on the setting and the policy evaluation framework, as discussed above in Section 4.1.

Mitigating risk leads to clear private adaptation gains, as seen in studies of index insurance (Hill et al., 2019), conditional credit or cash transfers (Lane, 2024), and technology transfer (Dar et al., 2013). In most contexts, then, private incentives to invest in risk mitigation are undistorted, and private markets will supply risk-reducing financial instruments. However, in two important cases, public intervention in risk management is warranted. First, many climate related shocks come in the form of natural disasters that create highly correlated risk. In this case, domestic markets may not be able to insure against aggregate shocks without international reinsurance. Access to these international markets is often costly (perhaps justifiably so), driving up domestic insurance prices, and is sometimes prohibited by regulation (Boomhower et al., 2024). A common solution in these situations is public supply of disaster relief, which has been shown to mitigate the damages from weather shocks in both high and low income settings (e.g., Gallagher et al., 2023; Tarquinio, 2022). However, this solution is imperfect, prone to public liquidity constraints and political distortions (del Valle et al., 2020; Tarquinio, 2022); it also creates moral hazard (see Section 4.3). While not a solution to the latter concern, sovereign insurance products have begun to offer a solution to the former two (del Valle, 2024; del Valle et al., 2020), though their use remains limited and additional research on optimal design, efficiency, and impacts of these products is needed. Second, insurance markets are often incomplete, unreliable, or subject to high levels of basis risk. Behavioral biases or credit and liquidity constraints may also undermine take up. In these cases, individuals may not insure against weather shocks without public intervention, even when the social benefits from insurance clearly outweigh the (undistorted) cost of provision (Casaburi and Willis, 2018; Cole et al., 2013). Policy may directly intervene by fixing insurance pricing or subsidizing premiums, or it may provide shock-contingent relief such as weather indexed cash transfers.[35] We discuss the potential moral hazard concerns associated with public provision of insurance or post-disaster transfers in Section 4.3, but note that these may be outweighed in many contexts by the welfare benefits of buffering vulnerable populations from negative weather shocks. Further evidence on these potential trade-offs is needed.

Credit and other financial market frictions will also distort private adaptation decisions. In the case of ex ante adaptation investments with high fixed costs, the higher the interest rate or transaction cost of credit access, the lower adoption will be. Of course, high interest rates may simply reflect high costs to lenders. However, better contract enforcement, credit tracking, and risk screening can all bring down these costs, resulting in better credit availability. The innovations that facilitate these improvements in credit markets often require government intervention. Rather than repairing the entire credit market (or the courts), subsidizing some forms of credit that provide particularly large adaptation benefits may be justified. For example, Lane (2024) and Collier et al. (2024) find that emergency credit improves ex post coping with weather shocks and increases ex ante investment in Bangladesh and in the U.S., respectively. In both cases, the emergency credit line is offered as a public intervention, implying that high

[35] A large literature evaluating cash transfer programs finds little evidence of wasteful spending (Banerjee et al., 2024).

costs of administering loans, a lack of collateral, or some other friction prevents the private market from supplying emergency credit at a sufficient scale.[36] Of course, it is not enough to show that subsidies deliver benefits when markets are incomplete; clear articulation of the market failure and accounting of costs and benefits is important for justifying policy intervention. Land and labor market may operate imperfectly as well, particularly in developing country contexts, with implications for adaptation investment and justifying some forms of policy intervention, such as land titling.

4.2.2 Policy intervention can be justified on equity grounds

Private adaptation typically requires diverting resources away from other needs. Low-income households, with a high marginal value of consumption, will thus spend less on adaptation, all else equal, than will high income households. Depending on the market, this unequal investment in adaptation can have further impacts on the poor through pecuniary externalities (Abajian et al., 2024; Hsiao, 2024). As discussed above, a growing body of empirical work shows that higher income households and/or populations are better insulated against a wide range of climate risks, including heat-related mortality (Burgess et al., 2017; Carleton et al., 2022), heat impacts on student learning (Park et al., 2021), heat effects on crime and conflict (Carleton et al., 2016), and heat impacts on the workforce (Behrer et al., 2021; Rode et al., 2022). Further exacerbating these inequities, the countries or regions that have the highest income or wealth today have contributed disproportionately to the stock of greenhouse gases that drive climate change (Callahan and Mankin, 2022).

These concerns about equity and moral responsibility underlie a second, welfare-based motivation for policy intervention *even in the absence of market failures*. Specifically, we consider two potential social welfare functions that justify policy action on climate adaptation: *(i)* distributional preferences or inequality aversion and *(ii)* moral responsibility or "polluter pays" preferences. The first is more familiar to economists, though the second has long stymied climate negotiations and serves to motivate much international adaptation spending, such as the Loss and Damage Fund. Either provides justification for policy intervention in a wider range of situations than those justified by market inefficiencies defined under neoclassical welfare assumptions (Section 4.2.1).

4.2.2.1 Equity weights

To the extent that local, national, and/or international planners have a distaste for inequality, intervention on adaptation can be justified on the grounds of reducing inequality (Saez and Stantcheva, 2016). While the equity implications

[36] Lane (2024) calculates positive profits to the implementer from the intervention.

of mitigation have been well studied (e.g., Diffenbaugh and Burke (2019); Prest et al. (2024)), the equity implications of adaptation and equity-motivated adaptation policy have received far less attention.

Even in the absence of inefficient markets, public spending to support adaptation may reduce inequality if it lowers the cost of adaptation in a way that flattens the income gradient in adoption, or if the benefits are disproportionately targeted to the poor. To the extent that adaptation is a normal good and marginal benefits of adaptation are decreasing, even untargeted policy support for adaptation will tend to disproportionately help the poor. Targeting might arise because benefits of take up are larger for lower income households, leading them to adopt more, or because of explicit or implicit policy design. For example, cooling centers might be more heavily utilized by low-income households if they have few available substitutes (e.g., in-home air conditioning), or if centers are strategically located in low-income neighborhoods.

While mounting evidence shows that relaxing budget constraints can flatten the damage curve for low-income households (see Section 3.2), one often voiced concern with scaling such insights is that economic growth itself is carbon intensive (Rozenberg et al., 2015). While the current carbon intensity of GDP does not support such an argument from a cost-effectiveness standpoint, it has also been argued that growth can increase inequality rather than lessen it (Aghion et al., 1999; Rubin and Segal, 2015). Thus, more targeted interventions, to increase the income of the poorest, may provide similar access to adaptation while being simultaneously fiscally feasible and less carbon intensive than economy-wide growth. For example, Chancel et al. (2023) calculate that bringing the entire global population living below $5.50/day (nearly half of the global population) up to that level would increase global emissions by one-third of the amount that the top 10 % of global emitters produce annually.

Of course, not all adaptation policy will reduce inequality. Infrastructure investments can create winners and losers, disaster relief or insurance payouts may miss households that do not fill in necessary paperwork, and public spending on adaptation may crowd out resources devoted to other forms of social protection. Private adaptation choices may also have distributional implications. For example, Hsiao (2024) studies how migration decisions in response to sea level rise in Jakarta affect land values. Wealthier households move, while poorer households stay behind; reduced demand lowers land prices, resulting in a decrease in the value of low-income households' assets and thus imposing a pecuniary externality. For factors with inelastic supply, these pecuniary externalities are likely to be strongest, and while these price signals are not necessarily distorted, they do have distributional implications. Similarly, in the Cape Town water case discussed in Abajian et al. (2024), as richer households adopted groundwater as a substitute for surface water during drought, more of the fiscal burden of financing the water supply was shifted onto the middle and lower class.

4.2.2.2 Moral responsibility

Policy motivated by economic efficiency considerations alone may fail to gain policy traction. Arguably, one of the main reasons that international climate agreements have repeatedly failed to get necessary global buy-in is a tension between high income countries that argue for an efficiency-based approach and low and middle income countries that demand attention to past and current contributions to atmospheric carbon concentrations. This tension is exacerbated by the inequities in damages and adaptation capacity discussed above. Thus, moral responsibility serves as an alternative justification for policy intervention in private adaptation decisions – that is, nations whose historical emissions have contributed the most to current and future climate change are argued to be obliged to expand budget constraints for adaptation in the world's poorest and most climate vulnerable nations (Okereke and Coventry, 2016).

Justifications for public spending on adaptation based on historical emissions contributions to climate damages have featured prominently in international discussions of a "Loss and Damage" fund. Burke et al. (2023) propose one approach to calculating contributions to damages that incorporate both past and future emissions and that aligns with the methodologies employed by social cost of carbon calculations. While transfers under such a fund need not be spent on adaptation per se, adaptation benefits of such transfers are generally an important part of the motivation (Okereke and Coventry, 2016). Transfers between countries will only address a portion of the inequality in both contributions and damages. Within-country inequality in emissions has overtaken between-country differences (Chancel et al., 2023), requiring transfers both domestically and internationally. One proposed approach would, for example, tax the world's richest corporations or individuals and transfer the revenue to the poorest using direct cash transfers.[37] As discussed in Section 3.2, there is growing evidence that cash transfers reduce sensitivity to weather shocks, implying potential adaptation benefits from such proposals.

4.3 Potential inefficiencies from public provision of climate adaptation

While there is substantial scope for public policy to correct market failures and address inequities in climate adaptation, much of the adaptation literature has focused on the potential pitfalls of public intervention in private adaptation markets. We highlight three important considerations: crowd out, moral hazard, and political economy. In forming optimal policy, these costs must be weighed against the many benefits of intervention: if the underlying distortion to socially optimal adaptation is large relative to any potential inefficiencies an

[37] For example, the poorer half of the Chinese population only generates 17 % of total carbon emissions in China while the top emitters are responsible for almost half of them (Chancel et al., 2023).

intervention creates, then welfare will still be improved and careful policy design can minimize the inefficiencies. While many studies quantify the costs or the benefits of adaptation interventions, few (including Fried, 2022) holistically weigh the market-correcting benefits of intervention against its possible distortionary effects.

Even in the best case, where public and private adaptation investments are substitutes and neither is distorted relative to the first best, the cost of raising public funds to pay for adaptation may justify leaving adaptation up to private markets. If public spending crowds out private adaptation with a sufficiently high substitution elasticity, and the marginal cost of public funds is also high, then adaptation may be best left up to private markets. Of course, equity concerns or distortions in private markets will offset the marginal cost of public funds, meaning that the justification for policy intervention will depend on the specific case. Numerous instances of crowd out have been documented in the literature (Annan and Schlenker, 2015; Baylis and Boomhower, 2021; Boustan et al., 2012; Fried, 2022; Kousky et al., 2016; Kousky et al., 2018; Peltzman, 1975), but presence of such a distortion does not constitute a full welfare accounting.

One important channel that erodes the effectiveness of public adaptation spending is moral hazard. A number of papers have documented increases in costs or damages when the public sector takes on environmental risks. For example, in the U.S., federal fire protection increased development in high hazard areas (Baylis and Boomhower, 2023) and subsidized crop insurance and farm aid reduce private investments in insurance and agricultural inputs, lowering crop revenue and increasing vulnerability to extreme temperatures (Annan and Schlenker, 2015; Deryugina and Kirwan, 2018). Similarly, the National Flood Insurance Program has been shown to increase the population living in high risk areas (Peralta and Scott, 2024) and to exhibit adverse selection (Wagner, 2022). Past reforms aimed at phasing out subsidies on flood insurance premiums in the National Flood Insurance Program increase the flood insurance price but decrease both property prices and insurance demand, showing potential trade-offs (Hennighausen et al., 2023). Coastal erosion mitigation programs increase building and eventual storm damages (Li et al., 2024). Similar moral hazard issues arise in disaster relief; if the government provides disaster aid after an adverse event, it will slow private investment in adaptation, such as inland migration (Kydland and Prescott, 1977; Hsiao, 2024).

Policy, of course, is subject to capture, and adaptation interventions are no exception. For example, Schneider and Kunze (2023) and Tarquinio (2022) show that disaster relief in the U.S. and India is mistargeted, with allocations that are influenced by reelection concerns. Similarly, Mahadevan and Shenoy (2023) find that water scarcity creates an opening for political capture of voters. While policy has the potential to correct market distortions, it can also exacerbate them if, for example, they concentrate market power among preferred market actors, as shown in agricultural markets in India (Kochhar and Song, 2023). Policymakers may also distort information about climate change to justify preferred policies or favor certain groups (Weill, 2023), or may respond to shocks in ways that create jurisdictional externalities (Hsiao et al., 2024). The literature on the political economy of climate adaptation is still nascent, and represents an important area for research as investments in adaptation increase (Bobonis et al., 2022; Cole et al., 2012; Fitch-Fleischmann and Kresch, 2021).

Some unintended consequences of public adaptation may be positive. For example, the Great Plains Shelterbelt increased tree cover across the American Midwest following the Dust Bowl, and led to increased precipitation and decreased temperatures due to local evapotranspiration effects. This, in turn, increased agricultural activity in nearby areas (Grosset et al., 2023; Li, 2021). This suggests that private adoption of nature-based adaptation may be too low given that benefits accrue at a scale beyond that of the individual decision-maker (Baylis and Boomhower, 2021; Das and Vincent, 2009; Edmondson et al., 2016; Menéndez et al., 2020). At the same time, evidence suggests that adaptation infrastructure can undermine these positive spillovers by, for example, damaging wetlands and estuaries (Gittman et al., 2016; Rodríguez et al., 2017; Tognin et al., 2021).

5 Priorities for future research on adaptation

As this chapter has demonstrated, the literature on adaptation to climate change is diverse and rapidly growing, though major holes remain. Here, we provide guidance for this emerging body of research in two areas. First, we make methodological recommendations that may help improve the quality and depth of current lines of questioning, whether the intent is better estimation of climate damages as reviewed in Section 3.1 or understanding the efficacy of adaptation interventions as reviewed in Section 3.2. Second, we lay out a set of priority areas for new research that we believe will help this literature better guide adaptation policy. To date, most adaptation research has focused on assessing whether and how adaptation is taking place. Prioritizing research on practical policy considerations will allow rapidly developing adaptation policy to draw more directly on research findings and evidence.

5.1 Methodological recommendations

Throughout Sections 3.1 and 3.2, we have noted methodological challenges facing the climate adaptation literature. Here, we provide recommendations aimed at helping surmount some of these challenges in future research. We discuss the two literatures together, both because many empirical challenges cut across them and because some areas for improvement lie at their intersection.

5.1.1 *Improving econometric identification of ex ante adaptation at scale*

The largest contribution of the climate damages literature to our understanding of adaptation is its ability to assess, at scale, the extent of ex ante adaptation to long-run climate change without needing to enumerate individual adaptive margins (of which there are likely too many to identify). Yet, many of the econometric contributions in this area leverage cross-sectional or long-run variation in the climate, which is rarely exogenous to other determinants of adaptation. Identification of ex ante climate adaptation can be improved by following the few studies seeking to identify plausibly random spatial discontinuities in long-run climate (e.g., Blakeslee et al., 2020; Druckenmiller and Hsiang, 2018; Hagerty, 2022; Hornbeck and Keskin, 2014) or by evaluating natural experiments that introduce plausibly random shocks to long-run climate risk information, such as climate change reporting or the release of new scientific consensus reports. In the literature on adaptation interventions, exploiting these sources of variation can also better inform what specific ex ante adaptation strategies are used and their efficacy.

5.1.2 *Theoretical and/or empirical justification for the functional form of climate and weather*

Many reduced form econometric studies make ad hoc choices about the functional form of long-run variation in the climate or of short-run weather shocks. As noted in Section 3, these modeling choices impose implicit assumptions on the expectations that underlie ex ante adaptation. For example, do populations update beliefs based on the long-run average daily temperature (e.g., Carleton et al., 2022) or long-run average cooling degree days (e.g., Rode et al., 2021)? Are expectations formed based on mean conditions or historical weather variability (e.g., Roth Tran, 2023)? How many years constitute the "long-run," and how should that historical record be weighted when constructing these variables? Similar questions arise around the functional form on shocks, particularly where data are too limited to allow fully non-parametric approaches (Fig. 1). These critical modeling decisions should be informed by the growing body of evidence on expectation formation and belief updating (e.g., Kala, 2017; Patel, 2024; Zappalà, 2024), as well as considerations of relevant decision horizons affecting, e.g., capital stock turnover. When such evidence is lacking, discussion of how climate variation relates to assumptions about belief formation and decision horizons can aid interpretation, and exploration of the sensitivity of results to alternative characterizations of the long-run climate can inform robustness of the results to alternative assumptions.

5.1.3 Robustness tests when short-run weather variation is limited

A related challenge is limited available variation in weather conditions. This affects long panel studies, but is particularly problematic in small-*N* studies where the variation in weather is constrained by the number of time periods or cross-sectional units. The proliferation of studies that interact existing interventions with weather variation and claim insights about climate adaptation are particularly prone to this problem. To combat this challenge, we first recommend that studies investigate and report the residual weather variation used to identify coefficients of interest. In particular, if the variation used for identification is far less than the variation relevant to long-run climate change, this should be communicated transparently. Beyond transparency, a set of robustness checks, many of which have been applied in the climate damages literature, can be conducted to assess reliability of results recovered with limited weather variation. These include: robustness to exclusion of weather outliers; placebo checks in which weather time series are randomly reshuffled; and placebo checks in which current outcomes are regressed on future weather shocks. When researchers have control over the roll out of an intervention – through, for example, an RCT – the variation in the intervention should aim to maximize variation in weather over space and/or time. For example, randomization can be stratified by climate zone or historical climate variation, across regions with documented differences in the distribution or nature of shocks (e.g., on either side of a rain shadow or at different elevations of a mountain range), or across periods forecasted to be on opposite ends of the El Niño Southern Oscillation cycle.

5.1.4 Studying adaptation to moderate weather conditions in addition to extremes

In small-*N* studies with limited weather variation, researchers generally focus on empirically identifying the impacts of, and adaptation to, extreme weather shocks (e.g., annual rainfall less than two standard deviations below the long run mean; see Fig. 1). This emphasis on extremes emerges because the (presumably) larger treatment effects of more extreme conditions are easier to statistically recover in small samples. However, moderate weather conditions are critical to understanding the welfare impacts of climate change and of adaptation interventions, since most weather will, by construction, be moderate. For example, 66 % of global population-weighted daily average temperatures fall between the moderate temperatures of 12.5°C and 27.5°C; this share is projected to fall to 42 % by end-of-century under high emissions climate change (Abajian et al., 2023). Thus, understanding how people and firms respond to these changes in moderate temperature exposure is critical to assessing adaptation today and under future climate change. This need is underscored by the many climate damage studies that have uncovered response functions in which even moderate temperatures or rainfall variations have economically meaningful impacts, for example on mortality

(Carleton et al., 2022), energy consumption (Wenz et al., 2017), and crop yields (Schlenker and Roberts, 2009). As discussed above, when researchers control data collection, sampling design can be used to maximize variation in the weather so that such moderate effects can be statistically recovered even when sample sizes are small. In some cases, estimating average effects of an intervention without exploiting weather variation may also be informative (e.g., Aker and Jack, 2023), but closer attention to mechanisms and evidence of maladaptation in the absence of the intervention is necessary.

5.1.5 Improving relevance to future climate change

Like other case studies, many papers documenting the adoption and/or efficacy of specific adaptation margins lack external validity. When applied to climate adaptation, relevance of empirical results to future time periods is particularly important (in particular, future years in which climate change has already unfolded). To improve such external validity, the definition of weather shocks investigated in historical data should be chosen based on forecasted weather under anthropogenic climate change. As discussed above, while this is relevant for large panel data settings, it is particularly challenging in small-*N* analyses, where the number of relevant weather realizations is limited, and in the study of rainfall, as projected rainfall patterns differ substantially across the globe (Lee et al., 2021). To make insights regarding resilience to short-run shocks relevant to potential adaptation benefits under long-run climate change, shocks that are projected to increase in frequency and/or intensity should be prioritized in observational data.

Relatedly, this literature would benefit from careful consideration of how responses to short-run shocks will change under long-run climate change due to ex ante adaptation. The climate damages literature reviewed in Section 3.1 has emphasized that ex ante adaptation decisions shaped by slow-moving climate change fundamentally change the effect of short run weather variation. The adaptation interventions literature, on the other hand, has largely ignored the fact that gradual climate change is likely to alter results based on current weather variation. Actionable steps to be taken in this regard include: quantitative assessment of how responses to short-run shocks differ across heterogeneous climates observed within a single sample (similar to Rosenzweig and Udry, 2020); comparison of results across studies with different climates; and investigation of whether results change when repeated shocks are experienced, relative to isolated events.

5.1.6 Leveraging long-run forecast information

The adaptation literature increasingly leverages weather forecasts to estimate climate damages inclusive of ex ante adaptation decisions that are informed not only by past experience but also by forecast information (e.g., Shrader et al., 2023). While these studies are valuable in their ability to demonstrate the returns to ex ante adaptation over daily to seasonal time scales, the literature has placed relatively less emphasis on the impact of longer-run climate risk information on adaptation decision-making.[38] To the extent that key adaptation decisions require multi-year planning, such as home remodels, public infrastructure investments, and migration, projections of long-run climate change (and its associated uncertainty) are the relevant source of information to guide ex ante adaptive choices. Forecasts are also increasingly used to understand ex ante belief formation and its impact on specific adaptation strategies (e.g., Burlig et al., 2024). Methods developed for short-run forecasts should be adapted to deliver insights regarding the extent and nature of ex ante adaptation to long-run climate projections.

5.1.7 *Integration of empirical evidence into integrated modeling*

The reduced form econometrics of adaptation has developed largely in isolation from the evolution of adaptation within quantitative general equilibrium models, IAMs, and process-based models. There is substantial scope for better integration of econometric results – either those that implicitly account for ex ante adaptation as reviewed in Section 3.1 or those that explicitly assess specific adaptation margins at scale as reviewed in Section 3.2 – into the parameterization of structural models of climate change damages.

5.2 Improving the literature's ability to inform adaptation policy

Although the literature reviewed in Section 3.2 is generally motivated by the need to inform adaptation interventions and policy, both it and the climate damages literature reviewed in Section 3.1 are not always well-suited to emerging adaptation policy needs. Here we list six lines of questioning that may help better align adaptation research with policy demand.

5.2.1 *How to evaluate and adapt adaptation policy?*

The net benefits and cost effectiveness of existing policies will change under climate change. While standard cost benefit analysis accounts for future uncertainty about states of the world, the uncertainty posed by climate change is unusual insofar as it is highly correlated across sectors, i.e., it has a high "project beta" (Gollier, 2021). As a result, forward looking policy evaluation (in any sector) should account for climate risks and for the risk reduction associated with effective adaptation policy. Theoretical work on how to appropriately evaluate climate policy remains an active area of work (e.g., Millner and Heal, 2023); however, most work has emphasized mitigation policy over adaptation policy, though parallels are presumably considerable. Practical guidance on applications to adaptation policy will increase the likelihood that these insights influence policy.

[38] Long-run climate risk information has been studied most extensively in the context of flood risk in the U.S. (e.g., Gibson and Mullins, 2020; Addoum et al., 2024).

As discussed in Section 4, policy must adapt to facilitate climate adaptation. However, evidence on the costs and benefits of relevant policy interventions remains very scarce. For example, anticipatory cash transfers receive a lot of policy attention as a tool to facilitate adaptation, yet numerous design alternatives and targeting approaches remain unstudied. The U.S. Occupational Safety and Health Administration recently released guidelines on worker protections during heatwaves built from scant evidence on impacts such regulations may have on worker health and productivity or on costs to employers. Information about cooling centers are a ubiquitous part of emergency messaging during heatwaves, but evidence on take up, targeting, and effectiveness is missing. Without evidence on these and other increasingly common adaptation policies, policy makers are left to improvise, potentially at a high public cost.

5.2.2 *What is the scope for adaptation benefits in a given sector and/or region?*

By quantifying climate change damages both with and without ex ante adaptation, the climate damages literature reviewed in Section 3.1 can indicate the potential for adaptation to lower the damages from climate change. Because these studies generally leverage large-scale datasets cutting across many regions, time periods, and even sectors of the economy, their findings can be used to prioritize where and for whom possible adaptation interventions may be most valuable. This is particularly true when policy is being guided by the more narrow framing discussed in Section 4.1, in which avoided climate damages are the only relevant criterion..

However, because this literature has been focused on climate damages and not directly on isolating adaptation, econometric and/or structural estimates of climate damages can be better leveraged to elucidate potential adaptation returns. Specifically, while Tables 1 and 2 list some studies that quantify returns to adaptation directly, many more studies do not report such results. Using existing methodologies, whether they are reduced form or structural, researchers can report differences in welfare-relevant impacts of climate change when ex ante adaptations are included versus when they are shut down. While this exercise is generally not feasible for ex post adaptations, as they are difficult to empirically isolate from direct climate damages (see Section 3.1 for details), providing such information for ex ante adaptation will help prioritize both research agendas and policy discussions regarding where and for whom specific interventions may have highest impact.

5.2.3 *How constrained is ex ante adaptation?*

While large-*N* studies of climate damages can help assess the scope for adaptation, such analyses often rely heavily on unrealistic assumptions regarding perfect markets and information. As the literature discussed in Sections 3.2 and 4.2.1 makes clear, in reality, many market imperfections and frictions constrain ex post and ex ante adaptation decisions, possibly explaining observed "adaptation gaps" between regions and/or time periods (Carleton and Hsiang, 2016). The literature providing large-scale assessments of climate damages inclusive of adaptation costs and benefits must confront such constraints to generate results that are relevant for adaptation policy.

There are multiple routes for doing so, particularly within the reduced form econometric literature. First, climate damage studies that aim to account for ex ante adaptation can investigate whether indicators of market frictions or constraints – such as infrastructure quality, credit market function, and market power – explain heterogeneity in weather dose-response functions. While this has been done to some extent – e.g., credit access lowers the mortality effects of heat (Burgess et al., 2017) and the cyclone impacts on economic growth (McDermott et al., 2014; Noy, 2009), while market power in agricultural markets restricts farmer adaptation (Kochhar and Song, 2023) – such constraints are rarely explicitly modeled in estimates of long-run climate damages. Integrating best available data on key market frictions into large-scale climate damage studies can help ensure that insights regarding the scope of potential adaptation (discussed above) include relevant real-world constraints.

Second, climate damage estimates that assume perfect ex ante adaptation decisions generate residual variation that can be exploited to better understand adaptation constraints. Specifically, studies that use long-run variation in climate to explain sensitivity to short-run weather shocks undoubtedly fail to perfectly fit the data. Researchers can use residual variation from such regressions to unpack where and for whom weather sensitivity falls above (or even below) that predicted by a model that assumes perfect ex ante adaptation based on long run climate. Such investigations set the stage for more context-specific analysis of specific adaptation interventions that may help explain or alter constraints to adaptation.

5.2.4 *Through which mechanisms do adaptation interventions operate?*

Many evaluations of adaptation interventions do not unpack the mechanisms through which treatment effects operate. This omission limits the literature's ability to either inform targeted adaptation interventions, or to asses the holistic costs and benefits of interventions that influence adaptation as well as other socially relevant outcomes.

This opportunity to improve the literature's policy relevance comes in at least three forms. First, some studies fail to assess how much of an intervention's overall treatment effect operates through reduced damages from adverse weather events. For example, if cash transfers are found to improve agricultural profits, it is likely some share of that recovered treatment effect is due to improved resilience to adverse weather events. If authors decompose treatment effects into components driven by weather resilience versus those driven by actions or outcomes unrelated to climate change, these studies can directly inform the ranking of potential interventions based on their adaptation potential alone. Without such a decomposition, it is difficult to use such analyses to inform adaptation policy choice. However, we also note several methodological considerations for the growing list of papers that interact development interventions with weather shocks, in the name of climate adaptation (see Section 5.1).

Second, many studies show that an adaptation intervention successfully lowers the damages caused by an adverse weather event (i.e., that $\delta \neq 0$ in Equation (5)), but fail to uncover which actions $\boldsymbol{b}$ or $\boldsymbol{k}$ are being taken by which agents in order to realize those resilience benefits (i.e., do not estimate Equation (6)). If survey data collection can be designed and exploited to enable researchers to estimate *both* Equations (5) and (6) (that is, identify effects on welfare but also the key actions or investments changed by the intervention), policymakers can learn not just that an intervention lowers damages, but which constraints to adaptation were alleviated by the treatment. Elucidating such mechanisms is critical to identifying targeted policies that effectively alleviate binding constraints to adaptation. Moreover, uncovering the actions or investments taken in response to an intervention will allow researchers to assess the full costs and benefits of an intervention, as each mechanism (e.g., increased air conditioning use) may entail different social or economic spillover effects beyond the measured effects on adaptation (e.g., increased greenhouse gas emissions from associated energy use).

Third, constraints to adaptation may exist in combination, such that addressing one does not change outcomes because another constraint continues to bind. An example is information and credit constraints. Informing households about future climate change may be insufficient to spur ex ante adaptation investments if households cannot access credit. Conversely, simply addressing frictions in the credit market may fail to unlock adaptation if individuals have overly optimistic beliefs about future climate. Addressing both constraints in tandem may have multiplicative benefits for adaptation. Similarly, correcting misinformation or biased beliefs in one domain (e.g., upcoming heat waves) may be ineffective if individuals are uninformed in related domains (e.g., the health damages from heat, the location of cooling centers, or the cost of accessing the centers). To date, the literature has tended to focus on single interventions in isolation, rather than understanding the adaptation decision process and potentially interacting constraints to optimal adaptation.

5.2.5 Should the government intervene, and how?

As articulated in Section 4, justifying adaptation interventions on social welfare grounds either requires a careful assessment of market failures *or* explicit delineation of a social welfare function that merits redistribution. While a growing number of studies econometrically assess or structurally model impacts of public policies on adaptation and associated welfare outcomes, these studies rarely ground their assessment of a public policy in a clear justification for intervention. For example, while Baylis and Boomhower (2021) estimate the disaster risk benefits of mandated regulations on wildfire-resilient building materials in California, it is unclear which market failures justify the blunt command-and-control intervention. Whether or not such a costly adaptation policy ought to be rolled out more broadly hinges critically on whether it was correcting an existing market failure or simply requiring homeowners to invest in more adaptation than was privately (and socially) optimal. Analogously, Pople et al. (2021) show that anticipatory cash transfers in Bangladesh reduced food insecurity impacts of flooding. The justification for this intervention appears to be an implicit equity motive on the part of the planner, but the policy justification is not made explicit. In this regard, Hovekamp and Wagner (2023) show that minimum elevation requirements for housing built in high-risk flood areas in the U.S. is efficient because adaptation benefits are not fully capitalized into house prices. Going forward, research aiming to inform policy ought to ground studied interventions with clear theoretical justifications, elucidating the relevant market failure or explicitly characterizing a social welfare function if no market failure motivates the intervention.

Of course, it is not necessary to elucidate the justifications for intervention if a study aims only to inform the more narrow policy agenda of ranking adaptation interventions based on their cost effectiveness (Section 4.1). In this case, researchers should be clear about the link between their work and policy, noting that a comprehensive welfare assessment is not feasible, nor is it the goal.

5.2.6 *Do the inefficiencies of public adaptation outweigh its benefits?*

Throughout this review, we have highlighted the critical role of the public sector in facilitating adaptation, particularly when market frictions or imperfections impede optimal adaptation decisions. However, we have also noted cases where public adaptation interventions are inefficient and distortionary (see Section 4.3). To date, literatures speaking to each side of this coin have largely been independent from one another. This means that in most contexts, it remains unclear whether the benefits of public adaptation interventions outweigh their possible inefficiencies or unintended consequences.

To inform welfare-enhancing adaptation policy, research is needed to carefully assess when the benefits of intervention exceed their costs. Undoubtedly, the answer to this question will vary across contexts. For example, as private insurance markets function relatively well in the United States, the inefficiencies of subsidized crop insurance quantified by Annan and Schlenker (2015) likely outweigh any benefits realized by correcting market failures. But in low and middle income country contexts where accessing actuarially fair insurance policies is nearly impossible, and where an equity motive for lowering damages to smallholder farmers exists, subsidized crop insurance may be welfare-improving. Research that can elucidate when intervention is justified, accounting both for benefits and possible costs of public action, is urgently needed.

Appendix A

TABLE A1 Studies of adaptation interventions and their definitions of weather anomaly used in Fig. 1.

Reference	Variable	Climate baseline period	Length of climate baseline (years)	Shock type	Percentile used as shock cutoff	Uses fixed effects
Adhvaryu et al. (2024)	Precipitation	Varies by birth year	10	Positive	84 (1σ)	Yes
Asfaw et al. (2017)	Precipitation	1983–2010	27	Positive	97.5 (2σ)	No
Björkman Nyqvist et al. (2023)	Precipitation	1983–2013	20	Continuous		No
Christian et al. (2019)	Precipitation	1979–2016	37	Continuous		Yes
Christian et al. (2019)	Precipitation	1951–2013	62	Continuous		Yes
Corno and Voena (2023)	Precipitation	1981–2010	29	Continuous		Yes
Deryugina (2013)	Temperature	1949–2000	51	Negative	5, 10, 25	Yes
				Positive	75, 90, 95	
Hirvonen et al. (2023)	Precipitation	1990–2020	30	Continuous		Yes
Jayachandran (2006)	Precipitation	1956–1987	31	Negative	20	Yes
				Positive	80	
Kazianga and Udry (2006)	Precipitation	1965–1985	20	Continuous		Yes
Lin et al. (2021)	Precipitation	1950–2014	64	Continuous		Yes
Mobarak and Rosenzweig (2014)	Precipitation	1999–2006	7	Continuous		Yes

Continued

TABLE A1 Studies of adaptation interventions and their definitions of weather anomaly used in Fig. 1.—Cont'd

Reference	Variable	Climate baseline period	Length of climate baseline (years)	Shock type	Percentile used as shock cutoff	Uses fixed effects
Moore et al. (2019)	Temperature	1981–1990	10	Continuous		Yes
Paxson (1992)	Precipitation	1951–1985	34	Continuous		Yes
Ponnusamy (2022)	Precipitation	2000–2014	14	Negative	16 (-1σ)	Yes
				Positive	84 (1σ)	
Premand and Stoeffler (2022)	Precipitation	1970–2011	41	Negative	10, 11, ..., 35	No
Riley (2018)	Precipitation	Not stated	15	Positive	84 (1σ)	Yes
Rocha and Soares (2015)	Precipitation	1938–2008	70	Continuous		Yes
				Negative	16 (-1σ)	
Rosenzweig and Udry (2014)	Precipitation	1950–2010	60	Continuous		Yes
				Negative	49 (Realization-norm ratio is < 1)	
Schlenker and Taylor (2021)	Temperature	2001–2020	19	Continuous		Yes[1]

Notes: The table lists all studies represented in Fig. 1 in the main text. Included studies are those that normalize weather variation with respect to a long-run climate norm when investigating the adoption or efficacy of specific adaptation technologies or strategies. Positive and negative shock definitions measured in standard deviations have been assigned percentile values using properties of the normal distribution, such that a positive shock threshold at 1 standard deviation (σ) above the mean is assumed to fall at the 84th percentile. Note that Moore et al. (2019) include an analysis that compares the number of temperature anomalies identified using a shifting versus a fixed 30-year baseline, but we do not report it in Fig. 1 or in this table as it is auxiliary from the authors' main analysis. [1]In Schlenker and Taylor (2021), fixed effects are included in separate specification from that which uses weather anomalies.

TABLE A2 Studies of adaptation interventions used in Fig. 3, their source of exogenous variation, and sector of focus.

Reference	Variation type	Exogenous variation	Adaptation intervention	Sector
Adhvaryu et al. (2024)	Income	Transfer*	Conditional cash transfer program (PROGRESA/ Oportunidades)	Cross-cutting
Adhvaryu et al. (2020)	Price	Ex post technology (*p*)	Roll-out of LED lighting in factories	Labor
Aker and Jack (2023)	Price	Ex ante technology (*r*)	Rainwater harvesting technique training (demi-lune)	Agriculture
Asfaw et al. (2017)	Income	Transfer+	Unconditional cash transfer	Cross-cutting
Balana et al. (2023)	Income	Transfer*	Anticipatory cash transfer	Cross-cutting
Banerjee and Maharaj (2020)	Price	Ex post technology (*p*)	Community health care worker program;	Health
	Income	Transfer+	Workfare program (NREGA)	
Baysan et al. (2019)	Income	Transfer*	Conditional cash transfer program (PROGRESA/ Oportunidades)	Health
Beaman et al. (2021)	Price	Ex ante technology (*r*)	Agricultural technology training (pit planting)	Agriculture
Bhandari et al. (2022)	Decision environment	Market structure	Technology subsidies for groundwater extraction	Agriculture
Björkman Nyqvist et al. (2023)	Price	Ex ante technology (*r*)	Deployment of community health care workers	Health

Continued

TABLE A2 Studies of adaptation interventions used in Fig. 3, their source of exogenous variation, and sector of focus.—Cont'd

Reference	Variation type	Exogenous variation	Adaptation intervention	Sector
Boucher et al. (2021)	Decision environment	Markets' frictions	Index insurance;	Agriculture
	Price	Ex ante technology (*r*)	Drought-tolerant seeds	
Brooks and Donovan (2020)	Decision environment	Market structure	New bridge construction	Agriculture
Burgess and Donaldson (2010)	Decision environment	Markets' frictions	Rural bank expansion program	Health
Burlig et al. (2024)	Decision environment	Information/ beliefs	Provision of monsoon forecast;	Agriculture
	Decision environment	Markets' frictions	Index insurance	
Christian et al. (2019)	Income	Transfer*	Conditional cash transfer (Program Keluarga Harapan)	Health
Christian et al. (2019)	Income	Transfer*	Staggered roll-out of Odisha Rural Livelihoods Program	Cross-cutting
Cohen and Dechezleprêtre (2022)	Price	Ex post technology (*p*)	Health care expansion policy	Health
Cole et al. (2017)	Decision environment	Markets' frictions	Rainfall insurance provision	Agriculture
Collier et al. (2024)	Decision environment	Markets' frictions	Contingent loan offerings	Cross-cutting

Colmer and Doleac (2023)	Price	Ex post technology (*p*)	Gun control policies	Health
Dar et al. (2013)	Price	Ex ante technology (*r*)	Flood-tolerant rice variety	Agriculture
Downey et al. (2023)	Decision environment	Information/ beliefs	Change in forecast quality	Labor
Emerick et al. (2016)	Price	Ex ante technology (*r*)	Flood-tolerant rice variety	Agriculture
Fetzer (2020)	Income	Transfer[+]	Workfare program (NREGA)	Cross-cutting
Garg et al. (2020)	Income	Transfer[+]	Workfare program (NREGA)	Cross-cutting
Garg et al. (2020)	Income	Transfer*	Conditional cash transfer program (PROGRESA/ Oportunidades)	Cross-cutting
Gibson and Mullins (2020)	Decision environment	Information/ beliefs	Biggert-Waters Flood Insurance Reform Act; Hurricane Sandy; Floodplain maps	Housing
Gunnsteinsson et al. (2022)	Price	Ex post technology (*p*)	Vitamin A supplement provision	Health
Hill et al. (2019)	Decision environment	Markets' frictions	Index insurance	Agriculture
Hino and Burke (2021)	Decision environment	Information/ beliefs	Updated floodplain maps	Housing
Hirvonen et al. (2023)	Income	Transfer[*+]	Ultra-poor graduation program (Productive Safety Net Program)	Cross-cutting

Continued

TABLE A2 Studies of adaptation interventions used in Fig. 3, their source of exogenous variation, and sector of focus.—Cont'd

Reference	Variation type	Exogenous variation	Adaptation intervention	Sector
Hou (2010)	Income	Transfer*	Conditional cash transfer program (PROGRESA/ Oportunidades)	Cross-cutting
Janzen and Carter (2019)	Decision environment	Markets' frictions	Index-based livelihood insurance pilot project	Cross-cutting
Jones et al. (2022)	Decision environment	Markets' frictions	Hillside irrigation canal construction	Agriculture
Knippenberg and Hoddinott (2019)	Income	Transfer*+	Social protection program (Productive Safety Net Program)	Cross-cutting
Kochhar and Song (2023)	Decision environment	Market structure	Variation in state-level laws governing agricultural transactions	Agriculture
Lane (2024)	Decision environment	Markets' frictions	Contingent loan offerings	Agriculture
Lee (2023)	Decision environment	Information/ beliefs	Homeseller Disclosure Requirement	Housing
Lemoine and Kapnick (2024)	Decision environment	Information/ beliefs	Change in forecast quality	Cross-cutting
Macours et al. (2022)	Income	Transfer*	Conditional cash transfer with vocational training or a productive investment grant	Agriculture
Mobarak and Rosenzweig (2014)	Decision environment	Markets' frictions	Index insurance offering	Agriculture

Mogge et al. (2024)	Income	Transfer*	Anticipatory cash transfer	Cross-cutting
Molina and Rudik (2023)	Decision environment	Information/ beliefs	Change in hurricane forecast quality	Cross-cutting
Mulder (2022)	Decision environment	Information/ beliefs	Improved flood risk classification	Cross-cutting
Mullins and White (2020)	Price	Ex post technology (*p*)	Health care expansion through Community Health Centers	Health
Patel (2023)	Price	Ex ante technology (*r*)	Salinity-tolerant seeds	Agriculture
	Decision environment	Information/ beliefs	Information on salinity levels	
Pople et al. (2021)	Income	Transfer*	Anticipatory cash transfer	Cross-cutting
Premand and Stoeffler (2022)	Income	Transfer*	Unconditional cash transfer	Cross-cutting
Riley (2018)	Decision environment	Markets' frictions	Roll-out of mobile money providers	Cross-cutting
Rosenzweig and Udry (2013)	Decision environment	Information/ beliefs	Change in forecast quality	Agriculture
Shr and Zipp (2019)	Decision environment	Information/ beliefs	Updated floodzone mapping	Housing
Shrader et al. (2023)	Decision environment	Information/ beliefs	Change in forecast quality	Health

Continued

TABLE A2 Studies of adaptation interventions used in Fig. 3, their source of exogenous variation, and sector of focus.—Cont'd

Reference	Variation type	Exogenous variation	Adaptation intervention	Sector
Song (2024)	Decision environment	Information/ beliefs	Change in forecast quality	Labor
Stoeffler et al. (2022)	Decision environment	Markets' frictions	Index insurance	Agriculture
Weill (2023)	Decision environment	Information/ beliefs	Updated flood maps after Hurricane Katrina	Housing

Notes: The table lists all studies represented in Fig. 3 in the main text. In the "Exogenous variation" column, p indicates a price intervention targeting an ex post adaptation technology, while r indicates a price intervention targeting an ex ante adaptation technology, following the notation from Section 2 in the main text. Additionally, superscripts $^{+}$ denote income interventions designed to affect the *mean* of income, while superscripts * denote those designed to affect the *variance*. For example, income interventions designed to affect the mean include unconditional cash transfers and workfare programs made available to all households in a given region, while those that target only the most vulnerable households (e.g., the poorest or the most shock-exposed) are designed to reduce variance.

References

Aaheim, A., Amundsen, H., Dokken, T., Ericson, T., Wei, T., 2009. A macroeconomic assessment of impacts and adaptation to climate change in Europe. CICERO Report.

Aaheim, A., Amundsen, H., Dokken, T., Wei, T., 2012. Impacts and adaptation to climate change in European economies. Global Environmental Change 22 (4), 959–968.

Abajian, A., Cole, C., Jack, B.K., Meng, K.C., Visser, M., 2024. Dodging Day Zero: Drought, Adaptation, and Inequality in Cape Town. Working Paper.

Abajian, A.C., Carleton, T., Meng, K.C., Deschenes, O., 2023. The Climate Adaptation Feedback. Working Paper.

Addoum, J.M., Eichholtz, P., Steiner, E., Yönder, E., 2024. Climate change and commercial real estate: evidence from Hurricane Sandy. Real Estate Economics 52 (3), 687–713. https://doi.org/10.1111/1540-6229.12435

Adhvaryu, A., Kala, N., Nyshadham, A., 2020. The light and the heat: productivity co-benefits of energy-saving technology. The Review of Economics and Statistics 102 (4), 779–792.

Adhvaryu, A., Molina, T., Nyshadham, A., Tamayo, J., 2024. Helping children catch up: early life shocks and the PROGRESA experiment. The Economic Journal 134 (657), 1–22.

Aghion, P., Caroli, E., Garcia-Penalosa, C., 1999. Inequality and economic growth: the perspective of the new growth theories. Journal of Economic Literature 37 (4), 1615–1660.

Aker, J.C., Jack, B.K., 2023. Harvesting the rain: the adoption of environmental technologies in the Sahel. The Review of Economics and Statistics 1–52.

Allen, T., Atkin, D., 2022. Volatility and the gains from trade. Econometrica 90 (5), 2053–2092. https://doi.org/10.3982/ECTA14411

Annan, F., Schlenker, W., 2015. Federal crop insurance and the disincentive to adapt to extreme heat. American Economic Review 105 (5), 262–266.

Aragón, F.M., Oteiza, F., Rud, J.P., 2021. Climate change and agriculture: subsistence farmers' response to extreme heat. American Economic Journal: Economic Policy 13 (1), 1–35.

Asfaw, S., Carraro, A., Davis, B., Handa, S., Seidenfeld, D., 2017. Cash transfer programmes, weather shocks and household welfare: evidence from a randomised experiment in Zambia. Journal of Development Effectiveness 9 (4), 419–442. https://doi.org/10.1080/19439342.2017.1377751

Auci, S., Barbieri, N., Coromaldi, M., Michetti, M., 2021. Climate variability, innovation and firm performance: evidence from the European agricultural sector. European Review of Agricultural Economics 48 (5), 1074–1108.

Auffhammer, M., 2018. Quantifying economic damages from climate change. Journal of Economic Perspectives 32 (4), 33–52.

Auffhammer, M., 2022. Climate adaptive response estimation: short and long run impacts of climate change on residential electricity and natural gas consumption. Journal of Environmental Economics and Management 114, 102669.

Auffhammer, M., Aroonruengsawat, A., 2011. Simulating the impacts of climate change, prices and population on California's residential electricity consumption. Climatic Change 109 (1), 191–210.

Auffhammer, M., Schlenker, W., 2014. Empirical studies on agricultural impacts and adaptation. Energy Economics 46, 555–561.

Ayres, A.B., Meng, K.C., Plantinga, A.J., 2021. Do environmental markets improve on open access? Evidence from california groundwater rights. Journal of Political Economy 129 (10), 2817–2860.

Adaptation & Resilience Investors Collaborative, 2024. Assessing Adaptation & Resilience Impact in Private Investments: A measurement framework for investors. Technical report.

Bakkensen, L., Barrage, L., 2018. Climate Shocks, Cyclones, and Economic Growth: Bridging the Micro-Macro Gap. NBER Working Papers, 24893. National Bureau of Economic Research.

Bakkensen, L., Phan, T., Wong, R., 2023. Leveraging the Disagreement on Climate Change: Theory and Evidence. Working Paper.

Bakkensen, L.A., Barrage, L., 2022. Going underwater? Flood risk belief heterogeneity and coastal home price dynamics. The Review of Financial Studies 35 (8), 3666–3709.

Bakkensen, L.A., Mendelsohn, R.O., 2016. Risk and adaptation: evidence from global hurricane damages and fatalities. Journal of the Association of Environmental and Resource Economists 3 (3), 555–587.

Balana, B., Adeyanju, D., Clingain, C., Andam, K.S., de Brauw, A., Yohanna, I., Olarewaju, O., Schneider, M., 2023. Anticipatory cash transfers for climate resilience: findings from a randomized experiment in northeast Nigeria. The International Food Policy Research Institute.

Balboni, C., 2023. In Harm's Way? Infrastructure Investments and the Persistence of Coastal Cities. Working Paper.

Balboni, C., Berman, A., Burgess, R., Olken, B.A., 2023. The economics of tropical deforestation. Annual Review of Economics 15 (1), 723–754.

Balboni, C., Boehm, J., Waseem, M., 2023. Firm Adaptation in Production Networks: Evidence from Extreme Weather Events in Pakistan. Structural Transformation and Economic Growth CEPR.

Baldauf, M., Garlappi, L., Yannelis, C., 2020. Does climate change affect real estate prices? Only if you believe in it. The Review of Financial Studies 33 (3), 1256–1295.

Banerjee, A., Hanna, R., Olken, B.A., Sverdlin Lisker, D., 2024. Social Protection in the Developing World. NBER Working Papers, 32382. National Bureau of Economic Research.

Banerjee, R., Maharaj, R., 2020. Heat, infant mortality, and adaptation: evidence from India. Journal of Development Economics 143, 102378.

Bardhan, P., Udry, C., 1999. Development Microeconomics. OUP, Oxford.

Bareille, F., Chakir, R., 2023a. The impact of climate change on agriculture: a repeat-Ricardian analysis. Journal of Environmental Economics and Management 119, 102822.

Bareille, F., Chakir, R., 2023b. Structural identification of weather impacts on crop yields: Disentangling agronomic from adaptation effects. American Journal of Agricultural Economics, n/a(n/a). https://doi.org/10.1111/ajae.12420.

Barrage, L., Furst, J., 2019. Housing investment, sea level rise, and climate change beliefs. Economics Letters 177, 105–108.

Barreca, A., Clay, K., Deschenes, O., Greenstone, M., Shapiro, J.S., 2016. Adapting to climate change: the remarkable decline in the US temperature-mortality relationship over the twentieth century. Journal of Political Economy 124 (1), 105–159.

Barwick, P.J., Donaldson, D., Li, S., Lin, Y., Rao, D., 2022. Improved Transportation Networks Facilitate Adaptation to Pollution and Temperature Extremes. NBER Working Papers, 30462. National Bureau of Economic Research.

Baylis, P., Boomhower, J., 2023. The economic incidence of wildfire suppression in the United States. American Economic Journal: Applied Economics 15 (1), 442–473.

Baylis, P.W., Boomhower, J., 2021. Mandated vs. Voluntary Adaptation to Natural Disasters: The Case of U.S. Wildfires. NBER Working Papers, 29621. National Bureau of Economic Research.

Baysan, C., Burke, M., González, F., Hsiang, S., Miguel, E., 2019. Non-economic factors in violence: evidence from organized crime, suicides and climate in Mexico. Journal of Economic Behavior & Organization 168, 434–452.

Beach, R.H., Cai, Y., Thomson, A., Zhang, X., Jones, R., McCarl, B.A., Crimmins, A., Martinich, J., Cole, J., Ohrel, S., DeAngelo, B., McFarland, J., Strzepek, K., Boehlert, B., 2015. Climate Change impacts on US agriculture and forestry: benefits of global climate stabilization. Environmental Research Letters 10 (9), 095004.

Beaman, L., BenYishay, A., Magruder, J., Mobarak, A.M., 2021. Can network theory-based targeting increase technology adoption? American Economic Review 111 (6), 1918–1943.

Behrer, A.P., Park, R.J., Wagner, G., Golja, C.M., Keith, D.W., 2021. Heat has larger impacts on labor in poorer areas*. Environmental Research Communications 3 (9), 095001.

Benetton, M., Emiliozzi, S., Guglielminetti, E., Loberto, M., Mistretta, A., 2022. Do House Prices Reflect Climate Change Adaptation? Evidence from the City on the Water. Working Paper.

Benonnier, T., Millock, K., Taraz, V., 2022. Long-term migration trends and rising temperatures: the role of irrigation. Journal of Environmental Economics and Policy 11 (3), 307–330.

Bento, A.M., Miller, N., Mookerjee, M., Severnini, E., 2023. A unifying approach to measuring climate change impacts and adaptation. Journal of Environmental Economics and Management 121, 102843.

Benveniste, H., Oppenheimer, M., Fleurbaey, M., 2020. Effect of border policy on exposure and vulnerability to climate change. Proceedings of the National Academy of Sciences 117 (43), 26692–26702.

Benveniste, H., Oppenheimer, M., Fleurbaey, M., 2022. Climate Change increases resource-constrained international immobility. Nature Climate Change 12 (7), 634–641.

Ben Yishay, A., Mobarak, A.M., 2019. Social learning and incentives for experimentation and communication. The Review of Economic Studies 86 (3), 976–1009.

Bernstein, A., Gustafson, M.T., Lewis, R., 2019. Disaster on the horizon: the price effect of sea level rise. Journal of Financial Economics 134 (2), 253–272.

Bhandari, H., Chakravorty, U., Emerick, K., Habib, M.A., 2022. Targeted Subsidies for Water Conservation in Smallholder Agriculture. Working Paper.

Bilal, A., Rossi-Hansberg, E., 2023. Anticipating climate change across the United States. NBER Working Papers, 31323. National Bureau of Economic Research.

Birol, D.F., 2018. The Future of Cooling. IEA, Paris.

Björkman Nyqvist, M., von Carnap, T., Guariso, A., Svensson, J., 2023. Weather Shocks, Child Mortality, and Adaptation: Experimental Evidence from Uganda. Working Paper.

Blakeslee, D., Fishman, R., Srinivasan, V., 2020. Way down in the hole: adaptation to long-term water loss in rural India. American Economic Review 110 (1), 200–224.

Blanc, E., Schlenker, W., 2017. The use of panel models in assessments of climate impacts on agriculture. Review of Environmental Economics and Policy 11 (2), 258–279.

Bobonis, G.J., Gertler, P.J., Gonzalez-Navarro, M., Nichter, S., 2022. Vulnerability and clientelism. American Economic Review 112 (11), 3627–3659.

Boomhower, J., Fowlie, M., Gellman, J., Plantinga, A., 2024. How Are Insurance Markets Adapting to Climate Change? Risk Selection and Regulation in the Market for Homeowners Insurance. NBER Working Papers, 32625. National Bureau of Economic Research.

Borensztein, E., Cavallo, E., Jeanne, O., 2017. The welfare gains from macro-insurance against natural disasters. Journal of Development Economics 124, 142–156.

Bosello, F., Roson, R., Tol, R.S.J., 2006. Economy-wide estimates of the implications of climate change: human health. Ecological Economics 58 (3), 579–591.

Bosello, F., Roson, R., Tol, R.S.J., 2007. Economy-wide estimates of the implications of climate change: sea level rise. Environmental and Resource Economics 37 (3), 549–571.

Bosetti, V., Carraro, C., Galeotti, M., Massetti, E., Tavoni, M., 2006. WITCH a world induced technical change hybrid model. The Energy Journal 27, 13–37.

Boucher, S., Carter, M., Flatnes, J.E., Lybbert, T., Malacarne, J., Marenya, P., Paul, L., 2021. Bundling Genetic and Financial Technologies for More Resilient and Productive Small-scale Agriculture. NBER Working Papers, 29234. National Bureau of Economic Research.

Boustan, L.P., Kahn, M.E., Rhode, P.W., 2012. Moving to higher ground: migration response to natural disasters in the early twentieth century. American Economic Review 102 (3), 238–244.

Bradt, J.T., Aldy, J.E., 2022. Private Benefits from Public Investment in Climate Adaptation and Resilience. Working Paper.

Brooks, W., Donovan, K., 2020. Eliminating uncertainty in market access: the impact of new bridges in rural Nicaragua. Econometrica 88 (5), 1965–1997.

Bruno, E.M., Hadachek, J., Hagerty, N., Jessoe, K., 2023. External Costs of Climate Change Adaptation: Agricultural Wells and Access to Drinking Water. Working Paper.

Buck, S., Auffhammer, M., Sunding, D., 2014. Land markets and the value of water: hedonic analysis using repeat sales of farmland. American Journal of Agricultural Economics 96 (4), 953–969.

Burgess, R., Deschenes, O., Donaldson, D., Greenstone, M., 2017. Weather, Climate Change and Death in India. Working Paper.

Burgess, R., Donaldson, D., 2010. Can openness mitigate the effects of weather shocks? Evidence from India's famine era. American Economic Review 100 (2), 449–453.

Burke, M., Emerick, K., 2016. Adaptation to climate change: evidence from US agriculture. American Economic Journal: Economic Policy 8 (3), 106–140.

Burke, M., González, F., Baylis, P., Heft-Neal, S., Baysan, C., Basu, S., Hsiang, S., 2018. Higher temperatures increase suicide rates in the United States and Mexico. Nature Climate Change 8 (8), 723–729.

Burke, M., Hsiang, S.M., Miguel, E., 2015a. Climate and conflict. Annual Review of Economics 7 (1), 577–617.

Burke, M., Hsiang, S.M., Miguel, E., 2015b. Global non-linear effect of temperature on economic production. Nature 527 (7577), 235–239.

Burke, M., Tanutama, V., 2019. Climatic Constraints on Aggregate Economic Output. NBER Working Papers, 25779. National Bureau of Economic Research.

Burke, M., Zahid, M., Diffenbaugh, N., Hsiang, S.M., 2023. Quantifying Climate Change Loss and Damage Consistent with a Social Cost of Greenhouse Gases. NBER Working Papers, 31658. National Bureau of Economic Research.

Burlig, F., Jina, A., Kelley, E.M., Lane, G., Sahai, H., 2024. Long-range forecasts as climate adaptation: Experimental evidence from developing-country agriculture. In: NBER Working Papers, 32173. National Bureau of Economic Research.

Burzyński, M., Deuster, C., Docquier, F., de Melo, J., 2022. Climate change, inequality, and human migration. Journal of the European Economic Association 20 (3), 1145–1197.

Butler, E.E., Huybers, P., 2013. Adaptation of US maize to temperature variations. Nature Climate Change 3 (1), 68–72.

Cai, R., Feng, S., Oppenheimer, M., Pytlikova, M., 2016. Climate variability and international migration: the importance of the agricultural linkage. Journal of Environmental Economics and Management 79, 135–151.

Callahan, C.W., Mankin, J.S., 2022. National attribution of historical climate damages. Climatic Change 172 (3), 40.

Cantelmo, A., Melina, G., Papageorgiou, C., 2023. Macroeconomic outcomes in disaster-prone countries. Journal of Development Economics 161, 103037.

Carleton, T., Crews, L., Nath, I., 2024. Is the world running out of fresh water? AEA Papers and Proceedings 114, 31–35.

Carleton, T., Greenstone, M., 2022. A guide to updating the US governmentas social cost of carbon. Review of Environmental Economics and Policy 16 (2), 196–218.

Carleton, T., Hsiang, S., Burke, M., 2016. Conflict in a changing climate. The European Physical Journal Special Topics 225 (3), 489–511.

Carleton, T., Jina, A., Delgado, M., Greenstone, M., Houser, T., Hsiang, S., Hultgren, A., Kopp, R.E., McCusker, K.E., Nath, I., 2022. Valuing the global mortality consequences of climate change accounting for adaptation costs and benefits. The Quarterly Journal of Economics 137 (4), 2037–2105.

Carleton, T.A., 2017. Crop-damaging temperatures increase suicide rates in India. Proceedings of the National Academy of Sciences 114 (33), 8746–8751.

Carleton, T.A., Hsiang, S.M., 2016. Social and economic impacts of climate. Science 353 (6304), aad9837.

Casaburi, L., Willis, J., 2018. Time versus state in insurance: experimental evidence from contract farming in Kenya. American Economic Review 108 (12), 3778–3813.

Castro-Vincenzi, J., 2023. Climate Hazards and Resilience in the Global Car Industry. Working Paper.

Castro-Vincenzi, J., Khanna, G., Morales, N., Pandalai-Nayar, N., 2024. Weathering the Storm: Supply Chains and Climate Risk. In: NBER Working Papers, 32218. National Bureau of Economic Research.

Cattaneo, C., Peri, G., 2016. The migration response to increasing temperatures. Journal of Development Economics 122, 127–146.

Chakravorty, U., Dar, M.H., Emerick, K., 2023. Inefficient water pricing and incentives for conservation. American Economic Journal: Applied Economics 15 (1), 319–350.

Chancel, L., Bothe, P., Voituriez, T., 2023. Climate Inequality Report 2023. World Inequality Lab Study 2023/1.

Chinowsky, P., Helman, J., Gulati, S., Neumann, J., Martinich, J., 2019. Impacts of climate change on operation of the US rail network. Transport Policy 75, 183–191.

Chinowsky, P.S., Price, J.C., Neumann, J.E., 2013. Assessment of climate change adaptation costs for the U.S. road network. Global Environmental Change 23 (4), 764–773.

Christian, C., Hensel, L., Roth, C., 2019. Income shocks and suicides: causal evidence from Indonesia. The Review of Economics and Statistics 101 (5), 905–920.

Christian, P., Kandpal, E., Palaniswamy, N., Rao, V., 2019. Safety nets and natural disaster mitigation: evidence from cyclone Phailin in Odisha. Climatic Change 153 (1), 141–164.

Château, J., Dellink, R., Lanzi, E., 2014. An Overview of the OECD ENV-Linkages Model: Version 3. *OECD Environment Working Papers*, No. 65, OECD Publishing, Paris.

Climate Impact Lab, 2023. Documentation for Data-driven Spatial Climate Impact Model (DSCIM).

Cohen, F., Dechezleprêtre, A., 2022. Mortality, temperature, and public health provision: evidence from Mexico. American Economic Journal: Economic Policy 14 (2), 161–192.

Cole, S., Giné, X., Tobacman, J., Topalova, P., Townsend, R., Vickery, J., 2013. Barriers to household risk management: Evidence from India. American Economic Journal: Applied Economics 5 (1), 104–135.

Cole, S., Giné, X., Vickery, J., 2017. How does risk management influence production decisions? Evidence from a field experiment. The Review of Financial Studies 30 (6), 1935–1970.

Cole, S., Healy, A., Werker, E., 2012. Do voters demand responsive governments? Evidence from Indian disaster relief. Journal of Development Economics 97 (2), 167–181.

Colelli, F.P., Emmerling, J., Marangoni, G., Mistry, M.N., De Cian, E., 2022. Increased energy use for adaptation significantly impacts mitigation pathways. Nature Communications 13 (1), 4964.

Collier, B.L., Howell, S.T., Rendell, L., 2024. After the Storm: How Emergency Liquidity Helps Small Businesses Following Natural Disasters. NBER Working Papers, 32326. National Bureau of Economic Research.

Colmer, J., 2021. Temperature, labor reallocation, and industrial production: evidence from India. American Economic Journal: Applied Economics 13 (4), 101–124.

Colmer, J., Doleac, J.L., 2023. Access to guns in the heat of the moment: more restrictive gun laws mitigate the effect of temperature on violence. The Review of Economics and Statistics 1–40.

Conte, B., 2023. Climate Change and Migration: The Case of Africa. CESifo Working Paper 9948.

Conte, B., Desmet, K., Nagy, D.K., Rossi-Hansberg, E., 2021. Local sectoral specialization in a warming world. Journal of Economic Geography 21 (4), 493–530.

Corno, L., Voena, A., 2023. Child marriage as informal insurance: empirical evidence and policy simulations. Journal of Development Economics 162, 103047.

Corugedo, E.F., Gonzalez, A., Guerson, A., Guerson, M.A.D., 2023. The Macroeconomic Returns of Investment in Resilience to Natural Disasters Under Climate Change: A DSGE Approach. In: IMF, WP/23/138. International Monetary Fund.

Costinot, A., Donaldson, D., Smith, C., 2016. Evolving comparative advantage and the impact of climate change in agricultural markets: evidence from 1.7 million fields around the world. Journal of Political Economy 124 (1), 205–248.

Cruz, J.L., 2021. Global warming and labor market reallocation. Working paper.

Cruz, J.-L., Rossi-Hansberg, E., 2023. The economic geography of global warming. The Review of Economic Studies 91 (2), 899–939.

Cui, X., 2020. Climate Change and adaptation in agriculture: evidence from US cropping patterns. Journal of Environmental Economics and Management 101, 102306.

Cui, X., Zhong, Z., 2024. Climate Change cropland adjustments, and food security: evidence from China. Journal of Development Economics 167, 103245.

Dar, M.H., de Janvry, A., Emerick, K., Raitzer, D., Sadoulet, E., 2013. Flood-tolerant rice reduces yield variability and raises expected yield, differentially benefitting socially disadvantaged groups. Scientific Reports 3 (1), 3315.

Das, S., Vincent, J.R., 2009. Mangroves protected villages and reduced death toll during Indian super cyclone. Proceedings of the National Academy of Sciences 106 (18), 7357–7360.

Davlasheridze, M., Fisher-Vanden, K., AllenKlaiber, H., 2017. The effects of adaptation measures on hurricane induced property losses: which FEMA investments have the highest returns? Journal of Environmental Economics and Management 81, 93–114.

De Bruin, K.C., Dellink, R.B., Tol, R.S.J., 2009. AD-DICE: an implementation of adaptation in the DICE model. Climatic Change 95 (1–2), 63–81.

del Valle, A., 2024. Saving Lives with Indexed Disaster Funds: Evidence from Mexico. American Economic Journal: Economic Policy 16 (2), 442–479.

del Valle, A., De Janvry, A., Sadoulet, E., 2020. Rules for recovery: impact of indexed disaster funds on shock coping in Mexico. American Economic Journal: Applied Economics 12 (4), 164–195.

Dell, M., Jones, B.F., Olken, B.A., 2012. Temperature shocks and economic growth: evidence from the last half century. American Economic Journal: Macroeconomics 4 (3), 66–95.

Dell, M., Jones, B.F., Olken, B.A., 2014. What do we learn from the weather? The new climate-economy literature. Journal of Economic Literature 52 (3), 740–798.

Dellink, R., Lanzi, E., Chateau, J., 2019. The sectoral and regional economic consequences of climate change to 2060. Environmental and Resource Economics 72 (2), 309–363.

Depsky, N., Bolliger, I., Allen, D., Choi, J.H., Delgado, M., Greenstone, M., Hamidi, A., Houser, T., Kopp, R.E., Hsiang, S., 2023. DSCIM-Coastal v1.1: an open-source modeling platform for global impacts of sea level rise. Geoscientific Model Development 16 (14), 4331–4366.

Deryugina, T., 2013. How do people update? The effects of local weather fluctuations on beliefs about global warming. Climatic Change 118 (2), 397–416.

Deryugina, T., 2017. The fiscal cost of hurricanes: disaster aid versus social insurance. American Economic Journal: Economic Policy 9 (3), 168–198.

Deryugina, T., Hsiang, S., 2017. The Marginal Product of Climate. NBER Working Papers, 24072. National Bureau of Economic Research.

Deryugina, T., Kirwan, B., 2018. Does the Samaritan's Dilemma Matter? Evidence from U.S. Agriculture. Economic Inquiry 56 (2), 983–1006.

Deschenes, O., 2022. The impact of climate change on mortality in the United States: Benefits and costs of adaptation. Canadian Journal of Economics/Revue canadienne d'économique 55 (3), 1227–1249.

Deschênes, O., Greenstone, M., 2007. The economic impacts of climate change: evidence from agricultural output and random fluctuations in weather. American Economic Review 97 (1), 354–385.

Deschênes, O., Greenstone, M., 2011. Climate change, mortality, and adaptation: evidence from annual fluctuations in weather in the US. American Economic Journal: Applied Economics 3 (4), 152–185.

Desmet, K., Kopp, R.E., Kulp, S.A., Nagy, D.K., Oppenheimer, M., Rossi-Hansberg, E., Strauss, B.H., 2021. Evaluating the economic cost of coastal flooding. American Economic Journal: Macroeconomics 13 (2), 444–486.

Desmet, K., Rossi-Hansberg, E., 2015. On the spatial economic impact of global warming. Journal of Urban Economics 88, 16–37.

Diaz, D., Moore, F., 2017. Quantifying the economic risks of climate change. Nature Climate Change 7 (11), 774–782.

Desmet, K., Rossi-Hansberg, E., 2024. Climate Change Economics over Time and Space. Annual Review of Economics 16, 271–304.

Diaz, D.B., 2016. Estimating global damages from sea level rise with the Coastal Impact and Adaptation Model (CIAM). Climatic Change 137 (1), 143–156.

Dietz, S., 2024. Introduction to integrated climate-economic modeling. Handbook of Climate Economics. vol. 1.

Dietz, S., Lanz, B., 2022. Growth and Adaptation to Climate Change in the Long Run. CESifo Working Paper 7986.

Dietz, S., Rising, J., Stoerk, T., Wagner, G., 2021. Economic impacts of tipping points in the climate system. Proceedings of the National Academy of Sciences 118 (34), e2103081118.

Diffenbaugh, N.S., Burke, M., 2019. Global warming has increased global economic inequality. Proceedings of the National Academy of Sciences 116 (20), 9808–9813.

Dorfleitner, G., Wimmer, M., 2010. The pricing of temperature futures at the Chicago Mercantile Exchange. Journal of Banking & Finance 34 (6), 1360–1370.

Downey, M., Lind, N., Shrader, J.G., 2023. Adjusting to rain before it falls. Management Science 69 (12), 7399–7422.

Druckenmiller, H., Hsiang, S., 2018. Accounting for Unobservable Heterogeneity in Cross Section Using Spatial First Differences. In: NBER Working Papers, 25177. National Bureau of Economic Research.

Du Puy, T., Shrader, J.G., 2024. Costs of Climate Adaptation: Evidence From French Agriculture. Working Paper.

Eboli, F., Parrado, R., Roson, R., 2010. Climate-change feedback on economic growth: explorations with a dynamic general equilibrium model. Environment and Development Economics 15 (5), 515–533.

Edmondson, J.L., Stott, I., Davies, Z.G., Gaston, K.J., Leake, J.R., 2016. Soil surface temperatures reveal moderation of the urban heat island effect by trees and shrubs. Scientific Reports 6 (1), 33708.

Emerick, K., De Janvry, A., Sadoulet, E., Dar, M.H., 2016. Technological innovations, downside risk, and the modernization of agriculture. American Economic Review 106 (6), 1537–1561.

Fetzer, T., 2020. Can workfare programs moderate conflict? Evidence from India. Journal of the European Economic Association 18 (6), 3337–3375.

Fitch-Fleischmann, B., Kresch, E.P., 2021. Story of the hurricane: Government, NGOs, and the difference in disaster relief targeting. Journal of Development Economics 152, 102702.

Flores, N.M., Northrop, A.J., Do, V., Gordon, M., Jiang, Y., Rudolph, K.E., Hernández, D., Casey, J.A., 2024. Powerless in the storm: severe weather-driven power outages in New York State, 2017–2020. PLoS Climate 3 (5) e0000364.

Fried, S., 2022. Seawalls and stilts: a quantitative macro study of climate adaptation. The Review of Economic Studies 89 (6), 3303–3344.

Fried, S., 2024. A Macro Study of the Unequal Effects of Climate Change. Federal Reserve Bank of San Francisco Working Paper 2024-18.

Gallagher, J., 2014. Learning about an infrequent event: evidence from flood insurance take-up in the United States. American Economic Journal: Applied Economics 6 (3), 206–233.

Gallagher, J., Hartley, D., Rohlin, S., 2023. Weathering an unexpected financial shock: the role of federal disaster assistance on household finance and business survival. Journal of the Association of Environmental and Resource Economists 10 (2), 525–567.

Garg, T., Jagnani, M., Taraz, V., 2020. Temperature and human capital in India. Journal of the Association of Environmental and Resource Economists 7 (6), 1113–1150.

Garg, T., McCord, G.C., Montfort, A., 2020. Can Social Protection Reduce Environmental Damages? Working Paper.

Gatti, N., Cecil, M., Baylis, K., Estes, L., Blekking, J., Heckelei, T., Vergopolan, N., Evans, T., 2023. Is closing the agricultural yield gap a "risky" endeavor? Agricultural Systems 208, 103657.

Gibson, M., Mullins, J.T., 2020. Climate risk and beliefs in New York floodplains. Journal of the Association of Environmental and Resource Economists 7 (6), 1069–1111.

Gillingham, K., Stock, J.H., 2018. The cost of reducing greenhouse gas emissions. Journal of Economic Perspectives 32 (4), 53–72.

Gine, X., Townsend, R.M., Vickery, J., 2015. Forecasting When it Matters: Evidence from Semi-Arid India. Working Paper.

Gittman, R.K., Scyphers, S.B., Smith, C.S., Neylan, I.P., Grabowski, J.H., 2016. Ecological consequences of shoreline hardening: a meta-analysis. BioScience 66 (9), 763–773.

Gollier, C., 2021. The welfare cost of ignoring the beta. FEEM Working Paper 003.2021, Fondazione Eni Enrico Mattei (FEEM).

Gouel, C., Laborde, D., 2021. The Crucial Role of International Trade in Adaptation to Climate Change.

Gouel, C., Laborde, D., 2021. The crucial role of domestic and international market-mediated adaptation to climate change. Journal of Environmental Economics and Management 106, 102408.

Gourevitch, J.D., Kousky, C., Liao, Y.P., Nolte, C., Pollack, A.B., Porter, J.R., Weill, J.A., 2023. Unpriced climate risk and the potential consequences of overvaluation in US housing markets. Nature Climate Change 13 (3), 250–257.

Graff-Zivin, J., Neidell, M., 2014. Temperature and the allocation of time: implications for climate change. Journal of Labor Economics 32 (1), 1–26.

Greenstone, M., Kopits, E., Wolverton, A., 2013. Developing a social cost of carbon for US regulatory analysis: a methodology and interpretation. Review of Environmental Economics and Policy 7 (1), 23–46.

Grosset, F., Papp, A., Taylor, C., 2023. Rain Follows the Forest: Land Use Policy, Climate Change, and Adaptation. Working Paper.

Gunnsteinsson, S., Molina, T., Adhvaryu, A., Christian, P., Labrique, A., Sugimoto, J., Shamim, A.A., West, K.P., 2022. Protecting infants from natural disasters: the case of vitamin A supplementation and a tornado in Bangladesh. Journal of Development Economics 158, 102914.

Guo, C., Costello, C., 2013. The value of adaption: climate change and timberland management. Journal of Environmental Economics and Management 65 (3), 452–468.

Hagerty, N., 2022. Adaptation to Surface Water Scarcity in Irrigated Agriculture. Working Paper.

Hahn, R.W., Hendren, N., Metcalfe, R.D., B. Sprung-Keyser, B., 2024. A Welfare Analysis of Policies Impacting Climate Change. NBER Working Papers, 32728. National Bureau of Economic Research.

Helo Sarmiento, J., 2023. Into the tropics: temperature, mortality, and access to health care in Colombia. Journal of Environmental Economics and Management 119, 102796.

Henderson, J., Rodgers, C., Jones, R., Smith, J., Strzepek, K., Martinich, J., 2015. Economic impacts of climate change on water resources in the coterminous United States. Mitigation and Adaptation Strategies for Global Change 20 (1), 135–157.

Hennighausen, H., Liao, Y., Nolte, C., Pollack, A., 2023. Flood insurance reforms, housing market dynamics, and adaptation to climate risks. Journal of Housing Economics 62, 101953.

Heutel, G., Miller, N.H., Molitor, D., 2021. Adaptation and the mortality effects of temperature across U.S. climate regions. The Review of Economics and Statistics 103 (4), 740–753.

Hill, R.V., Kumar, N., Magnan, N., Makhija, S., de Nicola, F., Spielman, D.J., Ward, P.S., 2019. Ex ante and ex post effects of hybrid index insurance in Bangladesh. Journal of Development Economics 136, 1–17.

Hinkel, J., Klein, R.J.T., 2009. Integrating knowledge to assess coastal vulnerability to sea-level rise: the development of the DIVA tool. Global Environmental Change 19 (3), 384–395.

Hinkel, J., Lincke, D., Vafeidis, A.T., Perrette, M., Nicholls, R.J., Tol, R.S.J., Marzeion, B., Fettweis, X., Ionescu, C., Levermann, A., 2014. Coastal flood damage and adaptation costs under 21st century sea-level rise. Proceedings of the National Academy of Sciences 111 (9), 3292–3297.

Hino, M., Burke, M., 2021. The effect of information about climate risk on property values. Proceedings of the National Academy of Sciences 118 (17), e2003374118.

Hirvonen, K., Gilligan, D.O., Leight, J., Tambet, H., Villa, V., 2023. Do ultra-poor graduation programs build resilience against droughts? Evidence from rural Ethiopia. IFPRI Discussion Paper 02206. The International Food Policy Research Institute.

Hogan, D., Schlenker, W., 2024. Empirical approaches to climate change impact quantification. Handbook of Climate Economics. vol. 1.

Hong, H., Li, F.W., Xu, J., 2019. Climate risks and market efficiency. Journal of Econometrics 208 (1), 265–281.

Hong, H., Wang, N., Yang, J., 2023. Mitigating disaster risks in the age of climate change. Econometrica 91 (5), 1763–1802.

Hope, C., Anderson, J., Wenman, P., 1993. Policy analysis of the greenhouse effect. Energy Policy 21 (3), 327–338.

Hornbeck, R., 2012. The enduring impact of the American dust bowl: short- and long-run adjustments to environmental catastrophe. American Economic Review 102 (4), 1477–1507.

Hornbeck, R., Keskin, P., 2014. The historically evolving impact of the ogallala aquifer: agricultural adaptation to groundwater and drought. American Economic Journal: Applied Economics 6 (1), 190–219.

Hou, X., 2010. Can drought increase total calorie availability? The impact of drought on food consumption and the mitigating effects of a conditional cash transfer program. Economic Development and Cultural Change 58 (4), 713–737.

Hovekamp, W.P., Wagner, K.R., 2023. Efficient adaptation to flood risk. AEA Papers and Proceedings 113, 304–309.

Hsiang, S., 2016. Climate econometrics. Annual Review of Resource Economics 8 (1), 43–75.

Hsiang, S.M., Burke, M., 2014. Climate, conflict, and social stability: what does the evidence say? Climatic Change 123 (1), 39–55.

Hsiang, S.M., Narita, D., 2012. Adaptation to cyclone risk: evidence from the global cross-section. Climate Change Economics 03 (02), 1250011.

Hsiao, A., 2024. Sea Level Rise and Urban Inequality. Working Paper.

Hsiao, A., Moscona, J., Sastry, K.A., 2024. Food Policy in a Warming World. Working Paper.

Hu, H., Lei, T., Hu, J., Zhang, S., Kavan, P., 2018. Disaster-mitigating and general innovative responses to climate disasters: evidence from modern and historical China. International Journal of Disaster Risk Reduction 28, 664–673.

Hultgren, A., Carleton, T., Delgado, M., Gergel, D.R., Greenstone, M., Houser, T., Hsiang, S., Jina, A., Kopp, R.E., Malevich, S.B., McCusker, K.E., Mayer, T., Nath, I., Rising, J., Rode, A., Yuan, J., 2022. Estimating Global Impacts to Agriculture from Climate Change Accounting for Adaptation. Working Paper.

Indaco, A., Ortega, F., Taspınar, A.S., 2021. Hurricanes, flood risk and the economic adaptation of businesses. Journal of Economic Geography 21 (4), 557–591.

Jack, W., Suri, T., 2014. Risk sharing and transactions costs: evidence from Kenya's mobile money revolution. American Economic Review 104 (1), 183–223.

Jagnani, M., Barrett, C.B., Liu, Y., You, L., 2021. Within-season producer response to warmer temperatures: defensive investments by Kenyan farmers. The Economic Journal 131 (633), 392–419.

Janzen, S.A., Carter, M.R., 2019. After the drought: the impact of microinsurance on consumption smoothing and asset protection. American Journal of Agricultural Economics 101 (3), 651–671.

Jayachandran, S., 2006. Selling labor low: wage responses to productivity shocks in developing countries. Journal of Political Economy 114 (3), 538–575.

Ji, X., Cobourn, K.M., 2021. Weather fluctuations, expectation formation, and short-run behavioral responses to climate change. Environmental and Resource Economics 78 (1), 77–119.

Jia, R., Ma, X., Xie, V.W., 2022. Expecting floods: firm entry, employment, and aggregate implications. NBER Working Papers, 30250. National Bureau of Economic Research.

Jones, M., Kondylis, F., Loeser, J., Magruder, J., 2022. Factor market failures and the adoption of irrigation in Rwanda. American Economic Review 112 (7), 2316–2352.

Jorgenson, D.W., Goettle, R.J., Hurd, B.H., Smith, J.B., 2004. U.S. market consequences of global climate change. Pew Center on Global Climate Change. Washington, DC.

Kahn, M.E., Mohaddes, K., Ng, R.N.C., Pesaran, M.H., Raissi, M., Yang, J.-C., 2021. Long-term macroeconomic effects of climate change: a cross-country analysis. Energy Economics 104, 105624.

Kala, N., 2017. Learning, Adaptation, And Climate Uncertainty: Evidence From Indian Agriculture. Working Paper.

Kalkuhl, M., Wenz, L., 2020. The impact of climate conditions on economic production. Evidence from a global panel of regions. Journal of Environmental Economics and Management 103, 102360.

Kazianga, H., Udry, C., 2006. Consumption smoothing? Livestock, insurance and drought in rural Burkina Faso. Journal of Development Economics 79 (2), 413–446.

Kelly, D.L., Kolstad, C.D., Mitchell, G.T., 2005. Adjustment costs from environmental change. Journal of Environmental Economics and Management 50 (3), 468–495.

Kelly, D.L., Molina, R., 2023. Adaptation infrastructure and its effects on property values in the face of climate risk. Journal of the Association of Environmental and Resource Economists 10 (6), 1405–1438.

Knippenberg, E., Hoddinott, J., 2019. Shocks, social protection, and resilience: evidence from Ethiopia. Gates Open Research 3 (702), 702.

Kochar, A., 1999. Smoothing consumption by smoothing income: hours-of-work responses to idiosyncratic agricultural shocks in rural India. Review of Economics and Statistics 81 (1), 50–61.

Kochhar, R., Song, R., 2023. Does Market Power in Indiaas Agricultural Markets Hinder Farmer Climate Change Adaptation? Working Paper.

Kolstad, C.D., Moore, F.C., 2020. Estimating the economic impacts of climate change using weather observations. Review of Environmental Economics and Policy 14 (1), 1–24.

Kousky, C., Luttmer, E.F.P., Zeckhauser, R.J., 2006. Private investment and government protection. Journal of Risk and Uncertainty 33 (1), 73–100.

Kousky, C., Michel-Kerjan, E.O., Raschky, P.A., 2018. Does federal disaster assistance crowd out flood insurance? Journal of Environmental Economics and Management 87, 150–164.

Krusell, P., Smith, J.A.A., 2022. Climate Change Around the World. Working Paper.

Kruttli, M.S., RothTran, B., Watugala, S.W., 2023. Pricing Poseidon: Extreme Weather Uncertainty and Firm Return Dynamics. Working Paper.

Kurukulasuriya, P., Mendelsohn, R., 2008. A Ricardian analysis of the impact of climate change on African cropland. African Journal of Agricultural and Resource Economics.

Kydland, F.E., Prescott, E.C., 1977. Rules rather than discretion: the inconsistency of optimal plans. Journal of Political Economy 85 (3), 473–491.

Lane, G., 2024. Adapting to climate risk with guaranteed credit: evidence from Bangladesh. Econometrica 92 (2), 355–386.

Larsen, P.H., Goldsmith, S., Smith, O., Wilson, M.L., Strzepek, K., Chinowsky, P., Saylor, B., 2008. Estimating future costs for Alaska public infrastructure at risk from climate change. Global Environmental Change 18 (3), 442–457.

Lee, J.-Y., Marotzke, J., Bala, G., Cao, L., Corti, S., Dunne, J.P., Engelbrecht, F., Fischer, E., Fyfe, J., Jones, C., Maycock, A., Mutemi, J., Ndiaye, O., Panickal, S., Zhou, T., 2021. Future global climate: scenario-based projections and near-term information. Climate Change 2021: The Physical Science Basis. Contribution of Working Group I to the Sixth Assessment Report of the Intergovernmental Panel on Climate Change, Number 4. Cambridge University Press, Cambridge, United Kingdom and New York, NY, USA, pp. 553–672.

Lee, S., 2023. Adapting to Natural Disasters through Better Information: Evidence from the Home Seller Disclosure Requirement. MIT Center for Real Estate Research Paper 21/17.

Lemoine, D., 2023. Estimating the Consequences of Climate Change from Variation in Weather. In: NBER Working Papers, 25008. National Bureau of Economic Research.

Lemoine, D., Kapnick, S., 2024. Financial markets value skillful forecasts of seasonal climate. Nature Communications 15 (1), 1–10.

Letta, M., Montalbano, P., Pierre, G., 2022. Weather shocks, traders' expectations, and food prices. American Journal of Agricultural Economics 104 (3), 1100–1119.

Li, T., 2021. Protecting the breadbasket with trees? The effect of the great plains shelterbelt project on agriculture. Land Economics 97 (2), 321–344.

Li, X., Gopalakrishnan, S., Klaiber, H.A., 2024. Local adaptation and unintended coastal vulnerability: the effect of beach nourishment on residential development in North Carolina. Journal of the Association of Environmental and Resource Economists 11 (3), 523–548.

Lin, Y., Liu, F., Xu, P., 2021. Effects of drought on infant mortality in China. Health Economics 30 (2), 248–269.

Linsenmeier, M., 2023. Temperature variability and long-run economic development. Journal of Environmental Economics and Management 121, 102840.

Liu, M., Shamdasani, Y., Taraz, V., 2023. Climate change and labor reallocation: evidence from six decades of the Indian census. American Economic Journal: Economic Policy 15 (2), 395–423.

Lobell, D.B., Schlenker, W., Costa-Roberts, J., 2011. Climate trends and global crop production since 1980. Science 333 (6042), 616–620.

Lorie, M., Neumann, J.E., Sarofim, M.C., Jones, R., Horton, R.M., Kopp, R.E., Fant, C., Wobus, C., Martinich, J., O'Grady, M., Gentile, L.E., 2020. Modeling coastal flood risk and adaptation response under future climate conditions. Climate Risk Management 29, 100233.

Lucas Jr, R.E., 1972. Econometric testing of the natural rate hypothesis. The Econometrics of Price Determination 50, 59.

Macours, K., Premand, P., Vakis, R., 2022. Transfers, diversification and household risk strategies: Can productive safety nets help households manage climatic variability? The Economic Journal 132 (647), 2438–2470.

Mahadevan, M., Shenoy, A., 2023. The political consequences of resource scarcity: targeted spending in a water-stressed democracy. Journal of Public Economics 220, 104842.

Mallucci, E., 2022. Natural disasters, Climate Change, and sovereign risk. Journal of International Economics 139, 103672.

Manne, A., Mendelsohn, R., Richels, R., 1995. MERGE: a model for evaluating regional and global effects of GHG reduction policies. Energy Policy 23 (1), 17–34.

Martinich, J., Crimmins, A., 2019. Climate damages and adaptation potential across diverse sectors of the United States. Nature Climate Change 9 (5), 397–404.

Marto, R., Papageorgiou, C., Klyuev, V., 2018. Building resilience to natural disasters: an application to small developing states. Journal of Development Economics 135, 574–586.

Massetti, E., Mendelsohn, R., 2018. Measuring climate adaptation: methods and evidence. Review of Environmental Economics and Policy 12 (2), 324–341.

McDermott, T.K., Barry, F., Tol, R.S., 2014. Disasters and development: natural disasters, credit constraints, and economic growth. Oxford Economic Papers 66 (3), 750–773.

McFadden, J.R., Smith, D.J., Wallander, S., 2022. Weather, Climate, and Technology Adoption: An Application to Drought-Tolerant Corn in the United States. NBER Working Papers, 30121. National Bureau of Economic Research.

McIntosh, C.T., Schlenker, W., 2005. Identifying Non-linearities In Fixed Effects Models. Working Paper.

McKenzie, D., 2012. Beyond baseline and follow-up: the case for more T in experiments. Journal of Development Economics 99 (2), 210–221.

Melvin, A.M., Larsen, P., Boehlert, B., Neumann, J.E., Chinowsky, P., Espinet, X., Martinich, J., Baumann, M.S., Rennels, L., Bothner, A., Nicolsky, D.J., Marchenko, S.S., 2017. Climate Change damages to Alaska public infrastructure and the economics of proactive adaptation. Proceedings of the National Academy of Sciences 114 (2), E122–E131.

Mendelsohn, R., Nordhaus, W.D., Shaw, D., 1994. The impact of global warming on agriculture: a ricardian analysis. The American Economic Review 84 (4), 753–771.

Mendelsohn, R.O., Massetti, E., 2017. The use of cross-sectional analysis to measure climate impacts on agriculture: theory and evidence. Review of Environmental Economics and Policy 11 (2), 280–298.

Menéndez, P., Losada, I.J., Torres-Ortega, S., Narayan, S., Beck, M.W., 2020. The global flood protection benefits of mangroves. Scientific Reports 10 (1), 4404.

Miao, Q., Popp, D., 2014. Necessity as the mother of invention: innovative responses to natural disasters. Journal of Environmental Economics and Management 68 (2), 280–295.

Millner, A., Heal, G., 2023. Choosing the future: markets, ethics, and rapprochement in social discounting. Journal of Economic Literature 61 (3), 1037–1087.

Mobarak, A.M., Rosenzweig, M., 2014. Risk, Insurance and Wages in General Equilibrium. NBER Working Papers, 19811. National Bureau of Economic Research.

Mogge, L., Röckert, J., Kraehnert, K., 2024. Impacts of anticipatory cash transfers in the context of weather disasters. Ruhr Economic Papers, No. 1065, RWI -. Leibniz- Institut für Wirtschaftsforschung, Essen.

Molina, R., Rudik, I., 2023. The Social Value of Hurricane Forecasts. NBER Working Papers, 32548. National Bureau of Economic Research.

Moore, F.C., 2017. Learning, adaptation, and weather in a changing climate. Climate Change Economics 08 (04), 1750010.

Moore, F.C., Diaz, D.B., 2015. Temperature impacts on economic growth warrant stringent mitigation policy. Nature Climate Change 5 (2), 127–131.

Moore, F.C., Lobell, D.B., 2014. Adaptation potential of European agriculture in response to climate change. Nature Climate Change 4 (7), 610–614.

Moore, F.C., Lobell, D.B., 2015. The fingerprint of climate trends on European crop yields. Proceedings of the National Academy of Sciences 112 (9), 2670–2675.

Moore, F.C., Obradovich, N., Lehner, F., Baylis, P., 2019. Rapidly declining remarkability of temperature anomalies may obscure public perception of climate change. Proceedings of the National Academy of Sciences 116 (11), 4905–4910.

Morduch, J., 1995. Income smoothing and consumption smoothing. Journal of Economic Perspectives 9 (3), 103–114.

Moscona, J., 2021. Environmental Catastrophe and the Direction of Invention: Evidence from the American Dust Bowl. Working Paper.

Moscona, J., Sastry, K.A., 2023. Does directed innovation mitigate climate damage? Evidence from U.S. agriculture. The Quarterly Journal of Economics 138 (2), 637–701.

Mosnier, A., Obersteiner, M., Havlík, P., Schmid, E., Khabarov, N., Westphal, M., Valin, H., Frank, S., Albrecht, F., 2014. Global food markets, trade and the cost of climate change adaptation. Food Security 6 (1), 29–44.

Muis, S., Güneralp, B., Jongman, B., Aerts, J.C.J.H., Ward, P.J., 2015. Flood risk and adaptation strategies under Climate Change and urban expansion: a probabilistic analysis using global data. Science of The Total Environment 538, 445–457.

Mulder, P., 2022. Mismeasuring Risk: The Welfare Effects of Flood Risk Information. Working Paper.

Mullins, J.T., White, C., 2020. Can access to health care mitigate the effects of temperature on mortality? Journal of Public Economics 191, 104259.

Murfin, J., Spiegel, M., 2020. Is the risk of sea level rise capitalized in residential real estate? The Review of Financial Studies 33 (3), 1217–1255.

Mérel, P., Gammans, M., 2021. Climate econometrics: can the panel approach account for long-run adaptation? American Journal of Agricultural Economics 103 (4), 1207–1238.

Mérel, P., Paroissien, E., Gammans, M., 2024. Sufficient statistics for climate change counterfactuals. Journal of Environmental Economics and Management 124, 102940.

Nath, I., 2023. Climate Change, The Food Problem, and the Challenge of Adaptation through Sectoral Reallocation. NBER Working Papers, 27297. National Bureau of Economic Research.

Neumann, J., Hudgens, D., Herter, J., Martinich, J., 2011. The economics of adaptation along developed coastlines. WIREs Climate Change 2 (1), 89–98.

Neumann, J.E., Emanuel, K., Ravela, S., Ludwig, L., Kirshen, P., Bosma, K., Martinich, J., 2015. Joint effects of storm surge and sea-level rise on US Coasts: new economic estimates of impacts, adaptation, and benefits of mitigation policy. Climatic Change 129 (1), 337–349.

Neumann, J.E., Price, J., Chinowsky, P., Wright, L., Ludwig, L., Streeter, R., Jones, R., Smith, J.B., Perkins, W., Jantarasami, L., Martinich, J., 2015. Climate Change risks to US infrastructure: impacts on roads, bridges, coastal development, and urban drainage. Climatic Change 131 (1), 97–109.

Nordhaus, W.D., 1992. An optimal transition path for controlling greenhouse gases. Science 258 (5086), 1315–1319.

Nordhaus, W.D., 1993. Optimal greenhouse-gas reductions and tax policy in the "DICE" model. The American Economic Review 83 (2), 313–317.

Noy, I., 2009. The macroeconomic consequences of disasters. Journal of Development Economics 88 (2), 221–231.

Noy, I., Strobl, E., 2023. Creatively destructive hurricanes: do disasters spark innovation? Environmental and Resource Economics 84 (1), 1–17.

Nyqvist, M.B., Carnap, T.V., Guariso, A., Svensson, J., 2023. Weather Shocks, Child Mortality, and Adaptation: Experimental Evidence from Uganda. Working Paper.

Okereke, C., Coventry, P., 2016. Climate justice and the international regime: before, during, and after Paris. WIREs Climate Change 7 (6), 834–851.

Ortiz-Bobea, A., 2020. The role of nonfarm influences in ricardian estimates of climate change impacts on US agriculture. American Journal of Agricultural Economics 102 (3), 934–959.

Ospital, A., 2023. Urban Policy and Spatial Exposure to Environmental Risk. Working Paper.

Ostriker, A., Russo, A., 2024. The effects of floodplain regulation on housing markets. Working Paper.

Pankratz, N.M.C., Schiller, C.M., 2024. Climate change and adaptation in global supply-chain networks. The Review of Financial Studies 37 (6), 1729–1777.

Park, R.J., Behrer, A.P., Goodman, J., 2021. Learning is inhibited by heat exposure, both internationally and within the United States. Nature Human Behaviour 5 (1), 19–27.

Park, R.J., Goodman, J., Hurwitz, M., Smith, J., 2020. Heat and learning. American Economic Journal: Economic Policy 12 (2), 306–339.

Patel, D., 2023. Learning about a Warming World: Attention and Adaptation in Agriculture. Working Paper.

Paxson, C.H., 1992. Using weather variability to estimate the response of savings to transitory income in Thailand. The American Economic Review 82 (1), 15–33.

Peltzman, S., 1975. The effects of automobile safety regulation. Journal of Political Economy 83 (4), 677–725.

Peralta, A., Scott, J.B., 2024. Does the national flood insurance program drive migration to higher risk areas? Journal of the Association of Environmental and Resource Economists 11 (2), 287–318.

Phan, T., Schwartzman, F.F., 2024. Climate Defaults and Financial Adaptation. European Economic Review 170, 104866.

Ponnusamy, S., 2022. Rainfall shocks, child mortality, and water infrastructure. Health Economics 31 (7), 1317–1338.

Pople, A., Hill, R., Dercon, S., Brunckhorst, B., 2021. Anticipatory cash transfers in climate disaster response. In: CSAE Working Paper Series 2021-07. Centre for the Study of African Economies, University of Oxford.

Premand, P., Stoeffler, Q., 2022. Cash transfers, climatic shocks and resilience in the Sahel. Journal of Environmental Economics and Management 116, 102744.

Prest, B.C., Rennels, L., Errickson, F., Anthoff, D., 2024. Equity weighting increases the social cost of carbon. Science 385 (6710), 715–717.

Price, J.C., Wright, L., Fant, C., Strzepek, K.M., 2016. Calibrated methodology for assessing climate change adaptation costs for urban drainage systems. Urban Water Journal 13 (4), 331–344.

Rafey, W., 2023. Droughts, deluges, and (river) diversions: valuing market-based water reallocation. American Economic Review 113 (2), 430–471.

Rajan, R., Ramcharan, R., 2023. Finance and Climate Resilience: Evidence from the long 1950s US Drought. In: NBER Working Papers, 31356. National Bureau of Economic Research.

Renard, D., Mahaut, L., Noack, F., 2023. Crop diversity buffers the impact of droughts and high temperatures on food production. Environmental Research Letters 18 (4), 045002.

Rennert, K., Errickson, F., Prest, B.C., Rennels, L., Newell, R.G., Pizer, W., Kingdon, C., Wingenroth, J., Cooke, R., Parthum, B., Smith, D., Cromar, K., Diaz, D., Moore, F.C., Müller, U.K., Plevin, R.J., Raftery, A.E., Ševčíková, H., Sheets, H., Stock, J.H., Tan, T., Watson, M., Wong, T.E., Anthoff, D., 2022. Comprehensive evidence implies a higher social cost of CO_2. Nature 610 (7933), 687–692.

Riley, E., 2018. Mobile money and risk sharing against village shocks. Journal of Development Economics 135, 43–58.

Rocha, R., Soares, R.R., 2015. Water scarcity and birth outcomes in the Brazilian semiarid. Journal of Development Economics 112, 72–91.

Rode, A., Baker, R.E., Carleton, T., D'Agostino, A., Delgado, M., Foreman, T., Gergel, D.R., Greenstone, M., Houser, T., Hsiang, S., Hultgren, A., Jina, A., Kopp, R.E., Malevich, S.B., McCusker, K., Nath, I., Pecenco, M., Rising, J., Yuan, J., 2022. Labor Disutility in a Warmer World: The Impact of Climate Change on the Global Workforce. Working Paper.

Rode, A., Carleton, T., Delgado, M., Greenstone, M., Houser, T., Hsiang, S., Hultgren, A., Jina, A., Kopp, R.E., McCusker, K.E., Nath, I., Rising, J., Yuan, J., 2021. Estimating a social cost of carbon for global energy consumption. Nature 598 (7880), 308–314.

Rodríguez, J.F., Saco, P.M., Sandi, S., Saintilan, N., Riccardi, G., 2017. Potential increase in coastal wetland vulnerability to sea-level rise suggested by considering hydrodynamic attenuation effects. Nature Communications 8 (1), 16094.

Rosenzweig, M., Udry, C.R., 2013. Forecasting Profitability. NBER Working Papers, 19334. National Bureau of Economic Research.

Rosenzweig, M.R., Binswanger, H.P., 1993. Wealth, weather risk and the composition and profitability of agricultural investments. The Economic Journal 103 (416), 56–78.

Rosenzweig, M.R., Udry, C., 2014. Rainfall forecasts, weather, and wages over the agricultural production cycle. American Economic Review 104 (5), 278–283.

Rosenzweig, M.R., Udry, C., 2020. External validity in a stochastic world: evidence from low-income countries. The Review of Economic Studies 87 (1), 343–381.

Roson, R., van der Mensbrugghe, D., 2012. Climate change and economic growth: impacts and interactions. International Journal of Sustainable Economy 4 (3), 270–285.

Roth Tran, B., 2023. Sellin' in the rain: weather, climate, and retail sales. Management Science 69 (12), 7423–7447.

Rozenberg, J., Davis, S.J., Narloch, U., Hallegatte, S., 2015. Climate constraints on the carbon intensity of economic growth. Environmental Research Letters 10 (9), 095006.

Rubin, A., Segal, D., 2015. The effects of economic growth on income inequality in the US. Journal of Macroeconomics 45, 258–273.

Rudik, I., Lyn, G., Tan, W., Ortiz-Bobea, A., 2024. The Economic Effects of Climate Change in Dynamic Spatial Equilibrium. Working Paper.

Saez, E., Stantcheva, S., 2016. Generalized social marginal welfare weights for optimal tax theory. American Economic Review 106 (1), 24–45.

Schlenker, W., 2017. Inter-annual Weather Variation and Crop Yields. Working Paper.

Schlenker, W., MichaelHanemann, W., Fisher, A.C., 2005. Will U.S. agriculture really benefit from global warming? Accounting for irrigation in the hedonic approach. American Economic Review 95 (1), 395–406.

Schlenker, W., Roberts, M.J., 2009. Nonlinear temperature effects indicate severe damages to U.S. crop yields under climate change. Proceedings of the National Academy of Sciences 106 (37), 15594–15598.

Schlenker, W., Roberts, M.J., Lobell, D.B., 2013. US maize adaptability. Nature Climate Change 3 (8), 690–691.

Schlenker, W., Taylor, C.A., 2021. Market expectations of a warming climate. Journal of Financial Economics 142 (2), 627–640.

Schneider, S.A., Kunze, S., 2023. Disastrous discretion: political bias in relief allocation varies substantially with disaster severity. The Review of Economics and Statistics 1–33.

Severen, C., Costello, C., Deschênes, O., 2018. A forward-looking ricardian approach: do land markets capitalize climate change forecasts? Journal of Environmental Economics and Management 89, 235–254.

Shayegh, S., 2017. Outward migration may alter population dynamics and income inequality. Nature Climate Change 7 (11), 828–832.

Shr, Y.-H.J., Zipp, K.Y., 2019. The aftermath of flood zone remapping: the asymmetric impact of flood maps on housing prices. Land Economics 95 (2), 174–192.

Shrader, J.G., 2023. Improving Climate Damage Estimates by Accounting for Adaptation. Working Paper.

Shrader, J.G., Bakkensen, L., Lemoine, D., 2023. Fatal Errors: The Mortality Value of Accurate Weather Forecasts. NBER Working Papers, 31361. National Bureau of Economic Research.

Sokolov, A.P., Schlosser, C.A., Dutkiewicz, S., Paltsev, S., Kicklighter, D.W., Jacoby, H.D., Prinn, R.G., Forest, C.E., Reilly, J.M., Wang, C., Felzer, B.S., Sarofim, M.C., Scott, J., Stone, P.H., Melillo, J.M., Cohen, J.B., 2005. MIT Integrated Global System Model (IGSM) Version 2:

Model Description and Baseline Evaluation. MIT Joint Program on the. Science and Policy of Global Change.
Song, Y., 2024. The value of weather forecasts: evidence from labor responses to accurate versus inaccurate temperature forecasts in China. Journal of Environmental Economics and Management 125, 102970.
Stoeffler, Q., Carter, M., Guirkinger, C., Gelade, W., 2022. The spillover impact of index insurance on agricultural investment by cotton farmers in Burkina Faso. The World Bank Economic Review 36 (1), 114–140.
Takakura, J., Fujimori, S., Hanasaki, N., Hasegawa, T., Hirabayashi, Y., Honda, Y., Iizumi, T., Kumano, N., Park, C., Shen, Z., Takahashi, K., Tamura, M., Tanoue, M., Tsuchida, K., Yokoki, H., Zhou, Q., Oki, T., Hijioka, Y., 2019. Dependence of economic impacts of climate change on anthropogenically directed pathways. Nature Climate Change 9 (10), 737–741.
Tambet, H., Stopnitzky, Y., 2021. Climate adaptation and conservation agriculture among Peruvian farmers. American Journal of Agricultural Economics 103 (3), 900–922.
Taraz, V., 2017. Adaptation to climate change: historical evidence from the Indian monsoon. Environment and Development Economics 22 (5), 517–545.
Tarquinio, L., 2022. The Politics of Drought Relief: Evidence from Southern India. Working Paper.
Tognin, D., D'Alpaos, A., Marani, M., Carniello, L., 2021. Marsh resilience to sea-level rise reduced by storm-surge barriers in the Venice Lagoon. Nature Geoscience 14 (12), 906–911.
Tol, R.S.J., 2006. Exchange rates and climate change: an application of fund. Climatic Change 75 (1), 59–80.
Tol, R.S.J., 2007. The double trade-off between adaptation and mitigation for sea level rise: an application of FUND. Mitigation and Adaptation Strategies for Global Change 12 (5), 741–753.
Tol, S.J.R., 1995. The damage costs of climate change toward more comprehensive calculations. Environmental and Resource Economics 5 (4), 353–374.
Townsend, R.M., 1994. Risk and insurance in village India. Econometrica 62 (3), 539–591.
Townsend, R.M., 1995. Consumption insurance: an evaluation of risk-bearing systems in low-income economies. The Journal of Economic Perspectives 9 (3), 83–102.
UNFCC, 2024. Introduction to adaptation and resilience / loss and damage.
US Environmental Protection Agency, 2022. Report on the social cost of greenhouse gases: Estimates incorporating recent scientific advances.
Van Der Straten, Y., 2024. Flooded House or Underwater Mortgage? The Implications of Climate Change and Adaptation on Housing, Income, and Wealth. Working Paper.
Wagner, K.R.H., 2022. Adaptation and adverse selection in markets for natural disaster insurance. American Economic Journal: Economic Policy 14 (3), 380–421.
Waldinger, M., 2022. The economic effects of long-term climate change: evidence from the little ice age. Journal of Political Economy 130 (9), 2275–2314.
Wang, J., Mendelsohn, R., Dinar, A., Huang, J., Rozelle, S., Zhang, L., 2009. The impact of climate change on China's agriculture. Agricultural Economics 40 (3), 323–337.
Weill, J., 2023. Flood Risk Mapping and the Distributional Impacts of Climate Information.Finance and Economics Discussion Series 2023-066. Board of Governors of the Federal Reserve System, Washington.
Wenz, L., Levermann, A., Auffhammer, M., 2017. North-south polarization of European electricity consumption under future warming. Proceedings of the National Academy of Sciences 114 (38), E7910–E7918.
Wobus, C., Small, E.E., Hosterman, H., Mills, D., Stein, J., Rissing, M., Jones, R., Duckworth, M., Hall, R., Kolian, M., Creason, J., Martinich, J., 2017. Projected Climate Change impacts on skiing and snowmobiling: a case study of the United States. Global Environmental Change 45, 1–14.

Wright, L., Chinowsky, P., Strzepek, K., Jones, R., Streeter, R., Smith, J.B., Mayotte, J.-M., Powell, A., Jantarasami, L., Perkins, W., 2012. Estimated effects of climate change on flood vulnerability of U.S. bridges. Mitigation and Adaptation Strategies for Global Change 17 (8), 939–955.

Yang, D., Choi, H., 2007. Are remittances insurance? Evidence from rainfall shocks in the Philippines. The World Bank Economic Review 21 (2), 219–248.

Yohe, G., Neumann, J., Marshall, P., Ameden, H., 1996. The economic cost of greenhouse-induced sea-level rise for developed property in the United States. Climatic Change 32 (4), 387–410.

Zappalà, G., 2023. Drought exposure and accuracy: motivated reasoning in climate change beliefs. Environmental and Resource Economics 85 (3), 649–672.

Zappalà, G., 2024. Adapting to climate change accounting for individual beliefs. Journal of Development Economics 169, 103289.

Zilberman, D., Zhao, J., Heiman, A., 2012. Adoption versus adaptation, with emphasis on climate change. Annual Review of Resource Economics 4 (1), 27–53.

Chapter 5

On international cooperation

Bård Harstad*
Stanford University, Stanford, California, United States
**Corresponding author. e-mail address: harstad@stanford.edu*

Chapter Outline

1 Introduction and overview

Amidst a number of tragic events, I find it to be a most fortunate coincidence that "international cooperation" is not only the most important topic to study, but it is also the most interesting one. All the major challenges humanities are facing

Handbook of the Economics of Climate Change, Vol. 1. https://doi.org/10.1016/bs.hesecc.2024.10.004

require international cooperation. In the very long run, the state of the world will hinge little on today's policies, except for how the countries manage to cooperate on climate change and nature conservation. But international cooperation is complicated, and interesting, because it requires a large number of very different nations to interact over time in a caotic situation with brute force and no world government. To understand international cooperation, we must understand laizzes faire, free riding, exernalities, dynamics, compliance, defections, punishments, negotiations, and renegotiations.

But when it comes to climate agreements, we do not have a lot of empirical observations to draw on. The Kyoto Protocol of 1997 was, essentially, the first global climate agreement and the Paris Agreement, of 2015, is another. Two data points are interesting, but not sufficient to deepen our understanding satisfactorily.

For these reasons, it is necessary to draw on theoretical models. An economic model simplifies the complicated world so that there are just one or a few mechanisms at play. The simplicity implies that the model is inaccurate, but that our thinking will be clear. A theoretical model that we can understand is helpful for our understandings of present policies, our exploration of alternatives, and the communication of our ideas.

This chapter employs simple models to shed light on climate policies without and with international cooperation. I include eight examples, or excercises, that can be solved by your undergraduate students, but the full analysis can be challenging for PhD students. Because while it is desirable to keep the models simple, they must still include a few features that are important when it comes to climate policies. First, the model obviously permits multiple countries. Second, policies must include both emissions, causing the problem, and technology investments, necessary for a solution. Third, the dynamics is essential: Greenhouse gases accumulate over time, the green technologies need time to develop, and one country's action might influence what others do in the future.

The three features are already making the models challenging, so I will abstract from many other important aspects (see below).

The basic framework is introduced in Section 2, and I will rely on it throughout the chapter, but the sections can be read independently of one another. After all, some readers might be interested in compliance and not contracts, for example.

Section 3 discusses dynamic common-pool problems and the so-called "business-as-usual" (BAU) scenario. In my view, it is important to begin with BAU to illustrate that the outcome with no cooperation can be much worse than what we would have thought based on static common-pool problems. In a static model, one country will abate too little, and emit too much, because it does not internalize the externality on the rest of the world. In a dynamic setting, a country might emit even more because the larger stock of greenhouse gases will induce other countries to emit less in the future. Similarly, it will invest less in technology, because by investing less it is expected to emit more, and then other countries will find it optimal to emit less and invest more themselves. The fact that the dynamic common-pool problem is especially costly should motivate the development of an international environmental agreement (IEA).

Nevertheless, IEAs can make things even worse. In Section 4, I refer to traditional findings in contract theory, where it is well-known that parties may under-invest prior to negotiations. The intuition is that if a party has already invested in, say, renewable energy, then this party will find it inexpensive to limit emissions and, in a bargaining game, that party will end up with a smaller emission allowance than parties that have invested less. Intuitively, parties that have invested less will find the IEA costly, and thus "hold up" the negotiations unless they obtain more favorable terms. When the hold-up problem is anticipated, investments fall. If investments fall by a lot, and they are important in order to deal with climate change, the parties can end up being worse off – even compared with BAU. The fact that short-term agreements can be harmful should motivate us to study in more detail how agreements ought to be designed.

Long-term agreements, analyzed next, specifies emission caps for such a long commitment period that the parties have time to invest and develop green technology. There might still be underinvestment problems, either because the agreement is finite while the technology is long-lasting, or because of technological spillovers. To motivate countries to invest more, the emission caps should and will be tighter, so that countries will need to invest in renewables in order to be able to consume satisfactory levels of energy.

The mechanisms just discussed suggest that a long-term agreement, or a long-lasting commitment period, is ideal in order to deal with the hold-up problem. The optimal length, discussed in Section 5, trades off the cost of short-termism with the fact that we do not really know what the caps ought to be several decades from now (Fig. 1).

Participation is the topic of Section 6. In contrast to districts within a country, the countries themselves are sovereign and free to decide whether they want to participate or free ride. This choice should be a part of the game, so that we can endogenize the size of the coalition. In much of the literature, the trade-off is as follows. The cost of participating is that one will be end up

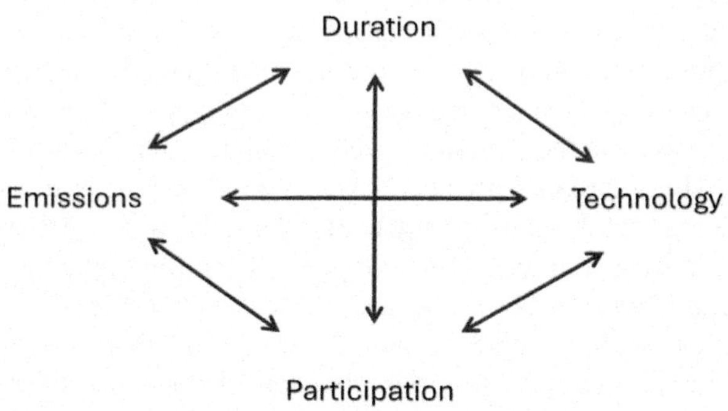

FIG. 1 Section 4 analyzes the two-way interaction between emission caps and investments in technology. Section 5 connects with the commitment period length and Section 6 connects with the coalition size.

contributing more, or emitting less, than what one could do as a free rider. The cost of free riding, however, is that the other members of the coalition cannot be influenced, and they cannot be expected to internalize the climate change harm experienced by the free rider. This trade-off implies that the equilibrium coalition size is relatively small: With linear-quadratic utility functions, for example, at most three countries will participate. When the coalition-formation game is embedded in a dynamic game with both investments and emissions, the results are more nuanced and interesting. In fact, the hold-up problem, reducing everyone's payoff in the earlier sections, can not be taken advantage off, and both the coalition and payoffs can be larger because of it. The intuition for this result is that when a coalition decides on the duration of the agreement, they find it optimal with a long-term agreement iff (i.e., if and only if) the number of members is large. If some countries free ride, however, the coalition might prefer a short-term agreement, hoping that the number of members will be larger in the future. Because the short-term agreements are associated with the hold-up problem, free riding becomes less attractive and, therefore, the coalition can be larger.

Compliance is studied in Section 7. Just as no world government can force a country to participate in an IEA, a participant might not necessarily comply with the pledges or promised that are made. The problem of motivating compliance is related to participation, but there are two major differences. First, while the membership decision is made at the beginning of a game, the decision about whether to comply or defect is made every day. Second, when a country defects, instead of complying, it can reasonably expect that the other members will stick to their promises up to the stage when the defection is observed. For this reason, compliance can be more challenging than participation. To study the limits of what a self-enforcing agreement can do, it is often assumed that the consequences of defection is severe. In many games, the most severe punishment is that everyone returns to BAU as soon as a single defection is observed. From the literature on repeated games, so-called folk theorems tell us that with this type of punishment, the first-best outcome can be sustained as an equilibrium iff the parties' weight on future payoffs (i.e., the discount factor) is sufficiently high. If the discount factor is smaller, the best self-enforcing IEA is inefficient. The inefficiency can be that the emission levels are higher than in the first best (FB), although still smaller than with BAU. This simple insight is derived and presented before we, once again, return to the game in which the parties are, in every period, both investing in technologies and emitting greenhouse gases. In this case, technology will have a strategic role that is different from the other scenaria studied in this chapter. After all, the temptation to defect not only depends on the discount factor, but also on the benefits of emitting. The temptation to emit is weakened if the party can consume energy from renewable energy sources, for example, instead of from fossil fuels. Thus, by investing more (and more than in the FB) in green technology, compliance at the emission stage will be credible. The more difficult it is to motivate countries to comply with the reduced emission levels, the larger are the equilibrium investment levels relative to the first-best levels. If, instead, it is difficult to motivate countries to comply with the high investments, then investments must be reduced relative to the first-best levels. In this case, the best self-enforcing IEA may require countries to be punished if they invest more, and as much as the first-best levels. The intuition for this result is that if countries were allowed to invest more, they would not find it optimal to emit a lot, and thus to punish, if it turns out that another country defects on its pledges.

Section 8 compares deep-but-narrow agreements with those that are broad-but-shallow. The difference can depend on, for instance, the choice between the top-down bargaining procedure associated with the Kyoto Protocol, and the bottom-up pledge-and-review bargaining procedure associated with the Paris Agreement. It is shown that "modesty may pay", as observed by Finus and Maus (2008), in that shallow agreements can attract a larger number of participants. Section 9 discusses how the various models can shed light on the Kyoto Protocol, the Paris Agreement, and the development from one to the other. I conclude by discussing "what's next".

What about everything else? It is reasonable to claim that it is a rather subjective judgement to think that exactly these three features are the most important ones: (1) Multiple countries, (2) green technology, (3) an infinite time horizon. This claim is supported by the fact that much of my own research, which I will draw on below, has investigated these aspects. But, at the least, this focus does make the chapter manageable to write and read.

My focus on feature 2 (technology) and 3 (dynamics) may be what separates this chapter from earlier overviews of international agreements. Those, of course, focus on aspects that I am abstracting from. For earlier overviews, one should consult with Kolstad and Toman (2005) on climate policy, Barrett (2005) on environmental agreements, Calvo and Rubio (2012) on the importance of the dynamics and the stocks, Benchekroun and Long (2012) on the game theory, Caparrós (2016) on the role of bargaining games, Buchholz and Sandler (2021) for the general public goods aspects, and Bellelli et al. (2023) on the empirical findings.

For other aspects, the readers are anyway better off looking elsewhere. Political economy forces are essential in the real world, of course, but those are emphasized in another book chapter that I am writing (Harstad, 2025). There, I emphasize the importance of heterogeneity, asymmetry, side transfers, elections, and time inconsistency. Thus, I view the two chapters as being complementary to one another. The importance of issue linkages is surveyed by Maggi (2016), disasters by Deryugina (2022), and, in this volume, you can learn more about integrated assessment models (Dietz, 2024), adaptation (Carleton et al., 2024), and domestic climate policies (Kotchen, 2024), for instance. The literate on trade agreements is also related and useful: See Maggi (2014), Grossman (2016), Bagwell and Staiger (2016). The literature on supply-side climate policies is still emerging and must be returned to in another volume.

2 Climate policies as dynamic games

The motivation to cooperate is that the non-cooperative outcome can be unattractive. Thus, to understand cooperation, we must understand its absence. When every country is free to decide on its policies unilaterally, the countries are playing a game against one another. One policy might influence the future policies of the other countries. When policies are made at multiple points in time, the game is dynamic. Thus, non-cooperative climate policies should be formalized as a dynamic game.

A formalized game will emphasize the strategic nature of the decisions, and it may abstract from a number of behaviors such as altruism and reciprocity preferences, inattention, and irrationality. While these characteristics are extremely important in the daily life of human beings, they are often harder to observe when it comes to hard-core policymaking at the international arena.

Dynamic games can be difficult to solve, however, so we might need to impose several simplifying assumptions. This section introduces a model where both the stock of greenhouse gases and the national stocks of technologies (or capacities to produce renewable energy) develop over time, depending on the choices of the countries. The model will be used throughout the section to illustrate the various aspects that are important to international cooperation.

In the game below, each country is represented by a benevolent decision maker that directly decides on both emission and investments. The idea is that voters might succeed electing a government acting on their behalf, and that this government can introduce national policies that implement the levels that are preferred by the government or the voters. In the chapter by Kotchen (2024), he explains how a government might introduce national climate policies to implement these quantities.

2.1 Greenhouse gases and technology stocks

The set of countries is $N := \{1, ..., n\}$. Each country is treated as one player, and I will assume that every $i \in N$ makes two decisions in every time period $t \in \{1, ..., \infty\}$. At the emission stage, all the i's are simultaneously deciding on the $g_{i,t}$'s, where $g_{i,t}$ measures i's emission of greenhouse gases. These emissions accumulate over time to the stock G_t, measuring the additional stock of CO2, for instance, caused by humans. Assuming that the fraction $q_G \in [0, 1]$ depreciates every period, G_t evolves according to:

$$G_t = q_G G_{t-1} + \sum_{i \in N} g_{i,t}. \tag{1}$$

As a substitute to emitting, and as a possible solution to climate change, let every i invest $r_{i,t}$ in "green technology". The investments accumulate to the stock $R_{i,t}$, which might depreciate by the factor $q_R \in [0, 1]$, so that it evolves as follows:

$$R_{i,t} = q_R R_{i,t-1} + r_{i,t}.$$

One interpretation of $R_{i,t}$ is that it represents i's capacity to abate, so that it emits only $g_{i,t} = y_{i,t} - R_{i,t}$, while still benefiting from $y_{i,t}$. van der Ploeg and de Zeeuw (1991) present one of the first climate-policy games with both emission and abatement decisions, and they formalize abatement in this way. Another interpretation of $R_{i,t}$, which I will stick with below, is that $R_{i,t}$ measures i's capacity to produce renewable energy, so that i's total consumption of energy, $y_{i,t}$, is such that the following inequality is satisfied:

$$y_{i,t} = g_{i,t} + R_{i,t}. \tag{2}$$

It will be useful to study the decisions on $g_{i,t}$ and $r_{i,t}$ separately, and thus to assume that they are made at different stages in period t. A period is defined so that it starts just before one investment stage and it ends just before the next investment stage. With an additive utility function, i enjoys the following utility at time t:

$$u_{i,t} = B(y_{i,t}) - C(G_t) - K(r_{i,t}, R_{i,t-1}). \tag{3}$$

The benefit of energy consumption is $B(y_{i,t})$, the cost of the greenhouse gas stock is $C(G_t)$, and the investment cost is given by the function $K(r_{i,t}, R_{i,t-1})$, which might depend on the stock developed so far.

The additive form of the utility function is not strictly necessary. If, instead, the utility was given by the Cobb-Douglas function $\widetilde{B}(y_{i,t})^c \widetilde{C}(G_t)^b \widetilde{K}(r_{i,t}, R_{i,t})^\gamma$, for example, we can use logarithmic maximization so that i would still maximize (3) if we define $B(y_{i,t}) = c \ln \widetilde{B}(y_i)$, $C(G_t) = -b \ln \widetilde{C}(G)$, and $K(r_{i,t}, R_{i,t-1}) = -\gamma \ln \widetilde{K}(r_{i,t}, R_{i,t})$.

At the beginning of a period, i would like to maximize its continuation value

$$v_{i,t} = \sum_{t' \geq t}^{\infty} \delta^{t'-t} u_{i,t} = u_{i,t} + \delta v_{i,t+1},$$

where $\delta \in (0, 1)$ is the discount factor. In general, the continuation values will depend on the stocks.

When the parties' actions influence the stocks, the game is called a differential game when time is continuous, and a difference game when time is discrete. These games are generally difficult to solve. Thus, it is common to simplify the functional forms. For example, one may assume that the functional forms are linear-quadratic. Engwerda (2005) provides a comprehensive overview of this literature and its methods. While a quadratic investment cost is introduced from Sections 6, Sections 3–5 assume that the investment cost is simply linear:

$$K(r_{i,t}, R_{i,t-1}) = kr_{i,t}. \tag{LK}$$

Evidently, we will abstract from how a country implements the chosen quantities domestically. Kotchen (2024) discusses alternative instruments. Because the countries are assumed to be identical, we also abstract from the importance of side transfers and international emission permit trading.

2.2 Equilibrium concept: SPE vs. MPE?

The choice of equilibrium concept is a part of the assumptions, and thus the model. In a static game, it would make sense to characterize all Nash equilibria (NEs). In a dynamic game with a finite time horizon, the typical choice would be subgame-perfect equilibrium (SPE). In a repeated game with infinite number of periods, there are typically a large number of SPEs. It is not clear, then, which SPE that will be most reasonable to focus on. At least two approaches seem to be reasonable.

One interpretations of international cooperation is that the talks are allowing the parties to coordinate on a good SPE. Thus, we may focus on what "best" SPE, given that all quantities must be self-enforcing (as an SPE). This is the approach taken in Section 7.

Alternatively, we can refine the equilibrium concept. When the game includes stocks that change over time, we have a dynamic game (but not a repeated game). To obtain sharp predictions, it is quite common to restrict attention to Markov-perfect equilibrium (MPE). The MPEs allow parties to form strategies that are contingent on stocks that are payoff relevant, but otherwise the strategies do not depend on the history. In lab experiments, subjects often play MPE strategies when the game is dynamic and complex (Vespa, 2011; Battaglini et al., 2015). Since these equilibria are relatively simple to characterize, we will begin by emphasizing the symmetric MPE from the next section (which turns out to be unique). In addition, Section 3 compares the MPE to the so-called "open loop" equilibrium, where the parties are not updating their actions after observing the actions of the others. This is not a reasonable equilibrium, of course, but by comparing that outcome to the MPE we will be able to understand why the dynamics of the climate policy game makes it especially inefficient.

None of the two approaches sheds light on everything, but both of them can be helpful. The choice will influence the type of treaty that will be considered. As mentioned, when we consider SPEs in Section 7, we study self-enforcing treaties. When treaties are discussed in Section 4–6, where we restrict attention to MPEs, we are explicitly ruling out self-enforcement mechanisms and, therefore, we will simply take as given that countries might be able to commit to certain actions (like short-term emission caps) but not to other actions (like technology investments). These analyses are especially relevant for so-called legally binding treaties, where there might be certain political costs associated with noncompliance.

If the countries are bargaining in a symmetric situation, it will be assumed that the outcome is both efficient and symmetric. This would apply if we employ the Nash Bargaining Solution (NBS), for example.

3 What if there is no cooperation?

If there is no agreement, we have "business as usual" (BAU). In this scenario, countries make decisions without internalizing the externality on the others.

This implies that countries will emit more than in the FB, and the stock of greenhouse gases will be larger than in the FB outcome.

What about the investments? If the emission levels were fixed, the investment levels would be first best when there are no technological spillover associated with the investments. The reason for this claim is simply that one country's investment level causes no externalities on the other countries: They don't care about the investment, per se.

Nevertheless, in the model of Section 2, countries will end up investing too little with BAU relative to the FB. The explanation for this finding is that emission levels are not fixed in the dynamic game – they are endogenous. If a country invests more, it will find it optimal to emit less later on. When this country emits less, the marginal cost of emission declines for everyone, and other countries will find it optimal to emit more. The larger emission levels by the others are anticipated by the investing country, who thus reduce the investments, relative to the situation in which this effect were not present.

In effect, one country's technology stock ends up being a public good, which benefits all the countries, even if there are no direct technological spillovers in this model.

This logic explains why the BAU outcome is even worse in this dynamic model than it would have been in a static model. To be precise, suppose every country i decided on the sequence of emission levels and investment levels once and for all, at the beginning of the game. When these decisions are made simultaneously, the game is static, and its Nash equilibrium (NE) is typically referred to as the open-loop equilibrium of the dynamic game. The NE is worse than the FB in that countries emit too much, but investments, conditional on the investment levels, are socially optimal. While this outcome is inefficient, the BAU outcome is even worse. With BAU, a country invests less also to induce other countries to emit less and invest more in the future. Furthermore, a country emits more because that induces the other countries to emit less and invest more in the next period. When all countries are adopting these strategies, they end up with more emission and lower payoffs than with the NE. The BAU outcome is thus especially harmful in a climate policy game – because it is dynamic.

This inefficiency should motivate us to study international cooperation in more detail, which we turn to after this section.

3.1 Example 1: Private windmills are public goods

As an example, consider the model of Section 2 but with only one period, period 1, and with quadratic functions for B and C:

$$B(y_i) = -\frac{b}{2}(\bar{y} - y_i)^2 \quad \text{and} \quad C(G) = \frac{c}{2}G^2 = \frac{c}{2}\left(q_G G_0 + \sum_{j \in N} g_j - R\right), \tag{Q}$$

where $R \equiv \Sigma_{i \in N} R_i$.

What is the SPE of this game?

Deriving the details are left as an exercise. Clearly, the SPE can be found by backward induction. At the emission stage, $B'(y_i) = C'(G)$, so every y_i is the same. The intuition is simply that, on the margin, one more unit of consumption leads to another unit of emission, when the renewable capacity is binding. Thus, R_i is, in effect, a public good, even when there are no technological spillovers.

With some algebra, we find that, at the emission stage,

$$y_i = \frac{\bar{y}b - cq_G G_0 + cR}{b + nc}, \quad \text{so} \tag{4}$$

$$g_i^{BAU}(\mathbf{R}) = \frac{\bar{y}b - cq_G G_0 + cR}{b + nc} - R_i, \tag{5}$$

where $\mathbf{R}$ is the vector of R_i's. Eq. (5) implies that if R_i is larger, i emits less, but country $j \neq i$ emits more. This is intuitive: A country does not need to emit if it can consume renewable energy, but when such a country emits less, C' declines, and other countries emit more. This is referred to as "carbon leakage." While carbon leakage here is the result of the convex $C(\cdot)$ function, carbon leakage can alternatively result from international trade (as in Kotchen, 2024).

All this is anticipated when i invests. Thus, i finds it optimal to invest until marginal benefits equal the marginal investment cost:

$$B'(y_i)(1 + \partial g_i/\partial R_i) - C'(G)\left(\sum_{j \in N} \partial g_j/\partial R_i\right) = k. \tag{6}$$

With (5), and some algebra, we get R:

$$R^{BAU} = n\bar{y} + q_G G_0 - \frac{(b + cn)^2}{cb(b + c)}k.$$

We refer to the above as BAU. The FB, in contrast, is given by the same equations if just c is replaced with nc. For example:

$$g_i^{FB}(\mathbf{R}) = \frac{\bar{y}b - ncq_G G_0 + ncR}{b + n^2 c} - R_i.$$

By comparison, emissions are larger with BAU than in the FB, and investments are lower. The reason is that j benefits if i invests more because with a larger R_i, i will emit less.

Another interesting comparison is with the Nash equilibrium (NE) of the static version of the game. If decisions were made simultaneously, j would *not* emit more if i changed its decisions. So, $\partial g_j/\partial R_i = 0$, and investments would be given by $B'(y_{i,t}) = k$, which equals the socially optimal level, conditional on the level of technologies. Because i's investment does not lead j to emit more, i would find it optimal to invest more in the NE than it does with BAU.

Regarding emission levels, (4)–(5) would continue to hold with the NE. By comparing all these conditions, we can conclude:

$$\begin{aligned} g_i^{BAU} &> g_i^{NE} > g_i^{FB}, \\ R^{BAU} &< R^{NE} < R^{FB}, \quad \text{so} \\ u_i^{BAU} &< u_i^{NE} < u_i^{FB}, \quad \forall i \in N. \end{aligned} \tag{7}$$

These inequalities tell us something important. With the NE, investment levels will be just right, conditional on those emission levels. But the NE is inefficient because emission levels will be too high: Country i will not take into account the externality on j, so the level of investments is smaller than in the FB. In BAU, investments are even lower than in the NE, because by investing less, other countries will emit less. When everyone invests less, total emission ends up being higher, and payoffs larger, than in the NE. Thus, the fact that the game is dynamic, and decisions are made sequentially, make the outcome even worse than it would be in the NE outcome, and the NE outcome is, in itself, also inefficient.

3.2 Business as usual

The basic insights from Example 1 survive in more general settings: all inequalities in (7) will hold, even when there is an infinite number of periods, and even if $B(\cdot)$ and $C(\cdot)$ are general concave and convex functions, respectively (for details, see the theorem in Harstad, 2012, 1534).

With the linear investment cost, (LK), introduced in Section 2, the analysis simplifies by a lot, even when we permit an infinite number of periods, and it can be shown that the continuation value will be linear in all the stocks. For this reason, the model is tractable, easy to solve, and there is a unique MPE.

Because $C(\cdot)$ is convex, it is more costly to emit when the stock G_t is large. Thus, every country emits less at time $t+1$ when G_t ends up being large. A country understands this, and thus that if i increases $g_{i,t}$, then, in equilibrium,

$$\frac{\partial g_{j,t+1}}{\partial g_{i,t}} < 0 \quad \text{and} \quad \frac{\partial r_{j,t+1}}{\partial g_{i,t}} > 0 \quad \forall j \in N. \tag{8}$$

Here, the second inequality says that the other countries will also invest more, if i emits more. This is natural, because when j finds it optimal to consume less energy from fossil fuels, it is beneficial to invest more in renewable energy, instead.

From this logic, it follows that if country i decides to invest more, then it will find it optimal to emit less and, because of that, other countries will emit more and invest less in the next period. Formally:

$$\frac{\partial g_{j,t+1}}{\partial r_{i,t}} > 0 \quad \text{and} \quad \frac{\partial r_{j,t+1}}{\partial r_{i,t}} < 0. \tag{9}$$

All these effects imply that other countries will take advantage of *i*'s "good" behavior. Because *i* prefers that another country, *j*, will emit less and invest more, *i* has an incentive to emit more and invest less than if *j* could not respond according to (8)–(9).

The situation in which *j* cannot respond to *i*'s policies is interesting in itself. Because dynamic games are complicated to solve, some scholars simplify by assuming that every party commits to a sequence of decisions at the very beginning of the game. When these commitments are made simultaneously, the game is essentially static, and the Nash equilibrium of the static game corresponds to the so-called open-loop equilibrium of the dynamic game. In this NE, *j*'s decisions will not change if *i* changes its policy, so (8) and (9) will not apply. Therefore, *i* finds it optimal to emit less, and invest more.

The NE is not first best, of course: Country *i* will not take into account the externality on *j*, when *i* decides on how much to emit. Because *i* finds it optimal to emit less if $R_{i,t}$ is large, *j* would have benefited if *i* invested more, so *i*'s equilibrium investment level is smaller than the first-best level. To summarize:

> The BAU outcome of the dynamic game is worse than the NE outcome of the static game.

In other words, while the static common-pool problem, characterized by the NE, is inefficient and provides lower utilities than in the first best, the BAU of the dynamic climate-change game is even worse.

The fact that dynamic common-pool problems are especially inefficient has been recognized a long time. Levhari and Mirman (1980) developed the insight in their study of fish wars, and van der Ploeg and de Zeeuw (1991, 1992) showed that the MPE outcome is worse than the NE in climate policy games. Although Dockner and Long (1993) show that MPEs in nonlinear strategies can be better, the simplest MPE, in linear strategies, is highly inefficient.

These inefficiencies should motivate us to search for agreements that can improve on the outcome.

4 Agreements as incomplete contracts

Because the BAU outcome is so inefficient, the countries may be quite motivated to sign an agreement.

As mentioned in Section 2, when it comes to international agreements, one sometimes distinguish between (legally) binding agreements and self-enforcing agreements. If an agreement is binding, a stakeholder can hold a government accountable if it does not comply. Now, it is not clear which stakeholders that will have this capacity, and it is also unclear what it means to "hold a government accountable": Both aspects may depend on the country in question. In the U.S., for example, ratifying an international treaty implies that it becomes law, so that a state, such as California, can sue the federal government if it does not comply. More generally, (IPCC, 2014, p. 1020) writes that "a more legally binding commitment … signals a greater seriousness by states … These factors increase the costs of violation (through enforcement and sanctions at international and domestic scales, the loss of mutual cooperation by others, and the loss of reputation and credibility in future negotiations)."

With this motivation, we start by considering legally binding agreements, where we abstract from the temptation to defect, but we return to that temptation, and self-enforcing agreements, in Section 7.

Contract theory is a branch of economic theory where binding agreements are analyzed. Bolton and Dewatripont (For textbook treatments, see, 2005). Two types of contracts can be relevant for climate change agreements. A "complete contract" is an agreement where the parties commit to all variables of interest. In the model of Section 2, the variables include every emission level and every investment level. With this possibility, the countries can and will agree on the first-best outcome, because they are symmetric, by assumption.

A complete contract is not realistic, of course. In the real world, there are a large number of political variables that influence the climate change outcome, and there is no hope that an international agreement can specify everything that is potentially relevant. The Kyoto Protocol, for example, emphasized emission levels, but left the countries' investment levels to be nationally determined. This approach has been confirmed by later agreements. According to article 114 of the 2010 Cancun Agreement, which was confirmed in Durban in 2011, "technology needs must be nationally determined, based on national circumstance and priorities."

There might be good reasons for why investment levels are left out. As argued by Golombek and Hoel (2006, p. 2), "it would hardly be feasible for a country (or some international agency) to verify all aspects of other countries' R&D policies".

Thus, a more realistic concept is "incomplete contract", where it is recognized that certain variables remain outside of the agreement. The literature on incomplete contracts literature was originally developed to study interaction between firms (see Hart, 1995). The literature recognizes that the variables that are not contracted on will be strategically chosen so as to influence the next round of (re)negotiations, but also that these variables may be influenced by the decisions that are committed to with the contract. In the climate policy game, this implies that there is a two-way interaction between the investment levels and the emission caps.

On the one hand, the agreed-upon emission levels are not exogenous, but the outcome of bargaining. At the time when the emission caps are negotiated, the countries that are ill-prepared for a treaty can "hold up" the countries that have already invested in green technology, and the laggards can demand to be granted larger emission quotas than the leaders who have invested more. When this hold-up problem is anticipated, countries might be reluctant to invest.

Thus, investments levels might be low, in equilibrium, when it is expected that the more one invest, then less one will be able to emit. If the investments are socially important, the hold-up problem associated with so-called short-term agreements can make them worse than BAU, it is argued in Section 4.1. The idea that technology investments can fall before climate negotiations go back to Buchholz and Konrad (1994).

There is evidence that the hold-up problem is important in reality. For example, The New York Times (17 October 2008, p. A4) reported that "Leaders of countries that want concessions say that nations like Denmark have a built-in advantage because they already depend more heavily on renewable energy."

On the other hand, because investing in renewables is a substitute to emission, a country will find it optimal to invest more if the emission cap is tight. By reducing the caps, the countries will be induced to invest more. Several papers have documented that regulation can motivate technological change in this way (Jaffe et al., 2003; Newell et al., 2006; Dugoua, 2023). This effect is likely to be important in so-called long-term agreements, where countries do have time to develop new technology between the negotiation stage and the emission stage.

By combining the two forces, we can arrive at the following insight. If an incomplete contract specifies emission levels for a large number of future periods, then countries will be less worried about the hold-up problem that might arise sometime in the future, and then investments will be first best iff the emission caps are first best. (After all, we have assumed away direct technological spillovers on the other countries.) When the current commitment period is about to end, and one thinks about the next round of bargaining, then the hold-up problem will begin to discourage investments in technology. To maintain the incentive to invest, also in this situation, the emission caps must be tighter, and more demanding. Consequently, the shorter is the duration of the commitment period, or the shorter it is until it expires, the more ambitious must the abatement levels be for investments to remain at the efficient level: See Sections 4.2 and 4.3.

4.1 Example 2: The strategic choice of technology

Buchholz and Konrad (1994) showed that technology investments might be strategically small, both in a situation without negotiations, and also if the negotiations are coming up. The title of this subsection is named after their article, although the formalization of the model is as in Harstad (2016).

To capture the basic insight, consider the one-period Example 1 in Section 3.1, but suppose the timing of a period is as given in Fig. 2, and that the g_i's are determined by the NBS. With this, the SPE of the game can be determined by backward induction. The details are left as an exercise.

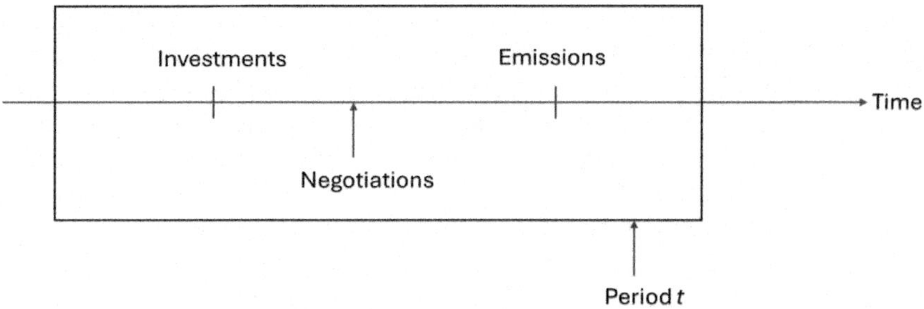

FIG. 2 With short-term agreements, the relevant technology has already been invested in.

As discussed after eq. (Q), differences in the R_i's are irrelevant at the emission stage. And when the technology stocks are given, the countries are, in effect, negotiating the y_i's. Countries have identical benefits and costs when it comes to the y_i's, and the threat point, given by y_i^{BAU}, is also the same for every i. With the NBS, therefore, all the y_i's will be the same, and they will be efficient, conditional on the technology level: $g_i^{ST}(\mathbf{R}^{ST}) = g_i^{FB}(\mathbf{R}^{ST})$. The investment levels are non-cooperative, and given by (6), as with BAU. However, in this equation, G will be different because of the negotiations: $g_i^{ST}(\mathbf{R}) < g_i^{BAU}(\mathbf{R})$. Thus, the marginal cost, C', will also be smaller, and the benefit from emitting even less, by investing, is reduced. Hence, equilibrium R is smaller when short-term agreements are expected, than with BAU: $\mathbf{R}^{ST} < \mathbf{R}^{BAU}$. The reduced technology level implies $g_i^{ST} < g_i^{FB}$, and that payoffs can be smaller too. With some algebra, we find:

$$\begin{aligned} g_i^{ST} &< g_i^{BAU}, \\ R^{ST} &< R^{BAU} < R^{NR} < R^{FB}, \\ u_i^{ST} &< u_i^{BAU} < u_i^{NE} < u_i^{FB} \quad \textit{iff } k > n/(n-1). \end{aligned}$$

4.2 Short-term agreements

Even if there is an infinite number of periods, it turns out that all the inequalities from Example 2 hold in this model, except that the condition is weakened as follows. (See Harstad, 2016, for details).

$$u_{i,t}^{ST} < u_{i,t}^{BAU} \quad \textit{iff } k > (1 - \delta q_R)n/(n-1). \tag{10}$$

Why can the countries be worse off when they negotiate emission caps, compared to with BAU?

To explain the intuition, remember that differences in the technologies (i.e., the $R_{i,t}$'s) turn out to be irrelevant when it comes to the benefits and costs of consumption levels (the $y_{i,t}$'s). These differences are also irrelevant in the BAU scenario, as observed after eq. (Q), and BAU serves as the threat point when the countries negotiate and decide on the quantities or, equivalently, the $y_{i,t}$'s.

Thus, the countries will sign an agreement which makes every $y_{i,t}$ the same, no matter differences in the technology stocks. While it is simple to show this mathematically, the intuition can be related to the hold-up problem: If a country invests a lot, then other countries, who invest less, can "hold up" the technology leader and demand that it takes on the lion's share of the total emission cuts. A country with a small $R_{i,t}$, in contrast, will find it costly to reduce $g_{i,t}$, and it can demand a larger $g_{i,t}$ in return for agreeing.

When this hold-up problem is anticipated at the investment stage, a country realizes that it will not be able to capture the full surplus of its investments. Thus, it invests less than the socially optimal level.

The investments before upcoming negotiations can be lower than with BAU.

The country also invested less than the socially optimal level in the BAU scenario. But the two situations are not identical. When party i expects that the countries will negotiate the emission levels, and thus to solve the climate change problem, to some extent, then it expects that the marginal cost, $C'(G_t)$, will be reduced. The reduced $C'(G_t)$ implies that it is less important that i invests in green technology as a way to solve the climate-change problem. The countries will, collectively, solve the problem anyway. For this reason, i might end up investing less when i expects that the countries will negotiate the $g_{i,t}$'s than i would have done in the BAU scenario.

The smaller investments are harmful to everyone, of course, because, even with BAU, investments are lower than the first-best levels. When the investments are further reduced, because of the reduced $C'(G_t)$, it is possible that the anticipation of the short-term agreements make everyone worse off, compared to BAU, because the cost of reduced investments might outweigh the benefit from reduced emission levels. As inequality (10) states, this will be the case when, for example, n is large, k is large, and q_R is large

The payoffs with short-term agreements can be lower than with BAU.

The intuition for why the inequality is weakened to (10) with many periods, so that it is more likely that $u_{i,t}^{ST} < u_{i,t}^{BAU}$, is that when some of the technology survives to another period ($q_R > 0$), then the under-investment problem, associated with the short-term agreements, is even costlier than in the one-period model (especially when the weight on the future, δ, is large).

Condition (10) is weakened further, so that it is more likely that $u_{i,t}^{ST} < u_{i,t}^{BAU}$, if there are technological spillovers associated with the investments. Thus, if intellectual property rights are weak or poorly enforced at the international level, it is more plausible that short-term agreements make everyone worse off, relative with BAU, because countries will be further discouraged from investing when they anticipate future negotiations.

It is worth returning to the possibility that payoffs are lower with agreements than without. In Section 2, we already concluded that the payoff in the BAU scenario was lower than in the static common-pool situation, which in turn was lower than the first-best payoffs. When payoffs in BAU are so low, it is worrisome that payoffs can be even lower when the countries are doing their best, negotiating caps on the emission levels. In this situation, the countries would have been better off if they committed to remain with BAU, before the investment decisions were made. After the investments are sunk, however, they all benefit from negotiating the emission levels. Thus, the countries are facing a time inconsistency problem, where they will find it optimal to negotiate later in the game, even though they could have been better off if they committed to not negotiate short-term agreements.

The details of this analysis are available in Harstad (2016), but, as mentioned, the idea goes back to Buchholz and Konrad (1994). In their model, the effect of the technology is multiplicative, and it reduces the per-unit cost of abatement effort. In the above model, in contrast, the effect of the technology is additive: see eq. (2). Furthermore, Buchholtz and Konrad permit a quite general utility function, although they consider only one period. Beccherle and Tirole (2011) also discuss the hold-up problem that arises when there is a delay in reaching an international agreement. Despite the differences between these models, the under-investment problem is present in all of them. This suggests that the result is quite robust.

The possibility that short-term agreements can be worse than BAU should motivate us to continue the search for a better design.

4.3 Example 3: Strategic emission caps

To introduce the benefits of a long-term agreement, return to Example 1 and 2, with only one period and quadratic $B(\cdot)$ and $C(\cdot)$. Assume, however, that the parties decide on the $g_{i,t}$'s at the beginning, and that the bargaining outcome is characterized by the NBS. What are the equilibrium emission caps and investment levels in this game?

The details are left as an exercise, but, of course, the SPE can be derived by backward induction. After g_i has been determined, country i can expect to benefit from consuming $g_i + R_i$ by investing. Thus, i invests as much as:

$$B'(g_i + q_R R_{i,0} + r_i) = k \Leftrightarrow$$
$$r_i = \bar{y} - k/b - g_i - q_R R_{i,0}.$$

The simple equation has three implications:

(1) Country i invests less if $g_{i,t}$ is large. Conversely, if the emission caps are tight, so that the $g_{i,t}$'s are small, then the parties find it optimal to invest more. In this way, the incomplete contract, which only specifies $g_{i,t}$, induce the parties to invest.

(2) Country i invests the socially optimal amount, conditional on $g_{i,t}$, no matter what $g_{i,t}$ is. This follows simply because there are, by assumption, no technological spillovers. Thus, as soon as the countries have pinned down the $g_{i,t}$'s, there is no need to negotiate the $r_{i,t}$'s, because countries will make those choices efficiently.
(3) Country i invests less if i starts out with a larger technology stock, so that $q_R R_{i,t-1}$ is large. At the negotiation stage, the countries anticipate all this. They know that every country will end up consuming $y_{i,t} = \bar{y} - k/b$ by investing $r_{i,t}$, that $g_{i,t}$ pins down r_i, and thus that negotiating the g_i's is equivalent to negotiating the induced r_i's. With the NBS, they agree on g_i's that are such that their costs, and thus the r_i's, will be the same. With simple algebra, we find:

$$g_i = (k - cqG_0)/nc + (R_0/n - R_{i,0})q_R/n.$$

With this, the first-best outcome is implemented. The g_i's are first best, by negotiation, and the r_i's are first best, because there are no spillovers associated with them.

4.4 Long-term agreements

With short-term agreements, the time distance between the negotiations and the compliance stage is too short for new technology to be developed. For a long-term agreement, instead, there will be time to develop new technology. The simplest way of capturing this situation is to assume that the emission caps are decided on at the very beginning of the period. The choice of emission caps will influence how much the countries will find it worthwhile to invest, and this influence can be taken into account by the countries when they decide on the emission caps.

Unfortunately, the efficient outcome in Example 3 does not survive when there is an infinite number of periods if each contract lasts only one period. The reason is, as in Section 4.1, that investments are inefficiently low when some of the technology survive to the next bargaining stage. To motivate countries to invest, even in this situation, it will be optimal to reduce the emission caps, below the ex post optimal level, because tight caps will motivate countries to invest more. (This is in line with point (1) in Example 3).

Formally, suppose the parties fix the $g_{i,t}$'s at the beginning of the period. Then, i can expect to consume one more unit of energy at time t by investing one more unit in technology. Furthermore, next period starts with q_R more units of technology. If the future $g_{i,t+1}$'s are not yet decided on, however, $R_{i,t}$ is, essentially, a public good, and all the n countries will invest less, as a consequence (just as in the previous subsection). When this is anticipated, i invests as much as:

$$B'(g_{i,t} + R_{i,t}) = (1 - \delta q_R/n)k \Leftrightarrow r_{i,t} = B'^{-1}(1 - \delta q_R/n) - g_{i,t} - q_R R_{i,t-1}.$$

Because the first-best investment level is

$$r_{i,t}^{FB} = B'^{-1}(1 - \delta q_R) - g_{i,t} - q_R R_{i,t-1},$$

we can make a few observations:

(1) As in Example 3, the country invests more if its emission allowance ($g_{i,t}$) is small. By playing around with the $g_{i,t}$'s, we can motivate i to invest any level that we want.

(2) If $\delta q_R > 0$, and $n > 1$, i invests less than the socially optimal level. The reason is that the other countries benefit when period $t+1$ starts with a larger $R_{i,t+1}$, because it will then be expected that this country will emit less.

Trade-off. Combining the two points, we realize that the parties will benefit from making the following trade-off. By reducing $g_{i,t}$ below the level that is ex post first best, the countries experience an inefficiency regarding the suboptimally low emission levels, but countries are induced to invest more, and that is beneficial in a situation in which the countries invest too little because of the hold-up problem. The optimal $g_{i,t}$'s will thus be smaller than the levels that are socially optimal, given the technology levels, because of the need to motivate additional investments. It can be shown that:

$$g_{i,t}(\mathbf{R}_t^{LT}) < g_{i,t}^{FB}(\mathbf{R}_t^{LT}),$$

where $\mathbf{R}_t^{LT}$ is the equilibrium technology vector under these types of long-term agreements. (See Harstad, 2012, for details).

We can do comparative static w.r.t. the length of the period. Suppose the *annual* depreciation rate is q_a, the annual discount rate is δ_a, and the number of years in a period is l. Then, $q_R = q_a^l$ and $\delta = \delta_a^l$, which both decrease in l. Thus, a more long-lasting agreement, where l is large, will motivate countries to make investments that are closer to the first-best levels, and thus it is optimal to negotiate emission caps that are close to the socially optimal level, as well. If, however, l is small, so that the agreement has a shorter duration, then δq_R is smaller, the investments are less than the first-best level, and to encourage more investments it is optimal to reduce the emission allowances relative to the level that is ex-post first best (given the equilibrium investment levels). In other words, an IEA that has a shorter duration, or commitment period, should be more ambitious and demanding, so that it will still motivate the parties to invest

The shorter the duration, the deeper the cuts must be.

4.5 Climate contracts over many periods

The situations above are quite stylized, of course. In reality, countries can negotiate emission caps for more than one period at the time. By allowing for this reasonable scenario, we will see how the insight from Sections 4.1 and 4.2 can be combined.

Suppose that the countries pin down the $g_{i,t}$'s for $t \in \{1,...,T\}$ at the beginning of period 1. Consider a period $t < T$. Party i knows that if i invests one unit more at time t, and q_R units less at time $t+1$, R_{t+1}, as well as the rest of the game, will remain unchanged. Thus, the cost of raising $R_{i,t}$ by one unit, in this way, is $(1 - \delta q_R)k$, so i invests to that:

$$B'(g_{i,t} + q_R R_{i,t-1} + r_{i,t}) = (1 - \delta q_R)k \Leftrightarrow$$
$$r_{i,t} = B'^{-1}((1 - \delta q_R)k) - g_{i,t} - q_R R_{i,t-1}.$$

Because there are no technological spillovers, i's investment is first best, conditional on $g_{i,t}$, regardless of what the $g_{i,t}$'s will be. Thus, the countries will negotiate and set the $g_{i,t}$'s equal to the optimal levels, and rest assured that the countries will invest the socially optimal amount. With this, the incomplete contract implements the first best outcome, just as in Example 3, even if countries decide on the investments independently.

This efficiency result is no longer true when we arrive at time T, however. Because the emission caps for the next period are not yet negotiated, the investments are as in the case with the one-period contract, and, thus, the optimal emission caps are less than the ex post socially optimal levels (conditional on the technology) in order to motivate countries to invest more. Consequently, the caps will be more demanding to comply with at the end.

With some algebra, we can compare the outcome with long-term (LT) agreements with the FB:

$$\text{For } t < T : g_{i,t}^{LT}(\mathbf{R}_t^{LT}) = g_{i,t}^{FB}(\mathbf{R}_t^{LT}), \quad \text{and} \quad R_t^{LT} = R_t^{FB}.$$
$$\text{For } t = T : g_{i,t}^{LT}(\mathbf{R}_t^{LT}) < g_{i,t}^{FB}(\mathbf{R}_t^{LT}), \quad \text{and} \quad R_t^{LT} < R_t^{FB}.$$

Technological spillovers. Based on the discussion so far, it may not be difficult to guess the consequences of introducing technological spillovers. If the spillovers are positive and large, countries are investing too little both because of the spillover, and because of the hold-up problem before new commitments are negotiated. The lower are the equilibrium investment levels relative to the socially optimal investment levels, the smaller should the $g_{i,t}$'s be, relative to the socially optimal $g_{i,t}$'s (conditional on the technology), because the tight emission caps will motivate the countries to invest more and thus closer to the socially optimal levels. In other words, when there are large technological spillovers, the caps should and will be more tighter so that they induce the countries to invest more. Technological spillovers are permitted in Harstad (2016) but the idea goes back to Golombek and Hoel (2005) who developed this insight in a finite game.

5 On the duration of agreements

An important aspect of an IEA is the commitment period length. This aspect defines the years for which the commitments are relevant, before they must be negotiated, once again. The first commitment period for the Kyoto Protocol was five years, 2008–2012. The second commitment period was eight years, 2013–2020. As observed by Bodansky et al. (2017, p. 203): "Parties disagreed on several issues including: the length of the commitment period—whether it should be five years (like the first commitment period) or eight years (to coincide with the scheduled launch of the 2015 agreement)." He continues: "the eight-year duration of the second commitment period was chosen so as to end when the Paris Agreement's NDCs were expected to take effect, and thus to avoid a commitment gap" (p. 205). The Paris Agreement has returned to the original commitment period length, and stipulates NDCs that are to be updated every five years.

There might be several important trade-offs involved when the optimal length is determined, but, unfortunately, we do not have a large literature on the optimal duration of a commitment period.

The title of this section is borrowed from Harris and Holmstrom (1987). They studied the optimal contract length in a situation in which they traded off the cost of uncertainty with a fixed cost of rewriting the contract. The larger is the uncertainty, the shorter is the optimal contract length. The larger is the cost of rewriting the agreement, or the cost of acquiring information, the longer is the optimal length. The authors did not have climate agreements in mind when analyzing their model, but their insight is relevant also in our context.

The "fixed" cost of negotiating new commitments might be related to the hold-up problem when it comes to international climate policies – as discussed above. That discussion emphasized the benefit of long-term commitments, because the parties will underinvest, due to the hold-up problem, when they approach a new round of negotiations. The benefit of increasing the commitment period from T to $T+1$ is that the hold-up problem is postponed. In Harris and Holmstrom (1987), the benefit is that the fixed cost can be postponed, but the shocks accumulate over time, so the uncertainty about the state of the world for time $T+1$ is greater than the uncertainty about the state for time T.

Uncertainty is crucial also when it comes to climate agreements. Thus, there are good reasons for why the commitment period is finite in reality. We do not really know what the emission caps ought to be 500 years from now. It would be rather stupid to tie our hands to certain actions so far in advance, because the world is more uncertain than what we have assumed in the simple model above. One uncertainty regards technology: If we ends up being positively surprised by technological breakthroughs, we might want to reduce the emission caps. Another uncertainty regards the cost of climate change. If the cost turns out to be larger than what we expect, the emission caps should be tightened. Either of these uncertainties is sufficient for the infinite-length conjecture to fail. The larger is the uncertainty, the smaller is the optimal T.

In our context, it is natural to assume that we are uncertain about the future amount of greenhouse gases and, thus, the marginal cost of emitting. This can be formalized by assuming:

$$G_t = q_G G_{t-1} + \sum_{i \in N} g_{i,t} + \theta_t. \tag{11}$$

The shock θ_t may be arbitrarily distributed with mean 0 and variance σ^2. The shock can reflect Nature's influence on G_t, and thus on the marginal cost of emission, $C'(G_t)$.

5.1 Example 4: The cost of commitments

Consider the model and timing of Example 3, with only one period, period $t = 1$, and with (11). What are the optimal g_i's if θ_t is known from the beginning, if it is not known, and what is the cost of deciding on the g_i's before learning θ_t?

The details are left as an exercise, but if θ_t is large, it will naturally be optimal to emit less, and invest more. Thanks to the linear investment cost, there is no cost associated with the stochastic θ_t, if just the realization is known before emission caps and investment levels are determined. If θ_t is not know, however, the additional cost will be $c\sigma^2/2$. Thus, $c\sigma^2/2$ represents the cost of committing to the g_i's before θ_t is realized.

5.2 The optimal commitment period length

Although the shocks are i.i.d. across periods, they have long-lasting impacts through their effect on G_t. Over time, the accumulated effects of the shocks can have large impacts on the marginal cost of emitting.

If the θ_t's are verifiable, so that the IEA can make the emission caps contingent on them, then the uncertainty does not matter and it remains optimal to agree on an infinite long commitment period, where the emission caps are functions of the history of shocks.

If the θ_t's are observable, but not verifiable, then it is difficult to write an IEA in which the caps are functions of the shocks. In this case, it might be simpler to negotiate new caps, once we have learned about the shocks and thus the cost of emitting. We are then left with a trade-off: It the length of the commitment period, T, is small, we benefit because we can update the caps once we have learned the shocks. By selecting a large T, however, incentives to invest will be larger. The optimal T, denoted T^*, trades off the two benefits. If the hold-up problem is more severe, because q_R is large (or because there are technological spillovers, making larger investments socially desirable), then T^* is larger. If the variance σ^2 is large, T^* is smaller.

With (LK) and (Q), we can calculate both the cost of the hold-up problem and also the cost of $g_{i,t}$'s that aren't reflecting the state of the world. It can then be shown that T^* is finite iff:

$$\sigma^2 > (q_R k)^2 \cdot [\delta(1 - q_G^2)(1 - \delta q_G^2)(1 - 1/n)^2 / bcq_G^2],$$

and, under this condition, T^* is smaller if the variance σ^2 is large, but T^* is larger if the hold-up problem is very costly (e.g., if $q_R k$ is large). The proof also allows for technological spillovers and show that, when these are larger, the hold-up problem is more costly, and T^* is larger. This comparative static implies that if the world suffers from weak protection of intellectual property rights (because the TRIPS agreement is not enforced, for example), then the optimal IEA should not only be more ambitious, but the commitment period should also be longer

> T^* is reduced when the uncertainty is large and the hold-up problem inexpensive.

While the proof of the above equation is in Harstad (2016), Schmidt and Strausz (2015) derive related results in a setting where two countries are asymmetric.

There are other concerns that determine T^*, of course. For example, if it turns out that many countries are free riding, then it might be wise to let the agreement expire relatively soon, so that it's easier to negotiate with a larger set of countries. We will return to this possibility in Section 6, where the possibility to free ride, instead of participating, is introduced and analyzed.

5.3 Updating and renegotiation design

Letting the commitments expire is actually not the best way of allowing the parties to update the agreement. Alternatively, the commitments can stay in place, as the default or threat point when the parties negotiate new commitments. In this way, the parties will take new information into account, but they will continue to have incentives to invest in new technology, because of this default outcome. The lower are the emission caps in the default, the larger are the incentives to invest, because being comfortable with the default is what gives a party bargaining power.

Chung (1991) and Aghion et al. (1994) have shown that "renegotiation design" can be beneficial when contracts are incomplete. The idea is that the terms will anyway be optimal, ex post, when the parties renegotiate. Thus, the initial, default agreement can be used to provide incentives to invest.

Edlin and Reichelstein (1996) showed that the first-best is achieved by initially contracting on the expected optimal quantity and thereafter allowing for renegotiation. Segal and Whinston (2002) introduced technological spillovers and found that the larger the spillover associated with the investments, the larger is the optimal default quantity, compared with the expected ex post first-best quantity. To ensure ex post efficiency, it is then necessary to renegotiate, also on the equilibrium path.

Applied to our dynamic climate policy game, it would work as follows. Suppose the agreement is only one period, as in Section 4.1. The countries start by agreeing on low default emission levels, but, after the investment stage, they renegotiate and permit the caps to be larger (and equal to the ex post optimal levels). The default levels should be low because, then, the countries that do not invest will be uncomfortable with the default outcome, they will desperately need to renegotiate, and this gives them a poor bargaining position, with an unattractive outcome. To obtain a better bargaining position, and a better outcome, a country will be incentivized to invest more if the default caps are low.

It is useful to return to the trade-off discussed in Section 4.2, and in the final period in Section 4.3. There, the emission caps traded off the benefits of larger investments, when g_i^{LT} was reduced, with the cost that the caps would be inefficiently small, ex post. When this cost vanishes, thanks to the renegotiation, then the "default caps", agreed to initially, can be further reduced. The optimal emission caps in the default (DE), and also the equilibrium levels, are characterized by tight caps, so that they motivate countries to invest the optimal levels. When $\delta q_R > 0$, then:

$$g_{i,t}^{DE}\left(\mathbf{R}_t^{LT}\right) < g_{i,t}^{LT}\left(\mathbf{R}_t^{LT}\right) < g_{i,t}^{FB}\left(\mathbf{R}_t^{LT}\right), \quad \text{and} \quad R_t^{DE} = R_t^{FB}.$$

In fact, any level of investment can be induced by selecting the appropriate default caps. If, for example, there are technological spillovers, and these are large, then it is beneficial to motivate more investments, and the default caps should be even smaller (see Harstad, 2012, for details).

By observing the procedure empirically, one might mistake it for being a time inconsistency problem. In every period, the countries pledge to limit emission by a lot but, later on, they renegotiate and allow themselves to emit more. Although this procedure is, empirically, similar to a time inconsistency problem, it can implement the first best.

6 Participation and coalition formation

There is no world government. Every country is free to decide whether or not to participate in an international agreement. Freedom to choose is generally a good thing, but this freedom also implies that it can be challenging to motivate appropriate actions when there are international externalities.

In reality, the level of participation varies quite a lot between agreements. The Kyoto Protocol, of 1997, distinguished between Annex I and Annex II countries, where only Annex II countries were expected to commit to reductions in their emission levels. In the end, only 37 countries committed to reduce emissions and one of them, Canada, withdrew in 2011. The Paris Agreement, in contrast, includes nearly every country in the world. The level of participation also varies for other types of international agreements, ranging from defence to international trade.

There is a large literature in economics that endogenizes the size and composition of coalitions. Much of this literature draws on how collusions among subset of firms have been modeled in the literature on industrial organization. Seminal papers include those of d'Aspremont et al. (1983) and

Palfrey and Rosenthal (1984). A major result in this literature is that equilibrium agreements are predicted to include a very small number of countries (Hoel, 1992; Carraro and Siniscalco, 1993; Carraro et al., 2006; Barrett, 1994; Dixit and Olson, 2000). With linear-quadratic utility functions, the coalition size is, at most, three! The contrast between the theoretical prediction and actual coalitions, which are often much larger, has been referred to as the "Paradox of International Agreements" (Kolstad and Toman, 2005).

In this section, I first illustrate the small-coalition result based on a simple two-stage participation game that is often used in the literature. The game is as follows:

(1) Every $i \in N$ decides whether to free ride or be a member.
(2) (a) The set of members, $M \subseteq N$, decides the terms of the agreements while (b) the free riders act noncooperatively.

When the members have symmetric preferences, it is typically, and reasonably, assumed that they select contributions to maximize the sum of the members' payoffs.

In this game, M is an equilibrium coalition if there is a subgame-perfect equilibrium in which (i) every $i \in M$ prefers to be a member, while (ii) every $i \notin M$ decides to free ride, anticipating (13). Part (i) is sometimes referred to as "internal consistency", because it requires that every that are inside the coalition is satisfied with their choice. Part (ii) is often referred to as "external consistency", because it requires that those external to the coalition are satisfied with their choice.

In Section 6.2, we embed the participation game in the dynamic game that we are used to by now, where countries both emit and invest in green technologies. If the coalition can also decide on the duration of the agreement (as in Section 5), then it turns out that the coalition can be larger.

If contracts were complete, so that countries could make agreements on both emission levels and investment levels, the small-coalition result would emerge for the same reasons as before.

With incomplete contracts, however, the coalition can be much larger. With incomplete contracts, the members cooperate on emission levels but investments are decided on noncooperatively. In fact, incomplete contracts turn out to be beneficial because of the large coalitions, and because of the hold-up problem (which will not be present on the equilibrium path). This result emerges if the countries can also decide on the duration of the agreement. When they can, they prefer a long-term agreement because it avoids the hold-up problem, but a short-term agreement if one of the members deviates by not participating in a given period. When it is expected that this free rider will return to the equilibrium and participate at the next round, the coalition prefers to have a short-term agreement instead of locking in a smaller coalition. When the short-term agreement comes along with the costly hold-up problem, the temptation to deviate is weakened, and a larger coalition can be sustained. In other words, the hold-up problem, which was problematic in the previous sections, is here beneficial. The hold-up problem arises only off the equilibrium path, if one of the members deviates by free riding, so that the coalition opt for a short-term agreement until the country returns. The cost of the hold-up problem implies that it is more attractive to participate, so that the coalition will be large enough for it to sign a long-term agreement.

At the end of this section, we will discuss other aspects that influence the coalition size. In particular, if we move away from the two-stage game, and countries are farsighted, they may cooperate because they would be worried that if they do not, then other countries will also opt out of the coalition later on.

6.1 Example 5: The result "m = 3"

Suppose there is one period, no investments, and country i's payoff from emitting g_i is:

$$-\frac{b}{2}(\overline{y} - g_i)^2 - c \sum_{j \in N} g_j,$$

What are the emission levels and the payoffs for the free riders and the coalition members? What is the equilibrium coalition size?

With BAU, g_i is $g_i^{BAU} = \overline{y} - c/b$. The FB is given by the same equation if just c is replaced with nc, while M's best policy requires c to be replaced with mc.

If we define i's abatement or contribution as $x_i := g_i^{BAU} - g_i$, we can write

$$u_i = -bx_i^2/2 + c \sum_{j \in N \setminus i} x_j, \tag{12}$$

plus a constant. With this, we find:

$$\begin{aligned} x_i &= (m-1)c/b, \quad i \in M, \\ x_i &= 0, \quad i \notin M. \end{aligned} \tag{13}$$

Thus, by free riding, a member reduces x_i to 0, but each of the other members reduces x_i by c/b. Thus, a member is better off participating iff:

$$\begin{aligned} -b[x_i(m)]^2/2 + c \sum_{j \in N \setminus i} x_i(m) &\geq c \sum_{j \in N \setminus i} x_i(m-1) \Leftrightarrow \\ m &\leq 3. \end{aligned}$$

Formally, M^* is an equilibrium coalition if and only if $m^* = |M^*| \in \{0, 2, 3\}$.

The coalition cannot include more than three countries. For every larger coalition, the contributions would be so costly for a member that its payoff would be larger by free riding. If $m = 3$, each member is exactly indifferent between participating and free riding, and thus $m = 2$ is also an equilibrium. In addition, $m = 0$ is an equilibrium, because every country will set exactly the same policy noncooperatively as if it enters and creates a coalition alone. Note that $m = 1$ is *not* an equilibrium, because a free rider would be better off by entering the coalition with one other member

In Example 5, at most three countries participate in the coalition.

Two aspects are striking about this result. First, the parameters (c and b) do not influence the equilibrium. The reason is that each parameter, such as c, will both raise the cost of participation, and also the benefit of participating: With the equilibrium x_i, both terms in (12) will be quadratic in c. (Similarly, both terms will be proportional to $1/b$.) Thus, the parameter cancels out when the payoffs are compared.

Second, the equilibrium coalition is very small. When m is large, both the benefit of dropping out, and the cost when the other $m-1$ members respond, are large. In this model, where the cost of contributing is convex while the benefit of the others' contribution is large, a large m will imply that the benefit of dropping out increases faster in m than does the cost. This comparison limits how large m can be, in equilibrium. In the two-stage participation game, the benefit of free riding is large also because it is assumed that the remaining coalition, with one less member, will simply continue as normal (although with lower x_i's).

6.2 Participation – with fixed duration

To generalize the model in Section 6.1, consider the dynamic game in Section 2 but with the following simplifying functional forms:

$$\begin{aligned} B(y_{i,t}) &= -\frac{b}{2}(\bar{y}-y_{i,t})^2, \\ C(G_t) &= \underline{c}G_t, \quad \text{and} \end{aligned} \tag{14}$$

$$K(R_{i,t}, R_{i,t-1}) = \frac{\underline{\kappa}}{2}(R_{i,t}^2 - q_R R_{i,t-1}^2), \tag{15}$$

where $K(\cdot)$ is the investment cost. The linear $C(\cdot)$ implies that the present-discounted cost of emitting one more unit at time t is $c \equiv \sum_{\tau=t}^{\infty}(\delta q_G)^{\tau-t}\underline{c} = \underline{c}/(1-\delta q_G)$. With the linear $C(\cdot)$, we get interior solutions only if the investment cost is convex. With (15), the cost is simply quadratic if $q_R = 0$, but the cost of reaching $R_{i,t}$ is smaller if $R_{i,t-1}$ and q_R are large. The net marginal investment cost is, say, $\kappa R_{i,t}$, iff $\kappa \equiv (1-\delta q_R)\underline{\kappa}$. With these functional forms, first-best investment, conditional on $g_{i,t}$, is

$$R_i^{FB}(g_{i,t}) = (\bar{y} - g_{i,t})b/(b+\kappa). \tag{16}$$

Because the first-best emission level is $g_i^{FB}(R_{i,t}) = \bar{y} - R_{i,t} - nc/\kappa$, we have

$$R_{i,t} = nc/\kappa,\ y_{i,t} = \bar{y} - nc/b, \quad \text{and} \quad g_{i,t} = \bar{y} - nc/b - nc/\kappa.$$

The coalitional decisions are the same if just n is replaced by m, while a free-rider's decisions are the same if just n is replaced by 1.

As a start, suppose the countries play the two-stage participation game before the emission stage in period 1. With this model, M's policies are "payoff-irrelevant" for the nonparticipant, and vice versa. That is, every free-riding country has a dominant strategy, so that its optimal policies are independent of what M will decide. For these reasons, the outcome of the game is the same whether M's decisions are before, after, or simultaneous with the decisions of the free riders (i.e., (a) and (b) at stage 2 in the participation game, described above).

The coalition members negotiate the $g_{i,t}$'s for period $t \in \{1, ..., T\}$, while later emission caps may be negotiated just before the emission stage in period $T+1$. The $r_{i,t}$'s are decided on noncooperatively, and i will find it optimal to set $\kappa R_{i,t} = b(\overline{y} - y_{i,t})$, which is socially optimal, in every $t \in \{2, ..., T\}$, but $\kappa R_{i,t} = c$ at $t = 1$, and $t = T + 1$, etc, i.e., just before the next emission stage. As before, the intuition is that before future caps are to be negotiated, i's technology is, essentially, a public good, because it motivates i to emit less, and i captures only a fraction of this benefit.

With these investments, as a function of the $g_{i,t}$'s, the coalition will negotiate the first-best $g_{i,t}$'s. The details are left as an exercise, but, by comparing the payoff for member i with what i can obtain from opting out, we learn that i is willing to participate iff the coalition includes at most three countries. Thus, the three-member result holds, also in this setting: M^* is an equilibrium coalition if and only if $m^* = |M^*| \in \{0, 2, 3\}$.

As discussed in Section 5, the duration of the commitment period may also be endogenous. When the coalition size is endogenous, it may depend on the coalition size.

6.3 Example 6: Endogenous duration

Consider the same payoffs as in Section 6.1, so that we abstract from investment levels, but let there be many periods. After M is formed, M can not only negotiate the caps, but also the duration. Then, the optimal duration depends on number of members at the time being, m, and how this compares to the equilibrium number, m^*. In particular, let M^* denote an equilibrium coalition of size $m^* \equiv |M^*|$ and consider a realized coalition $M \subseteq M^*$, with $m = |M| \leq m^*$. M finds it optimal to contract for $T(m)$ periods, where:

$$T(m) = \begin{cases} 1 & \text{if } m < m^* \\ \{1, ..., \infty\} & \text{if } m = m^* \end{cases}.$$

That is, if few countries participate at time t, they prefer to sign a one-period agreement so that the coalition can return to the larger, equilibrium size in the next period. If, in contrast, $M = M^*$, which will be the case on the equilibrium path, every $T \geq 1$ is equally good to the coalition. The reason is that after T periods, the same coalition will form again, in equilibrium, and they will contribute exactly the same when it comes to emission cuts and investments. The choice of T is thus irrelevant.

6.4 Participation – with endogenous duration

When we return to the model with investments, it is rather different.

Duration. When deciding on T, there is, as in Example 6, an incentive to reduce T when the actual number of participants, m, is small relative to the equilibrium number, m^*, so that the larger coalition can be formed soon. However, the reduced T is now coming along with a cost. The cost is that every member invests less before the next bargaining stage because of the hold-up problem. When investments are lower, emission levels will be larger at the next bargaining stage. Therefore, when $m = m$, the members strictly prefer a long-lasting agreement. (With complete contracts, they were indifferent.) If it turned out that a member deviated, so that the coalition right now is just $m^* - 1$, then the remaining coalition faces a dilemma. Should it "lock in" the coalition and sign a long-term agreement with the smaller coalition? Or should it sign a short-term agreement, where the benefit is that the coalition size can be expected to be m^* next period, but the cost is that investments will be small, in the meantime, because of the hold-up problem associated with short-term agreement?

Naturally, the answers also depend on how much it matters to include just one more country. If m^* is large, it may not be worthwhile that $m^* - 1$ countries should invest little, just to get another country on board. If m^* is small, one more member is relatively important. The threshold is given by:

$$m^* \leq m_M(\chi) \equiv 1 + \frac{1}{1 - \sqrt{(\chi + \delta)/(\chi + 1)}}, \qquad \text{where } \chi \equiv \frac{\kappa}{b}. \tag{17}$$

That is, M finds it worthwhile to sign a one-period contract is a single member deviates by free riding iff $m^* \leq m_M(\chi)$. (For details, see Battaglini and Harstad, 2016).

The answers to the two questions also depend on how costly the hold-up problem is. In this model, the hold-up problem is larger if κ/b is small. The reason is that if κ is small, or b is large, then the climate change problem is, most of all, relying on new technology, rather than reduced energy consumption. So, if κ/b is small, it is costly to sign a short-term agreement, and threshold $m_M(\chi)$ is small.

Participation. The cost of the hold-up problem is faced also by members considering to free ride. If (17) holds, a supposed-to-be member that deviates and free rides will cause the remaining coalition to sign a one-period agreement. Then, free riding comes along with the cost that the members will invest exactly as in BAU.

The additional cost makes free riding less attractive, and a member benefits from staying in the coalition for a larger set of parameters than when contracts are complete.

Here, is $m_I(\chi)$ the largest coalition size such that a member is better off participating rather than free riding for one period, given that investments will be as in BAU during that period. Because the cost of participating is convex in m^*, $m_I(\chi)$ is limited, especially when the hold-up problem is not that expensive for a member considering to free ride. By comparing one's alternative payoffs, we can show that a member is better off participating iff:

$$m^* \leq m_I(\chi) \equiv 3 + \frac{2\delta}{\chi - \delta}$$

When $\kappa \to \infty$, and therefore $\chi \to \infty$, $m_I(\chi) \to 3$, as in the case without any investment. Thus, for a large κ and, thus, χ, m^* is severely constrained by $m_I(\chi)$. By comparison, for a small χ, we had that m^* was severely constrained by $m_M(\chi)$. In combination, m^* is an equilibrium coalition size iff $m^* \leq \min\{m_I(\chi), m_M(\chi)\}$. Thus, m^* will be limited by $m_M(\chi)$ when χ is small, and by $m_I(\chi)$ if χ is large. If χ is moderate, m^* can be quite large, as illustrated in Fig. 3.

In other words, the hold-up problem associated with short-term incomplete contracts disciplines and motivates coalition members to participate

> The hold-up problem, as an out-of-equilibrium threat, can motivate a larger coalition to form.

6.5 Further reading and farsightedness

On the one hand, Eichner and Kollenbach (2023) showed that the possibility for the above hold-up problem is indeed important to generate large coalitions. They consider a timing of the game that leads to no hold-up problem, even for short-term agreements, and they find that, in this case, the coalition is small, just as when contracts are complete. Participation can also be low if investments are made prior to the participation stage (Helm and Schmidt, 2015).

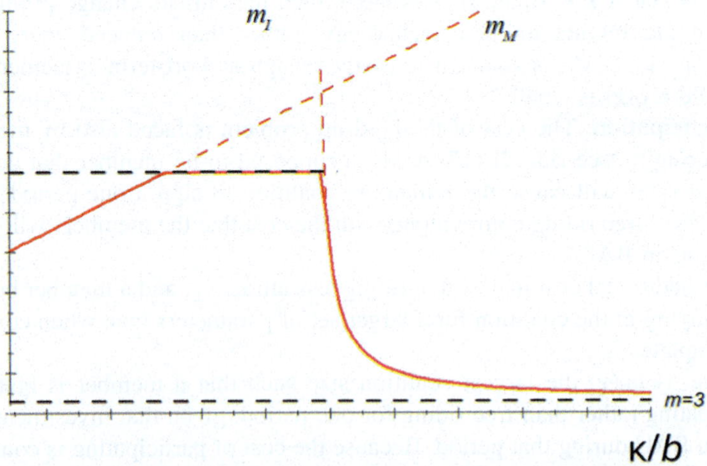

FIG. 3 The coalition size can be large, depending on the cost of the hold-up problem.

On the other hand, there are other reasons for why the coalition can be large, of course. Kováč and Schmidt (2012) show that if the remaining coalition cannot sign one-period agreements, the coalition will be large, even without the hold-up problem. The result that the small-coalition result gives the number 3 in the static model is, moreover, because of the linear-quadratic functional forms. Karp and Simon (2013) develop a non-parametric approach to the problem, and they identify conditions under which the equilibrium coalition size can be large, depending on the functional forms.

Altruistic preferences at the participation stage can lead to larger coalitions, but altruism at the emission-setting stage can reduce the equilibrium coalition size, because free riders can take advantage of the coalition's benevolent behavior (Schopf, 2024).

Heterogeneous preferences often reduce the equilibrium coalition size, but (therefore) increasing the effectiveness of adaptation in highly vulnerable countries can help supporting an IEA, when this reduces the heterogeneity (Li and Rus, 2019). When countries remain heterogeneous, transfers might be helpful to motivate some of the countries to participate (Dutta and Radner, 2020; Kotchen, 2020; Okada, 2023). Barrett (1997) analyzed how the coalition can be larger if the members could impose sanctions on the free riders. While Hoel and Schneider (1997) show that transfers can be harmful, and lead to more emissions, Barrett (2001) showed that if the countries are very asymmetric, transfers can be necessary for a large coalition to form. When the heterogeneity is private information, transfers are a natural part of the optimal mechanism (Martimort and Sand-Zantman, 2016). Besides explicit side payments, there can be various forms of favors or issue linkages (Maggi, 2016), including trade liberalization (Nordhaus, 2015), that can also motivate participation.

The two-stage participation game gives a lot of power to free riders. By opting out, the coalition is reduced by one party, even if it turns out that the remaining parties might also get second thoughts. It might be more realistic to allow other players to also reach and change their decision.

To capture this situation, it is sometimes assumed that other parties can also leave. When this is anticipated, and a potential free rider is "farsighted", then opting out might be less attractive. When free riding is less attractive, the coalition can be larger.

To illustrate, suppose that countries can only leave the coalition, and that free riders can not change their mind and join later on. Based on the above analysis, we know that, in the simple example of Section 6.1, a coalition of size 3 is farsightedly stable: A third member does not strictly want to leave, no matter what the other countries are doing. Therefore, a coalition of size 4 is not stable, because one member can leave without triggering other countries to leave. But because the size 4 is not stable, a coalition of size 5 will be stable: A member would anticipate that if it opts out, then the coalition will not end up being of size 4, which is unstable, but of size 3. That reduction in the coalition size will motivate all five countries to participate. Given this, a coalition of size

6 is not stable, because if a single country deviates, the remaining coalition, with five countries, is stable. Thus, the next larger stable coalition consists of eight participants, then 13, and so 20. There can be many coalition sizes that are farsightedly stable, and some of them can be quite large. The numbers from the example with linear-quadratic utility functions are from Ray and Vohra (2001). (But see also Chwe, 1994; Ray and Vohra, 1999; Ray, 2007; Osmani and Tol, 2009; Diamantoudi and Sartzetakis, 2018; Vosooghi et al., 2024).

Instead of a game where countries can only leave the coalition, one could study a game where countries can only join. These games are studied in the literature on ratification (see, for instance, Wagner, 2016) and when there are minimum participation thresholds (Black et al., 1993; Harstad, 2006; Carraro et al., 2009; Weikard et al., 2015), ignored in this chapter.

Another strong assumption that is imposed in most of the literature is that there is, at most, one environmental coalition. The assumption does not match well with the real world, however, because we observe a large number of coalitions in many other settings, including the environment, and international trade. Theoretically, this is also an unreasonable assumption: In Example 5, for instance, there might be only three countries in a coalition, but there can be a large number of coalitions that are active, side by side. Thus, Asheim et al. (2006) show that two agreements can sustain more: They find that a regime with two agreements can Pareto dominate a regime based on a single global treaty.

7 Compliance with self-enforcing treaties

What happens if a country does not comply with its pledges?

There is no world government that can force a sovereign country to comply. Thus, an IEA must be self-enforcing, and designed in a way so that countries will comply voluntarily. The IPCC (2014, 1015) states that: "*From a rationalist perspective, compliance will occur if the discounted net benefits from cooperation (including direct climate benefits, co-benefits, reputation, transfers, and other elements) exceed the discounted net benefits of defection.*"

This motivation, however, may not always be sufficiently strong. During the first commitment period of the Kyoto Protocol, for example, Canada found it costly to comply and, in 2011, it simply withdrew.

It is arguably more difficult to motivate compliance than to induce countries to participate in the first place: If a country does not participate, the other coalition members will contribute less; if a country participates but defects at the emission stage, the other coalition members will, in equilibrium, contribute just as expected. By comparison, the temptation to participate and defect might be stronger than the temptation to free ride from the very beginning.

This section studies the incentive to comply and derives conditions under which an IEA is self-enforcing. To check the boundaries of what self-enforcement can accomplish, it is often assumed that the punishment following noncompliance is as severe as possible. The harshest punishment when there is a single defecting country is that the other countries take actions that minimizes the maximal payoff for the defecting country, when this country maximizes its own payoff, given the punishment that it faces: These are the min-max strategies, often referred to in the literature on repeated games (for a textbook treatment, see Mailath and Samuelson, 2006).

A simpler punishment is that the cooperative arrangement breaks down, and that the countries return to the business-as-usual outcome. This punishment is also symmetric, and thus achievable if, and even if, it cannot be observed which country that is responsible to the higher-than-agreed-upon pollution level. This type of punishment is typically considered in the literature on self-enforcing agreements: see Barrett (1994, 2006), Dutta and Radner (2004, 2006), and Kerr et al. (2024), among others.

In some cases, the BAU strategies coincides with the min-max strategies. That will be the case in the simple benchmark model that I start out with below. This model is useful to illustrate the key factors that determine whether an agreement is self-enforcing: The discount factor must be large, and contributions must be modest. Thereafter, we return to the dynamic game, also used in the previous section, where countries are both emitting and investing in green technologies. In this model, the technology will take on a new, strategic role. When the temptation to defect at the emission stage is large, the temptation can be reduced if a country is endowed with green technology that reduces the need to emit. For this reason, the best self-enforcing treaty might require countries to invest more than in the first best, only to reduce the temptation to defect. This situation arises when first-best climate policies place a larger emphasis on the reduction of energy consumption rather than the development of new, green technology. In the reverse case, where investments are the most important ingredient, then countries might be more tempted to defect at the investment stage, instead of at the emission stage. In this situation, the best self-enforcing treaty permits and, in fact, requires the countries to invest less, even though they are expected to reduce the energy consumption by a lot. In equilibrium, a country would be tempted to invest more at the investment stage, but higher investments must be punished by the other members. The intuition for this result is that if a country did indeed invest more, it would find it optimal to emit less in the future, also in the event in which another country has defected. That is, it is not credible that defection will be punished sufficiently by the other countries, unless investments are kept low.

7.1 Example 7: A repeated game with trigger strategies

As a start, consider the payoffs in Example 6, given by (12), and assume that, if any country contributes another amount than x^*, all contributions will forever after be 0 (i.e., BAU). With this as the threat point, the most tempting defection is to set $x_i = 0$, but compliance with x^* is better than defection if and only if the following compliance constraint holds:

$$c(m-1)x^* - \frac{b}{2}(x^*)^2 \geq (1-\delta)c(m-1)x^* \Leftrightarrow$$

$$\delta \geq 1 - \frac{c(m-1)x^* - \frac{b}{2}(x^*)^2}{c(m-1)x^*} = \frac{bx^*}{2c(m-1)} \Leftrightarrow$$
$$x^* \leq 2\delta c(m-1)/b.$$

Thus, an IEA with contributions x^* can be self-enforcing iff x^* is small, δ is large, and m is large.

This inequality has several interpretations. First, it is defining a lower boundary for what the discount factor can be for countries to be willing to comply with x^*. Second, for any give discount factor, the inequality defines the largest contribution level that a coalition of size m is willing to comply with. The larger is the coalition, the larger is the threshold for the contribution x^*. Third, for any given δ and x^* , the inequality is requesting m to be large for compliance to be worthwhile. Hence, free riding can be discouraged if just the coalition is sufficiently large. This contrasts the findings in the previous section, where the incentive to free ride was stronger when m was large.

Part of the explanation for this difference is that, in the previous section, x^* was endogenous. We know that the coalition prefers countries to set $x^* = c(m-1)/b$. With these contributions, the inequality simplifies to:

$$\delta \geq \frac{bx^*}{2c(m-1)} = \frac{1}{2}.$$

If this condition fails, the contributions must be reduced below the first-best level for the agreement to be self-enforcing.

This simple analysis can be extended in several directions. For example, suppose that if a country defects, it will be observed and punished only with probability $q \in [0, 1]$. Furthermore, suppose the punishment phase will last only $T \leq \infty$ periods, before the coalition will renegotiate and re-start its cooperation phase. With these two generalizations, compliance is attractive only if:

$$v = c(m-1)x^* - \frac{b}{2}(x^*)^2 \geq (1-\delta)c(m-1)x^* + (1-q)\delta v + q\delta^{T+1}v.$$

If q or T is small, the right-hand side is larger, and thus x^* might need to be reduced for compliance to remain attractive. Vice versa: If the coalition can improve on its ability to monitor, so that q increases, then also contributions can increase, without violating the countries's compliance constraints

With better monitoring technology, the cuts can be deeper.

7.2 Compliance technology and self-enforcing agreements

Consider now the model in Section 6.2. A symmetric stationary self-enforcing agreement is now a pair (g_i, R_i), so that the countries prefer to comply and stick with (g_i, R_i) forever rather than to defect. Because the two variables are determined at different points in time, there are two types of compliance constraints that must be satisfied: One for the investment stage, and another for the emission stage. Each compliance constraint will require that the payoff is larger if one selects the agreed-upon level than if one defects. If a country defects, it will find it optimal to select the BAU level. For simplicity, it will be assumed that from the subsequent stage, all countries revert to the BAU outcome. With this, the two compliance constraints require that a country's payoff from complying forever is larger than if a country returns to its BAU strategy, before the other countries return to BAU at the next stage.

In general, for every pair (g_i, R_i), the compliance constraint at the investment stage will hold if $\delta \geq \delta^{R_i}(\mathbf{g}, R)$, while the compliance constraint at the emission stage holds iff $\delta \geq \delta^{g}(\mathbf{g}, R)$. With the first-best pair (g_i^{FB}, R_i^{FB}), the two compliance constraints can be written as follows. (For details, see Harstad et al., 2022).

$$\delta \geq \overline{\delta}^{R_i} \equiv \delta^{R_i}(\mathbf{g}^{\mathbf{FB}}, \mathbf{R}^{FB}) = \frac{b-\kappa}{2b}, \tag{CC-r}$$

$$\delta \geq \overline{\delta}^{g} \equiv \delta^{g}(\mathbf{g}^{\mathbf{FB}}, \mathbf{R}^{FB}) = \frac{\kappa}{b+2\kappa}. \tag{CC-g}$$

If δ is larger than both thresholds, the first best is attainable. If δ is smaller, the type of distortion depends on which compliance constraint that is binding first.

If investments are relatively costly (so that κ/b is large), investment levels are low, even in the first best. The low investment levels reduce the temptation to defect at the investment stage so, when δ is smaller, the first compliance constraint to bind is the one at the emission stage (i.e., $\delta \geq \overline{\delta}^{R_i}$). When (CC-g) binds, the emission level must be limited, and smaller than the first best, in order to motivate compliance. This is replicating the insight developed in Section 7.1.

When δ falls further, the best self-enforcing agreement moves along the horizontal arrow in Fig. 4: g_i will be permitted to increase, but there is no reason to reduce the investment levels, so the best self-enforcing agreement continues to require $R_i = R_i^{FB}$. Consequently, R_i is larger than the ex post first-best investment level, given g_i. When g_i increases, it is ex post optimal that R_i falls, in line with (16). The best agreement, however, requires countries to invest more, and too much, relative to the ex post optimal level. The intuition for this result is that if countries were allowed to invest less, and as little as $R_i^{FB}(g_i)$, the temptation to defect at the emission stage would be greater. To motivate compliance, g_i would need to fall even further. The inefficiently high investment levels reduces the need to consume fossil fuel, and thus they reduce the temptation to emit more. For this reason, the best self-enforcing treaty requires countries to invest more than what is socially optimal, given the emission level that is associated with the agreement. If the country implements the decision with taxes and subsidies, the outcome is that if δ falls, the country must reduce the tax on emission (below the Pigouvian level) but raise the subsidy on the investments, even if there are no technological spillover associated with the technology.

If κ/b is small, so that investments are inexpensive and thus important, then the first compliance constraint that binds when δ becomes smaller is the one at the investment stage. When the first best can no longer be supported as a self-enforcing agreement, the distortion that is necessary in the best self-enforcing agreement is that countries must be allowed to invest less. There is no reason to distort the energy consumption level, $y_{i,t}$, however, so $y_{i,t}$, will remain at the level that is first best. Because $y_{i,t}$ is constant, while R_i is smaller, g_i must be larger. If the discount factor falls, the best pair (g_i, R_i) moves along the downward-sloping line in Fig. 4. This implies that R_i is not optimal conditional on the g_i that will be chosen. Instead, $R_i < R_i^{FB}(g_i)$. This may be surprising, because countries would volunteer to invest as much as $R_i^{FB}(g_i)$ when they know that they must or will, in any case, emit g_i. (After all, there are no technological spillovers associated with the investments.) Thus, the best agreement requires that countries invest less than what they would prefer, given g_i. The intuition for this policy is that if countries were allowed to invest more, it would be too tempting to defect at the investment stage because, for those high investment levels, the other countries would be unable or unwilling to emit a lot as a punishment in this period. Thus, the large investment levels would reduce the credibility of punishment, and countries will find it beneficial to defect at the investment stage. If the country implements the decision with taxes and subsidies, the outcome is now that if δ falls, the country must tax investments in green technology.

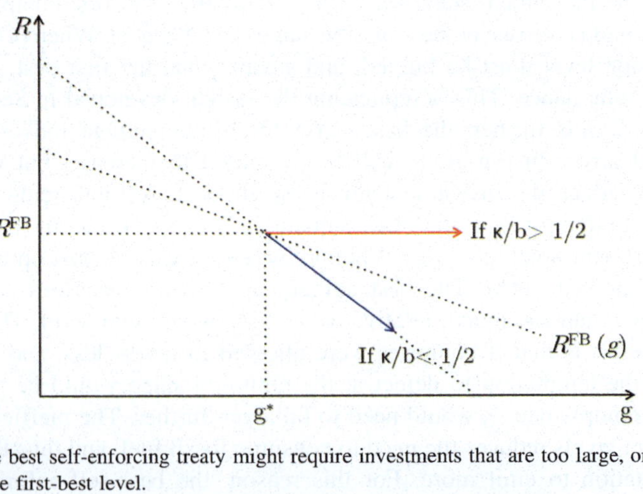

FIG. 4 The best self-enforcing treaty might require investments that are too large, or too small, relative to the first-best level.

7.3 Technologies, thresholds, and transfers

While green technology can help to motivate compliance, "brown technology", which can be strategic complements to emissions, can raise the temptation to emit. Thus, for an agreement to be self-enforcing, it might be necessary to limit how much countries can be permitted to invest in brown technologies. (These limits can justify taxes on the investments in drilling technologies, even when there are taxes also on the emission levels.) In Harstad et al. (2019), brown technology is permitted, and it is shown that even investments in adaptation technology might need to be regulated. If the temptation to defect is strong, then compliance will be credible only for countries that invest less in adaptation.

In general, our insight on self-enforcement draws on the literature on repeated games (for a textbook-treatment, see Mailath and Samuelson, 2006). Dutta and Radner (2009) allow strategies to be conditioned on the stock of greenhouse gases (even thought it is not "payoff relevant"), so that all countries emit little as long as the threshold is not crossed, but the countries revert to BAU when the threshold is crossed. These types of trigger strategies can motivate the countries to emit less, under some conditions. If countries are asymmetric, Kerr et al. (2024) show how transfers, and technology transfers, can help the agreement to be self-enforcing.

8 Narrow-but-deep vs. broad-but-shallow

The emission cuts for the Annex II signatories in the Kyoto Protocol (KP) faced substantial legally binding emission cuts. However, only 37 countries ended up with such commitments. The Paris Agreement (PA), in contrast, include 195 signatories, but the pledges are nationally determined, and they are not legally binding. By comparison, one may argue that the KP was narrow but deep, while the PA is broad but shallow.

Ideally, an international environmental agreement (IEA) should be both broad and deep, but this can be difficult because of the problems discussed in the earlier sections. When only second-best IEAs are possible, the debate regards whether it is worse to give up on depth vs. breadth. Aldy et al. (2003) and Aldy and Stavins (2007, 2009) include several chapters studying and comparing alternative climate agreement designs, and the trade-off arises in many of them.

The trade-off is especially natural when we take into account that countries are heterogeneous, as in Example 8. If the IEA is ambitious, only the most eager countries might be willing to pay the (high) cost of contributing. If it is important to get the most reluctant countries to cooperate, as well, it may be necessary to give up on ambition, and accept that contributions are less impressive.

Now, there is not always such a trade-off. A treaty can be broad because it is good, or it can be deep because it is broad. In Sections 4–6, the endogenous emission cuts were larger when the number of participants was larger, because the externalities on a larger number of countries were internalized. In Section 7, the incentive to defect, rather than to comply, was stronger when the cuts were deep, but weaker when the number of participants was large. Thus, a larger coalition can make it possible to deepen the emission cuts, without making it tempting for the countries to defect and emit more. When it is possible to make an IEA both broader and deeper, the members would to advantage of this possibility. After these possibilities have been taken advantage of, one might be left with a trade-off.

8.1 Example 8: Two types of countries

As a simple illustration, suppose n_S countries are willing to contribute $\underline{x}$, while n_N would be willing to contribute $\overline{x}$. With the utility functions in Example 6 and 7, the n_N countries are better off with the broad but shallow agreement iff:

$$(n_N - 1)c\overline{x} - b\overline{x}^2/2 < (n_N + n_S - 1)c\underline{x} - b\underline{x}^2/2 \Leftrightarrow$$
$$n_S > \frac{(n_N - 1)c(\overline{x} - \underline{x}) + b(\underline{x}^2 - \overline{x}^2)/2}{c\underline{x}},$$

which holds if n_S is large (relative to n_N) and if $(\overline{x} - \underline{x})$ is small, for example. The optimal design thus depends on how many more countries one can persuade, and what the cost of persuasion would be. (A better design can be that n_S contributes $\underline{x}$ while n_N contributes $\overline{x}$. This is referred to as common but differentiated responsibilities.).

8.2 Pledge-and-review bargaining

Even without heterogeneity, this trade-off can be important. To shed light on it, we must understand what makes the cuts deep vs. shallow, and that brings us to the choice of bargaining procedure.

In applications, the outcome of a bargaining game is often approximated by the NBS. One reason for this is that the NBS satisfies reasonable axioms. In addition, the NBS is the outcome of standard noncooperative games. When the parties are symmetric, the NBS predicts that the outcome is first best for the parties involved. With the linear-quadratic utility function (12), from Section 6.1, for example, the NBS predicts $x_i = (m - 1)c/b$, so that all externalities from the other members are fully taken into account.

In reality, negotiations might be less efficient than what is predicted by the NBS.

First, transaction costs typically arise when the parties are not fully informed about the preferences of one another. There is a large literature on bargaining under incomplete information, and it typically predicts that the negotiations are delayed or the outcome is inefficient.

Second, the negotiations might be inefficient by design. The bargaining procedure used in the PA was very different from that used for the KP. The PA relies on "nationally determined contributions" which are decided "bottom-up" rather than "top-down", one may argue.

With nationally determined contributions, one may fear that a country will just propose the contribution it prefers anyway. But if it is uncertain whether the other participants will bother to accept, ratify, or comply with the treaty, then a country might be willing to raise its contribution a little, just to reduce the risk. When all countries are doing so, the agreement is more valuable, and it makes sense to further raise one's contribution since the risks are costly when the agreement is valuable. The equilibrium of such a game can imply that the contributions are larger than in BAU, but lower than with the NBS, so that each contribution maximizes a weighed sum of payoffs, where the relative weight placed on others' payoffs is positive but less than 1. (See Harstad, 2023a, for details).

For such reasons, we may expect that the relative weight on others' payoffs, w, is less than 1, when the countries employ the P&R procedure:

$$u_i + w \sum_{j \in M \setminus i} u_j,$$

With the NBS, and symmetric utility functions, $w = 1$.

With the utility, (12), described in Section 6.1, the equilibrium contribution becomes:

$$\begin{aligned} x_i &= w(m-1)c/b, \quad i \in M, \\ x_i &= 0, \quad i \notin M, \end{aligned} \tag{18}$$

The immediate effect of $w < 1$ is that contributions will be less ambitious. Thus, an agreement that is "shallow", rather than "deep", may be associated with a smaller w. By adapting the P&R bargaining procedure, the world community might have moved to a game in which w was smaller for the PA than it was in the KP.

Naturally, the P&R procedure has been criticized by policymakers and scholars. Keohane and Oppenheimer (2016, p. 142) speculated that: "Many governments will be tempted to use the vagueness of the Paris Agreement, the discretion that it permits, to limit the scope or intensity of their proposed actions", while Tirole (2017, p. 209) wrote that: "The strategy of voluntary commitments has several significant defects, and is an inadequate response to the climate change challenge."

8.3 Modesty may pay

Suppose the members are deciding on the contributions using a bargaining procedure associated with a smaller w. For a given coalition size, m, the effect of a smaller w is that countries will emit more, and be worse off. The coalition size might change with w, however.

In fact, the effect of w on the equilibrium coalition size might be more important than the effect on the contribution level. Because the cost of participating is less when w is small, a member may be satisfied being a member even if m is large. By comparing the utility of a member to the utility this member could obtain from free riding, we get that it is better to participate if and only if:

$$m \leq 1 + 2/w. \tag{19}$$

Thus, if w is small, m can be large. This is shown by Finus and Maus (2008), which motivated the title of this subsection. (See also Colombo et al., 2022; Barrett, 2002).

The prediction that m is larger when w is small fits well with the fact that many more countries contributed in a meaningful way to the Paris Agreement than in the Kyoto Protocol. The choice of bargaining procedure can thus lead to the trade-off studied in this section. By adopting the P&R procedure, the concern is that the cuts will be less deep, but the consequence is (also) that the coalition will be broader.

8.4 Institutional design

To understand the trade-off, we must analyze the welfare effects of both the level of the cuts as well as the size of the coalition.

With the utility function (12), it turns out that if m decreases in w as in eq. (19), then also the payoff of every member decreases in w, so that all members would prefer a bargaining procedure characterized by a smaller w, where the coalition would be larger. In fact, when w declines, the increase in m is, in itself, motivating the countries to contribute more. This effect is balancing the effect that the contributions are reduced when w is low, for a fixed m. (For details, see Harstad, 2023b).

In reality, however, m might not decrease in w exactly as predicted by (19). First, we might have a constraint $m \leq \overline{m}$, because, after all, there is a finite number of countries that are relevant when it comes to global climate policies. Second, countries are more heterogeneous than what the model above assumes. The heterogeneity implies, for example, that some countries might participate even if others strictly prefer not to: They might be "committed". The countries in the EU, for example, cannot easily opt out from a treaty in which the other EU countries participate. To recognize this situation, let $\underline{m}$ measure the number of committed countries, which participate even if w is large.

With boundaries on m, so that $m \in [\underline{m}, \overline{m}]$, a bargaining game associated with a small $\underline{w}$ gives a larger total payoff to the world community than does a game associated with $\overline{w} > \underline{w}$ if the constraints on m are not too severe. The condition for when the members prefer $\underline{w}$ (e.g., P&R) is given by

$$\frac{\min\{\overline{m} - 1, 2/\underline{w}\}}{\max\{\underline{m} - 1, 2/\overline{w}\}} > \Omega \equiv \sqrt{\frac{\overline{w}(1 - \overline{w}/2)}{\underline{w}(1 - \underline{w}/2)}} \in \left(1, \frac{\overline{w}}{\underline{w}}\right). \tag{20}$$

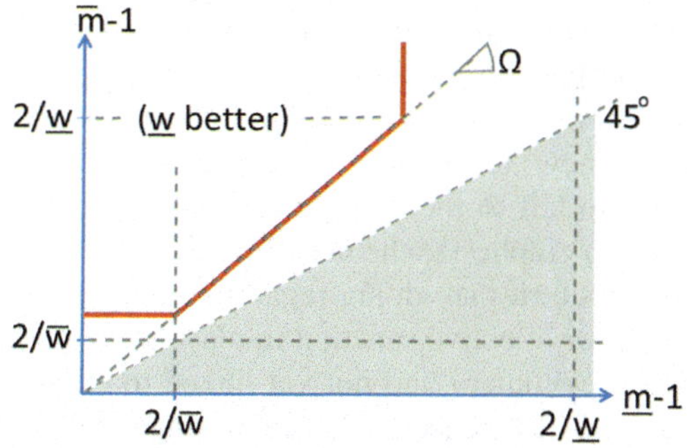

FIG. 5 A broad-but-shallow bargaining procudure is better top-left in the figure.

The inequality is derived and better explained elsewhere (Harstad, 2023b), and it can be illustrated easily in Fig. 5.

Thus, when we take into account that the constraints on m might bind, we are facing a trade-off. A broad but shallow agreement (associated with $\underline{w} < \overline{w}$) is better than a narrow but deep agreement (associated with $\overline{w} > \underline{w}$) iff there is a large number of potential members, and if the heterogeneity is limited, so that few of them are committed to participate regardless of the design.

Regarding compliance, a reduced w, and thus a reduced x^* or larger m, will also reduce the temptation to defect. From Section 7.1, we have that $x^* \le 2\delta c(m-1)/b$, and, with (18), the compliance constraint becomes

$$w(m-1)c/b \le \delta 2c(m-1)/b,$$

so, whether or not we endogenize m by (19), the compliance constraint becomes:

$$w \le 2\delta,$$

which is more likely to hold when w is small. Thus, emission cuts are more likely to be self-enforcing (so that they do not need to be "legally" binding) if they are the outcome of P&R bargaining rather than the top-down approach associated with the KP (were, we have argued, w might be larger).

The model above is simple, but the results hold in more general settings. With the models in Section 6.2, countries bargain contributions for a number of periods before they decide on investments or investment policies non-cooperatively. The investments will be functions of the contributions, and thus a country's continuation value can be written as a function of the x_i's. These continuation values are linear-quadratic, and can be written as (12), if just b and c are appropriately defined.

9 From Kyoto to Paris and beyond

United Nation's approach to climate change has evolved quite a lot over the last few decades. In 1997, only 37 countries were committed by the Kyoto

Protocol to limit emissions while, since 2015, nearly all countries in the world are participating in the Paris Agreement.

The two agreements have a lot in common. In both, the focus is on emission reduction, and while new technology is recognized as being crucial, the investment decisions are left to the individual countries and their market participants. The treaties also emphasize the need for transparency, so that it possible to observe how other countries are doing regarding their commitments. There is no world governments, or effective sanction in place if countries do not comply, and the participation is voluntary and not yet linked to explicit sanctions.

But there are several differences between the agreements. Not only is the number of committed countries quite different, but the bargaining procedure is also fundamentally different. The procedure under the KP has been referred to as "top-down", while the pledge-and-review procedure, associated with the PA, is described as "bottom-up". With P&R, we have nationally determined contributions. The commitments are also weaker in the sense that they are not legally binding, while they were legally binding under the KP. Finally, the two alternative designs were preferred at different moments in time. In the 1990s, the world community opted for the top-down approach but twenty years later, they opted for the bottom-up approach. That fact is, in itself, a puzzle that one must explain.

Empirical research on climate agreement is extremely important, but also challenging given the few data points that we have. Fortunately, economic theory also has a lot to contribute. In fact, several of the observation can be rationalized with game theory and contract theory. When international climate policies are decided on noncooperatively, we have a dynamic common-pool problem (formalized in Section 2), and the inefficiencies are even worse that in the game's static counterpart (Section 3). When we adopt the assumption that countries negotiate emission caps but not investment levels, then we can explain why we might see insufficient breakthroughs on the technology front, why countries might not invest enough, and how the investment levels can be influenced by the emission caps (Section 4). The so-called hold-up problem sheds light on why the commitment period is not annual, and how the optimal length trades off different inefficiencies when it is hard to predict how much one ought to emit in the future (Section 5).

The fact that the United Nation's approach does not ask countries to specify investment levels might be a puzzle in itself, given the costly hold-up problem, but this is consistent with the finding in Section 6 where we observed that the equilibrium coalition size can be larger when emission levels, but not as well investment levels, are negotiated. The need to motivate compliance, at a time without a world government, explains why peer pressure and transparent compliance are important for the treaties.

Economic theory can also shed light on the differences between the treaties. The benefit of P&R is that it is less expensive for a country to participate in the IEA. The lower expense explains why many more countries will participate with this type of procedure, and also why the emission cuts do not need to be legally binding in order to be credible. With these benefits, we can understand why the world community might be better off with P&R, rather than with the KP's top-down procedure. However, they are better off only if there is a large number of countries that are important to attract, and if few countries are sufficiently committed so that they will participate no matter what the procedure is. Both these conditions are more likely to be true in the 2010s, than they were in the 1990s. In the 1990s, many countries were less developed but some of them have since become emerging economies. This transition implies that the number of important potential members has grown. At the same time, some of the countries that were committed in the KP's first commitment period were not willing to remain committed to this type of treaty. Both changes suggest that the world might have moved from being located bottop-right in Fig. 5, to top-left in the same figure. If that is the case, economic theory can rationalize why the top-down procedure was optimal in the 1990s, while the bottom-up P&R procedure was more attractive in the 2010s.

Unfortunately, both the deep-but-narrow and the broad-but-shallow designs are second best. To deal with climate change successfully, the world needs to find a way to implement treaties that are both broad and deep. To achieve this, the cost of free riding and defecting on the treaty must be larger than what we have assumed above. Alternatively, the benefits of participating and complying need to be larger. The challenge is that there are not a lot of sticks or carrots that are available in world politics today. Economic sanctions tend to be ineffective, costly to impose, and thus not credible to sustain in the long run. Explicit monetary transfers are challenging for political reasons, and also because governments rarely have the necessary liquidity available. At the end of the day, perhaps market access and trade liberalization stand out among the few or only carrots that are possible to use. The idea to connect trade and environmental agreements is old and has been analyzed extensively by environmental economists (Barrett, 1997), trade economists (Copeland and Taylor, 2005), and Nobel laureates (Nordhaus, 2015), for example, and. Kotchen (2024) discuss carbon border adjustments elsewhere in this volume.

What about political economics? The normative approach to environmental policy and international agreements is challenged by the positive political economics approach. Political economics, as a field, sheds light on the political forces that exist and that can rationalize the inefficient policies that we actually observe in the world. At the least, policies and agreements must take these forces into account, for the policies to be feasible and effective. My companion chapter (Harstad, 2025) discusses the political economics of international public goods, how domestic political forces must be taken into account, and how the forces can actually strengthen international cooperation if the agreements are designed in the right way.

References

Aghion, P., Dewatripont, M., Rey, P., 1994. Renegotiation design with unverifiable information. Econometrica 62 (2), 257–282.

Aldy, J.E., Stavins, R.N., 2007. Architectures for Agreement. Cambridge University Press.

Aldy, J.E., Stavins, R.N., 2009. Post-Kyoto International Climate Polic. Cambridge University Press.

Aldy, J.E., Barrett, S., Stavins, R.N., 2003. Thirteen plus one: a comparison of global climate policy architectures. Climate Policy 3 (4), 373–397.

Asheim, G.B., Froyn, C.B., Hovi, J., Menz, F.C., 2006. Regional versus global cooperation for climate control. Journal of Environmental Economics and Management 51, 93–109.

Bagwell, K., Staiger, R.W., 2016. The design of trade agreements. Handbook of Commercial Policy 1, 435–529.

Barrett, S., 1994. Self-Enforcing International Environmental Agreements Oxford Economic Papers 46, 878–894.

Barrett, S., 1997. The strategy of trade sanctions in international environmental agreements. Resource and Energy Economics 19 (4), 345–361.

Barrett, S., 2001. International cooperation for sale. European Economic Review 45 (10), 1835–1850.

Barrett, S., 2002. Consensus treaties. Journal of Institutional and Theoretical Economics 158 (4), 529–547.

Barrett, S., 2005. The theory of international environmental agreements. Handbook of Environmental Economics 3, 1458–1493.

Barrett, S., 2006. Climate treaties and breakthrough technologies. American Economic Review, Papers and Proceedings 96 (2), 22–25.

Battaglini, M., Harstad, B., 2016. Participation and duration of environmental agreements. Journal of Political Economy 124 (1), 160–204.

Bellelli, F.S., Aftab, A., Scarpa, R., 2023. The participation dilemma: a survey of the empirical literature on international environmental agreement ratification. Review of Environmental Economics and Policy 17 (1), 2023.

Benchekroun, H., Long, N., 2012. Collaborative environmental management: a review of the literature. International Game Theory Review 14 (04).

Black, J., Levi, M.D., de Meza, D., 1993. Creating a good atmosphere: minimum participation for tackling the "greenhouse effect. Economica 60, 281–293.

Bolton, P., Dewatripont, M., 2005. Contract Theory. The MIT Press.

Buchholz, W., Konrad, K., 1994. Global environmental problems and the strategic choice of technology. Journal of Economics 60 (3), 299–321.

Buchholz, W., Sandler, T., 2021. Global public goods: a survey. Journal of Economic Literature 59 (2), 488–545.

Calvo, E., Rubio, S.J., 2012. Dynamic models of international environmental agreements: a differential game approach. International Review of Environmental and Resource Economics.

Caparrós, A., 2016. Bargaining and international environmental agreements. Environmental and Resource Economics 65, 5–31.

Carleton, T., Duflo, E., Jack, K., Zappala, G., 2024. Adaptation to climate change. Volume 1. Handbook of the Economics of Climate Change. Elsevier B.V.

Carraro, C., Siniscalco, D., 1993. Strategies for the international protection of the environment. Journal of Public Economics 52 (3), 309–328.

Carraro, C., Eyckmans, J., Finus, M., 2006. Optimal transfers and participation decisions in international environmental agreements. The Review of International Organizations 1 (4), 379–396.

Carraro, C., Marchiori, C., Oreffice, S., 2009. Endogenous minimum participation in international environmental treaties. Environmental and Resource Economics 42 (3), 411–425.

Chung, T.-Y., 1991. Incomplete contracts, specific investment, and risk sharing. Review of Economic Studies 58, 1031–1042.

Chwe, M.S.-Y., 1994. Farsighted coalitional stability. Journal of Economic Theory 63 (2), 299–325.

Colombo, L., Labrecciosa, P., Van Long, N., 2022. A dynamic analysis of international environmental agreements under partial cooperation. European Economic Review 143, 104036.

d'Aspremont, C., Jacquemin, A., Gabszewicz, J., Weymark, J., 1983. On the stability of collusive price leadership Canadian. Journal of Economics 16 (1), 17–25.

Deryugina, T., 2022. The Fiscal consequences of natural disasters. In: Skidmore, M. (Ed.), Handbook on the Economics of Disasters. Edward Elgar Publishing, pp. 208–228.

Diamantoudi, E., Sartzetakis, E.S., 2018. International environmental agreements—the role of foresight. Environmental and Resource Economics 71, 241–257.

Dietz, S., 2024. Introduction to Integrated Climate-Economic Modeling in Handbook of the Economics of Climate Change. Volume 1. Elsevier B.V.

Dixit, A., Olson, M., 2000. Does voluntary participation undermine the Coase Theorem? Journal of Public Economics 76 (3), 309–335.

Dockner, E.J., Long, N., 1993. International pollution control: cooperative versus noncooperative strategies. Journal of Environmental Economics and Management 25 (1), 13–29.

Dugoua, E., 2023. Induced innovation and international environmental agreements: evidence from the ozone regime. Review of Economics and Statistics 1–45.

Dutta, P.K., Radner, R., 2004. Self-enforcing climate-change treaties. Proceedings of the National Academy of Sciences of the United States of America 101, 4746–4751.

Dutta, P.K., Radner, R., 2006. A game-theoretic approach to global warming. Advances in Mathematical Economics 8, 135–153.

Dutta, P.K., Radner, R., 2009. A strategic analysis of global warming: theory and some numbers. Journal of Economic Behavior & Organization 71 (2), 187–209.

Dutta, P.K., Radner, R., 2020. The Paris Accord Can Be Effective if the Green Climate Fund is Effective, mimeo, New York University.

Edlin, A.S., Reichelstein, S., 1996. Holdups, standard breach remedies, and optimal investment. American Economic Review 86 (3), 478–501.

Eichner, T., Kollenbach, G., 2023. Participation and duration of environmental agreements: investment lags matter. Journal of the Association of Environmental and Resource Economists 10 (1), 33–53.

Engwerda, J., 2005. LQ Dynamic Optimization and Differential Games. Wiley.

Finus, M., Maus, S., 2008. Modesty May Pay!. JPET 10 (5), 801–826.

Golombek, R., Hoel, M., 2005. Climate policy under technology spillovers. Environmental and Resource Economics 31 (2), 201–227.

Golombek, R., Hoel, M., 2006. Second-best climate agreements and technology policy. Advances in Economic Analysis & Policy 6 (1) Article 1.

Grossman, G.M., 2016. The purpose of trade agreements. In: Bagwell, K., Staiger, R. (Eds.), Handbook of Commercial Policy 1, pp. 379–434.

Harris, M., Holmstrom, B., 1987. On the duration of agreements. International Economic Review 28 (2), 389.

Harstad, B., 2006. Flexible integration? Mandatory and minimum participation rules. Scandinavian Journal of Economics 108 (4), 683–702.

Harstad, B., 2012. Climate contracts: a game of emissions, investments, negotiations, and renegotiations. Review of Economic Studies 79, 1527–1555.

Harstad, B., 2016. The dynamics of climate agreements. Journal of the European Economic Association 14 (3), 719–752.

Harstad, B., 2023a. Pledge-and-review bargaining. Journal of Economic Theory 207, 105574.

Harstad, B., 2023b. Pledge-and-review bargaining: from Kyoto to Paris. The Economic Journal 133 (651), 1181–1216.

Harstad, B., 2025. The politics of global public goods, forthcoming. Handbook of Political Economy. Elsevier.

Harstad, B., Lancia, F., Russo, A., 2019. Compliance technology and self-enforcing agreements. Journal of the European Economic Association 917 (1), 1–29.

Harstad, B., Lancia, F., Russo, A., 2022. Prices vs. quantities for self-enforcing agreements. Journal of Environmental Economics and Management 111, 102595.

Hart, O., 1995. Firms, Contracts, and Financial Structure. Clarendon Press.

Helm, C., Schmidt, R.C., 2015. Climate cooperation with technology investments and border carbon adjustment. European Economic Review 75, 112–130.

Hoel, M., 1992. International environment conventions: the case of uniform reductions of emissions. Environmental and Resource Economics 2 (2), 141–159.

Hoel, M., Schneider, K., 1997. Incentives to participate in an international environmental agreement. Environmental and Resource Econ 9, 153–170.

IPCC, 2014. Climate Change 2014: Mitigation of Climate Change. Contribution of Working Group III to the Fifth Assessment Report of the Intergovernmental Panel on Climate Change. Cambridge University Press, Cambridge.

Jaffe, A.B., Newell, R.G., Stavins, R.N., 2003. Technological change and the environment. In: Mäler, K.-G., Vincent, J.R. (Eds.), Handbook of Environmental Economics Volume 1. Elsevier.

Karp, L., Simon, L., 2013. Participation games and international environmental agreements: a nonparametric model. Journal of Environmental Economics and Management 65 (2), 326–344.

Keohane, R., Oppenheimer, M., 2016. Paris: beyond the climate dead end through pledge and review? Politics and Governance 4 (3), 42–51.

Kerr, S., Lippert, S., Lou, E., 2024. Transfers in climate action teams. Economic Theory.

Kolstad, C.D., Toman, M., 2005. The economics of climate policy. Handbook of Environmental Economics 3, 1562–1593.

Kotchen, M., 2020. On the scope of climate finance to facilitate international agreement on climate change. Economics Letters 190, 109070.

Kotchen, M., 2024. Climate Policy Options in Handbook of the Economics of Climate Change, Volume 1. Elsevier B.V.

Kováč, E., Schmidt, R.C., 2012. A simple dynamic climate cooperation model. Journal of Public Economics 194, 104329.

Levhari, D., Mirman, L.J., 1980. The great fish war: an example using a dynamic cournot-nash solution. Bell Journal of Economics 11 (1), 322–334.

Li, H., Rus, H.A., 2019. Climate Change adaptation and international mitigation agreements with heterogeneous countries. Journal of the Association of Environmental and Resource Economists 6 (3), 503–530.

Maggi, G., 2014. International trade agreements. In: Gopinath, G., Helpman, E., Rogoff, K. (Eds.), Handbook of International Economics 4. Elsevier, pp. 317–390.

Maggi, G., 2016. Issue linkage. In: Bagwell, K., Staiger, R. (Eds.), Handbook of Commercial Policy, Vol. 1, pp. 513–564.

Mailath, G.J., Samuelson, L., 2006. Repeated Games and Reputations: Long-Run Relationships. Oxford University Press.

Martimort, D., Sand-Zantman, W., 2016. A mechanism design approach to climate-change agreements. Journal of the European Economic Association 14 (3), 669–718.

Newell, R.G., Jaffe, A.B., Stavins, R.N., 2006. The effects of economic and policy incentives on carbon mitigation technologies. Energy Economics 28, 563–578.

Nordhaus, W., 2015. Climate clubs: overcoming free-riding in international climate policy. American Economic Review 105 (4), 1339–1370.

Okada, A., 2023. A dynamic climate negotiation game achieving full cooperation. Journal of Economic Behavior and Organization 214, 657–669.

Osmani, D., Tol, R., 2009. Towards farsightedly stable international environmental agreements. Journal of Public Economic Theory 11 (3), 455–492.

Palfrey, T.R., Rosenthal, H., 1984. Participation and the provision of discrete public goods: a strategic analysis. Journal of Public Economics 24 (2), 171–193.

Ray, D., 2007. A Game-Theoretic Perspective on Coalition Formation. Oxford University Press.

Ray, D., Vohra, R., 1999. A theory of endogenous coalition structures. Games and Economic Behavior 26 (2), 286–336.

Ray, D., Vohra, R., 2001. Coalitional power and public goods. Journal of Political Economy 109 (6), 1355–1384.

Schmidt, R.C., Strausz, R., 2015. On the timing of climate agreements. Environmental and Resource Economics.

Schopf, M., 2024. Self-enforcing international environmental agreements and altruistic preferences. Environmental and Resource Economics 1–51.

Segal, I., Whinston, M.D., 2002. The mirrless approach to mechanism design with renegotiation. Econometrica 70 (1), 1–45.

Tirole, J., 2017. Economics for the Common Good. Princeton University Press.

van der Ploeg, F., de Zeeuw, A., 1991. A differential game of international pollution control. Systems & Control Letters 17 (6), 409–414.

van der Ploeg, F., de Zeeuw, A., 1992. International aspects of pollution control. Environmental and Resource Economics 2 (2), 117–139.

Vosooghi, S., Arvaniti, M., van der Ploeg, F., 2024. Climate Coalitions with Sophisticated Policy Makers CESifo Working Paper No. 9768.

Wagner, U., 2016. Estimating strategic models of international treaty formation. The Review of Economic Studies 83 (4), 1741–1778.

Weikard, H.-P., Wangler, L., Freytag, A., 2015. Minimum participation rules with heterogeneous countries. Environmental and Resource Economics 62, 711–727. https://doi.org/10.1007/s10640-014-9861-1

Chapter 6

Climate policy options☆

Matthew J. Kotchen*
Yale University and NBER
**Corresponding author. e-mail address: matthew.kotchen@yale.edu*

Chapter Outline

☆ I am grateful to several individuals for providing valuable feedback while refining the outline for this handbook chapter, including Joe Aldy, Lint Barrage, Chris Costello, Sol Hsiang, Stephen Holland, Sam Kortum, Giovanni Maggi, and Andy Yates. Any remaining errors or omissions are my sole responsibility.

Handbook of the Economics of Climate Change, Vol. 1. https://doi.org/10.1016/bs.hesecc.2024.10.003

1 Introduction

Nearly every market activity is directly or indirectly associated with greenhouse gas (GHGs) emissions that accumulate in the atmosphere and contribute to a changing climate. Yet while individual agents fully benefit from the private consequences of their chosen activities, they experience only an infinitesimally small fraction of the damages their emissions cause worldwide, and to future generations. From an economics perspective, the problem of climate change is a problem of market failure. In particular, private market activities are associated with a global externality: the full social cost of emissions is generally not taken into account when individual agents make decisions, and the result is excessive emissions and growing challenges of climate change. Correcting externalities—especially one that arises on a global scale—provides an economic rationale for policy interventions.

The aim of this paper is to provide and overview of climate policy options that work towards this objective. Some boundaries on what to cover are nevertheless necessary given the broad scope of potential topics. The policies covered here are those focused in particular on climate change mitigation, that is, policies that seek to directly reduce GHG emissions. This, of course, immediately excludes a large number of climate policies that are important, including but not limited to those focused on adaptation, finance, industrial policy, innovation, research and development, and international agreements. But one needs to start somewhere, and consistent with the externality motivation in the opening paragraph, the focus here is on policies that seek to internalize at least some portion of the external costs of GHG emissions.

Not surprisingly, the particular policies discussed in this paper also have an economics bent. In other words, they tend to affect incentives rather than imposing direct controls on economic activity. And the discussion will emphasize economic efficiency. This will sometimes mean efficiency in the broad sense of maximizing social net benefits, but it will more frequently mean efficiency in the narrower sense of cost effectiveness. Indeed, an important question to consider when designing and evaluating climate policy is the policy objective itself: is the economic objective to maximize social net benefits, or is it to achieve a given emissions target at the lowest possible cost? Although well-established theories of environmental policy tend to focus on the former objective, a distinguishing feature of climate policy, which is emphasized in what follows, is the frequency with which the latter (and more modest) objective applies.

There are, of course, other criteria upon which to evaluate climate policy, including political feasibility and distributional outcomes. While these perspectives are critically important—and justifiably an increasing focus in climate economics—they are not the primary emphasis here, although the topics are discussed in various places. It is, however, worth mentioning why efficiency itself remains of the upmost importance too. The scale of climate challenges the world faces are immense and growing more severe, but the resources available to address them are limited. Hence there is an increasingly urgent need for policies that address climate change, and that do so in a way that is efficient and cost effective. Quite simply, the challenges are too big and important to promote measures that waste resources.

Recognizing there are topics missing in what follows, some intentional and some surely not, let us briefly consider what the paper actually does cover. Without providing anything close to a comprehensive literature review, the paper seeks to provide an overview of what might be termed the standard economics "toolkit" of climate policies. They are standard in the sense that literature exists to study them because of desirable properties, that they have attracted attention because of frequent or large scale implementation in the real world, or both.

Before turning to particular policy instruments, however, Section 2 provides some high-level perspectives on the aims of climate policy. Some of the issues arise because of the way that sovereign nations not only set domestic policy, they face a global collective action problem of nothing less than maintaining a stable planetary climate. This raises questions about whether countries should seek to internalize the global damages of climate change, or perhaps only the domestic damages that affect them. Topics covered include efficient shadow pricing and different geopolitical scopes of the social cost of carbon (SCC). These approaches to setting and evaluating climate policy are then contrasted with the alternative of a target consistent approach, where the policy objective is taken as given, and the job of an economist shifts from evaluating overall efficiency to evaluating cost effectiveness.

Subsequent sections focus on particular climate policy instruments. Section 3 begins with the proverbial straw man of command-and-control regulations. The aim is to show how the information requirements for a regulator to deploy this approach cost effectively are exceedingly difficult to satisfy. Section 4 pivots to the pricing instruments of emissions taxes and subsidies. Although the advantages of these instruments compared to command and control are well-established, the discussion emphasizes the unique challenges and opportunities when applied to climate change. Section 5 develops the basic theory of cap-and-trade programs, where the standard framework is generalized a bit to allow some degree over which carbon offsets can count towards compliance. Section 6 considers the question of how uncertainty affects when a regulator might prefer taxing emissions or establishing a cap-and-trade program. This is the classic question of prices vs quantities, although the discussion adds a novel result about how the analysis applies not only to expectationally efficient policies, but even more generally to those that are expectationally equivalent with respect to emissions. Section 7 considers topics that arise in an open economy setting. This includes leakage, whereby policies to reduce emissions in one region have the side effect of increasing emissions elsewhere. There is also discussion of equivalence between optimal policy packages that simultaneously include two of the three instruments among production taxes, consumption taxes, and trade taxes. The framework enables straightforward analysis of a carbon border adjustment mechanism, which is a topic of increasing interest among researchers and policymakers alike. Finally, there is discussion of how the open economy setting provides a unilateral welfare rationale for green subsidies, which are typically considered only a second-best policy instrument.

The next two sections focus on climate policy instruments that are of interest primarily because of traction they have obtained in real world settings. Section 8 covers production and investment subsidies in the renewable energy sector, with a discussion about when one approach might be preferred over the other, along with empirical evidence. Section 9 provides a basic theory of performance based standards, which may include credit trading, followed by examples of their application in a variety of climate policy settings, including electricity sector emissions rates, renewable portfolio standards, low carbon fuel standards, and vehicle fuel economy standards. Section 10 provides a discussion of policy interactions that may arise because of overlapping policies, general equilibrium effects, and multiple objectives, including distributional and equity concerns. As the number of climate policies continue to grow and overlap, it is important to understand circumstances where policies can be mutually reinforcing or in conflict. What is more, climate policies that are big enough to have a meaningful impact are likely to affect a range of interacting markets and therefore require general equilibrium analysis to promote a complete understanding. And while economics has a long tradition of separating efficiency and distributional concerns when it comes to the design and evaluation of policy, recent changes in policy and guidance for official benefit-cost analysis, at least in the United States, are pushing economists to do more and opening new frontiers of analysis.

The final set of policies covered are those collectively referred to as voluntary and information based approaches. These policies seek to provide more complete information so that markets can adjust more efficiency and opportunities can emerge for voluntary actions to address climate change. The particular approaches discussed are information disclosure strategies, voluntary programs that offer certification or membership for meeting specific climate standards, and the strategic use of information to nudge behavior in ways that tap into social and psychological mechanisms. Finally, there is a brief discussion on the importance of understanding whether voluntary and information based approaches should serve a complements or substitutes for more centralized forms of climate policy. Section 12 concludes with some final observations about how the economics of climate policy raises new challenges and opportunities that are not already central to environmental economics. The section also includes some modest predictions about promising directions for future research.

2 Climate policy objectives

What should be the normative aim of climate policy? Even among economists, and at a theoretical level, this basic question generates different answers and controversy. This section illustrates different perspectives within a simple graphical framework. Distinctions are made between the optimal shadow price of emissions, the social cost of carbon (SCC), with global versus domestic perspectives, and a target consistent approach to valuing emission reductions for purposes of setting and evaluating climate policy.

2.1 Efficient shadow pricing

We begin with the most basic way to motivate the theory of environmental policy applied to climate change. To keep things simple, while focusing on the key ideas, consider the problem of climate change in a static setting. The horizontal axis of Fig. 1 represents global GHG emissions, and $\bar{E}$ denotes the business as usual (BAU) level of emissions, that is, the level that would occur in the absence of a policy intervention. The curve labeled *MAC* represents the marginal abatement costs of reducing emissions below $\bar{E}$ (the next section derives the *MAC* more formally). The curve labeled *MDF* represents the social marginal damage function of emissions. The marginal damages are global, monetized, and assumed in the figure to be increasing.

The standard efficiency objective of environmental policy is to find ways to set the level of emissions to equate the marginal damages with the marginal abatement costs, which occurs at E^*. At this level, P^* represents the nonmarket shadow price of emissions. As we will see, different policy instruments can be used to internalize P^* and therefore implement E^* as the equilibrium level of emissions. But should E^* be the objective of climate policy? It clearly would be in the hypothetical world of a global planner that seeks to maximize global efficiency. However, motivations for, and discussions about, climate policy often take place from a different perspective, and we will see how alternative viewpoints relate to the standard framework just described.

2.2 The social cost of carbon

The SCC is a fundamental concept in climate economics. It represents the marginal damages of emitting an additional ton of carbon dioxide (CO_2), or the CO_2 equivalent of another GHG. The SCC is an "ambitious" parameter, as it seeks to capture the marginal external costs of emissions over all future time and all space across the planet. Integrated assessment models (IAMs) are typically used to produce estimates of the SCC (Tol, 2023), though an expanding literature provides sector-specific estimates using observed data and econometric techniques (Rode et al., 2021; Rode et al., 2022; Carleton et al., 2022; Hultgren et al., 2022). The most recent estimate of the SCC for official use by the U.S. Environmental Protection Agency is $190 per metric ton in 2020, and increasing to $230 by 2030 (U.S. EPA, 2023). This estimate closely matches that in (Rennert et al., 2022), though a wide range of estimates can be found in recent reviews of the literature (Tol, 2023; Moore et al., 2024).

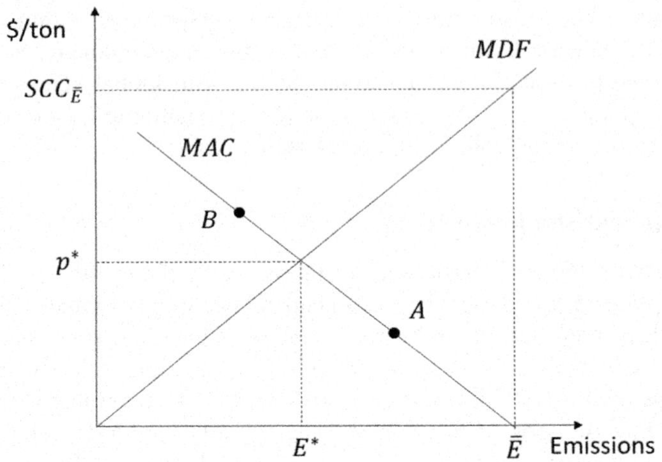

FIG. 1 Comparison of the efficient carbon price, the global social cost of carbon, and different target consistent prices.

Abstracting from the complexity of IAMs, we can ask how the SCC compares to the optimal shadow price of P^* in Fig. 1? The distinction between the two concepts becomes clear when one recognizes that the SCC represents the marginal damages at a given baseline level of emissions. With use of IAMs, the baseline is often an assumption of BAU emissions now and into the future. Econometric approaches are also estimated on the observed BAU baseline. In Fig. 1, the SCC therefore represents the shadow cost of emissions at the baseline of $\bar{E}$, shown as $SCC_{\bar{E}}$. It follows that with an increasing *MDF*, we have $P^* < SCC_{\bar{E}}$ because the later corresponds with a higher level of emissions, that is, $E^* < \bar{E}$.

Does the distinction matter empirically? Surprisingly few IAMs are able to produce estimates of both the optimal carbon price and the SCC, because they are typically built to estimate the marginal damages of emissions or the marginal costs of abatement, and not both. One exception is the DICE model developed over decades by William Nordhaus. In the most recent iteration, Barrage and Nordhaus (2024) report values of P^*, which is equivalent to the optimal carbon price, of \$50, \$59, and \$125 for the years 2020, 2030, and 2050, respectively. In contrast, their comparable estimates of the $SCC_{\bar{E}}$ are higher at \$66, \$78, and \$175. Beyond reinforcing the qualitative pattern in Fig. 1, the important takeaway of these numbers is recognition that the optimal carbon price and the SCC are not in general the same, and this is often a point of confusion in the literature and in policy discussions. But as can be seen in Fig. 1, they will be equal in the special cases where BAU is the efficient level of emissions, or where the *MDF* is constant, at least over the relevant domain.

What then is the use of the SCC, if it differs from the optimal shadow price? The answer is for benefit-cost analysis (BCA). Consider a policy that would reduce CO_2 emissions at a cost of $\$x$ per ton, and ask whether the benefits of the policy would exceed the costs? Assuming the policy is marginal relative to global emissions (or alternatively that the *MDF* is constant over the range of the emissions reduction), one need only compare the SCC to $\$x$. The global benefits of avoided climate damages exceed the policy costs if the SCC is greater than $\$x$. Indeed, this is precisely how the U.S. federal government currently uses the SCC for evaluating climate policy, along with many subnational levels of government and a handful of other countries, including Canada and Mexico. It is also how the SCC is used routinely among researchers in the academic literature to evaluate changes in emissions associated with climate policy.

2.3 The global vs domestic SCC

The conduct of BCA always requires a delineation between whose benefits and costs should count and whose should not. Typically, the jurisdiction of the regulatory agency for which the analysis is conducted determines the geographic scope of analysis. For example, a municipality considering investments in a local park will be concerned with the benefits and costs to those within its jurisdiction. The same logic does not apply, however, to conventional use of the SCC for evaluating climate policy.

Let's return to our example of a policy that would reduce GHG emissions at a cost of $\$x$ per ton. Assume the policy takes place in the United States. Standard practice for BCA is to compare this *domestic* cost per ton to the *global* SCC. Note how there is a mismatch between the geopolitical scope of the cost-benefit comparison: domestic costs to global benefits. Hence it is of both intellectual interest and policy relevance for us to examine this mismatch more carefully and to recognize how it is rationalized.

The fundamental issue can be understood with a simple prisoner's dilemma. Consider a setting with two identical countries that experience damages of $\alpha > 0$ per ton of emissions. This we can define as the domestic SCC. The global SCC with two identical countries is 2α. We can then ask, what marginal damages of emissions is individually rational for a country to internalize? The answer with this simple setup is of course α—the domestic SCC. The classic free-rider problem arises because both countries would be better off if they each internalized the global SCC of 2α. Put another way, it is individually rational for a country to only take account of its own *MDF* rather than the global *MDF* shown in Fig. 1, with the result being less stringent climate policy due to under-provision of the global public good. One could of course also sketch the domestic *MDF* in Fig. 1, as a downward shift (vertical subtraction), and show the domestic SCC, along with the domestically calibrated optimal level of emissions and shadow price.

How then does the United States, and other jurisdictions, rationalize use of global SCC as a normative benchmark for climate policy? There are at least two arguments that can be understood as potential ways out of the prisoner's dilemma. The first is that managing climate change is a repeated game, and the second is that international relations induce an element of reciprocity in how countries set their own climate policy. In these cases, it can be shown that a country's decision to internalize the global SCC can be individually rational (Kotchen, 2018). Although this topic is occasionally discussed in the literature, it does receive the attention is deserves (Sunstein, 2024). There appears to be an implicit assumption that countries should adopt cooperative behavior, because otherwise there appears to be is no way to solve the problem of global climate change.

The question of whether to use the global or domestic SCC is a topic that nevertheless generates controversy. There are legal questions that arise beyond the economic concerns (Gayer and Viscusi, 2016; Howard and Schwartz, 2019). Moreover, the official approach in the United States has flipped back and forth between the Obama, Trump, and Biden administrations (going from global to domestic and back to global), with significant consequences for how changes in GHG emissions are valued in federal policies. As of this writing, the U.S. approach is one that recognizes the importance of reciprocity on issues that affect global public goods, while emphasizing the importance of transparency and reporting results separately for global and domestic impacts (US OMB, 2023; Sunstein, 2024).

2.4 The target consistent approach

An alternative way to set the objectives of climate policy focuses on cost effectiveness rather than overall efficiency (Aldy et al., 2010). What has been referred to as the target consistent approach (TCA) begins with an intended target for reducing emissions, where the target is not necessarily chosen based on an efficiency criterion. An example is the internationally agreed upon target of keeping global average temperatures less the 2 degrees Celsius above pre-industrial levels. This translates into an emissions reduction target that, while perhaps considered critical from a scientific perspective, is not necessarily the result of balancing benefits and costs. Other examples occur at the level of national, subnational, and private governance. Governments at many levels around the world have commitments to reduce emissions by specific amounts and dates, and many of these commitments are part of country-level Nationally Determined Contributions (NDCs) for emissions reductions within the framework of the Paris Climate Agreement.

The next part of a TCA is to model the minimized marginal costs on a path toward meeting the target. The result is a *MAC* curve that alone determines carbon prices for evaluating climate policy, and these prices are used in place of the SCC. The basic idea can be illustrated is a static framework with reference back to Fig. 1. Consider a target that happens to be set at E^* . In this case, which also happens to be the efficient target, the marginal abatement costs are P^*. The TCA would use this price per ton to evaluate cost effectiveness of policies until the target is meet. A more lax target would set emissions to the right of E^* and have a lower price (consistent with point A), whereas a more stringent target to the left of E^* would have a higher price (consistent with point B). Kaufman et al. (2020) provide illustrative estimates. Assuming emissions pathways to net zero for the United States that would be accomplished in different years, 2040, 2050, or 2060, they find target consistent prices of \$93, \$52, and \$32, respectively, with lower prices reflecting the less ambitious target date. Given the corresponding targets, these estimates are intended to imply that policies with a cost per ton less than these amounts would be cost effective to implement.

It is important to emphasize how the TCA no longer entails a comparison of benefits and costs, but rather focuses on ensuring implementation of cost effective policies towards achieving a designated goal. The United Kingdom uses the TCA for evaluation of climate policy, which stands in contrast the U.S. approach based on the SCC (Aldy et al., 2021). Economists have employed different arguments in support of the TCA, including alignment with international objectives, ethics, and uncertainty (Kaufman et al., 2020; Stern and Stiglitz, 2021; Stern et al., 2022), and the approach is embedded in the way the Intergovernmental Panel on Climate Change (IPCC) uses IAMs to inform climate policy. One might also interpret Weitzman's (2009; 2011) "dismal theorem"—whereby a fat-tailed distribution over climate damages blunts the ability for BCA to inform decision-making—as an argument in support of the TCA. Others nevertheless caution against abandoning efficiency when it comes to setting climate policy objectives (Aldy et al., 2021b), in large part because without an objective normative criterion, political expedience can unduly sway the targets of the TCA.

3 Command and control

This section begins a transition to discussion of actual policy instruments, starting with the command-and-control (CAC) approach to regulation. The CAC approach is somewhat of a "straw man" against which to compare more efficient approaches to climate policy. The first step, however, is to consider abatement costs a bit more formally.

3.1 Abatement costs

Consider a setting with $i = 1, \ldots, n$ sources of emissions e_i. All are subject to the same regulatory authority. Each source benefits from emissions according to $b_i(e_i)$, measured in monetary units, where $b_i(0) = 0$, $b_i' > 0$, and $b_i'' < 0$. The unregulated level of emissions at each source satisfies $b_i'(\bar{e}_i) = 0$, and aggregate emissions without regulation are $\bar{E} = \sum_{i=1}^{n} \bar{e}_i$. This level of emissions corresponds with the unregulated, BAU level of emissions $\bar{E}$ in Fig. 1. Reducing emissions through abatement a_i means foregone benefits, and abatement costs can be written as $c_i(a_i) = b_i(\bar{e}_i) - b_i(\bar{e}_i - a_i)$ for any level of abatement $0 \leq a_i \leq \bar{e}_i$. It follows that $c_i(0) = 0$, $c_i' > 0$, and $c_i'' > 0$ for all i.

Let us now define the minimum costs for achieving any aggregate level of abatement A:

$$C(A) = \left\{ \min_{\{a_i\}_{i=1}^n} \sum_{i=1}^n c_i(a_i) : A = \sum_{i=1}^n a_i \right\}. \tag{1}$$

A consequence of this definition is that minimizing the cost of reaching any level of abatement (or equivalently a level of emissions $E = \bar{E} - A$) requires $c_i'(a_i) = c_j'(a_j)$ for all a_i, $a_j > 0$. In other words, the marginal abatement costs must be equalized across all sources with positive levels of abatement. What is more, the aggregate marginal abatement costs are equal to the individual marginal abatement costs such that $C'(A) = c_i'(a_i)$ for all $a_i > 0$. The function $C'(A)$ is simply a more formal statement of the *MAC* curve illustrated in Fig. 1.

3.2 Direct regulation

Now consider a regulator that seeks to reduce emissions to some level below $\bar{E}$, and this requires a level of aggregate abatement $A > 0$. Using a CAC approach, we can ask, how should the regulator assign required abatement levels across the different entities? One seemingly reasonably possibility is that a_i should be set equally across all i. Another is that abatement levels should be proportional to baseline emissions $\bar{e}_i$. In fact, there are an infinite number of possibilities, assuming there is more than one emitter. But there is only one distribution of abatement levels that achieves the overall objective at the least cost, and it is the one that satisfies equation (1).

Using direct regulation and minimizing compliance costs is nevertheless exceedingly difficult to achieve in practice because of the information requirements. The regulator would need to know the abatement cost function for all i sources of emissions, yet obtaining such information is challenging and unlikely to occur in a complete and unbiased way, due to information asymmetries and incentive compatibility issues with truthful reporting. The difficulty of having enough information to implement direct regulation in a cost effective way is one reason why economists tend to disfavor CAC approaches. The concern applies regardless of whether the level of aggregate abatement is set to maximize overall efficiency or some other criterion, though with efficiency additional information is needed about the marginal damages of emissions, that is, the *MDF* in Fig. 1.

Two additional question are worth considering at this point. First, are there policy instruments that can implement least-cost abatement without having complete information? The short answer is yes, as we will begin to see in the next section. Second, although economists often take it for granted, it is worth pausing for a moment to ask, why should we care so much about cost minimization? There are certainly other objectives of climate policy that people might care about, including different notations of equity, which might, for example, include forcing larger emitters pay more. But even in these cases the cost minimizing approach is a useful benchmark. As mentioned in the paper's introduction, resources are limited for addressing the growing challenges of climate change, so we should be cautious about pursuing GHG emissions reductions at higher costs than necessary. Moreover, to the extent that distributional concerns can be addressed separately through redistribution policy, all objectives can be accomplished to an even greater extent with cost minimization. For example, rather than forcing a large emitter with high marginal abatement costs to reduce emissions, a small emitter with lower marginal abatement costs can do it and receive a compensation payment from the high emitter. The result in this case will be lower costs of abatement and the potential for both emitters to be better off, that is, a Pareto improvement. Indeed, this is precisely the mechanism at work in cap-and-trade programs, as we will see in Section 5.

A final observation is that CAC approaches in practice are typically not as prescriptive as just described, although discussion of a regulator choosing abatement levels for all emitters is a useful way to illustrate the key ideas. Alternative CAC approaches might require firms to adopt a specific technology or to comply with a specified emissions rate, variants of which are discussed in Section 9. But the same general critique applies even in these cases. With a technology requirement, firms are not afforded the flexibility to choose their own way of reducing emissions, which in all likelihood would be lower cost. And emission rates applied uniformly across firms does not leverage the possibility that some firms can reduce emissions at a lower cost than others. Emission rates combined with tradable credits, however, do help somewhat, as will be discussed in Section 9.

4 Emissions taxes and subsides

We now turn to instruments of climate policy that directly target prices. These include emissions taxes, also referred to a carbon taxes, and subsidies. The discussion of subsidies will cover some of the potential benefits and challenges of carbon offsets, and the perverse incentives of inefficient fossil fuel subsidies.

4.1 Carbon taxes

When economists hear the word externality, it is almost a knee-jerk reaction to immediately recommend a Pigouvian tax. In the standard introductory setting, a Pigouvian tax is levied on a good in the amount equal the marginal external costs at the efficient quantity. The consequent internalization of the externality implements the efficient quantity of exchange as an equilibrium, and by assumption the tax revenue is returned lump sum. The standard way of modeling an emissions tax follows much the same logic if we think of emissions as an input for which there is demand and an associated externality. The reason for clarifying this point is that Pigouvian taxes are typically applied to a good, the production or consumption of which generates the externality, possibly through emissions. But emissions taxes are levied on the source of the externality itself, rather than indirectly on a good. One advantage of targeting the tax on emissions, rather than on the associated good, is that emissions taxes create incentives to find ways for reducing emissions beyond reducing exchange of the good itself.

Consider a carbon tax τ per unit of emissions, which we assume can be measured at each of the i emission sources. Let's remain agnostic for the moment about whether the tax is intended to maximize overall efficiency or is set at some other level, noting that only the former corresponds precisely with a Pigouvian tax. Each emitting entity will choose e_i to maximize $b_i(e_i) - \tau e_i$, with the first-order condition $b_i'(e_i) = \tau$ defining emissions as a function of the tax. In effect, $b_i'(e_i)$ is an inverse demand function for emissions, where τ is the price. We can equivalently write each entity's cost minimization problem as choosing a_i to minimize $c_i(a_i) + \tau(\bar{e}_i - a_i)$, with the first-order condition $c_i'(a_i) = \tau$. This defines the function $a_i(\tau)$ that is effectively each entity's supply function for abatement.

Aggregate abatement for a given tax is then $A(\tau) = \Sigma_{i=1}^{n} a_i(\tau)$, and it follows that $c_i'(a_i(\tau)) = c_j'(a_j(\tau))$ for all i and j. Hence the level of abatement is increasing in the level of the tax, and referring back to the conditions implied by the definition of $C(A)$ in (1), we find that aggregate abatement at any level of τ is implemented at the minimum cost. What is more, and important, the regulator need not know anything about the cost curves of each emitting entity.

There are nevertheless limitations. Without knowing anything about the aggregate abatement cost function, a regulator will have little sense about how much abatement will occur at a given tax rate. Thus far we have also said nothing about the regulator's objective function. Information about abatement costs is clearly needed if the aim is to use a carbon tax to meet some emissions reduction target. And if the objective is to set the target efficiently, additional information is needed about the marginal damages of emissions (i.e., the *MDF*), which as discussed previously could be calibrated to global or domestic damages.

Another important feature of carbon taxes is their potential to raise revenue. With our simple setup, the tax revenue is equal to $\tau(\bar{E} - A(\tau))$ and assumed to be returned lump sum. Estimates of the revenue from carbon taxes are large because of the broad base upon which they can be levied. In the United States, for example, a meta-analysis of 11 different energy and economy models finds that carbon taxes of \$25 and \$50 per ton would generate revenue of roughly \$103 and \$170 billion per year (Barron et al., 2018). Some have argued that the potential for raising revenue can make carbon taxes an attractive policy option (Bistline et al., 2025), whereas others point out that the comparison between tax revenue and welfare gains can affect political feasibility (Kotchen, 2025). Surveys suggest that how revenue is spent can have a significant affect on public support, showing greater support for carbon taxes when revenue is used to subsidize clean energy and to make direct transfers to those most adversely affected by climate change or the tax burden (Kotchen et al., 2017; Klenert et al., 2018; Dechezlepretre et al., 2022). To the extent that raising large amounts of revenue is a concern, nonlinear taxes are also possible, which can include exemptions over a range of emissions and for specific sectors. Such modifications to the tax policy can lower revenue while still creating the same incentives to reduce emissions.

The World Bank (2024a) maintains a comprehensive and updated list of carbon tax policies around the world, including those at the national and subnational levels. Nearly 30 countries currently have some form of a carbon tax in place, covering an estimated 6 % of global emissions. The prices per ton range widely, from less than \$1 in Ukraine to \$167 in Uruguay. Countries with carbon taxes over \$60 per ton are Ireland, Netherlands, Finland, Norway, Sweden, and Switzerland. Across these and others, however, there is a wide range in the share of GHG emissions covered. A review of studies that evaluate the impacts of implemented carbon taxes can be found in Metcalf (2021) and Timilsina (2022), although given the emphasis that economists place on carbon taxes, this is an area in need of more research.

4.2 Subsidies and carbon offsets

Now consider an abatement subsidy s that is paid to each polluting entity for every ton of emissions reductions below $\bar{e}_i$. We can again think of each polluting entity's decision problem in two ways. The first is to chose emissions to maximize benefits $b_i(e_i) + s(\bar{e}_i - e_i)$. The second is to chose abatement to minimize costs $c_i(a_i) - sa_i$. Focusing on the later, the first-order condition, $c_i'(a_i) = s$, defines abatement as a function of the subsidy, $a_i(s)$. It is immediately clear that the solution for all i is the same as that for the tax when $s = \tau$. Hence, like the emissions tax, an abatement subsidy can reduce aggregate emissions at the minimum abatement costs.

The potential for Coasian bargaining provides an intuitive way to understand why an abatement subsidy and an emissions tax, with $s = \tau$, induces the same equilibrium. Coase's (1960) fundamental insight is that bargaining between parties can result in the efficient resolution of an externality if property rights are well-established and there are zero transaction costs. Implementing a tax or subsidy effectively satisfies both conditions. Property rights are established by delineating who pays (the emitters or the public), and the level of the tax or subsidy eliminates transaction costs associated with how much to pay (i.e., there is no need to bargain). If the tax or subsidy is set at the efficient level, then both instruments will implement the efficient equilibrium. Although Coasian bargaining is typically invoked in cases where policy interventions are unnecessary to resolve externalities (Deryugina et al., 2021), we can see here that the same logic applies to the symmetry between emissions taxes and abatement subsides. Distributional implications are the primary difference between the two instruments, as the assignment of property rights determines whether emitters must pay or get paid.

There are other differences between emissions taxes and abatement subsidies. The payment of subsidies requires raising revenue through other means, likely taxes, and these can be distortionary. The analysis of subsidies might therefore need to account for the marginal cost of public funds. The two instruments can also differ in the long run because of differential effects on entry and exit. Another important way the policies differ is the information required for implementation. The tax applies to emissions, which we have assumed is observable. In contrast, the subsidy applies to emissions reductions, and implementation requires observation not only e_i, but also $\bar{e}_i$ for all i.

There are nevertheless difficulties identifying the baseline because it is inherently an unobservable counterfactual, and this contributes to the "additionality" problem in markets for carbon offsets, which are effectively abatement subsidies. Recent studies in the energy and forestry sectors highlight how additionality is a growing concern (Calel et al., 2024; West et al., 2023). Full additionality would occur if none of the emissions reductions below $\bar{e}_i$ would occur for entity i without the subsidy payment. But upon observing e_i, there is asymmetric information about what $\bar{e}_i$ would have been, and truthful reporting about baselines is generally not incentive compatible.

4.2.1 *Baselines and additionality*

There is something that can be done to help allay concerns about additionality. By adjusting the baseline, a regulator can decrease the subsidy cost per ton and stretch a fixed budget to induce greater emissions reductions. Assume the subsidy per ton must remain constant, the regulator does not observe $\bar{e}_i$, but can choose a baseline to which the subsidy applies, denoted $\tilde{e}_i$. Regardless of what baseline the regulator chooses, conditional on accepting the subsidy s, the emitter will chose a level of emissions $e_i(s) = \bar{e}_i - a_i(s)$. The question is then, how low can the baseline be set to still induce uptake? The answer is the lowest $\tilde{e}_i$ that satisfies $s(\tilde{e}_i - e_i(s)) \geq b(\bar{e}_i) - b_i(e_i(s))$. That is, the total subsidy payment must be greater than the foregone private benefit of reducing emissions optimally conditional on uptake, and the solution will be some baseline greater than $e_i(s)$ and less than $\bar{e}_i$.

While lowering the baseline is appealing and potentially useful, it is unfortunately not a "free pass" for eliminating non-additionality or extracting all rents, as accomplishing both requires knowing $\bar{e}_i$ and the marginal abatement cost curve. Another approach to help address additionality that has gained traction in practice, particularly with international forest offsets, is to assign group-level baselines (van Benthem and Kerr, 2013). This is an application of group-level approaches to environmental policy that have been employed in a range of other settings (Kotchen and Segerson, 2019, 2020).

4.2.2 Accounting for transfers

That a portion of subsidy payments are likely to represent a transfer from the government's budget to the emitting entities raises an additional topic about how to evaluate efficiency or cost effectiveness. When evaluating subsidy programs, it is typical for analysts to estimate the subsidy cost per ton of emissions reductions. While that is how the subsidy is set in the simple model here, subsidies in practice often target actions that subsequently affect emissions. Examples include subsidies for home weatherization to improve efficiency, the installation of heat pumps or solar panels, and the purchase of electric vehicles.

When evaluation of such programs entails estimates of a subsidy cost per ton, whether or not the transfer portion of the subsidy should be included in the ratio depends on the question the analysis intends to answer. If the benchmark is efficiency, whereby the subsidy cost per ton is compared to an estimate of the SCC, then the relevant comparison is the cost per ton *net* of the transfer—that is, the transfer portion of the subsidy should not be included as part of the cost. If, however, the analysis is intended to inform cost effectiveness—as would be the case for a government seeking to maximize emissions reductions with a given budget—then the transfer portion of the subsidy payment should be included in the subsidy cost per ton ratio. But in this case, the ratio should be used to make comparisons across potential subsidy alternatives, rather than be compared to the SCC. Finally, an alternative approach that nests both comparisons is to evaluate subsidy programs based on the marginal value of public funds (MVPF) (Hahn et al., 2024). The MVPF for a particular policy is the ratio of beneficiaries' willingness to pay for the policy to the net cost to the government. In this case, transfers are included in both the numerator and denominator, so MVPF ratios greater than unity pass a benefit-cost test, and the magnitude of ratios can be used to compare cost effectiveness.

4.3 Fossil fuel subsidies

The elimination of fossil fuel subsidies warrants consideration as a climate policy option because of their global scale and the way they are precisely counter productive to the emissions taxes and abatement subsidies just discussed. They lower the price of emitting GHGs and make it more difficult for clean energy substitutes to compete. Back in 2009, the Group of 20 (G-20) nations, comprising the largest developed and developing countries, agreed to the phase-out of inefficient fossil fuel subsides (G-20 Leaders, 2009). While the commitment has been repeated in multiple international fora every year since, there has been very little (if any) progress. The International Energy Agency (IEA, 2023) estimates explicit, global fossil fuel subsidies at nearly $1.1 trillion in 2022, almost double the estimate in 2010.

The International Monetary Fund (IMF) has advanced an influential research program to broaden thinking about fossil fuel subsides. The IMF work begins with the distinction between explicit and implicit subsidies. Explicit subsides are the familiar notion of a subsidy, based on fiscal costs that lower prices. The IEA estimates just mentioned are an example. In contrast, implicit subsidies arise because of the absence of efficient pricing, which gives rise to social costs not reflected in the market for fossil fuels. The IMF has drawn attention to implicit subsidies, and one way to think about them is a Coasian reframing of missing Pigouvian taxes: if the public has a property right to an emissions-free environment, than the absence of efficient pricing is an implicit subsidy to the fossil fuel sector. The IMF considers externalities associated with climate change, local air pollution, and road use, along with foregone tax revenue. The most recent estimates put the total fossil fuel subsidies at roughly $7 trillion in 2022, equivalent to about 7 % of global GDP (Black et al., 2023), and implicit subsidies due to climate damages account for 30 % of this amount, assuming a global SCC of $60 per ton.

To promote progress on phasing-out fossil fuel subsides, arguments are made about the importance of considering the distributional consequences (Rentschler and Bazilian, 2017) and instituting mechanisms for monitoring and review (Aldy, 2015). Political economy also plays a role: the fossil fuel sector has a lot at stake and wields significant political influence. Expanding on the IMF approach, Kotchen (2021) illustrates the importance of considering the incidence of implicit fossil fuel subsidies. In particular, the producer incidence indicates how much the fossil fuel sector stands to lose with the phase-out of implicit subsidies. In 2018, for example, the direct benefit to fossil fuel producers in the United States was estimated at $62 billion (Kotchen, 2021), helping to explain lobbying on the part of fossil fuel suppliers and one reason why reform is difficult.

5 Cap-and-trade programs

The cap-and-trade mechanism is a central instrument of environmental policy. Dales (1968) is given credit for first developing the idea. The academic literature on cap-and-trade is expansive, and the approach to reducing emissions has take hold in practice. The United States has a history of using cap-and-trade to regulate air pollution under the Clean Air Act. There are cap-and-trade programs to regulate CO_2 emissions in California and among states in the northeastern United States. The largest program is the European Union's Emissions Trading System (EU ETS), accounting for 2.6 % of global GHG emissions. While China's emissions trading system is sometimes referred to as a cap-and-trade, it is actually a tradable performance standard, which will be discussed in Section 9. The World Bank (2024a) dashboard on carbon pricing around the world provides details on all cap-and-trade programs, and the accompanying report includes additional country-specific information (World Bank, 2024b).

5.1 The basic mechanism

Consider a regulator that seeks to limit aggregate emissions at level $\hat{E}$. The cap-and-trade mechanism begins with issuance of tradable emissions permits totaling this amount, which we assume is a binding constraint. There is the question of how the permits are initially allocated, and assume for the moment they are auctioned off to the n emitting entities. Assume further that an auction mechanism is employed such that the resulting price, denoted p, exactly clears the market for permits. Before turning to the price that emerges, consider the optimization problem of each emitting entity for a given p. Each entity chooses its level of emissions to maximize $b_i(e_i) - pe_i$, with the first-order condition, $b_i'(e_i) = p$, defining demand for emissions, $e_i(p)$. Notice how this problem has an identical structure to that for the emissions tax, with the only difference being replacement of τ with p. Aggregate demand for emissions, for a given p, can be written as $E(p) = \sum_{i=1}^{n} e_i(p)$. The market clearing price must then satisfy $\hat{E} = E(\hat{p})$. Assuming an interior solution for all emitting entities, it follows that $\hat{p} = b_i'(\hat{e}_i) = c_i'(\hat{a}_i)$ for all i. Hence, referring again back to the implications of (1), we find that the cap-and-trade mechanism implements the cost minimizing solution for reducing emissions down to the regulator's chosen level. Importantly, this solution is obtained without the regulator having any information about marginal abatement costs. This is similar to the result we found for the emissions tax, but now the regulator is choosing a quantity of emissions at $\hat{E}$ rather than a price on emissions at τ.

Let us now revisit the initial allocation mechanism with an alternative. The "grandfathering" of permits occurs when they are allocated based on some predetermined, entity-specific characteristics, such as previous levels of emissions. Although the precise way that permits are grandfathered can create inefficient incentives in a dynamic setting, it has long been established that grandfathering and auctioning have the same efficiency consequences in the short-run, assuming no other market failures (Montgomery, 1972). To see why, let $\check{e}_i$ denote any initial allocation to entity i where it continues to hold that $\hat{E} = \sum_{i=1}^{n} \check{e}_i$. For a given permit price, each entity chooses emissions to maximize $b_i(e_i) - p(e_i - \check{e}_i)$, and the first-order condition is identical to that shown previously. Hence the conditions identifying an equilibrium—all i first-order conditions and the market clearing condition—remain unchanged.

This establishes an important result about cap-and-trade programs: they implement emission reductions at least cost, and the result does not depend on how permits are initially allocated. The result does, however, rely on the assumption that b_i does not depend on the allocation of allowances, and that all

i are price takers in the permit market. Numerous papers in the literature have considered various implications of market power, with an early and influential contribution by Hahn (1984).

It is nevertheless important to recognize that the allocation mechanism does have distributional consequences, as it effectively assigns valuable property rights. With the auction mechanism, no entity has the right to pollute, so they all must purchase permits for each unit of emissions. In contrast, with grandfathering of freely allocated permits, entities are given a property right for emissions, and each unit has value $\hat{p}$. Clearly an entity would prefer to have a free allocation, or a higher $\check{e}_i$, where it can sell any excess permits. Accordingly, with the static basic setup and through the allocation of permits, cap-and-trade programs are able to separate efficiency and distributional concerns, and this has a potential advantage when it comes to political economy. The use of grandfathering is more widely adopted in practice compared to auctions, presumably because regulators can build political support through concessions to influential stakeholders, adversely impacted entities, or both. When accounting for dynamic settings, however, allocation mechanisms can induce strategic behavior that is distortionary, and this should be taken into account as part of program design (Harstad and Eskeland, 2010).

We have thus far been silent about how the regular chooses the emissions cap $\hat{E}$. The mechanism will be cost effective for any chosen target. But additional information is required if the regulator seeks to set the target with an efficiency goal in mind. Recall that the efficient level of emissions E^* is shown in Fig. 1 at the intersection of the MAC and MDF curves. Information about both curves is necessary to set an efficient emissions cap, and with respect to climate change, there is also the question of which MDF a regulator might seek to internalize (e.g., global or domestic damages).

A further nuance that can affect the efficiency of cap-and-trade programs in general is whether the pollutant is uniformly mixing or whether the marginal damages differ by the source of emissions. GHG emissions ultimately have the same impact on climate change regardless of where they are emitted, but the same does not apply for local pollutants. With local pollutants, the cap-and-trade approach may be subject to "hot spots"—i.e., locations where emissions are more highly concentrated—that can affect overall efficiency of the instrument, in addition to it distributional consequences.

5.2 Empirical research

There is a literature focused on program evaluation of cap-and-trade programs. Schmalensee and Stavins (2017) and Haites et al. (2018) provide reviews. Studies have evaluated various aspects of the European Union ETS that was adopted in 2003 and covers about half of EU CO_2 emissions in 31 countries. Others examine California's cap-and-trade system (AB-32) that began in 2013 and covers all electricity generating units and large scale manufacturing, and the Regional Greenhouse Gas Initiative (RGGI) that focuses on emissions of the electric power sector in northeastern states of the United States. Finally, while hotspots are not a concern for cap-and-trade programs focused on CO_2 emissions—at least with respect to the regulated pollutant—studies have begun to examine the distributional consequences of changes in the levels and distribution of co-pollutants that have local effects on public health (Hernandez-Cortes and Meng, 2023; Sheriff, 2024).

5.3 The allowance of offsets

Many cap-and-trade programs for reducing GHG emissions have provisions that allow emitting entities to use offsets in place of permits for compliance. Examples include the Clean Development Mechanism (CDM) as part of the EU ETS, and the Compliance Offset portion of California's cap-and-trade program. Allowing offsets is not without controversy, however. Advocates argue in favor of lower costs of compliance, whereas detractors question whether offsets actually deliver equivalent emission reductions, pointing to concerns about additionality, impermanence, uncertainty, and measurement.

We can see the basic issues at play with a simple graphical illustration. Fig. 2 includes an aggregate marginal abatement cost curve, *MAC* as previously discussed, with the unregulated level of emissions at $\bar{E}$. Without the use of offsets for compliance, a cap on emissions $\hat{E}$ induces the market clearing price of permits at $\hat{p}$. Total abatement costs are given by the area $\bar{E}\hat{E}A$.

Now consider what happens if offsets are allowed for compliance in place of permits. Assume offsets are available at constant marginal cost $c_o > 0$. Begin with the case where there is no limit to the number offsets that can be used. The maximum willingness to pay for an offset is $\hat{p}$, and the *MAC* to the right of $\hat{E}$ represents the demand for offsets. Emissions in the regulated sector will increase up to E', where the marginal willingness to pay for offsets equals their marginal cost, and the permit price decreases to $\hat{p}' = c_o$. In principle, the increase in emissions in the regulated sector, $\hat{E}$ to E', is offset by an equal amount of emissions reductions in the offset sector. A further consequence is the total abatement costs decline to area $\bar{E}\hat{E}BC$. In practice, however, cap-and-trade programs limit the amount of offsets that can be used for compliance. With a binding constraint, the market clearing permit price $\hat{p}''$ will remain higher than c_o, and assuming rents denoted by the shaded areas accrue to the offset providers, total abatement costs will be area $\bar{E}\hat{E}DF$, which is lower than without the offset option but greater than with unlimited offsets. This is the argument is favor of allowing offsets: the same emissions reduction target can be achieved at a lower cost.

Two other observations are worth making. First, if offsets are available, each permit has less value. This may be important because it lowers the potential revenue a regulator can raise through the auctioning of permits. Second, and important, there are concerns about the validity of offsets, which

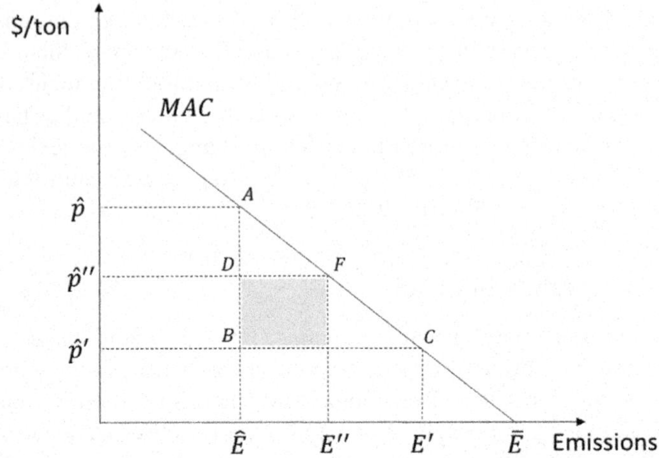

FIG. 2 Total abatement costs with a cap-and-trade program and the possibility of using offsets for compliance.

have been questioned in both the CDM and California's program (Calel et al., 2024; Stapp et al., 2023). In the extreme case where offsets are fully "hot air," emissions will increase by the full amount of offset purchases. But interestingly, even if offsets are not perfect, they can still play a role if we have an estimate of their success probability η. A regulator can make adjustments based on the expected tons. The key ratio is $1/\eta$ so that if, for example, the offset has a success probability of $\eta = .5$, it takes two offsets to count towards a single permit. As a consequence, the price of an offset effectively doubles (and appropriately so), which means that the permit price would not be as low, emissions in the regulated sector would not increase by as much, and the total abatement costs would be higher, though more realistic. Recent work on the social value of offsets (Groom and Venmans, 2023) can help provide guidance on potential success probabilities.

6 Prices vs quantities

Should climate policy take the form of an emissions tax or a cap-and-trade program? Arguments often center on political feasibility, seeking to advance whichever instrument is more likely for actual implementation. But there are cases where one policy can be more economically efficient than the other, and when they are equivalent. We have already seen a circumstance where they are equivalent. The previous sections show how setting a cap on emissions at $\hat{E}$ is associated with a permit price of $\hat{p}$, and the same level of emissions would arise if instead an emission tax were set at $\tau = \hat{p}$. Both instruments also generate the same revenue assuming the permits are auctioned rather than freely allocated. The two instruments can nevertheless differ when taking account of uncertainty.

6.1 Weitzman's central result

Let us begin with Weitzman's (1974) seminal analysis, framed as prices vs quantities. The regulator seeks to maximize overall welfare and must choose between and emissions tax or a cap-and-trade, where each is set optimally in expectation. The tax sets the emissions price with certainty, whereas the cap-and-trade sets the emissions quantity with certainty. There is uncertainty about the marginal abatement costs, perhaps because of asymmetric information, and the question is which instrument can take better account of the different possible outcomes.

Clear and direct results emerge with assumed linearity of the *MAC* and *MDF* curves, as shown in Fig. 1. In this setting, it is helpful (and with no consequence) to redefine the *MAC* as the marginal benefit of emissions. Noting that $E = \bar{E} - A$, we can write the expected marginal benefits of emissions as $MB(E) = \varphi - \kappa E$, and the realized marginal benefits are $MB(E) \pm \delta$, where δ captures the uncertainty. In the high-benefit state of the world, the marginal benefit shifts up by δ, which we assume occurs with probability.5, and in the low-benefit state of the world, it shifts down by δ with probability.5. The marginal damages of emissions are given by $MD = \varphi + \gamma E$, which are known with certainty. Although unrealistic, this assumption is justified in the basic setup because of a welfare invariance between policy instruments with uncertainty about marginal damages, which does not (on its own) affect the level of pollution with either the tax or cap. Indeed, Weitzman (1974) pays little attention to uncertainty about the marginal damages of emissions because it "affects price and quantity modes equally adversely" (p. 485).

The central result of Weitzman (1974) is that when choosing each instrument optimally ex ante, the welfare advantage of the tax compared to the cap is

$$\Delta^{\tau} = \frac{\delta^2(\kappa - \gamma)}{2\kappa^2}. \tag{2}$$

This expression is based on a comparison between the expected, deadweight loss of each instrument, assuming the uncertainty is not large enough to cause corner solutions. It makes clear that taxes and caps deliver equivalent welfare in the absence of uncertainty ($\delta = 0$), or if the slopes of the marginal benefit and damage functions are the same ($\kappa = \gamma$). More generally, the preferred instrument depends on the relative slopes of the marginal benefit and damage functions. The tax is preferred, for example, if the marginal damage function is flatter than the marginal benefit function, that is, if $\kappa - \gamma > 0$.

There are many ways to gain intuition for the result in equation (2), though perhaps the simplest is to focus on the slope of the marginal damages. If marginal damages are nearly constant ($\gamma \to 0$), an emissions tax can set nearly the right incentive regardless of the marginal benefits of emissions. If, however, the marginal damages are very step ($\gamma \to \infty$), the efficient quantity of emissions is relatively constant, so a cap that ensures this result is preferred to a tax. Fig. 3 illustrates a case where the tax is preferred, as the expected deadweight loss with the tax (the sum of the shaded areas) is smaller than that for the cap (the sum of the hashed areas).

When applied to climate change, many have argued that the framework favors taxes. The argument is based on the way that GHGs are a stock (rather than flow) pollutant, and hence marginal damages are relatively less responsive than marginal abatement costs to changes in emissions over what is considered the policy-relevant range and duration (Metcalf, 2023). Others have nevertheless argued recently in favor of cap-and-trade programs, based on extensions of the setup that accounts for technology and pollution shocks that are persistent over time (Karp and Traeger, 2024).

6.2 Extensions and hybrid approaches

Weitzman's analysis has given rise to an expansive literature that investigates whether or not the basic result holds up with modifications to the original setup. Although not the focus of their paper, Pizer and Prest (2020) provide a nice review of the literature. Some papers explore how regulators can seek better information from firms to address information asymmetries. Other papers examine different forms of uncertainty, including correlated uncertainty between marginal benefits and damages, market power, non-linearities, and how the choice of policy instrument affects other outcomes. Pizer and Prest (2020) also contribute to a literature that considers Weitzman-type results with policy updating in a multi-period setting. They categorize papers on this topic by the way they differentially account for uncertainty, intertemporal trading of permits, policy updating, and welfare analysis.

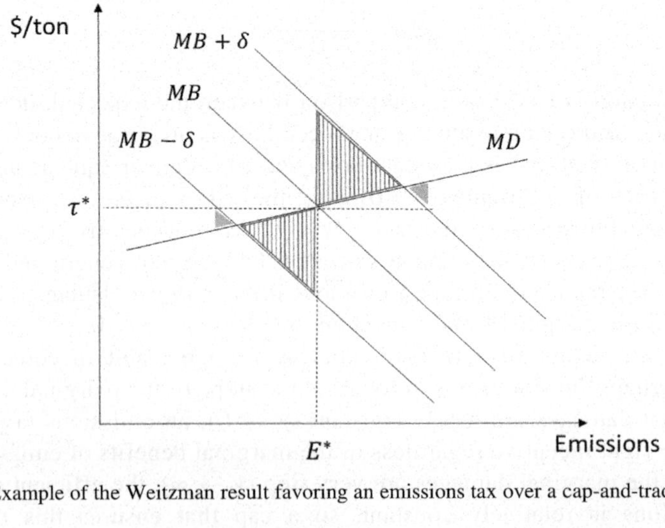

FIG. 3 Example of the Weitzman result favoring an emissions tax over a cap-and-trade program.

The framework has also given rise a number of papers that examine the design of hybrid instruments. For cap-and-trade programs, these include price containment mechanisms that may, for example, include a price ceiling on allowances or an additional reserve that can be released if permit prices get too high (Roberts and Spence, 1976; Pizer, 2002; Newell et al., 2005; Murray et al., 2009). It turns out that in practice, most cap-and-trade programs include some form of a price containment mechanism to help alleviate political concerns about significant price uncertainty (Brooks and Keohane, 2020). In many cases, however, allowance prices that are too low, meaning the cap is less binding, is a greater concern than ones that are too high (Burtraw and Keyes, 2018). More recently, research and specific policy proposals have focused on ways to employ emissions taxes with additional mechanisms to reduce uncertainty about the associated level of emissions (Aldy 2017; Hafstead and Williams, 2020; Metcalf, 2020). An example, consistent with the design of Switzerland's carbon tax, is a case where the tax rate is designed to increase over time, but the rate of increase is faster if emissions reductions fall short of intended annual targets.

6.3 A generalization

The Weitzman result in equation (2) captures the expected welfare benefit (or cost) of an emissions tax compared to an emissions cap-and-trade when both instruments are chosen optimally ex ante. That is, both instruments are chosen at levels that maximize the expected welfare gain. But what if the instruments are not chosen with the objective of maximizing efficiency? We have considered in this paper how the efficiency criterion is not always the objective of climate policy. It turns out that the result in equation (2) is even more general and can inform policy instrument choice under a broader set of circumstances: it shows the welfare advantage of the tax for any pair of price-quantity instruments where both are set to implement the same level of emissions in expectation. While a potentially useful result in the context of climate policy, it is one that appears to have not been shown in the existing literature.

Fig. 4 provides a graphical illustration. Recall that the tax and cap in Fig. 3 were selected optimally in expectation, that is, the levels of each policy satisfy $MB(E^*) = MD(E^*) = \tau^*$. In contrast, the policy levels in Fig. 4 need only satisfy the same level of emissions in expectation, that is, $MB(\hat{E}) = \hat{\tau}$. All other assumptions of the setup remain the same. The sum of the shaded areas still represents the expected deadweight loss with the tax, and the sum of the hashed areas still represents the expected deadweight loss with the cap. Here again, with the same curves, we find that the expected deadweight loss is lower with the tax. In fact, a few lines of algebra comparing the magnitudes will show that the welfare advantage of the tax is precisely equation (2). What is more, assuming the deadweight loss triangles do not hit a corner, the result holds when comparing any pair of policies with the same level of emissions in expectation. Fig. 4 shows just a single example, where the policies are less stringent than the ex ante efficient levels.

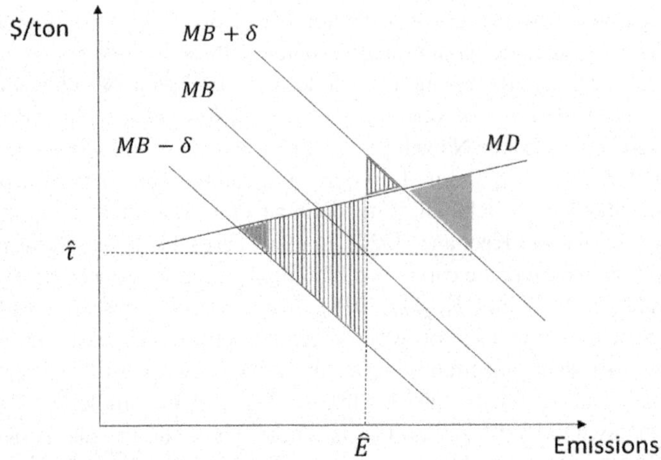

FIG. 4 Generalization of the prices vs quantities result to emissions equivalent instruments in expectation, which need not be efficient in expectation.

We find, therefore, that the prices vs quantities logic can inform policy instrument choice in what might be a more realistic setting for climate policy: when the primary objective is to reach what can be an arbitrarily set emissions target, the preferred instrument still depends on the relative slopes of the marginal damages and benefits of emissions. And it does so in precisely the same way as the standard result.

7 Climate policy in an open economy

Let us now turn to climate policy in an open economy setting. The perspective is important at a high level because of the way GHG emissions create a global externality, and economies are linked through trade. This gives rise to several topics covered here. The first is "leakage," which occurs when policies to reduce emissions in one region (or sector) have the side effect of increasing emissions elsewhere. The second is how climate policy can include a broad set of potential tax policy instruments, including production, consumption, and trade taxes. Third is how carbon border adjustments are a special case of trade taxes. The final set of observations relate to the different role green subsidies can play in open and closed economies.

7.1 Basic setup

The model used here is a simplified version of that in Kotchen and Maggi (2024), and it is closely related to the basic setup in Weisbach et al. (2023). Begin with the closed economy to establish a baseline. There are two final goods sectors: A is energy, and B is a numeraire. The numeraire is produced one-for-one with labor, which is in fixed supply. In this simple setup, energy is assumed to come from only one source that generates GHG emissions (the possibility for zero-emissions energy is discussed below). Energy is produced with a specific factor and labor, with constant returns to scale. Let y denote the production of energy, which causes marginal damages $\alpha > 0$, with a climate externality denoted $D = \alpha y$. We can think of energy as measured in units of its CO_2 emissions, in which case α is the domestic social cost of carbon. Preferences are quasilinear of the form $U(c^A) + c^B - D$, where $U' > 0$, $U'' < 0$, and c^j is consumption of good $j = A, B$.

Now consider demand, supply, and the market clearing condition for energy at price p. Demand, denoted $d(p)$, is defined implicitly from $U'(c^A) = p$. Consumer surplus is $CS(p)$, and it follows that $\frac{dCS(p)}{dp} = -d(p)$. On the supply side, total returns to the energy sector will depend only on p and the fixed wage $w = 1$. We can therefore write these returns as $\pi(p)$ and interpret the expression as producer surplus. The supply of energy can be written as $y(p) = \frac{d\pi}{dp}$, where the equality follows by Hotelling's lemma. Finally, market clearing requires $d(p) = y(p)$.

We begin with climate policy in the form of a production tax t on energy. As noted previously, there can be an equivalence between price and quantity instruments, so much of what follows can be translated into other forms of climate policy (e.g., a cap-and-trade program with auctioned permits), although the discussion focuses on taxes. Letting p and q denote consumer and producer prices, respectively, we have the price wedge $q = p - t$, and market clearing must satisfy $d(p) = y(p - t)$. Solving the welfare maximization problem—a special case of maximizing equation (3) below—one finds the intuitive solution of $t = \alpha$ in a closed economy. This is simply the benchmark Pigouvian tax.

7.2 A unilateral tax with leakage

Now assume there are two countries, Home and Foreign, and both have economies structured as just described. There is trade in energy with no trade costs. To illustrate the basic ideas, let's focus on Home's unilaterally optimal policies, assuming Foreign is passive with no policies of its own in place. The welfare of Home can be defined as aggregate indirect utility: $CS + \pi + R - D$, where R is government revenue, and we can ignore labor income because it is fixed. Letting ρ denote the world price of energy, Home's welfare function can be written as

$$W = CS(p) + \pi(q) + R - \alpha[y(q) + y^*(\rho)], \tag{3}$$

where $R = ty(q)$ is the production tax revenue, and asterisks are used to denote Foreign, so y^* is Foreign's production of energy, which depends on the world price. Note that the externality Home experiences depends on energy production in both countries, and we have assumed Home cares only about its own domestic SCC. Home's problem is to choose t to maximize W, where the market clearing condition is now $d(p) + d^*(\rho) = y(q) + y^*(\rho)$ with $p = \rho$ and $q = p - t$.

The first-order condition for the solution to Home's problem can be written as

$$\frac{\partial W}{\partial t} = -m\frac{\partial p}{\partial t} + (t - \alpha)y'\frac{\partial q}{\partial t} - \alpha y^{*\prime}\frac{\partial p}{\partial t} = 0, \tag{4}$$

where $m = d - y$ denotes Home's imports or exports of energy, and the primes denote derivatives. Totally differentiating the market clearing condition, we can substitute out the price changes and solve for Home's unilaterally optimal production tax:

$$t = \alpha - \frac{m + \alpha y^{*\prime}}{y^{*\prime} - d^{*\prime} - d'}. \tag{5}$$

It is immediately clear that without trade ($m = 0$) and no Foreign supply response ($y^{*\prime} = 0$), the solution is $t = \alpha$, which is the closed economy solution. More generally, the open economy introduces two additional effects that alter the level of the tax, both of which can be seen in the first-order condition and (5). First is the terms of trade (TOT) effect, which pushes down the tax if Home is an importer of energy. Second is leakage, whereby the increase in the world price of energy caused by the tax increases the Foreign supply of energy, and this in turn causes Home to choose a lower tax because of the climate damages it experiences as a consequence. In order to focus on the climate externality, it is helpful to assume that if $m > 0$, it is not large enough to turn the tax into a subsidy.

Leakage is a potentially important side effect of climate policy, and the type of leakage just described is often referred to as leakage through the "competitiveness channel." It occurs because regulation at Home increases costs, so production shifts abroad where regulation is more lax. Markusen (1975) is an early paper that identifies the leakage effect in the context of transboundary pollution, Hoel (1994) considers the issue specifically in the context of climate change, and other papers examine various aspects of leakage (Hoel, 1996; Fowlie, 2009; Böhringer et al., 2014; Holladay et al., 2018; Fowlie and Reguant, 2022; Weisbach et al., 2023). Branger and Quiron (2014) review studies with international estimates, primarily based on computational general equilibrium models, and find leakage ranges between 5 % and 20 %. See also Yu et al. (2021) for a meta-analysis with estimates of the same magnitude or greater. Finally, it is worth noting that the mechanism underlying leakage is related to another concept known as the pollution haven hypothesis, based on the idea that more lax environmental regulations within a region promotes comparative advantage for more pollution-intensive production in that region (Copeland et al., 2022).

7.3 Combining multiple tax instruments

Let us now examine what happens if we allow Home to deploy a fuller set of tax policies. Begin with the possibility for a consumption tax, in addition to the production tax. Recall that in a closed economy, production and consumption taxes are equivalent, but the equivalence no longer holds in an open economy setting, as the instruments have different effects on the world price. We have already discussed how the production tax increases the world price of energy, and this increases Foreign's supply, which causes leakage through the competitiveness channel. In contrast, a consumption tax at Home will decrease the world price of energy and therefore stimulate Foreign's demand. This effect is another unintended consequence also referred to as leakage in the literature, but this time through the "fuel price channel." Hence, while both instruments decrease the externality at Home, neither is without leakage effects in an open economy setting. A question worth considering, therefore, is how Home might choose the optimal balance between instruments, taking account of the different leakage effects, when setting its own unilateral policies (Weisbach et al., 2023).

Let θ denote Home's consumption tax on energy. The market clearing condition remains identical to that specified previously, but prices are now related according to $p = \rho + \theta$ and $q = \rho - t$. There is also an additional source of government revenue, so in this case $R = ty(q) + \theta d(p)$ in (3). Solving Home's maximization problem yields two first-order conditions, $\frac{\partial W}{\partial t} = \frac{\partial W}{\partial \theta} = 0$, which together define the optimal, unilateral policy package. Using the market clearing condition and the price identities, we can once again substitute the price changes out of the first order conditions (not shown) and solve for the optimal production and consumption taxes:

$$t = \alpha - \theta \quad \text{and} \quad \theta = \frac{m + \alpha y^{*\prime}}{y^{*\prime} - d^{*\prime}}. \tag{6}$$

In general, both instruments will be used, and the sum of the production and consumption tax equals α. This means that the climate externality is fully internalized from Home's perspective. Assuming m is sufficiently small also ensures that both taxes are positive.

How does Home split the incentive between the two instruments? Using the expressions in (6), we can write the ratio of the production tax to consumption tax as

$$\frac{t}{\theta} = -\frac{m + \alpha d^{*\prime}}{m + \alpha y^{*\prime}}. \tag{7}$$

It is clear from (7) that the ratio depends on the relative slope of Foreign's demand and supply for energy. The intuition is that Home seeks to avoid taxing in ways that provoke greater Foreign responsiveness, which causes leakage. To see this clearly, let's assume for the moment that $m = 0$. Then, to the extent that Foreign's demand for energy is more responsive than its supply, Home will favor the production tax, as leakage through the competitiveness channel (which depends on Foreign supply) is less of a concern than through the fuel price channel (which depends on Foreign demand). On the other hand, Home will favor a consumption tax when Foreign's demand is less responsive than its supply. Weisbach et al. (2023) describe the optimal ratio between the taxes as balancing these concerns, although their result differs from equation (7) because they restrict Home's policies to Pareto improvements, and this eliminates TOT effects by construction.

What about other combinations of tax instruments? There is a general equivalence in trade theory between the equilibria implied by the optimally chosen policy packages of (*i*) production and consumption taxes, (*ii*) production and trade taxes, and (*iii*) consumption and trade taxes. We just considered (*i*) and now turn to (*ii*), as trade taxes in various ways are increasingly a focal point in climate policy.

Letting μ denote the trade tax, the price relationships are now $p = \rho + \mu$ and $q = \rho - t + \mu$. What differs between this scenario and the one considered previously is that while $q = p - t$ continues to hold, the trade tax can be used to regulate the level of the world price ρ, because it directly shifts both p and q. Choosing t and μ to maximize (3), where in this case $R = ty(q) + \mu[d(p) - y(q)]$, yields two first-order conditions that, following the same steps outlined above, can be used to solve for the optimal, unilateral policies:

$$t = \alpha \quad \text{and} \quad \mu = \frac{m + \alpha y^{*'}}{y^{*'} - d^{*'}}. \tag{8}$$

In this case, the production tax is equal to the full marginal climate damages α, and the trade tax is equal in magnitude to the consumption tax in equation (6). Equivalence between the two optimally chosen policy packages, cases (*i*) and (*ii*), means they implement the same allocations, and generate the same level of government revenue. Although not a focus here, it is worth noting for completeness that case (*iii*), involving consumption and trade taxes, also implements the same allocation with $\theta = \alpha$, and $\mu = \frac{m + \alpha d^{*'}}{y^{*'} - d^{*'}}$. In effect, trade taxes are used to affect the world price, while the production or consumption taxes are used to internalize the externality at Home.

Many papers in the literature explore these relationships in far greater detail, allowing for a blend of different instruments, more comprehensive setups with goods that vary in their emissions intensities, and calibrated simulations. Examples that cover these topics in various ways include Markenson (1978), Hoel (1994, 1996), Jakob et al. (2013), Böhringer et al. (2014, 2017), Kortum and Weisbach, 2022, and Weisbach et al. (2023).

7.4 Carbon border adjustments

There are, of course, limits to the policy instruments available to regulators in practice. Constraints may arise because of challenges due technical feasibly (perhaps because of measurement), political economy, or as a matter of law. For example, the World Trade Organization (WTO) imposes limits on trade taxes. Seeking to find ways to implement trade taxes that are WTO compliant, economists and policymakers are increasingly focused on carbon border adjustments (Böhringer et al., 2022; Jakob, 2022). The most prominent example is the European Commission's Carbon Border Adjustment Mechanism (CBAM) that entered transitional implementation in 2023. Border adjustments are trade taxes that take the form of an import tariff (or possibly an export subsidy) calibrated specifically to the difference in the climate policy costs borne by domestic- and foreign-produced products. The rationale is to not disadvantage domestic producers and ultimately seek to leverage other countries into adopting more stringent climate policies.

Added to the basic setting here—with a production tax at Home and no Foreign climate policy (Section 7.2)—a border adjustment would entail a tariff on energy imports equal to the production tax t, or a subsidy on exports of the same magnitude. To keep things simple, assume Home is an importer, so the border adjustment would be a trade tax satisfying $\mu = t$. But of course the solution in (8) does not in general satisfy this condition. Indeed, it is important to recognize that in the previous section, we solved for the optimal unilateral production and trade tax, without any constraint on their relative magnitudes. A carbon border adjustment is therefore a constrained special case of a trade tax.

This distinction raises an interesting question: If Home knows the trade tax must satisfy the border adjustment constraint ($\mu = t$), what is Home's optimal unilateral choice of the production tax? In this case, we have the same price relationships as in the previous section, but the added constraint implies $q = \rho$, so the price wedge occurs only between the consumer price at Home and the world price. Interestingly, this setup is isomorphic to a problem where Home is solving for the optimal consumption tax, when a consumption tax is the only available instrument. Let us therefore use the notation for a consumption tax θ and write the price wedge as $p = \rho + \theta$. Solving this problem by choosing θ to maximize (3), with $R = \theta d(p)$, yields a single first-order condition that we can use to solve for

$$\theta = t|_{\mu=t} = \alpha + \frac{m + \alpha d^{*\prime}}{y^{*\prime} - d^{*\prime} + y^{\prime}}. \tag{9}$$

It is straightforward to see that without the TOT effect, the tax is less than α. This reflects the way that leakage still occurs, but this time through the fuel price channel, rather than the competitiveness channel.

Many of the papers cited previously examine various aspects of carbon border adjustment mechanisms. Another to mention is Kortum and Weisbach (2017) because they provide a nice discussion about how a border tax adjustment effectively shifts the tax from production to consumption at Home, which is the insight of equation (9). In effect, the production tax, without a border adjustment, taxes production at Home regardless of where energy is consumed, whereas adding the border adjustment taxes consumption at home regardless of where energy is produced. It follows that the question of whether Home would want to use a border adjustment, along with a production tax, is equivalent to asking whether Home would prefer a consumption tax to a production tax.

7.5 Green subsidies

What happens if a zero-emissions source of energy (i.e., green energy) is also available? This is the more general setting that Kotchen and Maggi (2024) consider. They find that if production instruments are available, the regulator will choose to subsidize green energy, while taxing the emitting source of energy, albeit at a lower level than when green energy is not available. The underlying mechanism is that green subsidies provide an additional channel through which a country can lower the world price of GHG emitting sources of energy. Green subsidies are also associated with a "reverse leakage" effect: subsidizing green energy at Home lowers its world price, and this causes a decrease in demand for conventional energy for both Home and Foreign. But it is the effect on Foreign that motivates the green subsidy, as the tax on conventional energy is a more targeted instrument for reducing the quantity demanded and supplied at Home. Indeed, focusing on only the climate externality, Kotchen and Maggi (2024) find a unilateral welfare rationale for a green subsidies in an open economy setting. This result stands in contrast to that in a closed economy, where green subsidies serve only as second-best instruments.

8 Renewable energy subsidies

World leaders agreed to triple global renewable energy capacity by 2030 (UNFCCC, 2023), and in line with this goal, renewable energy subsidies are among the favored instruments of climate policy. There are different rationales for green subsidies based on different market failures (Armitage et al., 2024; Gillingham and Stock, 2018), including the open economy scenario covered in the previous section. But regardless of the motivation, green subsidies are substantial, often comprising a central part of the recent trend toward green industrial policy. Direct subsidies to renewable sources of energy were estimated at $166 billion worldwide in 2017, and forecasts for 2030 reach $192 billion (Taylor, 2020). Not included in this estimate, however, is the U.S. Inflation Reduction Act (IRA) of 2022, which includes provisions initially estimated at $271 billion for renewable energy subsides over 10 years, with more recent estimates putting the magnitudes at $700 billion or more (Bistline et al., 2023).

8.1 Investment vs production subsidies

Renewable energy subsides often take the form of either decreasing the costs of investment or increasing the benefits of production. Examples include the investment and production tax credits (the ITC and PTC, respectively) in the

United States and the European Union's Renewable Energy Financing Mechanism. Given the scale of these different approaches, it is worth considering the circumstances under which subsidies should target investment or production.

One consideration is the precise market failure the subsidy seeks to address. In some settings, there might be barriers to getting renewable energy projects up and running. These can range from a lack of well-developed capital markets to provide financing, political and institutional risk, and a shortage of technical experience and expertise. These barriers often provide the rational for multilateral financing of renewable energy projects that focus on lowering investment costs, along with that for green banks at the international, national, and subnational levels. The idea is that by demonstrating successful projects and promoting learning-by-doing, the implicit and explicit costs of future projects will be lower.

In other cases, the market failure is more generally the under-provision of clean energy, which does not generate a negative climate externality. Hence the objective is to scale up generation. While intuition might suggest a production subsidy would be preferred to an investment subsidy, there are additional factors to consider. Parish and McLaren (1982) consider a static setup with perfect competition and ask how much of an input or output subsidy would be needed to induce the same increase in output. The answer depends on whether the inputs are used more intensively on average or on the margin. They focus on how an investment subsidy is more cost effective at increasing output when production has decreasing returns to scale. But it turns out that their static setup misses some important features that can affect the preference between investment or production subsides. Consumers and investors may discount future payments too much, thereby providing a reason to favor the up-front investment subsidy (De Groote and Verboven, 2019; Bartlett, 2023). One the other hand, conditional on project construction, production subsides create continuing incentives to maintain and improve operations and management that can boost production (Aldy et al., 2023). Finally, the efficiency of a production subsidy will also depend on its duration, and when limited, a combination of investment and production subsides can be optimal (Ricks and Kay, 2024).

Aldy et al. (2023) provide empirical evidence comparing the ITC and PTC for wind energy in the United States. They find that installations claiming the investment subsidy were between 10 % and 12 % less productive than they would have been under the production subsidy. Moreover, they estimate that the amount of wind power attributed to the investment subsidy could have be achieved with a cost reduction of 29 % if an output subsidy were used instead.

There are also efficiency concerns to consider beyond cost effectiveness when doing a full comparison between investment and production subsides. The subsidies will affect the production costs and value of electricity generation is ways that are distortionary (Bartlett, 2023), and future research that takes these effects into account would be useful. Investment subsidies can raise the costs of electricity production by encouraging excessive spending on capital costs or by inadequately incentivizing operations and maintenance. In contrast, production subsidies that are set irrespective of prices, can incentivize lower valued electricity production. This arises because the subsidy takes no account of how the value of electricity can differ with the timing of generation and the location. For example, production subsidies can encourage greater electricity generation when prices are negative (Aldy et al., 2023). Furthermore, subsidies, when set at fixed and uniform rates, are not calibrated to the way that displaced marginal emissions from fossil sources of electricity generation differ by location, time of day, and therefore social value (Graff Zivin et al., 2014; Holland et al., 2022).

8.2 Feed-in tariffs

Another form of production subsidies for electricity generated from renewable source of energy is a feed-in tariff (FIT). FITs are long-term contracts that guarantee an above market price for electricity generation form renewable sources of generation. The guaranteed price can differ by source, depending on the costs of generation, and FITs differ from the type of production subsidies previously discussed because they establish a price rather than a fixed subsidy amount. FITs promote renewable generation because they not only provide a subsidy, they protect producers from price uncertainty. As with any production subsidy, FITs can result in inefficiencies because the incentives are not calibrated to the socially optimal timing and location of generation. They may also raise concerns politically because the potential costs to the regulator can be unbounded, though the same concern potentially applies to all subsidies unless limits are set.

FITs have been implemented around the world in developed and developing countries, at both the national and subnational levels. Jenner et al. (2013) provide an evaluation of program effectiveness among Eurpean Union countries along with a literature review. Germany is often pointed to as having the most impactful FIT program, contributing to the country's significant increase in the share of renewable sources of energy for electricity generation, from roughly 8 % in 2000 to 46 % in 2020 (Energy Information Administration, EIA, 2024). Despite the significant shift in Germany's generation profile, there are critics of Germany's FIT design and cost effectiveness (Frondel et al., 2010).

9 Performance based standards

A common form of climate policy, and environmental policy more generally, is a performance based standard. Performance based standards apply a benchmark for compliance at a per unit level of output for a regulated entity, or perhaps an entity's average across units of output. Examples include limits on the emissions per megawatt of electricity generation, and the average fuel economy of vehicles sold. Two features of many performance based standards contribute to their ability to lower compliance costs. First is how regulated entities have flexibility about how to comply, and second is the allowance of tradable credits for compliance. Nevertheless, performance based standards are generally not efficient or cost effective compared to other instruments. This section briefly illustrates why, followed by specific examples of how of performance based standards have been applied in different climate policy settings.

9.1 Basic theory

The potential inefficiency of performance (or sometimes intensity) standards has been well established for quite some time (Helfand, 1991). To convey the basic issues that arise, let's consider a simplified version of the setup in Holland et al. (2009). Focus on electricity generation, and assume there are two sources of fuel for generation: q_l and q_h are associated with low and high emissions rates, respectively. Specifically, the marginal CO_2 emissions rates are β_l and β_h, with $0 < \beta_l < \beta_h$. Consider a single, representative price taking firm with strictly increasing and strictly convex costs of generation from each fuel of $c_l(q_l)$ and $c_h(q_h)$. We can think of q_i in units of embodied energy that maps into different emissions rates, and the cost functions represent the respective costs of generating perfectly substitutable electricity that sells at a fixed price p. Finally, let α denote the marginal social damages of emissions.

Without any regulatory intervention, electricity producing firms will choose q_i to maximize $pq_i - c_i(q_i)$ for both fuels, where the solution (assuming it is interior) will satisfy $p - c_i'(q_i) = 0$ for both i. A welfare maximizing regulator, however, will account for the marginal external costs associated with each fuel, $\alpha\beta_i$, and the socially optimal levels of each will satisfy $p - c_i'(q_i) = \alpha\beta_i$. As discussed in Section 4.1, one way to implement the efficient quantity of each fuel is for the regulator to impose a carbon tax equal to α, which results is a differential tax for each fuel depending on its emission rate.

But we can also consider a more general set of tax levels that need not be set to maximize social welfare. The total emissions will be decreasing in the carbon tax level, and we know from our previous discussion that the emissions reductions associated with each are implemented at least cost. Taking the ratio of the first-order conditions with any tax yields the following useful condition:

$$\frac{p - c_l'(q_l)}{p - c_h'(q_h)} = \frac{\beta_l}{\beta_h}. \tag{10}$$

This tells us that the ratio of the private net benefits between fuels must equal the ratio of their relative emissions rates, and this is equivalent to the ratio of the taxes for each fuel that the producer internalizes. Equation (10) is useful because it identifies a necessary and sufficient condition for cost effective emissions reductions, which is of course also necessary for overall efficiency.

Let us now define a performance standard as an upper limit σ on the producer's average emissions per unit of electricity generation:

$$\frac{\beta_l q_l + \beta_h q_h}{q_l + q_h} \leq \sigma \tag{11}$$

Assuming the standard is binding and feasible means that the equation will hold with equality and that $\beta_l < \sigma < \beta_h$. Substituting (11) into the firms profit maximization problem, and solving for the first-order conditions, we find the following necessary condition for the solution:

$$\frac{p - c_l'(q_l)}{p - c_h'(q_h)} = \frac{\beta_l - \sigma}{\beta_h - \sigma}. \tag{12}$$

The right-hand side represents the ratio of the policy induced costs the firm faces between fuels. Because $\beta_l - \sigma < 0$ and $\beta_h - \sigma > 0$, the standard effectively subsidizes q_l while taxing q_h. Intuitively, there is an incentive to use more of the low emissions fuel because it relaxes the performance constraint.

The key insight comes from a comparison between equations (10) and (12). With the setup here, and assuming the standard causes a reduction in emissions, it can never be cost effective (or efficient). Expression (10) shows how this requires taxing both fuels, whereas (12) shows how the performance standard taxes one and subsidizes the other. The result is an increase in q_l and a decrease in q_h. What is more, it is possible for emissions to increase with the performance standard relative to no policy at all. Intuition for this counterproductive result can be seen right from the standard itself, as one way to comply is to increase output, which can increase emissions even if the average emissions rate declines.

Holland et al. (2009) generalize the basic framework in many ways. They account for price endogeneity, different ways of defining the performance standard to accommodate a range of potential settings, and trading of credits among regulated entities that reduces compliance costs. It is worth noting, however, that unlike a cap-and-trade program the number of credits is not fixed with a performance based standard. While the simple setup described here produces the stark result that performance based standards are less efficient than an emissions tax, others have identified particular circumstances where this need not be the case, and performance standards can be efficient or preferable to taxes in a second-best setting. These results depend on existence of a zero emissions option, perfectly inelastic demand, and whether or not there is leakage or market power (Holland, 2009; Holland et al., 2009; Holland, 2012; Fell et al., 2017).

9.2 Electricity sector emission rates

China commenced operation of an emissions trading program in 2021 with coverage of the electric power sector. The program is a performance based standard with tradable credits, and it is the largest emissions trading program in the world, covering an estimated 9.3 % of global emissions (World Bank, 2024a). Long and Goulder (2023) provide a detailed description of the particular features of China's program, including the preceding pilot programs that began in 2013. An important feature of the program is the use of different benchmark emissions rates for different types of electricity generators. While intended to address distributional concerns at the regional level, the different benchmark standards further limit the program's potential cost effectiveness. Studies have found that employing a single benchmark would reduce compliance costs significantly, and the compliance costs of the emissions trading system itself far exceed what they could have been with an emissions equivalent cap-and-trade program (Goulder et al., 2022, 2023).

Although never implemented in the United States, the Obama administration's Clean Power Plan was intended as a performance based policy to reduce CO_2 emissions in the U.S. electricity sector. An interesting feature of the policy design is that states were afforded the flexibility to choose between the performance based approach, which many believed was anchored in the statutory basis of the Clean Air Act, or an emissions equivalent cap-and-trade program. While both approaches sought to promote the efficiency gains of emissions trading, they were designed subject to different legal constraints, whereby the cap-and-trade approach would be more cost effective, but states needed to opt in (U.S. EPA, 2015). The most recent iteration of U.S. federal regulations to reduce CO_2 emissions from the use of fossil fuels in the electricity sector adopts neither approach and reverts back to a command-and-control type of direct regulation on the emission rates of particular electricity generating units (U.S. EPA, 2024).

9.3 Renewable portfolio standards

Renewable portfolio standards (RPS) seek to increase the generation of electricity from renewable sources of energy in order to reduce emissions. In general, a RPS requires that suppliers of electricity meet a minimum share of electricity generation (i.e., a rate based requirement) from approved renewable sources by a specified date. Another feature of many RPS programs is the establishment of trading systems based on renewable energy credits (RECs). Electricity suppliers that use more renewable sources of generation than the RPS requires can earn RECs that can be sold to others that fall short of the RPS requirement. There is wide variability in the particular design features of RPS programs, and many countries have implemented a RPS in various ways, including the United Kingdom, China, Mexico, Australia, and the majority of states in the United States. Deschenes and Malloy (2023) and Feldman and Levinson (2023) review the literature that seeks to estimate a causal effect of U.S. state RPS programs on various outcomes and provide estimates of their own. The results are generally mixed across studies, but most find state RPS programs have reduced GHG emissions, increased wind generation, and increased electricity prices. In another study, Greenstone and Nath (2024) estimate the cost of CO_2 emissions reductions across U.S. RPS programs as ranging between \$80 and \$210 per ton.

9.4 Low carbon fuel standards

Low carbon fuel standards (LCFS) seek to reduce the average carbon intensity of transportation fuels. A LCFS sets an industry-wide intensity target, and producers or importers of carbon intensive fuels can meet the target through two potential mechanisms. The first is to blend into their supply lower carbon intensity fuels (e.g., biofuels), and the second is to purchase credits from fuel suppliers with lower carbon intensities that fall under the target. The LCFS credits are then traded through a market mechanism that creates incentives to meet the overall, industry-wide intensity target at least cost. In the United States, California's LCFS has been in place since 2007, while Oregon and Washington have more recently followed. Several other states also have pending or recently failed LCFS policies. Other countries and regions with an LCFS are the United Kingdom, the European Union, and British Columbia, Canada. Yeh et al. (2016) provide a detailed overview and evaluation of California's LCFS, its interaction with other policies, and comparisons to other programs. Holland et al. (2009) simulate the effects of a national LCFS in the United States to explore the effects on emissions, efficiency, and cost effectiveness of different program designs.

While the United States does not have a federal LCFS that targets emissions intensity, there is a federal Renewable Fuel Standard (RFS) that was first enacted in 2005 and requires a blending of biofuels into the vehicle fuel supply, with a system of tradable compliance permits referred to as Renewable (fuel) Identification Numbers (RINs). The RFS is effectively a tax on petroleum fuels and a subsidy on biofuels that is revenue neutral. Much of the research focused on the RFS has nevertheless focused on the unintended environmental consequences that occur through shifts in agricultural production (Lark et al., 2022) and on the pass-through of RIN prices to fuel markets (Knittel et al., 2017).

9.5 Vehicle fuel economy standards

Vehicle fuel economy standards are another area were performance based standards have been applied. Two economic rationales motivate these policies: reducing fuel consumption, and therefore emissions, and correcting the behavioral market failure whereby consumers misperceive the benefits of improved energy efficiency (Anderson et al., 2011). Since 1975, the United States has had a Corporate Average Fuel Economy (CAFE) standard, and the particulars of the program have changed over time. The basic contours of the program in place now include an average fuel economy standard that manufactures must meet for a specific category of vehicle, and the creation of tradable credits when a manufacturer exceeds the standard. Other countries have fuel economy standards with a similar structure, including China, Canada, India, Mexico, and the Eurpean Union (Cazzola et al., 2023). There is a large literature with research that evaluates various aspects of CAFE standards. Interest focuses on the benefits and costs that include how the standards affect vehicle prices, sales, composition, attributes, miles traveled, externalities, distributional effects, and implications on the used car fleet along with comparisons to other policy instruments (Austin and Dinan, 2005; Klier and Linn, 2012; Jacobsen, 2013; Bento et al., 2020).

9.6 Feebates

A pricing instrument can also be used to implement a performance based standard. A "feebate" is a combination fee (or tax) on units of output that do not meet a performance standard and a rebate (or subsidy) on those that do. For example, Gillingham (2013) shows an equivalence between CAFE standards and an appropriately calibrated feebate that penalizes and rewards low- and high-fuel economy vehicles, respectively. Underlying this result is a mechanism similar to the price and quantity equivalence we encountered earlier between an emissions tax and a cap-and-trade program when there is no uncertainty. Indeed, accounting for uncertainty, Wang et al. (2022) show that a modified Weitzman (1974) rule can be used to compare feebates and tradable performance standards, with applications to China's emissions trading system and California's LCFS.

10 Policy interactions

We have thus far considered climate policy options one at a time and in isolation, ignoring the possibility for overlapping instruments, objectives, or both. Much of the academic literature and policy implementation in the real world proceeds with the same simplifying assumption. But there are a growing number of instances where climate policies overlap, and understanding how they interact is increasingly important as the number of policies continues to grow. At the same time, many policies seek to accomplish more than one objective, including the reduction of GHG emissions and the promotion of equity and environmental justice. This section provides a discussion of overlapping policies, general equilibrium approaches, and recent policy shifts that encourage greater consideration of distributional and equity effects.

10.1 Overlapping policies

There are many examples of overlapping climate policies. At the most general level, policies that seek to price fossil fuels to internalize externalities are often layered over an entrenched set of preexisting fossil fuel subsidies that push prices in the opposite direction. In the electricity sector, there are policies that subsidize renewable sources of generation, while others mandate their use, price emissions intensive alternatives, or both. With transportation fuels, we have biofuel subsidies concurrent with mandates for their use in low carbon fuel standards. A final example is that we subsidize low emissions vehicles, including electric vehicles (EVs), at the some time there are CAFE standards and targets that mandate future EV sales.

When it comes to overlapping climate policies, issues and opportunities arise across subnational, national, and international levels (Goulder and Stavins, 2011; Shobe and Burtraw, 2012; Metcalf and Weisbach, 2012). The mix of different instruments is sometimes referred to as a "belts and suspenders" approach (Levinson, 2012), and a key question is whether, and the degree to which, policies can be mutually reinforcing or in conflict. Policies can be reinforcing when there is more than one market failure or when the administrative costs differ across instruments. Conflicts might arise when, for example, a cap-and-trade program is layered on top of an existing standard. In these cases, an important condition is whether the permit price is greater than or less than the marginal cost of complying with the standard. If the permit price is lower, the standard is binding and cost effectiveness of the cap-and-trade program will be limited. Levinson (2012) suggests even this simple comparison might sound a note of caution for cap-and-trade programs, as permit prices are often lower than predicted. Empirical studies of overlapping policies have, for example, examined how complementary policies affect emissions permit prices (Borenstein et al., 2019), how the presence of both fuel economy and emissions standards can distort credit trading markets (Leard and McConnell, 2017), and how renewable energy subsides can increase co-pollutants in a cap-and-trade program (Novan, 2017).

Constructing a general framework that accounts for overlapping policies is difficult in part because the underlying rationales are often complex, involving a mix of political economy. Perino et al. (2023) nevertheless make progress on a framework to evaluate the emissions consequences of policies that overlap an existing carbon pricing system. Their framework, which includes empirical illustrations, considers how different policy features create deviations from two extreme cases where an overlapping policy will have no effect. The first is "internal carbon leakage," where a product-market shift causes an offsetting decrease and increase in demand for tradable emissions permits. The second is the "waterbed effect" in the carbon market, where a system-wide decrease in demand for permits only lowers the permit price with no change in emissions because the total allocation is fixed. An immediate result, for example, is that the waterbed effect no longer holds with a carbon tax instead of a cap-and-trade program.

While empirical evaluations of policy in the academic literature often take great care to control for the confounding effects of other policies, more attention in theoretical work to the cases where overlapping policies might be important is an area of need. Finally, with respect to management of overlapping policies in practice, there is a need for more institutionalization of reporting, especially in the domain of clean energy subsidies, where a complicated patchwork of incentives potentially undermines the effectiveness of clean energy subsidies (Aldy et al., 2022).

10.2 General equilibrium approaches

Climate policies will have broad effects on the economy, if they are big enough to meaningfully reduce GHG emissions. In these cases, partial equilibrium perspectives will be limited in their ability to fully inform policy design and evaluation. Much progress has been made over the last three decades on general equilibrium analysis of environmental policies. An important insight of the literature is recognition of how large scale policies, such as those seeking to address climate change, will interact with pre-existing tax distortions. Questions about the "double dividend hypothesis" have spurred research is this area.

Might there be two distinct benefits (i.e., dividends) of imposing a revenue-raising climate policy, such as a carbon tax or a cap-and-trade system with auctioned permits? That a welfare gain occurs because of the reduction in emissions is clear. More subtle is the potential for a second dividend, whereby tax revenue from the climate policy can be used to reduce other distortionary taxes such as those on labor or capital. The second dividend's possibility captures imagination because, if true, it means that climate policy is beneficial even without concern for the environmental benefits.

The direct mechanisms underlying the two dividends are referred to as the "Pigouvian welfare" effect and the "revenue recycling" effect. Complicating matters, however, is a third mechanism that might arise because of interactions between a newly imposed climate policy and pre-existing distortionary taxes, referred to as the "tax interaction" effect. Early research cast doubt on the existence of the second dividend, finding that a negative tax interaction effect is likely to outweigh the beneficial revenue recycling effect (Bovenberg and de Mooij, 1994; Parry, 1995). Subsequent analyses have found grounds for more optimism (Bovenberg and Goulder, 1997; Parry and Bento, 2000). Bento (2024) provides a recent overview of how different assumptions affect results in the literature and their empirical importance, and Freire-González (2018) provides a detailed meta-analysis. Although evidence on the double dividend is mixed, two things are clear: the environmental rational for climate policy is robust, and recognizing that policy formation takes place in a second-best setting can affect instrument choice (Parry et al., 1999; Fullerton and Metcalf, 2001; Bovenberg and Goulder, 2002).

General equilibrium approaches have also been used recently to examine the distributional effects of climate policy. Goulder et al. (2019) provide an example. They consider how an economy-wide carbon tax in the United States will affect households, accounting for both use-side and source-side effects. Use-side effects arise because changes in prices affect purchasing power, and source-side effects are due to changes in income. Goulder et al. (2019) confirm the results of previous studies showing that use-side effects are regressive, source-side effects are progressive, and the net effect appears to be progressive or at least close to proportional. A further contribution of their analysis is estimation of the efficiency sacrifices necessary to avoid distributional outcomes that adversely affect low income households.

10.3 Distributional effects and equity objectives

Economics has a long tradition of separating efficiency and distributional concerns when is comes to the design and evaluation of policy. But as concerns about equity and distributional impacts continue to grow, economists are being pushed to do more, and appropriately so. The shift in focus is evident in research on climate policy, where an increasing number of papers characterize the distributional consequences of both proposed and actual policies. The Goulder et al. (2019) paper just discussed provides and example of a proposed policy. More generally, studies have considered the distributional consequences of a range of policies, including gasoline taxes, cap-and-trade programs, fuel economy standards, building codes, and renewable energy subsides. Borenstein and Davis (2024) provide a recent example that is typical, although they consider several different policies. They examine the distributional impacts of U.S. tax credits for heat pumps, solar panels, and electric vehicles. The overall finding, consistent with others in the literature, is that tax credits disproportionately benefit higher-income households. The results illustrate how policies that aim to address climate change, and therefore promote efficiency, often have undesirable distributional consequences.

The causality can also run in the other direction, when policies that aim to address distributional concerns have an efficiency cost. Arthur Okun (1975) famously characterizes the general tradeoff with the analogy of a leaky bucket: accomplishing redistribution goals comes with an efficiency loss, with the bucket representing redistribution efforts and having less water (because of the leak) the efficiency cost. Climate policies are nevertheless increasingly designed with equity in mind. In an international context, multilateral climate funds, such those part of the Green Climate Fund and the Global Environmental Facility, establish windows of funding for particular countries or regions rather than allocating funds globally to maximize impact. The Justice40 Initiative in the United States is another example, where 40 % of the benefits of climate, clean energy, and other public investments are to be directed towards regions specifically designated as disadvantaged. Rudik et al. (2025) provide estimates of the equity-efficiency tradeoff of the Justic40 Initiative on climate related spending of the 2021 U.S. Bipartisan Infrastructure Law.

More research along these lines is surely forthcoming, as equity goals of climate policy are becoming more explicit and major climate regulations establish more of a track record. While these tradeoffs are important to identify and evaluate, questions of interpretation are open to debate. There is an argument for why linking climate and equity objectives makes both harder to accomplish (Levinson and Fullerton, 2022), the thrust of which is that regulation should focus on expanding the size of the pie, and redistribution should be left to the tax system. But these arguments assume feasibility of separate policies to accomplish different objectives, and whether this counterfactual is possible is itself likely to be its own source of debate.

Also likely to further scholarly interest in equity and distributional issues are recent revisions to the U.S. official guidance on how to conduct federal benefit-cost analysis (US OMB, 2023). In particular, the guidance opens the door for federal agencies to use distributional weights for the impacts on different groups based on estimates of diminishing marginal utility of income. While many might find the approach appealing because it up-weights impacts on lower income groups, questions and concerns arise because weighted benefit-cost analysis no longer has the same basis in welfare economics (Adler, 2016; Banzhaf, 2023). The approach also raises questions that are likely to become more important for climate policy in particular. Distributional weighting is already used in some cases for estimation of the SCC (Anthoff and Emmerling, 2019). But will countries choose to apply the same inequality aversion across countries as they do within their own country? We have already discussed in Section 2.3 questions about whether countries will seek to internalize domestic or global climate damages, and equity weighting adds another dimension in need of even further research. Indeed, when discussing distributional weighting, the new guidance focuses on domestic benefits and costs, and there is relatively little mention of international impacts, other than to state that altering the approach "may be appropriate when analyzing regulations with international scope" (US OMB, 2023, p. 67).

11 Voluntary and information based approaches

Voluntary and information based approaches (VIBAs) to climate policy seek to provide more complete information so that markets can adjust more efficiently and opportunities can emerge for voluntary actions to address climate challenges. This final section includes discussion about information disclosure, voluntary programs, and the ways that VIBAs might serve as complements or substitutes for other climate policies.

11.1 Disclosure strategies

One source of market failure with respect to climate change is incomplete or asymmetric information. Market participants are often unaware, or are unable to observe, how their consumption and production choices affect emissions, or how investments face different policy or climate risks. Markets will not function efficiently with such incomplete information. Individuals who want to reduce their personal carbon footprint may prefer goods and services with lower carbon intensities, but they can only find the low-carbon alternatives if the information is available or at least not too costly to obtain. Moreover, investors believing more stringent climate policies are forthcoming will only know which firms are most exposed if information on emissions is available. Nevertheless, the provision of complete and accurate information is rarely incentive compatible and suffers from further under-provision because it is a public good.

Information disclosure policies seek to solve these market failures through the improved provision of information, which in turn can promote efficiency through various adjustments in product, capital, and labor markets, as well as by spurring the potential for judicial and legislative action. Tietenberg (1998) identifies information disclosure policies as the "third wave" of environmental policy, following the first wave of command-and-control regulations and the second wave of market-based instruments.

Policies that mandate climate related disclosures are beginning to gain traction, requiring that companies report their GHG emissions along with information about climate-related risks. Prominent examples, both scheduled to take effect in 2026, are recent legislation in California applicable to companies doing business in the state, and the U.S. Securities and Exchange Commission's requirements for all publicly traded companies reporting in U.S. markets. These follow the EU's Corporate Sustainability Reporting Directive that commenced in 2024 and has specific requirements related to emissions, risks, and company policies. While it is too early to tell how these disclosure policies will affect markets and emissions, research to answer these questions is sure to be forthcoming. Greenstone et al. (2023) provide an early indication of what the reporting might look like based on a third-party data set of global companies. They make comparisons across industries and countries, focusing not only on emissions, but also on the economic value of damages in accordance with the notion of implicit subsides discussed in Section 4.3.

11.2 Voluntary programs

While the policies just discussed implement mandatory disclosure, there are many voluntary disclosure programs around the world that focus on reporting emissions and climate risk. Examples include the Carbon Disclosure Project (CDP) and the Global Reporting Initiative (GRI). Many of the voluntary programs exist not only to report information, but to signal environmental and climate commitments such that participants gain reputational benefits. For example, the Net-Zero Banking Alliance is a United Nations convened program of global banks that receive membership through commitments to activities that promote reaching net-zero GHG emissions. Another example is the Climate Neutral Certification that companies can obtain if they comply with the third-party protocol of the Climate Impact Partners, which stipulates specific measures to reduce emissions.

There is an environmental economics literature focused on voluntary programs. In an early theoretical contribution, Segerson and Miceli (1998) consider, for example, how the threat of future regulation can induce participation in a voluntary program, with potentially positive or negative consequences for environmental quality. Voluntary programs can be designed to tap into consumer willingness to pay for impure public goods, which combine a private benefit with provision of an environmental public good (Kotchen, 2006). A paper by van't Veld and Kotchen (2011) shows how club theory can illuminate the understanding of voluntary programs, as membership provides a non-rival and excludable benefit, and the program's sponsor (e.g., government, industry, or a nongovernmental organization) will affect the expected program impacts. A number of studies have sought to evaluate the effectiveness of voluntary programs (Morgenstern and Pizer, 2007; Borck and Coglianese, 2009), and perhaps unsurprisingly, the results are quite mixed. Only some find significant effects on environmental outcomes, and the results differ by industry and phases of the program. Many studies also face empirical challenges owing to the way that voluntary participation is endogenous to the outcomes of interest, and programs are likely to have spillover effects (Zhou et al., 2020).

11.3 Behavioral approaches

Another form of climate policy is the strategic use of information to nudge behavioral change in ways that tap into social and psychological mechanisms. There is large literature on the topic that employs both observational and experimental methods, with many applications to energy conservation and the adoption of renewable energy technologies. One approach is the use of social comparisons that report information along with a normative signal about what constitutes pro-social behavior. Opower Home Energy Reports are a prominent example, whereby electric utilities notify households of their own electricity consumption in comparison to those of other similar households, indicating that lower consumption (i.e., efficiency) is a pro-social behavior. Allcott (2011) and Allcott and Rogers (2014) find that the Opower messaging decreases electricity consumption, persistency of the notifications matter, and some long-term (although smaller) behavioral adjustments remain even after notifications cease. Others have examined the effect of moral suasion to induce conservation behavior and compared its effects to pricing instruments (Reiss and White, 2008; Ito et al., 2018). Peer effects also exert a positive influence on energy and climate related behaviors, with evidence in particular on the adoption of residential solar photovoltaic panels (Gillingham and Bollinger 2012), and information about behavioral motives is being used to develop programs that promote participation in renewable energy programs (Jacobsen et al., 2013; Carattini et al., 2014).

11.4 Complements or substitutes

The appeal of VIBAs from a policy perspective is their potential for relatively low cost and cost-effective interventions. But because of the global public goods nature of the climate change problem, VIBAs are unlikely to be effective substitutes for more direct and centralized forms of climate policy on a large scale. Even the most successful VIBAs still face powerful disincentives for private provision of GHG emission reductions—a global public good. That is, while VIBAs may help mitigate emissions in many settings, the instances in which they themselves will produce economically efficient outcomes in practice are likely to be few and far between.

The ways in which VIBAs can serve as complements or substitutes for other forms of climate policy is an important question. In the United States, for example, fuel economy labels on new vehicle purchases reinforce fuel economy standards, and certified energy efficient appliances through the EnergyStar program also qualify for rebates. In other settings, however, the pursuit of a VIBAs can crowd out policies that might be more effective, as VIBAs are less likely to face political opposition compared to alternative policies that impose new taxes or regulatory standards. Finally, a recent strand of research focuses on how recognizing the presence of voluntary behaviors interacts with centralized policies and can affect instrument choice (Costello and Kotchen, 2022; Chan, 2024; Kaufmann et al., 2024). This provides another example of the ways in which researchers are increasingly focused on policy interactions as discussed in Section 10.

12 Conclusion

The aim of this paper has been to provide an overview of the standard economics "toolkit" of climate policy instruments. As mentioned at the outset, the focus has been on policies that create incentives for the internalization of at least some portion of the external costs associated with GHG emissions. Important topics that are missing, but will be covered in other chapters, include but are not limited to adaptation, finance, industrial policy, innovation, research and development, and international agreements. While a bit of formal modeling has been inserted at points, the discussion has been primarily narrative and intended to convey basic ideas and on-ramps to the literature where readers can find more advanced and detailed treatments in both theoretical and empirical papers. The preceding discussion has also sought to provide real-world examples of the different policy instruments. Efforts have been made to reference examples from around the world, yet there is an unmistakable bias towards those in the United States, reflecting only the author's greater familiarity.

All of the policy instruments discussed here apply not only to the problem of climate change, but also environmental problems more generally. Hence it is reasonable to ask: what, if anything, is different about the economics of climate policy that is not already covered in the economics of environmental policy? A theme of this paper, which provides and answer by way of emphasis, is that climate change is ultimately a problem of global collective action. This means that when it comes to climate change, regulators do not have authority to set policy that covers the full scope of the problem, which also includes future generations. In this way, climate change is fundamentally different from most other environmental problems. This often means that climate policy is not set with overall efficiency as the objective, and this differs from the typical focus of environmental economics on the design of policy to maximize efficiency. While this feature of climate policy poses significant real-world challenges, it also creates new frontiers for research.

What are the promising directions for future research? While making predictions is a risky business, some of the topics covered here may provide insight in at least a few areas. First, there is a need for more scholarly attention on the question of what should be the objectives of climate policy. Tremendous effort is focused on estimating various aspects of the SCC, but how policy-makers should use these estimates in the formation of climate policy is a more nuanced question than scholars often recognized or acknowledge. Moreover, to the extent that target consistent approaches gain traction, there will be an increasing need for estimates of economy-wide marginal abatement costs. Second, we can expect a surge of interest in empirical research that evaluates the cost effectiveness of green subsidy policies given the scale of these programs as part of an emergence of green industrial policy in the United States and other countries. This research is important to provide insight on how to use public resources most effectively. Third, research is needed on how to improve markets for carbon offsets—accounting for measurement, verification and pricing—because these markets, troubled as they may seem, provide opportunities for gains from trade that can significantly reduce the costs of lowering GHG emissions. Finally, an important area of emerging climate policy research focuses on open economies and trade policy. This is fundamentally important because of the way that stabilizing the climate is a global public good and economies are linked through trade. While advances have been made to the understanding of emissions taxes in these settings, which are typically the favored instrument of economists, little attention has been given to the role of subsidies, which are increasingly a favored instrument of policymakers.

References

Adler, M.D., 2016. Benefit–cost analysis and distributional weights: an overview. Review of Environmental Economics and Policy 10, 264–285.

Aldy, J.E., 2015. Policy surveillance in the G-20 fossil fuel subsidies agreement: lessons for climate policy. Climatic Change 144, 97–110.

Aldy, J.E., Atkinson, G., Kotchen, M.J., 2021. Environmental benefit-cost analysis: a comparative analysis between the United States and the United Kingdom. Annual Review of Resource Economics 13, 267–288.

Aldy, J.E., Burtraw, D., Fischer, C., Fowlie, M., Williams, R.C., Cropper, M.L., 2022. How is the U.S. pricing carbon? How could we price carbon? Journal of Benefit-Cost Analysis 13, 310–334.

Aldy, J.E., Gerarden, T.D., Sweeney, R.L., 2023. Investment versus output subsidies: implications of alternative incentives for wind energy. Journal of the Association of Environmental and Resource Economists 10, 981–1018.

Aldy, J.E., Kotchen, M.J., Stavins, R.N., Stock, J.H., 2021b. Keep climate policy focused on the social cost of carbon. Science 373, 850–852.

Aldy, J.E., Krupnick, A.J., Newell, R.C., Parry, I.W.H., Pizer, W.A., 2010. Designing climate mitigation policy. Journal of Economic Literature 48, 903–934.

Allcott, H., 2011. Social norms and energy conservation. Journal of Public Economics 95, 1082–1095.

Allcott, H., Rogers, T., 2014. The short-run and long-run effects of behavioral interventions: experimental evidence from energy conservation. American Economic Review 104, 3003–3037.

Anderson, S.T., Parry, I.W.H., Sallee, J.M., Fischer, C., 2011. Automobile fuel economy standards: impacts, efficiency, and alternatives. Review of Environmental Economics and Policy 5, 89–108.

Anthoff, D., Emmerling, J., 2019. Inequality and the social cost of carbon. Journal of the Association of Environmental and Resource Economists 2, 243–273.

Armitage, S., Bakhtian, N., Jaffe, A., 2024. Innovation market failures and the design of new climate policy instruments. Environmental and Energy Policy and the Economy 5, 4–48.

Austin, D., Dinan, T., 2005. Clearing the air: the costs and consequences of higher CAFE standards and increased gasoline taxes. Journal of Environmental Economics and Management 50, 562–582.

Banzhaf, H.S., 2023. Distribution and disputation: net benefits, equity, and public decision-making. Journal of Benefit-Cost Analysis 14, 205–229.

Barron, A., Fawcett, A., Hafstead, M., McFarland, J., Morris, A., 2018. Policy insights from the EMF 32 study on U.S. carbon tax scenarios. Climate Change Economics 9, 1–37.

Barrage, L., Nordhaus, W., 2024. Policies, projections, and the social cost of carbon: results from the DICE-2023 model. Proceedings of the National Academy of Sciences 121, e2312030121.

Bartlett, J., 2023. Beyond subsidy levels: the effects of tax credit choice for solar and wind power in the Inflation Reduction Act, Resources for the Future Report 23–20, Washington, DC.

Bento, A.M., 2024. Environmental Policy and the Double Dividend Hypothesis. Oxford Research Encyclopedia of Environmental Science.

Bento, A.M., Jacobsen, M.R., Knittel, C.R., van Benthem, A.A., 2020. Estimating the costs and benefits of fuel-economy standards. Environmental and Energy Policy and the Economy 1, 129–157.

Bistline, J., Clausing, K.A., Mehorotra, N.R., Stock, J.H., Wolfram, C., 2025. Climate policy reform options in 2025, Environmental and Energy Policy and the Economy, forthcoming.

Bistline, J.E.T., Mehrotra, N.R., Wolfram, C., 2023. Economic implications of the climate provisions of the inflation reduction act. Brookings Papers on Economic Activity, Spring 77–157.

Black, S., Liu, A.A., Parry, I., Vernon, N., 2023. IMF fossil fuel subsidies data: 2030 update, IMF Working Paper WP/23/169, Washington, DC.

Böhringer, C., Fischer, C., Rosendahl, K.E., Rutherford, T.F., 2022. Potential impacts and challenges of border carbon adjustments. Nature Climate Change 12, 22–29.

Böhringer, C., Lange, A., Rutherford, T.F., 2014. Optimal emission pricing in the presence of international spillovers: decomposing leakage and terms-of-trade motives. Journal of Public Economics 110, 101–111.

Böhringer, C., Rosendahl, K.E., Storrøsten, H.B., 2017. Robust policies to mitigate carbon leakage. Journal of Public Economics 149, 35–46.

Borck, J.C., Coglianese, C., 2009. Voluntary environmental programs: assessing their effectiveness. Annual Review of Environment and Resources 34, 305–324.

Borenstein, S., Bushnell, J., Wolak, F.A., Zaragoza-Watkins, M., 2019. Expecting the unexpected: emissions uncertainty and environmental market design. American Economic Review 109, 3953–3977.

Borenstein, S., Davis, L., 2024. The distributional effects of U.S. tax credits for heat pumps, solar panels, and electric vehicles, Energy Institute at Haas Working Paper 348R.

Bovenberg, A.L., de Mooij, R., 1994. Environmental levies and distortionary taxation. American Economic Review 94, 1085–1089.

Bovenberg, A.L., Goulder, L.H., 1997. Costs of environmentally motivated taxes in the presence of other taxes: general equilibrium analyses. National Tax Journal 50, 59–87.

Bovenberg, A.L., Goulder, L.H., 2002. Chapter 23 – Environmental taxation and regulation. In: Auerbach, A.J., Feldstein, M. (Eds.), Handbook of Public Economics. 3. Elsevier, pp. 1471–1545.

Branger, F., Quiron, P., 2014. Climate policy and the "carbon haven" effect. Wiley Interdisciplinary Reviews: Climate Change 5, 53–71.

Brooks, S.A., Keohane, N.O., 2020. The political economy of hybrid approaches to a U.S. carbon tax: a perspective from the policy world. Review of Environmental Economics and Policy 14, 67–75.

Burtraw, D., Keyes, A., 2018. Recognizing gravity as a strong force in atmosphere emissions markets. Agricultural and Resource Economics Review 47, 201–219.

Calel, R., Colmer, J., Dechezlepretre, A., Glachant, M., 2024. Do carbon offsets offset carbon? American Economic American Economic Journal: Applied Economics, forthcoming.

Carattini, S., Gillingham, K., Meng, X., Yoeli, E., 2014. Peer-to-peer solar and social rewards: evidence from a field experiment. Journal of Economic Behavior and Organization 219, 340–370.

Carleton, T., Jina, A., Delgado, M., Greenstone, M., Houser, T., Hsiang, S., Hultgren, R., Kopp, R., McCusker, K., Nath, I., Rising, J., Rode, A., Seo, H., Viaene, V., Yuan, J., Zhang, A., 2022. Valuing the global mortality consequences of climate change accounting for adaptation costs and benefits. Quarterly Journal of Economics 137, 2037–2105.

Cazzola, P., Paoli, L., Teter, J., 2023. Trends in the global vehicle fleet 2023, Global Fuel Economy Initiative. UC Davis Institute of Tranformation Studies. https://doi.org/10.7922/G2HM56SV

Chan, N.W., 2024. Pigouvian policies under behavioral motives. Journal of the Association of Environmental and Resource Economists 11, 97–135.

Coase, R.H., 1960. The problem of social cost. Journal of Law and Economics 3, 1–44.

Copeland, B.R., Shapiro, J.S., Taylor, M.S., 2022. Chapter 2 – Globalization and the environment. In: Gopinath, G., Helpman, E., Rogoff, K. (Eds.), Handbook of International Economics. Elsevier, pp. 61–146 Volume 5.

Costello, C., Kotchen, M.J., 2022. Policy instrument choice with Coasean provision of public goods. Journal of the Association of Environmental and Resource Economists 9, 947–980.

Dales, J.H., 1968. Pollution, Property, and Prices. University of Toronto Press, Toronto.

De Groote, O., Verboven, F., 2019. Subsidies and time discounting in new technology adoption: evidence from solar photovoltaic systems. American Economic Review 109, 2137–2172.

Dechezlepretre, A., Fabre, A., Kruse, T., Planterose, B., Chico, A.S., Stantcheva, S., 2022. Fighting climate change: international attitudes toward climate policies, NBER Working Paper 30265, Cambridge, MA.

Deryugina, T., Moore, F., Tol, R.S.J., 2021. Environmental applications of the Coase Theorem. Environmental Science and Policy 120, 81–88.

Deschenes, O., Malloy, C., McDonald, 2023. Causal effects of Renewable Portfolio Standards on renewable investments and generation: the role of heterogeneity and dynamics. Resource and Energy Economics 75, 101393.

Energy Agency (IEA), 2023. Fossil Fuels Consumption Subsidies 2022, IEA, Paris https://www.iea.org/reports/fossil-fuels-consumption-subsidies-2022, Licence: CC BY 4.0.

Energy Information Administration, EIA, 2024. Energy System of Germany, Accessed online July 25, at https://www.iea.org/countries/germany.

Feldman, R., Levinson, A., 2023. Renewable portfolio standards. The Energy Journal 44, 1–20.

Fell, H., Kaffine, D., Steinberg, D., 2017. Energy efficiency and emissions intensity standards. Journal of the Association of Environmental and Resource Economists 4, S201–S226.

Fowlie, M.L., 2009. Incomplete environmental regulation, imperfect competition, and emissions leakage. American Economic Journal: Economic Policy 1, 72–112.

Fowlie, M.L., Reguant, M., 2022. Mitigating emissions leakage in incomplete carbon markets. Journal of the Association of Environmental and Resource Economists 9, 307–343.

Freire-González, J., 2018. Environmental taxation and the double dividend hypothesis in CGE modelling literature: a critical review. Journal of Policy Modeling 40, 194–223.

Frondel, M., Ritter, N., Schmidt, C.M., Vance, C., 2010. Economic impacts from the promotion of renewable energy technologies: the German experience. Energy Policy 38, 4048–4056.

Fullerton, D., Metcalf, G.E., 2001. Environmental controls, scarcity rents, and pre-existing distortions. Journal of Public Economics 80, 249–267.

G-20Leaders, 2009. G-20 Leaders' Declaration, Pittsburgh G-20, September.

Gayer, T., Viscusi, W.K., 2016. Determining the proper scope of climate change policy benefits in U.S. regulatory analyses: domestic versus global approaches. Review of Environmental Economics and Policy 10, 245–263.

Gillingham, K., 2013. The Economics of Fuel Economy Standards Versus Feebates. Working Paper. National Energy Policy Institute, Washington, DC.

Gillingham, K., Stock, J.H., 2018. The cost of reducing greenhouse gas emission. Journal of Economic Perspectives 32, 53–72.

Goulder, L.H., Hafstead, M.A.C., Kim, G., Long, X., 2019. Impacts of a carbon tax across US household income groups: what are the equity-efficiency tradeoffs? Journal of Public Economics 175, 44–64.

Goulder, L.H., Long, X., Lu, J., Morgenstern, R.D., 2022. China's unconventional nationwide CO_2 emissions trading system: cost-effectiveness and distributional impacts. Journal of Environmental Economics and Management 111, 102561.

Goulder, L.H., Long, X., Qu, C., Zhang, D., 2023. China's nationwide CO_2 emissions trading system: a general equilibrium assessment, NBER Working Paper 31809, Cambridge, MA.

Goulder, L.H., Stavins, R.N., 2011. Challenges from state-federal interactions in US climate change policy. American Economic Review 101, 253–257.

Graff Zivin, J., Kotchen, M.J., Mansur, E.T., 2014. Spatial and temporal heterogeneity in marginal emissions: implications for electric cars and other electricity-shifting policies. Journal of Economic Behavior and Organization 107, 248–268.

Greenstone, M., Leuz, C., Breuer, P., 2023. Mandatory disclosure would reveal corporate carbon damages. Science 381, 837–840.

Greenstone, M., Nath, I., 2024. Do renewable portfolio standards deliver cost-effective carbon abatement? Working Paper No. 2019–62, Energy Policy Institute at the University of Chicago.

Groom, B., Venmans, F., 2023. The social value of offsets. Nature 619, 768–773.

Hafstead, M.A.C., Williams, R.C., 2020. Designing and evaluating a U.S. carbon tax adjustment mechanism to reduce emissions uncertainty. Review of Environmental Economics and Policy 14, 95–113.

Hahn, R.W., 1984. Market power and transferable property rights. Quarterly Journal of Economics 99, 753–765.

Hahn, R.W., Hendren, N., Metcalf, R.D., Sprung-Keyser, B., 2024. A welfare analysis of policies impacting climate change, NBER Working Paper 32728, Cambridge, MA.

Haites, E., Maosheng, D., Gallagher, K.S., Mascher, S., Narassimhan, E., Richards, K.R., Wakabayashi, M., 2018. Experience with carbon taxes and greenhouse gas emissions trading systems. Duke Environmental Law & Policy Forum 29, 109–182.

Harstad, B., Eskeland, G.S., 2010. Trading for the future: signaling in permit markets. Journal of Public Economics 94, 749–760.

Helfand, G.E., 1991. Standards versus standards: the effects of different pollution restrictions. American Economic Review 81, 622–634.

Hernandez-Cortes, D., Meng, K.C., 2023. Do environmental markets cause environmental injustice? Evidence from California's carbon market. Journal of Public Economics 217, 104786.

Hoel, M., 1994. Efficient climate policy in the presence of free riders. Journal of Environmental Economics and Management 27, 259–274.

Hoel, M., 1996. Should a carbon tax be differentiated across sectors? Journal of Public Economics 59, 17–32.

Holladay, J.S., Mohsin, M., Pradhan, S., 2018. Emissions leakage, environmental policy and trade frictions. Journal of Environmental Economics and Management 88, 95–113.

Holland, S.P., 2009. Taxes and trading versus intensity standards: second-best environmental policies with incomplete regulation (leakage) or market power, NBER Working Paper 15262, Cambridge, MA.

Holland, S.P., 2012. Emissions taxes versus intensity standards: second-best environmental policies with incomplete regulation. Journal of Environmental Economics and Management 63, 375–387.

Holland, S.P., Hughes, J.E., Knittel, C.R., 2009. Greenhouse gas reductions under low carbon fuel standards? American Economic Journal: Economic Policy 1, 106–146.

Holland, S.P., Kotchen, M.J., Mansur, E.T., Yates, A.J., 2022. Why marginal CO_2 emissions are not decreasing for US electricity: estimates and implications for climate policy. Proceedings of the National Academy of Sciences 119, e2116632119.

Howard, P., Schwartz, J., 2019. Think global: international reciprocity as justification for a global social cost of carbon, Columbia. Journal of Environmental Law 42 (S). https://doi.org/10.7916/cjel.v42iS.3734

Hultgren, A., Carleton, T., Delgado, M., Gergel, D., Greenstone, M., Houser, T., Hsiang, S., Jina, A., Kopp, R., Malevich, S., McCusker, K., Mayer, T., Nath, I., Rising, J., Rode A., Yuan, J., 2022. Estimating global impacts to agriculture from climate change ac-counting for adaptation, Working Paper available at https://doi.org/10.2139/ssrn.4222020.

Ito, K., Ida, T., Tanaka, M., 2018. Moral suasion and economic incentives: field experimental evidence from energy demand. American Economic Journal: Economic Policy 10, 240–267.

Jacobsen, G.D., Kotchen, M.J., Clendenning, G., 2013. Community-based incentives for environmental protection: the case of green electricity. Journal of Regulatory Economics 44, 30–52.

Jacobsen, M.R., 2013. Evaluating US fuel economy standards in a model with producer and household heterogeneity. American Economic Journal: Economic Policy 5, 148–187.

Jakob, M., 2022. How trade policy can support the climate agenda. Science 376, 1401–1403.

Jakob, M., Marschinski, R., Hübler, M., 2013. Between a rock and a hard place: a trade-theory analysis of leakage under production- and consumption-based policies. Environmental and Resource Economics 56, 47–72.

Jenner, S., Groba, F., Indvik, J., 2013. Assessing the strength and effectiveness of renewable electricity feed-in tariffs in European Union countries. Energy Policy 52, 385–401.

Karp, L., Traeger, C., 2024. Taxes versus quantities reassessed. Journal of Environmental Economics and Management 125, 102951.

Kaufman, N., Barron, A.R., Krawczyk, W., Marsters, P., Haewon, M., 2020. A near-term to net zero alternative to the social cost of carbon for setting carbon prices. Nature Climate Change 10, 1010–1014.

Kaufmann, M., Andre, P., Kőszegi, B., 2024. Understanding markets with socially responsible consumers. Quarterly Journal of Economics 139, 1989–2035.

Klenert, D., Mattauch, L., Combet, E., Edenhofer, O., Hepburn, C., Rafaty, R., Stern, N., 2018. Making carbon pricing work for citizens. Nature Climate Change 8, 669–677.

Klier, T., Linn, J., 2012. New-vehicle characteristics and the cost of the Corporate Average Fuel Economy standard. RAND Journal of Economics 43, 186–213.

Knittel, C.R., Meiselman, B.S., Stock, J.H., 2017. The pass-through of RIN prices to wholesale and retail fuels under the renewable fuel standard. Journal of the Association of Environmental and Resource Economists 4, 1081–1119.

Kortum, S., Weisbach, D.A., 2022. Optimal Unilateral Carbon Policy, Working Paper. Yale University.

Kotchen, M.J., 2006. Green markets and private provision of public goods. Journal of Political Economy 114, 816–834.

Kotchen, M.J., 2018. Which social cost of carbon? A theoretical perspective. Journal of the Association of Environmental and Resource Economists 5, 673–694.

Kotchen, M.J., 2021. The producer benefits of implicit fossil fuel subsidies in the United States. Proceedings of the National Academy of Sciences 118, e2011969118.

Kotchen, M.J., 2025. Taxing externalities: revenue vs. welfare gains with an application to U.S. carbon taxes, Review of Environmental Economics and Policy, forthcoming.

Kotchen, M.J., Maggi, M., 2024. Carbon Taxes and Green Subsidies in a World Economy, Working Paper. Yale University.

Kotchen, K.J., Segerson, K., 2019. On the use of group performance and rights for environmental protection and resource management. Proceedings of the National Academy of Sciences 116, 5285–5292.

Kotchen, K.J., Segerson, K., 2020. The use of group-level approaches to environmental and natural resource policy. Review of Environmental Economics and Policy 14, 173–193.

Kotchen, M.J., Turk, Z.M., Leiserowitz, A.A., 2017. Public willingness to pay for a US carbon tax and preferences for spending the revenue. Environmental Research Letters 12, 094012.

Kortum, S., Weisbach, D.A., 2017. The design of border adjustments for carbon prices. National Tax Journal 70, 421–446.

Lark, T.J., Hendricks, N.P., Smith, A., Gibbs, H.K., 2022. Environmental outcomes of the U.S. Renewable Fuel Standard. Proceedings of the National Academy of Sciences 119, e2101084119.

Leard, B., McConnell, V., 2017. New markets for credit trading under U.S. automobile greenhouse gas and fuel economy standards. Review of Environmental Economics and Policy 2, 207–226.

Levinson, A., 2012. In: Fullerton, D., Wolfram, C. (Eds.), Belts and Suspenders: Interactions Among Climate Policy Regulations, Chapter 8 in The Design and Implementation of US Climate Policy. Oxford University Press.

Levinson, A., Fullerton, D., 2022. Linking climate and social justice makes both harder, VOX EU, CEPR.

Long, X., Goulder, L.H., 2023. Carbon emission trading systems: a review of systems across the globe and a close look at China's national approach, China. Economic Journal 16, 203–216.

Markusen, J.R., 1975. International externalities and optimal tax structures. Journal of International Economics 5, 15–29.

Metcalf, G.E., 2020. An emissions assurance mechanism: adding environmental certainty to a U.S. carbon tax. Review of Environmental Economics and Policy 14, 114–130.

Metcalf, G.E., 2021. Carbon taxes in theory and practice. Annual Review of Resource Economics 13, 245–265.

Metcalf, G.E., 2023. Five myths about carbon pricing. Oxford Review of Economic Policy 39, 680–693.

Metcalf, G.E., Weisbach, D., 2012. Linking policies when tastes differ: global climate policy in a heterogeneous world. Review of Environmental Economics and Policy 6, 110–129.

Montgomery, W.D., 1972. Markets in licenses and efficient pollution control programs. Journal of Economic Theory 5, 395–418.

Moore, F.C., Drupp, M.A., Rising, J., Dietz, S., Rudik, I., Wagner, G., 2024. Synthesis of evidence yields high social cost of carbon due to structural model variation and uncertainties, NBER Working Paper 32544, Cambridge, MA.

Morgenstern, R.D., Pizer, W.A., 2007. Reality Check: The Nature and Performance of Voluntary Environmental Programs in the United States, Europe and Japan (eds.). Resources for the Future Press, Washington, DC.

Murray, B.C., Newell, R.G., Pizer, W.A., 2009. Balancing cost and emissions certainty: an allowance reserve for cap-and-trade. Review of Environmental Economics and Policy 3, 84–103.

Newell, R., Pizer, W., Zhang, J., 2005. Managing permit markets to stabilize prices. Environmental and Resource Economics 31, 133–157.

Novan, K., 2017. Overlapping environmental policies and the impact on pollution. Journal of the Association of Environmental and Resource Economists 4, S153–S199.

Okun, A., 1975. Equality and Efficiency, the Big Tradeoff. Brookings Institution, Washington, D.C.

Parish, R.M., McLaren, K.R., 1982. Relative cost-effectiveness of input and output subsidies. Australian Journal of Agricultural Economics 26, 1–13.

Parry, I.W.H., 1995. Pollution taxes and revenue recycling. Journal of Environmental Economics and Management 29, S64–S77.

Parry, I.W.H., Bento, A., 2000. Tax deductions, environmental policy, and the 'double dividend' hypothesis. Journal of Environmental Economics and Management 39, 67–96.

Parry, I.W.H., Williams, R.C., Goulder, L.H., 1999. When can carbon abatement policies increase welfare? The fundamental role of distorted factor markets. Journal of Environmental Economics and Management 37, 52–84.

Perino, G., Ritz, R.A., van Benthem, A.A., 2023. Overlapping Climate Policies, Working Paper. University of Pennsylvania.

Pizer, W.A., 2002. Combining price and quantity controls to mitigate global climate change. Journal of Public Economics 85, 409–434.

Pizer, W.A., Prest, B.C., 2020. Prices versus quantities with policy updating. Journal of the Association of Environmental and Resource Economists 7, 483–518.

Reiss, P.C., White, M.W., 2008. What changes energy consumption? Prices and public pressures. The RAND Journal of Economics 39, 36–663.

Rennert, K., Errickson, F., Prest, B., Rennels, L., Newell, R., Pizer, W., Kingdon, C., Wingenroth, J., Cooke, R., Parthum, B., Smith, D., Cromar, K., Diaz, D., Moore, F., Móller, U., Plevin, R., Raftery, A., Ševčíková, H., Sheets, H., Stock, J., Tan, T., Watson, M., Wong, T., Anthoff, D., 2022. Comprehensive evidence implies a higher social cost of CO_2. Nature 610, 687–692.
Rentschler, J., Bazilian, M., 2017. Principles for designing effective fossil fuel subsidy reforms. Review of Environmental Economics and Policy 11, 138–155.
Ricks, M.D., Kay, O., 2024. Time-Limited Subsidies: Optimal Taxation with Implications for Renewable Energy Subsidies, Working Paper. University of Nebraska.
Roberts, M.J., Spence, M., 1976. Effluent charges and licenses under uncertainty. Journal of Public Economics 5, 193–208.
Rode, A., Baker, R., Carleton, T., D'Agostino, A., Delgado, M., Foreman, T., Gergel, D., Greenstone, M., Houser, T., Hsiang, S., Hultgren, A., Jina, A., Kopp, R., Malevich, S., McCusker, K., Nath, I., Pecenco, M., Rising, J., Yuan, J., 2022. Labor disutility in a warmer world: the Impact of climate change on the global workforce, Working Paper Available at doi: https://doi.org/10.2139/ssrn.4221478.
Rode, A., Carleton, T., Delgado, M., Greenstone, M., Houser, T., Hsiang, S., Hultgren, A., Jina, A., Kopp, R., McCusker, K., Nath, I., Rising, J., Yuan, J., 2021. Estimating a social cost of carbon for global energy consumption. Nature 598, 308–314.
Rudik, I., Lemoine, D., Marcheva, A., 2025. Equity and efficiency in the bipartisan infrastructure law's adaptation investments. Environmental and Energy Policy and the Economy (forthcoming).
Schmalensee, R., Stavins, R., 2017. Lessons learned from three decades of experience with cap and trade. Review of Environmental Economics and Policy 11, 59–79.
Segerson, K., Miceli, T.J., 1998. Voluntary environmental agreements: good or bad news for environmental protection? Journal of Environmental Economics and Management 36, 109–130.
Sheriff, G., 2024. California's GHG cap-and-trade program and the equity of air toxic releases. Journal of the Association of Environmental and Resource Economists 11, 137–170.
Shobe, W.H., Burtraw, D., 2012. Rethinking environmental federalism in a warming world. Climate Change Economics 3, 1250018.
Stapp, J., Nolte, C., Potts, M., Baumann, M., Haya, B.K., Butsic, V., 2023. Little evidence of management change in California's forest offset program. Communications Earth & Environment 4, 331.
Stern, N., Stiglitz, J., 2021. The social cost of carbon, risk, distribution, market failures: An Alternative Approach, NBER Working Paper 28472, Cambridge, MA.
Stern, N., Stiglitz, J., Taylor, C., 2022. The economics of immense risk, urgent action and radical change: towards new approaches to the economics of climate change. Journal of Economic Methodology 29, 181–216.
Sunstein, C.R., 2024. The economic constitution of the United States. Journal of Economic Perspectives 38, 25–42.
Taylor, M., 2020. Energy Subsidies: Evolution in the Global Energy Transformation to 2050, International. International Renewable Energy Agency, Abu Dhabi.
Tietenberg, T., 1998. Disclosure strategies for pollution control. Environmental and Resource Economics 11, 587–602.
Timilsina, G.R., 2022. Carbon taxes. Journal of Economic Literature 60, 1456–1502.
Tol, R., 2023. Social cost of carbon estimates have increased over time. Nature Climate Change 13, 532–536.

UNFCCC, 2023. Conference of the Parties Serving as the Meeting of the Parties to the Paris Agreement Fifth Session: First Global Stock Take, United Arab Emirates, FCCC/PA/CMA/2023/L.17.

U.S. Environmental Protection Agency (EPA), 2015. Regulatory impact analysis for the clean power plan final rule, EPA-452/R-15-003, Washington, DC.

U.S. Environmental Protection Agency (EPA), 2023. Report on the social cost of greenhouse gases: estimates incorporating recent scientific advances, National Center for Environmental Economics, Office of Policy, and Climate Change Division, Office of Air and Radiation.

U.S. Environmental Protection Agency (EPA), 2024. Regulatory impact analysis for the new source performance standards for greenhouse gas emissions from new, modified, and reconstructed fossil fuel-fired electric generating units; emission guidelines for greenhouse gas emissions from existing fossil fuel-fired electric generating units; and repeal of the affordable clean energy rule, EPA-452/R-24-009, Washington, DC.

U.S. Office of Management and Budget (OMB), 2023. Circular No. A-4, Washington, DC, https://www.whitehouse.gov/wp-content/uploads/2023/11/CircularA-4.pdf.

van Benthem, A., Kerr, S., 2013. Scale and transfers in international emissions offset programs. Journal of Public Economics 107, 31–46.

van't Veld, K., Kotchen, M.J., 2011. Green clubs. Journal of Environmental Economics and Management 62, 309–322.

Wang, B., Pizer, W.A., Munnings, C., 2022. Price limits in a tradable performance standard. Journal of Environmental Economics and Management 116, 102742.

Weisbach, D.A., Kortum, S., Wang, M., Yao, Y., 2023. Trade, leakage, and the design of a carbon tax. Environmental and Energy Policy and the Economy 4, 43–90.

Weitzman, M.L., 1974. Prices vs. quantities. The Review of Economic Studies 41, 477–491.

Weitzman, M.L., 2009. On modeling and interpreting the economics of climate change. Review of Economics and Statistics 91, 1–19.

Weitzman, M.L., 2011. Fat-tailed uncertainty in the economics of catastrophic climate change. Review of Environmental Economics and Policy 5, 275–292.

West, T.A.P., Wunder, S., Sills, E.O., Borner, J., Rifai, S.W., Neidermeier, A.N., Frey, G., Kantoleon, A., 2023. Action needed to make carbon offsets from forest conservation work for climate change mitigation. Science 381, 873–877.

World Bank, 2024a. State and Trends of Carbon Pricing Dashboard. Wold Bank Group accessed July 31, 2024 at https://carbonpricingdashboard.worldbank.org.

World Bank, 2024b. 2024 Sate and Trends of Carbon Pricing. World Bank Group, Washington, DC.

Yeh, S., Witcover, J., Lade, G.E., Sperling, D., 2016. A review of low carbon fuel policies: principles, program status and future directions. Energy Policy 97, 220–234.

Yu, B., Zhao, Q., Wei, Y.-M., 2021. Review of carbon leakage under regionally differentiated climate policies. Science of The Total Environment 782, 146765.

Zhou, R., Bi, X., Segerson, K., 2020. Evaluating voluntary environmental programs with spillover effects. Journal of the Association of Environmental and Resource Economists 7, 145–180.

Chapter 7

Uncertainty in climate-economic modeling☆

Svenn Jensen[a] **and Christian Traeger**[b,*]
[a]*Oslo Business School, Oslo Metropolitan University, Oslo, Norway,* [b]*Department of Economics, University of Oslo, Oslo, Norway*
Corresponding author. e-mail address: traeger@uio.no

Chapter Outline

1 Introduction

Uncertainty permeates all aspects of climate change, influencing the physical climate system, the socio-economic system, and our policy response. Uncertainties governing the climate include the critical concept of climate sensitivity—the uncertain response of global temperatures to greenhouse gas emissions (See Figure 3 in Chapter 1). In addition to climate sensitivity, carbon

☆ CT gratefully acknowledges support by the Norwegian Research Council under grant 315878.

Handbook of the Economics of Climate Change, Vol. 1. https://doi.org/10.1016/bs.hesecc.2024.10.005

cycle dynamics and the possibility of tipping points such as ice sheet collapse or permafrost thaw add uncertainty and layers of complexity to the challenge. These physical uncertainties are deeply intertwined with socio-economic uncertainties, such as uncertain economic growth, which significantly affect the optimal level of the social cost of carbon (SCC).

Understanding the nature of uncertainty and its quantification is only the first step in economic models. We must describe not only the uncertainty itself but also its consequences for decision making. Whereas simulations of possible futures can deliver valuable insights, the true challenge of decision making under uncertainty lies in our response. Fig. 1 illustrates a decision maker who has to decide how to spread her investments between consumption, physical capital building, and emission reductions under the threat of various climate tipping points. How future decision makers can (or cannot) respond to different events can have crucial implications already for today's optimal decisions and the SCC. We will see that the difference in how we expect future decision makers to respond to realizations of high or low growth or high or low climate sensitivity can, in some cases, even affect the sign of the risk premium. If the reader is willing to take two messages away from this article, then let it be those. First, the policy response to uncertainty is generally not driven by risk aversion. The welfare loss crucially depends on risk aversion, but policies depend on marginal trade-offs, not the level of welfare. Second, it matters whether and how we optimize policies. Simple Monte Carlo simulations are great tools to explore possible futures based on complex models, but they cannot readily analyze how we should respond to uncertainty. And once we analyze optimal policy, it generally matters whether future policy makers respond to the resolution of uncertainty.

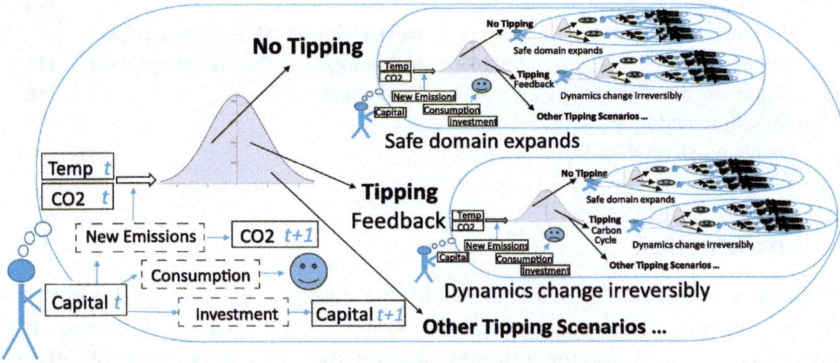

FIG. 1 The schematic illustrates how our response to uncertainty today depends on how we (i) affect future outcomes and (ii) the impact today's choices have while living in different future worlds. The schematic is replicated from Lemoine and Traeger (2016a), who analyze a "tipping point domino". Given tipping either happens or not, the decision tree is still somewhat modest as compared to "simple" growth or climate sensitivity uncertainty, where we we face a continuum of (intertemporally correlated) outcomes in every period.

Climate change uncertainty differs from a simple objective coin-toss lottery. First, the uncertainty we face is often difficult to translate into probabilities and sometimes merely relies on experts' subjective (gu)estimates. Second, the climate and economic systems are complex, sometimes nonlinear, and feature long delays between actions and impacts. Third, the interaction between multiple uncertainties, such as temperature feedbacks, economic damges, and growth can amplify or mitigate each other in ways that are difficult to predict without formal modeling. Fourth, the way we as a society evaluate these uncertainties through our preferences greatly influences policy recommendations.

The focus of this chapter is on pricing carbon, as it provides the clearest signal across different models on how uncertainty affects the incentives and urgency of climate policy. Rather than concentrating on the level of the SCC itself–which varies widely across models (Moore et al., 2024)–we are primarily interested in how uncertainty alters the SCC. This impact closely mirrors its effect on abatement decisions. Given the limited scope of this chapter, we will not cover how firms and individuals respond to "policy uncertainty," i.e., how governments may set or revise climate policies. While this is an important topic, we anticipate that future volumes will offer dedicated chapters on such second-best settings. For similar reasons, we also abstract from the debate over taxes versus quantities, instead focusing on first-best policy solutions. Even under regulatory delays and uncertainty, price signals or cap-and-trade systems can be adjusted to optimally spread uncertainty between firms and the environment, making the choice between cap-and-trade or carbon taxes less central (Karp and Traeger, 2024).

That said, much of the conceptual analysis in the first sections applies equally well to firms and asset managers, who must consider how future uncertainty should inform their decisions. By exploring how uncertainty shapes the optimal policy response, we provide a framework for understanding the broader implications for both public policy and private decision making in the face of uncertain climate risks.

A chapter on uncertainty in climate change economics must navigate between providing generic insights on how uncertainty affects decisions and those more specific to climate-economic models. We begin by outlining the general types of uncertainty and discussing approaches for their evaluation further below. Section 2 moves straight into outlining the general structure of current integrated climate-economic models. While more stylized models can offer valuable insights, many of the uncertainties in more structured climate-economic models have more nuanced effects, sometimes altering predictions in ways that overly simple models cannot capture. Section 3 discusses general analytic insights, which we consider the most valuable guide for a reader entering this quickly expanding field, where the quantitative estimates for the SCC's risk premium sill vary from negligible to a doubling or tripling of the optimal carbon tax, and also change sign across papers. Section 4 surveys numeric approaches and papers. Again, our emphasis will be less on numbers than on the conceptual approach. The division into analytic and numeric approaches is far from perfect. Our analytic discussions will include comments on magnitudes and signs and some references to numeric approaches, and the papers we discuss in Section 4 will also offer interesting analytic insights and extensions such as the analysis of tipping points and decision making under model uncertainty and robustness.

Interest in the role of uncertainty in climate change has grown rapidly in recent years. While Pindyck's (2007) and Heal's (2017) general surveys still call for more work on the economic modeling of climate change uncertainty, recent surveys on such uncertainty with a somewhat different focuses include Golub et al. (2014), Rudik and Lemoine (2017), and Cai (2021). We also wish to honor the pioneers of this field, who were far ahead of their time. Heal (1984) introduced a stylized analytic assessment of climate change with tipping points 40 years ago. Pizer (1999) applied a log-linear approximation of the DICE model to analyze optimal abatement under uncertainty, finding that uncertainty modestly increases emission reductions. Perhaps most impressively, Kelly and Kolstad (1999) examined a fully stochastic version of the DICE model using neural network approximations of the value function 25 years ago. These early studies have set the stage for contemporary research. We are thrilled to finally see an explosion of the field, including the deployment of many state of the art modeling approaches.

1.1 Fundamental classifications of uncertainty

Risk vs Ambiguity (hard uncertainty). One way of classifying different uncertainties is in terms of their probabilistic nature. If a decision maker can assign (unique) probabilities to all events *and* the probabilities are known, then we generally speak of risk. Otherwise, we commonly speak of ambiguity or hard uncertainty. There are many different models of ambiguity. Some assign ranges or sets of probabilities to events, and others replace the concept of a probability distribution with more general concepts. The most common extension of probabilities uses capacities to describe the uncertain world. Capacities are non-additive set functions that are harder to interpret than probabilities. The non-additivity refers to the implication that the probability of two disjoint events no longer has to add up, which implies that the temperature increase by 2100 can be below 2° or it can be above 2° or, well, it can be something else. This difficulty in interpretation explains why this somewhat common model of ambiguity has not found much application in more applied fields such as climate change economics. Yet, certain decision models built on capacities are equivalent to decision models that assign non-unique probabilities to events, a conceptualization of hard uncertainty that is more intuitive and has been prominently applied in the climate change literature.

Objective vs Subjective Probabilities. In situations where we are willing to characterize the world probabilistically, we can interpret probabilities as either objective or subjective. The classical definition of objective probabilities is based on the limit of observing an arbitrarily large frequency of repeated events or on symmetry reasoning (like in the case of a die or a coin). Outside of a casino, such definitions are rarely helpful, and modern probability theory is based on Kolmogoroff's (1933) axioms declaring the existence of a non-negative additive set function normalized to unity where the probabilities of disjoint events add up. These probabilities can be interpreted as (more or less) objective if we have good knowledge of the likelihood of each outcome or as subjective if we do not. Objective probabilities are rare in climate change economics. The best example is the stochasticity of month-to-month or year-to-year temperature fluctuations after detrending, which leads us to the next distinction.

Stochasticity vs Epistemological Uncertainty. A common distinction between uncertainties, which overlaps with the categorizations above, is the following. Stochasticity, or aleatory uncertainty, describes nature's fluctuations of frequent events. We have no way to forecast the exact outcomes because nature's processes are "intrisically stochastic". Given our current forecasting abilities, our best forecast of next month's average temperature will remain the same probabilistic forecast even if we were to observe another ten years of monthly temperature fluctuations. Therefore, stochasticity is also considered an irreducible uncertainty. By contrast, epistemological uncertainty governs a decision maker's lack of knowledge. As discussed aleady in Chapter 1, scientists are uncertain about the climate's sensitivity to atmospheric CO_2 concentrations. Once we observe the medium-run temperature response to a doubling of atmospheric CO_2, we know the answer and, if still relevant, can predict a similar event deterministically in the future. In this case, nature's process is not stochastic, or at least that's not the most relevant part of the unceraintу. Nature will respond to our added CO_2 in a particular way; we just do not know yet how exactly.

Learning. Connecting immediately to the two classifications above is the idea of learning. Many of the interesting probabilities in climate change economics are neither objective nor do they qualify as stochasticity. As a result, we can learn from observation. The most common modeling approach, which is likely also the most theoretically convincing, is Bayesian learning. It is generally interpreted as combining both subjective uncertainty and objective uncertainty (or stochasticity) in a single framework. In our prime example, we are subjectively uncertain how global average surface temperature responds to a change in atmospheric CO_2 concentrations. Every year, we observe a new temperature response to altered greenhouse gas concentrations. At the same time, temperatures fluctuate naturally from year to year, even without changes in greenhouse gases. This latter stochasticity prevents us from easily learning the temperature response. What we can do in such situations is to follow Bayes rule and update our probabilistic believe over the climate sensitivity based on the observed realization, taking into account the fluctuating nature of annual temperatures (likelihood function). In order to model Bayesian learning, we have to pick an initial guess for climate sensitivity, the prior. Based on (potentially historic) observations, we use our knowledge of the likelihood function governing annual temperature fluctuations and the particular observation to update the Bayesian prior into a posterior. This posterior will then serve as our new prior. Over time, the prior shrinks. Under some assumptions, it shrinks every period; under other assumptions, it can also increase in response to unexpected observations.

Objective *and* Subjective Probabilities. The idea of combining objective and subjective probabilities links closely to not only Bayesian learning but also a prominent model of (smooth) ambiguity aversion and second-order risk aversion. Here we can associate likelihood functions and objective utilities with objective risk that is evaluated at a lower level of risk aversion and a Bayesian prior with subjective uncertainty that is potentially subject to higher risk aversion as in, e.g., the prominent smooth ambiguity model (Klibanoff et al., 2005, 2009), which we discuss further below and in Section 4.4.

Endogenous vs exogenous uncertainty. It often matters for decisions whether uncertainty is endogenous or exogenous to the decision problem. In our running example, annual temperature fluctuations (deviations from a trend) are mostly exogenous to our anthropogenic doings. By contrast, the uncertainty governing the temperature trend is endogenous to decisions governing emissions or carbon taxation, at least on a global level. Without anthropogenic greenhouse gases, there is no (or far less) uncertainty about the future climate. As we increase our emissions, we increase the uncertainty governing the future.

Ignorance. Ignorance describes a situation where decision makers are unaware of potential outcomes. Even though this could be debated, we include not only the famous "unknown unknowns", but also the "known unknowns" in this class, where the decision maker is aware that he or she is ignorant about some possible outcomes. Given we do not even conceive these outcomes, they also defy assigning probabilities (or capacities) and a valuation. Arguably, there is a lot of ignorance governing the detailed implications of climate change. Scientists are constantly discovering new implications for ecosystems that defy even the imagination of most of us and clearly that of our models. Yet, by their very nature of not being conceived, it is very hard to build such uncertainties into our models. The decision-theoretic literature has built a language to talk about such "known unkowns" and "unknown unknowns" in terms of logical operators (Fagin and Halpern, 1987; Dekel et al., 1998; Heifetz et al., 2013). However, most questions in climate change economics require trade-offs, and trade-offs usually require some form of quantification beyond binary operators or possibilities, which makes it hard to apply these theories in climate change economics.

1.2 Crucial uncertainties in the climate and economic systems

There are many interacting uncertainties in both the climate and economic systems. One of the most important sources of climate uncertainty is how global temperatures will respond to greenhouse gas emissions. This uncertainty is captured by the so-called *climate sensitivity*, which refers to the long-term increase in global average surface temperature resulting from a doubling of atmospheric CO_2 concentrations. Climate sensitivity is a key determinant of future climate change, as it encompasses a wide range of feedback effects. For example, feedbacks such as water vapor, cloud-formation, ice melting and its impact on our planet's reflectivity, as well as more intricate change such as modifications of the vertical temperature profile in the atmosphere (lapse rate). The IPCC's Sixth Assessment Report estimates the likely range of climate sensitivity to be between 2.5 and 4 degrees Celsius, with a best estimate of 3 degrees Celsius (IPCC, 2021). Some probability distributions still carry substantial wait in the tails making it hard to rule out even substantially stronger temperature responses. Figure 3 in Chapter 1 presents a set of distributions that estimates the climate sensitivity.

Another significant uncertainty in the climate system concerns carbon flows, particularly the future behavior of carbon sinks, such as oceans and terrestrial ecosystems. The ability of these sinks to absorb CO_2 is critical to determining future atmospheric carbon concentrations, which cause the greenhouse effect. The precise mechanics of current carbon flows are still part of active research and the absorptive capacity may decline at higher levels of carbon concentration or temperature, leading to further warming (Denning, 2022).

In recent years, attention has increasingly focused on the potential for tipping points–nonlinear processes that could trigger abrupt and potentially irreversible changes in the climate system. Examples include the collapse of the Greenland ice sheet, the thawing of permafrost, or the dieback of the Amazon rainforest. Each of these events could have cascading impacts on global climate, making tipping points another major source of climate uncertainty (Armstrong McKay et al., 2022). We will focus on the economic response to such threshold-crossing uncertainties in a dedicated Section on tipping points (Section 4.3).

Economic growth and technological advances are another crucial and deeply uncertain component in modeling the interaction between human activity and climate change. They affect both, our emissions that alter the climate system and the impact of climate change feeding back into the economy and human well-being. For example, heatwaves may reduce workers' productivity, sea-level rise may destroy infrastructure, and extreme weather events may cause the loss of agricultural output. Increased average temperatures may make regions uninhabitable and lead to migration or conflict. The extent of these impacts remains highly uncertain, as does the effectiveness of future adaptation efforts. While significant progress has been made in refining the empirical foundations of damage functions, see Chapters 2 and 5, these impacts remain highly uncertain for the foreseeable future (Carleton et al., 2022; Rode et al., 2021).

While some uncertainties are epistemic and may be reduced with better data and models, others are irreducible. The global economy is in constant flux, shaped by innovation, societal changes, and evolving institutions, implying that forecast of economic growth are highly uncertain and will likely remain uncertain (Müller et al., 2022). Policy decisions affect both the climate and the economy and are particularly hard to predict. As climate change is a global externality, mitigating its effects relies heavily on policies enacted at global, regional, and local levels of governance. A key source of uncertainty is how much future decision makers will prioritize climate action by committing to and enforcing effective policies. This uncertainty also extends to how various stakeholders—voters, firms, and governments—will respond to policies or their uncertain anticipation. As we noted above, we will have to save a more careful survey of the response to second-best policy uncertainty to a future volume of the handbook. Section 4 will survey some of the literature that develop future scenario analysis incorporating such reasoning, and we will discuss how the assumed policy response by future policy makers affects today's optimal course of action.

1.3 Uncertainty evaluation

The question of uncertainty evaluation has several dimensions. Some of the early assessments, as well as some prominent present examples of more complex models, use probabilities for a more structured exploration of possible future scenarios. These scenario explorations prescribe a particular policy and explore the possible consequences. They can also randomly draw policies or policy scenarios making them part of the uncertain future. The climate economic literature generally labels this approach *Monte Carlo analysis* as it is based on relatively straightforward Monte Carlo simulations that are easily implemented in most integrated assessment models (IAMs). We discuss this method in detail in Section 4.1. The upside is that we can use any deterministic IAM to sample future worlds. The downside is that there is no uncertainty inside the model itself. Hence, the model cannot properly address how we should respond to uncertainty.

At the other end of the spectrum is a policy maker who optimally responds to uncertainty. She takes decisions keeping in mind a decision tree that quickly branches out over the future. While she might not take future decisions herself, she has to take assumption over how future decision makers will respond to future information, e.g., that growth was lower that expected or the climate sensitivity higher than expected. This forward-looking policy maker also anticipates how today's decisions will influence future outcomes across different possible realizations of the probability distributions. To tackle the quickly unbranching decision tree given the time horizons necessary in a model of climate change the literature resorts to *stochastic dynamic programming* and closely related approaches. The recursive formulation of the optimization makes uncertainty quite tractable and can easily incorporate, e.g., anticipated future learning about the climate sensitivity based on temperature realizations. Yet, the challenge is that numeric dynamic programming struggles with the complexity of many IAMs for reasons we discuss in Section 4.2.

Under either approach, we have to decide how our model evaluates future outcomes, and how much a planner or a representative agent dislikes the uncertainty: we have to specify preferences. This chapter will not delve into the interesting debate of whether climate change should be evaluated normatively or descriptively. We will take the stand that our models should capture observed risk aversion reasonably well. Given we are interested in how decision makers should respond to uncertainty, we emphasize rational attractiveness over behavioral attractiveness. Unfortunately, there are many different perspectives on what constitutes rational behavior. Our main concern is that models do not give rise to foreseeable planning inconsistencies that imply an unnecessary waste of resources (e.g., Dutch books). The vast majority of literature agrees with these criteria, so they do not impose much of a constraint on our discussions.

The standard preference framework for evaluating uncertainty in economics is the *Expected Utility* model. Based on von Neumann and Morgenstern's (1944) aximatization it remains one of the benchmarks for rational decision making. In this model, the curvature of the instantaneous utility function captures the decision maker's attitude toward risk. Most models in climate economics assumes a constant relative risk aversion (CRRA) utility function, which implies decreasing absolute risk aversion as (per capita) consumption increases. Expected utility requires that we quantify uncertainty probabilistically. Thanks to Savage's (1954) alternative axiomatization, we can equally well employ the expected utility framework when probabilities are subjective (e.g., based on expert judgment) or objective (based on known frequencies).

Two criticisms have been raised against the use of expected utility in climate economics. First, in a dynamic setting, the CRRA function simultaneously captures two a priori distinct preference characteristics: the desire for a smooth consumption over time and aversion to risk. Conceptually distinct, they are both captured by the same parameter (or concavity) in the expected utility framework. This constraint can lead to serious difficulties calibrating both risk premia and discount rates to the data, both of which are particularly important in the climate change context. The second critique is that expected utility does not distinguish between different types of uncertainty. Whether a probability distribution reflects objective risk (stochasticity) or expert judgment about epistemic uncertainty, the decision maker treats them the same.

One way to disentangle preferences for consumption smoothing and risk aversion is through *Epstein-Zin-Weil* preferences, which allow for separate functional representations of these two preference dimensions. This formulation enables the decision maker to be intertemporally risk-averse. The use of Epstein-

Zin-Weil preferences has become increasingly common in climate economics over the past decade. Epstein-Zin-Weil preferences are recursively defined, requiring a recursive approach to the decision problem, typically solved using stochastic dynamic programming or related recursive methods.

Chapter 1's Figure 3 illustrates how different research groups, relying on various methods, have derived quite different probability distributions for climate sensitivity. From a Bayesian modeling perspective, the IPCC's estimate of the equilibrium climate sensitivity corresponds to a decision maker's subjective prior, and this prior might not even be unique. The subjectivity and multiplicity of distributional estimates raise the question of whether climate sensitivity uncertainty should be treated similarly to known risks or whether we need to treat "deeper uncertainty" differently from objective risk. More specifically, we may need to account for differences in how decision makers respond to ambiguity compared to objective risk, as the two may evoke different levels of aversion.

An extreme form of ambiguity aversion is captured by Gilboa and Schmeidler's (1989)'s *maxmin expected utility*. In this model, the decision maker considers a set of possible probability distributions, evaluates the expected value for each, and then focuses on the worst possible expected outcome. *Robust Control* is a related approach but interprets uncertainty differently, where the decision maker is uncertain whether the model itself is misspecified (Hansen and Sargent, 2001, 2008).

Klibanoff et al. (2005) introduce a model of *smooth ambiguity aversion*, which they later extend to a recursive dynamic framework in Klibanoff et al. (2009). Smooth ambiguity aversion can account for more moderate attitudes toward ambiguity compared to maxmin expected utility. While the normative implications of ambiguity aversion from a rational decision making perspective remain a matter of debate, Traeger (2010) shows that smooth ambiguity models are consistent with the von Neumann and Morgenstern (1944) axioms, provided we allow for distinguishing between different types of probabilities or degrees of confidence in probabilistic beliefs.[1]

2 Integrated climate-economic modeling

Section 2.1 summarizes the basic structure of what we consider an integrated climate-economic model. In presenting the model, we do not explicitly highlight uncertainty. In reality, every functional relationship and parameter described is uncertain. For practical purposes, later sections will focus on specific uncertainties. Section 2.2 outlines the basic objective function and explains how uncertainty will be incorporated into the formal model.

Our objective is recursively defined through the Bellman equation, which breaks up long and complex decision trees into a sequence of two-period

[1] See Section 4.4 and Berger and Marinacci (2020) for further discussion.

decision problems. This approach makes uncertainty more tractable but requires the introduction of a value function, which captures the maximum future welfare achievable through optimal management of the climate-economic system. For analytical solutions, the value function provides a useful and insightful tool. For numeric approaches, approximating the value function on a high-dimensional state space can be challenging, as discussed in Section 4.

2.1 General model layout

This section briefly lays out the crucial components of what we consider an integrated model of climate and the economy. Chapter 1 discusses a particular example, Nordhaus' DICE model, at some length. Aiming at general insights, we start out with a general model structure. Where needed, we will point out how some contributions rely on more specific assumptions. The present model structure is mainly borrowed from Traeger's (2015, 2023) Analytic Climate Economy (ACE) framework. For the moment, we do not pay explicit attention to uncertainty. The reader may think of any of these equations as featuring uncertain functional forms and picking up explicit stochastic parameters. In the later applications, the state variables below will be stochastic, either because the functional form is uncertain or because the inputs themselves are uncertain, e.g., an uncertain temperature increase implies uncertain future production. Gross output is a function of capital $\boldsymbol{K}_t$, labor $\boldsymbol{N}_t$, energy inputs $\boldsymbol{E}_t$, and the commonly exogenously evolving technology $\boldsymbol{A}_t$.[2] Bold letters indicate that these inputs are generally vectors characterizing the inputs of a multi-sector economy. We assume that climate damages can be characterized as a function of the current atmospheric surface temperature increase above 1900 levels, $T_{1,t}$. Net production is

$$Y_t = F(\boldsymbol{A}_t, \boldsymbol{N}_t, \boldsymbol{K}_t, \boldsymbol{E}_t, T_{1,t}). \tag{1}$$

We assume that the production function $F(\cdot)$ is homogeneous (of arbitrary degree) in capital. This functional form covers the production and abatement structure of several common IAMs such as Golosov et al. (2014) and Nordhaus (2017) as well as a more complex production structure relying on several sectors and energy inputs with distinct and time-changing degrees of energy substitutability (Traeger, 2022, 2023).

A common assumption is that a multiplicatively separable damage function can capture the impacts of climate change, and the most common functional form is DICE's quadratic damage function where

$$F(\cdot, T_{1,t}) = F^{gross}(\cdot)\frac{1}{1 + aT^2} \quad \text{or} \quad F(\cdot, T_{1,t}) = F^{gross}(\cdot)(1 - aT^2).$$

[2] Endogenous technological progress with aggregate uncertainty is an interesting challenge to take on in these climate-economic models, which introduces another (set of) equation(s) of motion.

The first version is normalized so that damages do not exceed output.[3] Two calibrations of such damage functions based on Barrage and Nordhaus's (2024) and Howard and Sterner's (2017) are depicted in Fig. 2. The other damage function in the figure is fitted to Rennert et al.'s (2022) GIVE model using the double-exponential (Traeger, 2021)

$$F(\cdot, T_{1,t}) = F^{gross}(\cdot)\exp(-\xi_0(\exp(\xi_1 T_t) - 1)). \tag{2}$$

The figure also illustrates the large uncertainty governing the loss of GDP at a given temperature level based on ten thousand simulations by Rennert et al. (2022) and the difference between two prominent quadratic damage estimates (DICE 2023 and HS).

Following Golosov et al. (2014), we assume that the first d entries of the energy vector $\boldsymbol{E}_t$ are fossil-fuel-based and measure their energy content in terms of CO_2. Then emissions are summarized by $E_t \sum_{i=1}^{d} E_{i,t} + E_t^{other}$, where E_t^{other} captures emissions from land conversion, forestry, and agriculture, often treated as exogenous. Emissions accumulate in the atmosphere where they cause a greenhouse effect. Over time, some of the added atmospheric CO_2 moves on to other reservoirs, like the oceans or the biosphere (plant matter and soils). Therefore, most models keep track of CO_2 in the different reservoirs, requiring a vector of carbon concentrations that follows the equation of motion

$$\boldsymbol{M}_{t+1} = M(\boldsymbol{M}_t, E_t). \tag{3}$$

In most models, including DICE, equation (3) models a carbon cycle, where the function $M(.)$ is fully characterized by a carbon transition equation Φ, i.e., $\boldsymbol{M}_{t+1} = \Phi \boldsymbol{M}_t + \boldsymbol{e}_1 E_t$.[4] Another popular model, based on Joos et al. (2013), uses several boxes merely for atmospheric carbon. These boxes decay at different rates and mimick the atmospheric impulse response of large climate models.

Increased atmospheric carbon causes radiative forcing, modeled by

$$Q_t = \eta \frac{\log \frac{M_{1,t} + G_t}{M_{pre}}}{\log 2}. \tag{4}$$

where η defines the greenhouse effect's strength and G_t captures the radiative forcing from other, exogenous greenhouse gases in CO_2 equivalents. Radiative forcing is the technical term for the greenhouse effect, colloquially compared to putting a lid on the pot (which is being heated by the incoming solar

[3] The DICE model versions frequently swap between the different formulations, sometimes even between text and code. Whereas damages could, in principle, exceed damages, they would also quickly after exceed the total capital stock. Of course, we hope we never reach those temperatures.

[4] The first unit vector $\boldsymbol{e}_1$ implies that we emit into the atmosphere, the first reservoir of the vector $\boldsymbol{M}_t$. Hänsel et al. (2024) extend DICE to include explicit temperature feedbacks into the diffusion coefficients in the carbon cycle, an extension now also imported into the latest official DICE update (Barrage and Nordhaus, 2024). In this case, equation (3) generalizes to $\boldsymbol{M}_{t+1} = M(\boldsymbol{M}_t, E_t, T_{1,t})$.

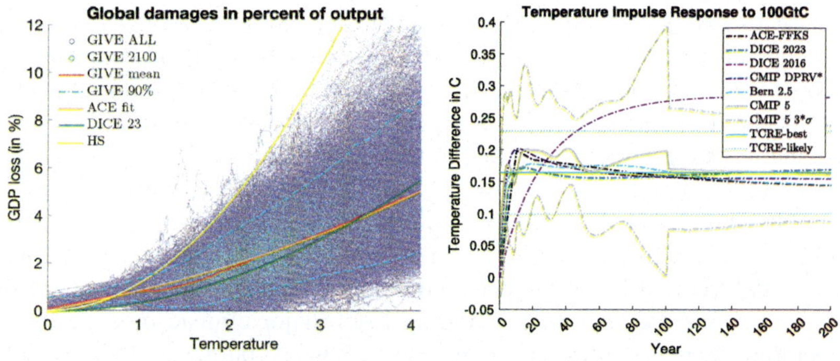

FIG. 2 Left panel illustrates the uncertainty governing climate damages based on the GIVE model by Rennert et al. (2022), see Section 4.1. It shows the GDP loss along ten thousand scenarios from the present until 2300 over the temperature increase since 1900. It also shows Traeger's (2021) ACE fit to the mean, using a double-exponential damage function, and the quadratic damage functions of Barrage and Nordhaus's (2024) DICE 2023 model and Howard and Sterner's (2017) preferred estimate from their meta-review. The right panel illustrates the uncertain warming response to today's emissions. It depicts the warming response from emitting a 100Gt carbon pulse into the atmosphere today, based on the IPCC's (2013) model comparison study (CMIP 5), showing the mean response and a three-sigma interval around it (Joos et al., 2013). The uncertainty seems to fall 100 years into the future only because some models drop out of the sample for longer horizons. The graph also depicts the impulse response following the approach of Dietz et al. (2021), a ten year time step version of the ACE model (combining a non-linear temperature system with Folini et al.'s (2024) three reservoir carbon cycle), and the DICE 2016 and 2023 models. The TCRE model approximates these responses with a straight line. The Figure is based on Traeger (2021).[5]

radiation not absorbed by CO_2). Fortunately, the oceans keep cooling our planet substantially for the moment. Therefore, most models keep track of at least one more temperature in addition to atmospheric temperature $T_{1,t}$. We denote the equation of motion for the temperature vector by

$$\boldsymbol{T}_{t+1} = T(\boldsymbol{T}_t, Q_t), \tag{5}$$

which closes the model's feedback loop between production and climatic change.

An increasingly popular shortcut for modeling temperature dynamics is based on Matthews et al. (2009), Allen et al. (2009), Dietz et al. (2018) and Dietz and Venmans (2019). The so-called TRCE model (transient climate

[5]The right panel also depicts the impulse response of the DICE 2016 model to illustrate some of the recent improvements in connecting climate-economic modeling with the climate sciences. The depicted DICE 2023 impulse response has been modified to align initial conditions to CMIP 5. (Barrage and Nordhaus, 2024). "CMIP DPRV*" follows Dietz et al.'s (2021) approach approximating CMIP 5 using Geoffroy et al.'s (2013) linear approximation of the CMIP 5 results. Based on code kindly provided by the authors, Traeger (2023) adjusted this fit for a 3 °C climate sensitivity. ACE's temperature calibration depicted here was not calibration to CMIP 5′s impulse experiment but Magicc 6.0 and the IPCC's stochastic transient climate response. We thank Lisa Rennels, Fortunat Joos, David Anthoff, Frank Venmans, and Lint Barrage for their contributions to these graphs.

response to cumulative emissions) simplifies equations (3)–(5) by assuming that temperatures are linear in cumulative historic emissions. In essence, a ton of CO_2 added to the atmosphere today induces radiative forcing and contributes to atmospheric warming over a long period. Similar to heating a large pot of soup, the warming effect takes time to manifest. Meanwhile, some of the CO_2 moves into the oceans and biosphere. Large climate models show that most of the temperature increase from an additional ton of carbon occurs relatively quickly, within a decade or so, and then remains nearly constant over a long time (as delayed warming balances with slow CO_2 removal). This simplified intuition reflects the "empirical" finding from major climate models that the temperature increase from emissions can, for many purposes, be reasonably approximated by replacing equations (3)–(5) with this simpler model:

$$\boldsymbol{T}_{1,t+1} = \alpha \sum_{t=\text{preindustrial}}^{t} E_t, \tag{6}$$

and $\alpha \approx 0.165°C$ per 100 Giga tons carbon (GtC) emitted. We currently emit around $10GtC$ per year globally. Thus, every year of emissions warms our planet by approximately $0.017°C$. Fig. 2 presents the temperature response to a $100GtC$ emission impulse at today's climate conditions based on Joos et al.'s (2013) model comparison project for the 5th IPCC report (CMIP 5). It depicts the mean response as well as the 3σ interval from these studies (which falls after 100 years because some models left the sample). The figure also depicts an approximation to Geoffroy et al.'s (2013) linearization of the model results following Dietz et al.'s (2021) (CMIP DPRV*, see Footnote 5), and a ten year time step illustration based on combining ACE's non-linear temperature system with Folini et al.'s (2024) reference carbon cycle calibration.

On the economic side, we still need to model capital accumulation. Almost all stochastic models assume that there is only one generic capital stock $K_t = \Sigma_i \boldsymbol{K}_{i,t}$ that is spread across different sectors in every period. It follows the usual equation of motion for capital

$$K_{t+1} = Y_t - C_t + (1 - \delta_k)K_t. \tag{7}$$

Some slightly more complex models such as ACE, or some runs of DICE, also incorporate the potential scarcity of fossil fuels by keeping track of the non-negativity constraint of resource stocks in the ground, which follow the simple equation of motion

$$\boldsymbol{R}_{t+1} = \boldsymbol{R}_t - \boldsymbol{E}_t^d. \tag{8}$$

2.2 Information and objective function

For convenience, we now summarize all of our physical state variables in the vector $\boldsymbol{X}_t = (k_t, \boldsymbol{T}_t, \boldsymbol{M}_t, \boldsymbol{R}_t, \boldsymbol{A}_t)$. We note that output Y_t, consumption C_t, and energy use and emissions E_t are flow variables (rather than states). They derive from the state $\boldsymbol{X}_t$ given our policy decisions. When the decision maker does not have full knowledge of the dynamic processes governing the economy and/or climate system the dynamic equations are stochastic. Even if only a single equation, say equation (5) for temperature, becomes uncertain, all other equations become stochastic because temperature affects output through equation (1), which then affects all other variables of the model. If shocks are iid, we can merely add a stochastic parameter into any of the equations above to explicitly incorporate the source of the uncertainty. Eg., we can change equation (5) to the form $\boldsymbol{T}_{t+1} = T(\boldsymbol{T}_t, Q_t, \tilde{\varepsilon})$, where $\tilde{\varepsilon}$ specifies an iid distributed temperature shock.

Most interesting shocks are serially correlated. E.g., annual shocks to global average temperature are highly serially correlated. Similarly, growth shocks are generally serially correlated either because of business cycles or because of long-run growth uncertainty. If shocks are serially correlated, then we need to keep track of past shocks as well, or, we have to add informational state variables to the system that capture past information. In the case of a simple AR(1) shock process, such an informational variable can simply be ϵ_t, i.e., last period's realization of the shock. In a Bayesian learning model governing the climate sensitivity, the informational variables will characterize the distribution of the Bayesian prior. We further discuss such structural learning in Section 4.2. For now, we merely collect such information states by a vector $\boldsymbol{I}_t$, adding another equation of motion.[6]

$$\boldsymbol{I}_{t+1} = I(\boldsymbol{I}_t, \boldsymbol{X}_t).$$

Stochastic dynamic programming formulates the objective function recursively. Let us assume that the objective is to maximize the sum of discounted future utility. Let us furthermore assume that the policy maker controls consumption C_t and energy use $\boldsymbol{E}_t$, which by construction includes fossil fuel use and CO_2 emissions, as well as the labor $\boldsymbol{N}_t$ and capital $\boldsymbol{K}_t$ distributions across sectors, which are subject to the obvious availability constraint that we suppress (shares summing to unity). We collect those variables in the control vector $\boldsymbol{a}_t = (C_t, \boldsymbol{E}_t, \boldsymbol{K}_t, \boldsymbol{N}_t)$. Neglecting uncertainty for a moment, we can define the maximal achievable welfare given the current state of the system as

$$V(\boldsymbol{X}_t, \boldsymbol{I}_t) = \max_{a_{t,\in\{0,1,2\ldots\}}} \sum_{t=0}^{\infty} \beta^t u(C_t) \tag{9}$$

where β is the utility discount factor expressing pure time preference, and the optimization is subject to the constraints formulated in equations (1)–(8). Under certainty, we can cut off the time horizon in a few hundred years and solve this problem solving for consumption and energy inputs of every period,

[6] Formally, all states and decisions have to be measurable with respect to the filtration generated by the stochastic shocks. Practically, it just means that we cannot base decisions on information we have not received, yet.

already a daunting task for many sector problems. Under uncertainty, we would have to solve future control variables conditional on future information, which, for most problems, becomes quickly infeasible as the number of control variables explodes. Even if every period only branches out based on two possible stochastic realizations, the number of possible time paths and conditional decision variables in period t evolves with 2^t. If we assume a time step of 10 years, and a binary realization of uncertainty every 10 years, the number of possible time paths 150 years from today is 2^{15}, exceeding 30,000. Counting the number of (information-conditioned) control variables in 150 years, we still have to multiply that number by the number of physical control variables in the model, a bare minimum of 2 in the most aggregated IAMs such as DICE.

We hope this crude reasoning fleshes out the beauty of Bellman's (1966) insight that we can break up the problem above into a sequence of simple two-period problems of the form

$$V(\boldsymbol{X}_t, \boldsymbol{I}_t) = \max_{\boldsymbol{a}_t} u(C_t) + \beta \mathbf{E}_t [V(\boldsymbol{X}_{t+1}, \boldsymbol{I}_{t+1}) | \boldsymbol{X}_t, \boldsymbol{I}_t, \boldsymbol{a}_t], \tag{10}$$

again subject to equations (1)–(8). Instead of a quickly unfolding decision tree, the decision maker trades off between current consumption value and future value captured by the value function $V(\boldsymbol{X}_t, \boldsymbol{I}_t)$, which under uncertainty also includes the informational states. The insight is that the problem tomorrow looks exactly the same as the problem today, *conditional* on being in the same state of the world. If the world is changing, we merely add a description of this change explicitly to the state vector.

The crucial difference between solving the Bellman equation (10) and the sum over time (9) is that we only need to solve a single, simple maximization problem, though we do not know the value function $V(\cdot)$ a priori. The key advantage of the Bellman equation is that we no longer have to worry about the branching out of decision trees. Thus, the main challenge becomes finding the value function. If the problem can be solved analytically, the value function immediately provides insight into the shadow values of the various state and information variables. If an analytic solution is not possible, we must approximate the value function, which will be discussed in Section 4.

The Bellman equation (10) explicitly shows that we take the expectation over period $t+1$ using information available in period t. This setting accounts for the fact that future decision makers can incorporate information revealed between today and the time they need to make their decisions. Merely adding an expectation in front of the sum in equation (9) would be somewhat ambiguous as to whether expectations are formed already in period 0 or whether future decisions can incorporate information that is revealed later.

We note that equations (10) and (9) above evaluate the utility of total consumption in the economy. It is more common to maximize per capita consumption, characterizing a representative consumer. Some models also use population-weighted per capita consumption. As noted by Jensen and Traeger

(2014), we can usually accommodate labor-weighting and/or per capita consumption by simply renormalizing the discount factor β, which may become time-dependent.[7] For the purpose of this chapter, we abstract from such an induced time dependence of β.

3 Analytic modeling and insights

This section derives general analytical insights into the SCC's response to various uncertainties. It integrates key concepts from the literature, drawing in particular from Jensen and Traeger's (2021) "Pricing Climate Risk." We begin with a simple formula for the social cost of carbon (SCC) under uncertainty and proceed to analyze how different uncertainties translate into a risk premium on the optimal carbon tax or SCC. Our primary examples will include uncertainties stemming from economic growth and temperature feedback processes in the climate system, which are generally found to generate the largest risk premiums. Growth uncertainty is particularly interesting for analytical discussion because it can generate both positive and negative risk premiums, depending on the model specification.

The section also briefly relates to Chapter 3 in this handbook, discussing some of the implications of using Epstein-Zin-Weil preferences. Most of the section uses general functional forms, which most clearly identify the drivers of the risk premium. As we will see, parameters of specific utility functions can be potentially misleading as they often conflate conceptually different drivers of the risk response. A discussion using general functional forms allows us to understand the economic meaning of the drivers of the uncertainty effect and to sign the risk premium. We close the section with a quantitative model that has a closed-form solution.

3.1 A simple SCC formula

To keep the initial model simple, we summarize the climate system in one equation. The preferred interpretation of this model is the TCRE model following equation (6), where global average surface temperature is proportional to cumulative historic emissions. We keep track of M as cumulative historic emissions rather than T. Alternatively, the model can be interpreted as a simplified model where M denotes atmospheric carbon. Later in Section 3.5, we will revert to this interpretation and explicitly reintroduce the non-linear

[7] This is true for using power utility (constant relative risk aversion) or Epstein-Zin-Weil preferences. See, e.g., Traeger (2023) for a discussion of the implications of increasing the weight on more populous future generations. In particular, an often overlooked implication is that, if we interpret the model descriptively, population weighting increases the rate of pure time preference. If the rate of population growth falls, then population weighting gives a lower rather than higher SCC.

relation between atmospheric carbon M and temperature dynamics T into the model. In such a model, Jensen and Traeger (2014) show that the SCC is[8]

$$SCC_0 = \mathbf{E}_0 \sum_{t=1}^{\infty} \beta^t \frac{u'(c_t)}{u'(c_0)} \underbrace{\left(-\frac{\partial F_t}{\partial M_t}\right)}_{\equiv d(\cdot)} \frac{\partial M_t}{\partial E_0}. \tag{11}$$

The SCC captures the impact of a marginal ton of CO_2 released into the atmosphere. Reading the expression from right to left, a marginal increase in emissions affects the cumulative stock of CO_2, which in turn leads to a temperature rise resulting in a marginal loss in production. The production loss causes a proportional change in consumption (see footnote 9), which is then evaluated using marginal utility. The discount factor β^t reflects the utility discount rate applied across time, and we use a lowercase c_t to denote per capital consumption.[9]

Here, uncertainty simply introduces the expected value operator. We abbreviate marginal damages with respect to an increase in CO_2 and, thus, temperature in a given period by $d(\cdot)$, suppressing time indices. The marginal addition of emissions to the stock of CO_2, $\frac{\partial M_t}{\partial E_0}$, is unity in the TCRE model where M_t captures cumulative historic emissions, and this term would fall over time if we were to interpret M_t as the atmospheric CO_2 concentration.

Growth uncertainty plays a particularly interesting (and complex) role for the SCC. Therefore, it helps to briefly review how economic growth affects the SCC under certainty. Let us introduce the common Arrow-Pratt measure of relative risk aversion

$$\text{RRA}(u, c) = -\frac{u''(c)}{u'(c)}c,$$

as the measures of our utility function's curvature. In a deterministic world, it really only expresses an aversion to intertemporal substitution and is the inverse of the elasticity of intertemporal substitution. The constant intertemporal elasticity of substitution (CIES) utility function, $u(c) = \frac{c^{1-\eta}}{1-\eta}$, as used in DICE, gives $\text{RRA}(u, c) = \eta$. Similarly, we define the elasticity of marginal damages with respect to changes in production as

$$\text{Dam}_1(d, y) = \frac{d'(y)}{d(y)}y.$$

---

[8] Jensen and Traeger (2014) assume a constant consumption rate in the derivation, just like Dietz et al. (2018) discussed further below. Lemoine (2021), also discussed below, uses a more reduced form model without production where $\frac{\partial c_t}{\partial M_t}$ would replace $\frac{\partial F_t}{\partial M_t} = \frac{\partial y_t}{\partial M_t}$.

[9] Under population-weighted per capita consumption, such as in DICE, the discount factor β acquires a time index, as explained in Jensen and Traeger (2014).

It measures the percentage increase in marginal damages when production rises by 1 %. In the DICE model discussed in Chapter 1, we have $\text{Dam}_1(d, y) = 1$ because damages are proportional to production. This damage sensitivity term relates closely to what Lemoine (2021) later labels the damage scaling effect.

Jensen and Traeger (2014) show that a growth increase raises the SCC if and only if

$$\text{RRA}(u, c) < \text{Dam}_1(d, y) \quad \Leftrightarrow \quad \eta < 1 \quad \text{in DICE}. \tag{12}$$

Technological growth increases the SCC if, and only if, the rise in physical damages (represented by $\text{Dam}_1(d, y)$) outweighs the decrease in the marginal value of damages caused by growing wealth, which is captured by the aversion to intertemporal substitution ($\text{RRA}(u, c)$).

The fact that lower aversion to intertemporal substitution increases the social cost of carbon in the context of economic growth is often framed in terms of the social discount rate. Specifically, reducing the aversion to intertemporal substitution lowers the consumption discount rate, thereby giving more weight to future damages. Additionally, a greater sensitivity of marginal damages to production further supports a stronger optimal abatement effort.

3.2 Uncertainty–covariance decomposition and the climate beta

The literature has suggested various approaches to analyzing how uncertainty changes the SCC and optimal abatement while maintaining some analytic tractability. We start with a simple covariance decomposition as, suggested by, e.g., Lemoine (2021). This step allows us to connect to Chapter 3's discounting perspective on climate change. For this purpose, we split up the expectation over a single period's contribution to the SCC focusing on the covariance of marginal utility and marginal damages, i.e., the terms $u'(c)$ and $d(\cdot)$ in equation (11). Marginal utility evaluates the damages caused by an additional ton of CO_2. When marginal utility is high in scenarios where marginal damages are also high, the two effects reinforce each other. This occurs when damages are severe in situations where the representative agent is relatively poor. Conversely, if marginal utility is low when marginal damages are high, the impact of climate damage on welfare is less severe, as those damages occur in scenarios where we are relatively better off to begin with.

Following the asset pricing literature, we can formalize this idea mathematically using the covariance formula for the joint expectation of marginal utility and marginal damages.

$$\mathbf{E}u'(c)d(\cdot) = \mathbf{E}u'(c)\mathbf{E}d(\cdot) + \mathbf{Cov}(u'(c), d(\cdot)), \tag{13}$$

where we suppress time indices and proportionality constants (including $\frac{\partial M_t}{\partial E_0}$). The covariance term states that the valuation of marginal damages is higher if marginal utility and marginal damages are positively correlated. Because marginal utility is not observable, the asset pricing literature frequently approximates marginal utility by consumption, an approximation that is exact under either quadratic utility or normally distributed uncertainty. Assuming a normal distribution of both marginal utility and marginal damages, Stein's Lemma states that $\mathbf{Cov}(u'(c), d(\cdot)) = \mathbf{E}u''(c)\mathbf{Cov}(c, d(\cdot))$. Because marginal utility falls ($u''(c) < 0$) in consumption, the valuation in the consumption-based formulation is higher if consumption and marginal damages are negatively correlated.

Lemoine (2021) labels the second term in equation (13) an "insurance" term, and Dietz et al. (2018) focus on it in the context of a "climate beta", a name motivated by the consumption-based capital asset pricing model (CCAPM) presented in Chapter 3. Apart from the risk premium, the crucial determinant of an asset's value in the CCAPM is its correlation with consumption (or consumption growth).[10] Regressing an asset's return on consumption gives rise to the regression coefficient $\beta^{asset} = \frac{\mathbf{Cov}(c, d(\cdot))}{\mathbb{V}\mathrm{ar}(c)}$, referred to as the asset's β. In the present context, we think of the asset as a small mitigation project that avoids a ton of CO_2 emissions. Its value equals the stream of avoided marginal damages. Section 3.4 will analyze this covariance for a climate-economic model, after a brief intermission relating our reasoning to some of the insights from the discounting literature.

3.3 A note on discounting

Let us, for a moment, assume that marginal damages $d(\cdot)$ are independent of the state of the world so that we can neglect the uncertainty governing $d(\cdot)$. Adding back the time preference discount factor β and time subscripts, equation (13) simplifies to $\beta^t\mathbf{E}u'(c_t)d(\cdot) = d(\cdot)\beta^t\mathbf{E}u'(c_t)$. The term $\beta^t\mathbf{E}u'(c_t)$ captures the marginal value of a deterministic future consumption unit. This expression is the source of Weitzman's (1998) and Weitzman's (2001) famous publications arguing that we should discount future environmental damages at a falling discount rate, an argument that triggered the UK to implement falling discount rates for cost-benefit analysis (Treasury, 2003) and still enjoys some popularity in the field.

By Jensen's inequality, uncertainty increases an expectation if and only if the argument is convex in the stochastic variable. Here, the argument is marginal utility. Marginal utility is convex in consumption if the decision maker is prudent, a common assumption that assumes a positive third derivative of the utility function (more below). Assuming prudence, the expected value falls as uncertainty grows. Thus, as uncertainty grows over time, uncertainty increases our valuation of a future consumption unit. Faced with such an uncertain future, Weitzman offers us the first deterministic consumption unit to ensure safe baseline consumption. Our marginal willingness to pay for this first safe

[10] The CCAPM can be formulated either in terms of consumption itself or consumption growth, both models are mere reformulations of each other.

unit grows large with the uncertainty. We will return to this reasoning further below in the climate context. The crucial insight for the moment is that such reasoning relies on the assumption that the future is uncertain, but our environmental payoff is not. Yet, environmental payoffs are generally uncertain as well, in which case Weitzman's reasoning is too simple. Gollier (2004) points out how a seemingly related argument could be construed to turn Weitzman's argument upside down, arguing for an increasing rather than falling discount rate ("Weitzman-Gollier puzzle"). The full equation (13) shows that, in general, the valuation of uncertainty crucially depends on the correlation between the project's payoff and the evolution of the overall economy, a point emphasized by Traeger (2013).

Equation (11) states the SCC in present value terms. It discounts using pure time preference and, otherwise, values marginal damages based on marginal utility. We chose this approach because it makes the interaction between overall consumption, marginal damages, and the impact of emissions on warming explicit. Connecting to the discount rate more generally, we could define the pure rate of time preference ρ and the average consumption growth rate g_t over the time horizon t to transform our factor $\beta^t \frac{u'(c_t)}{u'(c_0)} \approx \exp(-(\rho + \text{RRA}\, g_t)t)$ to a form explicitly containing the Ramsey formula's discount rate $\rho + \text{RRA}\, g_t$. As explained in Chapter 3, this rate picks up a prudence term under uncertainty, an alternative way to understand Weitzman's argument. Yet, once again, it is important to realize that this consumption discount rate is generally correlated with our mitigation project's payoff (and, in particular, marginal damages). Traeger (2014) shows how to take the mitigation project's payoff correlation into account under standard preferences, Epstein-Zin-Weil preferences, ambiguity aversion, and in the case of an unknown correlation (uniform prior over the correlation coefficient). Some climate-economy simulations employ consumption discount rates straight to marginal damages to calculate the SCC. When running stochastic simulations with these essentially deterministic models (as discussed in Section 4 on Monte Carlo simulations), it becomes clear that we cannot simply apply a uniform consumption discount rate across all scenarios: even in a deterministic model the consumption discount rate should adjust according to the Ramsey equation ($\rho + \text{RRA}\, g_t$). Recognizing this limitation, most models adjust the consumption discount rate to at least account for this (essentially deterministic) variation, which recently was labeled 'endogenous discounting' by some authors. We note that this term may be somewhat misleading, as it more commonly refers to methods that incorporate a hazard rate into the discount rate and where the decision maker is fully aware of the uncertainty (Tsur and Zemel, 2009). This chapter primarily relies on formulations like equation (11), where all components of future value are captured explicitly, rather than separating them into a price and a correlated stochastic discount rate. If we were to split them this way, the time profile of the discount rate, known as the term structure, can be of interest in the context of climate change valuation (Gollier, 2013; Traeger, 2014; Bansal et al., 2019; Newell et al., 2022; Bauer and Rudebusch, 2023).[11]

3.4 Growth uncertainty – a negative risk premium?

We now proceed to tie the impact of uncertainty on the SCC more closely to our climate-economy model. It is well known that shocks increase an expectation if and only if an upward shock causes a greater positive deviation in the expression than the negative deviation caused by a downward shock of the same magnitude. To analyze this asymmetry in the impact of shocks, it is necessary to examine the curvature of the expression, which indicates how the marginal response differs between positive and negative shocks. We already used this argument above arguing that the expected value increases the expectation if the underlying argument is convex in the stochastic variable.

Section 3.1 explained that the drivers of the SCC's response to a change in growth are changes in marginal utility and marginal damages. In particular, the final term in equation (11) is not affected by economic growth uncertainty. Measuring the curvature of marginal utility, which values marginal damages, we define the relative prudence measure following Kimball (1990)

$$\text{Prud}(u, c) = -\frac{u'''(c)}{u''(c)}c.$$

In precautionary savings, prudence characterizes the savings response to income uncertainty. For a CIES utility function, Prud(u, c) $= 1 + \eta = 3$ is always positive, expressing that decision makers' risk aversion (or desire to smooth consumption over time) falls as they grow wealthier.[12] In the same fashion, we introduce a measure of the convexity of *marginal* damage in production

$$\text{Dam}_2(d, y) = \frac{d''(y)}{d'(y)}y.$$

In the DICE model, where damages are proportional to production, $\text{Dam}_2(d, y) = 0$.

We now calculate the approximate risk premium of the SCC. We define this risk premium as the difference between the SCC under uncertainty and the SCC under certainty, where under certainty, consumption and output are fixed to their expected levels denoted by $\bar{c}$ and $\bar{y}$. This risk premium represents the difference in the SCC obtained from upgrading a deterministic IAM by

[11] It's important to note that a falling term structure (declining interest rate) does not necessarily lead to a higher SCC, as marginal damages could increase even faster as a result of the same uncertainty, and correlation effects must be considered. The term structure is particularly interesting when relating the evaluation directly to capital markets.

[12] We note that for a risk averse decision maker $u''(c) < 0$, hence risk aversion, which is proportional to $-u''(c)$ falls if $u'''(c) > 0$.

incorporating uncertainty, while calibrating both models to the same expected trends. Following Jensen and Traeger (2014), the second-order terms of a Taylor expansion of the expressions in equation (13) delivers period t's contribution to the SCC's risk premium.[13]

$$\text{Prud}(u,\, c)\text{RRA}(u,\, c) + \text{Dam}_1(d,\, y)\,\text{Dam}_2(d,\, y) - \underbrace{2\,\text{Dam}_1(d,\, y)\text{RRA}(u,\, c)}_{\propto\,\mathbf{Cov}(u'(c), d(y))}. \tag{14}$$

Under a small risk approximation, this contribution from period t to the SCC's risk premium is proportional to the variance[14] and, of course, the impact of emissions on warming $\left(\frac{\partial M_t}{\partial E_0} \approx 1.65 * 10^{-15}{}^{\circ}C/GtC\right.$ under the TCRE model identifying T with cumulative historic emissions $\left.M\right)$. Under the assumptions of our IAM, equation (14) pins down the covariance in equation (13) analytically. Under proper normalization, the sought-for covariance is given by the risk-aversion-weighted elasticity of marginal damages to output. Given an approximately constant consumption rate, RRA measures how production shocks reduce marginal utility, and $\text{Dam}_1(d, y)$ measures how they increase marginal damages. Together they characterize the covariance.

The first two terms in equation (14) characterize prudence and the convexity of marginal damage in output. Both derive from the first term on the right side of equation (13), which also gives rise to the deterministic contribution that gets dropped in the characterization of the risk premium. Before interpreting the equation further, we note that even without a small risk approximation, Jensen's inequality tells us that period t's contribution to the SCC is positive if and only if the right side of equation (14) is positive. Following Jensen and Traeger's (2014) rearrangement of the equation, we find that growth uncertainty increases period t's contribution to the SCC if and only if

$$\text{Prud}(u,\, c) > 2\,\text{Dam}_1(d,\, y) - \frac{\text{Dam}_1(d,\, y)}{\text{RRA}(u,\, c)}\,\text{Dam}_2(d,\, y). \tag{15}$$

In a model where damages are proportional to output, $\text{Dam}_2(d, y) = 0$ and we can neglect the final contribution. Then, uncertainty causes a positive risk premium if and only if prudence dominates twice the sensitivity of marginal damages to output. The prudence term results from the expectation $\mathbf{E}u'(c)$; we discussed in Section 3.3 how it captures an increase in the valuation of marginal damages (and consumption in general) under uncertainty. Yet, we also have to account for the fact that growth uncertainty additionally translates into the uncertainty of

[13] The first-order terms of the Taylor expansion merely deliver the deterministic contribution, which we subtract again to obtain the risk premium.

[14] Jensen and Traeger (2014) and Dietz et al. (2018) assume proportionality of production and consumption, thus all terms share the same variance that can either be expressed in terms of output or consumption. Lemoine (2021) only models consumption.

marginal damages, where $\text{Dam}_1(d, y)$ captures that higher output scales up marginal damages.

Under CRRA preferences, $\text{Prud}(u, c) = 1 + \eta$. In models like DICE and ACE where damages are proportional to output $\text{Dam}_1(d, y) = 1$ (and $\text{Dam}_2(d, y) = 0$). Then, condition (15) turns into $\eta > 1$, which happens to be the exact opposite of equation (12): growth uncertainty reduces the SCC whenever deterministic growth increases the SCC. Even though these two equations look the same under the assumption of CRRA utility, their economic intuition differs. The uncertainty effect is driven by prudence, and the deterministic effect is driven by a desire for consumption smoothing (measured by RRA).

In models where damages scale non-linearly in production, we also find a contribution to the risk premium from the convexity of marginal damages in output (final term in equations (14) and (15)). If the damage done by the marginal cost of CO_2 increases more strongly for a positive growth shock than it falls for a negative growth shock, $\text{Dam}_2(d, y)$ further increases the risk premium. In equation (15), this term is scaled by the ratio of the damage elasticity to production and the desire to smooth consumption over time. By equation (12), this ratio is larger than one, amplifying the risk premium if and only if growth itself increases the SCC.

Thus far, our discussion of equation (11) has focused on the contribution to the SCC's risk premium from a single period. Yet, past shocks also affect future periods' marginal damages, particularly if shocks are serially correlated. As a result, serially correlated shocks amplify the risk premium. This effect is particularly prominent in, e.g., Nordhaus's (2008) analysis. Using a Monte Carlo setting, the growth rate is either high or low in all periods, and we have a perfect correlation of uncertainty over time and a strong correlation between the realization of the growth rate and temperatures. The study uses DICE to sample 100 Monte Carlo runs featuring eight different uncertainties. Nordhaus finds that growth uncertainty is by far the most important uncertainty in his setting and that uncertainty slightly reduces the SCC. Akin a "climate beta" analysis, Nordhaus shows a positive correlation between high output (low marginal utility) and high temperatures. This now common reasoning is similar to the damage scaling argument embedded in our $\text{Dam}_1(d, y)$, but relies directly on the intertemporal correlation.

What this reasoning overlooks is that higher carbon emissions resulting in higher temperatures do not necessarily increase the marginal damage from another ton of carbon. While the marginal damages increase in temperature, the marginal impact of another ton of CO_2 on warming falls with the prevailing concentration, see equation (4) for radiative forcing. As a result the marginal damages from CO_2 do not necessarily increase in cumulative emissions and temperature (Golosov et al., 2014; Traeger, 2023). Nordhaus does not explicitly analyze the correlation of output with marginal damages, which is done in

Dietz et al.'s (2018) more complex Monte Carlo analysis who find a "climate beta" approximately equal to unity.

Dietz et al. (2018) complement their numeric Monte Carlo study with a simple model that addresses intertemporal correlation through a "timeless model," where the same output realization simultaneously drives current consumption and past emissions since the preindustrial era, thereby affecting current temperature. In this parametric example, they demonstrate how incorporating this (admittedly extreme) intertemporal correlation impacts the $\text{Dam}_1(d, y)$ term in equation (14). Focusing on the climate beta, Dietz et al. (2018) do not sign the overall uncertainty effect.

Our derivations above, as well as the Monte Carlo studies, assume that future policy remains fixed. However, it is reasonable to expect that future policy-makers will adjust their strategies in response to new information. For example, policymakers can modify emission targets based on whether they are on a high or low growth trajectory. Assuming that future policymakers respond optimally to incoming information, Jensen and Traeger's (2014) solve the forward-looking problem using the Bellman equation (10) and the methods discussed in Section 4.2. They find, in a slightly simplified version of DICE,[15] that under Nordhaus's (2008) parametrization, growth uncertainty increases rather than reduces the SCC, which aligns with the analytical results in equation (15). In addition to incorporating the optimal response of future decision makers, the model also features stochastic growth processes rather than a one-time growth shock. This result is shown in Fig. 3, where the dashed line represents $\text{RRA}(u, c) = \eta = 2$, capturing both the agents' preference for consumption smoothing and their risk aversion. The other graphs increase risk aversion while keeping the preference for consumption smoothing fix, a preference specification we will discuss in Section 3.6, and increase persistence of the growth shock. All graphs depict the future policies conditional on drawing the expected growth realization in every period. These graphs emphasize that even in a world where nature happens to always draw the expected realization, time paths look different based on the uncertainty anticipated by the decision maker.

Finally, we note an alternative decomposition of the expectation in equation (13) by Lemoine (2021). Lemoine uses a parametric setting where damages are proportional to consumption, and utility is isoelastic. In this case, it can make sense to alternatively evaluate the covariance $\mathbf{Cov}\left(cu'(c), \frac{d(\cdot)}{c}\right)$, which shifts all consumption dependence to the left because, by assumption, $\frac{d(\cdot)}{c}$ is independent of consumption. Of course, this rearrangement also affects the overall decomposition in equation (13).

[15] Jensen and Traeger (2014) use their own version of a simple climate model, rather than DICE's carbon cycle and temperature module. Unlike the TCRE model, which assumes zero decay of cumulative carbon emissions, their model calibrates a small gradually declining decay rate.

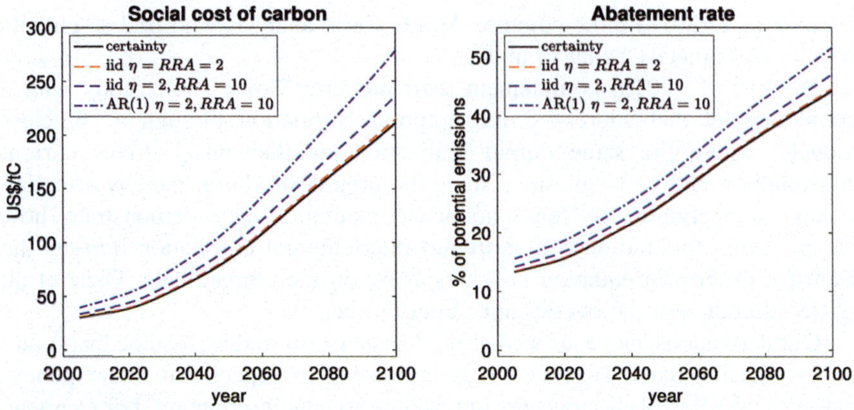

FIG. 3 Illustrates the effect of uncertainty on the SCC. The red dashed lines represents uncertainty under standard preferences and the blue dashed lines under Epstein-Zin-Weil preferences. The dash-dotted line shows that shock persistence increases the policy's risk premium. All graphs assume an aversion to intertemporal substitution of $\eta = 2$. For the case of Epstein-Zin-Weil the measure of Arrow-Pratt risk averison is RRA $= 10$. For future dates, the paths represent future policy conditional on the expected draws of the growth shocks. The Figure is replicated from Jensen and Traeger (2014).

Having shifted the consumption dependence out of the marginal damage term, Lemoine finds an additional term that he labels the "damage scaling" term. Using our general functional forms, this damage scaling term precisely picks up our $\text{Dam}_1(d, y)$ contribution above, originally attributed to the "climate beta", leaving the altered covariance term to pick up correlations that are independent of consumption scaling (and absent in our current setting of mere growth uncertainty). In this section, we focused on a simple growth shock that alters output as a mean-zero shock. Appendix A of Jensen and Traeger (2014) relaxes this assumption and shows that alternative growth processes add a term to equations (14) and (15) that accounts for the possible non-linearities in the growth process.

3.5 Climate uncertainty

The Monte Carlo studies by Nordhaus (2008) and Dietz et al. (2018) both identify temperature uncertainty as the second-most important factor for the SCC's risk premium, after growth uncertainty. Furthermore, similar to Jensen and Traeger (2013), they find that uncertainty regarding the temperature response to emissions unambiguously increases the SCC.

We follow Jensen and Traeger (2021), explaining how an uncertain climate response changes the reasoning in the previous section somewhat fundamentally. This general analytic reasoning also explains why a simple stochastic process that makes temperatures uncertain, as in the case of growth uncertainty, would overlook crucial contributions to the climate risk premium. More generally, it makes the point that climate change and weather shocks are fundamentally different, not only by nature but also in their contributions to the SCC.

For reasons we further explain in Section 3.7, we abandon the TCRE model in our study of temperature uncertainty and use Jensen and Traeger's (2021) formula for the SCC, which explicitly distinguishes between the impact of emissions on the carbon concentration, $\frac{\partial M_\tau}{\partial E_0}$, and the impact of the atmospheric carbon on atmospheric temperature, $\frac{\partial T_t}{\partial M_\tau}$.[16] Then, the sum in equation (11) has to be replaced by a double sum:

$$SCC_0 = \mathbf{E}_0 \sum_{t=1}^{\infty} \sum_{\tau=1}^{t} \beta^t \frac{u'(c_\tau)}{u'(c_0)} \frac{\partial F}{\partial T_t} \frac{\partial T_t}{\partial M_\tau} \frac{\partial M_\tau}{\partial E_0}. \tag{16}$$

An additional ton of carbon today increases atmospheric CO_2 in all future periods giving rise to the sum over τ. In addition, because warming is an autoregressive delay equation, an increase in atmospheric CO_2 and radiative forcing in some period τ causes an increase in temperature in all subsequent periods τ.

The response of the average global surface temperature to our emissions is governed by a parameter called the climate sensitivity, see Section 1.2. In a properly calibrated model, it governs both the medium and long-run response to our emissions. A high realization of climate sensitivity increases marginal damages and reduces consumption. These mechanics give rise to a negative correlation of consumption and marginal damages, which is the opposite of the relation discussed above for a growth shock, where a positive growth shock increases consumption while increasing marginal damages (positive correlation).

Jensen and Traeger's (2021) show that this reasoning gives rise to the same formulas as above. Marginal damages are now $d(T) = \frac{\partial F}{\partial T_t}$, where we emphasize temperatures are the crucial argument,[17] and we define

$$\text{Dam}_1(d, T) = \frac{d'(T)}{d(T)} T \quad \text{and} \quad \text{Dam}_2(d, T) = \frac{d''(T)}{d'(T)} T.$$

In addition, uncertainty now governs climate sensitivity rather than output and consumption directly. As a result, we have to introduce elasticities $\epsilon_{T,s}$ and $\epsilon_{c,s}$ that translate climate sensitivity uncertainty into temperature uncertainty and consumption uncertainty, see Jensen and Traeger (2021) for details. As we

[16] For the purpose of analytic tractability with general function forms, the only endogenous climate states are atmospheric carbon and atmospheric temperature. Ocean cooling is approximated exogenously, and atmospheric carbon is removed at an exogenously fitted time-dependent rate.

[17] Of course, marginal damages depend on all the arguments of the production function. We merely emphasize that we are now analyzing how marginal damages respond to a change in temperature. Here we have $\text{Dam}_1(d, T) = \frac{\partial^2 F_t}{\partial T_t^2} \Big/ \frac{\partial F}{\partial T_t} T_t$.

reasoned above, the covariance contribution now switches sign, implying that prudence and $\text{Dam}_1(d, T)$ work in the same direction, both increasing the risk premium.[18] In the climate sensitivity context, the contribution $\text{Dam}_2(d, T)$ captures the convexity of marginal damages, i.e., the change in damage convexity as temperatures increase. Even with damages proportional to output, this term is, in general, no longer zero. While it can initially be positive, it will eventually become negative to ensure that damages cannot outstrip overall production (and/or capital), see Jensen and Traeger (2021) for a discussion.

The major conceptual difference for signing climate uncertainty is, however, the insight that, in the presence of climate change uncertainty, it is no longer enough to analyze the correlation between marginal utility and marginal damages, the reasoning underlying the discussion above and governing equations (13) to (15). Climate sensitivity not only affects the overall temperature and consumption levels, but it also changes how the marginal ton of carbon emitted translates into warming. In equation (16), marginal utility $u'(c_\tau)$, marginal damages $d(T) = -\frac{\partial F}{\partial T_t}$, and marginal warming $\frac{\partial T_t}{\partial M_\tau}$ all depend simultaneously on climate sensitivity. Thus, we need to account for the correlation between all three terms. The climate sensitivity can be defined as the proportionality factor between temperature increase and the radiative forcing from a doubling of CO_2 concentrations. Then, the temperature resulting from a given marginal ton of CO_2 emitted covaries linearly with climate sensitivity. Jensen and Traeger (2021) show that, as a consequence, period t's contribution to the risk premium is proportional to the variance of climate sensitivity and the following sum

$$\underbrace{\text{RRA}\epsilon_{c,s}}_{\substack{\text{direct}\\ \text{risk}\\ \text{aversion}}}[2+\underbrace{\text{Prud}\epsilon_{c,s}}_{\substack{\text{welfare}\\ \text{prudence}}}+\underbrace{3\text{Dam}_1(d,T)\epsilon_{T,s}}_{\substack{\text{welfare}\\ \text{economy}\\ \text{interaction}}}]+\underbrace{\text{Dam}_1(d,T)\epsilon_{T,s}}_{\substack{\text{direct}\\ \text{damage}\\ \text{convexity}}}[2+\underbrace{\text{Dam}_2(d,T)\epsilon_{T,s}}_{\substack{\text{economy}\\ \text{prudence}}}]$$

Strikingly, the risk premium is directly proportional to risk aversion. Usually, risk aversion causes a loss in welfare, but prudence is responsible for the policy response to uncertainty. The reason why risk aversion directly causes a risk premium under climate sensitivity is because of its interaction with climate sensitivity's simultaneous impact on marginal warming (it's a covariance with a linearly changing term). For the same reason, the convexity of the damage function, $\text{Dam}_1(d, T)$, directly increases the risk premium–without interacting with risk aversion as in equation (14). Jensen and Traeger (2021) show that this direct impact of the damage convexity implies by far the biggest risk premium under any model specification. We emphasize that any model featuring climate change

[18] The sign of $\text{Dam}_1(d, T)$ stays the same, but the response of consumption to an increase in climate sensitivity is now negative, which can either be captured by defining the elasticities $\epsilon_{T,s}$ and $\epsilon_{c,s}$ with their proper signs (first positive, second negative), or by defining the elasticities to be positive and literally switching the sign in front of the $\text{Dam}_1(d, T)$ term in equations (14) and (15).

uncertainty as an exogenous stochastic process governing temperatures will overlook this most substantial contribution to the SCC under climate uncertainty.

The Monte Carlo assessments by Nordhaus (2008), Dietz et al. (2018), and Lemoine (2021) all pick up the combined effects above and find that temperature uncertainty has a substantial impact, but that the magnitude of the SCC's risk premium is dominated by growth uncertainty.[19] Jensen and Traeger (2021) split up the different uncertainty channels above. They find that the damage convexity channel by far dominates all the other channels. On second place, with approximately equal contributions, are the direct risk aversion effect and the "welfare-economy interaction", a term that captures the interplay of risk aversion and damage convexity and reflects the covariance between marginal utility and marginal damages. For more convex damage functions, such as a cubic-in-temperature specification, "economy prudence" comes in second place, outpacing risk aversion and the welfare-economy interaction. Economy prudence captures the change in damage convexity, just like conventional welfare prudence captures the change in risk aversion. Its contribution reflects that an increasing convexity of the damage function adds to the incentive to cut back on emissions under uncertainty, where convexity reduces expected output in the economy.

Once more, the above reasoning and Monte Carlo studies relied on keeping policies fixed. Jensen and Traeger (2021) show that this assumption exaggerates the risk premium by comparing the formula's output (and the Monte Carlo result) to the solution to the forward-looking problem where policy adapts to (anticipated) learning over climate sensitivity. They also show that the main effects of policy response can be captured by adjusting the (endogenous) temperature elasticity to changes in climate sensitivity $\epsilon_{T,s}$, which has to pick up that optimal policy fights the warming more intensely if climate sensitivity turns out to be high rather than low in the future.

3.6 Epstein-Zin-Weil preferences

Climate change assessments need to account for both time and risk preferences. The well-known risk-premium puzzle in asset pricing demonstrates that standard utility functions struggle to explain observed behavior under risk without significantly increasing risk aversion, which, in turn, leads to inconsistencies with observed risk-free rates. In typical models, raising risk aversion to capture risk premia also intensifies intertemporal consumption smoothing, effectively increasing the discounting of the future. To address this issue, the long-run risk literature emphasizes the importance of distinguishing between risk attitude and intertemporal substitution, as these two factors influence decision making in different ways.

[19] Using somewhat more extreme uncertainty specifications, Lemoine finds that damage uncertainty has an even stronger impact.

Empirical evidence supports the idea that individuals are much more averse to risk than they are to intertemporal substitution. The literature estimates the coefficient of relative risk aversion for a representative household to be between approximately 6 and 10 (Vissing-Jorgensen and Attanasio, 2003; Bansal and Yaron, 2004; Bansal et al., 2010, 2012; Chen et al., 2013; Nakamura et al., 2013; Bansal et al., 2014; Collin-Dufresne et al., 2016; Nakamura et al., 2017). Simply increasing the curvature of the utility function to account for such a risk attitude would lead to excessively high risk-free discount rates, a result at odds with market observations (known as the risk-free rate puzzle), and would discount away any concern for climate change in economic models. The assumption that attitude to risk coincides with the aversion to intertemporal consumption change is embedded in the intertemporally additive expected utility model, yet it is not a necessary result of von Neumann and Morgenstern's (1944) axioms (Traeger, 2019). Hence, this section analyzes how the SCC's risk premium changes if we distinguish risk attitude from the propensity to smooth consumption over time. The most prominent example of such preferences are those by Epstein and Zin (1989, 1991) and Weil (1990).

Ha-Duong and Treich (2004) analyze Epstein-Zin-Weil preferences in an early two-period pollution control problem, and Crost and Traeger (2014) introduce them into a recursive stochastic DICE-based IAM with infinite planning horizon and stochastic damages. Here, we follow Jensen and Traeger (2014), who incorporate Epstein-Zin-Weil preferences into the growth uncertainty setting we already discussed above. The authors follow Traeger's (2007) reformulation of Epstein-Zin-Weil preferences, rewriting the Bellman equation as

$$V(\boldsymbol{X}_t, \boldsymbol{I}_t) = \max_{\boldsymbol{a}_t} u(C_t) + \beta f^{-1}(\mathbf{E}_t[fV(\boldsymbol{X}_{t+1}, \boldsymbol{I}_{t+1})|\boldsymbol{X}_t, \boldsymbol{I}_t]) \qquad (17)$$

where the concavity of u continues to capture aversion to intertemporal substitution, and the function f picks up risk aversion above and beyond the mere desire to smooth consumption over time. Traeger (2007, 2019) gives an axiomatic characterization of this additional risk aversion as intrinsic or intertemporal risk aversion. In the Epstein-Zin-Weil case, f is a power function. The difference between Traeger's formulation and that of Epstein and Zin (1989, 1991) and Weil (1990) is that our Bellman equation above is additive in the time step, which makes it more obvious that u captures consumption smoothing and the generalized mean $f^{-1}(\mathbf{E}_t f[\cdot])$ captures additional aversion to risk (in the deterministic case, where $\mathbf{E}_t$ is degenerate, f and f^{-1} cancel).

Borrowing from Traeger's (2011) formulation in the discounting context, Jensen and Traeger (2014) show that Epstein-Zin-Weil preferences change equation (11) for the SCC under uncertainty to the form

$$SCC_0 \propto \mathbf{E}_0 \sum_{t=0}^{\infty} \beta^t \underbrace{\left\{\prod_{j=0}^{t-1} \Pi_j P_j\right\}}_{\text{EZW-preferences}} \frac{u'(c_t)}{u'(c_0)} \left(-\frac{\partial F_t}{\partial M_t}\right) \frac{\partial M_t}{\partial E_0}. \qquad (18)$$

This equation still represents the social cost of carbon as the discounted sum of future marginal damages. The term $\Pi_{j=0}^{t-1}\Pi_j P_j$ introduces the additional adjustment for (intertemporal) risk aversion inherent in Epstein-Zin-Weil preferences. In this context, Π_j captures intertemporal prudence, and P_j represents pessimism, which biases the decision maker toward giving more weight to bad outcomes. Under standard preferences with certainty, both Π_j and P_j would equal one. We now explain these contributions in more detail and how they affect the SCC's risk premium.

The intertemporal prudence term Π_t is defined as

$$\Pi_t = \frac{\mathbf{E}_t f'(V_{t+1})}{f'(f^{-1}\mathbf{E}_t f(V_{t+1}))}.$$

This term compares the expected marginal value of future welfare, $\mathbf{E}_t f'(V_{t+1})$, to the marginal value at the expected future welfare, $f'(f^{-1}\mathbf{E}_t f(V_{t+1}))$ (where expected future welfare is taken using the generalized mean).

For mean-zero shocks to future welfare, the prudence term usually increases the right-hand side of equation (18), raising the SCC (as also more generally investment under uncertainty). More precisely, it does so if, and only if, absolute intertemporal risk aversion, given by $-\frac{f''}{f'}$, decreases as welfare increases (Traeger, 2011). In simpler terms, this condition means that as future welfare improves, the decision maker becomes less averse to risk, which encourages more precautionary saving. We can express this condition as Prud $(f, V) > \text{RRA}(f, V)$, meaning that the third derivative of f (representing intertemporal prudence) dominates the second derivative (representing intertemporal risk aversion). In this case, prudence is strong enough to encourage additional saving in response to uncertainty. This condition, known as decreasing absolute intertemporal risk aversion, is satisfied for the standard parametrization of Epstein-Zin-Weil preferences. However, with growth uncertainty, mean-zero technology shocks do not necessarily result in mean-zero welfare shocks. As a result, the overall response of the intertemporal prudence term is slightly more complicated and we refer the interested reader to Jensen and Traeger (2014) for more details.

The quantitatively dominating correction of the SCC under Epstein-Zin-Weil preferences results from the pessimism weighting term defined as

$$P_t = \frac{f'(V_{t+1})}{\mathbf{E}_t f'(V_{t+1})}.$$

The term P_t represents a normalized weight referred to as a pessimism bias. This name reflects that, for a concave risk aversion function f, low welfare outcomes receive a higher weight through P_t, while high welfare outcomes receive a lower weight. In other words, the decision maker effectively places greater emphasis on the likelihood of bad outcomes, thus skewing the perceived probabilities toward worse scenarios.

In the context of growth uncertainty, the pessimism effect shifts the focus toward worse technological outcomes, increasing the weight on scenarios where economic growth is slower and future welfare is lower. If we were to keep aversion to intertemporal substitution at $\eta = 2$, as in Nordhaus' original DICE scenario discussed above, low technology realizations lead to a higher marginal value of climate capital. In particular, Jensen and Traeger (2014) show that the increase in the marginal value of climate capital is more than three times greater than the increase in the marginal value of produced capital. As a result, the overall opportunity cost of abatement decreases, and uncertainty drives a significant increase in the optimal level of abatement and, correspondingly, the SCC. We reproduce the corresponding result in Fig. 3's blue lines (with and without shock persistence) where $\eta = 2$ and RRA $= 10$.

Yet, the standard calibration of Epstein-Zin-Weil preferences suggestest a quite different value of the intertemporal elasticity of substitution. Once we disentangle it from risk aversion, the long run risk literature in asset pricing finds that aversion to mere intertemporal fluctuations is closer to $\eta = \frac{2}{3}$ than to $\eta = 2$. In contrast, relative risk aversion in these estimates becomes much larger and closer to values of RRA $\in [6, 10]$. In these scenarios, as the result of the low η, the pessimism term reduces the expected value of abatement, while simultaneously increasing the expected value of produced capital. This dynamic causes the expected opportunity cost of abatement to rise, and the pessimism weighting reduces the optimal level of abatement in this scenario. Here, the decision maker is more focused on preserving produced capital rather than investing in abatement, given that the relative value of climate capital is lower in these pessimistic states. We depict this result in the left panel of Fig. 4. The right panel shows how the SCC and, thus, the risk premium changes as a function of the aversion to intertemporal substitution under Epstein-Zin-Weil preferences.

Fig. 4 also shows that, despite the negative risk premium, the SCC increases w.r.t. to the original $\eta = 2$ scenario. As pointed out by Crost and Traeger (2014), this is a recalibration effect resulting from the lower growth discounting under Epstein-Zin-Weil preferences. These preferences split the aversion embedded in the unique utility function of the standard additive expected utility model into a lower aversion to intertemporal substitution and a higher aversion to risk. In a scenario with expected growth, aversion to intertemporal substitution increases the marginal utility of the present generation who have to pay for the abatement, relative to the marginal utility of the future generations who benefit from the abatement. Reducing η, therefore, reduces the valuation of the cost and increases the valuation of the benefits of abatement (reducing the growth discounting term of the consumption discount rate). Thus, Epstein-Zin-Weil preferences increase the SCC despite the negative risk premium they imply in the context of growth uncertainty. Epstein et al. (2014) point out that the common calibration of Epstein-Zin-Weil preferences can cause a rather high willingness to pay for an early resolution of uncertainty (even in the absence of any instrumental value). Traeger (2019)

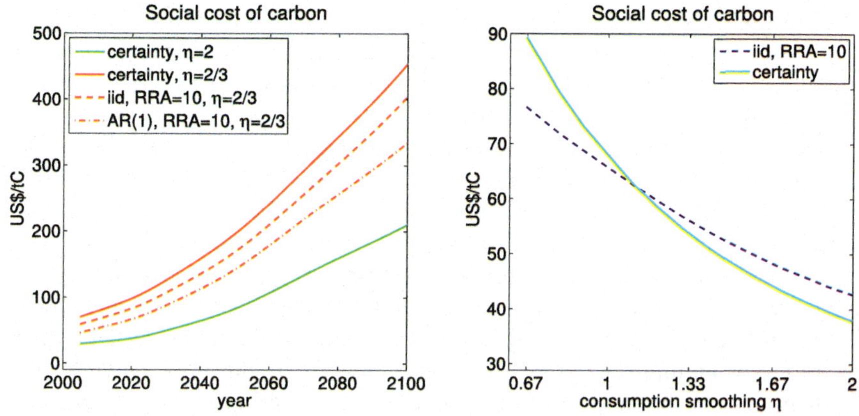

FIG. 4 Left panel shows the SCC's response to iid (dashed) and more persistent (dash-dotted) growth shocks in red. Here, aversion to intertemporal substitution is $\eta = 2/3$ and uncertainty causes a negative risk premium. Both panels employ Epstein-Zin-Weil preferences with an Arrow-Pratt coefficient of relative risk aversion of 10. The upward shift from the green to the red solid line under certainty represents the recalibration of the intertemporal consumption smoothing parameter under Epstein-Zin-Weil preferences, which is also reflected in the falling green solid line in the right panel. The right panel shows that the SCC's risk premium is negative under a low aversion to intertemporal substitution η and switches sign for η slightly above unity. The Figure is replicated from Jensen and Traeger (2014).

explains that the standard calibration and $\eta \leq 1$ can be explained by an artefact of isoelastic Epstein-Zin-Weil preferences, which behave somewhat counter-intuitively for $\eta > 1$. This reasoning makes a choice of unity for the intertemporal elasticity of substitution under Epstein-Zin-Weil preferences somewhat attractive, in combination with a substantially higher coefficient or relative risk aversion. In the next section, we discuss how to solve the climate-economy model presented in Section 2.1 in closed form for this particularly attractive version of Epstein-Zin-Weil preferences. We note that, under growth uncertainty, Epstein-Zin-Weil preferences also imply a precautionary savings effect and refer to Jensen and Traeger (2014) for details.

3.7 Closed-form solutions

Hoel and Karp (2001, 2002) inspired what we might call the first generation of dynamic climate-economic models that analyze uncertainty using closed-form solutions. These "linear-quadratic" models feature a quadratic objective function and exclude an explicit production function. The climate system is simplified to a model of atmospheric carbon, although this limitation had been mitigated by the introduction of the TRCE model. These authors, along with many who followed, primarily used the framework to study issues related to Weitzman's (1974)'s analysis of prices versus quantities in a dynamic climate change context, concluding that in most cases, taxes are more effective than quotas.

In a highly stylized dynamic analytic climate-economy model, Weitzman (2009) derives a dismal theorem, effectively stating that we should dedicate all of our resources to combating climate change. This reasoning largely relies on a mitigation project being the only option to deliver a certain unit of consumption into a hugely uncertain future. Unfortunately, the "fait-tails" paper uses this interesting argument to discredit cost-benefit analysis in the climate context and to argue that uncertainty is more important than time preference when evaluating the climate problem. This reasoning has caused a lot of confusion in the field, so we briefly elaborate on the core intuition of the model, even if the model is far more stylized than the other models that we are discussing here. First, Weitzman starts out by describing the uncertainty over the future by an improper prior, whose expectations are infinity by assumption. Such priors can be helpful to analyze where a Bayesian parameter estimate bunches up its mass. Yet, by assumption, they defy an expected utility representation of preferences.[20] We could find alternative preference representations, such as lexicographic preferences that give immediate priority to one particular outcome. We could also interpret Weitzman's infinity as such a priority given to climate change. Yet, his model's priority really only applies to passing the first safe consumption unit into the future. Afterwards, we can resume standard cost-benefit analysis. Alternatively, if we believe that doomsday climate scenarios make it impossible to pass a safe consumption unit into the future, the value of the mitigation project merely changes the uncertainty and might well be finite.

The decision-theoretic literature offers several maxi-min type representations where we are very focused on a particular doomsday scenario. Yet, keeping in mind that climate change is not the only challenge humanity is facing on this planet, we are somewhat skeptical of how useful it is to abandon the type of trade-offs that more carefully structured and normalized models allow us to do. In general, such trade-offs can be well-represented by cost-benefit analysis, which, of course, has to include proper treatments of uncertainty. Section 4.4 surveys models that pay attention to maxi-min-related ideas, including model misspecification and ambiguity aversion, and still deliver well-defined trade-offs. We interpret Weitzman's work instead as a call to better incorporate uncertainty analysis into cost-benefit analysis (rather than defying cost-benefit analysis). Costello et al. (2010) show that placing an upper bound on the temperature distribution renders a well-behaved model that is not particularly sensitive to the temperature cut-off. We refer to Millner (2013) for interesting variations of Weitzman's dismal theorem and a somewhat different

[20] Most axiomatizations of expected utility theory assume in addition to the von Neumann-Morgenstern axioms that utility is bounded and that probabilities are properly normalized and integrate to unity. Both of these assumptions are violated in Weitzman's base model. We can permit unbounded utility at the expense of restricting how utility/consumption is permitted to change over time.

critique. We further discuss learning under fat-tails in the context of Kelly and Tan's (2015) work in Section 4.2, and we re-examine the conjecture that uncertainty dominates time preference further below in a more structured model.

Van den Bremer and van der Ploeg (2021) take the discussion of the previous sections into the continuous time framework and introduce a new and promising solution technique, common in the sciences, into climate change economics. The starting point is a simple AK-model with a known closed-form solution. This one state model has no climate but an analytic solution even in the case of their adopted Epstein-Zin-Weil preferences. The authors then introduce climate as a first order perturbation to the system. Given climate change damages are generally small, such a first-order perturbation gives a closed-form solution that can be conjectured a good approximation of the underlying AK-climate economy. The nice feature is that this first-order perturbation is itself a nonlinear function of the climate. While the abatement policy is exogenous, the authors can derive a complex parametric SCC formula discussing several of the phenomena of the previous sections jointly in parametric form (some as part of the discount rate and some as part of the price of carbon). In addition, they introduce exogenous correlations between different stochastic processes that give rise to a set of 'climate betas'. The authors find that growth uncertainty dominates the SCC's risk premium, which is positive in their base runs assuming $\eta > 1$. They also point out that growth uncertainty turns their SCC risk premium negative when calibrating η accordingly to the asset pricing literature ($\eta = \frac{2}{3}$).

Golosov et al. (2014) sparked a new wave of interest in closed-form IAMs. Under an assumption of full capital depreciation and logarithmic utility, the authors show how to solve the optimal energy allocation problem in an economy with explicit production and a CES-substitutability between coal, oil, and renewable energy. For this purpose, they simplify the climate system to equation (3) governing the carbon cycle and argue that the strong concavity of the radiative forcing equation (4) cancels the convexity of damages in temperature. What this reasoning overlooks is that warming from atmospheric carbon happens with a substantial delay, which actually reduces the SCC, see below.[21]

Golosov et al.'s (2014) model has been criticized for ignoring capital in energy production, arguably one of the most important inputs in fossil and renewable energy production. Traeger (2015, 2023) shows that the model can also be solved with the general production function from equation (3), which

[21] There has been some confusion on this point, resulting from equation (6)'s TCRE model. Cumulative historic emissions can be a good approximation for warming (under certainty), and the equation suggests that there is no warming delay. However, the approximation merely cancels the delayed warming resulting from *atmospheric* carbon's radiative forcing in the temperature equation with the slow removal of carbon from the atmosphere in the equation characterizing carbon dynamics.

includes capital in energy production and can also vary energy substitutability by sector (Traeger, 2022). This Analytic Climate Economy (ACE) also relaxes Golosov et al.'s (2014) full depreciation assumption, which would replace the capital accumulation equation (7) by $K_{t+1} = I_t$. Such a full depreciation assumption has two main shortcomings: (i) it misses the remaining capital from previous periods, and (ii) it fails to account for how current investments increase future capital availability. ACE uses instead the equation

$$K_{t+1} = I_t \left[\frac{1 + g_{k,t}}{\delta_k + g_{k,t}} \right], \tag{19}$$

which provides a "quick fix" using a correction factor that relies on an exogenous approximation of the growth rate of capital $g_{k,t} = \frac{K_{t+1}}{K_t} - 1$ and falls in the rate of capital depreciation δ_k. Traeger shows that equation (19) coincides with the standard capital accumulation equation (7) if the exogenous capital growth approximation is accurate (or if $\delta_k = 1$).[22]

In the context of uncertainty, Golosov et al. (2014) employ their analytic framework to evaluate the impact of a damage coefficient that, in some future year, will either jump up or down to a given value reflecting high or low damages. Motivated by the reasoning discussed in the preceding section, Traeger (2015) integrates Epstein-Zin-Weil preferences with an arbitrary degree of risk aversion into the framework, while keeping aversion to intertemporal substitution equal to unity. It is this difference between aversion to risk and to intertemporal substitution that is exploited by the asset pricing literature to explain observed risk premia. Moreover, Traeger (2015) points out that Golosov et al.'s (2014) damage function over CO_2 is slightly concave, making it less well suited for an analysis of uncertainty given that the damage function's convexity in temperature plays an important role as we saw in Section 3.5. Thus, he shows how to solve the IAM with a more comprehensive climate model following the standard equations (3)–(5) explained in Section 2.1. While it employs a standard carbon cycle or impulse response model for the carbon cycle, Traeger shows that an analytic solution requires a non-linear model for temperature dynamics, whose impulse response compares nicely with other models and CMIP 5 (see Fig. 2).

Using the damage function presented in equation (2), Traeger (2015, 2021) shows how to solve climate-economic models of the form presented in Section 2.1 under the assumptions above if the underlying uncertainty is governed by affine stochastic processes. Affine stochastic processes belong to a class of stochastic processes that have a particular structure: an additive

[22] We note that most IAMs calibrate an exogenous rate of technological progress incorporated into $\boldsymbol{A}_t$ to observed growth, making this exogeneity less of an issue than one might think. Yet, one has to be careful when calibrating the model for short time steps.

decomposition of the cumulant generating function. Cumulants are close relatives to the standard central moments of a probability distribution. The first cumulant is the expected value, the second the variance, the third captures skewness, the fourth kurtosis, and so on. Examples of affine stochastic processes include autoregressive processes with somewhat arbitrary shock distributions or a normal-normal learning model. Affine processes have been widely used in asset pricing models due to their analytical tractability.

Lemma 1 in Traeger (2021) transforms Section 2's recursive stochastic dynamic programming problem on the state space into a system of (nonlinear) algebraic equations for the shadow values, making the numeric problem significantly easier to solve. For some specifications, these algebraic equations can be solved in closed form, providing valuable analytic insights into the impact of uncertainty. Relating back to Weitzman (2009), the paper shows that a simple additive autoregressive shock model describing carbon flow uncertainty leads to the following expression for welfare loss:

$$\Delta W \sim \sum_{l=1}^{\infty} \frac{1}{l!}\kappa_l \left(\frac{\beta}{1-\gamma\beta} \alpha\varphi_{M,1} \right)^l ,$$

where γ is the autoregressive coefficient, which measures the persistence of shocks over time, β is the discount factor, and $\alpha\varphi_{M,1}$ is the (intertemporal) risk-aversion weighted shadow value of atmospheric carbon under certainty. In this equation, κ_l represents the cumulants ($\approx$moments) of the underlying shock distribution. First, we observe how the persistence of the shocks increases the welfare loss. This equation emphasizes that, in the context of climate change, we are worried mostly about long-term growth uncertainty and less about business cycles. In contrast to persistent shocks, iid shocks to emissions and carbon flows are smoothed out over the long time horizons relevant for climate change. Shock persistence derives naturally in the case of epistemological uncertainty, i.e., those situations where uncertainty is merely reflecting our ignorance of the true system dynamics rather than nature's stochasticity (Traeger, 2015). Then, observing a high realization in some period, also makes it more likely to observe a high realization in future periods.

Second, we observe the close interaction between time preference and the order l of the moment of the distribution. For autoregressive shocks, $\left(\frac{\beta}{1-\gamma\beta}\right)^l$ can be large and grows with l. Thus, time preference plays a particularly crucial role in the context of higher moments and the contribution from "fat-tails". Unfortunately, uncertainty does not make our models less sensitive to the heated debate about the right calibration of time preference, but rather more sensitive.

Turning towards the impact of uncertainty on the SCC, Traeger (2021) models three different stochastic processes governing temperature, carbon dynamics, and damages. Each of these processes reflect epistemological uncertainty implying autoregression of the shocks and an endogenous evolution of the uncertainty. For example, the stochastic carbon dynamics can be reasonably well approximated with a common stochastic process in the long-run risk literature on asset pricing. For temperature uncertainty, the model requires an autoregressive gamma process to match the climate response adequately.[23]

In the absence of uncertainty, the model's deterministic social cost of carbon is

$$SCC_t^{det} = \frac{\beta Y_t^{net}}{M_{pre}} \xi_0 \underbrace{[(\mathbf{1} - \beta \boldsymbol{\sigma})^{-1}]_{1,1} \sigma^{forc}}_{\text{temperature dynamics}} \underbrace{[(\mathbf{1} - \beta \boldsymbol{\Phi})^{-1}]_{1,1}}_{\text{carbon dynamics}}, \tag{20}$$

where $[\cdot]_{1,1}$ refers to the first element of the inverted matrix. The formula depends on several key factors. Its base is the discounted (net of climate damages) output of the economy Y_t^{net} multiplied by the damage (semi-)elasticity ξ_0 and divided by the the preindustrial carbon concentration M_{pre}. The part $\sigma^{forc}(\mathbf{1} - \beta \boldsymbol{\sigma})^{-1}$ captures the temperature dynamics and the term $(\mathbf{1} - \beta \boldsymbol{\Phi})^{-1}$ describe the persistence of carbon dynamics, respectively.[24] The temperature dynamics multiplier reduces the optimal carbon tax by approximately 20–40 % because ocean cooling provides a delay in warming, whereas the carbon dynamics multiplier increases the carbon tax by a factor of 4 and more depending on the rate of time preference as a result of long life-time of atmospheric carbon (Traeger, 2023).

Here, we are interested in how uncertainty increases this SCC. Let $\theta_i(z_i)$ denote the percentage increase of the SCC as a result of adding uncertainty $i \in \{T, M, d\}$ to either temperature dynamics, carbon flow dynamics, or damage and damage-adaptation dynamics. Then, adding an individual uncertainty to the model, we have

$$SCC^{unc} = SCC^{det}(1 + \theta_i(z_i)).$$

We will not reproduce the detailed formulas for each uncertainty here, but summarize the main findings and use the model to discuss the interaction of multiple uncertainties.

The relative risk premium $\theta_T(z_T)$ from temperature uncertainty is a generally increasing and convex function of the risk aversion weighted shadow value of carbon under certainty. Thus, the *relative* importance of risk is larger,

---

[23] Interestingly, the main reason is not so much the long-run skewed equilibrium climate sensitivity, but the non-linearities of the temperature system and the necessity to match expected temperature dynamics to those of the deterministic model for a fair evaluation of the risk premium.

[24] As explained in Traeger (2023), a Neumann series expansion of $(1 - \beta \boldsymbol{\Phi})^{-1} = \sum_{i=0}^{\infty} \beta^i \boldsymbol{\Phi}^i$ shows that the expression in square brackets characterizes the discounted sum of carbon that remains in or returns to the atmosphere over an infinite time horizon while cycling through the different reservoirs, and similarly for the heat exchange matrix $\boldsymbol{\sigma}$.

the larger the level of the SCC. As we discussed for welfare above, also the SCC increases strongly with the shock persistence and discount factor (= reduction of the rate of pure time preference). Pure time preference is far more important than the general discount rate because growth discounting is canceled by a proportional damage increase. Moreover, the SCC's risk premium from temperature uncertainty can be divided into two contributions. The first stems directly from the convexity of the damage function in temperature, and the second interacts these damages with the type of risk aversion encapsulated in the Epstein-Zin-Weil preferences (intertemporal risk aversion).

The relative risk premium $\theta_M(z_M)$ from carbon flow uncertainty is also increasing and convex in the risk aversion weighted shadow value of carbon under certainty, with the same implication that the SCC's relative risk premium grows convexly in the level of SCC^{det}. However, in contrast to the risk premium from temperature uncertainty, for carbon flow shocks, the damage function's convexity channel is mostly canceled by the strong concavity in equation (4), which translates CO_2 emissions into radiative forcing. As a result, carbon flow uncertainty has a somewhat negligible impact on the SCC, a finding emphasized by Traeger (2021) as follows. The persistence of CO_2 in the atmosphere implies that, under certainty, the main multiplier of the SCC in equation (20) is the carbon dynamics multiplier whereas temperature's warming delay reduces the SCC. By contrast, under uncertainty, the concavity of the radiative forcing equation implies that carbon flow uncertainty delivers an almost negligible risk premium whereas temperature uncertainty contributes substantially.

This finding on the relative importance of temperature uncertainty and the relative unimportance of carbon flow uncertainty explains why we decided to switch away from the TRCE model when we started discussing climate uncertainty in Section 3.5. The TRCE model gives us a convenient approximation for the temperature response to emissions. However, it masks the different non-linearities that play a crucial role for understanding the impacts of different uncertainties in the climate system.

Finally, damage uncertainty results in a related relative risk premium θ_d. We want to focus now on the interaction of these three different climate uncertainties. Incorporating the implications of these three uncertainties jointly into the model delivers

$$SCC^{unc} = SCC^{det} \cdot (1 + \theta_d) \cdot (1 + \theta_T(z_T \cdot (1 + \theta_d))) \cdot (1 + \theta_M(z_M \cdot (1 + \theta_T(z_T \cdot (1 + \theta_d))))). \quad (21)$$

While each uncertainty type independently raises the SCC, their interaction causes an even larger increase. First, uncertain damages also increase the impact of an uncertain temperature as seen in the new relative temperature risk premium $\theta_T(z_T \cdot (1 + \theta_d))$ whose argument is amplified directly by the damage uncertainty multiplier $(1 + \theta_d)$. Similarly, temperature and damage uncertainty both amplify the social cost of carbon fluctuations, leading to the final multiplier in equation (21). Recalling that the functions $\theta_T(\cdot)$ and $\theta_M(\cdot)$ are generally increasing and convex in their arguments, these relative risk premia grow in the case of joint uncertainties. In addition, the mere fact that these relative risk premia interact multiplicatively implies another mutual aggravation of the uncertainty premia, which is also convex in the sense that $(1+x\%)^3$ is marginally larger than $3x$ for small x, but substantially larger than the sum of the individual contributions if each contribution by itself is already large. Traeger finds that only the temperature premium is individually sizable. The mutual aggravation of the premia is noticeable, but only substantial in the case of low rates of pure time preference.

4 Numeric modeling and insights

Most quantitative studies use numeric methods as the set of models with closed-form solutions is limited. The majority of studies exploring uncertainty started out with scenario analysis that eventually was expanded into what we label "Monte-Carlo simulations" discussed in Section 4.1. Incorporating optimization and forward-looking behavior generally requires numeric dynamic programming, an approach that we will discuss together with some of the literature's insights on anticipated learning in Section 4.2. Thus far, we have discussed smooth and reversible stochastic events. Section 4.3 on tipping points discusses the modeling, literature, and results governing large-scale irreversible climate phenomena that can be triggered by global warming. Section 4.4 takes a closer look at a literature where modelers have been weary to assume given probabilities or unique models to analyze climate economics. Finally, Section 4.5 gives a very brief introduction to a recent approach that harnesses the power of machine learning to solve more complex dynamic programming problems.

4.1 Monte-Carlo simulations

Monte Carlo simulations are the simplest and, at times, the only feasible way to introduce uncertainty into complex policy-oriented IAMs. These studies draw a large number of separate worlds and compare results statistically. The simulations generally assume some given policy regime and simulate the IAM forward. They introduce uncertainty by drawing realization from a joint probability distribution representing uncertainty about multiple model parameters. Repeated drawing and simulation generate distributions of how the future might look under a given policy. In these models, the SCC is commonly calculated by running the model twice for each draw of the parameter distribution: once for the given policy scenario and a second time with an additional 'pulse' of CO_2 emissions. The SCC is then determined by comparing the economic loss generated by an additional ton of carbon. Like for all outcome variables, Monte Carlo simulations also generate a distribution over the SCC. Its average value is often interpreted as the SCC under uncertainty.

The strength of the Monte Carlo approach is that it is relatively simple to implement and permits the introduction of multiple uncertainties into complex IAMs using realistic climate modules and detailed, disaggregated representations of the world economy. Such complexity is challenging to handle with stochastic dynamic programming approaches. The results explore possible futures and indicate the relative importance of different uncertainties and the overall sensitivity to parameter changes.

The downside of the Monte Carlo approach is that it cannot optimize policies. In a similar vein, future policymakers do not respond to the resolution of uncertainty, which can introduce a sort of 'negativity bias' into the simulated futures. This contrasts sharply with Bellman's approach characterized by equation (10) in Section 2.2, where the policy maker optimizes in every period conditional on the given information set (we might well consider this the optimistic extreme). Sometimes, modelers try to "fix" the lack of optimization by simply optimizing the policy of each run by itself. As shown by Crost and Traeger (2013), this approach is generally a bad idea. In their example of damage uncertainty, it can result in the wrong sign of the uncertainty effect. The issue is that, in such an approach, each decision maker lives in her own separate world, knows her particular future with certainty, and optimizes accordingly, which is quite different from optimizing in the face of uncertainty where decisions have to trade off the consequences across all possible futures.[25]

The trouble with deriving a distribution of SCCs is that setting today's policy requires a unique policy recommendation. As we know from Section 3, the optimal response to uncertainty is not equal to the average response. It is based on optimizing expectations, as done by the Bellman equation (10). This always gives rise to a unique SCC conditional on current information.

Already the Stern Review (Stern, 2007) includes Monte Carlo simulations carried out with the PAGE IAM (Hope, 2006). Nordhaus (2008) uses this approach for his DICE model. Using the baseline scenario (no emission reduction policy), he first draws randomly 100 times from the iid normal distributions of eight parameters[26] separately. He simulates the (slightly simplified) DICE model for each set of realizations. In this exercise, he finds that the quantitatively most important variables are productivity growth and climate sensitivity - a one standard deviation from their mean value has the largest impact on outcomes. He then repeats the exercise with 100 runs of the parameters being jointly uncertain to find the overall impact of the eight uncertainties and analyze potential interactions. Again productivity uncertainty

[25] As we discussed in Section 3.4, it can also happen with standard (non-optimizing) Monte Carlo analysis that the sign differs between a world where policies are optimized and respond to uncertainty and where we merely simulate an expected SCC along a fixed policy trajectory. Yet, the issue with (simplistically) optimizing policy is that decisions can only be based on the current information set (see Footnote 7), which is violated when letting each decision maker foresee its actual future.

[26] The eight parameters are: growth in factor productivity, rate of decarbonization, equilibrium climate sensitivity, damage coefficient, backstop technology price, asymptotic population, transfer coefficient in carbon cycle and total fossil fuel resources.

dominates in his analysis and leads to a negative risk premium. Gillingham et al. (2018) run and compare Monte-Carlo simulations for six common IAMs[27] for uncertainty about productivity growth, population growth, and the equilibrium climate sensitivity. Using 125 runs for each model, they reproduce Nordhaus's earlier result that productivity growth has the largest impact of the three parameters. They also conclude that the parametric uncertainty is more important than the differences between the six models, which they interpret as model uncertainty.

Most prominently, the Monte Carlo method has been used to calculate distributions, percentiles, and a mean SCC for US government agencies to evaluate the emission impact of large projects and new regulations in governmental cost-benefit analysis. In 2010, 2013, 2016 and 2021, the Interagency Working Group on the Social Cost of Carbon[28] simulated three IAMs (DICE, FUND, and PAGE) to create distributions of the social cost of carbon for three different discount rates and five different socio-economic scenarios with 10,000 draws from a probability distribution for the climate sensitivity.[29] The latest official set of numbers can be found in EPA (2023), which is based on input from the following two studies.

Rennert et al. (2022) introduce a new IAM, GIVE, with the explicit purpose of updating the SCC (and other SC-GHGs) used by US government agencies. The GIVE model improves earlier models along several dimensions. First, building on Rennert et al. (2021), they substantially improve the representation of economic uncertainty. Rennert et al. (2021) combine recent empirical work with expert elicitation to generate long-term probabilistic projections of population dynamics, economic growth, and emissions. Additionally, rather than drawing parameters once before a run, these simulations generate 'stochastic paths' for some of the uncertain variables. In addition to the probabilistic projections, the 10,000 Monte Carlo draws in Rennert et al. (2022) also incorporate a wide range of climatic and damage-related uncertainties. Second, the authors develop bottom-up country-level damage functions based on recent empirical work on damages from agriculture, mortality, sea-level rise, and energy. Third, they use the reduced complexity climate model FAIR as their climate module.

In parallel, the researchers of the The Climate Impact Lab (2023) developed their own high-resolution IAM, DSCIM. Their model also uses the probabilistic projections by Rennert et al. (2021) and the FAIR climate model, deploying Monte Carlo simulations similarly as outlined above. The Climate

[27] DICE (Nordhaus and Sztorc, 2013), FUND (Anthoff and Tol, 2013), GCAM (Calvin et al., 2011), MERGE (Manne et al., 1995), IGSM (Webster et al., 2012), and WITCH (Bosetti et al., 2006).

[28] Interagency Working Group on Social Cost of Carbon (2010, 2013, 2016); Interagency Working Group on Social Cost Greenhouse Gases (2021).

[29] For PAGE and FUND, also additional model parameters are uncertain in those simulations.

Impact Lab has made outstanding econometric efforts to empirically estimate the impacts of climate change, with the aim of putting the damage function on the best empirical foundations possible. For (so far) five impacts (health, and mortality, agriculture, labor, energy, and coastal impacts), they use highly granular temperature and outcome data from around the globe and state-of-the-art econometric methods to estimate and simulate the damages (Burke et al., 2015; Hsiang et al., 2017; Rode et al., 2021; Carleton and Greenstone, 2022; Carleton et al., 2022). All of these studies demonstrate the large uncertainties surrounding climate change and the SCC.

4.2 Classic numeric stochastic dynamic programming and learning

In recent years, numeric stochastic dynamic programming has become the most widely adopted approach to analyze optimal climate policies under uncertainty and learning. This approach's popularity is due to two main reasons. First, only a limited number of problems can be solved analytically in closed form (Section 3.7). Second, the simpler Monte Carlo method described in Section 4.1) does not optimize policy or permit future policy makers to respond to new information. As a result, they serve better for stochastic scenario exploration than to pin down the optimal policy in the face of uncertainty. A seminal paper by Kelly and Kolstad (1999) translated the DICE model into a recursive numeric stochastic dynamic programming model already 25 years ago. It took more than a decade until their pioneering approach became more widely adopted in the field of climate change economics.

The crucial challenge of dynamic programming is finding the value function. Numerically, we approximate the value function using a set of basis functions, which represent the value function as a linear combination of simpler, predefined functions. These basis functions are often polynomials or splines. The value function is then expressed as $V(\boldsymbol{X}) \approx \sum_{i=1}^{n} \theta_i \phi_i(\boldsymbol{X}) \equiv V_\theta(\boldsymbol{X})$, where θ_i are coefficients to be determined and $\phi_i(\boldsymbol{X})$ are the basis functions. Using the approximation of the value function, the Bellman equation from Section 2.2 reads

$$V_{t,\theta}(\boldsymbol{X}_t) = \max_{\boldsymbol{a}_t} u(C_t) + \beta\, \mathbf{E}_t[V_{t+1,\theta}(\boldsymbol{X}_{t+1})|\boldsymbol{X}_t], \tag{22}$$

subject to the climate-economic equations of Section 2.1. Here, we made the informational states $\boldsymbol{I}_t$ part of the state vector $\boldsymbol{X}_t$ for notation convenience.

With a finite time horizon, the value function becomes period-dependent and picks up a time index, $V_{t,\theta}$, which we already added to equation (22). In the final period T, the value function is simply the utility from consuming whatever is left/available based on the system state $\boldsymbol{X}_T$. We can then iterate backwards using equation (22). For this purpose, we have to define at which points to evaluate the value function. Unfortunately, numeric evaluation at all points is computationally infeasible, and we do not yet know where the optimally controlled system will arrive in the final period. Therefore, we must define a reasonably large state space that should cover the relevant possible states, e.g., based on some (stochastic) steady state reasoning or by starting with a large state space and refining it later. On this state space, we have to decide on a grid of points at which we evaluate the right side of equation (22), called the interpolation nodes. Evaluation at these grid points should give us a somewhat dense evaluation of the right side of equation (22), sufficiently so to get enough evaluation points allowing us to then fit the previous period's value function $V_{t,\theta}(\boldsymbol{X}_t)$ with reasonable precision. We obtain the basis coefficients of θ by some form of projection method, e.g., least squares, or if the number of coefficients equals that of the gridpoints, we obtain them from a simple matrix inversion (called collocation). This way, we can work our way backwards to the present and, in principle, are done. In practice, we want to carefully check the quality of our solution using a variety of methods going beyond this out chapter.

The crucial step we skipped above is how to evaluate the uncertainty. Here, we can use a Monte Carlo method, merely drawing a set of realizations and calculating expectations. More computationally efficient is usually the approximation of the uncertainty distribution by so-called Gauss-Legendre nodes that satisfy certain properties, ensuring a good approximation of the distributional moments with as few evaluations as possible. Because we only have to calculate ahead one period at a time, the uncertainty evaluation is simple, and solving the stochastic problem is hardly more difficult than solving a deterministic problem.

With an infinite time horizon, we do not require the time index on the value functions because all periods look the same. If some equations of motion are non-stationary, we can always include the state representing the underlying change explicitly (which could be population, the technology level, or even time itself). Finding an approximation to the value function is still similar to the case of a finite time horizon. Instead of a last period, we start with a guess of the value function, which could simply be zero. Then, as before, we choose (i) the intervals over which to approximate the value function (relevant state space), (ii) the interpolation nodes at which we evaluate the optimization problem in the Bellman equation, and (iii) the basis functions with which to approximate the value function.[30] We then iterate the Bellman equation until we (hopefully) converge to a solution where the right side equals the left side of the Bellman equation up to a small approximation error.

The convergence of this solution approach is guaranteed in theory, conditional on a well-behaved model that implies a contraction mapping. However,

[30] We generally choose the basis functions and interpolation nodes jointly. Eg., Chebyshev polynomials should better be evaluated at the Chebyshev nodes. Combining Chebyshev polynomials with equidistant nodes might give rise to Runge's phenomenon: large approximation errors at the boundaries of the state space.

the theoretical convergence results assume that we evaluate the system everywhere in our state space and do not approximate the value function either.[31] Yet, in practical terms, convergence might fail. We only approximate the function with a limited number of basis functions and only over a subset of the state space. In particular, potential 'kinks' in the value function can be hard to approximate, and sometimes transitions lead us out of the approximated state space where our value function evaluation becomes quite error-prone. The upside of value function iteration in the infinite time horizon setting is that if the algorithm converges, we generally have a reasonable solution conditional on checking some robustness criteria.

The main drawback of (classical) numeric stochastic dynamic programming is the curse of dimensionality, limiting how detailed a climate-economy model we can represent. To capture climate and economic dynamics faithfully requires several state variables. In addition, uncertainty and learning require informational states. In the standard approach, increasing the number of state variables increases the computational burden exponentially. Suppose we have three ($n = 3$) state variables: capital, carbon stock, and time (to capture exogenous processes). Suppose we use a fifth-order Chebyshev polynomial in each dimension, including all interaction terms, and, accordingly, use five interpolation nodes along each dimension ($m = 5$) to approximate the value function. Then, for each iteration, we must approximate the value function at $m^n = 125$ grid points and optimize the Bellman equation 125 times. Adding states with the same polynomial order leads quickly to prohibitively large computations. For our example, doubling the number of states to six requires 15, 625 nodes, a 125-fold increase in nodes. Adding another three states would require 1, 953, 125 nodes, and so on. A similar increase in the computational burden happens if we want to improve the precision of the approximation by adding to the order of the Chebyshev polynomials for one or more states.[32] There are a variety of methods to reduce the computational burden of the dynamic programming problem. For example, using Smolyak grids or endogenous grids reduces the computational burden to only grow polynomially in the state space and Howard's method suggests that we don't have to reoptimize the right side of the Bellman equation in every period. We also note that dynamic programming is particularly well-suited for parallization as the optimization problem can be easily spread out over different computation nodes. We refer the reader to Judd (1996) and Stachurski (2009) for more details and

[31] Stachurski (2009) gives sufficient conditions for convergence under a linear approximation of the value function.

[32] For six states, adding one node in one state space dimension adds 3125 total grid points; increasing by one node in each state space dimension requires a total of 46, 656 grid points. Several approaches to circumvent the constraints imposed by computational power exist, and we discuss them and their characteristics in section 4.5.

briefly summarize one of the most promising recent approaches based on machine learning techniques in Section 4.5.

Kelly and Kolstad (1999) and Kelly and Kolstad (2001) use neural nets to approximate the value function to solve the stochastic DICE model in 24 h. For using a Sun Spark 20 with 75mHz at the time, they use an impressive grid of 57,600 points, and, yet, the policy function approximation using the neural network is a bit coarse, and even the sign of the optimal policy response is not quite obvious. Traeger (2012) finds that a similar DICE-based model with the same amount of state variables as in Kelly and Kolstad's (1999) original implementation can be solved to high precision using fewer grid points employing either Chebychev polynomials or splines for the value function approximation. Given the smoothness of the solution, Chebychev polynomials performed the best.

Starting with Kelly and Kolstad (1999), the stochastic DICE model has been recognized as a helpful framework to investigate the dynamics of learning over model parameters and, in particular, the equilibrium climate sensitivity. These models commonly assume that the optimizing decision maker employs Bayesian updating. The decision maker holds an initial belief (a prior) governing the climate sensitivity and updates this belief using Bayes' Theorem (generating a posterior or updated prior). The prior is a subjective probability distribution over all the possible values of the equilibrium climate sensitivity. If this original prior is (or can be approximated by) a so-called conjugate prior, the updated prior has the same distribution as the original one. Then, we can fully describe the uncertainty using this distribution's parameters. For a normally distributed prior, for example, the epistemological uncertainty is fully captured by two informational state variables, the prior's mean and variance. The updating process depends on how new information about the parameter arrives. Suppose the decision maker observes stochastic temperature realizations and knows the structure of the temperature equation and the distribution of temperature shocks out. Then, with every temperature observation, she can infer an estimate of the 'realized' equilibrium climate sensitivity and update her prior.

Kelly and Kolstad (1999) investigate how long it takes to learn the 'true' value of equilibrium climate sensitivity, which is about 90 years in their framework, and for their definition of the 'true' value. They point out that learning speed positively (if weakly) depends on emissions. Given limited numeric precision, the authors discuss learning more than the optimal uncertainty response of the policy, which in their plots would likely suggest a negative risk premium from climate uncertainty under learning. Karp and Zhang (2006) investigate learning in the linear-quadratic model with a mostly analytic solution. They find that anticipated learning in their setup decreases the optimal level of abatement relative to a situation with uncertainty only uncertainty. Leach (2007) introduces a second uncertain variable, the persistence of temperature changes, into the model by Kelly and Kolstad (1999) and shows that learning slows down significantly - by hundreds of years. His findings suggest that the decision maker increases emissions to accelerate learning. Jensen and Traeger (2013) revisit uncertainty about the climate sensitivity in the DICE model, using Traeger's (2012) insights on numeric precision. They find a positive risk premium and precautionary emission reductions and no emission response to the ability to learn (no 'wait-and-see'). Daniel et al. (2019) build a stylized model with Epstein-Zin-Weil preferences and uncertainty. The DICE-inspired framework features six time periods, six possible states of the climate, and technological progress. They find that the SCC declines over time as uncertainty declines, a finding they attribute to learning under Epstein-Zin-Weil preferences. We note that Jensen and Traeger (2013) also feature runs using Epstein-Zin-Weil preferences in a more comprehensive implementation of DICE with Bayesian learning and find the usual increase of the SCC over time.

Inspired by Weitzman (2009), Kelly and Tan (2015) introduce fat-tailed uncertainty over climate sensitivity into the DICE model. They find that learning the true value of climate sensitivity is also a comparatively slow process in their model, confirming results from Kelly and Kolstad (1999) for a normal climate sensitivity prior. However, they also find that Bayesian learning from observed temperatures leads the decision maker to quickly discard the fat tail of the distribution (if the underlying true climate sensitivity is not in the tail). They also investigate the impact of uncertainty *without* learning in a counterfactual model in which the decision maker does not update their prior despite new information. The risk optimal present-day SCC is higher under uncertainty and learning than under certainty (for the expected value of the climate sensitivity), and much higher still under uncertainty without learning. Like Kelly and Tan (2015), Hwang et al. (2017) analyze learning under fat-tailed risk. They use a somewhat different DICE-based model, a different solution method, and a different learning definition. They find that anticipated learning lowers the optimal SCC compared to a situation with uncertainty but no learning. They also find that the optimal policy is less sensitive to the uncertain variable's true value than in the pure uncertainty case. Their solution method is somewhat idiosyncratic. The authors assume that the value function is an additively separable combination of logarithms in each dimension, which mostly eliminates the usual computational burden.

In Rudik (2020), the decision maker is uncertain about the damage function coefficient and exponent. She does not learn about the coefficient but about the exponent. Immediate learning is hindered by stochastic multiplicative shocks to damages. The decision maker learns the exponent value over time from observing realized output (net of damages) and temperatures. Overall, the contributions of damage uncertainty and learning to the present-day optimal SCC are small but positive. Kelly et al. (2024) investigate uncertainty and learning about two parameters simultaneously: the effectiveness of solar geoengineering and the climate feedback parameter. Their main numeric finding is that at the optimal level of solar geoengineering deployment[33] uncertainty slows learning about solar geoengineering effectiveness and climate sensitivity. They explain this effect analytically. In principle, a 'large' deployment of solar geoengineering can cause big temperature changes that speed up learning. However, a 'small' optimal deployment makes overall temperature changes smaller, and the joint uncertainty reduces the learning signal of the temperature observation. Meier and Traeger (2023) examine solar geoengineering in an extension of the ACE model that distinguishes long-run persistent uncertainty governing climate and some aspects of solar radiation management from quickly resolving components of the uncertainty governing the efficiency of and damage from solar geoengineering. They find that the quickly resolving uncertainty slightly lowers optimal initial deployment and that the conditional deployment after uncertainty varies widely depending on the realized learning, including large probabilities on no further deployment but also on quite high deployment.

4.3 Tipping point models

In the realm of climate change, tipping points refer to situations where small changes in environmental conditions can lead to significant and often irreversible shifts in the Earth's climate system. Such regime shifts in the climate dynamics are generally triggered at an unknown threshold (if they occur at all). Unlike gradual change, these thresholds require IAMs to model discrete and irreversible changes in their system dynamics. This section explores the economic implications of tipping points, the role of uncertainty, and their policy implications.[34] Examples of tipping points include the melting of permafrost, releasing methane into the atmosphere; the release of methane hydrates from the ocean; an Amazon rainforest dieback, which releases stored CO_2; and the melting of the Greenland ice sheet, which could raise sea levels by about 7 m. The collapse of the Western Antarctic ice sheet could add about 2–3 m to sea levels, while a weakening of the Atlantic Meridional Overturning Circulation, a crucial ocean current, could substantially alter weather patterns over Europe and around the globe. Climate change could also alter the Indian summer

[33] The optimal level is a 'small' deployment leading to a four percent reduction in radiative forcing (at expected effectiveness and climate sensitivity values). The paper relates closely to Heutel et al. (2018) who introduce solar geoengineering into a DICE-based model and quantify the impacts of climate sensitivity uncertainty (increasing optimal deployment) and uncertain damages from solar geoengineering (decreasing optimal deployment). They use an approximate dynamic programming method to solve their model under uncertainty.

[34] In environmental economics, the careful modeling of tipping points likely began with the study of Skiba points, which emerged in the context of shallow lakes. This research explored how the sustained use of fertilizers can cause a lake to suddenly tip into a eutrophic state–a condition where the lake becomes oxygen-deprived, smelly, and largely devoid of life (e.g., Skiba, 1978; Brock and Starrett, 2003; Mäler et al., 2003; Wagener, 2003).

monsoon, whose timing is crucial for agricultural production, and alter carbon uptake by soils and the biosphere.

Uncertainty is particularly crucial in the context of modeling tipping points. If we were to know the tipping threshold, the optimal policy would simply be to stay underneath the threshold if worthwhile or cross it otherwise. While the question of whether or when to cross the threshold might still be of interest, we have not encountered any example in the climate system where the threshold is known. As a result, the task of managing tipping points becomes one of managing the hazard rate, i.e., managing the risk of tipping into a different climate regime. Following early literature on stylized tipping models (Heal, 1984; Clarke and Reed, 1994; Tsur and Zemel, 1996; Brock and Starrett, 2003), Keller et al. (2004) introduce a tipping point into the DICE model. Crossing a known threshold triggers a decline in the North Atlantic circulation impacting Northern Europe, which the authors represent as a damage whose magnitude is stochastic. Most importantly, they introduce uncertainty over the climate sensitivity implying that avoiding the threshold is a question of reducing the tipping hazard. The authors show that the optimal abatement rate increases in the presence of a tipping point. However, uncertainty might not lead to a larger reduction than if we could deterministically steer clear of the tipping point.

Keller et al. (2004) use the classic implementation of the deterministic DICE model and jointly optimize over an ensemble of DICE runs. Pathbreaking at the time, this approach significantly limits the informational structure of the decision maker and uncertainty cannot smoothly unfold over time. In their scenario where the decision maker can learn and respond to uncertainty resolution, he can only do so in the year 2085, learning that climate sensitivity takes on one of three different values. These shortcomings can be resolved using the dynamic programming approach of Sections 2.2 and 4.2, extending the approach to include tipping points. In the IAM context, this approach was first implemented by Lemoine and Traeger (2014) in a recursive implementation of the DICE model. Extending Kelly and Kolstad's (1999) pioneering implementation of the stochastic DICE model, the authors consider two possible regime shifts in the climate system. The first regime shift triggers temperature feedbacks that increase the climate sensitivity; the second regime shift reduces the carbon sinks. The authors model one of these tipping points at a time. The simple trick is to first solve the post-tipping regime the way described in Section 4.2, where post-tipping means that we are in a world where the irreversible change in climate system dynamics has already occurred. Let us call the resulting value function $V_1(\cdot)$. Then we move back to solve the optimal policy in the pre-tipping world using the modified Bellman equation

$$\begin{aligned} V_0(\boldsymbol{X}_t) \;=\; & \max_{a_t} \{u(C_t) + \beta_t \mathbf{E}_t[[1 - h(\boldsymbol{X}_t, \boldsymbol{X}_{t+1})]\, V_0(\boldsymbol{X}_{t+1}) \\ & + h(\boldsymbol{X}_t, \boldsymbol{X}_{t+1})\, V_1(\boldsymbol{X}_{t+1})]\} \end{aligned} \tag{23}$$

which we solve subject to the pre-tipping system dynamics. Neglecting the expectations operator for a moment, the hazard probability $h(\boldsymbol{X}_t, \boldsymbol{X}_{t+1})$ gives the (endogenous) probability of tipping. This probability depends on both the warming over the course of the period and past information capturing potential learning, captured by the states at time t and their change w.r.t. period $t+1$. E.g., Lemoine and Traeger (2014) model learning as an updating of a uniform Bayesian prior over the possible threshold locations, information that can be inferred from the current state of the physical system, avoiding the need for an additional (costly) state variable. Learning is important because it implies that, with some probability, we can avoid tipping by stabilizing temperatures at, say, 2°C, a number promoted in the Paris Accord and closely based on the idea of trying to avoid dangerous tipping points.

The Bellman equation (23) states that our current value is composed of our current consumption utility plus the future value. The future value is now a combination of the hazard-weighted future value if we tip into the regime shift and the future value if we avoid tipping for another period as captured by the value function $V_0(\cdot)$. We stay in the pre-tipping regime precisely with the probability $1 - h(\boldsymbol{X}_t, \boldsymbol{X}_{t+1})$. The expectation operator governs other non-tipping uncertainties and not the tipping hazard that is explicitly captured by $h(\cdot)$. In the examples of Lemoine and Traeger (2014) such uncertainty governs temperature stochasticity.[35]

The power of a recursive formulation of the tipping point problem is that it allows us to model the possibility of tipping in any possible period and to let the decision maker respond to a potential tipping or learn that she is in a safe region. It also allows us to combine tipping points with other stochastic events, such as temperature uncertainty, all of which would be unfeasible if we actually had to calculate through all the possible trajectories of the corresponding decision tree (see Fig. 1).

Lemoine and Traeger (2014) distinguish between two drivers of the pre-tipping policy. First, the presence of a tipping hazard implies that today's optimal policy has to be tailored to its implications in both scenarios, tipping and remaining in the pre-tipping regime. As compared to a world without tipping, this reasoning adds a new term proportional to $DWI \equiv h\left[\frac{\partial V_0}{\partial \boldsymbol{X}_{t+1}} - \frac{\partial V_1}{\partial \boldsymbol{X}_{t+1}}\right]\frac{\partial \boldsymbol{X}_{t+1}(e_t^*)}{\partial e_t}$ to the SCC, which the authors label the *differential welfare impact (DWI)*. An additional unit of emissions changes the future state of the system. With the hazard $h(\cdot)$ of tipping, we have to evaluate the effect of this change in the post rather than the pre-tipping regime. For example, if the tipping point suppresses the natural carbon sinks, then the welfare cost of increasing the CO_2 concentration today is worse in the

[35] The authors assume that weather fluctuations during a period cannot trigger a tipping point, but only if they persist into the next period

post-tipping regime than in the current regime. Then, accounting for the differential welfare impact makes the decision maker more precautionary.

The second factor changing the SCC in the face of a possible tipping point is what Lemoine and Traeger (2014) call the *marginal hazard effect*. It accounts for the policy's implication on the hazard of tipping and is proportional to $\frac{h(X_t, X_{t+1}(E_t))}{\partial E_t}[V_0 - V_1]$. As long as temperatures are on the rise, increasing emissions increases the future temperature and, thus, increases the likelihood of future tipping. The difference $V_0 - V_1$ multiplies this hazard with the cost of tipping, i.e., the future value loss of the regime shift (evaluated at the given system state).

Lemoine and Traeger (2014) find that either tipping point increases the optimal current carbon tax (or SCC) by approximately 25 %, which varies depending on the precise strength of the tipping point and support of the uniform prior. The authors also find that neglecting learning doubles the estimate of the risk premium. The marginal hazard effect, i.e., emissions' increase of the tipping probability by far outweighs the differential welfare impact, i.e., accounting for the policy's marginal welfare impact in the post-tipping regime.[36]

Lemoine and Traeger (2014) only model one tipping point at a time. Lemoine and Traeger (2016a) and Cai et al. (2016), and Cai and Lontzek (2019) model interactions between multiple tipping points. Lemoine and Traeger (2016a) model three tipping points, where one alters the climate system's temperature feedbacks, a second increases the residence time of atmospheric carbon by reflecting warming-induced changes in oceans, soil carbon dynamics, and standing biomass, and a third tipping point increases the convexity of the DICE damage function encapsulating direct economic impacts from warming caused by, e.g., sea level rise resulting from a collapse of one of the major ice sheets, or a weakening of the Northern Atlantic Ocean currents. In Cai et al. (2016) and Cai and Lontzek (2019), all tipping points are represented as a level change of the DICE damage function calibrated to the possible consequences of tipping points in the climate system. A nice novelty of Cai et al. (2016) is that they model a slow delayed onset of the economic impacts of their tipping points in order to be able to better represent crossing a non-convex threshold in the climate system when projecting them straight onto an economic damage function. The solutions of these models are similar to the algorithm suggested above. Lemoine and Traeger (2016a) solve the infinite time-horizon problem recursively in state space for all possible combinations of tipping regimes, starting with the situation where all tipping points have occurred. The social planner eventually solves the

36 We note that this decomposition analyzes the add-on to a given period's carbon tax from the immanent possibility of tipping, which still employs the future value functions. As a result, this decomposition cannot be compared directly to the comprehensive analytic discussion in Section (3), where we recursively eliminate the future value function to explain the full risk premium and account for the interactions of different value function derivatives over time.

present-day policy where she is aware that these irreversible tipping points can occur at any point and in any order, and she understands that her emission and investment decisions affect the tipping hazard. Cai et al. (2016) and Cai and Lontzek (2019) solve the model recursively in finite time, starting from a last period long into the future. Apart from the nature of the tipping points, the main differences between the two approaches are that (i) Lemoine and Traeger (2016a) include learning and (ii) Cai et al. (2016) and Cai and Lontzek (2019) use Epstein-Zin-Weil preferences. Both sets of authors recalibrate DICE's climate system, but Cai et al. (2016) and Cai and Lontzek (2019) retain more state variables and use a supercomputer to solve the model. Interestingly, despite their many differences, Lemoine and Traeger (2016a) and Cai and Lontzek (2019) both find that three interacting tipping points imply a doubling of the optimal present day carbon tax.[37]

Even more interesting, such a doubling of the optimal carbon tax as a result of tipping points is precisely what Nordhaus (2008) finds as a result of a back-of-the-envelope calculation when calibrating his damage coefficients. Based on a survey about different tipping points, their approximate probabilities, and crude impact guesstimates, Nordhaus approximately doubles the damage coefficients in DICE's damage function. Amazingly, both groups of researchers effectively come up with the same doubling after running through the hoops of complex recursive dynamic programming. In absolute terms, Lemoine and Traeger's (2016a) optimal present-day SCC matches DICE's SCC because the authors removed Nordhaus' tipping point correction to avoid double-counting. Cai and Lontzek (2019) find double the SCC because they retained Nordhaus' original correction in addition to their explicit modeling of tipping points, which is likely closer to today's perspective on the magnitude of climate change damages.

At first sight, we would expect that the inclusion of learning should lead to lower estimates in Lemoine and Traeger (2016a), whereas the use of Epstein-Zin-Weil preferences should lead to a higher estimate in Cai and Lontzek (2019). Fig. 5 from Lemoine and Traeger (2016a) provides a possible explanation as to why these two quite different approaches result in a similar correction of the SCC. The figure depicts the probability of eventually triggering the second threshold-crossing after a first threshold has already been crossed. This probability falls over time: if we have not crossed the second tipping point in a later year with a higher temperature, we have expanded the safe temperature range, and, given we are closer to the temperature peak, the probability of eventually tipping has decreased. The red lines show the probability of triggering the second tipping point conditional on holding policy fixed. The

[37] Cai and Lontzek (2019) simultaneously include growth uncertainty, which, as discussed in Section 3.6 causes a negative risk premium but increases the SCC based on the calibration effect implied by Epstein-Zin-Weil preferences.

thick black line shows the counterfactual scenario where tipping points would not interact. The dotted red line shows the drastic increase in the tipping hazard after the first tipping point has activated the temperature feedbacks. The same emissions now lead to more warming making it more likely to cross the next tipping threshold, a domino effect. The long dashes represent the increased tipping hazard if the first tipping point activates the reduction in CO_2 sequestration from the atmosphere. Also such a reduction in CO_2 sequestration increases the warming and, hence, the likelihood of tipping. Finally, the narrowly dotted line lies right on top of the counterfactual, stating that, given a fixed policy, the damage tipping point does not alter the probability of tipping at all because it does not affect emissions. The corresponding blue lines turn on the optimal policy response. Having tipped implies that the same emissions now lead to either higher warming or higher damages. Either of these implications increases the policy maker's optimal carbon abatement, reducing the tipping hazard as compared to the fixed policy world. If the tipping points alter climate dynamics, the tipping probabilities are still higher also when accounting for the optimal policy response. If the tipping point merely affects economic output, the likelihood of tipping is even smaller after the first tipping point has occurred because higher damages increase optimal abatement and, given the lack of an explicit climate system consequence, an abatement reduction unambiguously reduces the likelihood of tipping. Lemoine and Traeger (2016a) find that the interaction of the temperature feedback tipping point with the damage tipping point contributes the largest "domino" premium to the SCC, followed by the interaction of the carbon sink reduction with the damage tipping point and a triple-interaction premium.

Recognizing that Cai and Lontzek (2019) directly model the economic implications of tipping points, the domino effect in their model is substantially smaller than in Lemoine and Traeger (2016a). In fact, every tipping point occurring in Cai and Lontzek (2019) reduces the likelihood of the next tipping point. Probably, it reduces the likelihood somewhat less than in Fig. 5 because the tipping points in Cai and Lontzek (2019) only affect the damage level, whereas the damage tipping point in Lemoine and Traeger (2016a) focuses more on the convexity of damages. The idea of a tipping point increasing damages more at higher temperatures conjectures that, e.g., sea-level rise interacts with the general economic and environmental pressure from global warming. In this case, also the marginal damages from a ton of CO_2 are higher in the post-tipping regime (and more so at higher temperatures). For mere jumps in the damage level, crossing a tipping threshold has severe welfare impacts but triggers less of an ex-post policy response and, thus, less strongly a reduction of the tipping hazard. We note that the absence of learning in Cai and Lontzek (2019) implies that we would not literally be able to plot an analog of Fig. 5 in their setting because eventual tipping happens with certainty, and all lines would be unity independent of the policy response. It is probably fair to say that quickly

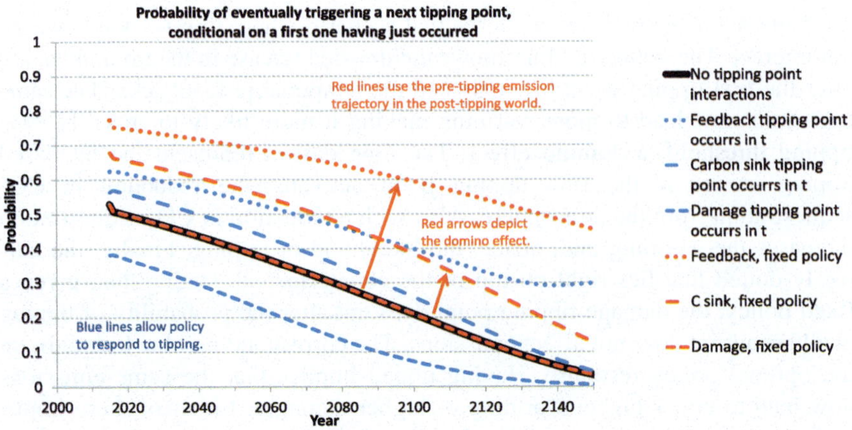

FIG. 5 The probability of eventually triggering a next tipping point, conditional on having just triggered a first tipping point (out of three potential ones) in a given year. The black line depicts the case in which tipping points do not interact through system dynamics or policy. The red lines combine the pre-tipping emission trajectory with post-tipping dynamics. The change from the black to the red lines gives each tipping point's (physical) domino effect. The blue lines allow policy and the economy to respond to having tipped. Triggering one of the two climate regime shifts substantially increases the probability of triggering a further tipping point. In contrast, triggering the economic damage tipping point does not increase the probability of triggering another tipping point. The optimal policy response to tipping reduces the domino effect. Replicated from Lemoine and Traeger (2016a).

learning whether a tipping point has occurred at a given temperature, as in Lemoine and Traeger (2014), might be the opposite extreme of no learning, and the truth lies somewhere in between (and requires more state variables to model). Related is a scenario by Lemoine and Traeger (2016a), which assumes that the policymaker cannot respond directly to a tipping threshold without delay. They find that the inability to respond directly to a tipping point comes at a substantial welfare loss, which is much larger than a generic policy delay in the absence of tipping points (or when at least coordinating on optimal policy once the first tipping point has occurred).

Cai et al. (2015) introduce environmental amenities as an explicit part of the welfare function and model a tipping point (primarily) affecting these environmental amenities. Given limited substitutability in consumption between environmental amenities and produced goods, such a tipping point can have a particularly strong repercussion on the SCC for an elasticity of substitution below unity, in line with work analyzing direct damages on environmental amenities under limited substitutability in consumption in the DICE model (Sterner and Persson, 2008; Drupp and Hänsel, 2021). Most papers find negligible precautionary savings effects in the face of tipping points (unless they omit economic growth). Van der Ploeg and de Zeeuw (2018) find a more notable precautionary savings effect and discuss that the savings response to a potential tipping point can be positive or negative, comparing stable saddle paths before and after tipping. Their paper also takes the tipping point discussion in IAMs to a continuous time framework that they solve using log-linearization. Also in continuous time, Brausmann and Bretschger's (2024) AK-model sets the stage for modeling tipping points as simple Poisson shocks to economic output, an idea also taken up by Van Den Bremer et al. (2023) in a paper comparing approximate analytic to numeric solutions.

Dietz et al. (2021) integrate all seven tipping point examples mentioned in the introduction into an economic IAM, plus an ice-albedo feedback governing the melting of Arctic sea ice that reduces our planet's reflectivity, further increasing warming. Their calibration of tipping hazards and economic impacts is arguably the most careful we have seen in the literature. Interestingly, their study finds that these eight interactive tipping points increase the SCC by "only" 25 %. While their model is not a full-fledged IAM, it accounts for impacts at the country level. Production grows exogenously, but tipping points have immediate and lagged effects on output using a simple lag equation. The fact that policies are exogenous should only increase the impacts of the tipping points on today's SCC. We are not aware of an explanation for why this study differs as much from the earlier publications and try to at least give a possible explanation with respect to Lemoine and Traeger's (2016a) doubling of the SCC. The earlier authors were motivated by a slightly different question. The Copenhaguen and Paris Accord's $2°C$ target was largely based on avoiding dangerous tipping points. Yet, the interaction of tipping points had not previously been analyzed in an integrated climate-economic model. The authors analyze whether, everything else equal, the presence and potential domino-like interaction of tipping points can indeed bring DICE's optimal peak temperature down to $2°C$. For this purpose, the authors consciously picked somewhat extreme tipping point parameterizations and found that, yet, the explicit modeling of tipping points alone will not imply that baseline DICE gives rise to a $2°C$ peak temperature unless we alter other parameters (which very much stands to reason). In fact, the authors found that, all they could achieve was reproducing what Nordhaus had already built into DICE as a damage correction for missing tipping points. The second difference is that Lemoine and Traeger (2016a) explicitly eliminated the earlier tipping point correction of DICE's damage function, which implies a much lower overall SCC in their study. In absolute terms, Dietz et al.'s (2021) Monte Carlo study does indeed find a larger risk premium on the SCC than Lemoine and Traeger (2016a), who somewhat optimistically incorporate optimal policy response and learning. From this perspective, in absolute terms, also Dietz et al. (2021) study somewhat confirms how well our environmental economics Nobel laureate Bill Nordhaus did with his relatively simple back-of-the-envelope adjustment of the damage coefficient in DICE for missing tipping points back in the day.[38]

In a model of damage tipping points, Taconet et al. (2021) find that the main effect of tipping points in IAMs is merely their impact on expected damages. This finding might explain why Nordhaus might have done so well with his back-of-the-envelope correction. From this perspective, it stands to reason to merely incorporate the expected damages of tipping points into a much easier-to-solve model with smooth damages. Another reason why the simpler "smooth damages" approach is plausible is the extended time span over which climate tipping points gradually unfold their impacts. Even a rapid ice sheet disintegration will take at least several decades, more likely centuries. From this perspective, the main issue of tipping points for economic IAMs is less the speed of the change and more its irreversibility. However, most current climate change and policy scenarios aim to stabilize temperatures at a reasonable degree of warming. In this case, the irreversible nature of climate change is less important for our models because we are not currently foreseeing that we will bring temperatures back to the current or even pre-industrial level at any time in the reasonably near future.

From this perspective, the relevance of explicitly modeling tipping points might be twofold. First, we need such modeling to better estimate the actual impact of tipping points on economic activity and welfare, which requires the explicit integration of tipping points in the climate system with an integrated climate-economic model that can translate the physical tipping processes into output loss. Once we have these estimates and their temperature dependence, it seems reasonable to integrate them into standard IAMs, complementing sectorial bottom-up damage estimates or macroeconomic top-down estimates that will miss out on the impacts of future tipping points. Of course, the tipping points' economic impacts depend directly on the damage functions in the economy, and updates of these non-tipping damage functions will also require us to rerun models like that of Dietz et al. (2021), or models including at least some policy response to update the damage function's tipping component. Second, the irreversible nature of tipping points becomes essential again in models and policy trajectories that foresee a substantial overshooting and that use carbon dioxide removal to substantially lower temperatures again after crossing a peak.

4.4 Ambiguity aversion & robust control

Climate change uncertainty often falls into the realm of deep uncertainty, where probability distributions are neither unique nor well-defined, and

[38] It is unclear to what degree these adjustments are still part of the most recent versions of DICE. Moreover, neither of these studies uses Epstein-Zin-Weil preferences, which, apart from no learning, can at least partially explain the higher SCC estimates in Cai et al. (2016) and Cai and Lontzek (2019), even in the absence of domino-type interactions.

objective risk assessments are seldom possible. For example, Figure 3 in Chapter 1 of this handbook illustrates that scientists have derived a range of probability distributions for climate sensitivity using various approaches, including energy balance models, historical data, and large-scale computational simulations. When we modeled growth uncertainty in Jensen and Traeger (2014), we were surprised to find that no reasonable long-term forecasts of economic growth existed for the time horizons required by IAMs. At the time, we turned to the long-run risk model from asset pricing, which had resolved long-standing asset pricing puzzles by positing small but persistent shocks in the consumption process–a clear leap of faith. When Gillingham et al. (2018) faced the same issue in their study, they conducted an expert elicitation (Christensen et al., 2018). Later, for the Rennert et al. (2021) scenarios mentioned in Section 4.1, Müller et al. (2022) produced the most rigorous econometric study to date, estimating a long-run growth process. However, when RFF first proposed the need for a stochastic forecast spanning over a century, one of the authors humorously compared the task to reading tea leaves.

Behaviorally, there is some evidence based on, e.g., Ellsberg's (1961) famous paradox that individuals indeed distinguish between situations with known probabilities and other situations. Ellsberg (1961) famous publication was merely a smart thought experiment based on careful contemplation, suggesting more than just limited rationality. The decision-theoretic literature has axiomatized a variety of models for decision making under situations with ambiguous probabilities and "hard" or "deep" uncertainty, most of them with a behavioral motivation. From a normative perspective, we might argue that von Neumann and Morgenstern's (1944) axioms still hold the key to how to make rational decisions. Yet, Traeger (2010) shows that even under Neumann and Morgenstern's (1944) axioms, risk aversion can depend on the level of confidence in probabilistic beliefs once we are willing to distinguish different classes of probabilistic descriptions of the world. The most widely applied ambiguity model in the climate change context falls precisely into this category. The recursive smooth ambiguity framework by Klibanoff et al. (2009) builds a dynamically consistent version of the smooth ambiguity preferences originally axiomatized by Klibanoff et al. (2005). In this framework, ambiguity is represented as a probability distribution. The smooth ambiguity model proposes that decision makers value subjective priors differently from objective risk.

From a different perspective, Nobel laureate Lars Hansen worries about the fact that most of our models are misspecified in one way or another, promoting a robust control approach (Hansen and Sargent, 2001, 2008). As the authors show, this approach can be formally related to maximin expected utility by Gilboa and Schmeidler (1989), which is an extreme limit of smooth ambiguity aversion. However, the perspective of model misspecification differs regarding what can be learned from observation. Robust control and smooth ambiguity aversion have been the most prominent frameworks to assess deep uncertainty in the climate change literature.

Starting with smooth ambiguity aversion, we can interpret such a model in terms of a subjective prior governing the distribution over climate sensitivity and weather shocks that are predicted by well-known probabilities (risk).

$$V(\mathbf{X}_t, \mathbf{I}_t) = \max_{\mathbf{a}_t} u(C_t) + \beta f^{-1}\left\{\int f\ \mathbf{E}_t[V(\mathbf{X}_{t+1}, \mathbf{I}_{t+1})|\mathbf{X}_t, \mathbf{I}_t]\mathrm{d}\,\theta_t\right\} \tag{24}$$

Equation (24) modifies the general stochastic dynamic programming equation incorporating an additional aversion to subjective risk. We already wrote the Epstein-Zin-Weil model in equation (17) in a formulation emphasizing the similarity. The difference to the earlier formulation is that equation (24) contains two expectations, and only the subjective prior is evaluated with the additional aversion to risk. Here, θ_t captures this prior uncertainty, and the additional aversion to ambiguity is captured by a concave function f. Temperature shocks or other objective uncertainty are taken care of by the expected value operator $\mathbf{E}_t$ and are not subject to the additional aversion. The decision maker first takes expectations over the future value and then integrates over the subjective prior. In general the prior evolves over time as the decision maker learns.

Lange and Treich (2008) integrate such a model into a simple stylized two- and three-period framework to sign the effects of ambiguity aversion and learning. Millner et al. (2013) apply the recursive smooth ambiguity aversion model evaluating of simulated consumptions paths using the DICE model, representing twenty different distributions for climate sensitivity. The decision maker faces ambiguity about which distribution is correct and assigns equal weight to all of them. They examine two policy scenarios from DICE: simulations using business-as-usual emissions and simulations aiming at limiting CO_2 concentrations to twice the preindustrial level. Their results show that ambiguity aversion increases the value of emission reductions. The effect is sizable for a low rate of pure time preference and highly convex damages. Lemoine and Traeger (2016b) use ambiguity aversion to evaluate tipping points, where the decision maker's deep uncertainty governs the distribution of the tipping threshold. In this framework, the decision maker chooses policy optimally and updates a uniform prior governing the location of the tipping point as temperatures rise, learning whether a threshold has been crossed. Numerically, they find that ambiguity aversion leads to a rather moderate increase in emission reductions. Analytically, they discuss how ambiguity aversion affects the *marginal hazard effect* and the *differential welfare impact* discussed in Section 4.3.

Berger et al. (2017) apply a two-period version of the smooth ambiguity preferences developed by Marinacci (2015) in a theoretical exploration of how ambiguity affects optimal emission reductions when there is uncertainty regarding the probability of crossing a 'catastrophic' tipping point, which would result in a loss of future consumption. In this stylized setting, they identify two conditions under which ambiguity increases optimal abatement. First, the decision maker must exhibit decreasing absolute ambiguity aversion (i.e., ambiguity prudence). Second, the structure of model uncertainty must be such that the disagreement between models does not increase as abatement increases.[39] The authors numerically analyze the impact of smooth ambiguity aversion using their own adaptation of the DICE model. They introduce a tipping point that could occur in the year 2100, at which time the decision maker learns exogenously whether the 'catastrophe' - a 20 % reduction in GDP - has occurred. To evaluate welfare, they use preferences that disentangle risk, ambiguity, and intertemporal substitution. Their results show that, in this setting, ambiguity aversion increases abatement by approximately one-fourth to one-half of the effect of risk aversion.

We now turn to robust control, the second prominent approach addressing deep uncertainty in climate economics. It is worth noting that the majority of robust control problems are formulated in continuous time, and often multiple alternative mathematical formulations exist. Whether one uses discrete or continuous time is generally a matter of convenience; for some specific problems, the analysis is more straightforward in one format than the other. As mentioned above, this approach is often motivated by model misspecification and, therefore, also called model uncertainty. In this framework, the decision maker has a preferred or 'best-guess' model but also considers a set of alternative models that might be correct. This set consists of models that are within a certain 'distance' from the preferred one.[40] In an ambiguity context, the size of this set can relate to both the level of ambiguity (i.e., how much the model might be misspecified) and the degree of aversion to this uncertainty. When choosing a policy, the decision maker accounts for the possibility that her preferred model could be wrong.

Let p_t denote the probability distribution governing the decision maker's best-guess model, and let $D_t(p_{t+1}|q_{t+1})$ measure the distance between this best-guess model and an alternative, possibly correct model q_{t+1}. Here, the "model" is captured by the probability distributions governing our equations of motion.

A helpful way to think about this framework is by considering a fictitious adversary, often referred to as 'nature.' Nature aims to minimize the decision maker's welfare. We can formulate a game between the decision maker maximizing welfare by choosing a_t, and nature choosing p_t to minimize the payoff

$$V(\boldsymbol{X}_t, \boldsymbol{I}_t) = \min_{q_t}\left(\max_{\boldsymbol{a}_t} u(C_t) + \beta\left\{\int [\psi D_{t+1}(p_{t+1}|\, q_{t+1}) + V(\boldsymbol{X}_{t+1}, \boldsymbol{I}_{t+1})]dq_{t+1}\right\}\right). \tag{25}$$

[39] Alternatively, if the decision maker exhibits constant absolute ambiguity aversion, the uncertainty must decrease with greater abatement.

[40] Formally, this distance is measured using an entropy metric, often referred to as an entropy ball.

Equation (25) is adapted from Rudik (2020). Being precautions, the decision maker evaluates the future for all possible models q_{t+1}. She then assumes somewhat pessimistically that nature draws the worst of these possible futures with one twist: the term $\psi D_{t+1}(p_{t+1}|q_{t+1})$ increases the value under the integral for models that are far from the best-guess. As a result, nature will be less prone to pick a model with moderately lower payoffs if it is far away from the best-guess model. The nonnegative parameter ψ is often called the penalty parameter.

Hennlock (2009) and Athanassoglou and Xepapadeas (2012) were among the first to apply robust control preferences in the context of climate change analysis. Hennlock (2009) introduces uncertainty around equilibrium climate sensitivity and derives an analytic solution to his model by making several simplifying assumptions, such as linear damages and an additively separable objective function. His findings suggest that robust control preferences generally lead to increased abatement efforts. Athanassoglou and Xepapadeas (2012), on the other hand, utilize a linear-quadratic utility framework and simple carbon stock dynamics to introduce uncertainty. These assumptions allow them to obtain an analytical solution to a partial equilibrium problem. While their theoretical results show that increased uncertainty does not necessarily result in greater emission reductions, their numerical calibrations consistently indicate that uncertainty leads to higher abatement.

Anderson et al. (2014) use a simplified version of Golosov et al.'s (2014) model with only one energy source and improve the climate model by using the TCRE model discussed in Section 2.1. In addition to providing analytic solutions, they also solve a more complex version of their model numerically. Their model incorporates three simultaneous uncertainties: temperature, damages, and total factor productivity. One of their key insights is that introducing robust control preferences can either increase or decrease optimal emissions, depending on whether the consumption smoothing parameter is greater or less than one. Li et al. (2016) focus on damage uncertainty, also using a model based on Golosov et al. (2014). They find that increasing the decision maker's concern about misspecification leads to a higher optimal carbon tax, a concern that increases with carbon emissions.

Barnett et al. (2020) develop a framework for climate economics that addresses model misspecification and model uncertainty separately—capturing ambiguity both *within* models and *between* models. Using decision-theoretic and asset pricing tools, their model incorporates the preference specification by Hansen and Miao (2018), which separates aversion to model misspecification and model uncertainty into distinct parameters. Much like standard robust control preferences, there is a cost to deviating from the preferred model specification, both within and between models. The decision maker is uncertain about climate sensitivity and the damage function, with damages either affecting output or growth. They find that uncertainty governing climate sensitivity and damages is multiplicative. The authors show how uncertainty preferences can be expressed as adjustments to probabilities. Their numerical illustrations suggest that model uncertainty has a modest impact on the optimal social cost of carbon when damages reduce GDP but a much larger impact when damages reduce growth. Barnett et al. (2022) extend the framework and analysis in Barnett et al. (2020), introducing uncertainty in the carbon cycle and decomposing the contributions of the three uncertainties to the optimal carbon tax.

Rudik (2020) introduces uncertainty in the damage parameters into a stochastic dynamic programming version of the DICE model and evaluates it using robust control preferences. By analytically decomposing the optimal carbon tax using a Taylor expansion, Rudik (2020) identifies a channel he refers to as "misspecification insurance," which affects the tax. He finds that this channel increases the optimal carbon tax in the absence of learning but decreases it when learning is introduced. His numerical results suggest that robust control preferences do not significantly alter the optimal tax.

4.5 Approximate dynamic programming and machine learning

This final section slightly differs from the preceding sections with what we consider a motivational methodological outlook into the future. Given the recent success of and interest in machine learning approaches, we want to briefly motivate how these techniques can be made useful for dynamic programming and the challenge of solving more complex IAMs numerically. In the climate change context, this approach is pioneered by Friedl et al. (2023). In our discussion of classical dynamic programming, we focused on solving the Bellman equation by iterating on the value function, where the right-hand side of the Bellman equation (22) is evaluated and used to update the left-hand side. This iterative process often relies on contraction mappings and function approximation techniques like Chebyshev polynomials. However, this method can become computationally expensive, especially in high-dimensional state spaces typical in climate change economics. Alternatively, we can directly iterate on the Euler equation. The "machine learning" approach picks up ideas from approximate dynamic programming using such a forward simulation (Bertsekas et al., 2011), neural networks for function approximation, and stochastic gradient descent for parametric updates of the approximation.

The forward simulation approach involves generating simulated paths of the state variables over time rather than iterating directly on the Bellman equation. These simulated paths allow us to explore the dynamics of the system under uncertainty, often using Monte Carlo methods. Monte Carlo simulation involves generating multiple possible future trajectories of the state variables, given initial conditions and stochastic elements like random shocks to the economy or the climate system. The simulation uses the current guess of the control rule for, e.g., consumption and emission policy. The control rules can be approximated by the same neural network that is used to estimate the value function. This is a significant departure from the approach we discussed previously, where the control variables are optimized explicitly at each step or iteration of the Bellman equation.[41]

We can simulate forward using a policy function that the neural network approximates alongside the value function. By jointly approximating both, the neural network allows us to simulate the system dynamics without re-solving the optimization problem at each step, leading to significant computational savings. However, to accurately capture the uncertainties in the problem, we must simulate an event tree that branches out over time with sufficient density to reflect the stochastic nature effectively, which can require breaking up the forward simulation into different batches (see also Footnote 43). To further enhance the efficiency of forward simulation, directly applying the Euler equations governing the optimal controls can be advantageous. The Euler equations characterize the optimal trade-off between current and future utility, offering a direct method for updating the policy function, which can lead to faster convergence and more accurate approximations.

For each simulated trajectory, we compute the immediate utility and an estimate of the future value function based on the current policy or control strategy. The difference between the current estimate of the value function and the value function estimated from the forward simulation provides the basis for updating the model. This approach differs from the traditional Bellman iteration by not requiring the direct computation of the value function at every possible state, thus reducing the computational burden.

Stochastic Gradient Descent is the optimization algorithm used to update the parameters of the neural network. Its goal is to minimize the error between the current estimate of the value function and the observed outcomes from the forward simulation, which in this economic context is the difference between current and future utility. The temporal difference error, which drives the updates, is computed as

$$\delta_t = u(C_t) + \beta V_\theta(\boldsymbol{X}_{t+1}) - V_\theta(\boldsymbol{X}_t),$$

where $\boldsymbol{X}_{t+1}$ is the next state obtained from the forward simulation. The parameters θ describe the parameters defining the neural network (the value function approximation) and are updated using the gradient of this error

$$\theta_{t+1} = \theta_t - \alpha_t \nabla_\theta \delta_t,$$

[41] Howard's method, mentioned above in the context of classical dynamic programming, similarly avoids re-optimization at every iteration. However, because the classical method solves the problem at every grid point–potentially using a set of Gauss-Legendre points for stochastic realizations–it does not require Monte Carlo forward simulation. Even if Monte Carlo methods are used instead of Gauss-Legendre grid points, the classical approach only requires simulation for one period at a time, thereby avoiding the extensive branching out of the decision tree that occurs in the multi-period forward simulation employed in approximate dynamic programming.

where α_t is the learning rate. The learning rate controls the size of the steps the algorithm takes when updating the neural network's parameters. If the learning rate is set too high, the algorithm may take steps that are too large, causing it to overshoot the optimal solution. This can lead to instability or divergence, where the algorithm fails to converge to a solution. On the other hand, if the learning rate is set too low, the algorithm will take very small steps, resulting in slow convergence and potentially requiring an excessive number of iterations to reach a good solution.[42]

Neural networks in these models are typically composed of multiple layers of interconnected neurons, known as deep neural networks. Each neuron in the network can be thought of as a simple function that takes inputs and produces an output, contributing to the network's overall "decision making process".[43] The network consists of an input layer, several hidden layers, and an output layer. The input layer takes in the state variables $\boldsymbol{X}_t$, while the hidden layers transform these inputs through weighted sums and nonlinear activation functions. These transformations enable the network to capture complex, nonlinear relationships between the state variables and the value function. The output layer provides the estimated value function $V_\theta(s_t)$ or the policy decision. The depth of the network (i.e., the number of hidden layers) allows it to model intricate patterns and dependencies that would be difficult to capture with simpler models.

As we discussed above, a crucial challenge in dynamic programming is the curse of dimensionality, where the computational complexity can grow exponentially (or at a high polynomial rate) with the number of state variables. While neural networks do not universally solve this problem, they offer practical advantages in many cases. Specifically, deep neural networks can learn to represent high-dimensional data in a more compact form through hierarchical or multiscale representations, which can help mitigate the effects of dimensionality. Additionally, under certain conditions, such as in the approximation of smooth functions with bounded derivatives (as shown in Barron's theorem), the number of parameters required by a neural network can grow only polynomially with dimensionality rather than exponentially. In general, neural networks seem capable of approximating complex functions with far fewer parameters than traditional grid-based methods.

Speed and convergence to local optima might be the most important characteristics setting the method apart from classical dynamic programming. One of the major strengths of the approach is its computational efficiency. Modern

---

[42] To check whether the learning rate is well-chosen, you can monitor the convergence behavior of the algorithm. If the loss function (or error measure) decreases steadily and smoothly, the learning rate is likely appropriate. If the loss function fluctuates wildly or increases, the learning rate may be too high. Conversely, if the loss function decreases very slowly or appears to plateau early, the learning rate may be too low. In practice, one can experiment with different learning rates or use adaptive methods like Adam, which adjust the learning rate dynamically.

[43] More specifically, a neuron in a neural network takes one or more inputs, applies a weighted sum to these inputs, adds a bias term, and then passes the result through a nonlinear activation function.

implementations of neural networks leverage highly optimized libraries like TensorFlow or PyTorch, which are designed to perform the necessary tensor algebra operations at high speed. These operations can be parallelized and executed on GPUs, significantly reducing computation time compared to CPU-based implementations. This makes the approach not only scalable to large problems but also fast, allowing for the analysis of more complex climate-economic models in far less time than required by traditional methods.

While the approach offers significant advantages, it is important to acknowledge that there is no underlying theory guaranteeing global convergence. Stochastic gradient descent is a local optimization method, meaning it is possible and also common to converge to a local optimum rather than the global optimum. However, with careful tuning of the learning rate, network architecture, and training process, it is often possible to achieve satisfactory solutions that are close to the global optimum. Experience has shown that the approach often produces high-quality solutions. The flexibility and power of neural networks, combined with their efficiency in connection to simulation-based stochastic gradient descent, make this approach one of the most promising methods for exploring the solution space of high-dimensional dynamic programming problems, even though it does not guarantee the absolute best solution. However, as many of us have seen with large language models that use related methods, there is a risk of what is commonly referred to as "hallucinations." While the hope is that well-defined economic problems with sufficiently smooth objective functions will yield more reliable results in economics, it remains crucial to carefully validate the outcomes when using these methods.

5 Concluding summary

This chapter has underscored the profound influence of uncertainty on climate policy, particularly in shaping the cost of CO_2 emissions and guiding optimal decision making. Several key insights have emerged from both numeric and analytic modeling. Unfortunately, one such insight is that there is no simple, uniform rule on how to respond to uncertainty in the climate context. Growth uncertainty affects the optimal carbon price differently than climate uncertainty, and studies often disagree on even the direction of the overall risk premium. For this reason, we have devoted considerable attention to discussing the individual drivers of policy risk premia, and then discussed the models that evaluate their relative importance. We explained the core assumptions of various modeling approaches, such as Monte Carlo simulations versus models of decision making under uncertainty and learning.

We have shown that the impact of uncertainty on optimal policy depends on how it interacts with time preference, risk preferences, and the various convexities and correlations within climate-economic models. To summarize a few key insights: time preference and uncertainty strongly interact, especially with respect to the higher moments of probability distributions. A related important result is that the risk premium increases convexly in relation to components of the deterministic SCC, making uncertainty more significant when more is at stake.

As is well known, a higher elasticity of intertemporal substitution increases the deterministic SCC (by lowering growth discounting). By contrast, it reduces the risk premium, which can even turn negative. Disentangling the elasticity of intertemporal substitution from risk aversion helps clarify the distinct roles these preference characteristics play in shaping climate policy. This distinction is also critical for more accurate calibration of climate-economic models to both risk-free discount rates and risk premia.

It is crucial to note that it is not risk preferences alone, but the interaction between various model convexities, that plays a decisive role in determining the policy response to risk. Classical prudence arguments from the precautionary savings literature appear to play a more minor role in the climate context. It is moreover important to capture that climate risk is largely endogenous–driven by human activity. Additionally, we expect to learn more about the true climate sensitivity over time. While the precise impact of learning varies across models, we feel comfortable ruling out that wait-and-see is a reasonable response to anticipated learning.

The influence of model uncertainty and ambiguity aversion also varies depending on the model and approach chosen. A potential conjecture is that the results may not differ as much from those under an 'objective risk' framework as one might expect. The interaction of different uncertainties often amplifies the need for stronger policy responses. This is true for both smooth, reversible uncertainties and potential tipping points. While the direct impact of irreversible damages can be captured through an increase in expected damages, translating the potential interactions between tipping points into economic damages requires more complex climate-economic models.

This chapter has explored the strengths and limitations of various modeling approaches, each offering valuable insights into climate-economic uncertainties and their implications for current policy. Analytic models help identify the drivers of the uncertainty premium, while numeric models assess their relative importance. We hope that new machine learning-based solution methods will enable the analysis of even more complex stochastic interactions, guided by the analytic insights we have discussed. One particularly promising area for future research is the interaction of uncertainty across heterogeneous regions–an issue we hope to see addressed in a future handbook chapter.

Declaration of AI and AI-assisted technologies in the writing process

During the preparation of this work, the authors used ChatGPT and Grammarly to improve the writing style. After using these tools/services, the authors reviewed and edited the content as needed and take full responsibility for the content of the publication.

References

Allen, M.R., Frame, D.J., Huntingford, C., Jones, C.D., Lowe, J.A., Meinshausen, M., Meinshausen, N., 2009. Warming caused by cumulative carbon emissions towards the trillionth tonne. Nature 458 (7242), 1163–1166.

Anderson, E., Brock, W., Hansen, L.P., Sanstad, A.H., 2014. Robust analytical and computational explorations of coupled economic-climate models with carbon-climate response. RDCEP Working Paper 13–05.

Anthoff, D., Tol, R.S., 2013. The uncertainty about the social cost of carbon: a decomposition analysis using fund. Climatic Change 117, 515–530.

Armstrong McKay, D.I., Staal, A., Abrams, J.F., Winkelmann, R., Sakschewski, B., Loriani, S., Fetzer, I., Cornell, S.E., Rockström, J., Lenton, T.M., 2022. Exceeding 1.5c global warming could trigger multiple climate tipping points. Science 377 (6611), eabn7950.

Athanassoglou, S., Xepapadeas, A., 2012. Pollution control with uncertain stock dynamics: when, and how, to be precautious. Journal of Environmental Economics and Management 63 (3), 304–320.

Bansal, R., Kiku, D., Ochoa, M., 2019. Climate change risk. Federal Reserve Bank of San Francisco Working Paper.

Bansal, R., Kiku, D., Shaliastovich, I., Yaron, A., 2014. Volatility, the macroeconomy, and asset prices. The Journal of Finance 69 (6), 2471–2511.

Bansal, R., Kiku, D., Yaron, A., 2010. Long-run risks, the macro-economy and asset prices. American Economic Review: Papers & Proceedings 100, 542–546.

Bansal, R., Kiku, D., Yaron, A., 2012. An empirical evaluation of the long-run risks model for asset prices. Critical Finance Review 1, 183–221.

Bansal, R., Yaron, A., 2004. Risks for the long run: a potential resolution of asset pricing puzzles. The Journal of Finance 59 (4), 1481–1509.

Barnett, M., Brock, W., Hansen, L.P., 2020. Pricing uncertainty induced by Climate Change. The Review of Financial Studies 33 (3), 1024–1066.

Barnett, M., Brock, W., Hansen, L.P., 2022. Climate Change uncertainty spillover in the macroeconomy. NBER Macroeconomics Annual 36 (1), 253–320.

Barrage, L., Nordhaus, W., 2024. Policies, projections, and the social cost of carbon: results from the dice-2023 model. Proceedings of the National Academy of Sciences 121 (13), e2312030121.

Bauer, M.D., Rudebusch, G.D., 2023. The rising cost of climate change: evidence from the bond market. Review of Economics and Statistics 105 (5), 1255–1270.

Bellman, R., 1966. Dynamic programming. Science 153 (3731), 34–37.

Berger, L., Emmerling, J., Tavoni, M., 2017. Managing catastrophic climate risks under model uncertainty aversion. Management Science 63 (3), 749–765.

Berger, L., Marinacci, M., 2020. Model uncertainty in climate change economics: a review and proposed framework for future research. Environmental and Resource Economics 1–27.

Bertsekas, D.P., et al., 2011. vol. ii. Dynamic Programming and Optimal Control, third ed. Athena Scientific, Belmont, MA, pp. 1.

Bosetti, V., Carraro, C., Galeotti, M., Massetti, E., Tavoni, M., 2006. A world induced technical change hybrid model. The Energy Journal 27 (2_suppl), 13–37.

Brausmann, A., Bretschger, L., 2024. Escaping damocles' sword: endogenous climate shocks in a growing economy. Environmental and Resource Economics 1–48.

Brock, W., Starrett, D., 2003. Managing systems with non-convex positive feedback. Environmental and Resource Economics 26 (4), 575–602.

Burke, M., Hsiang, S.M., Miguel, E., 2015. Global non-linear effect of temperature on economic production. Nature 527 (7577), 235–239.

Cai, Y., 2021. The role of uncertainty in controlling climate change. Oxford Research Encyclopedia of Economics and Finance. Oxford University Press Published online: 23 February 2021.

Cai, Y., Judd, K.L., Lenton, T.M., Lontzek, T.S., Narita, D., 2015. Environmental tipping points significantly affect the cost- benefit assessment of climate policies. Proceedings of the National Academy of Sciences 112 (15), 4606–4611.

Cai, Y., Lenton, T.M., Lontzek, T.S., 2016. Risk of multiple interacting tipping points should encourage rapid CO2 emission reduction. Nature Climate Change 6 (5), 520–525.

Cai, Y., Lontzek, T.S., 2019. The social cost of carbon with economic and climate risks. Journal of Political Economy 127 (6), 2684–2734.

Calvin, K., Patel, P., Clarke, L., Asrar, G., Bond-Lamberty, B., Hejazi, M., Kyle, P., Wise, M., DiVittorio, A., Edmonds, J., 2011. GCAM Documentation. Joint Global Change Research Institute, College Park, MD.

Carleton, T., Greenstone, M., 2022. A guide to updating the us government's social cost of carbon. Review of Environmental Economics and Policy 16 (2), 196–218.

Carleton, T., Jina, A., Delgado, M., Greenstone, M., Houser, T., Hsiang, S., Hultgren, A., Kopp, R.E., McCusker, K.E., Nath, I., et al., 2022. Valuing the global mortality consequences of climate change accounting for adaptation costs and benefits. The Quarterly Journal of Economics 137 (4), 2037–2105.

Chen, X., Favilukis, J., Ludvigson, S.C., 2013. An estimation of economic models with recursive preferences. Quantitative Economics 4, 39–83.

Christensen, P., Gillingham, K., Nordhaus, W., 2018. Uncertainty in forecasts of long-run economic growth. Proceedings of the National Academy of Sciences 115 (21), 5409–5414.

Clarke, H.R., Reed, W.J., 1994. Consumption/pollution tradeoffs in an environment vulnerable to pollution-related catastrophic collapse. Journal of Economic Dynamics and Control 18 (5), 991–1010.

Collin-Dufresne, P., Johannes, M., Lochstoer, L.A., 2016. Parameter learning in general equilibrium: the asset pricing implications. American Economic Review 106 (3), 664–698.

Costello, C.J., Neubert, M.G., Polasky, S.A., Solow, A.R., 2010. Bounded uncertainty and Climate Change economics. Proceedings of the National Academy of Sciences 107 (18), 8108–8110.

Crost, B., Traeger, C.P., 2013. Optimal climate policy: uncertainty versus Monte-Carlo. Economic Letters 120 (3), 552–558.

Crost, B., Traeger, C.P., 2014. Optimal CO_2 mitigation under damage risk valuation. Nature Climate Change 4, 631–636.

Daniel, K.D., Litterman, R.B., Wagner, G., 2019. Declining CO_2 price paths. Proceedings of the National Academy of Sciences 116 (42), 20886–20891.

Dekel, E., Lipman, B.L., Rustichini, A., 1998. Recent developments in modeling unforeseen contingencies. European Economic Review 42 (3–5), 523–542.

Denning, A.S., 2022. Where has all the carbon gone? Annual Review of Earth and Planetary Sciences 50 (1), 55–78.

Dietz, S., Gollier, C., Kessler, L., 2018. The climate beta. Journal of Environmental Economics and Management 87, 258–274.

Dietz, S., Rising, J., Stoerk, T., Wagner, G., 2021. Economic impacts of tipping points in the climate system. Proceedings of the National Academy of Sciences 118 (34), e2103081118.

Dietz, S., van der Ploeg, F., Rezai, A., Venmans, F., 2021. Are economists getting climate dynamics right and does it matter? Journal of the Association of Environmental and Resource Economists 8 (5), 895–921.

Dietz, S., Venmans, F., 2019. Cumulative carbon emissions and economic policy: in search of general principles. Journal of Environmental Economics and Management 96, 108–129.

Drupp, M.A., Hänsel, M.C., 2021. Relative prices and climate policy: how the scarcity of non-market goods drives policy evaluation. American Economic Journal: Economic Policy 13 (1), 168–201.

Ellsberg, D., 1961. Risk, ambiguity and the savage axioms. Quarterly Journal of Economics 75, 643–669.

EPA, 2023. Report on the social cost of greenhouse gases: estimates incorporating recent scientific advances.

Epstein, L.G., Farhi, E., Strzalecki, T., 2014. How much would you pay to resolve long-run risk? The American Economic Review 104, 2680–2697.

Epstein, L.G., Zin, S.E., 1989. Substitution, risk aversion, and the temporal behavior of consumption and asset returns: a theoretical framework. Econometrica 57 (4), 937–969.

Epstein, L.G., Zin, S.E., 1991. Substitution, risk aversion, and the temporal behavior of consumption and asset returns: an empirical analysis. Journal of Political Economy 99 (2), 263–286.

Fagin, R., Halpern, J.Y., 1987. Belief, awareness, and limited reasoning. Artificial Intelligence 34 (1), 39–76.

Folini, D., Friedl, A., Kübler, F., Scheidegger, S., 2024. The climate in climate economics. Review of Economic Studies, rdae011.

Friedl, A., Kübler, F., Scheidegger, S., Usui, T., 2023. Deep uncertainty quantification: with an application to integrated assessment models. Technical report, Working Paper University of Lausanne.

Geoffroy, O., Saint-Martin, D., Olivié, D.J., Voldoire, A., Bellon, G., Tytéca, S., 2013. Transient climate response in a two-layer energy-balance model. Part I: Analytical solution and parameter calibration using CMIP5 AOGCM experiments. Journal of Climate 26 (6), 1841–1857.

Gilboa, I., Schmeidler, D., 1989. Maxmin expected utility with non-unique prior. Journal of Mathematical Economics 18 (2), 141–153.

Gillingham, K., Nordhaus, W., Anthoff, D., Blanford, G., Bosetti, V., Christensen, P., McJeon, H., Reilly, J., 2018. Modeling uncertainty in integrated assessment of climate change: a multi-model comparison. Journal of the Association of Environmental and Resource Economists 5 (4), 791–826.

Gollier, C., 2004. Maximizing the expected net future value as an alternative strategy to gamma discounting. Finance Research Letters 1 (2), 85–89.

Gollier, C., 2013. Pricing the Planet's Future: The Economics of Discounting in an Uncertain World. Princeton University Press.

Golosov, M., Hassler, J., Krusell, P., Tsyvinski, A., 2014. Optimal taxes on fossil fuel in general equilibrium. Econometrica 82 (1), 41–88.

Golub, A., Narita, D., Schmidt, M.G., 2014. Uncertainty in integrated assessment models of climate change: alternative analytical approaches. Environmental Modeling & Assessment 19 (2), 99–109.

Ha-Duong, M., Treich, N., 2004. Risk aversion, intergenerational equity and climate change. Environmental and Resource Economics 28 (2), 195–207.

Hänsel, M.C., 2020. Climate economics support for the UN climate targets. Nature Climate Change 10 (8), 781–789.

Hansen, L.P., Miao, J., 2018. Aversion to ambiguity and model misspecification in dynamic stochastic environments. Proceedings of the National Academy of Sciences 115 (37), 9163–9168.

Hansen, L.P., Sargent, T.J., 2001. Robust control and model uncertainty. American Economic Review 91 (2), 60–66.

Hansen, L.P., Sargent, T.J., 2008. Robustness. Princeton University Press.

Heal, G., 1984. Interactions between economy and climate: a framework for policy design under uncertainty. Volume 3 In: Smith, V.K., White, A.D. (Eds.), Advances in Applied Microeconomics. JAI Press, Greenwich, CT, pp. 151–168 Volume 3.

Heal, G., 2017. The economics of the climate. Journal of Economic Literature 55 (3), 1046–1063.

Heifetz, A., Meier, M., Schipper, B.C., 2013. Unawareness, beliefs, and speculative trade. Games and Economic Behavior 77 (1), 100–121.

Hennlock, M., 2009. Robust control in global warming management: an analytical dynamic integrated assessment. RFF Workding Paper (DP 09–19).

Heutel, G., Moreno-Cruz, J., Shayegh, S., 2018. Solar geoengineering, uncertainty, and the price of carbon. Journal of Environmental Economics and Management 87, 24–41.

Hoel, M., Karp, L., 2001. Taxes and quotas for a stock pollutant with multiplicative uncertainty. Journal of Public Economics 82, 91–114.

Hoel, M., Karp, L., 2002. Taxes versus quotas for a stock pollutant. Resource and Energy Economics 24, 367–384.

Hope, C., 2006. The marginal impact of CO_2 from PAGE2002: an integrated assessment model incorporating the IPCC's five reasons for concern. The Integrated Assessment Journal 6 (1), 19–56.

Howard, P.H., Sterner, T., 2017. Few and not so far between: a meta-analysis of climate damage estimates. Environmental and Resource Economics 68, 197–225.

Hsiang, S., Kopp, R., Jina, A., Rising, J., Delgado, M., Mohan, S., Rasmussen, D.J., Muir-Wood, R., Wilson, P., Oppenheimer, M., et al., 2017. Estimating economic damage from climate change in the United States. Science 356 (6345), 1362–1369.

Hwang, I.C., Reynès, F., Tol, R.S., 2017. The effect of learning on climate policy under fat-tailed risk. Resource and Energy Economics 48, 1–18.

Interagency Working Group on Social Cost Greenhouse Gases, U. S. G., 2021. Technical support document: Social cost of carbon, methane, and nitrous oxide interim estimates under executive order 13990. Department of Energy.

Interagency Working Group on Social Cost of Carbon, U. S. G., 2010. Technical support document: social cost of carbon for regulatory impact analysis under executive order 12866. Department of Energy.

Interagency Working Group on Social Cost of Carbon, U. S. G., 2013. Technical support document: Technical update of the social cost of carbon for regulatory impact analysis under executive order 12866. Department of Energy.

Interagency Working Group on Social Cost of Carbon, U. S. G., 2016. Technical support document: Technical update of the social cost of carbon for regulatory impact analysis under executive order 12866 (Department of Energy).

IPCC, 2013. Climate Change 2013: The Physical Science Basis. Contribution of Working Group I to the Fifth Assessment Report of the Intergovernmental Panel on Climate Change. Cambridge University Press, Cambridge, United Kingdom and New York, NY, USA.

IPCC, 2021. Climate Change 2021: The Physical Science Basis. Contribution of Working Group I to the Sixth Assessment Report of the Intergovernmental Panel on Climate Change. Cambridge University Press, Cambridge, United Kingdom and New York, NY, USA.

Jensen, S., Traeger, C., 2013. Optimally climate sensitive policy: a comprehensive evaluation of uncertainty & learning. Department of Agricultural and Resource Economics, UC Berkeley.

Jensen, S., Traeger, C.P., 2014. Optimal climate change mitigation under long-term growth uncertainty: stochastic integrated assessment and analytic findings. European Economic Review 69 (C), 104–125.

Jensen, S., Traeger, C.P., 2021. Pricing climate risk.

Joos, F., Roth, R., Weaver, A.J., 2013. Carbon dioxide and climate impulse response functions for the computation of greenhouse gas metrics: a multi-model analysis. Atmos. Chem. Phys. 13, 2793–2825.

Judd, K.L., 1996. Approximation, perturbation, and projection methods in economic analysis. Handbook of Computational Economics 1, 509–585.

Karp, L., Traeger, C., 2024. Smart cap. Journal of the European Economic Association, jvae030.

Karp, L., Zhang, J., 2006. Regulation with anticipated learning about environmental damages. Journal of Environmental Economics and Management 51, 259–279.

Keller, K., Bolker, B.M., Bradford, D.F., 2004. Uncertain climate thresholds and optimal economic growth. Journal of Environmental Economics and Management 48, 723–741.

Kelly, D.L., Heutel, G., Moreno-Cruz, J.B., Shayegh, S., 2024. Solar geoengineering, learning, and experimentation. Journal of the Association of Environmental and Resource Economists 11, 6.

Kelly, D.L., Kolstad, C.D., 1999. Bayesian learning, growth, and pollution. Journal of Economic Dynamics and Control 23, 491–518.

Kelly, D.L., Kolstad, C.D., 2001. Solving infinite horizon growth models with an environmental sector. Computational Economics 18, 217–231.

Kelly, D.L., Tan, Z., 2015. Learning and climate feedbacks: optimal climate insurance and fat tails. Journal of Environmental Economics and Management 72, 98–122.

Kimball, M.S., 1990. Precautionary saving in the small and in the large. Econometrica 58 (1), 53–73.

Klibanoff, P., Marinacci, M., Mukerji, S., 2005. A smooth model of decision making under ambiguity. Econometrica 73 (6), 1849–1892.

Klibanoff, P., Marinacci, M., Mukerji, S., 2009. Recursive smooth ambiguity preferences. Journal of Economic Theory 144, 930–976.

Kolmogoroff, A., 1933. Grundbegriffe der wahrscheinlichkeitsrechnung.

Lange, A., Treich, N., 2008. Uncertainty, learning and ambiguity in economic models on climate policy: some classical results and new directions. Climatic Change 89, 7–21.

Leach, A.J., 2007. The climate change learning curve. Journal of Economic Dynamics and Control 31, 1728–1752.

Lemoine, D., 2021. The climate risk premium: how uncertainty affects the social cost of carbon. Journal of the Association of Environmental and Resource Economists 8 (1), 27–57.

Lemoine, D., Traeger, C., 2016a. Economics of tipping the climate dominoes. Nature Climate Change 6, 514–519.

Lemoine, D., Traeger, C.P., 2014. Watch your step: optimal policy in a tipping climate. American Economic Journal: Economic Policy 6 (1), 1–31.

Lemoine, D., Traeger, C.P., 2016b. Ambiguous tipping points. Journal of Economic Behavior & Organization 132, 5–18.

Li, X., Narajabad, B., Temzelides, T., 2016. Robust dynamic energy use and climate change. Quantitative Economics 7 (3), 821–857.

Manne, A., Mendelsohn, R., Richels, R., 1995. Merge: a model for evaluating regional and global effects of ghg reduction policies. Energy Policy 23 (1), 17–34.

Marinacci, M., 2015. Model uncertainty. Journal of the European Economic Association 13 (6), 1022–1100.

Matthews, H.D., Gillett, N.P., Stott, P.A., Zickfeld, K., 2009. The proportionality of global warming to cumulative carbon emissions. Nature 459 (7248), 829–832.

Meier, F.D., Traeger, C.P., 2023. Uncertain remedies to fight uncertain consequences: the case of solar geoengineering.

Millner, A., 2013. On welfare frameworks and catastrophic climate risks. Journal of Environmental Economics and Management 65 (2), 310–325.

Millner, A., Dietz, S., Heal, G., 2013. Scientific ambiguity and climate policy. Environmental and Resource Economics 55, 21–46.

Moore, F.C., Drupp, M.A., Rising, J., Dietz , S., Rudik , I., Wagner, G., 2024. Synthesis of evidence yields high social cost of carbon due to structural model variation and uncertainties. Technical report, CESifo.

Müller, U.K., Stock, J.H., Watson, M.W., 2022. An econometric model of international growth dynamics for long-horizon forecasting. Review of Economics and Statistics 104 (5), 857–876.

Mäler, K., Xepapadeas, A., de Zeeuw, A., 2003. The economics of shallow lakes. Environmental and Resource Economics 26 (4), 603–624.

Nakamura, E., Sergeyev, D., Steinsson, J., 2017. Growth-rate and uncertainty shocks in consumption: cross-country evidence. American Economic Journal: Macroeconomics 9 (1), 1–39.

Nakamura, E., Steinsson, J., Barro, R., Ursua, J., 2013. Crises and recoveries in an empirical model of consumption disasters. American Economic Journal: Macroeconomics 5 (3), 35–74.

Newell, R.G., Pizer, W.A., Prest, B.C., 2022. A discounting rule for the social cost of carbon. Journal of the Association of Environmental and Resource Economists 9 (5), 1017–1046.

Nordhaus, W., 2008. A Question of Balance: Weighing the Options on Global Warming Policies. Yale University Press.

Nordhaus, W., Sztorc, P., 2013. Dice 2013r: Introduction and user's manual.

Nordhaus, W.D., 2017. Revisiting the social cost of carbon. Proceedings of the National Academy of Sciences 114 (7), 1518–1523.

Pindyck, R.S., 2007. Uncertainty in environmental economics. Review of Environmental Economics and Policy.

Pizer, W.A., 1999. The optimal choice of climate change policy in the presence of uncertainty. Resource and Energy Economics 21 (3–4), 255–287.

Rennert, K., Errickson, F., Prest, B.C., Rennels, L., Newell, R.G., Pizer, W., Kingdon, C., Wingenroth, J., Cooke, R., Parthum, B., et al., 2022. Comprehensive evidence implies a higher social cost of CO2. Nature 610 (7933), 687–692.

Rennert, K., Errickson, F., Prest, B.C., Rennels, L., Newell, R.G., Pizer, W., Kingdon, C., Wingenroth, J., Cooke, R., Parthum, B., Smith, D., Cromar, K., Diaz, D., Moore, F.C., Müller, U.K., Plevin, R.J., Raftery, A.E., Ševčíková, H., Sheets, H., Stock, J.H., Tan, T., Watson, M., Wong, T.E., Anthoff, D., 2022. Comprehensive evidence implies a higher social cost of CO_2. Nature 610 (7933), 687–692.

Rennert, K., Prest, B.C., Pizer, W.A., Newell, R.G., Anthoff , D., Kingdon, C., Rennels , L., Cooke, R., Raftery , A.E., Ševčíková, H., Errickson, F., 2021. The social cost of carbon: advances in long-term probabilistic projections of population, gdp, emissions, and discount rates. Working Paper 21–28, Resources for the Future.

Rode, A., Carleton, T., Delgado, M., Greenstone, M., Houser, T., Hsiang, S., Hultgren, A., Jina, A., Kopp, R.E., McCusker, K.E., Nath, I., Rising, J., Yuan, J., 2021. Estimating a social cost of carbon for global energy consumption. Nature 598 (7880), 308–314.

Rudik, I., 2020. Optimal climate policy when damages are unknown. American Economic Journal: Economic Policy 12 (2), 340–373.

Rudik, I., Lemoine, D., 2017. Managing climate change under uncertainty: recursive integrated assessment at an inflection point. Annual Review of Resource Economics 9, 117–142.

Savage, L.J., 1954. The Foundations of Statistics. Wiley, New York.

Skiba, A.K., 1978. Optimal growth with a convex-concave production function. Econometrica 46 (3), 527–539.

Stachurski, J., 2009. Economic Dynamics: Theory and Computation. MIT Press.

Stern, N., 2007. The Economics of Climate Change: The Stern Review. Cambridge University Press, Cambridge, UK.

Sterner, T., Persson, M., 2008. An even sterner review: introducing relative prices into the discounting debate. Review of Environmental Economics and Policy 2 (1), 61–76.

Taconet, N., Guivarch, C., Pottier, A., 2021. Social cost of carbon under stochastic tipping points: when does risk play a role? Environmental and Resource Economics 78, 709–737.

The Climate Impact Lab, 2023. Documentation for Data-driven Spatial Climate Impact Model (DSCIM) Version092023-EPA. The Climate Impact Lab.

Traeger, C., 2007. Theoretical aspects of long-term evaluation in environmental economics. Ph.D. thesis, University of Heidelberg. Published online at http://www.ub.uni-heidelberg.de/archiv/7049.

Traeger, C., 2010. Subjective risk, confidence, and ambiguity. CUDARE working paper 1103.

Traeger, C., 2014. Why uncertainty matters – discounting under intertemporal risk aversion and ambiguity. Economic Theory 56 (3), 627–664.

Traeger, C.P., 2011. Discounting and confidence. CUDARE working paper 1117.

Traeger, C.P., 2012. A 4-stated dice: quantitatively addressing uncertainty effects in climate change. Environmental and Resource Economics 59, 1–37.

Traeger, C.P., 2013. Discounting under uncertainty: disentangling the weitzman and the gollier effect. Journal of Environmental Economics and Management 66 (3), 573–582.

Traeger, C.P., 2015. Closed-form integrated assessment and uncertainty. CESifo Working Paper 5464. Split into Traeger (2021) and Traeger (2023).

Traeger, C.P., 2019. Capturing intrinsic risk aversion. SSRN Working Paper 3462905.

Traeger, C.P., 2021. Uncertainty in the analytic climate economy. CEPR Discussion Paper DP16065.

Traeger, C.P., 2022. IAMs and CO_2 emissions – an analytic discussion. Technical report. www.traeger.eu.

Traeger, C.P., 2023. ACE – analytic climate economy. American Economic Journal: Economic Policy 15 (3), 372–406.

Treasury, H., 2003. The Green Book – Appraisal and Evaluation in Central Government. HM Treasury, London.

Tsur, Y., Zemel, A., 1996. Accounting for global warming risks: resource management under event uncertainty. Journal of Economic Dynamics and Control 20 (6-7), 1289–1305.

Tsur, Y., Zemel, A., 2009. Endogenous discounting and climate policy. Environmental and Resource Economics 44, 507–520.

van den Bremer, van der Ploeg, 2021. The risk-adjusted carbon price. American Economic Review 2782–2810.

Van Den Bremer, T., Hambel, C., der Ploeg, R.V., 2023. Three reasons to price carbon under uncertainty: Accuracy of simple rules. Available at SSRN 4666508.

Van der Ploeg, F., de Zeeuw, A., 2018. Climate tipping and economic growth: precautionary capital and the price of carbon. Journal of the European Economic Association 16 (5), 1577–1617.

Vissing-Jørgensen, A., Attanasio, O.P., 2003. Stock-market participation, intertemporal substitution, and risk-aversion. The American Economic Review 93 (2), 383–391.

von Neumann, J., Morgenstern, O., 1944. Theory of Games and Economic Behaviour. Princeton University Press, Princeton.

Wagener, F.O.O., 2003. Skiba points and heteroclinic bifurcations, with applications to the shallow lake system. Journal of Economic Dynamics and Control 27 (9), 1533–1561.

Webster, M., Sokolov, A.P., Reilly, J.M., Forest, C.E., Paltsev, S., Schlosser, A., Wang, C., Kicklighter, D., Sarofim, M., Melillo, J., et al., 2012. Analysis of climate policy targets under uncertainty. Climatic Change 112, 569–583.

Weil, P., 1990. Nonexpected utility in macroeconomics. The Quarterly Journal of Economics 105 (1), 29–42.

Weitzman, M., 1974. Prices versus quantities. Review of Economic Studies 41 (4), 477–491.

Weitzman, M.L., 1998. Why the far-distant future should be discounted at its lowest possible rate. Journal of Environmental Economics and Management 36, 201–208.

Weitzman, M.L., 2001. Gamma discounting. The American Economic Review 91 (1), 260–271.

Weitzman, M.L., 2009. On modeling and interpreting the economics of catastrophic climate change. The Review of Economics and Statistics 91 (1), 1–19.

Printed and bound by CPI Group (UK) Ltd, Croydon, CR0 4YY
06/08/2025
01931568-0002